MODELS OF TEACHING

SEVENTH EDITION

MODELS OF TEACHING

Bruce Joyce
Booksend Laboratories

Marsha Weil
ETR Associates

with *Emily Calhoun*
The Phoenix Alliance

Boston   New York   San Francisco
Mexico City   Montreal   Toronto   London   Madrid   Munich   Paris
Hong Kong   Singapore   Tokyo   Cape Town   Sydney

Executive Editor: Steve Dragin
Series Editor: Traci Mueller
Editorial Assistant: Krista E. Price
Marketing Manager: Elizabeth Fogarty
Manufacturing Buyer: Andrew Turso
Composition and Prepress Buyer: Linda Cox
Cover Administrator: Linda Knowles
Editorial-Production Service: Omegatype Typography, Inc.
Electronic Composition: Omegatype Typography, Inc.

For related titles and support materials, visit our online catalog at
www.ablongman.com.

Between the time Website information is gathered and then published, it is not
unusual for some sites to have closed. Also, the transcription of URLs can result in
unintended typographical errors. The publisher would appreciate notification
where these errors occur so that they may be corrected in subsequent editions.

Library of Congress Cataloging-in-Publication Data

Joyce, Bruce R.
    Models of teaching / Bruce Joyce, Marsha Weil with Emily Calhoun.—7th ed.
      p. cm.
    Includes bibliographical references (p.) and index.
    ISBN 0-205-38927-9
    1. Education—Experimental methods. 2. Educational innovations. 3. Teaching.
  I. Weil, Marsha. II. Calhoun, Emily. III. Title.

  LB1027.3.J69 2004
  371.39—dc21

                                       2003048046

Printed in the United States of America

10 9 8 7 6 5 4 3 2   HAM   08 07 06 05 04

CONTENTS

Preface   *xiii*

PART I
FRAME OF REFERENCE   1

We begin with the idea of giving students the tools that increase their learning ability. The primary role of education is to increase student capacity for personal growth, social growth, and academic learning.

CHAPTER 1
BEGINNING THE INQUIRY
Creating Communities of Expert Learners   3

Schools divide students into classes that need to be developed into learning communities and provided with the models of learning that result in expert learners. Those students strive for knowledge and enjoy the companionship of their peers as they try to understand the world.

CHAPTER 2
WHERE MODELS OF TEACHING COME FROM
Multiple Ways of Constructing Knowledge   23

The history of teacher researchers comes to us in the form of models of teaching that enable us to construct vital environments for our students.

PART II
THE INFORMATION-PROCESSING FAMILY OF MODELS   39

How can we best acquire information, organize it, and explain it? There are several ways of making those things happen. We now look at some of the most important ones.

CHAPTER 3
LEARNING TO THINK INDUCTIVELY
Forming Concepts by Collecting and Organizing Information   41

Human beings are born to build concepts. The vast intake of information is sifted and organized and the conceptual structures that guide our lives are developed. The inductive model builds on and enhances the inborn capacity of our students.

CHAPTER 4
ATTAINING CONCEPTS
Sharpening Basic Thinking Skills   59

Students can develop concepts. They also can learn concepts developed by others. Concept attainment teaches students how to learn and use concepts and develop and test hypotheses.

CHAPTER 5
THE PICTURE-WORD INDUCTIVE MODEL
Developing Literacy across the Curriculum   77

Built on the language experience approach, the picture-word inductive model enables beginning readers to develop sight vocabularies, learn to inquire into the structure of words and sentences, write sentences and paragraphs, and, thus, to be powerful language learners. In Chapter 19 the outstanding results from primary curriculums and curriculums for older struggling readers are displayed.

CHAPTER 6

SCIENTIFIC INQUIRY AND INQUIRY TRAINING
The Art of Making Inferences   **101**

From the time of Aristotle, we have had educators who taught science-in-the-making rather than teaching a few facts and hoping for the best. We introduce you to a model of teaching that is science on the hoof, so to speak. This model has had effects, among other things, on improving the capacity of students to learn.

CHAPTER 7

MEMORIZATION
Getting the Facts Straight   **131**

Memorization has had something of a bad name, mostly because of deadly drills. Contemporary research and innovative teachers have created methods that not only improve our efficiency in memorization, but also make the process delightful.

CHAPTER 8

SYNECTICS
The Arts of Enhancing Creative Thought   **155**

Creative thought has often been thought of as the province of a special few, and something that the rest of us can not aspire to. Not so. Synectics brings to all students the development of creative capacity.

CHAPTER 9

LEARNING FROM PRESENTATIONS
Advance Organizers   **187**

Learning from presentations has almost as bad a name as learning by memorization. Ausubel developed a system for creating lectures and other presentations that will increase learner activity and, subsequently, learning.

PART III
THE SOCIAL FAMILY OF MODELS   **203**

Working together might just enhance all of us. The social family expands what we can do together and generates the creation of democracy in our society in venues large and small. In addition, the creation of learning communities can enhance the learning of all students dramatically.

CHAPTER 10
PARTNERS IN LEARNING
From Dyads to Group Investigation   **205**

Can two students who are paired in learning increase their learning? Can students organized into a democratic learning community learn to apply scientific methods to their learning? You bet they can.

CHAPTER 11
THE STUDY OF VALUES
Role Playing and Public Policy Education   **229**

Values provide the center of our behavior, helping us get direction and understand other directions. Policy issues involve the understanding of values and the costs and benefits of selecting some solutions rather than others. In these models, values are central.

PART IV
THE PERSONAL FAMILY OF MODELS   **265**

The learner always does the learning. His or her personality is what interacts with the learning environment. How do we give the learner centrality when we are trying to get that same person to grow and respond to tasks we believe will enhance growth?

CHAPTER 12

NONDIRECTIVE TEACHING
The Learner at the Center   **267**

How do we think about ourselves as learners? As people? How can we organize schooling so that the personalities and emotions of students are taken into account? Let us inquire into the person who is the center of the education process.

CHAPTER 13

DEVELOPING POSITIVE SELF-CONCEPTS
The Inner Person of Boys and Girls,
Men and Women   **283**

If you feel great about yourself, you are likely to become a better learner. But you begin where you are. Enhancing self concept is a likely avenue.

PART V

THE BEHAVIORAL SYSTEMS FAMILY OF MODELS   **295**

We are what we practice. So how do we learn to practice more productive behaviors? Let's explore some of the possibilities.

CHAPTER 14

LEARNING TO LEARN FROM MASTERY LEARNING   **303**

Bit by bit, block by block, we climb our way up a ladder to mastery.

CHAPTER 15

DIRECT INSTRUCTION   313

Why beat around the bush when you can just deal with things directly? Let's go for it! However, finesse is required, and that is what this chapter is all about.

CHAPTER 16

LEARNING FROM SIMULATIONS
Training and Self-Training   323

How much can we learn from quasi-realities? The answer is, a good deal. Simulations enable us to learn from virtual realities where we can experience environments and problems beyond our present experience. Presently, they range all the way to space travel, thanks to NASA and affiliated developers.

PART VI

INDIVIDUAL DIFFERENCES, DIVERSITY, AND CURRICULUM   335

The rich countryside of humanity makes up the population of our schools. The evidence suggests that diversity enhances the energy of schools and classrooms. However, some forms of teaching make it difficult for individual differences to flourish. We emphasize the curriculums and models of teaching that enable individual differences to thrive.

CHAPTER 17

LEARNING STYLES AND MODELS OF TEACHING
Making Discomfort Productive   337

By definition, learning requires knowing, thinking, or doing things we couldn't do before the learning took place. Curriculums and teaching need to be shaped to take us where we haven't been. The trick is to develop an optimal mismatch in which we are pushed but the distance is manageable.

CHAPTER **18**

EQUITY
Gender, Ethnicity, and Socioeconomic
Background **351**

The task here is to enable differences to become an advantage. The best curriculums and models of teaching do just that. In other words, if differences are disadvantages, it is because of how we teach.

CHAPTER **19**

ATTACKING THE LITERACY PROBLEM
WITH MODELS OF TEACHING **371**

We examine two studies in which rich and multidimensional curriculums reach students thought to be unreachable. In one case the curriculum reaches overage beginning readers, that is, students who failed to learn to read effectively in the primary grades. In the second study, kindergarten students learn to read better than most first grade students usually do.

CHAPTER **20**

CREATING CURRICULA
The Conditions of Learning **389**

Robert Gagné's framework for building curriculums is discussed and illustrated. This content is not simple, but it is powerful.

CHAPTER **21**

INQUIRIES
A Research Brief **401**

We provide an introduction to the rich literature on models of teaching, exploring the effects that can be expected when they are used and their limitations.

A P P E N D I X

PEER COACHING GUIDES   427

Related Literature and References   *479*

Index   *519*

PREFACE

Models of Teaching was conceived to connect teacher candidates and teachers to a variety of well-developed ways of teaching, to models that not only had a strong rationale but also had lines of research into their workings and into what one could expect if they were used. Thus, those models represent a base for professional teaching—*professional* meaning "using research to guide practice."

Years ago there was an expectation that research on curriculum and instruction would result in a single model that was superior for all types of educational objectives. However, that was not the case when we began writing *Models of Teaching*, and it is not the case today. Excellent teaching is made up of a repertoire of models that are very good for particular purposes but need to be assembled to generate a top-drawer curriculum.

Three important developments have enhanced teaching over the last thirty years. One is the continued research on particular models and the development of new ones. Refinements have enhanced their effectiveness. The second is the development of combinations of models into curricula that have great power. We have very good curricula in all the curricula areas and, in literacy, curricula that bring virtually all students into reading and writing and reach older students who did not learn to read and write effectively. Third is the development of electronic technologies that enlarge the library and bring massive amounts of information into the classrooms of the youngest children. In modern classrooms, hundreds of books—fiction and nonfiction—surround the students, and electronic media provide encyclopedias and dictionaries that represent a real advance over print media. In addition, masses of information are available over the Internet. Tens of thousands of cities and towns are connected through their web pages. The Eisenhower networks, among others, provide a remarkable array of information and experiments in science. NASA provides information about space exploration that was available to only a few people a dozen years ago. ScienceFriday.com is delightful. E-mail enables any class to be connected with classes in many of the countries of the world. Young children can follow Jane Goodall's career from her earliest studies to the development of the worldwide organization of children and adults who work together to create a better environment for all living things (including ourselves).

In other words, developed models of teaching have grown stronger and stronger year by year both in their own right and because support materials, both print and electronic, have become richer.

Yet the field of education is being fiercely criticized at this time in history. Governmental agencies are pressing schools with unprecedented force because current examinations of student learning, particularly the national studies of educational progress, have indicated serious problems. One such problem is that a third or more of our students are not learning to read and write effectively. How can that be, when teaching strategies and learning resources are developing so well?

The reason is that those powerful models of teaching are unknown to many educators and are not widely used. They need to be known, learned, and used. This book and the resources connected to it can enable new and experienced teachers to broaden their repertoires, develop rich curricula, and enable all students to succeed. Our cause is passionate. Education is not only present life; it is also the life of the future. As time passes, all of these models of teaching will be radically changed or replaced by better ones. For now, let's give the students the best that we know.

Bruce Joyce
Emily Calhoun
Saint Simons Island, GA

ACKNOWLEDGMENTS

We would like to thank the following reviewers: Amy P. Dietrich, The University of Memphis, and Kent Freeland, Morehead State University.

MODELS OF TEACHING

PART I

FRAME OF REFERENCE

We survey a selection of the most useful models of teaching, examine them as models of learning for students, and consider how to build communities of learners. We find that education can greatly affect learning capacity and that these tools we call *models of teaching* are one way to organize intelligence-oriented education, giving our children the means to educate themselves. The key to the effectiveness of models of teaching is to teach students to become more powerful learners. The key to our work is to build on research on models of teaching to give students learning skills. Their intelligence as learners increases.

BEGINNING THE INQUIRY

Creating Communities of Expert Learners

This book could have been called Models of Learning. *Real teaching is teaching kids how to learn.*

—Emily Calhoun to Bruce Joyce, hundreds of times

Let's begin by visiting two first-grade and two tenth-grade classrooms at 9:00 on the first day of school.

S C E N A R I O

In one first-grade classroom, the children are gathered around a table on which a candle and jar have been placed. The teacher, Jackie Wiseman, lights the candle and, after it has burned brightly for a minute or two, covers it carefully with the jar. The candle grows dim, flickers, and goes out. Then she produces another candle and a larger jar, and the exercise is repeated. The candle goes out, but more slowly. Jackie produces two more candles and jars of different sizes, and the children light the candles, place the jars over them, and the flames slowly go out. "Now we're going to develop some ideas about what has just happened," she says. "I want you to ask me questions about those candles and jars and what you just observed." The students begin. She gently helps them rephrase their questions or plan experiments. When one asks, "Would the candles burn longer with an even bigger jar?," Jackie responds, "How might we find out?" Periodically, she will ask them to dictate to her what they know and questions they have and will write what they say on newsprint paper. Their own words will be the content of their first study of reading.

Jackie is beginning her year with the model of teaching we call *inquiry training* (Chapter 6). The model begins by having the students encounter what will be, to them, a puzzling situation. Then, by asking questions and conducting experiments, they build ideas and test them. Jackie will study their inquiry and plan the next series of activities to build a community whose members can work together to explore their world.

S C E N A R I O

Next door the children are seated in pairs. In front of them is a pile of small objects. Each pair of children also has a large nail, wires, and a battery. Their teacher, Jan Fisher, smiles at them and explains that they are going to study magnetism. "The first thing I want each pair to do is to put your nail next to each of the things I have set in front of you. Then, let's discuss what we learn."

The students take turns exploring the objects with the nail. Each pair reports that nothing happens as the nail passes near to or touches the objects.

Then she shows them how to wrap the insulated wire around the nails and attach the uninsulated ends to the batteries through a switch. They connect the ends and turn on the switches. "Now, find out what happens when you bring it close to or touch the things in front of you with it. And sort the objects according to what happens." The students soon have two piles of objects in front of them, one with items that have been pulled to the nail and stuck to it and one with items that have not.

Jan has begun with the model we call *inductive thinking* (Chapter 3). That model begins by presenting the students with a data set or having them build one, helping them study the items in the set, and classify those items. As they develop categories—in this case noting how the objects respond to a magnetic field—they will build hypotheses to test. Jan will study how the students think, what they see and don't see and will help them learn to attack this and other content areas as a community of inductive thinkers. Their discovery of how to create an electromagnet will lead to a wide variety of other possible explorations.

S C E N A R I O

Marilyn Hrycauk's 10th-grade social studies class begins with a videotape taken in a California courtroom, where litigation is being conducted over whether a mother can prevent a father and their 12-year-old son from having time together. The parents are divorced and have joint custody of their son, who lives with the mother.

The tape presents the opening arguments in the case. Marilyn asks the students to generate, individually, the issues as they see them and to request further information about the situation. She then urges them to share their ideas and also asks each student to accumulate the ideas and questions that all the students share under the headings of "issues" and "questions." They find it necessary to develop another category called "positions and values" because many of the students articulated positions during the sharing exercise.

The inquiry will continue by watching more segments of the tape and analyzing several abstracts of similar cases that Marilyn has collected for them. One such case is their first homework assignment. Gradually, through the week, Marilyn will lead the students to develop sets of policy statements and the values that underlie the various possible policies. As the exercise proceeds, she will be studying how well the students are able to clarify facts, distinguish value positions from one another, and discuss differences between seemingly opposing values and policy positions. She, too, is beginning the development of a learning inquiry and is herself an inquirer into her students and their learning.

Marilyn has opened her class with the *jurisprudential model* of teaching (Chapter 11), which is designed to lead students to the study of public policy issues and their own values.

S C E N A R I O

Marilyn's class then moves to Shirley Mills's English course, which opens with a scene from the film *The Milagro Beanfield War*. The students share their reactions to the setting, action, and characters. They express a variety of viewpoints, but when they want to defend their interpretations or argue against the ideas of others, Shirley announces that, for the time being, she wants to preserve their differences so that they can inquire into them. She then passes out copies of the novel of the same name by the author John Nichols and asks them to begin reading it. During the week she will encourage them to explore the social issues presented by the book and film and to compare the devices used by the author and filmmakers. She will watch closely what issues and devices students see and don't see as she works with them to build an inquiring community.

Shirley has introduced her students to the *group investigation model* (Chapter 10), a powerful cooperative learning model she has used to design her course. The model begins by having students confront information that will lead to an area of inquiry. They then inquire into their own perceptual worlds, noting similarities and differences in perception as the inquiries proceed.

Education continuously builds ideas and emotions. The flux of human consciousness gives the process of education its distinctive character and makes teaching and learning such a wondrous, ever-changing process, as thoughts and feelings are built and rebuilt. The children come to school filled with experiences stored in their memories, including complex patterns of behavior that will be built on as they mature. We try to peer inside to find out what learning has taken place and what readiness there is for new learning. But teachers cannot crawl inside and look around—we have to infer what is inside from what we see and hear. Our educated guesses are the substance of our trade as we try, continually, to construct in *our* minds the pictures of the minds of our students. The never-ending cycles of arranging environments, providing tasks, and building pictures of the minds of the students make teaching—the continuous inquiry into mind and environment—a business that is never complete. The process occurs in elementary and secondary education and in the university. Teachers and professors of physics arrange environments, provide tasks, and try to learn what is going on in those wondrous and unique minds in parallel cadence with the teacher who first introduces reading and writing to the students.

To teach well is to embrace the adventure of limitless learning about how ideas and emotions interact with environments and become transformed. We are never finished with this adventure, never satisfied with the arts and sciences of making those inferences, never done with the construction of models of learning and teaching that are built on the guesses we make about what is going on in those minds. We are caught up in an inquiry that has no end.

Models of teaching are the product of the teachers who have beaten a path for us and hacked out some clearings where we can start our own inquiries. All teachers create a repertoire of practices as they interact with their students and shape environments intended to educate them. Some of these practices become the objects of formal study—they are researched and polished and become models we can use to develop the professional skills that we bring to the tasks of teaching.

In this book we introduce some of these models, discuss their underlying theories, examine the research that has tested them, and illustrate their uses. As educators we survey these models and select ones we will master to develop and increase our own effectiveness. We use them, study our students' responses, and adapt them. To become competent to use these teaching strategies comfortably and effectively requires much study and practice, but by concentrating on one or two at a time we can easily expand our repertoires. The key to getting good at a model is to use it as a tool of inquiry. We provide environments, study our students' responses, and learn from the experience—next time around will be a little different, a little better.

MODELS OF LEARNING

Models of teaching are really models of *learning*. As we help students acquire information, ideas, skills, values, ways of thinking, and means of expressing themselves, we are also teaching them how to learn. In fact, the most important long-term outcome of instruction may be the students' increased capabilities to learn more easily and effectively in the future, both because of the knowledge and skill they have acquired and because they have mastered more learning processes.

How teaching is conducted has a large impact on students' abilities to educate themselves. Successful teachers are not simply charismatic and persuasive presenters. Rather, they engage their students in robust cognitive and social tasks and teach the students how to use them productively. For example, although we need to learn to lecture clearly and knowledgeably, the students does the learning from the lecture; successful lecturers teach students how to mine the information in the talk and make it their own. Effective learners draw information, ideas, and wisdom from their teachers and use learning resources effectively. Thus, a major role in teaching is to create powerful learners.

The same principle applies to schools. Outstanding schools teach the students to learn. Thus, teaching becomes more effective as the students progress through those schools because, year by year, the students have been taught to be stronger learners. We measure the effects of various models of teaching not only by how well they achieve the specific objectives toward which they are directed (for example, self-esteem, social skill, information, ideas, creativity) but also by how well they increase the ability to learn, which is their fundamental purpose.

Students will change as their repertoire of learning strategies increases, and they will be able to accomplish more and more types of learning more effectively. Inquiries into various models of teaching and teachers who are consistently effective have explored two basic questions: how rapidly students can be taught to learn more effectively and the extent to which all students can be taught to learn more powerfully. Let's look at two examples of research that explored both of these questions.

THE RAPID RESPONSE TO CHANGES IN INSTRUCTION

A group of secondary school teachers in Israel, led by Shlomo Sharan and Hana Shachar (1988), demonstrated the rapid acceleration in states of growth when they studied and first began to use the group investigation model, a complex form of cooperative learning. They worked with classes in which the children of the poor (referred to as "low-SES," which is shorthand for "lower socioeconomic status") were mixed with the children of middle-class parents (referred to as "high-SES," for "higher socioeconomic status"). In a year-long social studies course, the teachers gave pretests of knowledge to the students as well as final examinations. This way they could measure students' gains in academic learning and compare them with those of students taught by the "whole-class" format most common in Israeli schools. Table 1.1 shows the results.

You can make several interesting comparisons as you read the table. First, in the pretests the lower-SES students scored significantly lower than their higher-SES counterparts. Typically, socioeconomic status is related to the knowledge students bring to the instructional situation, and these students were no exception. Then the lower-SES students taught by group investigation achieved average gains nearly two and a half times those of the lower-SES students taught by the whole-class method and exceeded the scores made by the higher-SES students taught with the whole-class format. In other words, the "socially disadvantaged" students taught with group investigation learned at rates above those of the "socially advantaged" students taught by teachers who did not have the repertoire provided by group investigation. Finally, the "advantaged" students also learned more through group investigation. Their average gain was *twice* that of their whole-class counterparts. Thus, the model was effective by a large margin for students from both backgrounds.

These examples should get us thinking about making a big difference for our students. As we will see, other models also can help students increase their learning capability, sometimes modestly and sometimes dramatically. The important point is that teaching can make a big difference

TABLE 1.1   **EFFECTS OF COMPLEX COOPERATIVE LEARNING IN A HISTORY COURSE BY SES**

	Cooperative Learning (Treatment)		Whole Class Control	
	High SES	**Low SES**	**High SES**	**Low SES**
Pretest				
M	20.99	14.81	21.73	12.31
SD	9.20	7.20	10.53	7.05
Posttest				
M	62.60	50.17	42.78	27.03
SD	10.85	14.44	14.40	13.73
Mean Gain	41.61	35.36	21.05	14.92

Source: S. Sharan and H. Shachar, *Language and Learning in the Cooperative Classroom.* N.Y.: Springer-Verlag, 1988.

to students at both the classroom and school levels. Knowing this is the *core* of effective teaching, because effective teachers are confident that they can make a difference and that the difference is made by tooling up their learning community. Then they study student learning closely and shape the learning environment to accelerate growth. Throughout the book we will use examples of this type. The bottom line is that students can increase their learning abilities quite rapidly—the essence of our work as teachers.

DESIGNING THE SCHOOL WHERE EVERYBODY CAN LEARN

Imagine a school where the various models of teaching are not only intended to accomplish a range of curriculum goals (learning to read; to compute; to understand mathematical systems; to comprehend literature, science, and the social world; and to engage in the performing arts and athletics) but are also designed to help the students increase their power as learners. As students master information and skills, the result of each learning experience is not only the content they learn, but the increased ability they acquire to approach future learning tasks and to create programs of study for themselves.

In our school the students acquire a range of learning strategies because their teachers use the models of teaching that require them. Our students learn models for memorizing information (Chapter 7). They learn how to attain concepts (Chapter 4) and how to invent them (Chapters 3, 5, and 8). They practice building hypotheses and theories and using the tools of science to test them (Chapter 6). They learn how to extract information and ideas from lectures and presentations (Chapter 9), how to study social issues (Chapter 11), and how to analyze their own social values (Chapter 11).

Our students also know how to profit from training and how to train themselves in athletic, performing arts, mathematical, and social skills. They know how to make their writing and problem solving more lucid and creative. Perhaps most important, they know how to take initiative in planning personal study, and they know how to work with others to initiate and carry out cooperative programs of inquiry. These students are both challenging and exhilarating to teach because their expanded learning styles enable us to teach them in the variety of ways that are appropriate for the many goals of education.

When we visited the four teaching/learning episodes at the beginning of the chapter, we saw those teachers and students beginning to develop the learning communities that would work together throughout the year to educate themselves. Schools and classes are communities of students, brought together to explore the world and learn how to navigate it productively. We have high hopes for these little units of our society. We hope their members will become highly literate, that they will read omnivo-rously and write with skill and delicacy. We hope they will understand their social world, be devoted to its improvement, and develop the dignity, self-esteem, and sense of efficacy to generate personal lives of high quality. These aspirations are central to the study of teaching and guide the re-search that has resulted in the rich array of models of teaching that give tools of learning to our students and stimulate our inquiry. Can we design such schools and classrooms? You bet we can! Can we do it by using the developed teaching strategies as formulas? No we can't! Do we have to study the kids' responses and continuously adapt the ways we teach? You bet we do! So, let's continue our inquiry. As we prepare to do so, let's again visit some teachers who are beginning to organize their learning commu-nities and reflect on their confidence in their students.

S C E N A R I O

Evelyn Burnham's fifth-grade class enters the classroom on the first day of school. They find all the computers turned on. On each screen is the same message: "Please check a book out of the classroom library. Select a desk, which will be yours for the time being, and begin reading the book silently. If you come across a word you can't figure out, write it on a card in your Words to Learn box."

The kids are a bit confused, but, looking around the room, they sort out from the tables of science paraphernalia and video equipment, the book-shelves that are labeled "Classroom Library." They find cards on one of the shelves and sign out their books, locate a desk, and begin to read. Evelyn moves about the room, introducing herself to the students and making name tags for them.

S C E N A R I O

Bonnie Brigman's second-grade class enters the classroom on the first day of school. They find that their desks have been labeled with their names, and a note on the blackboard asks them to find their desk and to begin read-ing a set of sentences that are on the desks. Bonnie also asks them to write down any words they have trouble pronouncing or understanding.

Like Evelyn, Bonnie moves about the room, introducing herself to the children. She invites parents who have brought their children to stay, and asks them to read a description of the Just Read program that she has run off for them.

After about 20 minutes, Bonnie asks the kids to share any words they had difficulty reading. When a child indicates a word, Bonnie asks how many others had difficulty reading the same word. She has her clipboard on her knee, with a list of the kids' names, and she records the words they have trouble with. The sentences are constructed to include words representing most phonetic combinations, and in each sentence there is a word that she is fairly sure will be new reading vocabulary to them, so that they have to use context clues to comprehend the word.

S C E N A R I O

Bruce Hall's eighth-grade social studies class enters the room on the first day of school, and the students find name tags on the desks and locate their seats. He gives them a minute to get settled, introduces himself, and flips on the video recorder. A scene from the film *Gandhi* appears and the students watch while Gandhi delivers the famous speech on passive resistance. When the scene is over, Bruce asks the children to write their impressions of the film. "I want us to get started on our study of the world. I also want to get a look at how you write."

"Is this an English class?" asks one of the students.

"Well, it's called social studies, but all classes are about literacy. We'll write a lot this year."

All three teachers, working with students of quite different ages, do some similar things. All three let their children know, by the tasks they give them, that they are in a learning environment. They provide instructions and get things moving right away. They do not spend time telling the kids how to behave; they assume that the kids will follow their instructions. And they are right; the kids get right to work. In addition to taking the kids into the learning process without delay, they are kind and affirmative.

All three are studying the kids from the moment they enter the classroom. They are preparing to modulate as they get information on what the kids can do and how they do it.

All three assume that the kids can manage their own activities, checking out books, reading independently, and writing on demand.

All three expect independent reading and writing. They begin their Just Read programs the first day of school.

All three radiate confidence in themselves and the kids. They let the kids know that they are the adults in the teaching/learning transaction, but do not pretend they are gods. If the students get stuck, they say, "Well, let's try something else and see if it works." They let the kids see them as learners.

CONCEPTS OF LEARNING
THAT APPLY TO ALL MODELS _____

Through most of the book we discuss the models one by one, on their own terms, although we also study how to combine them to create learning environments and curriculums. That said, we need to recognize ideas that cross models—ways of thinking that help us think about our students and whatever models we are using and to better understand those models and how they work.

Current thought about students and educational environments include terms such as

- Constructivism
- Metacognition
- Scaffolding
- Optimal mismatches with tasks given to students (sometimes called the *zone of proximal development*)
- Roles of expert performance when developing goals

We want to unpack these terms and their underlying ideas and consider how we can use them. As you will find, they are relevant to how and why the models work as you attempt to create environments in which your students will flourish.

CONSTRUCTIVISM

We don't particularly like this term because the *ism* implies a political position about education leading to a "Are you a constructivist or not?" way of thinking. However, that said, one of the long-standing ways of thinking about education crosses a *fault line* where one side of the line emphasizes what is taught and the other side emphasizes how students learn to work together to reconstruct their current knowledge and, basically, to learn to be inquirers and build their learning capacity. Put simply, do we teach content to students (one side of the line), or teach them how to learn the content and how to learn new content? The fault line is in the mind, an either-or perception that may not be the best way to frame the question. For example, as we look at the various (and, on the surface, quite different) models of teaching, we find that all of them, if in different ways, depend on teaching the students to improve their capacity both to generate knowledge and to work together with their peers to create productive social and intellectual relationships—constructing knowledge in the academic, social, and personal domains simultaneously.

And, that's what constructivism is all about. It has various forms (for a detailed analysis see Phillips, 2000) that have emerged from a wide variety of sources for as long as education has been discussed. Plato and Aristotle developed positions about the nature of knowledge and how people construct it. John Dewey was the major spokesperson through much of the twentieth century. The Russian psychologist Lev Vygotsky has received much attention for his positions. Keeping in mind the variety of versions of constructivism, we believe the following ideas are at the core of most of the positions.

First is the idea that learning is the construction of knowledge. In the process of learning, the mind stores information, organizes it, and revises previous conceptions. Learning is not just a process of taking in new information, ideas, and skills, but the new material is reconstructed by the mind. If you think of the content of this book, where we concentrate on developing a repertoire of models of teaching, imagine how much reconstruction of knowledge is needed for people who approach teaching with the belief that there will be one teaching model that is superior for all purposes. The reality is that there are many models that generate particular types of learning and those models can be combined to help students with the various types of learning that are needed to master any given curriculum area.

Second, the mind operates from birth. The child learns the culture and the particular varieties that exist in the family and community of birth and early childhood. Raised in a given culture (note that we are born with the capacity to learn any language and absorb any culture), we develop, as small children, an enormous body of information and ideas, ways of interacting with others, and how to transmit our language and culture to children when our turn comes. New information is absorbed into that matrix and may well set in motion a reconstruction of the existing ideas. For a simple example, many novices at tennis assume that one hits the ball with a flat swing, parallel to the ground. Not so—the ball has to be lifted. Hit flat, gravity will pull the ball into the ground before it reaches the net. Without reconstructing the view of the swing, tennis will be no pleasure and competence will not be increased. For a more complex example, imagine that a child is reared in a home governed by combative ways of interacting, one in which conflict is accelerated by aggressive responses to challenge. In a collaborative learning environment, like a good school or classroom, students need to learn integrative ways of reacting to others. A major reconstruction of information is required.

Culture aside, the constructivist position is that knowledge is not just transmitted to the student by teachers or parents, but inevitably has to be created as the child responds to the information in the educational environment. However, teaching through discovery models is not the only way to facilitate the construction of knowledge. Well-designed direct methods can help students build knowledge (see Mayer, 1999, for a clear discussion). Also, see Chapter 9 where we examine the advance organizer model which is designed to help students learn from lectures and other forms of presentation by teaching them how to be active in what are apparently receptive situations.

METACOGNITION

A related concept is that the most effective learners are increasingly conscious of how they learn, they expand their tools, and they monitor their progress. In other words, they develop "executive control" over learning strategies rather than passively reacting to the environment. An illustration is how students respond to the task of comprehending what they read. As sad as it might seem, some students approach books or other text passively. They work through the material and let what sticks stick, but they are not actively constructing knowledge. Others attack the material consciously, building understanding by organizing information and building concepts as they read. The good news is that students can get better and better, provided that we design instruction to improve their skills—and we can do so right from the start, in kindergarten and grade one (see the extensive treatments by Pressley, 2002, and Gaskins and Eliot, 1992, and our discussion immediately below of reciprocal teaching).

You can easily see the relationship between the idea of constructivism and the concept of metacognition as they relate to curriculum and teaching. We can conduct teaching so that we attend continuously to the "learning how to learn" process. When we teach science, we can teach the students not only scientific thinking processes, but how to use those processes to learn, not just science, but other content as well. When we teach students to work inductively, we teach them to become better and better at inductive thinking. As Perkins (1992) puts it, speaking of "thinking skills" in all curriculum areas, the student is taught to acquire and retain knowledge, to understand it by constructing concepts, and then to apply it—to become a generative thinker. As we explore the models of teaching, we will pay close attention to teaching the model of learning that underlies each model—to help the students develop metacognitive control over each model—essentially trying to help them learn to construct knowledge as they learn.

SCAFFOLDING

S C E N A R I O

Mimi's class has been studying the Caribbean. They have been noticing that there are considerable differences in wealth in the larger islands. However, they don't know how to respond—what to do next to explain the differences. That task is, at the moment, beyond their capacity. Mimi suggests to them that they build a table indicating the differences in per capita income, size and population, and colonial history (length of and colonial country) and speculate about whether there are relationships among those variables. Mimi is trying to find a level where the students can understand the data and relationships so they can proceed with their inquiry. She is trying to reach the students' current capacity and elevate it. Will she succeed? We do not know, but her intent is the subject of this section, in which we deal with the concept of scaffolding.

Scaffolding refers to a variety of ways that we can help students acquire increasing metacognitive control. Within all models we do this by studying students' performance as learners and their development of learning strategies.

RECIPROCAL TEACHING OF READING COMPREHENSION

Many cooperative learning strategies are generic; they are designed for use in a wide variety of curriculum areas and a considerable range of goals while building interpersonal understandings and skills. Reciprocal teaching was designed specifically to teach listening and reading comprehension where comprehension is seen as a problem-solving process engaged in by inquiring groups (see Brown, 1985; Brown and Palincsar, 1989). In reading, the goals are to increase students' abilities to think about and understand extended text, and their ability to work together as inquirers.

Reading is a multidimensional thinking process. Expert readers have acquired large sight vocabularies and know how to add to them. They know how to attack unknown words using phonetic and structural analysis knowledge and skills. And, they squeeze meaning from words, sentences, paragraphs, and larger units of text—they work to comprehend the ideas the author presents to them. The field of reading has struggled with all of these, but comprehension has been particularly bedevilling, because reading without full or almost full comprehension is not reading at all. Therefore, developing techniques that improve comprehension is a high priority, and reciprocal teaching is one of the approaches that, hopefully, will help students develop better skills to unlock the meaning of words, sentences, and extended texts.

The approach is straightforward. Students read passages one paragraph at a time. The teacher models the use of four comprehension techniques: developing questions about the text, summarizing what is learned, attempting to clarify word meanings, and making predictions about what may be in the next paragraph. Then, the students take turns leading the group as the next paragraph or section is attacked. Listening to the students, the teacher provides help to lift and clarify the dialogue and will model the strategies again as needed. The teacher's role is modulated as the students become more proficient and are able to monitor their use of the strategies. The self-monitoring, based on the development of metacognitive control of the strategies, is a very important part of the teaching technique. The teacher provides the support needed, but diminishes his or her role as the students master the strategies. The dialogues around the questions help the students not only comprehend the text but also develop the awareness to guide their own inquiry. Rotating leadership causes the students to try to increase their control of the strategies as they lead and also as they observe the other students do so.

The principles of reaction—reading the students and providing enough but not too much support—is the key to successful execution of reciprocal teaching. The intervention is designed for about 20 days of instruction with small groups of elementary and middle school students who have problems comprehending text. Periodic maintainance sessions are provided.

Brown and Palincsar (1989) carried out some very careful evaluations of reciprocal teaching. When instruction began, the average student began with scores of about one-third on comprehension accuracy. By the end of the cycle, nearly all (98 percent) reached a level of 75 percent. Most maintained their level over time as they were assessed some weeks later. Generally, students' standard test results were modest (see the 1994 review by Rosenshine and Meister), but one doesn't expect a brief intervention that deals with one of the several dimensions of competence in reading to affect such general measures. It would be interesting to see what would happen if it were combined with interventions to increase amounts of independent reading and, say, development of vocabulary. Alfasi's (1998) study extended the application of reciprocal teaching to high schools in a socially difficult setting with the same general effects as those reported by the original experimenters.

Throughout *Models of Teaching* we will discuss and illustrate scaffolding with respect to applications of each model. Each model has what we call "principles of reaction," guidelines for how we can modulate to the students as we attempt to elevate their inquiries.

OPTIMAL MISMATCHES: ZONES OF PROXIMAL DEVELOPMENT

One of the aspects of teaching that is most challenging is to generate goals and processes that are in reach of the students but not beyond their grasp. If we work within what they know and can do, they will not learn more or develop more powerful strategies for learning. If we work too far outside their present knowledge and capacity, they will struggle too much to learn optimally.

The principle of optimal mismatch is quite simple on its surface but complex in implementation. An easy example is when you are teaching students to work in cooperative groups when classifying new information. First, students vary in the degree to which they can work effectively in groups of different sizes. The students in a given class may be able to function quite well in groups of two, but not in larger groups. An obvious solution is to organize those students into groups of two, and, if that is adequate for the purposes of a unit, all is well. However, if one wishes to help the students learn to work in larger groups, they need to have experience and instruction in, say, groups of three or four—groups of five or six may be too demanding. Similarly, the students may be just learning to classify information in data sets and need considerable support if they are to build categories effectively.

FINDING ZONES OF PROXIMAL DEVELOPMENT

At one time or another all of us experience tasks that are way over our heads. Similarly, we can take a course in which we are barely challenged at all. One of the most challenging parts of teaching is generating environments that pull the students forward without overwhelming them.

Sometimes content provides a key. Probably the trickiest part of reciprocal teaching is watching the students carefully and deciding when to model a comprehension skill one more time (or several times). If the students are laboring at making predictions about what will come next in a passage, the teacher steps in and models making predictions, trying to pull the students to a higher level of skill.

The first days of the school year pull a tremendous amount of energy from teachers and a major reason stems from the task of figuring out what the students know and don't know and what they can do easily and what is hard for them.

Even more complex than seeking content matches that will work for a given class is learning the students' developmental stages of growth—their general intellectual and emotional levels. Several frames of reference have been developed to guide us as we try to "read" the students. Within the constructivist framework, Vygotsky invented the term *zone of proximal development* to capture the problem of understanding the student's level of development and then arranging the cognitive tasks or the social demands of the environment to pull the student toward growth. Piaget's framework is used to understand stages of development and prescribe environments that will enable the students to function adequately while enabling them to grow without undue stress.

To illustrate concretely, let us consider an interpersonal relations situation. Natalie would tend to respond to ideas that conflict with hers either by incorporating them into her own as if there were no difference, or by rejecting them completely. Will would dissect the ideas, balancing them against his own, perhaps rejecting portions and accepting others, perhaps modifying his own. Thus, it is easier for Will to be productive in complex social models, for he can more easily receive ideas from others and more easily adapt his expressions to meet the frame of reference of the others. Natalie will need much more guidance to develop the capacity that Will has come by through natural development.

OPTIMAL ENVIRONMENTS

The best procedure for inducing an individual to progress toward complexity and flexibility is to match that person's present stage of personality development to an environment tailored to the characteristics of that stage, but in such a way as to pull the individual toward the next stage of development (Harvey, Hunt, and Schroeder, 1961). The following chart summarizes four conceptual levels and indicates in general terms a matching educational environment:

CHARACTERISTICS OF STAGE

I. This stage is characterized by extremely fixed patterns of response. The individual tends to see things evaluatively—that is, in terms of rights and wrongs—and he or she tends to categorize the world in terms of stereotypes. The individual prefers unilateral social relationships—that is, those that are hierarchical and in which some people are on top and others are on the bottom. The individual also tends to reject information that does not fit in with his or her present belief system or to distort the information in order to store it in existing categories.

OPTIMAL ENVIRONMENT

To produce development from this stage, the environment needs to be reasonably well structured, because this kind of person will become even more concrete and rigid in an overly open social system. At the same time, however, the environment has to stress delineation in such a way that the individual develops a self-image separate from his or her beliefs and begins to recognize that different people, including himself or herself, have different vantage points from which they look at the world, and that the rights and wrongs in a situation and the rules in a situation can be negotiated. In summary, the optimal environment for this individual is supportive, structured, and fairly controlling, but with an emphasis on self-delineation and negotiation.

II. In this stage the individual breaks away from the rigid rules and beliefs that characterized his or her former stage. He or she is in a state of active resistance to authority and tends to resist control from all sources, even nonauthoritative ones. This person still tends to dichotomize the environment. He or she has difficulty seeing the points of view of others and difficulty in maintaining a balance between task orientation and interpersonal relations.

The delineation of self that is suggested is now taking place, and the individual needs to begin to reestablish ties with others, to begin to take on the points of view of others, and to see how they operate in situations. Consequently, the environment needs to emphasize negotiation in interpersonal relations and divergence in the development of rules and concepts.

III. At this stage, the individual is beginning to reestablish easy ties with other people and to take on the point of view of the other. In his or her new-found relationships with other people, this person has some difficulty maintaining a task orientation because of a concern with the development of interpersonal relations. He or she is, however, beginning to balance alternatives and to build concepts bridging differing points of view and ideas that apparently contradict each other.

The environment at this point should strengthen the reestablished interpersonal relations, but an emphasis should also be placed on tasks in which the individual as a member of the group has to proceed toward a goal as well as maintain himself or herself with other individuals. If the environment is too protective at this point, the individual could be arrested at this stage, and although he or she might continue to develop skills in interpersonal relations, the person would be unlikely to develop further skill in conceptualization or to maintain himself or herself in task-oriented situations.

IV. The individual is able to maintain a balanced perspective with respect to task orientation and interpersonal relations. He or she can build new constructs and beliefs, or belief systems, as these are necessary in order to adapt to changing situations and new information. In addition, this individual is able to negotiate with others the rules or conventions that will govern behavior under certain conditions, and he or she can work with others to set out programs of action and to negotiate with them conceptual systems for approaching abstract problems.

Although this individual is adaptable, he or she no doubt operates best in an interdependent, information-oriented, complex environment.

If we learn to read these stages, we will both understand why our students respond as they do and be able to push them to greater development. Expanding their conceptual flexibility is a serious goal of education.

Think for a moment of a teacher who is working with students at different levels of development. Imagine a first grade in which most of the students are operating at Stage I. They will want high structure and need it. They are happy with boot camp! Yet, if high structure is their total diet, they are unlikely to grow to higher stages—we'll be growing little authoritarians! Let's now switch to the upper elementary grades or early middle school grades. If the students are progressing, they can see more alternative frames of reference and manage the ambiguity of inquiry. At this stage, too much structure will seem repressive to them. On the other hand, if they are to progress, they need to be challenged to generate greater ability to see alternative views and respect the opinions of others. (Debating a public issue, they can push hard for their position and see the positions of anothers clearly enough to challenge them. But true integrative complexity is in their future.) At the more advanced stages, students will resent being overcontrolled but will be responsive to strong, challenging leadership.

THE ROLE OF EXPERT PERFORMANCE IN SELECTING OBJECTIVES

How do we decide on objectives? A problem involves whether to have levels of objectives (first-grade students should be able to do this; second-grade students to do that, and so on). Or, should we have a vision of top-level importance that is used at all levels as the overall expert performance that is desired? The expert-performance frame of reference places high-level performance as the goal at all educational levels rather than stages of development for each phase of education. Essentially, we try to find out how experts behave and design the curriculum to model, for all students at every age, how experts operate.

Essentially, it comes down to whether we build baby-steps curriculums that are designed to help children up ladders of competence or whether we introduce students to top-level performance early, while recognizing that their "expert" behavior will be limited by their developed capability. The behavior of the expert provides a model toward which the student progresses, moving up a continuum of competence.

Using the behavior of experts to help define objectives can be applied to all curriculum areas. For example

• In reading, we can study how expert readers approach text, identify words, seek comprehension, and build their vocabularies (see Ehri, 1999; Calhoun, 1998), and arrange the curriculum to help the students develop those competencies.

• In writing, we can lead the students to study how authors develop titles, introduce topics and characters, structure sentences, and so on. First-grade students getting ready to write can use the titles in their picture books to help them frame titles.

• In social studies, students can gather and organize information about social groups, neighborhoods, and communities using the tools that scholars in sociology, economics, and the other social sciences use. They can compare societies using versions of the concepts that social scientists use (as in the scenario on pages 14–15 where a fifth-grade class is using concepts like per capita income to compare nations).

To do these things, the material has to be within reach of the students (nuclear physics is not a great topic for the second grade, but the seesaw provides a fine beginning for the study of leverage). And, teachers need to be willing to push their own development—for many, using the model of the expert writer for their own writing will be a first-time experience even as they introduce the students to the idea. Looking at the community with sociological concepts may be a new experience.

On first encountering the expert model concept, a familiar reaction is that it violates the optimal mismatch principle—that, say, asking first-grade students to make comparisons between their community and one in a far away part of the world is simply beyond their capability. The counterargument is that expert behavior is elegant and direct and in a certain sense easier than the awkward fumbling of the novice. When comparing countries, knowing to look for economic indicators such as per capita income provides a place to start, a conceptual handle that gets the inquiry going. Without concepts and inquiry tools, the novice can just flounder about.

When writing, one of the most difficult tasks is to frame the first sentences of paragraphs and longer pieces—the ones in which the topic is announced and the theme is introduced. If the novice is acquainted with a half dozen ways that expert writers solve that problem, the introduction to writing becomes much easier.

The issue of elegance is an important one and can be seen clearly in sports. If we were introducing five or six year olds to play tennis, we would find that the service motion of the expert enables little people to get the ball over the net and into the court whereas flailing at the ball does not. The expert is not just bigger and stronger and more fit. Experts get more out of their bodies.

The expert model concept is seriously challenging the baby steps approach to curriculum where content in the early grades is kept within the experience of the child rather than expanding it. A familiar example in the social studies is where first- and second-grade students study the community they live in—a step that ends up five years later with the study of unfamiliar societies—rather than starting right away with comparative analysis of, say, one's own community and one in England, France, or another country.

We should emphasize that using the expert model does not imply a heavy, force-feeding approach to education. It does imply high goals and aspirations for the students, but, if the processes are really more elegant, then learning may be quite a bit easier as well as more challenging.

GUIDELINES

The concepts we have been discussing add up to a package of guidelines for teaching. Let's see if we can boil this considerable mass of information into a clear set of practices that we can use across models.

From constructivism comes the powerful idea that, as we think of our students, we think of them less as absorbers of information and more as builders of knowledge. And, just as important, we think of them as people who have to reorganize knowledge as they proceed. They come with knowledge and they inevitably have to rebuild it. In its own way, each model of teaching helps students generate new ways of creating and recreating the information and ideas that add up to an educated person.

From metacognition we see the students as people who become continuously more aware of how to learn, creating more strategies of learning and how to use them. Student success within each model depends on mastering the model of learning that underlies it—becoming aware of how to be successful and to monitor one's performance when using the model.

From the work on scaffolding we see our work as studying our students' responses and moving to elevate their skills, including their metacognitive understanding of performance. We *modulate* to them, reading where they are and trying to boost their performance.

From the idea of optimal mismatch we get a guideline for pulling the students to better performance by working just slightly above their developmental level. If the students need more structure, we provide it, but not so much that they don't need to learn to work independently. In some ways we imagine we have a rubberband attached to their capability. If they need more help, we pull the rubberband a bit, but not so hard that they cannot keep up.

From the concept of expert performance we understand goals better. There are two messages from the concept. One is to set high expectations, pulling our students to the best levels of performance we know. The second is to teach expert performance at all levels.

Throughout the book we will integrate these ideas as we discuss each model and how they can be brought together to generate strong curriculums.

CHAPTER 2

WHERE MODELS OF TEACHING COME FROM

Multiple Ways of Constructing Knowledge

This work is more than worthwhile. It's transporting. The satisfaction when the veil lifts and someone realizes that the only barriers to growth are imaginary and self-imposed is almost unbearable. It must be like watching the birth of a species.

—Fritz Perls to Bruce Joyce, Spring 1968

S C E N A R I O

A day in the life of Section 4A in the Simons Elementary School. (The events are referenced to chapters in this book.)

8:30. Traci Poirier's fifth-grade class assembles and find their places in the big horseshoe where their desks are arranged. This week they are organized in groups of three. The members of each group share something they have done or thought about since leaving class yesterday. Some share books they have read or films or television programs they have seen, places they have gone or conversations with their family. All are responsible for sharing some current news event (see Chapter 10).

8:45. Traci asks whether any students wish to share an item that was shared with them. Andy shares that Sharon reported that her sister was getting married on Saturday and wonders if they could send her a "best wishes" card. They agree to do so and Andy volunteers to make a card in PrintShop. Then Nancy shares that Billy had received an email from his pen pal in the Taipei Market School in Hong Kong (their recently adopted class which uses them to study life in America as they study life in Hong Kong). Billy's friend has wondered how many brothers and sisters they have. Everyone writes down his or her number of siblings and passes it to Billy so he can reply.

9:00. Literacy until 10:30. The first inquiry is to get information from a picture of the downtown of Taipei Market. The class members take turns identifying items in the picture (see Chapter 5) and Traci draws lines from the items to chart paper that surrounds the picture, writes and spells the words, and Andy enters them into the computer. Later they will be printed out on cards for each member of the class. About 30 items are identified.

The words are then compared with a set of items they have generated from a picture of the downtown area in their town. To their amazement, about 25 words from each picture are the same. Only three items in the Taipei Market picture are unfamiliar to them. The items are similar although their representations may be different (as a sign in Chinese and English contrasts with a sign only in English). Sharon agrees to circle them on the digital picture in their email computer and send it to the Hong Kong class for identification.

9:30. Independent reading. For most students this means looking through the encyclopedias for information about Hong Kong, taking notes, and developing questions to explore (see Chapter 10). Traci tests two students using the Gray Oral Reading Test, looking for fluency and comprehension, searching for clues for her next sessions on comprehension skills for all the students.

10:00. Writing. Using the words they have used to describe the information in the two pictures, the students write, comparing the two downtown areas. Traci models opening sentences for them, concentrating on how titles and first lines work together to establish topic and theme. She picks up on a prior session where the students classified opening sentences in trade books (see Chapter 3). Tomorrow they will use synectics (see Chapter 8) to explore analogies to structure their writing.

It's only 10:30, but Traci has already designed activities using cooperative learning strategies, the picture-word inductive model, group investigation, and the inductive model, and has planned a follow-up lesson using synectics. As the day progresses, she will begin a unit on plants in their vicinity, using the scientific inquiry model (Chapter 6), and continue a unit where the properties of number systems are the focus.

Traci has a good-sized repertoire of models of teaching and knows that success for the students depends on their mastery of the models of learning that are embedded in each model of teaching.

LEARNING ENVIRONMENTS AND MODELS OF TEACHING

The classic definition of teaching is the design of environments. Students learn by interacting with those environments and they study how to learn

(Dewey, 1916). A model of teaching is a description of a learning environment, including our behavior as teachers when that model is used. These models have many uses, ranging from planning lessons and curriculums to designing instructional materials, including multimedia programs.

For years we have conducted a continuous search for promising approaches to teaching. We visit schools and classrooms and study research on teaching and learning. We also study teaching in settings other than K–12 schools, such as therapists and trainers in industrial, military, and athletic settings. We have found models of teaching in abundance. Some have broad applications, while others are designed for specific purposes. They range from simple, direct procedures that get immediate results to complex strategies that students acquire gradually from patient and skillful instruction.

For this book we selected models that constitute a basic repertoire for schooling. That is, with these models we can accomplish most of the common goals of schools—and a good many goals that only outstanding schools aspire to achieve. Using them in combination we can design schools, curriculums, units, and lessons. The selection includes many, but not all, of the major philosophical and psychological orientations toward teaching and learning. All have a coherent theoretical basis—that is, their creators provide us with a rationale that explains why we expect them to achieve the goals for which they were designed. The selected models also have long histories of practice behind them: they have been refined through experience so that they can be used comfortably and efficiently in classrooms and other educational settings. Furthermore, they are adaptable: they can be adjusted to the learning styles of students and to the requirements of many curriculum areas.

In addition to being validated by experience, all are backed by some amount of formal research that tests their theories and their abilities to gain effects. The amount of related research varies from model to model. Some are backed by a few studies, while others have a history of hundreds of items of research. As we discuss each model we will provide key references—ones that provide access to the research literature.

We have grouped the models of teaching we have discovered into four families whose members share orientations toward human beings and how they learn. These are

- The information-processing family
- The social family
- The personal family
- The behavioral systems family

Parts II to V of the book present the models selected for each family. In Part VI we examine several important applications of combinations of models: increasing equity in education by reducing gender, ethnic, and socioeconomic inequities; creating curricula; building environments for seriously at-risk students; and edging students of various learning styles into higher states of growth. Let us look briefly at the models we selected for inclusion.

THE INFORMATION-PROCESSING FAMILY _____

Information-processing models emphasize ways of enhancing the human being's innate drive to make sense of the world by acquiring and organizing data, sensing problems and generating solutions to them, and developing concepts and language for conveying them. Some models provide the learner with information and concepts, some emphasize concept formation and hypothesis testing, and still others generate creative thinking. A few are designed to enhance general intellectual ability. Many information-processing models are useful for studying the self and society, and thus for achieving the personal and social goals of education.

Eight information-processing models are discussed in Part III. Table 2.1 displays the developers and redevelopers of those models.

TABLE 2.1   **INFORMATION-PROCESSING MODELS**

Models	Developers (Redevelopers)
Inductive thinking (classification-oriented)	Hilda Taba (Bruce Joyce)
Concept attainment	Jerome Bruner (Fred Lighthall) (Tennyson and Cocchiarella) (Bruce Joyce)
The Picture-Word Inductive Model	Emily Calhoun
Scientific inquiry	Joseph Schwab
Inquiry training	Richard Suchman (Howard Jones)
Mnemonics (memory assists)	Michael Pressley Joel Levin Richard Anderson
Synectics	Bill Gordon
Advance organizers	David Ausubel (Lawton and Wanska)

INDUCTIVE THINKING (CHAPTER 3)

The ability to analyze information and create concepts is generally regarded as the fundamental thinking skill. The model presented here is an adaptation from the work of Hilda Taba (1966) and of many others (Schwab, 1965; Tennyson and Cocchiarella, 1986) who have studied how to teach students to find and organize information and to create and test hypotheses describing relationships among sets of data. The model has been used in a wide variety of curriculum areas and with students of all ages—it is not confined to the sciences. Phonetic and structural analysis depend on concept learning, as do rules of grammar. The structure of the field of literature is based on classification. The study of communities, nations, and history requires concept learning. Even if concept learning were not so critical in the development of thought, the organization of information is so fundamental to curriculum areas that inductive thinking would be a very important model for learning and teaching school subjects. The model as presented is based on the recent adaptations by Joyce and Calhoun (1996, 1998), and Joyce, Hrycauk, and Calhoun (2001) in programs designed to accelerate student ability to learn.

CONCEPT ATTAINMENT (CHAPTER 4)

This model, built around the studies of thinking conducted by Bruner, Goodnow, and Austin (1967), is a close relative of the inductive model. Designed both to teach concepts and to help students become more effective at learning concepts, concept attainment provides an efficient method for presenting organized information from a wide range of topics to students at every stage of development.

THE PICTURE-WORD INDUCTIVE MODEL (PWIM) (CHAPTER 5)

Developed by Emily Calhoun, this model was designed from research on how students acquire print literacy, particularly reading and writing, but also how listening-speaking vocabularies are developed. PWIM incorporates the inductive thinking and concept attainment models as students study words, sentences, and paragraphs. The model is the core of some very effective curriculums where kindergarten and primary students learned to read and older beginning readers and writers were engaged in "safety net" programs for upper elementary, middle school, and high school students.

SCIENTIFIC INQUIRY (CHAPTER 6)

Of the several models that engage students in scientific inquiry, we use as the primary example the work of the Biological Sciences Curriculum Study (BSCS), led by Joseph Schwab (1965). From the beginning, the student is brought into the scientific process and helped to collect and analyze data, check out hypotheses and theories, and reflect on the nature of knowledge construction. The model can be used to introduce young children to science (Metz, 1995) and has a substantial effect on equity in learning, virtually eliminating gender differences (Parker and Offer, 1987), and greatly reduces socioeconomic differences. BSCS continues to revise the curriculum and develop curriculums for younger students. The Web has a great deal of information about inquiry-oriented science curriculums. The Eisenhower network in particular is packed with ideas, and space simulations are available through the Eisenhower and NASA outlets.

INQUIRY TRAINING (CHAPTER 6)

Designed to teach students to engage in causal reasoning and to become more fluent and precise in asking questions, building concepts and hypotheses, and testing them, this model was first formulated by Richard Suchman (1962). Although originally used with the natural sciences, it has been applied in the social sciences and in training programs with personal and social content. It is included here because of its value for teaching students how to make inferences and build and test hypotheses.

MNEMONICS (MEMORY ASSISTS) (CHAPTER 7)

Mnemonics are strategies for memorizing and assimilating information. Teachers can use mnemonics to guide their presentations of material (teaching in such a way that students can easily absorb the information), and they can teach devices that students can use to enhance their individual and cooperative study of information and concepts. This model also has been tested over many curriculum areas and with students of many ages and characteristics. We include variations developed by Pressley, Levin, and Delaney (1982), Levin and Levin (1990), and popular applications by Lorayne and Lucas (1974) and Lucas (2000). Because memorization is sometimes confused with repetitious, rote learning of obscure or arcane terms and trivial information, people sometimes assume that mnemonics deal only with the lowest level of information. That is by no means true. Mnemonics can be used to help people master interesting concepts, and in addition, they are a great deal of fun.

SYNECTICS (CHAPTER 8)

Developed first for use with "creativity groups" in industrial settings, synectics was adapted by William Gordon (1961a) for use in elementary and secondary education. Synectics is designed to help people "break set" in problem-solving and writing activities and to gain new perspectives on topics from a wide range of fields. In the classroom it is introduced to the students in a series of workshops until they can apply the procedures individually and in cooperative groups. Although designed as a direct stimulus to creative thought, synectics has the side effect of promoting collaborative work and study skills and a feeling of camaraderie among the students.

ADVANCE ORGANIZERS (CHAPTER 9)

During the last 40 years this model, formulated by David Ausubel (1963), has become one of the most studied in the information-processing family. It is designed to provide students with a cognitive structure for comprehending material presented through lectures, readings, and other media. It has been employed with almost every conceivable content and with students of every age. It can be easily combined with other models—for example, when presentations are mixed with inductive activity.

THE SOCIAL FAMILY: BUILDING THE LEARNING COMMUNITY

When we work together, we generate a collective energy that we call synergy. The social models of teaching are constructed to take advantage of this phenomenon by building learning communities. Essentially, "classroom management" is a matter of developing cooperative relationships in the classroom. The development of positive school cultures is a process of developing integrative and productive ways of interacting and norms that support vigorous learning activity. Table 2.2 identifies the models and several of the developers and redevelopers of the social models.

TABLE 2.2 **SOCIAL MODELS**

Models	Developers (Redevelopers)
Partners in learning	
Positive interdependence	David Johnson
	Roger Johnson
	Margarita Calderon
	Elizabeth Cohen
Structured inquiry	Robert Slavin
	(Aronson)
Group investigation	John Dewey
	Herbert Thelen
	(Shlomo Sharan)
	(Bruce Joyce)
Role playing	Fannie Shaftel
Jurisprudential inquiry	Donald Oliver
	James Shaver

PARTNERS IN LEARNING (CHAPTER 10)

In recent years there has been a great deal of development work on co-operative learning, and great progress has been made in developing strategies that help students work effectively together. The contributions of three teams—led respectively by Roger and David Johnson, Robert Slavin, and Shlomo Sharan—have been particularly notable, but the entire cooperative learning community has been active in exchanging information and techniques and in conducting and analyzing research (see, for example, Johnson and Johnson, 1999). The result is a large number of effective means for organizing students to work together. These range from systems for teaching students to carry out simple learning tasks in pairs to complex models for organizing classes and even organizing whole schools into learning communities that strive to educate themselves.

Cooperative learning procedures facilitate learning across all curriculum areas and ages, improving self-esteem, social skill and solidarity, and across academic learning goals ranging from the acquisition of information and skill through the modes of inquiry of the academic disciplines.

In Chapter 10 we begin with the simpler forms of cooperative learning, especially as they are combined with other models of teaching. We end with the most complex model, group investigation, which combines preparation for life in a democratic society with academic study.

GROUP INVESTIGATION

John Dewey (1916) was the major spokesperson for the idea—extended and refined by a great many teachers and shaped into powerful definition by Herbert Thelen (1960)—that education in a democratic society should teach the democratic process directly. A substantial part of the students' education should be by cooperative inquiry into important social and academic problems. Essentially, the model also provides a social organization within which many other models can be used when appropriate. Group investigation has been used in all subject areas, with children of all ages, and even as the core social model for entire schools (Chamberlin and Chamberlin, 1943; Joyce, Calhoun, and Hopkins, 1999). The model is designed to lead students to define problems, explore various perspectives on the problems, and study together to master information, ideas, and skills—simultaneously developing their social competence. The teacher organizes the group process and disciplines it, helps the students find and organize information, and ensures that there is a vigorous level of activity and discourse. Sharan and his colleagues (1988) and Joyce and Calhoun (1998) have extended the model and combined it with recent findings on the development of inquiring groups.

ROLE PLAYING (CHAPTER 11)

Role playing is included next because it leads students to understand social behavior, their role in social interactions, and ways of solving problems more effectively. Designed by Fannie and George Shaftel (1982) specifically to help students study their social values and reflect on them, role playing also helps students collect and organize information about social issues, develop empathy with others, and attempt to improve their social skills. In addition, the model asks students to "act out" conflicts, to learn to take the roles of others, and to observe social behavior. With appropriate adaptation, role playing can be used with students of all ages.

JURISPRUDENTIAL INQUIRY (CHAPTER 11)

As students mature, the study of social issues at community, state, national, and international levels can be made available to them. The jurisprudential model is designed for this purpose. Created especially for secondary students in the social studies, the model brings the case-study method, reminiscent of legal education, to the process of schooling (Oliver and Shaver, 1966, 1971; Shaver, 1995). Students study cases involving social problems in areas where public policy needs to be made (on issues of justice and equality, poverty and power, for example). They are led to identify the public policy issues as well as options available for dealing with them and the values underlying those options. Although developed for the social studies, this model can be used in any area where there are public policy issues, and most curriculum areas abound with them (ethics in science, business, sports, and so on).

THE PERSONAL FAMILY _____

Ultimately, human reality resides in our individual consciousnesses. We develop unique personalities and see the world from perspectives that are the products of our experiences and positions. Common understandings are a product of the negotiation of individuals who must live and work and create families together.

The personal models of learning begin from the perspective of the selfhood of the individual. They attempt to shape education so that we come to understand ourselves better, take responsibility for our education, and learn to reach beyond our current development to become stronger, more sensitive, and more creative in our search for high-quality lives.

The cluster of personal models pays great attention to the individual perspective and seeks to encourage productive independence, so that people become increasingly self-aware and responsible for their own destinies. Table 2.3 displays the models and their developers.

NONDIRECTIVE TEACHING (CHAPTER 12)

Psychologist and counselor Carl Rogers (1961, 1982) was for three decades the acknowledged spokesperson for models in which the teacher

TABLE 2.3   **PERSONAL MODELS**

Models	Developers (Redevelopers)
Nondirective teaching	Carl Rogers
Enhancing self-esteem	Abraham Maslow
	(Bruce Joyce)

plays the role of counselor. Developed from counseling theory, the model emphasizes a partnership between students and teacher. The teacher endeavors to help the students understand how to play major roles in directing their own educations—for example, by behaving in such a way as to clarify goals and participate in developing avenues for reaching those goals. The teacher provides information about how much progress is being made and helps the students solve problems. The nondirective teacher has to actively build the partnerships required and provide the help needed as the students try to work out their problems.

The model is used in several ways. First, at the most general (and least common) level, it is used as the basic model for the operation of entire educational programs (Neill, 1960). Second, it is used in combination with other models to ensure that contact is made with the students. In this role, it moderates the educational environment. Third, it is used when students are planning independent and cooperative study projects. Fourth, it is used periodically when counseling students, finding out what they are thinking and feeling, and helping them understand what they are about. Although designed to promote self-understanding and independence, it has fared well as a contributor to a wide range of academic objectives (see Aspy and Roebuck, 1973; Chamberlin and Chamberlin, 1943).

ENHANCING SELF-ESTEEM (CHAPTER 13)

The influential work of Abraham Maslow has been used to guide programs to build self-esteem and self-actualizing capability for 40 years. We explore the principles that can guide our actions as we work with our students to ensure that their personal image functions as well as possible. Recent adaptations to the study of teachers as they expand their repertoire of teaching models have provided a means by which teachers can study their learning styles and processes (Joyce and Showers, 2002). The personal, social, and academic goals of education are compatible with one another. The personal family of teaching models provides the essential part of the teaching repertoire that directly addresses the students' needs for self-esteem and self-understanding and for the support and respect of other students.

THE BEHAVIORAL SYSTEMS FAMILY _____

A common theoretical base—most commonly called *social learning theory,* but also known as *behavior modification, behavior therapy,* and *cybernetics*— guides the design of the models in this family. The stance taken is that human beings are self-correcting communication systems that modify behavior in response to information about how successfully tasks are navigated. For example, imagine a human being who is climbing (the task) an unfamiliar staircase in the dark. The first few steps are tentative as the foot reaches for the treads. If the stride is too high, feedback is received as the foot encounters air and has to descend to make contact with the surface. If a step is too low, feedback results as the foot hits the riser. Gradually behavior is adjusted in accordance with the feedback until progress up the stairs is relatively comfortable.

Capitalizing on knowledge about how people respond to tasks and feedback, psychologists (see especially Skinner, 1953) have learned how to organize task and feedback structures to make it easy for human beings' self-correcting capability to function. The result includes programs for reducing phobias, learning to read and compute, developing social and athletic skills, replacing anxiety with relaxation, and learning the complexes of intellectual, social, and physical skills necessary to pilot an airplane or a space shuttle. Because these models concentrate on observable behavior and clearly defined tasks and methods for communicating progress to the student, this family of teaching models has a firm research foundation. Behavioral techniques are appropriate for learners of all ages and for an impressive range of educational goals. Table 2.4 displays the models and their developers.

MASTERY LEARNING AND PROGRAMMED INSTRUCTION (CHAPTER 14)

The most common application of behavioral systems theory for academic goals takes the form of what is called *mastery learning* (Bloom, 1971). First, material to be learned is divided into units ranging from the simple to the complex. The material is presented to the students, generally working as individuals, through appropriate media (readings, tapes, activities). Piece by piece, the students work their way successively through the units of materials, after each of which they take a test designed to help them find out what they have learned. If they have not mastered any given unit, they can repeat it or an equivalent version until they have mastered the material.

Instructional systems based on this model have been used to provide instruction to students of all ages in areas ranging from the basic skills to highly complex material in the academic disciplines. With appropriate adaptation, they have also been used with gifted and talented students, students with emotional problems, and athletes and astronauts.

TABLE 2.4   **BEHAVIORAL MODELS**

Models	Developers (Redevelopers)
Mastery learning	Benjamin Bloom James Block
Direct instruction	Tom Good Jere Brophy Carl Bereiter Ziggy Engleman Wes Becker
Simulation	Carl Smith Mary Smith
Social learning	Albert Bandura Carl Thoresen Wes Becker
Programmed schedule (task performance reinforcement)	B. F. Skinner

DIRECT INSTRUCTION (CHAPTER 15)

From studies of the differences between more and less effective teachers and from social learning theory, a paradigm for instructing directly has been assembled. Direct statements of objectives, sets of activities clearly related to the objectives, careful monitoring of progress, and feedback about achievement and tactics for achieving more effectively are linked with sets of guidelines for facilitating learning.

LEARNING FROM SIMULATIONS: TRAINING AND SELF-TRAINING (CHAPTER 16)

Two approaches to training have been developed from the cybernetic group of behavior theorists. One is a theory-to-practice model and the other is simulation. The former mixes information about a skill with demonstrations, practice, feedback, and coaching until the skill is mastered. For example, if an arithmetic skill is the objective, it is explained and demonstrated, practice is given with corrective feedback, and the student is asked to apply it with coaching from peers or the instructor. This variation is commonly used for athletic training.

Simulations are constructed from descriptions of real-life situations. A less-than-real-life environment is created for the instructional situation. Sometimes the renditions are elaborate (for example, flight and spaceflight simulators or simulations of international relations). The student engages in activity to achieve the goal of the simulation (to get the aircraft off the ground, perhaps, or to redevelop an urban area) and has to deal with realistic factors until the goal is mastered.

USING THE TEACHING REPERTOIRE: A FIRM YET DELICATE HAND

Although we gain personal satisfaction as teachers by expanding our repertoire of tools, and although teaching is made easier by teaching students strategies for learning, all of the creators of the various models of teaching have designed them to increase student learning and thus to help us become more effective professionals.

As we consider when and how to use various combinations of models and, therefore, which learning strategies will get priority for particular units and lessons and groups of students, we take into account the types and pace of learning likely to be promoted. We draw on the research to help us determine the sizes and kinds of effects each model has had in its history so that we can estimate its productivity if we use it properly.

As you study the four families of teaching models, you will want to accumulate a mental picture of what each model is designed to accomplish and whether, under certain conditions, one is likely to have a larger effect than another.

Sometimes decision making is relatively easy because one model just stands out as though it was crafted for a given purpose. For example, the jurisprudential model is designed to teach students to analyze public issues in the high school. It is not appropriate for use with young children, but then neither is the study of complex national and international political and economic issues. However, a high school course that has the analysis of public issues as a major objective can give major attention to the model, which can actually be used to design a whole course or part of one. The model serves other objectives (students learn information and concepts while studying issues, and the model promotes cooperative skills), but those are its nurturant rather than its primary objectives.

More complicated decisions occur when several models can achieve the same objective. For example, information can be acquired through inductive inquiry or from readings and lectures developed around advance organizers. Or the two models can be blended. While the coordination of models with objectives when designing curricula, courses, and activities cannot be thoroughly addressed until the four families have been studied, we need to keep in mind as we study each model that it eventually becomes part of a repertoire that we draw on as we design programs of learning.

As we study the research base, we learn to estimate the magnitude of effects we can get when we teach the students any given model in comparison with some other possible procedure. The cognitive and social tasks that each model of teaching provides to students are designed to create energy that will result in particular kinds of learning. The *effects* of each model are the types of learning prompted by the model in comparison to a condition in which that model or some equivalent one is not being used. For example, we can ask, "Are certain kinds of learning enhanced when students study together *compared* to when they study alone?" Notice that this is a question of comparison. Clearly students can learn under either condition. The question when choosing models is which will probably pay off best in certain courses, units, or episodes. Also, we have to keep in mind that there are many kinds of learning and that some may be enhanced through cooperative study whereas others may not.

Placement of models in a program of study is important, as is blending them appropriately. Consider a program to teach students a new language. One of the early tasks when learning a new language is to develop an initial vocabulary. The link-word method has been dramatically successful in initial vocabulary acquisition, in some cases helping students acquire and retain words as much as twice as fast as normal (Pressley, Levin, and Delaney, 1982), making it a good choice for use early in the program. Students need to acquire skills in reading, writing, and conversation that are enhanced by an expanded vocabulary; then other models that generate practice and synthesis can be used.

To make matters more complicated, we have to acknowledge, thankfully, that students are not identical. What helps one person learn a given thing more efficiently may not help another as much. Fortunately, there are few known cases where an educational treatment that helps a given type of student a great deal has serious damaging effects on another type, but differences in positive effects can be substantial and need to be taken into account when we design educational environments. Thus, we pay considerable attention to the "learning history" of students, how they have progressed academically, their self-image, their cognitive and personality development, and their social skills and attitudes.

Students will change, both as communities and as individuals, as their repertoire of learning strategies increases. As they become a more powerful learning community, they will be able to accomplish more and more types of learning more effectively. Thus, the remedy for students needing above average help is to increase learning capability.

In assessing the research, we are concerned with the general educational effects of each model and the specific, "model-relevant" effects for which it was designed. For example, the inductive models were designed to teach students the methods of science. That is their primary, direct mission. Research clearly indicates that those models achieve those effects very well, but that traditional, "chalk-and-talk" methods of teaching science are poor instruments for teaching the scientific method (Bredderman, 1983; El-Nemr, 1979; Gabel, 1994). Just as important, scientific inquiry increases the amount of information students learn, encourages their development of concepts, and improves their attitudes toward science. What is of interest to us is that those models both achieve their primary goals and have general educational benefits, including gains in student aptitude to learn.

We are satisfied when some models achieve small but consistent effects that accumulate over time. The advance organizer model, which is designed to increase the acquisition and retention of information from lectures and other kinds of presentations such as films and readings, achieves its results when the "organizers" are properly used (Joyce and Showers, 1995). Consider the thousands of hours of presentations and readings to which students are exposed as part of their education: lectures, written assignments, and films and other media are so pervasive as educational tools that even relatively modest increments of knowledge from specific uses of organizers can add up to impressive increases in learning.

Perhaps the most interesting research has resulted when several models have been combined to attack multifaceted educational problems. Robert L. Spaulding, for example, developed a program for economically poor, socially disruptive, low-achieving children that used social learning theory techniques based on knowledge from developmental psychology and inductive teaching models. That program succeeded in improving students' social skills and cooperative learning behavior, induced students to take more responsibility for their education, substantially increased students' learning of basic skills and knowledge, and even improved students' performance on tests of intelligence (Spaulding, 1970).

Spaulding's work illustrates the importance of combining models in an educational program to pyramid their effects and achieve multiple objectives. Effective education requires combinations of personal, social, and academic learning that can best be achieved by using several appropriate models. In Chapter 5 you will see cases where there were dramatic effects on student competence in reading and writing because the Picture-Word Inductive Model was combined with other models.

Also, although many models have been designed to promote specific kinds of learning, they do not necessarily inhibit other objectives. For example, because inductive teaching methods are designed to teach students how to form concepts and test hypotheses, it is sometimes assumed that they will inhibit the "coverage" of information. Tests of these models have found that they are also excellent ways of helping students learn information. In addition, the information so learned is likely to be retained longer than that learned by the recitation and drill-and-practice methods that are so common in schools (see Chapter 21).

Methods designed for particular kinds of content can often be adapted successfully for others. Inductive methods, for example, were designed for academic content in the sciences and social sciences, but they can also be used for studying literature and social values. It would be a mistake to assume that, because a particular model is effective, it should be used exclusively. Inductive models illustrate this point. If they are used relentlessly for all purposes, they achieve less-than-optimal results. Creativity is valuable, and the creative spirit should pervade our lives and Synectics (Chapter 8) enhances it. But much learning requires noncreative activity. Memorization is important, too, but to build all of education around memorization would be a serious mistake.

A few models of learning can have dramatic effects in specific applications. The link-word method, one of several models that assist memorization, has increased rates of learning two to three times in a series of experiments. Essentially, this means that students learned given amounts of material two to three times faster when they used the link-word method than they would have if they had used customary procedures for memorizing words (Pressley, Levin, and Delaney, 1982). However, such dramatic effects should not lead us to attempt to achieve all objectives with the link-word method. It is one of the models of choice when rapid acquisition of information is the objective, but it is not the sole answer to the problems of education. On the other hand, it should not be sold short. It has been shown to be useful to teach hierarchies of concepts in science (Levin and Levin, 1990), addressing one of the important and most complex instructional goals. It also nurtures academic self-confidence—more rapid and confident learning almost always helps students feel better about themselves.

Thus, as we study the tested alternative models of teaching, we find no easy route to a single model that is superior for all purposes, or even that should be the sole avenue to any given objective. However, we do find powerful options that we can link to the multiple educational goals that constitute a complete educational diet. The message is that the most effective teachers (and designers) need to master a range of models and prepare for a career-long process of adding new tools and polishing and expanding their old ones.

Satisfaction from personal and professional growth and exploration should be reason enough for teachers to set as a goal not one or two basic models to use for all purposes, but a variety that they explore for the potential they hold for pupils and teachers alike.

The world we hope to see is one in which children (and older students) will experience many models of teaching and learn to profit from them. As teachers increase their repertoires, so will students increase theirs and become more powerful and multifaceted learners. That is the raison d'être of *Models of Teaching*.

PART II

THE INFORMATION-PROCESSING FAMILY OF MODELS

When the creators of these models look at a human being, they "see" information being processed, decisions being made, intellectual capacity developing, and creativity being expressed and enhanced. These model-builders *cannot* just watch—they simply have to seek ways of helping us process information better and carry our increased capacity around with us as we try to understand the world and solve problems and teach our students.

These scholar-practitioners go about their business in what at first appear to be quite different ways. Some help us design courses where students organize information and build concepts and test those concepts against those of experts. Others lay out concepts so that the students can examine them and build structures that hold information. Some help us memorize existing information while others help us create new ideas.

Their common objective is to help students become more powerful learners.

We can't imagine a classroom where several of these models are not in active use in every curriculum area. The models included here apply to every subject and are useful to all students, providing the tools for learning that help them when they are growing up and through their adult lives.

CHAPTER 3

LEARNING TO THINK INDUCTIVELY

Forming Concepts by Collecting and Organizing Information

Thinking inductively is inborn and lawful. This is revolutionary work, because schools have decided to teach in a lawless fashion, subverting inborn capacity.

—Hilda Taba to a group sitting on the steps of the Lincoln Memorial, 1966.

SCENARIO

At the Motilal Nehru School of Sports in the state of Haryana, India, two groups of 10th-grade students are engaged in the study of a botany unit that focuses on the structure of plant life. One group is studying the textbook with the tutorial help of their instructors, who illustrate the structures with plants found on the grounds of the school. We will call this group the presentation-cum-illustration group. The other group, which we will call the inductive group, is taught by Bharati Baveja, an instructor at Delhi University. This group is presented with a large number of plants that are labeled with their names. Working in pairs, Bharati's students build classifications of the plants based on the structural characteristics of their roots, stems, and leaves. Periodically, the pairs share their classifications and generate labels for them.

Occasionally, Mrs. Baveja employs concept attainment (Chapter 4) to introduce a concept designed to expand the students' frame of reference and induce more complex classification. She also supplies the scientific names for the categories the students invent. Eventually Mrs. Baveja presents the students with some new specimens and asks them to see if they can predict the structure of one part of the plant from the observation of another part (as predicting the root structure from the observation of the leaves). Finally, she asks them to collect some more specimens and fit them to the categories they have developed so they can determine how comprehensive their categories have become. They discover that most of the new plants will fit into existing categories but that new categories have to be invented to hold some of them.

After two weeks of study, the two groups take a test over the content of the unit and are asked to analyze more specimens and name their structural characteristics.

The inductive group has gained twice as much on the test of knowledge and can correctly identify the structure of eight times more specimens than the presentation-cum-illustration group.

S C E N A R I O

Jack Wilson is a year one teacher in Cambridge, England. He meets daily for reading instruction with a group of children who are progressing quite well. He is studying how his students attack unknown words. He believes that they do well when they sound out words and recognize them as being in their listening–speaking vocabulary. For example, when they find "war" they are fine. However, a word like "postwar" appears to stop them. He decides that they have trouble with morphological structures where elements like prefixes and suffixes add to the root meanings of words. So, he plans the following sequence of lessons.

Jack prepares a deck of cards with one word on each card. He selects words with particular prefixes and suffixes, and he deliberately puts in words that have the same root words but different prefixes and suffixes. He picks prefixes and suffixes because they are very prominent morphological structures—very easy to identify. (He will later proceed to more subtle features.) Jack plans a series of learning activities over the next several weeks using the deck of cards as a data set. Here are some of the words:

set	reset	heat	preheat	plant	replant
run	rerun	set	preset	plan	preplan

When the group of students convenes on Monday morning, Jack gives several cards to each student. He keeps the remainder, intending to gradually increase the amount of information. Jack has each student read a word on one of the cards and describe something about the word. Other students can add to the description. In this way the structural properties of the word are brought to the students' attention. The discussion surfaces features like initial consonants (begins with an "s," vowels, pairs of consonants ("pl"), and so on.

After the students have familiarized themselves with the assortment of words, Jack asks them to put the words into groups. "Put the words that go together in piles," he instructs. The students begin studying their cards, passing them back and forth as they sort out the commonalities. At first the students' card groups reflected only the initial letters or the meanings of the words, such as whether they referred to motion or warmth. Gradually, they noticed the prefixes, how they were spelled, and looked up their meanings in the dictionary, discovering how the addition of the prefixes affected the meanings of the root words.

When the students finished sorting the words, Jack asked them to talk about each category, telling what the cards had in common. Gradually, because of the way Jack had selected the data, the students could discover the major prefixes and suffixes and reflect on their meaning. Then he gave them sentences in which words not in their deck began and ended, using those same prefixes and suffixes, and asked them to figure out the meanings of those words, applying the concepts they had formed to help them unlock word meanings. He found that he had to teach them directly to identify the root word meaning and then add the meaning of the prefix or suffix.

By selecting different sets of words, Jack led the students through the categories of consonant and vowel sounds and structures they would need to attack unfamiliar words, providing students with many opportunities to practice inductive learning. Jack studied their progress and adjusted the classification tasks to lead them to a thorough understanding and the ability to use their new knowledge to attack unfamiliar words.

S C E N A R I O

Eight-year-old Seamus is apparently playing in the kitchen. In front of him are a number of plates. On one is a potato, cut in quarters. Another contains an apple, similarly cut. The others contain a variety of fruits and vegetables. Seamus pushes into the segments of potato a number of copper and zinc plates which are wired together and to a tiny light bulb. He nods with satisfaction when the bulb begins to glow. He disconnects the bulb, attaches a voltmeter, examines it briefly, and then reattaches the bulb. He repeats the process with the apple, examining the bulb and voltmeter once again. Then come the raspberries, lemon, carrot, and so on. His father enters the room and Seamus looks up. "I was right about the raspberries," he says, "we can use them as in a battery. But, some of these other things. . . ."

Seamus is, of course, classifying fruits and vegetables in terms of whether they can interact with metals to produce electric current.

S C E N A R I O

Diane Schuetz provided her first-grade students with sets of tulip bulbs which they classified. The students formed groups according to size, whether two were joined together ("Some have babies on them"), whether they had "coats," or whether they had the beginnings of what looks like roots. Now the students are planting their bulbs, trying to find out whether the variation in attributes they identified will affect how the tulips grow. ("Will the big ones [bulbs] grow bigger?" "Will the babies grow on their own?" and so on.) She has designed the science curriculum area around the basic processes of building categories, making predictions, and testing their validity.

S C E N A R I O

Dr. Makibbin's social studies class is examining data from a large demographic base on the nations of the world. One group of students is looking at the base on Africa, another is studying Latin America, and the others are poring over the data from Asia and Europe. They are searching for correlations among variables, such as trying to learn whether per-capita income is associated with life expectancy and whether educational level is associated with rate of increase in population, and so on. As they share the results of their inquiry, they will compare the continents, trying to learn whether the correlations within each are comparable to the others.

These five scenarios show inductive thinking and the inductive model of teaching at work. The teachers use essentially the same process with content from several curriculum areas and with primary and secondary school children. In each case, the process objectives (learning to build, test, and use categories) are combined with the content objectives (inquiring into and mastering important topics in the curriculum).

We stress that students are natural conceptualizers. Humans conceptualize all the time, comparing and contrasting objects, events, emotions—everything. To capitalize on this natural tendency, we arrange the learning environment and give tasks to students to increase their effectiveness in forming and using concepts, and we help them consciously develop their skills for doing so. Over the years we have generated guidelines for shaping the environment and creating tasks that facilitate concept formation. As students become more skilled in inductive learning, we modulate our behavior, helping them create appropriate environments and tasks. Learning how to think inductively is the critical goal and the students need to practice it, not just be led through it. The guidelines for shaping the environment (designing lessons and units) are straightforward.

One is *focus*—helping the students concentrate on a domain (an area of inquiry) they can master, without constricting them so much that they can't use their full abilities to generate ideas. At first we do this by presenting the students with data sets that provide information in the domain that will be the focus of the lesson or unit and by asking them to study the attributes of the items in the set. A simple example is to present kindergarten or first grade students with cards containing several letters from the alphabet and ask them to examine them closely and describe their attributes. The domain is *the alphabet: letters and their names.* Another example is to present fifth or sixth grade students with a data set containing statistical data on the countries from a region of the world, say, Latin America, and ask the students to study the data on each country carefully. The domain is *Latin American countries,* with the subdomain of *statistical data.*

Second is *conceptual control*—helping the students develop conceptual mastery of the domain. In the case of the alphabet, the goal is to distinguish the letters from one another, and to develop categories by grouping letters that have many, but not all, attributes in common. The students will learn to see the alphabet in terms of similarities and differences. They will also find those letters in words and, when they have made categories of letters with the same shape (as putting a half-dozen B's together), will learn the names of those letters as we supply them. The letters will be placed on charts in the classroom along with words that contain them. In the case of the Latin American countries, the students will classify the countries according to the demographic data provided in the set, moving from single-attribute categories such as population and per capita income to multiple-attribute categories such as determining whether variables like education levels, fertility, and income are related. They will be able to see Latin America in terms of those categories, a step toward the conceptual control that will emerge as they add more data to their set and develop advanced categories, gaining *meta-control* by developing hierarchies of concepts to gain further mastery of the domain.

The third guideline is converting conceptual understanding to *skill.* In the case of the alphabet, this is exploring letter–sound relationships and how to use them in reading and spelling, where recognition evolves to conscious application in word identification. In the case of the Latin American countries, the skills are in the development of multiple-attribute categories and generating and testing hypotheses (such as studying whether per capita income is related to fertility rates or education levels).

The environment is made up of the development of the learning community, the creation of the data sets, and the learning tasks—classification, reclassification, and development of hypotheses. Also, the teacher observes the students and scaffolds their inquiry by helping them elaborate and extend their concepts. In the alphabet example, tasks like "which letters are most like the 'A' and are most likely to be confused with it" would be generated. In the Latin American example, tasks like "what other variables might be correlated with levels of literacy" would be generated.

As the students learn to build and extend categories (concepts), they take on increased responsibility for the process. For example, they learn to build data sets that are relevant to the domains being studied. Our kindergarten/first grade students use their word charts to develop data sets, at first with explicit guidance ("Here are three words that begin the same. Can you add to my list?") and later by looking at the list and sorting the words independently according to how they begin and end. Our young scholars on Latin America learn to add variables to the data base using statistical sources and expository sources like encyclopedias. As their study of nations proceeds, they will be able to create data sets on regions and sets that enable them to compare and contrast entire regions.

The inductive model causes students to collect information and examine it closely, to organize the information into concepts, and to learn to manipulate those concepts. Used regularly, this strategy increases students' abilities to form concepts efficiently and increases the range of perspectives from which they can view information.

RESEARCH

Although quite a bit of the research on information-processing models has been focused on how to increase students' ability to form and use concepts and hypotheses, a number of questions asked by both practitioners and laymen are particularly relevant here. Essentially, the questions reflect a concern that a concentration on thinking might inhibit the mastery of content.

Teachers put the question something like this: "I have much content to cover. If I devote energy to the teaching of thinking, won't the students miss out on the basic skills and content that are the core of the curriculum?" Several reviews of research have addressed this question.

El-Nemr (1979) concentrated on the teaching of biology as inquiry in high schools and colleges. He looked at the effects of student achievement on the development of process skills and on attitudes toward science. The experimentally-oriented biology curriculums achieved positive effects on all three outcomes. Bredderman's (1983) analysis included a broader range of science programs and included the elementary grades. He also reported positive effects for information acquisition, creativity, and science process. In addition, he reported effects on intelligence tests where they were included. Hillocks's (1987) review of the teaching of writing produced similar results. Essentially, the inductive, inquiry-oriented approaches to the teaching of writing produced average effect sizes of about .60 compared to treatments that covered the same material, but without the inductive approaches to the teaching/learning process.

Some other researchers have approached the question of "coverage" in terms of the transfer of the teaching of thinking from one curriculum to another, and have found that inquiry-oriented curriculums appear to stimulate growth in other, apparently unconnected, areas. For example, Smith's (1980) analysis of aesthetics curriculums shows that the implementation of the arts-oriented curriculums was accompanied by gains in the basic skills areas.

The question of time and efficiency has been addressed recently in a number of large-scale field studies in the basic curriculum areas. An example has been provided by the 190 elementary school teachers of an Iowa school district. The teachers and administrators in this district focused on improving the quality of their students' writing by using the inductive model of teaching to help students explore the techniques used by published authors to accomplish such tasks as introducing characters, establishing settings, and describing action. Teachers collected samples of the children's writing and those samples were scored by experts who did not know the identity of the children.

By the end of the year, student writing had improved dramatically. The example of the fourth grade illustrates how much they improved. (See Table 3.1.) Their end-of-year scores for writing quality were higher than the end-of year scores for eighth grade students the previous year! Students had made greater gains in one year than were normally achieved by comparable students over a period of four years. Moreover, students at all levels had improved substantially—from the ones who started with the poorest writing skills to the ones who began with the most developed skills. A gender gap in writing (males often lag behind females in developing writing skills) narrowed significantly (Joyce, Calhoun, Carran, Simser, Rust, & Halliburton, 1994, 1996).

Table 3.1 compares the means for the two periods (fall 1992 and spring 1993) for the three dimensions for which quality was assessed (Focus/

TABLE 3.1   **MEAN GRADE FOUR SCORES ON EXPOSITORY WRITING FOR FALL 1992 AND SPRING 1993**

	Dimensions		
Period	**Focus/Org.**	**Support**	**Grammar/Mech.**
Fall			
Mean	1.6	2.2	2.11
SD	0.55	0.65	0.65
Spring			
Mean	2.8	3.2	3.0
SD	0.94	0.96	0.97

Organization, Support, and Grammar/Mechanics). In the fall, the correlation coefficient between the dimensions of Focus/Organization and Support was 0.56. Between the dimensions of Focus/Organization and Grammar/Mechanics, the correlation coefficient was 0.61, and between the dimensions of Support and Grammar/Mechanics it was 0.63. In the spring, these were 0.84, 0.65, and 0.74, respectively.

Effect sizes were computed for fall and spring scores. For Focus/Organization the effect size was 2.18; for Support, 1.53; and for Grammar/Mechanics, 1.37. (See Appendix A for an explanation of *effect size* and how to interpret it.) All these are several times the effect sizes calculated for a year's gain for the national sample and of the baseline gains determined from the 1991–1992 analyses. For Focus/Organization, the differences are so great that in the spring the average student reached the top of the fall distribution, something that does not happen nationally during the entire time from grades four to twelve.

It is surprising to many people that the same model of teaching reached all the students, but it is a typical finding in studies of teaching and teaching strategies. Teachers who "reach" the students with poor histories of learning and help them out of their rut also propel the best students into higher states of growth than they have been accustomed to.

SYNTAX

The concept we refer to as *syntax* depicts the structure of a model—its major elements or phases and how they are put together. Some models, such as concept attainment, have relatively fixed structures within which some of the elements or phases need to follow each other for maximum effectiveness. Others have a rolling or wavelike structure in which phases are recycled. The inductive model has a rolling structure that evolves over time; inductive inquiries are rarely brief. The essence of the inductive process is the continual collecting and sifting of information; the construction of ideas, particularly categories, that provide conceptual control over territories of information; the generation of hypotheses to be explored in an effort to understand relationships better or provide solutions to problems; and the conversion of knowledge into skills that have practical application.

Think about the scenarios at the beginning of the chapter as you review the four phases of the inductive model of teaching and learning. The phases of the inductive model include (1) identifying and enumerating the data that are relevant to a topic or problem; (2) grouping these items into categories whose members have common attributes; (3) interpreting the data and developing labels for the categories so that they can be manipulated symbolically; and (4) converting the categories into skills or hypotheses.

To engage students in inductive activities, Taba (1966, 1967) invented teaching moves in the form of tasks given to the students, and we follow her example. For instance, asking students to "Look up the data on per capita income and population growth for 12 countries from each of the major regions of the world" will induce the students to create a data file. The task "Decide which countries are most alike" is likely to cause students to group those things that have been listed. The question, "What would we call these groups?" begins a task likely to induce students to develop labels or categories. Asking the students to correlate income and growth leads to further interpretation and the development of hypotheses (they will find that there is an inverse correlation between per capita income and population growth and wonder why). An example of the development of skill is where students have classified ways that authors introduce characters and then experiment with those classifications, learning multiple ways *they* can introduce characters.

The teacher moves the model along by means of eliciting questions to guide the student from one phase of activity into the next at the appropriate time. For example, the grouping of data would be premature if the data had not been identified and enumerated. But to delay too long before moving into the next phase would be to lose opportunities for learning and could decrease students' cognitive interest.

To teach students to respond to the model, we advise teachers to begin by leading the students through activities based on data sets that are presented to them, and in later lessons to teach students how to create and organize data sets.

THE DATA COLLECTION AND PRESENTATION PHASE

Inductive operations involve organizing data and pulling it apart and reorganizing it in the search for ideas. Thus, collecting data occurs early, but new data may be added or discarded as an inquiry proceeds. While teaching students to work inductively, we often present sets of otherwise unorganized data to the students, and we will always do so on occasion when we want to select the substance for their initial inquiry. However, we will teach them to collect data and create data sets, and many inductive inquiries begin with a collection phase. Data sets are developed from substantive domains that are identified for academic purposes. Domains are arbitrary boundaries for study and are quite various—they are territories to be explored. They can be defined geographically ("Let's study everything in the town center") or by general categories (the economic systems of all nations, or the nations of Asia; poems written last year by Chinese women), and are selected for the reason that we believe it will be productive to study them. Essentially, they need to be significant by some academic standard. In fact, the academic territories have developed over the years (the study of quality in writing, romance poets, optics, algebraic equations—an enormous list). Thus, although trivial things *can* be studied and classified, we usually do not spend valuable curricular time on them. However, serious inquiry can turn the apparently trivial into something quite significant. Irving Goffman's book, *Gender Advertisements* explores how images are formed in our public mind. George Gerbner's studies of how print and film media shape views of teachers are others.

THE PHASE OF EXAMINING AND ENUMERATING DATA

The data need to be examined closely, whether rocks or poems or philosophies, and labelled or tagged so we can identify them as we move them around. Rocks can have numbers or tags of different colors, poems have names and can have numbers as well, philosophies can be named after the philosophers. Items in the data set also need to be studied very carefully so that their attributes are teased out richly. This phase needs to be done carefully, or the inquiry will be superficial. We have found that many teachers tend to rush this phase, which is almost always a mistake.

THE FIRST PHASE OF CLASSIFYING

To be really productive, we generally classify data several times. The first phase is important, but we have a tendency to classify on gross characteristics and on just one or two attributes or confine ourselves to one-way classifications; we are just getting started. When classifying poems, we rely on the more obvious differences in subject matter, mood, and device. However, the first pass at building and sharing categories gets us going.

Sometimes after the first exercise in classification, we find we want to add some more data to our set or that we are seeing things we didn't pay attention to when we were studying and enumerating the data. In those cases, we cycle back and collect or examine again, or both.

THE FURTHER PHASES OF CLASSIFYING

Digging into our data again, we reclassify, refine or collapse categories, experiment with two- and three-way schemes, and categories emerge and are shared. We gradually get control of our data. Sometimes we alternate classification with a further search for data.

THE PHASE OF BUILDING HYPOTHESES AND GENERATING SKILLS

Just having categories is educative. When we classify character sketches drawn from novels and short stories, we discover ways that authors introduce characters. Those ways enable us to read with a more refined eye. However, if we keep pushing at the categories, we can milk them for hypotheses and convert some of them into useful skills. Suppose we discovered that women writers used analogies more frequently than male writers when introducing characters: we might hypothesize that women would use analogies more in all phases of their writing. We can develop a new inquiry to test that hypothesis. If we pursue the subject, we can try to find out why.

Building skills from categories requires learning what to do to produce something that fits the category. Suppose that we discover metaphors as a device used by our poets. If we want to produce metaphors, we need to practice and to compare our products with the metaphors generated by expert writers.

THOUGHTS ON DESIGNING THE LEARNING ENVIRONMENT

Very important to current classroom use of the inductive model was the work of Hilda Taba cited earlier (1966, 1967). Taba was largely responsible for popularizing the term *teaching strategy* and for shaping the inductive model so that it could be conveniently used to design curriculums and lessons.

SOCIAL SYSTEM

The atmosphere of the classroom is cooperative, with a good deal of pupil activity. Since the teacher is generally the initiator of phases, and the sequence of the activities is determined in advance, he or she begins in a controlling, though cooperative, position. However, as the students learn the strategies, they assume greater control.

PRINCIPLES OF REACTION

Taba provides the teacher with rather clear guidelines for reacting and responding within each phase. When using cognitive tasks within each strategy, the teacher must be sure that the cognitive tasks occur in optimum order, and also at the "right" time. Regulating the tasks requires that studying the data set is done thoroughly before categorization proceeds and that seeking for relationships follows thorough categorization. The teacher's primary mental task in the course of the strategies is to monitor how students are processing information and then to use appropriate eliciting questions. The important task for the teacher is to sense the students' readiness for new experience and new cognitive activity with which to assimilate and use those experiences.

SUPPORT SYSTEM

The model can be used in any curricular area that has large amounts of raw data that need to be organized. For example, in studying the economic aspects of various nations, students would need large quantities of data about the economics of those countries and statistics about world affairs. Then the teacher's job is to help them process the data in increasingly complex ways and, at the same time, to increase the general capacities of their systems for processing data.

APPLICATION

The primary application of the model is to develop thinking capacity. However, in the course of developing thinking capacity, the strategies obviously require students to ingest and process large quantities of information. The model can be used in every curriculum area and from kindergarten through high school. Inducing students to go beyond the given data is a deliberate attempt to increase productive or creative thinking. Inductive processes thus include the creative processing of information, as well as the convergent use of information to solve problems.

The concept formation model can be used with students of all ages, from nursery school through graduate study.

The model causes students to collect information and examine it closely, to organize it into concepts, and to learn to manipulate those concepts. Used regularly, the strategy increases the students' abilities to form concepts efficiently and also the perspectives from which they can view information.

For example, if a group of students regularly engages in inductive activity, the group can be taught more and more sources of data. The students can learn to examine data from many sides and to scrutinize all aspects of objects and events. Imagine students studying communities, for instance. We can expect that at first their data will be superficial, but their increasingly sophisticated inquiry will turn up more and more attributes that they can use for classifying the data. Also, if a classroom of students works in groups to form concepts and data, and then the groups share the categories they develop, they will stimulate each other to look at the information from different perspectives.

The students can learn to categorize categories, too. Imagine students who have classified poems or short stories. They can build concepts that further cluster those categories.

Another example may serve to pull these ideas together in practical terms. As we have discussed, sometimes we create and organize data sets for our students to classify, and sometimes we help them create and organize sets. In the following example we have organized a set from writing samples produced by the students themselves.

S C E N A R I O

ADVERBS: AN INDUCTIVE EXERCISE INVOLVING STUDENT WRITING

The students have watched a scene from the film *Out of Africa* in which three new friends amuse themselves with witty conversation and telling anecdotes and stories. Then the students were instructed to create a sentence about the scene, beginning each sentence with an adverb. (They are studying the use of adverbs because it was discovered that they are more awkward using adverbs than adjectives.)

They opened their sentences in the following ways (the rest of the sentences are omitted to create a focus on the use of adverbs in openings):

1. Profoundly looking into one another's eyes . . .
2. Intently listening to one another's words . . .
3. Wonderingly and as if by magic the love began to flow . . .
4. With relaxed and forthright honesty they shared a part of themselves . . .
5. Anxiously the husband watched as his normally taciturn wife . . .
6. Passionately I gazed at my two companions . . .
7. Playfully at first, but with growing intensity . . .
8. Tentatively, like three spiders caught in the vortex of the same web, . . .
9. With heated anticipation, the three formed a web of mystery and emotion.
10. Quietly listening they were engulfed by the tale.
11. With awe and a certain wonderment . . .
12. Tenderly, in the midst of warm candlelight, they . . .
13. Skillfully she met the challenge . . .
14. Boldly they teased one another with their mutual love of language.
15. Effortlessly her practiced mind . . .
16. Awkwardly, like children just learning to walk . . .
17. Softly, slowly, but glowing like the candles about them, they negotiated . . .
18. Boldly she drew them into the fabric of her story.
19. Suspended by the delicate thread of her tale . . .
20. Instinctively she took his cue . . .

Before reading further, read the passages and make notes about the attributes of the writing. Then classify the sentences. (If you are alone or in a small group studying the model, classify them independently. If you are in a group of eight or more, classify them with a partner. Then share your classifications, discussing the basis each of you used and the attributes you focused on.)

Now, let's turn to some of the categories developed by our class.

One group classified the sentences by the form of the adverbs, placing single words together (such as *profoundly* from number 1, *anxiously* from 5), phrases together (such as "with relaxed and forthright honesty" from 4), and the single clause (number 19) by itself. A second group reported that it had classified them according to the mood or tone that was evoked. For example, numbers 12, 17, 19, 11, 3, and 7 were placed together because the group members decided that they all shared the creation of a gentle, loving mood, whereas 5 and 16 emphasized the awkwardness of strangers.

The class then used their categories to experiment with writing, changing single words into phrases and clauses and vice versa, substituting words to change the mood evoked, and so on. For example, one pair experimented with 6, trying "with passion," and "passion flowed as I gazed. . . ." Another changed number 8 to "tentatively and spiderlike" and decided the change altered the mood. One changed *boldly* to *skillfully* in number 18 and judged that it helped the development of the mood.

The episode was followed by a foray into several books of short stories, and the members of the class created a data set of sentences in which authors had made use of adverbs. Classifying them, they proceeded to create categories of adverb use by expert writers and to experiment with them in their own writing.

Thus, the phases of the model built on one another to generate more and more complex mental activity and to increase the likelihood that the study of language would have a yield for their skill in writing. The second inductive activity built on the first as the students added the study of expert writers and tried to learn from them.

The model is adaptable to a wide range of learning styles. Hunt, Joyce, and their associates (1981) explored inductive processes with both relatively rigid and flexible students; they found that both groups were able to engage in the inductive process but that the more flexible students made the greatest gains initially. More important, they found that practice and training increased effectiveness and that the students could learn to carry on inductive activity independently.

Tips for Teaching Inductively

Here are a number of tips for teaching inductively that Bruce Joyce wrote to a group of teachers a few years ago:

1. Practice, practice, practice—anxiety reduces practice—let go and have fun. Build a learning community around the model—designing a weekly lesson won't accomplish that.

2. Study how the kids think—the process gives us a bit of a window into their minds. The better the handle on their minds, the more we can adjust what we do.

3. Keep up front that we are trying to help the kids learn to learn. A common mistake in teaching is to ask questions without teaching the kids how to answer them—or, even better, to ask them themselves and then seek the answers. Teaching comprehension in reading is an example. Many folks ask the kids questions about what they have read to learn if they have comprehended—or ask them to make predictions. Neither teaches the kids *how* to comprehend or make predictions based on understanding. They need models to follow—exposing how we comprehend and make predictions.

4. The inductive process brings kids into the exploration of a domain as a learning community trying to master that domain. For example, suppose that initial consonants is the domain for beginning readers. They need to explore a heap of initial consonants, distinguishing the letters and sounds from one another. Giving them a set with the "letter of the week" in it and hoping they will focus on that letter subverts the inquiry. We learn phonics by comparing and contrasting letters and their associated sounds—learning them one at a time without comparison makes life difficult for them. Remember that the customary ways of teaching reading leave 30 percent of the kids virtually unable to read. They need to inquire actively into phonetic and structural analysis and comprehension skills.

5. Except for very specific concentration on phonetic elements and newly learned vocabulary, words should be presented in sentences that provide context clues and a kind of "cloze" activity carried on to ensure that meaning is established. We are producing a nation of "word callers" who don't know how to extract meaning from text or who give up easily in the face of demanding text.

6. Use the model in the curriculum areas—to teach substance. Not a rainy day activity.

7. Make sure the data set has the attributes present, both for concept formation and concept attainment. I probably overuse the example of "food groups." Kids can memorize what food goes in what group and take our word for the meaning of nutrition. They *cannot* use inductive methods to discover the groups. Biochemists can. However, if the data presented are rich enough they can, by the fourth grade, classify the nations of the world by demographic characteristics because no arcane scientific knowledge or process is indicated.

8. Be careful how you teach "complete" and "incomplete" sentences. Teach subject and predicate first. A complete sentence is simply an expression that has an explicit or implied subject and predicate.

9. Distinctions between fact and opinion are probably not appropriate for short explorations—data sets containing each will only work if the kids already know which are facts and opinions—in which case there is no new learning. The distinction requires inference from context or, more often, verification from an authoritative source.

10. In science, try to concentrate on stuff where the kids can collect raw data. With respect to rocks, for example, they can study density, hardness, pH, and homogeneity by visual inspection, but they have to consult authoritative sources to find out how the rocks got that way. They can't tell whether a rock was produced from a volcanic process unless they already know or get the information from an authoritative source.

Suggestion for the "forest unit." Find a nearby grove with variety in it and have the kids observe the trees for a year, building categories as they go. They can also consult resource books for data about other trees, using the ones they have observed as "anchors" for information gained through print and other media sources.

11. Yes! Kids can create or attain multiple-attribute categories.

12. Teaching concepts like *adverb, adjective, phrase, clause*—remember that there are many subcategories of all of these. If a data set contains one each of five or six categories of adverbs, it can be tough for the kids. Consider sets where they discover the various subcategories.

13. "Squeeze" the meaning out of complex sets, such as poems. The kids want to approach these with the idea of learning *everything* about them.

14. Studying attributes of things like characters in stories provides interesting problems. Usually, learning what a character is like involves mining the context. You might consider data sets where clues referring to various characteristics are concentrated on—such as physical description and temperament. Again, teach the kids how to answer the question.

15. Back on characters—if they are going to classify characters, they need 20 or so in the set.

16. Figure out the higher-order objective at the beginning. A good example is the log describing an exercise where the kids classified pictures of clouds and then were given the scientific terms for clouds that have particular appearances. The question was "how do I know when we're done?" That question is not unique to the inductive model—it would apply to a unit taught in any fashion. The answer is to figure out what they are going to do with their newfound knowledge and design an application task that starts them on their way. For example, have them take a minute at the beginning of several days to look at the sky and write or dictate a description. Or have them look up information about weather or examine a number of weather forecasts and find concepts in them.

INSTRUCTIONAL AND NURTURANT EFFECTS _____

The inductive model of learning and teaching is designed to instruct students in concept formation and, simultaneously, to teach concepts, and the application of concepts/generalizations. It nurtures attention to logic, attention to language and the meaning of words, and attention to the nature of knowledge. Figure 3.1 displays the instructional and nurturant effects of the inductive model.

It is sometimes thought that higher-order thinking is reserved for the mature. Not so. Students of all ages can process information richly. Although the content of primary education needs to be rich with concrete experience,

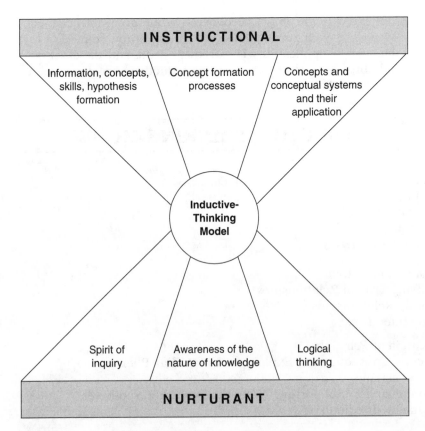

FIGURE 3.1   Instructional and nurturant effects of the
inductive-thinking model.

little kids can learn to think well. Similarly, complex, inquiry-oriented models of instruction have turned out to be the best educational medicine for students who start school slowly or who later have the poorest learning histories.

Good thinking combines discipline with flexibility. If we are to help children become more powerful and flexible thinkers, we have to master the paradox and create environments that offer challenge and strong support without smothering the very characteristics we seek to nurture.

THE SYNTAX OF INDUCTIVE PROCESS IN SUM

The accompanying summary chart outlines elements of the inductive model. The model has a relatively clear syntax, with the reactions of the teacher coordinated with the phases, a cooperative but (at first) teacher-centered social system, and support systems that require ample sources of raw ungrouped data. Their applicability is extremely wide, and the classroom teacher should consider a repertoire of basic inductive strategies such as these to be an essential tool.

SUMMARY CHART ► INDUCTIVE-THINKING MODEL

Syntax

Concept Formation
Enumeration and Listing
Grouping
Labeling, Categorizing

Interpretation of Data
Identifying Critical Relationships
Exploring Relationships
Making Inferences

Application of Principles
Predicting Consequences, Explaining Unfamiliar Phenomena,
    Hypothesizing
Explaining and/or Supporting the Predictions and Hypotheses
Verifying the Prediction

Social System

The model has high to moderate structure. It is cooperative, but the teacher is the initiator and controller of activities.

Principles of Reaction

Teacher matches tasks to students' level of cognitive activity, determines students' readiness.

Support System

Students need raw data to organize and analyze.

Instructional and Nurturant Effects

The inductive-thinking model (Figure 3.1) is designed to instruct students in concept formation and, simultaneously, to teach concepts. It nurtures attention to logic, to language and the meaning of words, and to the nature of knowledge.

4

ATTAINING CONCEPTS
Sharpening Basic
Thinking Skills

What that kid did made the point so everybody could hear it. Four times last
week he was in concept attainment lessons taught by the student teachers.
So he said we owed him one. If we'd get him some second-graders to teach,
he'd make a data set and teach the same kind of lesson. And he wanted to be
videotaped like the student teachers were. So we got him the kids and he
taught the lesson and he did a great job. So now everybody understands that
the whole point is to teach the kids the model, and practice will do it.

—Kay Vandergrift to Bruce Joyce, November 1969

S C E N A R I O

We happen on a classroom in Hong Kong. Dr. Ora Kwo is teaching a lesson on English to her students. She has a chart in the front of the room. We
will follow her as she leads her students through an exercise that employs
it. The headings on the chart are:

Positive Exemplars   Negative Exemplars

She puts the following two words under the headings on the chart:

clean   help

"Take a look at these two words. How are they alike and how are they different? *Clean* has the attributes of our category. *Help* does not." She places
cards containing two more words on the chart.

clear   trim

"Now examine this pair. *Clear* has the attributes we are concerned with.
Trim does not. What do *clear* and *clean* have in common that help and trim
do not?"

Dr. Kwo asks the students to work alone during this phase of the exercise. She presents two more words and asks the students to compare and contrast them, trying to discover what the positive exemplars have in common that they do not share with the negative exemplars.

clip   hip

"Now, what do you see? Please write down your hypothesis at this point. What attributes do you think the 'positive' words have in common that they do not share with the words I have identified as 'negative'?" After a few seconds, she proceeds to the next pair of words.

clap   lap

"Did any of you have to change your ideas?" She looks around the room and finds that several did. Then, in the same fashion, she presents several other pairs of words:

cling   ring
climb   limb
club   tree

Dr. Kwo continues until she has presented a dozen more pairs. Then she presents a word and asks the students whether they believe, on the basis of their hypothesis, that it is positive or negative.

lip

Of the students, 30 correctly identify the word as a negative exemplar. Six do not. She infers that the 30 were concentrating on the "cl," while the others were still not sure whether having either a "c" or an "l" would qualify it. Therefore, she presents the following series to them:

clue   flue
clarify   rarify
clack   lack

Then she asks the question again. "What do you think of this one?"

crack

All the students identify the word as negative. Thus, she presents the next one.

clank

They all identify it as positive. She proceeds to present them with a half dozen positive and negative exemplars and, when they can identify them correctly, asks them to share their current hypotheses. ("The positives begin with 'cl' and sound like [imagine the sound].") She has them identify what is not critical (meanings, endings, and so on) and then asks them how they would make negatives positive (transforming "an" to "clan" and so forth, until she is satisfied that the idea is clear). Dr. Kwo then sends them to scour a couple of stories, looking for positive exemplars, and gives them a list of words to classify on the basis of the attributes of the category.

We have, of course, looked in on a phonics lesson for students for whom English is a second language. The lesson is designed according to the concept attainment model of teaching and teaches concepts useful in both writing and spelling.

S C E N A R I O

Mrs. Stern's eighth-grade class in Houston, Texas, has been studying the characteristics of the 14 largest cities in the United States. The class members have collected data on size, population, ethnicity, types of industry, location, and proximity to natural resources.

Working in committees, the students have collected information and summarized it on a series of charts now pasted up around the room. One Wednesday in November, Mrs. Stern says, "Today let's try a series of exercises designed to help us understand these cities better. I have identified a number of concepts that help us compare and contrast them. I am going to label our charts either yes or no. If you look at the information we have and think about the populations and the other characteristics, you will identify the ideas that I have in mind. I'm going to start with a city that's a yes and then one that's a no, and so forth. Think about what the yeses have in common. Then write down after the second yes the idea that you think connects those two places, and keep testing those ideas as we go along." "Let's begin with our own city," she says. "Houston is a yes."

The students look at the information about Houston, its size, industries, location, ethnic composition. Then she points to Baltimore, Maryland. "Baltimore is a no," she says. Then she points to San Jose, California. "Here is another yes," she comments. The students look for a moment at the information about San Jose. Two or three raise their hands.

"I think I know what it is," one offers.

"Hold on to your idea," she replies. "See if you're right." She then selects another yes—Seattle, Washington; Detroit, Michigan, is a no. Miami, Florida, is a yes. She continues until all students think they know what the concept is, and then they begin to share concepts.

"What do you think it is, Jill?"

"The yeses all have mild climates," says Jill. "That is, it doesn't get very cold in any of them."

"It gets pretty cold in Salt Lake City," objects another.

"Yes, but not as cold as in Chicago, Detroit, or Baltimore," another student counters.

"I think the yeses are all rapidly growing cities. Each one of them increased more than 10 percent during the last 10 years." There is some discussion about this.

"All the yeses have lots of different industries," volunteers another.

"That's true, but almost all of these cities do," replies another student.

Finally the students decide the yeses are all cities that are growing very fast and have relatively mild climates.

"That's right," agrees Mrs. Stern. "That's exactly what I had in mind. Now let's do this again. This time I want to begin with Baltimore, Maryland, and now it is a yes."

The exercise is repeated several times. Students learn that Mrs. Stern has grouped the cities on the basis of their relationship to waterways, natural resources, ethnic composition, and several other dimensions.

The students are beginning to see patterns in their data. Finally she says, "Now, each of you try to group the cities in a way that you think is important. Then take turns and lead us through this exercise, helping us to see which ones you place in which category. Then we'll discuss the ways we can look at cities and how we can use different categories for different purposes. Finally, we'll use the inductive model and you can see how many relationships you can find."

In this scenario Mrs. Stern is teaching her students how to think about cities. At the same time she is teaching them about the process of categorizing. This is their introduction to the model of teaching we call concept attainment.

CATEGORIZING, CONCEPT FORMATION, AND CONCEPT ATTAINMENT

Concept attainment is "the search for and listing of attributes that can be used to distinguish exemplars from nonexemplars of various categories" (Bruner, Goodnow, and Austin, 1967, p. 233). Whereas *concept formation*, which is the basis of the inductive model described in the previous chapter, requires the students to decide the basis on which they will build categories, concept attainment requires a student to figure out the attributes of a category that is already formed in another person's mind by comparing and contrasting examples (called *exemplars*) that contain the characteristics (called *attributes*) of the concept with examples that do not contain those attributes. To create such lessons we need to have our category clearly in mind. As an example let us consider the concept *adjective*. Adjectives are words, so we select some words that are adjectives (these become the positive exemplars) and some that are not (these become "negative" exemplars—the ones that do not have the attributes of the category adjective). We present the words to the students in pairs. Consider the following four pairs:

triumphant	triumph
large	chair
broken	laugh
painful	pain

It is probably best to present the words in sentences to provide more information, because adjectives function in the context of a sentence. For example:

Yes: Our *triumphant* team returned home after winning the state championship.
No: After her *triumph*, Senator Jones gave a gracious speech.
Yes: The *broken* arm healed slowly.
No: His *laugh* filled the room.
Yes: The *large* truck backed slowly into the barn.
No: She sank gratefully into the *chair*.
Yes: The *painful* separation had to be endured.
No: He felt a sharp *pain* in his ankle.

To carry on the model, we need about 20 pairs in all—we would need more if the concept were more complex than our current example, *adjectives*.

We begin the process by asking the students to scrutinize the sentences and to pay particular attention to the underlined words. Then we instruct them to compare and contrast the functions of the positive and negative exemplars. "The positive exemplars have something in common in the work they do in the sentence. The negative exemplars do different work."

We ask the students to make notes about what they believe the exemplars have in common. Then we present more sets of exemplars and ask them whether they still have the same idea. If not, we ask what they now think. We continue to present exemplars until most of the students have an idea they think will withstand scrutiny. At that point we ask one of the students to share his or her idea and how he or she arrived at it. One possible response is as follows: "Well, at first I thought that the positive words were longer. Then some of the negatives were longer, so I gave that up. Now I think that the positive ones always come next to some other word and do something to it. I'm not sure just what."

Then other students share their ideas. We provide some more examples. Gradually the students agree that each positive exemplar adds something to the meaning of a word that stands for an object or a person, or qualifies it in some way.

We continue by providing some more sentences and by asking the students to identify the words that belong to our concept. When they can do that, we provide them with the name of the concept (*adjective*) and ask them to agree on a definition. The final activity is to ask the students to describe their thinking as they arrived at the concepts and to share how they used the information given.

For homework we ask the students to find adjectives in a short story we assign them to read. We will examine the exemplars they come up with to be sure that they have a clear picture of the concept.

This process ensures that the students learn the attributes that define a concept (the defining attributes) and can distinguish those from other important attributes that do not form the definition. All the words, for example, are composed of letters. But the presence of letters does not define the parts of speech. Letters are important characteristics of all items in the data set, but are not critical in defining the category we call *adjective*. The students learn that it is the function of the word that is the essence of the concept, not what it denotes. *Pain* and *painful* both refer to trauma, but only one is an adjective.

As we teach the students with this method, we help them become more efficient in attaining concepts. They learn the rules of the model. Let us look at another example, this time language study for beginning readers.

S C E N A R I O

Teacher: (Presents 6-year-old students with the following list of words labeled *yes* or *no*.)

fat	Yes
fate	No
mat	Yes
mate	No
rat	Yes
rate	No

I have a list of words here. Notice that some have yes by them and some have no by them. (The children observe and comment on the format. The teacher puts the list aside for a moment.) Now, I have an idea in my head, and I want you to try to guess what I'm thinking of. Remember the list I showed you. (Picks up the list.) This will help you guess my idea because each of these is a clue. The clues work this way. If a word has a yes by it (points to first word), then it is an example of what I'm thinking. If it has a no by it, then it is not an example.

(The teacher continues to work with the students so that they understand the procedures of the lesson and then turns over the task of working out the concept to them.)

Teacher: Can you come up with a name for my idea? Do you know what my idea is? (The students decide what they think the teacher's idea is. She continues the lesson.)

Teacher: Let's see if your idea is correct by testing it. I'll give you some examples, and you tell me if they are a yes or a no, based on your idea. (She gives them more examples. This time the students supply the nos and yeses.)

kite	No
cat	Yes
hat	Yes

Well, you seem to have it. Now think up some words you believe are yeses. The rest of us will tell you whether your example is right. You tell us if we guessed correctly.

(The exercise ends with the students generating their own examples and telling how they arrived at the concept.)

In this lesson if the children simply identified the concept as the /at/ vowel-consonant blend and correctly recognized *cat* and *hat* as a yes, they had attained the concept on a simple level. If they verbalized the distinguishing features (essential attributes) of the *at* sound, they attained the concept on a higher level. Bruner outlines these different levels of attainment: correctly distinguishing examples from nonexamples is easier than verbalizing the attributes of the concept. Students will probably be able to distinguish examples correctly before they will be able to explain verbally either the concept name or its essential characteristics.

Concept teaching provides a chance to analyze the students' thinking processes and to help them develop more effective strategies. The approach can involve various degrees of student participation and student control, and material of varying complexity.

RATIONALE

We have used terms such as *exemplar* and *attribute* to describe categorizing activity and concept attainment. Derived from Bruner's study of concepts and how people attain them, each term has a special meaning and function in all forms of conceptual learning, especially concept attainment.

EXEMPLARS

Essentially the exemplars are a subset of a collection of data or a data set. The category is the subset or collection of samples that share one or more characteristics that are missing in the others. It is by comparing the positive exemplars and contrasting them with the negative ones that the concept or category is learned.

ATTRIBUTES

All items of data have features, and we refer to these as *attributes*. Nations, for example, have areas with agreed-on boundaries, people, and governments that can deal with other nations. Cities have boundaries, people, and governments also, but they cannot independently deal with other countries. Distinguishing nations from cities depends on locating the attribute of international relations.

Essential attributes are attributes critical to the domain under consideration. Exemplars of a category have many other attributes that may not be relevant to the category itself. For example, nations also have trees and flowers, but these are not relevant to the definition of nation—although they, too, represent important domains and can be categorized and subcategorized as well. However, with respect to the category "nation," trees and flowers are not essential.

Another important definition is that of *attribute value*. This refers to the degree to which an attribute is present in any particular example. For instance, in any given situation, everyone has some rationality and irrationality mixed together. The question is when is there enough rationality that we can categorize someone as "rational" or enough irrationality that "irrational" is an appropriate description. For some types of concepts—triangle, for example—attribute values are not a consideration. For others, they are.

When creating a data set for instruction, it is wise to begin with exemplars where the value of the attribute is high, dealing with the more ambiguous ones after the concept has been well established. Thus, when classifying nations according to wealth, beginning with the very rich and the very poor makes it easier for the students. As we categorize things, we have to deal with the fact that some attributes are present to various degrees. We have to decide whether any amount of presence of an attribute is sufficient to place something in a particular category and what the range of density is that qualifies something to belong to a category. For example, consider the category *poisonous*. We put chlorine in water precisely because chlorine is poison. Yet we judge the amount that will kill certain bacteria and still not harm us. So tap water in a city is not an exemplar of poisonous water because it does not contain enough poison to harm us. But if we added enough chlorine, it would affect us. In this case, if the value of the attribute is low enough, its presence does not give the water membership in the category *poisonous to humans*.

Now consider the category *short person*. How short is short enough to be so categorized? People generally agree on a relative value, just as they do for tall. When is something cold? Hot? When is a person friendly? Hostile? These are all useful concepts, yet the categorization issue turns on matters of degree, or what we call *attribute value*.

In other cases, value is not a consideration. To be a telephone, an instrument simply must have certain characteristics. Yet there are degrees of quality. A question such as, "When is a sound machine a high-fidelity instrument?" puts us back into the consideration of attribute values.

Once a category is established, it is named so that we can refer to it symbolically. As the students name the categories, they should do so in terms of attributes. Thus, in the scenario at the very beginning of the chapter, they will describe the category as words beginning with "cl" and sounding like (imagine the sound of "cl" at the beginning of a word). Then, if there is a technical term (*adjective* in one of the other examples above), we supply it. However, the concept attainment process is not one of guessing names. It is to get the attributes of a category clear. Then the name can be created or supplied. Thus, the name is merely the term given to a category. *Fruit, dog, government, ghetto* are all names given to a class of experiences, objects, configurations, or processes. Although the items commonly grouped together in a single category may differ from one another in certain respects (dogs, for example, vary greatly), the common features cause them to be referred to by the same general term. Often we teach ideas that students already know intuitively without knowing the name itself. For instance, young children often put pictures of fruit together for the reason that they are "all things you can eat." They are using one characteristic to describe the concept instead of the name or label. If students know a concept, however, they can easily learn the name for it, and their verbal expressions will be more articulate. Part of knowing a concept is recognizing positive instances of it and also distinguishing closely related but negative examples. Just knowing terms will not suffice for this. Many people know the terms metaphor and simile but have never clarified the attributes of each well enough to tell them apart or apply them. One cannot knowingly employ metaphoric language without a clear understanding of its attributes.

Multiple attributes are another consideration. Concepts range from cases in which the mere presence of a single attribute is sufficient for membership in a category to those in which the presence of several attributes is necessary. Membership in the category *red-haired boys* requires the presence of maleness and red hair. *Intelligent, gregarious, athletic red-haired boys* is a concept that requires the presence of several attributes simultaneously. In literature, social studies, and science we deal with numerous concepts that are defined by the presence of multiple attributes, and sometimes attribute value is a consideration also. Consider the theatrical concept *romantic comedy*. A positive example must be a play or film, must have enough humor to qualify as a comedy, and must be romantic as well. Negative exemplars include plays that are neither funny nor romantic, are funny but not romantic, and are romantic but not funny.

To teach a concept, we have to be very clear about its defining attributes and about whether attribute values are a consideration. We must also select our negative exemplars so that items with some but not all the attributes can be ruled out.

We call concepts defined by the presence of one or more attributes conjunctive concepts. The exemplars are joined by the presence of one or more characteristics. Two other kinds of concepts need to be considered. Disjunctive concepts are defined by the presence of some attributes and the absence of others. Inert gases, for example, have the properties of all other gases but are missing the property of being able to combine with other elements. Bachelors, for instance, have the characteristics of other men, but are identified by an absence of something—a spouse. Lonely people are defined by an absence of companionship. Prime numbers are defined by the absence of a factor other than one and the number itself.

Finally, some concepts require connection between the exemplar and some other entity. Parasites, for example, have hosts, and the relationship between the parasite and its host is crucial to its definition. Many concepts of human relationships are of this type. There are no uncles without nephews and nieces, no husbands without wives, and no executives without organizations to lead.

STRATEGIES FOR CONCEPT ATTAINMENT ⎯⎯⎯⎯⎯⎯

What goes on in the minds of students when they are comparing and contrasting sets of exemplars? What kinds of hypotheses occur to them in the early stages and how do they modify and test them? To answer these questions, three factors are important to us. First, we can construct the concept attainment exercises so that we can study how our students think. Second, the students can not only describe how they attain concepts, but they can learn to be more efficient by altering their strategies and learning to use new ones. Third, by changing the way we present information and by modifying the model slightly, we can affect how students will process information.

The key to understanding the strategies students use to attain concepts is to analyze how they approach the information available in the exemplars. In particular, do they concentrate on just certain aspects of the information (*partistic strategies*), or do they keep all or most of the information in mind (*holistic strategies*)? To illustrate, suppose we are teaching concepts for analyzing literary style by comparing passages from novels and short stories. The first set of positive exemplars includes the following passage:

> A new country seems to follow a pattern. First come the openers, strong and brave and rather childlike. They can take care of themselves in a wilderness, but they are naive and helpless against men, and perhaps that is why they went out

in the first place. When the rough edges are worn off the new land, business-men and lawyers come in to help with the development—to solve problems of ownership, usually by removing the temptations to themselves. And finally comes culture, which is entertainment, relaxation, transport out of the pain of living. And culture can be on any level, and is. (Steinbeck, 1952, p. 249)

The students know that this passage will be grouped with the others to come, on the basis of one or more attributes pertaining to style.

Some students will concentrate on just one kind of attribute, say the use of declarative sentences or the juxtaposition of contrasting ideas about the opening of the frontier. Others will scan the details of the passage, noting the presence or absence of metaphors, the use of evocative language, the author's stance of being an observer of the human scene, and so on.

When comparing this passage with another positive one, a partist (someone who focuses on just one or two aspects of the use of language) will in some sense appear to have an easier task—just looking to see if the attribute present in the first is also present in the second, and so on. How-ever, if the student's focus does not work out, he or she must return to the earlier examples and scan them for something else on which to concentrate. A holist, on the other hand, has to keep many attributes in mind and has to eliminate nondefining elements one at a time. But the holistic strategy places the learner in a good position to identify multiple attribute concepts, and the loss of a single attribute is not as disruptive to the overall strategy.

There are two ways that we can obtain information about the way our students attain concepts. After a concept has been attained, we can ask them to recount their thinking as the exercise proceeded—by describing the ideas they came up with at each step, what attributes they were concen-trating on, and what modifications they had to make. ("Tell us what you thought at the beginning, why you thought so, and what changes you had to make.") This can lead to a discussion in which the students can discover one another's strategies and how they worked out.

Older students can write down their hypotheses, giving us (and them) a record we can analyze later. For example, in a study of the classification of plants conducted by Baveja, Showers, and Joyce (1985), students worked in pairs to formulate hypotheses as pairs of exemplars (one positive and one negative) were presented to them. They recorded their hypotheses, the changes they made, and the reasons they made them. The students who op-erated holistically, painstakingly generated multiple hypotheses and gradu-ally eliminated the untenable ones. The students who selected one or two hypotheses in the early stages needed to review the exemplars constantly and revise their ideas in order to arrive at the multiple-attribute concept that was the goal. By sharing their strategies and reflecting on them, the stu-dents were able to try new ones in subsequent lessons and to observe the ef-fect of the changes.

If we provide students with a large number of labeled exemplars (ones identified as positive and negative) to commence a lesson, they are able to scan the field of data and select a few hypotheses on which to operate. If we provide the exemplars pair by pair, however, the students are drawn toward holistic, multiple-attribute strategies.

Many people, on first encountering the concept attainment model, ask about the function of the negative exemplars. They wonder why we should not simply provide the positive ones. Negative exemplars are important because they help the students identify the boundaries of the concept. For example, consider the concept *impressionism* in painting. Impressionistic styles have much in common with other painting styles. It is important for students to "see" examples that have no traces of impressionism for them to be absolutely certain about the defining attributes. Likewise, to identify a group of words as a prepositional phrase, we need to be able to tell it from a clause. Only by comparing exemplars that contain and do not contain certain attributes can we identify the characteristics of the attributes precisely, and over time. The concept attainment model is designed to produce long-term learning. Having struggled our way, for example, to precise definitions of *prime number, element, developing nation, irony,* and so on, we should recognize members of their categories positively and surely when we encounter them in the future.

Tennyson and his associates (Tennyson and Cocchiarella, 1986) have conducted important research into concept learning and developed a number of models that can be used to improve instructional design. In the course of their explorations, they have dealt with a number of questions that can help us understand the model we are presenting in this chapter. They have compared treatments where students induce attributes and definitions, much as we have been describing the process with conditions where the definition is discussed before the list of exemplars is presented. In both cases the students developed clearer concepts and retained them longer when the examination of the exemplars *preceded* the discussion of attributes and definitions. Tennyson and Cocchiarella also discovered that the first positive exemplars presented should be the *clearest possible prototypes,* especially with multiple-attribute concepts. In other words, the teacher should not try to "fake out" the students with vague exemplars, but should take care to facilitate concept learning by arranging the data sets so that less-clear exemplars are dealt with in the phases where the principles are applied.

Tennyson and his associates also have concluded that students develop procedural knowledge (how to attain concepts) with practice, and also that the more procedural knowledge the students possess, the more effectively they attain and can apply conceptual knowledge. Thus, the analysis of thinking to facilitate learning the metacognitions of concept attainment appears to be very important.

The idea of learning concepts and then clarifying attributes and definitions runs counter to much current teaching practice. We have learned that some teachers, when first using concept attainment, have an urge to provide definitions and lists of attributes, and it is important to remember that the appropriate time for clarification is *after* the students have abstracted the concepts.

Data are presented to the students in the form of sets of items called *exemplars,* for instance, a set of poems. These are labeled "positive" if they have characteristics or attributes of the concept to be taught (for example, the sonnet form). The exemplars are labeled "negative" if they do not contain the attributes of the concept (for example, poems that do not have all the attributes of "sonnet").

By comparing the positive and negative exemplars, the students develop hypotheses about the nature of the category. They do not, however, share their hypotheses at this point. When most of the students have developed a hypothesis, some unlabeled exemplars are presented to them and they indicate whether they can successfully identify positive exemplars. They may be asked to produce some of their own (as by scanning a set of poems and picking out some positive and negative ones).

Then they are asked to share their hypotheses and describe the progression of their ideas during the process. When they have agreed on the hypotheses that appear most likely, they generate labels for them. Then the teacher supplies the technical label, if there is one (*sonnet,* for example).

To consolidate and apply the concept, the students then search for more items of the class (poems, in this case) and find which ones most closely match the concept they have learned.

THE MODEL OF TEACHING

The phases of the concept attainment model are outlined in Table 4.1.

SYNTAX

Phase one involves presenting data to the learner. Each unit of data is a separate example or nonexample of the concept. The units are presented in pairs. The data may be events, people, objects, stories, pictures, or any other discriminable units. The learners are informed that all the positive examples have one idea in common; their task is to develop a hypothesis about the nature of the concept. The instances are presented in a prearranged order and are labeled yes or no. Learners are asked to compare and justify the attributes of the different examples. (The teacher or students may want to maintain a record of the attributes.) Finally, learners are asked to name their concepts and state the rules or definitions of the concepts according to their essential attributes. (Their hypotheses are not confirmed until the next phase; students may not know the names of some concepts, but the names can be provided when the concepts are confirmed.)

In phase two, the students test their attainment of the concept, first by correctly identifying additional unlabeled examples of the concept and then by generating their own examples. After this, the teacher (and students)

TABLE 4.1   **SYNTAX OF THE CONCEPT ATTAINMENT MODEL**

Phase One: Presentation of Data and Identification of Concept	Phase Two: Testing Attainment of the Concept
Teacher presents labeled examples. Students compare attributes in positive and negative examples.	Students identify additional unlabeled examples as yes or no.
Students generate and test hypotheses.	Teacher confirms hypotheses, names concept, and restates definitions according to essential attributes.
Students state a definition according to the essential attributes.	Students generate examples.

Phase Three: Analysis of Thinking Strategies
Students describe thoughts. Students discuss role of hypotheses and attributes. Students discuss type and number of hypotheses.

confirm or disconfirm their original hypotheses, revising their choice of concepts or attributes as necessary.

In phase three, students begin to analyze the strategies by which they attain concepts. As we have indicated, some learners initially try broad constructs and gradually narrow the field; others begin with more discrete constructs. The learners can describe their patterns—whether they focused on attributes or concepts, whether they did so one at a time or several at once, and what happened when their hypotheses were not confirmed. Did they change strategies? Gradually, they can compare the effectiveness of different strategies.

SOCIAL SYSTEM

Prior to teaching with the concept attainment model, the teacher chooses the concept, selects and organizes the material into positive and negative examples, and sequences the examples. Most instructional materials, especially textbooks, are not designed in a way that corresponds to the nature of concept learning as described by educational psychologists. In most cases, teachers will have to prepare examples, extract ideas and materials from texts and other sources, and design them in such a way that the attributes are clear and that there are, indeed, both positive and negative examples of the concept. When using the concept attainment model, the teacher acts as a recorder, keeping track of the hypotheses (concepts) as they are mentioned and of the attributes. The teacher also supplies additional examples as needed. The three major functions of the teacher during concept attainment activity are to record, prompt (cue), and present additional data. In the initial stages of concept attainment, it is helpful for the examples to be very structured. However, cooperative learning procedures can also be used successfully (see Part III of this book).

PRINCIPLES OF REACTION

During the flow of the lesson, the teacher needs to be supportive of the students' hypotheses—emphasizing, however, that they are hypothetical in nature—and to create a dialogue in which students test their hypotheses against each others'. In the later phases of the model, the teacher must turn the students' attention toward analysis of their concepts and their thinking strategies, again being very supportive. The teacher should encourage analysis of the merits of various strategies rather than attempting to seek the one best strategy for all people in all situations.

SUPPORT SYSTEM

Concept attainment lessons require that positive and negative exemplars be presented to the students. It should be stressed that the students' job in concept attainment is not to invent new concepts, but to attain the ones that have previously been selected by the teacher. Hence, the data sources need to be known beforehand and the attributes visible. When students are presented with an example, they describe its characteristics (attributes), which can then be recorded.

APPLICATION

The use of the concept attainment model determines the shape of particular learning activities. For instance, if the emphasis is on acquiring a new concept, the teacher will emphasize through his or her questions or comments the attributes in each example (particularly the positive examples) and the concept label. If the emphasis is on the inductive process, the teacher might want to provide fewer clues and reinforce students for participating and persevering. The particular content (concept) may be less important than participating in the inductive process; it may even be a concept the students already know (as it was in Bruner's original experiments). If the emphasis is on the analysis of thinking, a short sample concept attainment exercise might be developed so that more time can be spent on the analysis of thinking.

The concept attainment model may be used with children of all ages and grade levels. We have seen teachers use the model very successfully with kindergarten children, who love the challenge of the inductive activity. For young children the concept and examples must be relatively simple, and the lesson itself must be short and heavily teacher-directed. The typical curriculum for young children is filled with concrete concepts that readily lend themselves to concept attainment methodology. The analysis-of-thinking phase of the strategy (phase three) is not possible with very young children, though most upper elementary students will be responsive to this kind of reflective activity.

When the model is used in early childhood education, the materials for examples are often available and require little transformation for their use as examples. Classroom objects, Cuisinaire rods, pictures, and shapes can be found in almost any early childhood classroom. Although helping children work inductively can be an important goal in itself, the teacher should also have more specific goals in mind in using this model.

As with all models, we encourage teachers to take the essence of this model and incorporate its features into their natural teaching styles and forms. In the case of concept attainment, it is relatively easy (and intellectually powerful) to incorporate Bruner's ideas about the nature of concepts into instructional presentations and assessment activities. We have seen our own students make these ideas a natural part of their concept teaching.

The concept attainment model is an excellent evaluation tool when teachers want to determine whether important ideas introduced earlier have been mastered. It quickly reveals the depth of students' understanding and reinforces their previous knowledge.

The model can also be useful in opening up a new conceptual area by initiating a sequence of individual or group inquiries. For example, a unit exploring the concept of culture could begin with a series of concept attainment lessons followed by a simulation activity, in which students experience the problems that persons of one culture have when they are first introduced to members of a different culture. From this experience, students would be prepared to read about different cultures.

Thus, the concept attainment model can not only introduce extended series of inquiries into important areas, but it can also augment ongoing inductive study. Concept attainment lessons providing important concepts in social studies units—concepts such as *democracy, socialism, capitalism,* and *due process*—can be interjected periodically into units that otherwise depend on student reading and reporting. If a concept is controversial, the teacher can present several interpretations of it, which the students can then debate. Debates are usually great motivators for further inquiry into any subject matter in question.

INSTRUCTIONAL AND NURTURANT EFFECTS

The concept attainment strategies can accomplish several instructional goals depending on the emphasis of the particular lesson. They are designed for instruction on specific concepts and on the nature of concepts. They also provide practice in inductive reasoning and opportunities for altering and improving students' concept-building strategies. Finally, especially with abstract concepts, the strategies nurture an awareness of alternative perspectives, a sensitivity to logical reasoning in communication, and a tolerance of ambiguity (see Figure 4.1).

Robert Gagné's 1965 article thoroughly discusses a similar approach to concept attainment. Merrill and Tennyson (1977) describe a similar approach without, however, an extensive analysis of the thinking processes. McKinney, Warren, Larkins, Ford, and Davis (1983) have reported a series of interesting studies comparing the Merrill/Tennyson approaches with Gagné's and a recitation procedure. Their work illustrates the complexity of designing studies to meaningfully compare sets of models built on the same premises but differing in details of execution. However, the differences in approach and the research to build better models are probably of less

FIGURE 4.1   Instructional and nurturant effects of the concept attainment model.

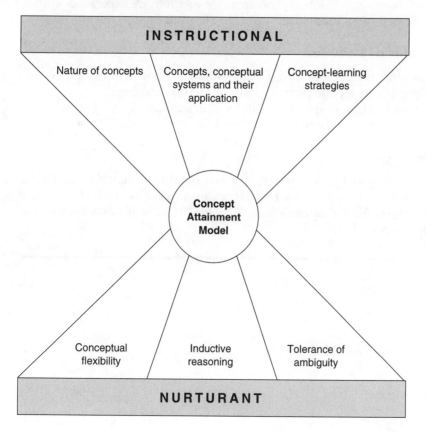

importance to teachers than the fact that there are models that do a good job of teaching concepts—ones more powerful than the way concepts have traditionally been taught—and therefore represent useful additions to the teaching/learning repertoire. The model we have been discussing is one of them.

SUMMARY CHART ▶

THE CONCEPT ATTAINMENT MODEL

Syntax

The syntax proceeds from presentation of the exemplars to testing and naming concepts to application.

Social System

The model has moderate structure. The teacher controls the sequence, but open dialogue occurs in the latter phases. Student interaction is encouraged. The model is relatively structured, with students assuming more initiative for inductive process as they gain more experience (other concept attainment models are lower in structure).

Principles of Reaction

1. Give support but emphasize the hypothetical nature of the discussion.
2. Help students balance one hypothesis against another.
3. Focus attention on specific features of examples.
4. Assist students in discussing and evaluating their thinking strategies.

Support System

Support consists of carefully selected and organized materials and data in the form of discrete units to serve as examples. As students become more sophisticated, they can share in making data units, just as in phase two they generate examples.

CHAPTER 5

THE PICTURE-WORD INDUCTIVE MODEL
Developing Literacy across the Curriculum

> *It's inquiry, INQUIRY, INQUIRY! Do I sound like a broken record?*
> *We must have students inquire into how language works.*
> *Thelen was right! It's inquiry, not activity!*
> —Emily Calhoun to Bruce Joyce, for the thousandth time

S C E N A R I O

We are in Lisa Mueller's first grade class. This narrative is taken from Lisa's log which describes a picture-word inductive model (PWIM) cycle in which her 23 students were engaged for 22 sessions, each 50 minutes long, during the second month of school, October 2–30.

The picture shows a marketplace in Kuala Lampur. At the beginning of the cycle, she asks the students to study the picture and take turns identifying items and actions. ("You have had a couple of days to look at the picture and identify things in it and things that are going on. Let's take turns putting words to some of the things you have found.") As each item is named, Lisa draws a line from the word to a place on the background paper where she prints it, spells it, and then has the students spell it and say it. The students review the words frequently, spelling them, saying them, and tracing the line from the word to the picture, learning how to use the chart as a picture dictionary. During the first session, 24 words (such as *banana, car, boy, flowers*) are shaken out of the picture.

These words are entered into the computer and printed out on cards, a set of which is given to each child. Three activities alternate during the next few days. First is a review of the words as a class: looking at the PWIM chart, selecting a word, tracing it to the element in the picture to which it refers, spelling the word, and so on to another word. ("Look at your cards, one by one. If you can say the word on a card, then look at the picture chart,

A common scene in Koala Lampur. Note how much is common to a North American scene.

find the word, trace it to the picture, and make sure you are right.") Second, each student looks at the cards, decides whether he or she recognizes the word correctly, and, if not, goes to the PWIM chart to figure it out. Third, each student classifies the words, manipulating his or her cards into groups containing common attributes. ("Look carefully at the words. Then make groups of ones that have something in common.") During classification, several categories of word families emerged, particularly words with common endings. Singulars and plurals also emerged (such as *car* and *cars*). Lisa prints some of those categories on large cards, and the students discuss what the words have in common and think of other words that might fit into the categories. An additional 16 words appear (among them are *to*, *two*, and *too*; *slight*, *might*, *tight*, and *night*).

At the beginning of the second week of the PWIM cycle, the children are asked to generate titles for the pictures. ("I'm going to show you some other pictures and titles I've made for them. Then I want you to make up a title for our picture. Try to make a title that would help a visitor find our picture from among the other pictures in the room.") Lisa models some sample titles and asks the students to examine the titles of several books as further models. Each student creates a title, and each title is printed on newsprint. Fourteen words are added to the list, and more families of words are discovered (*parking*, *carrying*, *watching*) as the students continue to study and classify their words. Throughout the second week, the children continue to study the words, using the picture-word dictionary and classifying the words on their word cards.

Kayla Nowicki explains her categories to Lisa Mueller in the Northern Lights, Alberta, school division.

At the end of the second week, Lisa and her teaching assistant, Cecile, check the students' knowledge of the words out of the context of the picture, the titles, and the sentences by presenting the words to the students on cards that show only one word. Nine students could correctly read 11 to 17 of the words and seven could read between 8 and 10. Six students correctly identified only 1 to 7 at the end of the second week.

At the beginning of the third week, Lisa presents a series of sentences she has written about the picture, modeling several sentence structures (such as, "We found a _____ in the picture.") During the week the students dictate their own sentences, using the words they shook out of the picture plus other words that are needed to make sentences (such as *the*). Altogether, 16 more words were identified as the sentences were dictated by the children. Many of these were "little useful words," such as *is, are, by,* and *from*.

The students continue to study the words and read the sentences. At the end of the week Lisa and Cecile test the recognition of the words again. During that week there was a considerable gain in words recognized; most students were able to read 20 or more. Only one student did not gain. Most students were able to read the titles and sentences without assistance.

During the last week, Lisa selected one of the titles and constructed a paragraph using modifications of the sentences the students had created. The paragraph was printed on a card program, making a booklet the students could take home and read to their parents.

Speaking of reading, the school participates in the school division's Just Read program (see Joyce and Showers, 2002). Each week this first grade class records the number of books that have been read to them, or that, as they learn to read, they read themselves. The goal is for the parents to read at least five books each week to their children. The average by the last three weeks in October was six books, but there was variance; in any given week two or three parents did not report any books or reported only one. However, the least number during the three-week period was three books—all students were being read to at least occasionally. There was no gender difference.

During the 2000–2001 school year, Lisa conducted several studies, including sight word acquisition and retention, an analysis of the degree to which high frequency words were included in the body of words, the development of phonetic and structural analysis skills, books read independently, and reading levels attained.

SIGHT WORDS

Altogether the students encountered 1,029 words during the year, aside from the words encountered by individuals in their reading. Of these, 377 words came from the initial weeks of the PWIM cycles. Retention of those words was assessed in May and again in September. On average, the students recognized 91 percent of the words in out-of-context assessments in May and September. The lowest student retained 59 percent.

SIGHT WORDS AS HIGH FREQUENCY WORDS

Lisa tested the students' recognition of the Dolch lists of the high frequency words appearing in typical books through grade three. On average, the students recognized 87 percent of the words, with a range of 49 to 100 percent. Fifteen of the 22 students recognized 90 percent of the words or more. This finding has importance because this curriculum does not introduce the sight words systematically according to predetermined lists. Despite that, the high frequency words appear regularly, which is logical, and these first grade students appear to be learning them at a good rate.

SKILL IN PHONICS

Again, this curriculum does not introduce phonetic skills one-by-one in a predetermined manner. The students analyze words and develop phonics concepts inductively or are led by the teacher to explore beginning and ending sounds and structural properties of words as words containing those attributes are encountered. In May, Lisa administered the Names Test to the students. (In the test, the students try to decode unfamiliar words that, among them, contain all the basic combinations). A perfect score on the test indicates that all basic letter–sound relationships have been used correctly when decoding the words. The average score was 81 percent. The lowest was 62 percent. Four students scored 95 percent or better. This picture is considerably better than the typical performance of first-grade classes assessed in this manner.

BOOKS READ DURING THE YEAR (MOST INDEPENDENTLY)

The number ranged from 60 (about two per week) to 300 or more. The average number of books read was about 200.

LEVELS OF READING ACHIEVED

By the end of the year, 22 students who had been enrolled throughout the year were administered the Alberta Diagnostic test, which provided estimates of reading achievement in terms of grade levels. Twelve of the students were well above the "ending grade 1" level. Two were at the mid-grade 6 level, three at mid-grade 4, six at beginning grade 3, and two at the end of grade 2. Six scored at ending grade 1 or beginning grade 2, and three at the mid-grade 1 level. The average was a little above the ending grade 2 level, where typical exiting grade 2 students score.

RATIONALE

Whereas many models of teaching have relatively long histories that have been refined through several "generations" of developers, there are only a handful of powerful new models that we consider for inclusion in *Models of Teaching* as we prepare each edition. The picture-word inductive model is a very interesting addition and is unusual for the breadth of its grounding and the width of its applications.

The grounding is in research in the field of literacy—how students develop literacy in general (particularly how they learn to read and write), *and* literacy in all curriculum areas, and cognitive development. The development of metacognitive control is central—learning how to learn is built in to the process. Emily Calhoun developed the model over a twenty year period and, as you will see, its applications have enabled students to increase their achievement substantially.

Central is the nature of student learning as students construct knowledge about printed language (phonetic and structural analysis) and develop the skills of extracting and organizing information in all curriculum areas. In some senses, this is the ultimate constructionist model because general literacy is the base on which curriculum-relevant literacy is developed.

To become an expert reader, people need to read a lot, develop large sight vocabularies, develop skill in phonetic and structural analysis, and learn to comprehend and use extended text. All these are essential as students learn to understand text across the curriculum areas, where the gathering, conceptualization, and application of information is at the core of achievement.

Let's begin with a series of propositions derived from studies of how students become literate.

First, children learn to listen and speak the languages spoken to them in a most natural way. In an Arabic speaking household, they would learn to hear and reproduce Arabic, and they would learn French in a French household. In homes where large vocabularies and complex syntaxes are used, they develop large vocabularies and complex syntaxes. Importantly, the process is *natural*.

Second, inductive thinking is built into our brains, as described in Chapter 3. Children classify from birth, sorting out the world. They are natural conceptualizers.

Third, children seek meaning. They want to understand their worlds by organizing what they perceive, and they reach toward language as a source of meaning.

Fourth, interaction with adults and peers is the natural avenue to socialization. Interaction through reading is an important part of socialization as the young reader encounters information and ideas. The depth of socialization is enormously affected by literacy. Nonreaders have a serious disadvantage in learning the culture and a serious deprivation of the pleasure that accompanies learning through interaction with authors.

All this is not to assert that reading and writing are natural biological processes, but to say that the natural ways children approach the learning of language might be capitalized on. A challenge for us is to design curriculums that will take advantage of these natural abilities so as to make the learning of reading and writing an extension of what our children are born to do.

The picture-word inductive model was designed to meet the challenge, and its conceptual underpinnings drew on the body of research about how literacy is acquired and on the bodies of research underlying several of the models of learning we have been describing in the previous chapters.

Although the model is useful in social studies and science, the concentration here will be on its application to the reading/writing curriculum in the early years of schooling. In Chapter 19, we will discuss its use as a dimension of a successful curriculum for older students who have not responded well to the prevailing curriculums in the language arts.

The model (Calhoun, 1999; Joyce and Calhoun, 1998) was designed to be a major component of language arts curriculums for primary-level beginning readers and older beginning- or early-stage readers. It resides within the information-processing family because much of the pedagogical focus is on structuring lessons so that students inquire into language and form and use generalizations about how letters, words, phrases, sentences, and longer text work to support communication within the English language arts. Based on several lines of research on instructional strategies and on promoting growth in reading and writing, the model also contains a number of tools to help teachers study students' progress as they come into literacy. In fact, using the picture-word inductive model effectively requires an action research frame of reference because you don't just adopt or buy into PWIM, you inquire into its theory and rationale, its structure, and its effects on your students.

SOURCES

As indicated previously, when Calhoun developed the model she drew on the basic and applied research on how children become literate (children's development of language, the process of learning to read and write, and the reading-writing connection) and the studies of several of the models of teaching, synthesizing these and adding to them her insights from her experience teaching students to read and write. This complex base differs somewhat from the bases under several models where specialists in one form of teaching and learning elaborated that base rather than synthesizing from a broader spectrum of lines of inquiry. Because the original concept of using pictures as a stimulus for language experience activities in the classroom was developed for application in the language arts, specifically for teaching young beginning readers to read and write (see, for example, Adams, Johnson, and Connors, 1980), we will approach the rationale first from the point of early literacy curriculum.

CHILDREN'S DEVELOPMENT OF LANGUAGE

The first source is children's natural acquisition of language. By the time most children in developed countries are five years old, they are able to listen to and speak between four- and six-thousand words with understanding, and have developed the basic syntactical structure of the language (Chall, 1983; Clark and Clark, 1977). They can listen with understanding to

Tracy Poirier leads the students in shaking out words in the picture at another Northern Lights School.

complex sentences and longer communications. They produce sentences that include prepositions and conjunctions and make causal connections like "If we go to the store now, we could watch *Thomas* when we get back." They gobble up words, play with them, and have conversations with stuffed animals and dolls—composing ideas and manipulating words very much like they will later when they write. Children's natural acquisition of language is one of the most exciting inductions into their culture and brings with it a great sense of personal power and satisfaction as these young learners receive communications and learn to put ideas into words.

In the structure of the picture-word inductive model, young children are presented with pictures of relatively familiar scenes. They "shake out" the words from the picture by identifying objects, actions, and qualities they recognize. A line is drawn from the object out to the chart paper, where the word or phrase is written, thus connecting the items they identified to words already in their naturally-developed listening/speaking vocabularies.

These connections between the items and actions in the picture and the children's language enable them to transition naturally from spoken (listened to and spoken) language to written (read and written) language. They see these transformations. They watch the words being spelled and spell them with the teacher. They connect something in the picture with a word and then watch that word appear in print. They can now read that word. Shortly, they learn that we always spell that word the same way. They identify a dog in the picture, see *dog* written, hear it spelled, spell it themselves, and on the way home from school they see a lost dog sign on the street corner and read *dog*.

Thus, a major principle of the model is to build on children's growing storehouse of words and syntactic forms and facilitate the transition to print. Most children want to "make sense" of the language around them, and they will engage with us eagerly in unlocking its mysteries. A corollary principle is that the approach respects the children's language development: their words are used and their ability to make connections is central. Mnemonic principles, especially the development of rich associations to generate long-term retention, are explicitly capitalized on as the vocabulary is developed.

THE PROCESS OF LEARNING TO READ AND WRITE

Much remains to be learned about the almost magical process whereby children make connections between their naturally developing language and the world of print, surely a cognitive marvel. Our understanding at this time is that several types of learning need to be accomplished as reading and writing develop.

To learn to read and write, children need to build a substantial "sight" vocabulary, that is, a storehouse of words they can recognize instantly by their spellings. About 400 to 500 words are necessary to bring children to the stage where picture storybooks are available to them, although, as we will see, even 100 to 150 words bring very simple books like *Go, Dog, Go*

(Eastman, 1961) and *Ten in the Bed* (Dale, 1988) within reach. Also, once students have about 50 sight words, their study of phonics is greatly facilitated, as are many other aspects of learning, including the development of more vocabulary (Graves, Watts, and Graves, 1994).

The picture-word inductive model approaches this development of sight vocabulary directly. First, the students read and spell the words as they are shaken out of the picture. Then, these words are placed on large vocabulary cards that they can look at and the teacher can use for group instruction. Students also get their own set of smaller vocabulary cards. They sort these words and consult the picture dictionary to check their understanding and refresh the meaning of the words. The students keep their word cards in "word banks" or word boxes, consulting them as they wish and eventually arranging them to compose sentences.

Today, it is again recognized that the development of sight vocabulary is an essential channel to literacy (Ehri, 1999). PWIM addresses this development as well as the problem of retention of words and how to move them into long-term memory and make them available for the study of how the English language alphabet works.

In order to learn to read and write, children must also build concepts about the conventions used in language to connect sounds and structures to print forms. With respect to sound/print (*phonetic*) forms (often called *sound/symbol* or *letter/sound* relationships), children need to learn that nearly all the words that begin with a particular sound begin with particular letters representing those sounds. Periodically, a teacher using PWIM will ask students to pull out all the words they have in their word bank that contain the letter *b* and they will concentrate on that letter for a while. Another time, all the words with *at* will get attention. After the students have learned to read most of the words on the picture chart, the teacher may ask them to pull out all the words in which they can hear an *s* sound.

With respect to the structure of words, students need to build an understanding of inflection, the change in form that words undergo to indicate number, gender, person, tense, case, mood, and voice. While it may seem impossible to believe, these structural conventions that have developed over time do eventually result in more rapid and accurate communication of their ideas. Students notice the similarities and differences between singular and plural words (as in how *book* and *books* are alike and different).

The picture-word inductive model induces students to classify their new words, building the concepts that will enable them to unlock words they have not seen before. The English language has about 44 sounds represented in more than 200 forms—some say as many as 250 forms (Morris, 1997)—because some sounds have multiple representations (*shut, nation*). As students work with their words, they will develop many categories: these words all begin like *boy,* these all have two d's in the middle like *ladder.* They will develop phonograms or rhyming families (*bat, cat, hat*) that they will use to read and spell words they have not memorized previously (*mat*). And, they will learn that the generalizations they make will enable them to un-lock about 70 percent of the new words they encounter.

Students will be amused at some of the ways we spell words (*ate*, *eight*), and, like the rest of us before them, they will sigh occasionally at our insistence that they learn the peculiarities our language has developed. They will be perplexed by *see* and *sea* and will want to know why we made them sound alike. At times, all we can say is what some of our teachers said to us: "You'll just have to memorize them."

In summary, the picture-word inductive model capitalizes on children's ability to think inductively. It enables them to build generalizations that form the basis of structural and phonetic analysis. And, it respects their ability to think. Thus, a major principle of the model is that students have the capability to make those generalizations that reveal to them the conventions of language.

THE READING/WRITING CONNECTION

As the students mine a picture for words, those words are spelled correctly by the teacher and written on the picture dictionary, which launches the students into the early stages of formal writing. Later the students will be asked to make up sentences about the picture, and with the help of the teacher, they begin to write longer pieces. Through much repetition, the words in the sentences are added to their storehouse of knowledge, and maybe even physically added to their word banks. Gradually, as they read more and more trade books, the students learn to analyze how other authors write, and they use the devices of these authors to enhance their ability to express themselves. Essentially, they come to use our great literature and prose base (the library of the world) as a model for learning even more about writing to share and communicate ideas. As they read more picture storybooks and short informative books, they will discuss them and make up sentences about the book they are reading or have just read. Many will come to feel that the reading of a book is not complete until they have said something about it in their own words, completing the communication loop between the writer and the reader in constructing meaning.

From kindergarten on, students and teachers work together building words and sentences and paragraphs and books. As they build paragraphs, they will select and discuss titles. The teacher will lead metacognitive discussions on why one title is chosen over another, talking to the students about which title is most comprehensive, which title might be most interesting to one audience or another, which sentences would go with one title, which with another. When writing a paragraph or creating a title, the teacher will help students focus on the essence of communication: what do we want to say to our readers, to ourselves? The students will use the reading/writing connection as the teacher has them think about what they want to share, what they most want the reader to know, how they will help the reader "get" this information, and, finally, to assess whether we shared what we wished.

The teacher will continue to work on this link until it becomes explicit and accessible for their use as independent learners.

Thus, another major principle at work in the picture-word inductive model is that reading and writing are naturally connected and can be learned simultaneously, and later can be used together to advance one's growth in language use rapidly and powerfully. Relational concepts are critical. If singular nouns are connected to singular verbs in speech, so should they be connected when writing. If authors write titles that promise readers particular content and approach to content, beginning writers learn to promise readers content and approach as they shape titles.

STRUCTURE

Each cycle of the picture-word inductive model uses a large photograph as a common stimulus for the generation of words and sentences. The teacher, working with the whole class or with small groups of students, uses the moves that comprise a PWIM cycle to support students' building vocabulary: forming and using phonetic and structural analysis generalizations; reading comprehension at the word, phrase, sentence, paragraph, and extended text levels; composing at the word, sentence, paragraph, and extended text levels; and observing and verifying data using reference sources.

MOVES OF THE MODEL

The picture-word inductive model structures cycles of inquiry by students, generally lasting two to six weeks. The sequence of lessons in a PWIM cycle begins with a picture, usually a photograph, for which the contents (both the central elements and details) include many things that students can describe using their developed listening-speaking language. The students study the picture and then *shake out* the words. This means that the students identify things they see in the picture, and the teacher draws a line from those things to a place outside the picture, reiterates the word, and writes and spells the word or phrase aloud. The students repeat the word and its spelling. What emerges is an illustrated picture-word dictionary. (See the photograph on page 88.)

The next phase of PWIM involves providing students with their individual sets of word cards. The students check whether they can recognize words immediately or decode them if necessary, using the picture-word dictionary if they have difficulty. It's easy to assess students' knowledge and skills as the teacher moves around among the students. As students begin to read the words, the next phase of the model comes into play: students classify the words in terms of phonetic, structural, or content properties and share their categories and why they put a particular set of words together. The categorization activity occurs several times during the PWIM cycle.

Dallas Fulk shows Lisa
Mueller how he can use
the picture dictionary.

The pace of lessons during a picture-word cycle depends on the reading level of the students and the curriculum objectives of the teacher, but after the classification of words, students are asked to generate factual sentences about the picture. New words from the sentences may be added to students' vocabulary banks, and the categorization activity can be repeated, maybe several times. As soon as students begin to read the sentences, they are asked to classify them (however they wish, by content or common patterns of syntax or structure) into groups and provide reasons for their classifications.

Next, the teacher selects one of the students' sentence categories (content) and models writing a well-organized paragraph, sharing her thinking about how she used the ideas in the sentences and modified the structures, if needed, to form the message about the picture that she wished to share with her readers. In whatever way is appropriate to the developmental level of the students (e.g., a combination of drawing and writing, pieces dictated to an older student buddy), students are asked to use other categories and generate their own paragraphs. The PWIM cycle ends anytime after the paragraph development.

S C E N A R I O

We drop in on Nancy Werner and her second grade class during the third week of school. Nancy has 22 students, eight of whom entered school with limited English proficiency. This is the students' second picture-word inductive model unit, and Nancy is still teaching them the moves of the model.

The first grade in Hempsill Hill school in Nottingham, England, responds to the picture-word model. In turn, they become a picture used in the United States and Canada.

Pinned to the bulletin board and centered in the middle of two large strips of light-blue paper is a 24 × 30 inch picture of a classroom where a group of children is gathered.

Nancy gathers the students in front of the picture. As they seat themselves on the rug, she says, "Make sure you have your personal space around you and that you can see the picture." She takes a minute to help students adjust their spaces. "We're going to work with this picture for the next few days, just like we did with the picture of the school. We'll shake a lot of words out, learn to read and spell those words, and maybe we'll write about the picture so we can practice our writing. Now, be ready to tell us something you recognize in the picture."

Nancy waits about a minute until most hands are up and calls on Dylan. "What's something you see in this picture?"

Dylan points to a necktie one of the children in the picture is wearing and says, "That's a necktie."

Nancy draws a line from the necktie to a spot on the paper and says "Necktie. Now, I want you to listen while I spell *necktie* first and then we'll spell it together so that you get lots of practice on your spelling." The children listen while Nancy says, "n-e-c-k-t-i-e," writing the letters as she says them. Then again, "n-e-c-k-t-i-e spells *necktie*. Now, all together."

The children chorus the spelling as the teacher points to each letter. "Now, that spells...?"

"Necktie!"

Nancy next calls on Marianna. Marianna points to a piece of tape in the picture and says, "tape." The teacher draws a line from the piece of tape to the paper and says, "Now, let's learn how to spell *tape*." She spells it, then has the students spell it as she points to each letter and says "Now, t-a-p-e spells . . . ?"

"Tape," the children say, almost in unison.

For the next 20 minutes, the group continues to shake words out of the picture. *Gold letters, books, whiteboard,* and *children* are quickly identified. Each time, the teacher spells the word and pronounces it again, and the children spell and pronounce it. As in their first unit, they are building a picture dictionary.

"T-shirt" is volunteered and Nancy spells it *tee shirt*. Harry bursts out with, "That's not T-shirt. It's spelled with a big T!" She adds *T-shirt* to the chart as well. She has students read both versions, but they only spell *shirt* with her. She says, "I'll have to check and see if both spellings are correct. See what you can find out too." Altogether, about 25 words appear.

Nancy reviews all the words with the children, then leads them into a discussion of the picture. "Now, several of you asked me where these children are. Where do *you* think they are?" She calls on Marta.

"School."

"How many of you agree with Marta? And what makes you think they are in school?"

"Well, it could be a family, but there are too many children."

One student asks, "Why are they all wearing red?" Nancy has them speculate for a while and ideas like "special class" and "their school makes them do it" surface.

Robert suggests that it's probably a school because there's a whiteboard, and most houses don't have whiteboards.

Francesca suggests that the presence of a big library corner makes it more likely that the picture is of a group of students at school.

Paul says it can't be a home because there are too many books. Anna adds, "And homes don't have bookcases." There's some discussion about this.

Finally, Nancy confirms that it is a school, that in this school students wear uniforms, that the school is in Nottingham, England, and that these are five-year-old students. She pulls the map down and asks Sarah to come up and put her hand on Nottingham.

"Tomorrow we'll continue with our picture. When you have a little time today, practice reading our words. If you have trouble reading a word, what do you do?"

"Trace the line to the picture," they chorus.

The next day the students gather around the picture at 9 A.M. and Nancy announces, "We're going to work on silent reading before I give you your set of new word cards." She points to a word and about half the children read it aloud. She says, "Let's all read it again . . . silently. Don't let any letter sounds or words escape your mouth. Here we go, just practice reading it in your mind." She points to a word, holding her hand against her lips. Everyone is silent. She traces the line, "Now, aloud."

And the process continues, with Nancy pointing to words, the students reading them silently; then she traces the line so they can check their reading, and they read the word aloud. Then she gives them their envelopes with the words from yesterday's work and says, "For the next 15 minutes I want everyone to work individually on reading your set of words. Use the picture chart when you need to."

They begin the third lesson the next morning with a quick review of the chart. After all the words are read, Nancy takes a number of pattern blocks in her hand and begins to prepare students for the process of classification. She picks up a yellow plastic bucket and shakes it. "What's this?" They respond: "Our math bucket." "Our pattern blocks." "Our shapes." Then she says, "I'm going to select some pattern blocks from this bucket. I'm going to sort out some and put them together. I want you to think about why I put them together. See if you can come up with at least two reasons." She pulls out five pattern blocks and holds them so students can see them. Then she calls on Kyrinas, who says, "You put them together because they're all red."

"How many of you agree with Kyrinas that these are all red?" Hands go up. "Does anyone have another reason?" Scott volunteers that they each have four sides. Again, Nancy asks who agrees. They all do. Serena then volunteers, "You put them together because they are red, have four sides, and are square." Nancy says, "Serena just gave us three reasons why I might have put these pattern blocks together. Who agrees with all three reasons?" Some students who saw only one attribute come to recognize that Nancy made her category one in which the objects have several attributes in common.

She says, "Now, let's switch to words. I want you to learn to study words carefully and put them together in groups based on how they are spelled or on what they mean." She places three word cards in the large pocket chart with the words turned away from the students. "I want you to do the same kind of detective work with these words that you just did with our pattern blocks." She turns the cards over. "Everyone read them silently." Then she demonstrates checking your reading by taking each card and placing it under the matching word on the chart and running her finger down the line to the item(s).

purple
person
pictures

"Now, why do you think I might have put these words together?"

She calls on Marloes, who shyly ventures that the reason is all three words begin with the letter *p*."

"Who agrees? These three words begin with the letter *p*." Nancy pauses for the students to study the words for a few seconds.

"Now, let's read the words together and see if you can come up with another reason why I might have put them together." They read them, first silently, then aloud, as she points to them. "Now, I am going to read them aloud and you listen. See if you can think of another reason. You were right; one reason was they all begin with the letter *p*."

She pronounces *purple, person,* and *pictures* carefully and several hands go up. She calls on Annelle.

"They all have *e* in them."

"That's correct. What else can you discover? Read them silently and think about them. Jueron?"

"Person and purple sound alike at the beginning, but they have different letters."

"Good thinking, Jueron. The *r* often works like that when it follows vowels. Here it makes the *er* and *ur* sound alike at the beginning of *person* and *purple*.

"Can you think of anything else?" Nancy calls on Christina.

"It's like they're two words."

"Say more about that, Christina. What do you mean when you say 'it's like they're two words'?"

"You know, like two parts, two pieces."

Nancy says, "Everyone listen carefully," and she pronounces the three words, slightly emphasizing the two syllables. "Good thinking. You discovered both reasons I put those words together: they all begin with *p* and they all have two parts or *syllables*. Would the word *paper* (writing it on the board as she says it) fit in this group?" The students assure her it would. "How about *pen*?" she asks as she writes it. There is some disagreement about whether *pen* would belong, so Nancy uses the difference between *pen* and *pencil* for a little more practice.

"Good detective work. Today, I want you to sort the words in your envelope any way you want to, and be prepared to share your groups and tell us why you put the words together." She passes out the envelopes, helps the students spread out, and they get to work. Nancy circulates, observing the groups being formed, checking to be sure the students can read the words, sending some students to the chart to check their reading, and asking students to tell her why they put words together.

Lots of categories emerge. As would be expected, many students have similar groups; however, there is much variety in what they "see" in the words and what they can articulate. Some students attend more to letters and sounds, some to the meanings of words, and some to a combination. Here are a few of their categories and the reasons expressed by the students:

- *book, boy, board* ("all begin with *b*"; "all have the same two first letters")
- *picture, people, person* ("all have *p*'s"; "all have *p*'s at the beginning"; "all haves *p*'s as the first letter and two parts"; "all have *p*'s at the beginning and they all have *e*'s")
- *girl, boy, child, children, people, person* ("They are all humans." "They are all names for people when we don't know their names." "They are all people.")

- *black book, yellow book, blue book* ("They all have *book*." "All have the color of the book." "They all have *book*, and they all have two *o*'s.")

Nancy ends this lesson by commenting on several categories then uses her large word cards to share the category with *book, board,* and *boy*. They discuss initial *b* sound and the varying sounds of *oo, oa,* and *oy*. Homework is to see if they can find at least six words that begin with the two letters *bo*, list them on a piece of paper, and drop them in the picture-word box in the morning.

On Thursday, they begin with a quick review of the words and add a few new words to the picture-word chart. Then Nancy selects some of the words from the homework papers for a short lesson on *oo, oa,* and *oy*. Part of the content generated by students during this segment includes a list of words that rhyme with *book* and *boy* and a discussion of the influence of *r* on vowels. Then she asks students to reclassify their words to see if they can identify any new groups, and to make sure they can read every word on the chart. Homework is to see if they can find any more words that stand for "people when we don't know their names."

During Friday's lesson, Nancy begins working on titles and sentences. As the students gather around the picture, she says, "Who remembers what a title does?" The responses circle around: "Names of books," "Names of stories," "Covers of books," "Tells us what the story's about." Then Nancy says, "Study our picture carefully. See if you can think of a good title for our picture." She gives them a minute to think, then collects about ten titles. As students volunteer titles, she asks them how the various titles relate to the picture. Some are comprehensive and accurate, some are less so, and some are sentences. Here are a few of their responses:

"I think the picture should be called 'all colors,' because there are so many colors in it."

"'Children in uniforms,' 'cause they're all wearing red uniforms."

"'Shiny books,' there are lots of shiny books in their school."

"'Kids in school.' They are *at* school."

After listening to a few of the titles, Nancy decides she wants to pull a few informative books—a couple she has read to them and a few new ones—and talk with them about length, content, and promises to the reader represented by informative titles. They move on to sentences for now.

Nancy writes the word *sentence* on the board and under it two of the sentences she heard during discussion:

1. The students are all wearing uniforms.
2. They're young kids all gathered around their teacher.

She asks the students to read the sentences silently, reading as many words as they can; then they read the sentences together.

"Remember, we helped Renata turn the first sentence into the title, 'Students Wearing Uniforms,' because Renata said 'The students are all wearing uniforms.' And George came up with 'Children around Their Teacher,' for sentence number two. Well that is good thinking. Later, we'll work on titles again. For journal time, you may want to write something that goes with your title."

"Study our picture sometime today and pretend you are going to write a letter describing the picture to someone who has not seen it. Be ready on Monday to share something from your pretend letter."

On Monday morning, when it's picture-word time, Nancy has the overhead projector set up near their work area. They begin the lesson with a quick reading of the picture-word chart, they work on two target sight words, and they add a few more *oo*, *oa*, and *oy* words to the wall charts. Then Nancy says, "All right. Sentence time. Who's ready?" They spend the next two days generating and recording sentences describing things in the picture.

The sentences cover most everything. Here are a few of them:

"Gold letters are on the uniform." (Began as "Gold letters." Nancy asks, "Where are the letters, Maryanne?" "On the uniform.")

"They like school because they're smiling."

"The tops of the uniforms are all alike, but the bottoms are different for boys and girls."

When students give something that is not obvious or that requires some interpretation, Nancy asks them for their evidence.

"The children are learning by listening to the teacher."

"Why do you say that?" Nancy asks.

"They are all being quiet, sort of leaning close to the teacher, and it doesn't look like they're talking."

Serena adds, "They are learning because they're good listeners and they read lots of books."

"They look like they are happy."

"Why do you think so?" asks Nancy.

"Most of them are smiling. They look like they're happy working together."

"These kids are learning how to read and write."

"How do you know? They could be getting ready for music," Nancy adds.

"I see their work, and they have a chart up too!"

On Wednesday, the students get copies of all the sentences printed front and back on light green paper. Their work time the next few lessons is on learning to read the sentences. As Nancy walks around listening to them read their sentences, she targets some high frequency words (*in*, *on*, *The/the*, *They/they*) to work on.

The following week they begin classifying their sentences. They work in partners, and they spend several days reading and classifying. At first, Nancy just observes and listens to their categories; she wants to find out how they are thinking and be sure their reasons for grouping are accurate. About half the students put sentences together based on how they are written: "These all begin with *They*." "These all begin with *They are*." One student describes her category as, "These all have five words and they all have our work word *the* in them." About half the students put sentences together based on a topic or what they are about: "These are about students in uniforms." "My sentences are all about what's in the room."

After the second session of reading sentences and classifying them however they wish, Nancy selects one of the topical categories she has seen several times and uses it as a demonstration of grouping sentences by content. She encourages every partnership to find at least one group of sentences that go together because of what they are about. Before they begin working as partners, she does a quick drill with them on *an, and, are, all*, high frequency words she's heard some students confuse and that she wants every student to master.

Nancy is preparing her students for work on writing informative paragraphs about a single topic and main idea, and how an accurate brief description of their category can provide a good title. For their next lesson, she will take one of their groups, put together a paragraph, and discuss how she put the paragraph together.

On Thursday, she begins the PWIM lesson by saying, "You've put together a number of good categories with our sentences. Some of you put together sentences about uniforms; some about all the colors in the picture; some about the books, where they were, and how they were being used; and some about what the students were doing. Several of you put together three or four different categories, and some of you have written your own piece about what you were most interested in."

"I took one of your groups and wrote a paragraph about our picture." She places four of their sentences one below the other in the large pocket chart. "Let's read these sentences; then I'll share my paragraph."

"The students have many talents."

"They are learning how to write words and spell."

"They are learning by listening to the teacher and by reading lots of books."

"They look like they are happy working together."

Nancy continues, "There are lots of good groups we could write about, but I selected this one because when I asked why you put them together, you talked about kids learning. And that's one of the things I think is special when I look at our picture, and that's what I wanted to write about."

Then, she displays this paragraph on the overhead projector:

ALL KIDS LEARNING
These young students have many talents. They're learning how to write words and how to spell. Reading lots of books and listening to the teacher helps them learn. They look like they're happy working together.

She gives students time to read the paragraph silently; then she reads it aloud and talks about how she structured the paragraph, telling the reader who (young students), what (learning happily), how (by reading lots of books, by listening to the teacher, by working together, and because they have many talents), and where (in a classroom).

She keeps the pace up but includes, among other things, why she changed the first *They* to *These young students*, why she added the second *how to* in the second sentence, and so forth. She puts her first draft on the projector as she talks about a couple of the changes she made in word order and sentence order, and students ask her about a few of the changes from the original sentences.

We have been visiting with Nancy and her students for three weeks of picture-word lessons. Most of the lessons lasted around 30 minutes, a few around 45 minutes. This picture-word cycle will continue for at least another week. They will write a group paragraph about uniforms because that is one of the more interesting topics to many of them, and students will write individual paragraphs about at least one of their groups. They will continue to add words to the chart and to their word wall, to work on spelling and phonics patterns, and Nancy will continue to listen to them, to observe what they are producing, and to model and demonstrate and talk about how the English language works.

SUMMARY: THE PICTURE-WORD INDUCTIVE MODEL OF TEACHING AND LEARNING

The picture-word inductive model is an inquiry-oriented model of teaching whose structure scaffolds the students to ever more complex tasks. Hopefully, the previous scenario illustrates how a teacher can use the picture-word inductive model to structure student inquiry into the English language and how it works.

The model provides a multidimensional curriculum for teaching beginning readers and writers (Calhoun, 1999). Full use of the model includes multiple opportunities for explicit instruction by the teacher and many opportunities, through structured inductive activities, for concept formation

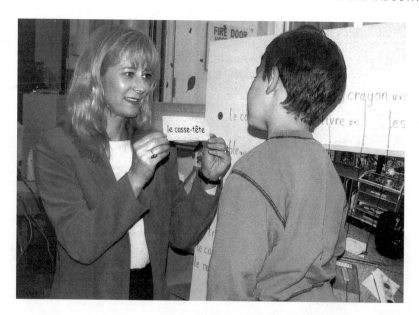

Carol Kruger checks out Brady Hite's new vocabulary in the French immersion kindergarten in Northern Lights.

by the students. At the primary grade levels, and for English as a second language students, its focus is on developing skills in reading and writing. However, it is also a useful model for teaching information and concepts in the social sciences when working with older students who are already reading on their own (Joyce and Calhoun, 1998).

REFLECTIONS

Teachers hold the keys to literacy for many students—the keys that provide access and choice. The more words students have in their listening and speaking vocabularies, the more understanding they have of the world around them. The more words they have in their reading and writing vocabularies, the more control and choice they have in life both in and out of school, along with greater access to knowledge and experience and greater potential for teaching themselves. The more understanding they have of how language works, the more powerful they are and can become as communicators and citizens.

SEQUENCE OF THE PICTURE-WORD INDUCTIVE MODEL FOR BEGINNING READING AND WRITING

LEARNING ABOUT SYMBOLS AND COMMUNICATION (THE RELATIONSHIPS AMONG "REAL THINGS," PICTURES, WORDS, LETTERS, SENTENCES, AND PARAGRAPHS)

1. Select a picture.

2. Have students identify what they see in the picture.

3. Label the picture parts identified. (The teacher draws a line from the picture to the word, says the word, spells the word and points to each letter with her/his finger or the marker, says the word again, students spell the word with the teacher.)

4. Read/review the picture-word chart.

5. Have students classify the words into a variety of groups. Identify common concepts in the words to emphasize with the class as a whole. The students "read" the words by referring to the chart if the word is not in their sight vocabulary.

6. Read/review the picture-word chart (say, spell, and say).

7. Add words, if desired, to the picture-word chart and to the word banks.

8. Have students think of a title for their picture-word chart. (The teacher leads students to think about the "evidence" and information in their chart and about what they want to say about this information.)

9. Have students generate a sentence, sentences, or a paragraph directly related to their picture-word chart. Students may classify group-generated sets of sentences. The teacher models putting the sentences together into a good paragraph.

10. Read/review the sentences or paragraphs.

PHONICS/GRAMMAR/MECHANICS/USAGE

1. Students hear the words pronounced correctly many times, and they have an immediate reference source to use (the picture-word chart) as they add these words to their sight vocabulary. At the teacher's discretion, almost any sound/symbol relationship can be emphasized (introduced or taken to mastery).

2. Students hear and see the letters identified correctly many times, and they see them formed correctly many times.

3. Students hear the words spelled correctly many times and participate in spelling words correctly.

4. In writing the sentences, the teacher uses standard English usage (transforming student sentences if necessary) and uses correct punctuation and mechanics (commas, capital letters, and so on).

INSTRUCTIONAL AND NURTURANT EFFECTS (WHAT THE MODEL IS DESIGNED TO TEACH STUDENTS TO DO)

1. Learn how to build their sight vocabularies

2. Learn how to inquire into word and sentence structures

3. Generate writing (titles, sentences, paragraphs)

4. Create an understanding of the reading/writing connection

5. Develop skill in phonetic and structural analysis

6. Develop interest and capacity to generate expressions through writing

7. Increase reading of nonfiction

8. Develop cooperative skills in working with others in the reading/writing area

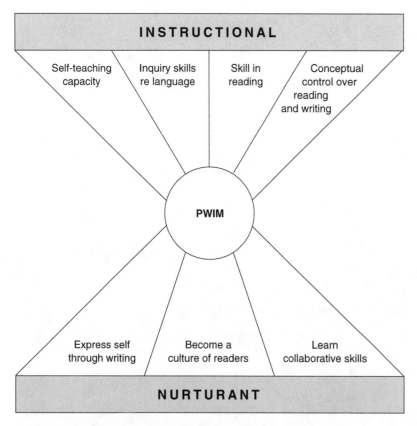

FIGURE 5.1   Instructional and nurturant effects of the picture-word
inductive model (PWIM).

The development of sight vocabulary is pivotal to the success of the
model.

In a series of recent studies, teachers in the Northern Lights School District #69 in Alberta, Canada, have collected data relevant to several of these
effects. With respect to the development of sight vocabulary, first grade
teachers in English and French immersion have studied words learned
when shaken out and have documented that their average student has, in
the course of a year, developed from 600 to 800 sight vocabulary words and
has retained them throughout the year (see Calhoun and others, 2000). In
Chapter 19 we will describe two studies in which the picture-word inductive model was part of a multidimensional curriculum for kindergarten students and for students in grades four through twelve who were struggling
readers.

SCIENTIFIC INQUIRY AND INQUIRY TRAINING

The Art of Making Inferences

There's an aesthetic dimension to everything. Every school environment, every teaching act, every setting you create to spend time in, enhances or diminishes the quality of life. Whether you're teaching science or art, the challenge is to make it beautiful.

—Eliot Eisner, to the Association for Supervision and Curriculum Development, Spring 1990

This chapter celebrates science as a teaching strategy. We will deal with the general model, illustrate it with biology, and follow that with another inquiry model that teaches students to develop hypotheses and reason causally. Let's begin in a classroom.

THE SCIENTIFIC INQUIRY MODEL

25 June, 2002. John Orr's fifth grade class has been browsing the *Science Times* section of the *New York Times* and come upon an extensive report on the genome mapping project in Iceland (Wade, 2002). John's school has a subscription to the electronic edition of the newspaper, and it is well-used in his class. He leads the students toward some stories that relate to parts of the world they have been studying or items of national and international news he believes they should be conversant with. Working in teams, they also browse sections of the paper, looking for items of interest. Often, as today, John projects an article on the screen, using an LCD monitor on the overhead projector, and reads the article with the class. Information is recorded on newsprint tablets and the major points in the article are summarized by the student "writing leaders of the day."

In this case, he asks the leaders to find a file where information from past forays into genome projects are summarized and he projects those summaries before turning to the June 25 article.

The students have been fascinated with the genome projects. They are amazed to find that 99.9 percent of human genomes are shared by everyone on the planet. The Web has been a fine resource, as have been the encyclopedias in the classroom CD-ROM collection, as John has led the class to study the concepts of race and gender. They have begun to realize how many differences are products of socialization.

Today's story arrests the students for three reasons:

1. One is that the researchers have genealogical information that goes back for 1,100 years with a population that has had little immigration over that period of time. Thus the research strategy differs from the other genomic projects in that the researchers can trace the lineage so far back. Thus, a unique strategy has been created.

2. Second are some of the preliminary findings. The project is disease-oriented and, in the case of asthma, the researchers have traced current asthmatics who are under treatment to a single common ancestor who was born in 1710.

3. Third is the composition of the population. In the 800s A.D. about 10,000 to 15,000 Norseman from Norway founded Iceland. They raided Northern Ireland and England for young women whom they captured and made into "slave wives." Altogether they enslaved 40,000 to 50,000 young females.

This item galvanizes the students. They have trouble coming to grips with it, and they become oriented toward the study of Iceland and Scandinavia. They set out to gather data, and the encyclopedias and data banks on nations serve them. They also come to realize that the "wife-raids" by the Vikings greatly depleted the female population in Ireland and England and wonder what effect that might have had. Eventually, they will be in touch with a scholar at Oxford who will offer his opinions about the subject.

The students are studying how science is made as well as its findings. Mr. Orr keeps making them aware of the how as well as the what. He keeps reminding them of Carl Sagan's premise, that "The method of science, as stodgy and grumpy as it seems, is far more important than its findings."

S C E N A R I O

In London, Ontario, Mr. Hendricks's fourth-grade students enter their classroom after lunch to find an array of glasses, bottles, bells, wooden boxes of different sizes (with holes in them), tuning forks, xylophones, and small wooden flutes. These objects are spread about the room, and the students spend a few minutes playing with them, creating a most horrendous sound. Mr. Hendricks watches.

After a few minutes the students begin to settle down and one of them asks, "What's going on here, Mr. Hendricks? It looks like you've turned the place into an orchestra."

"Well, in a way," he smiles. "Actually, for the next few weeks this is going to be our sound laboratory." He moves across the room and picks up an instrument made of wood and wires and plucks one of the wires. At the same time he uses a spoon to strike a soft drink bottle on the desk next to him. "Do you notice anything about these sounds?" he asks, and repeats his plucking and striking.

"Hey," says one of the girls, "they sound the same, but different."

"Do it again," suggests one of the students, and Mr. Hendricks obliges. Soon all of the students have noticed that the sound is at the same pitch or level.

"Your problem," explains Mr. Hendricks, "is to find out what makes sound vary and to describe that variation. Given the limitations of the devices we have in this room, I want you to organize yourselves to conduct some experiments and present me with sets of principles that you think describe the variations. When you're finished, I want you to be able to describe to me how you would design an instrument with certain capabilities. I'll tell you what I want the instrument to be able to do, and you can tell me how to make it. Then we'll begin to test your ideas. Now, I think we ought to organize ourselves into groups and decide how we're going to go about this. Does anybody have any ideas?"

"Well," Sally ventures, "I've noticed that the things are made out of five different kinds of materials. Maybe we could get into five groups, and each group would experiment with those for a while. Then we could share what we've learned and trade around and check out the thinking of the other groups. After that we could decide what to do next."

Someone joins in with another suggestion, and the class spends the next half hour planning how the study will begin.

From the early 1950s to the late 1960s, innovation in American education was propelled mainly by the Academic Reform movement, an effort to revise the conventional curriculum areas of the school around conceptions of the major ideas and research methods of the academic disciplines. In the area of mathematics, for example, the curriculum designers attempted to influence the way students would think about mathematics, both the major ideas and the methods they would use to inquire into mathematics. Similarly, the science curricula reflected both the major ideas of the sciences and the research methods and attitudes of the scientific community. In other words, curricula were built around the information-processing systems of the academic disciplines. Similar curricula continue to be developed, and research and development is active, especially in the sciences and social science education.

Two straightforward examples were the Biological Sciences Curriculum Study (BSCS) (Schwab, 1965), which produced curricular and instructional patterns for use in high school biology, and the Michigan Social Science Curriculum Project, which teaches the use of social psychology methods to study human relations (Lippitt, Fox, and Schaible, 1969a). In this chapter we use the BSCS model to represent the group of models. Incidentally, the BSCS organization is still alive and well, creating innovative curriculums for both high school and elementary school (see http://www.bscs.org/au_why.html).

ORIENTATION TO THE MODEL

The essence of the BSCS approach is to teach students to process information using techniques similar to those of research biologists—that is, by identifying problems and using a particular method to solve them. BSCS emphasizes content and process. The first emphasis is on human behavior in the ecology of earth:

> The problems created by growing human populations, by depletion of resources, by pollution, by regional development, and the like, all require intelligent government or community action. These are, in part at least, biological-ecological problems, and every citizen should have some awareness of their background. (Schwab, 1965, p. 19)

The second emphasis is on scientific investigation:

> Although one of the major aims of this version (of the course) is to describe the major contributions modern molecular biology has made to the general understanding of scientific problems, a second aim will also be apparent. Measured by almost any standard, science has been and continues to be a powerful force in our society. A difficulty has arisen, however. This difficulty, expressed by C. P. Snow in his book, *Two Cultures*, arises from the fact that although many people may understand the products of science, at the same time they may be very ignorant of the nature of science and its methods of inquiry. It is probably a safe generalization to say that the understanding of the products of science cannot be attained unless the process is also understood. It is apparent that in a free society such as ours, much will depend on the average citizen's evaluation of science. (Schwab, 1965, pp. 26–27)

To help students understand the nature of science, the strategies developed by the BSCS committee introduce students to the methods of biology at the same time that they introduce them to the ideas and facts. The committee put it rather pungently:

> If we examine a conventional high school text, we find that it consists mainly or wholly of a series of unqualified, positive statements. "There are so many

kinds of mammals." "Organ A is composed of three tissues." "Respiration takes place in the following steps." "The genes are the units of heredity." "The function of A is X."

This kind of exposition (the statement of conclusions) has long been the standard rhetoric of textbooks even at the college level. It has many advantages, not the least of which are simplicity and economy of space. Nevertheless, there are serious objections to it. Both by omission and commission, it gives a false and misleading picture of the nature of science.

By commission a rhetoric of conclusions has two unfortunate effects on the student. First, it gives the impression that science consists of unalterable, fixed truths. Yet, this is not the case. The accelerated pace of knowledge in recent years has made it abundantly clear that scientific knowledge is revisionary. It is a temporary codex, continuously restructured as new data are related to old.

A rhetoric of conclusions also tends to convey the impression that science is complete. Hence, the fact that scientific investigation still goes on, and at an ever-accelerated pace, is left unaccounted for to the student.

The sin of omission by a rhetoric of conclusions can be stated thus: It fails to show that scientific knowledge is more than a simple report of things observed, that it is a body of knowledge forged slowly and tentatively from raw materials. It does not show that these raw materials, data, spring from planned observations and experiments. It does not show that the plans for experiments and observations arise from problems posed, and that these problems, in turn, arise from concepts which summarize our earlier knowledge. Finally, of great importance, is the fact that a rhetoric of conclusions fails to show that scientists, like other men, are capable of error, and that much of inquiry has been concerned with the correction of error.

Above all, a rhetoric of conclusions fails to show that our summarizing concepts are tested by the fruitfulness of the questions that they suggest, and through this testing are continually revised and replaced.

The essence, then, of a teaching of science as inquiry, would be to show some of the conclusions of science in the framework of the way they arise and are tested. This would mean to tell the student about the ideas posed, and the experiments performed, to indicate the data thus found, and to follow the interpretation by which these data were converted into scientific knowledge. (Schwab, 1965, pp. 39–40)

The BSCS uses several techniques to teach science as inquiry. First, it uses many statements that express the tentative nature of science, such as, "We do not know," "We have been unable to discover how this happens," and "The evidence about this is contradictory" (Schwab, 1965, p. 40). Current theories, it is pointed out, may be replaced by others as time goes by. Second, in place of a rhetoric of conclusions, BSCS uses what is called a *narrative of inquiry*, in which the history of major ideas in biology is described and the course of inquiry in that area is followed. Third, the laboratory work is arranged to induce students to investigate problems, rather than just to illustrate the text. As they put it, "They [scientists] treat problems for which the text does not provide answers. They create situations in which the students can participate in the inquiry" (Schwab, 1965, p. 40). Fourth, the laboratory programs have been designed in blocks that involve the student in an investigation of a real biological problem. At first students may be presented with materials already familiar to scientists and problems whose solutions are already disclosed, but "as the series of problems progresses, they come nearer and nearer to the frontier of knowledge" (Schwab, 1965, p. 41). Thus, the student simulates the activity of the research scientist. Finally, there is the use of what are called *Invitations to Enquiry*. Like the functioning of the laboratory, the Invitations to Enquiry involve the student in activities that enable him or her to follow and participate in the reasoning related to a front-line item of investigation or to a methodological problem in biology.

In this chapter we present the Invitations to Enquiry as the model of teaching drawn from the BSCS materials.

INVITATIONS TO ENQUIRY

Credited to Schwab, this strategy was designed

> to show students how knowledge arises from the interpretation of data to show students that the interpretation of data—indeed, even the search for data—proceeds on the basis of concepts and assumptions that change as our knowledge grows . . . to show students that as these principles and concepts change, knowledge changes too . . . to show students that though knowledge changes, it changes for a good reason—because we know better and more than we knew before. The converse of this point also needs stress: The possibility that present knowledge may be revised in the future does *not* mean that present knowledge is false. Present knowledge is science based on the best-tested facts and concepts we presently possess. It is the most reliable, rational knowledge of which man is capable. (Schwab, 1965, p. 46)

Each Invitation to Enquiry (or lesson) is a case study illustrating either a major concept or a method of the discipline. Each invitation "poses example after example of the process itself [and] *engages the participation of the student in the process*" (Schwab, 1965, p. 47).

In each case a real-life scientific study is described. However, omissions, blanks, or curiosities are left uninvestigated, which the student is invited to fill: "This omission may be the plan of an experiment, or a way to control one factor in an experiment. It may be the conclusion to be drawn from given data. It may be an hypothesis to account for data given" (Schwab, 1965, p. 46). In other words, the format of the invitation ensures that the student sees biological inquiry in action and is involved in it, because he or she has to perform the missing experiment or draw the omitted conclusion.

The sets of invitations are sequenced in terms of difficulty to gradually lead the students to more sophisticated concepts. We can see this sequencing in the first group of Invitations to Enquiry, which focuses on topics related to methodology—the role and nature of general knowledge, data, experiment, control, hypothesis, and problems in scientific investigation. The subjects and topics of the invitations in Group 1 appear in Table 6.1.

TABLE 6.1 **INVITATIONS TO ENQUIRY, GROUP 1, SIMPLE ENQUIRY: THE ROLE AND NATURE OF GENERAL KNOWLEDGE, DATA, EXPERIMENT, CONTROL, HYPOTHESIS, AND PROBLEMS IN SCIENTIFIC INVESTIGATION**

Invitation	Subject	Topic
1	The cell nucleus	Interpretation of simple data
2	The cell nucleus	Interpretation of variable data
3	Seed germination	Misinterpretation of data
4	Plant physiology	Interpretation of complex data
Interim Summary 1, Knowledge and Data		
5	Measurement in general	Systematic and random error
6	Plant nutrition	Planning of experiment
7	Plant nutrition	Control of experiment
8	Predator-prey; natural populations	"Second-best" data
9	Population growth	The problem of sampling
10	Environment and disease	The idea of hypothesis
11	Light and plant growth	Construction of hypotheses
12	Vitamin deficiency	"If . . . , then . . ." analysis
13	Natural selection	Practice in hypothesis
Interim Summary 2, The Role of Hypothesis		
14	Auxins and plant movement	Hypothesis; interpretation of abnormality
15	Neurohormones of the heart	Origin of scientific problems
16	Discovery of penicillin	Accident in inquiry
16A	Discovery of anaphylaxis	Accident in inquiry

Source: Joseph J. Schwab, supervisor, BSCS, *Biology Teachers' Handbook* (New York: John Wiley & Sons, Inc., 1965), p. 52. By permission of the Biological Sciences Curriculum Study.

Invitation 3 in Group 1, an example of this model, leads students to deal with the problem of misinterpretation of data.

INVITATION 3
(Subject: Seed Germination)
(Topic: Misinterpretation of Data)
   (It is one thing to take a calculated risk in interpreting data. It is another thing to propose an interpretation for which there is no evidence—whether based on misreading of the available data or indifference to evidence. The material in this Invitation is intended to illustrate one of the most obvious misinterpretations. It also introduces the role of a clearly formulated *problem* in controlling interpretation of the data from experiments to which the problem leads.)

To the student: (a) An investigator was interested in the conditions under which seeds would best germinate. He placed several grains of corn on moist blotting paper in each of two glass dishes. He then placed one of these dishes in a room from which light was excluded. The other was placed in a well-lighted room. Both rooms were kept at the same temperature. After four days the investigator examined the grains. He found that all the seeds in both dishes had germinated.
   What interpretation would you make of the data from this experiment? Do not include facts that you may have obtained elsewhere, but restrict your interpretation to those from *this experiment alone.*

   (Of course the experiment is designed to test the light factor. The Invitation is intended, however, to give the students a chance to say that the experiment suggests that moisture is necessary for the sprouting of grains. Others may say it shows that a warm temperature is necessary. If such suggestions do not arise, introduce one as a possibility. Do so with an attitude that will encourage the expression of unwarranted interpretation, if such exists among the students.)
   (If such an interpretation is forthcoming, you can suggest its weakness by asking the students if the data suggest that corn grains require a glass dish in order to germinate. Probably none of your students will accept this. You should have little difficulty in showing them that the data some of them thought were evidence for the necessity of moisture or warmth are no different from the data available about glass dishes. In neither case are the data evidence for such a conclusion.)

To the student: (b) What factor was clearly *different* in the surroundings of the two dishes? In view of your answer, remembering that this was a deliberately planned experiment, state as precisely as you can the specific problem that led to this particular plan of experiment.

   (If it has not come out long before this, it should be apparent now that the experiment was designed to test the necessity of light as a factor in germination. As to the statement of the problem, the Invitation began with a very general question: "Under what conditions do seeds germinate best?" This is not the most useful way to state a problem for scientific inquiry, because it does not indicate where and how to look for an answer. Only when the "question" is made specific enough to suggest what data are needed to answer it does it become an immediately useful scientific problem. For example, "Will seeds germinate better with or without light?" is a question pointing clearly to what data are required.

A comparison of germination in the light with germination in the dark is needed. So we can say that a general "wonderment" is converted into an immediately useful problem when the question is made sufficiently specific to suggest an experiment to be performed or specific data to be sought. We do not mean to suggest that general "wonderments" are bad. On the contrary, they are indispensable. The point is only that they must lead to something else—a solvable problem.)

To the student: (c) In view of the problem you have stated, look at the data again. What interpretation are we led to?

(It should now be clear that the evidence indicates that light is not necessary for the germination of *some* seeds. You may wish to point out that light is necessary for some other seeds [for example, Grand Rapids Lettuce] and may inhibit the germination of others [for example, some varieties of onion].)

(N.B.: This Invitation continues to deal with the ideas of data, evidence, and interpretation. It also touches on the new point dealt with under paragraph (b), the idea of a *problem*. It exemplifies the fact that general curiosity must be converted into a specific problem.)

(It also indicates that the problem posed in an inquiry has more than one function. First, it leads to the design of the experiment. It converts a wonder into a plan of attack. It also guides us in interpreting data. This is indicated in (c), where it is so much easier to make a sound interpretation than it is in (a), where we are proceeding without a clear idea of what problem led to the particular body of data being dealt with.)

(If your students have found this Invitation easy or especially stimulating, you may wish to carry the discussion further and anticipate to some extent the topic of Invitation 6 [planning an experiment]. The following additions are designed for such use.) (Schwab, 1965, pp. 57–58)

The format of this investigation is fairly typical. The students are introduced to the problem the biologist is attacking, and they are given some information about the investigations that have been carried on. The students are then led to interpret the data and to deal with the problems of warranted and unwarranted interpretations. Next, the students are led to try to design experiments that would test the factor with less likelihood of data misinterpretation. This syntax—to pose a problem about a certain kind of investigation, and then to induce students to attempt to generate ways of inquiring that will eliminate the particular difficulty in the area—is used throughout the program.

Let's look at another Invitation to Enquiry—this time, with a more concept-oriented topic. The following illustration is from the Invitation to Enquiry group dealing with the concept of *function*. The topic has been structured so that it is approached as a methodological problem. How can we infer the function of a given part from its observable characteristics (what is the evidence of function)? In this model the question is not posed directly. Rather the student is guided through an area of investigation, which in this invitation has been framed to embed the methodological concern and the spirit of inquiry. Questions are then posed so that the student himself or herself identifies the difficulty and later speculates on the ways to resolve it.

INVITATION 32
(Subject: Muscle Structure and Function)
(Topic: Six Evidences of Function)
(We concluded Interim Summary 3 by pointing out that the concept of causal lines has no place for the organism as a whole. Instead, the concept treats the organism simply as a collection of such causal lines, not as an organization of them. Each causal line, taken separately, is the object of investigation. The web formed by these lines is not investigated. The conception of function is one of the principles of inquiry which brings the web, the whole organism, back into the picture.)

(This Invitation introduces the student to the idea of *function*. This concept involves much more than the idea of causal factor. It involves the assumption that a given part [organ, tissue, and so on] encountered in an adult organism is likely to be so well suited to the role it plays in the life of the whole organism that this role can be inferred with some confidence from observable characteristics of the part [its structure, action, and so on]. As we shall indicate later, this assumption, like others in scientific research, is a *working* assumption only. We do not assume that organs are invariably perfectly adapted to their functions. We do assume that most or many of the organs in a living organism are so well adapted [because of the process of evolution] that we proceed farther in studying an organ by assuming that it is adapted to its function than by assuming that it is not.)

To the student: (a) Which of the various muscle masses of the human body would you say is the strongest?

(Students are most likely to suggest the thigh muscles, or the biceps, on the grounds that they are large. If not, suggest the thigh muscle yourself, and defend your suggestion on grounds of size.)

To the student: (b) We decided that the thigh muscle was probably the strongest of our body muscles, using *size* as our reason for choosing it. Hence size seems to be the datum on which we base this decision. But why size, rather than color or shape? Behind our choice of size as the proper criterion, are there not data of another sort, from common experience, that suggest to us that larger muscles are likely to be stronger muscles?

(In considering this question students should be shown that their recognition and acceptance of this criterion of muscle strength is derived from associations from common experience. A kick sends a football farther than a forward pass (not always true, by the way), a weight lifter has bulkier musculature than a pianist, and so on.)

To the student: (c) Now a new point using no information beyond common experience. What can you say happens to a *muscle* when it contracts?

(The question here is *not* what a muscle does to other parts of the body, but what the muscle itself does—its change of shape in a certain way—becoming shortened, thicker, firmer by contraction. Have the students feel their arm muscles as they lift or grasp.)

To the student: (d) To the fact that the motion of muscle is as you have found it to be, add two further facts: Many muscles are attached to some other parts of the body, and many such muscles are spindle-shaped, long, narrow, and tapering. From these data alone, what do you think muscles do?

(The motion, attachment, and shape taken together suggest that muscles in general move one or all of the other parts of the body to which they may be attached. Such inferences about function are only probable. But so are practically all inferences in science. In (e) and later queries, we shall make a point of the doubtful character of functional inference.) (Schwab, 1965, pp. 174–176)

The example continues in this vein.

THE MODEL OF TEACHING

The essence of the model is to involve students in a genuine problem of inquiry by confronting them with an area of investigation, helping them identify a conceptual or methodological problem within that area of investigation, and inviting them to design ways of overcoming that problem. Thus, they see knowledge in the making and are initiated into the community of scholars. At the same time, they gain a healthy respect for knowledge and will probably learn both the limitations of current knowledge and its dependability (Schaubel, Klopfer, and Raghaven, 1991).

SYNTAX

The syntax takes a number of forms (see Table 6.2). Essentially it contains the following elements or phases, although they may occur in a number of sequences: In phase one, an area of investigation is posed to the student, including the methodologies used in the investigation. In phase two, the problem is structured so that the student identifies a difficulty in the investigation. The difficulty may be one of data interpretation, data generation, the control of experiments, or the making of inferences. In phase

TABLE 6.2 **SYNTAX OF BIOLOGICAL SCIENCE INQUIRY MODEL**

Phase One	Phase Two
Area of investigation is posed to students.	Students structure the problem.

Phase Three	Phase Four
Students identify the problem in the investigation.	Students speculate on ways to clear up the difficulty.

three, the student is asked to speculate about the problem, so that he or she can identify the difficulty involved in the inquiry. In phase four, the student is then asked to speculate on ways of clearing up the difficulty, by re-designing the experiment, organizing data in different ways, generating data, developing constructs, and so on.

SOCIAL SYSTEM

A cooperative, rigorous climate is desired. Because the student is to be welcomed into a community of seekers who use the best techniques of sci-ence, the climate includes a certain degree of boldness as well as humility. The students need to hypothesize rigorously, challenge evidence, criticize research designs, and so forth. In addition to accepting the need for rigor, students must also recognize the tentative and emergent nature of their own knowledge as well as that of the discipline, and in doing so develop a cer-tain humility with respect to their approach to the well-developed scientific disciplines.

PRINCIPLES OF REACTION

The teacher's task is to nurture the inquiry by emphasizing the process of inquiry and inducing the students to reflect on it. The teacher needs to be careful that the identification of facts does not become the central issue and should encourage a good level of rigor in the inquiry. He or she should aim to turn the students toward the generation of hypotheses, the interpre-tation of data, and the development of constructs, which are seen as emer-gent ways of interpreting reality.

SUPPORT SYSTEM

A flexible instructor skilled in the process of inquiry, a plentiful supply of "real" areas of investigation and their ensuing problems, and the required data sources from which to conduct inquiry into these areas provide the necessary support system for this model.

APPLICATION ─────────────────────────

A number of models for teaching the disciplines as processes of inquiry exist, all built around the concepts and methods of the particular disciplines.

The Michigan Social Science Curriculum Project, directed by Ronald Lippitt and Robert Fox, is based on an approach that is potentially very powerful but that is startling in its simplicity. The strategy is to teach the research techniques of social psychology directly to children using human relations content, including their own behavior. The result presents social psychology as a living discipline whose concepts and method emerge through continuous application to inquiry into human behavior. Another result is a direct demonstration of the relevance of social science to human affairs. This curriculum illustrates how elementary school children can use scientific procedures to examine social behavior.

Both the conception of social psychology held by these curriculum makers and their teaching strategy, which is essentially to lead the children to practice social psychology, are probably best illustrated by looking at their materials and the activities they recommend. They have prepared seven "laboratory units" developed around a resource book or text and a series of project books. The seven units begin with an exploration of the nature of social science, "Learning to Use Social Science," and proceed to a series of units in which the students apply social science procedures and concepts to human behavior: "Discovering Differences," "Friendly and Unfriendly Behavior," "Being and Becoming," "Influencing Each Other."

The first unit is structured to introduce students to social science methods such as:

1. "What Is a Behavior Specimen?" (How do we obtain samples of behavior?)
2. "Three Ways to Use Observation" (Introduces the children to description, inference, and value judgment, and the differences among them.)
3. "Cause and Effect" (Introduces the inference of cause, first in relation to physical phenomena, then in relation to human behavior.)
4. "Multiple Causation" (Teaches how to deal with several factors simultaneously. For example, the children read and analyze a story in which a central character has several motivations for the same action.) (Lippitt, Fox, and Schaible, 1969a, pp. 24–25)

The children compare their analyses of the samples so that they check observations and inferences against one another and come to realize problems of obtaining agreement about observations. They also learn how to analyze interaction through the technique of circular analysis.

Finally, a series of activities introduces the children to experiments by social psychologists that have generated interesting theories about friendly and unfriendly behavior and cooperation and competition.

This approach focuses the children's study on human interaction, provides an academic frame of reference and techniques for delineating and carrying out inquiry, and involves the student in the observation of his or her own behavior and that of those around him. The overall intention is that the student will take on some of the characteristics of the social scientist. Thus, the instructional values are in the interpersonal as well as the academic domain.

This model has wide applicability, but unfortunately it is dependent on inquiry-oriented materials (areas of investigation), which are rare in most classrooms, since the didactic text is the standard. However, every subject area has at least one text series that is inquiry-oriented or one that is easily adapted to this model. An instructor with a clear understanding of the model will easily discern instructional material that, with a little rearrangement, might provide suitable areas for investigation. Instructors who are quite knowledgeable in their particular disciplines can probably construct their own materials.

INSTRUCTIONAL AND NURTURANT EFFECTS

The biological science inquiry model (Figure 6.1) is designed to teach the processes of research biology, to affect the ways students process information, and to nurture a commitment to scientific inquiry. It probably also nurtures open-mindedness and an ability to suspend judgment and balance

FIGURE 6.1   Instructional and nurturant effects of the biological science inquiry model.

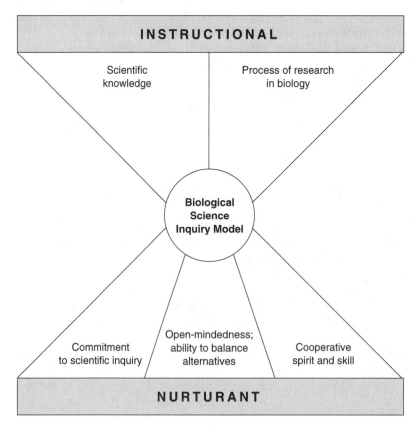

alternatives. Through its emphasis on the community of scholars, it also nurtures a spirit of cooperation and an ability to work with others.

Scientific-inquiry models have been developed for use with students of all ages, from preschool through college (Metz, 1995). The core purpose is to teach the essential process of science and, concurrently, major concepts from the disciplines along with the information from which these have been developed.

Research on these models has usually focused on entire curricula that have been implemented for one or more years, using the models consistently with appropriate materials of instruction. Two types of findings are of particular interest to us. The first is that teachers who would use them need to engage in intensive study both of the academic substance and of these models of teaching. Otherwise, they tend to withdraw from inquiry-based instruction. The second is that where these models have been well implemented with adequate attention to the teachers' study of academic content and teaching process, the results have been impressive (Bredderman, 1981; El-Nemr, 1979). The students have learned the scientific process, have mastered the major concepts of the disciplines, have acquired basic information about science, and have developed positive views of science. In Chapter 19 you will find detailed descriptions of curriculums that introduce literacy to young children and provide new avenues to older struggling readers, curriculums where inquiry is a major component. As you will see, these curriculums are very successful.

SUMMARY ► **BIOLOGICAL SCIENCE**
CHART **INQUIRY MODEL**

Syntax

Phase One: Pose Area of Investigation to Students

Phase Two: Students Structure the Problem

Phase Three: Students Identify the Problem in the Investigation

Phase Four: Students Speculate on Ways to Clear Up the Difficulty

Social System

The model has moderate structure and a cooperative, rigorously intellectual climate.

Principles of Reaction

Teacher nourishes inquiry, turning students toward inquiry process rather than identification efforts.

Support System

The model requires a flexible instructor skilled in the process of inquiry and a supply of problem areas of investigation.

THE FUTURE

A number of lines of inquiry are currently in progress that will probably advance thinking about how students can learn to build categories, make inferences, and develop more effective causal reasoning and synthesizing skills. Theories about "multiple intelligences" may give rise to other ways of thinking about thinking.

Computers are making large databases available to students that will make much more complex types of concept formation easier to research and will permit the development of more intricate and probably more powerful support systems. In the social studies the journal *Social Education* is a goldmine of topics and resources.

THE INQUIRY TRAINING MODEL: FROM FACTS TO THEORIES

S C E N A R I O

One morning, as Mrs. Harrison's fourth-grade students are settling down to their arithmetic workbooks, she asks for their attention. As they raise their eyes toward her, a lightbulb directly over Mrs. Harrison's desk blows out and the room darkens.

"What happened?" asks one child.

"Can't you see?" remarks another. "The lightbulb blew out."

"Yeah," inquires another, "but what does that mean?"

"What do you mean, 'What does that mean?' "

"Just that we have all seen a lot of lightbulbs blow out, but what does that really mean? What happens?"

Mrs. Harrison unscrews the lightbulb and holds it up. The children gather around, and she passes it among them. After she gets it back, she says, "Well, why don't you see if you can develop a hypothesis about what happened?"

"What's inside the glass?" asks one of the children.

"I'm afraid I can't answer that," she replies. "Can you put it another way?"

"Is there air inside the glass?" one questions.

"No," says Mrs. Harrison.

"Is there a gas inside?" asks another.

"Yes," says Mrs. Harrison. The children look at one another in puzzlement. Finally, one asks, "Is it inert?"

"Yes," nods Mrs. Harrison.

"What is that little wire made of?" asks another student.

"I can't answer that," says Mrs. Harrison. "Can you put it another way?"

"Is the little wire made of metal?"

"Yes," she responds.

Asking questions such as these, the children gradually identify the materials that make up the lightbulb and the events that took place. Finally, they begin to venture hypotheses about what happened. After they have generated four or five of these, they search through reference books in an effort to verify them.

Mrs. Harrison's class has been prepared to carry out a model of teaching that we call *inquiry training*. Normally, the class uses inquiry training to explore preselected areas. That is, either Mrs. Harrison organizes a unit of instruction, or the children identify a topic that they are going to explore. In this case, the children used the techniques of inquiry training to formulate theories about an event that was familiar to all of them and yet puzzled them, for none of them had previously developed ideas about what really went on when a lightbulb blew out.

Inquiry training was developed by Richard Suchman (1962) to teach students a process for investigating and explaining unusual phenomena. Suchman's model takes students through miniature versions of the kinds of procedures that scholars use to organize knowledge and generate principles. Based on a conception of scientific method, it attempts to teach students some of the skills and language of scholarly inquiry.

Suchman developed his model by analyzing methods employed by creative research personnel, especially physical scientists. As he identified the elements of their inquiry processes, he built them into the instructional model called inquiry training.

RESEARCH

Inquiry training is designed to bring students directly into the scientific process through exercises that compress the scientific process into small periods of time. What are the effects? Schlenker (1976) reported that inquiry training resulted in increased understanding of science, productivity in creative thinking, and skills for obtaining and analyzing information. He reported that it was not more effective than conventional methods of teaching in the acquisition of information, but that it was as efficient as recitation or lectures accompanied by laboratory experiences. Ivany (1969) and Collins (1969) reported that the method works best when the confrontations are strong, arousing genuine puzzlement, and when the materials the students use to explore the topics under consideration are especially instructional. Both elementary and secondary students can profit from the model (Voss, 1982). In an intriguing study, Elefant (1980) successfully carried out the model with deaf children, which suggests that the method can be powerful with students who have severe sensory handicaps.

ORIENTATION TO THE MODEL

GOALS AND ASSUMPTIONS

Inquiry training originated in a belief in the development of independent learners; its method requires active participation in scientific inquiry. Children are curious and eager to grow, and inquiry training capitalizes on their natural energetic explorations, giving them specific directions so that they explore new areas effectively. The general goal of inquiry training is to help students develop the intellectual discipline and skills necessary to raise questions and search out answers stemming from their curiosity. Thus, Suchman is interested in helping students inquire independently, but in a disciplined way. He wants students to question why events happen as they do and to acquire and process data logically, and he wants them to develop general intellectual strategies that they can use to find out why things are as they are.

Inquiry training begins by presenting students with a puzzling event. Suchman believes that individuals faced with such a situation are *naturally* motivated to solve the puzzle. We can use the opportunity provided by natural inquiry to teach the procedures of disciplined searching.

Like Bruner and Taba, Suchman believed that students can become increasingly conscious of their process of inquiry and that they can be taught scientific procedures directly. All of us often inquire intuitively; however, Suchman feels we cannot analyze and improve our thinking unless we are conscious of it.

Suchman believes, further, that it is important to convey to students the attitude that *all knowledge is tentative*. Scholars generate theories and explanations. Years later, these are pushed aside by new theories. There are no permanent answers. We can always be more sophisticated in our explanations, and most problems are amenable to several plausible explanations. Students should recognize and be comfortable with the ambiguity that genuine inquiry entails. They should also be aware that the point of view of a second person enriches our own thinking. The development of knowledge is facilitated by help and ideas from colleagues if we can learn to tolerate alternative points of view. Thus, Suchman's theory is that:

1. Students inquire naturally when they are puzzled.
2. They can become conscious of and learn to analyze their thinking strategies.
3. New strategies can be taught directly and added to the students' existing ones.
4. Cooperative inquiry enriches thinking and helps students to learn about the tentative, emergent nature of knowledge and to appreciate alternative explanations.

OVERVIEW OF THE TEACHING STRATEGY

Following Suchman's belief that individuals have a natural motivation to inquire, the inquiry training model is built around intellectual confrontations. The student is presented with a puzzling situation and inquires into it. Anything that is mysterious, unexpected, or unknown is grist for a discrepant event. Because the ultimate goal is to have the students experience the creation of new knowledge, the confrontation should be based on discoverable ideas. In the following example, bending a metallic strip held over a flame begins the inquiry cycle.

> The strip is made of a lamination of unlike strips of metal (usually steel and brass) that have been welded together to form a single blade. With a handle at one end it has the appearance of a narrow knife or spatula. When this apparatus is heated, the metal in it expands, but the rate of expansion is not the same in the two metals. Consequently, half of the thickness of this laminated strip becomes slightly longer than the other half and since the two halves are attached to each other the internal stresses force the blade to assume a curve of which the outer circumference is occupied by the metal which has expanded the most. (Suchman, 1962, p. 28)

Suchman deliberately selects episodes that have sufficiently surprising outcomes to make it difficult for students to remain indifferent to the encounter. Usually things that are heated do not bend into a big curve. When this metal strip does, the students *naturally* want to know *why*. The learners cannot dismiss the solution as obvious; they have to work to explain the situation, and the products of that work are new insights, concepts, and theories.

After the presentation of the puzzling situation, the students ask the teacher questions. The questions, however, must be answered by yeses or nos. Students may not ask the teacher to explain the phenomenon to them. They have to focus and structure their probes to solve the problem. In this sense, each question becomes a limited hypothesis. Thus, the student may not ask, "How did the heat affect the metal?" but must ask, "Was the heat greater than the melting point of the metal?" The first question is not a specific statement of what information is wanted; it asks the teacher to do the conceptualizing. The second question requires the student to put several factors together—heat, metal, change, liquid. The student had to ask the teacher to verify the hypothesis that he or she has developed (the heat caused the metal to change into a liquid).

The students continue to ask questions. Whenever they phrase one that cannot be answered by a yes or a no, the teacher reminds them of the rules and waits until they find a way of stating the question in proper form. Comments such as "Can you restate this question so that I can answer it with a yes or a no?" are common teacher responses when students slip out of the inquiry mode.

Over time, the students are taught that the first stage in inquiry is to verify the facts of the situation—the nature and identity of the objects, the events, and the conditions surrounding the puzzling event. The question "Was the strip made of metal?" helps verify the facts—in this case, a property of the object. As the students become aware of the facts, hypotheses should come to mind and guide further inquiry. Using their knowledge about the behavior of the objects, students can turn their questions to the relationships among the variables in the situation. They can conduct verbal or actual experiments to test these causal relationships, selecting new data or organizing the existing data in new ways to see what will happen if things are done differently. For example, they could ask, "If I turn the flame down, will the bend still occur?" Better yet, they could actually do this! By introducing a new condition or altering an existing one, students isolate variables and learn how they affect one another.

It is important for students and teachers to recognize the difference between questions that attempt to verify "what is" and questions or activities that "experiment" with the relationships among variables. Each of these is essential to theory development, but fact gathering should precede hypothesis raising. Unless sufficient information about the nature of the problem situation and its elements is verified, students are likely to be overwhelmed by the many possible causal relationships.

> If the child immediately tries to hypothesize complex relationships among all the variables that seem relevant to him, he could go on testing indefinitely without any noticeable progress, but by isolating variables and testing them singly, he can eliminate the irrelevant ones and discover the relationships that exist between each relevant independent variable (such as the temperature of the blade) and the dependent variable (which in this case is the bending of the blade). (Suchman, 1962, pp. 15–16)

Finally, the students try to develop hypotheses that will fully explain what happened. (For instance, "The strip was made of two metals that were fastened together somehow. They expand at different rates, and when they were heated, the one that expanded the most exerted pressure on the other one so that the two bent over together.") Even after lengthy and rich verification and experimentation activities, many explanations may be possible, and the students are encouraged not to be satisfied with the first explanation that appears to fit the facts.

Inquiry cannot be programmed, and the range of productive inquiry strategies is vast. Thus, students should

> experiment freely with their own questions, structuring and sequencing [the inquiry session]. Nevertheless, inquiry can be divided into broad phases which, on the whole, should be taken in logical order simply because they build upon one another. Failure to adhere to this order leads either to erroneous assumptions or to low efficiency and duplication of effort. (Suchman, 1962, p. 38)

The emphasis in this model is clearly on becoming aware of and mastering the inquiry process, not on the content of any particular problem situation. Although the model should also be enormously appealing and effective as a mode of acquiring and using information, the teacher cannot be too concerned with subject-matter coverage or "getting the right answer." In fact, this would violate the whole spirit of scientific inquiry, which envisions a community of scholars searching together for more accurate and powerful explanations for everyday phenomena.

THE MODEL OF TEACHING

SYNTAX

Inquiry training has five phases (see Table 6.3). The first phase is the student's *confrontation* with the puzzling situation. Phases two and three are the *data-gathering* operations of *verification* and *experimentation*. In these two phases, students ask a series of questions to which the teacher replies yes or no, and they conduct a series of experiments on the environment of the problem situation. In the fourth phase, students *organize* the information they obtained during the data gathering and try to *explain* the discrepancy. Finally, in phase five, students *analyze* the problem-solving strategies they used during the inquiry.

Phase one requires that the teacher present the problem situation and explain the inquiry procedures to the students (the objectives and the procedure of the yes/no question). The formulation of a discrepant event such as the bimetallic strip problem requires some thought, although the strategy can be based on relatively simple problems—a puzzle, riddle, or magic trick—that do not require much background knowledge. Of course, the ultimate goal is to have students, especially older students, experience the creation of new knowledge, much as scholars do. However, beginning inquiries can be based on very simple ideas.

The distinguishing feature of the discrepancy is that it involves events that conflict with our notions of reality. In this sense, not every puzzling situation

TABLE 6.3   **SYNTAX OF THE INQUIRY TRAINING MODEL**

Phase One: Confrontation with the Problem	Phase Two: Data Gathering—Verification
Explain inquiry procedures. Present discrepant event.	Verify the nature of objects and conditions. Verify the occurrence of the problem situation.

Phase Three: Data Gathering— Experimentation	Phase Four: Organizing, Formulating an Explanation
Isolate relevant variables. Hypothesize (and test) causal relationships.	Formulate rules or explanations.

Phase Five: Analysis of the Inquiry Process
Analyze inquiry strategy and develop more effective ones.

is a discrepant event. It may be puzzling because we do not know the answer, but we do not need new concepts to understand it, and therefore we do not need to conduct an inquiry. We mention this because occasionally teachers do not pick problems that are truly puzzling to the student. In these cases, the learning activity does not progress beyond a "20-questions" format. Even though the questioning activity has value for its own sake, it should not be confused with the notion of scientific inquiry.

Phase two, verification, is the process whereby students gather information about an event they see or experience. In experimentation, phase three, students introduce new elements into the situation to see if the event happens differently. Although verification and experimentation are described as separate phases of the model, the students' thinking and the types of questions they generate usually alternate between these two aspects of data gathering.

Experiments serve two functions: *exploration* and *direct testing*. Exploration—changing things to see what will happen—is not necessarily guided by a theory or hypothesis, but it may suggest ideas for a theory. Direct testing occurs when students try out a theory or hypothesis. The process of converting a hypothesis into an experiment is not easy and takes practice. Many verification and experimentation questions are required just to investigate one theory. We have found that even sophisticated adults find it easier to say, "I think it has something to do with . . . " than to think of a series of questions that will test the theory. Also, few theories can be discarded on the basis of one experiment. Although it is tempting to "throw away" a variable if the first experiment does not support it, it can be very misleading to do so. One of the teacher's roles is to restrain students whenever they assume that a variable has been disproven when it has not.

A second function of the teacher is to broaden the students' inquiry by expanding the type of information they obtain. During verification they may ask questions about objects, properties, conditions, and events. *Object* questions are intended to determine the nature or identity of objects. (Is the knife made of steel? Is the liquid water?) *Event* questions attempt to verify the occurrence or nature of an action. (Did the knife bend upward the second time?) *Condition* questions relate to the state of objects or systems at a particular time. (Was the blade hotter than room temperature when the teacher held it up and showed that it was bent? Did the color change when the liquid was added?) *Property* questions aim to verify the behavior of objects under certain conditions as a way of gaining new information to help build a theory. (Does copper always bend when it is heated?) Because students tend not to verify all aspects of the problem, teachers can be aware of the type of information needed and work to change the questioning pattern.

In phase four, the teacher calls on the students to organize the data and to formulate an explanation. Some students have difficulty making the intellectual leap between comprehending the information they have gathered and constructing a clear explanation of it. They may give inadequate explanations, omitting essential details. Sometimes several theories or explanations are possible based on the same data. In such cases, it is often useful to ask students to state their explanations so that the range of possible hypotheses becomes obvious. Together the group can shape the explanation that fully responds to the problem situation. Finally, in phase five, the students are asked to analyze their pattern of inquiry. They may determine the questions that were most effective, the lines of questioning that were productive and those that were not, or the type of information they needed and did not obtain. This phase is essential if we are to make the inquiry process a conscious one and systematically try to improve it.

SOCIAL SYSTEM

Suchman's intention is that the social system be cooperative and rigorous. Although the inquiry training model can be quite highly structured, with the social system controlled largely by the teacher, the intellectual environment is open to all relevant ideas; teachers and students participate as equals where ideas are concerned. Moreover, the teacher should encourage students to initiate inquiry as much as possible. As the students learn the principles of inquiry, the structure can expand to include the use of resource material, dialogue with other students, experimentation, and discussion with the teacher.

After a period of practice in teacher-structured inquiry sessions, students can undertake inquiry in more student-controlled settings. A stimulating event can be set up in the room, and students can inquire on their own or in informal groups, alternating between open-ended inquiry sessions and data gathering with the aid of resource materials. In this way, the students can move back and forth between inquiry sessions and independent study. This utilization of the inquiry training model is especially suited to the open-classroom setting, where the teacher's role is that of instructional manager and monitor.

In the initial stages of inquiry the teacher's role is to select (or construct) the problem situation, to referee the inquiry according to inquiry procedures, to respond to students' inquiry probes with the necessary information, to help beginning inquirers establish a focus in their inquiry, and to facilitate discussion of the problem situation among the students.

PRINCIPLES OF REACTION

The most important reactions of the teacher take place during the second and third phases. During the second phase the teacher's task is to help the students to inquire but not to do the inquiry for them. If the teacher is asked questions that cannot be answered by a yes or no, he or she must ask the students to rephrase the questions so as to further their own attempts to collect data and relate them to the problem situation. The teacher can, if necessary, keep the inquiry moving by making new information available to the group and by focusing on particular problem events or by raising questions. During the last phase, the teacher's task is to keep the inquiry directed toward the process of investigation itself.

SUPPORT SYSTEM

The optimal support is a set of confronting materials, a teacher who understands the intellectual processes and strategies of inquiry, and resource materials bearing on the problem.

APPLICATION ─────────────────────────────

Although inquiry training was originally developed for the natural sciences, its procedures are usable in all subject areas; any topic that can be formulated as a puzzling situation is a candidate for inquiry training. In literature, murder mysteries and science fiction stories or plots make excellent puzzling situations. Newspaper articles about bizarre or improbable situations may be used to construct stimulus events. One of the authors was at a Chinese restaurant not too long ago and puzzled over the question, "How is the fortune put into the fortune cookie, since it does not appear burned or cooked in any way?" It occurred to us that this would make an excellent inquiry-training topic for young children. The social sciences also offer numerous possibilities for inquiry training.

The construction of puzzling situations is the critical task, because it transforms curriculum content into problems to be explored. When objects and other materials are not available or appropriate to the problem situation, we recommend that teachers make up a *problem statement* for students and a *fact sheet* for themselves. The problem statement describes the discrepant event and provides the information that is shared initially with the students. The fact sheet gives the teacher further information about the problem, and the teacher draws on it to respond to the students' questions. Let's look at an example in the social studies.

S C E N A R I O

In anthropology, students have the problem of reconstructing cultural events. For a social studies class, an instructor composed a problem statement and a student fact sheet based on an anthropological issue. The teacher passed the following statement out to his students:

PROBLEM STATEMENT _____

This map shows an island in the middle of a lake. The island is connected to the shore by a causeway made of stones piled on the bottom of the lake until the pile reached the surface. Then smoothed stones were laid down to make a road. The lake is surrounded by mountains, and the only flat land

MAP 6.1

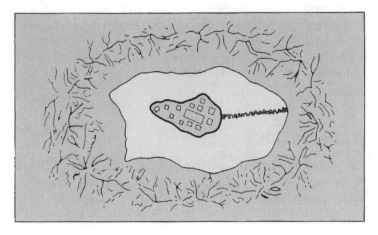

is near the lake. The island is covered with buildings whose walls are still standing, although the roofs are now gone. It is completely uninhabited.

Your task is to discover what happened to the people who lived there. What caused the place to be empty of human beings?

As the students conducted their inquiry, the instructor drew on the following fact sheet:

INSTRUCTOR FACT SHEET

1. The lake is 500 feet deep, 600 feet across.
2. The lake is 6,500 feet above sea level. The mountains rise to 11,000 feet.
3. The causeway is made of dumped rocks.
4. The houses are close together. Each one is about 20 by 25 feet and has more than one room. They are made of limestone blocks.
5. Some broken tools and pottery have been found in the homes.
6. The edifice in the center is made of marble and has three levels. At the bottom it is six times larger than the houses. At the top level of the edifice, you can sight the planets and stars through a hole slit in a stone. You can sight Venus at its lowest rise, which occurs on December 21.
7. There is evidence that the islanders fished with traps. They also had livestock such as sheep, cows, and chickens.
8. Apparently there was no art, but evidence of graphic writing has been found.
9. Cisterns have been found under limestone streets.
10. There is no habitation within 80 miles.
11. The island has been uninhabited for about 300 years.
12. The area was discovered in 1900.
13. It is located in a subtropical area of South America where there is plenty of drinking water and where every available area was farmed. There is evidence of irrigation but no evidence of crop rotation. In general, the land is marginal for farming.
14. There is a thin layer of topsoil over a limestone shelf.
15. About 1,000 to 1,500 people lived on the island.
16. The mountains around the island can be crossed, but with difficulty.
17. There is a stone quarry in nearby mountains and a burial ground across the lake.
18. Dead bodies with hands folded have been found.
19. There is no evidence of plague, disease, or war.

AGE-LEVEL ADAPTATION

Inquiry training can be used with children of all ages, but each age group requires adaptation. We have seen the method be successful with kindergarten children but encounter difficulty with third-graders. As with many other aspects of teaching, each group and each student are unique.

However, the model can be simplified in several ways until students are able to engage in all phases.

For very young children, it is best to keep the content of the problem simple—perhaps with more emphasis on discovery than on a principle of causation. Problem situations like "What is in this box?" or "What is this unusual thing?" or "Why does one egg roll differently from the other?" are appropriate. One teacher we know showed her students a picture of a flying squirrel from a magazine for science teachers. Since most of us believe mammals do not fly, this was truly a discrepant event. She asked the students to come up with an explanation for this phenomenon using inquiry procedures.

Bruce and Bruce (1992) provide a very large number of discrepant events for use in the social studies, items that can be used with all grades and over a wide range of common social studies topics. Numerous children's science books are filled with simple science experiments, many of them suitable for primary grades. Mystery stories and riddles work well as stimuli for young children. Another way to adapt inquiry training to young children is to use visual material—props giving clues—which simplifies the stimuli and lessens the requirements for memory. It is useful to aim for only one or two specific objectives in a single inquiry training session. Initially (with students of all ages) it is good to start off with a simple game that requires yes/no questions. This game will give students confidence that they can formulate questions and avoid direct theory questions. Some teachers we know use the mystery bag; others play "I'm thinking of something I'm wearing. Guess what it is." Simple guessing games like this also give the students practice in distinguishing theory questions ("Is it your shirt?") from attribute questions ("Is it made of cotton?"). We recommend that teachers introduce and stress each element of inquiry separately. At first the teachers could pose all yes/no questions. Then they can ask students to convert their theory questions into experiments. One by one the teachers can tighten the constraints of the inquiry as they teach the students each of the elements. Trying to explain and enforce all the elements at once will only frustrate both students and teachers.

At first, older students are better able to handle the inquiry process itself, and their subject matter—especially science—more readily lends itself to inquiry training. Although there are more suitable discrepant events in the upper elementary and secondary curricula, it is usually necessary for the teacher to convert available materials from an expository mode into the inquiry mode—that is, to create a discrepant event.

LEARNING ENVIRONMENT ADAPTATIONS

Like many other models, especially information-processing models, inquiry training can be taught in a teacher-directed setting or incorporated into more self-directed, learning-centered environments. Discrepant events can be developed through print, film, or audio means, and task cards directing students to respond according to the model can be developed. The inquiry can be conducted over a period of several days, and the results of other students' inquiries can be shared. Students should have access to appropriate resources, and they may work together in groups. Students may also develop discrepant events and conduct inquiry sessions for peers.

INSTRUCTIONAL AND NURTURANT EFFECTS

The model promotes strategies of inquiry and the values and attitudes that are essential to an inquiring mind, including:

> Process skills (observing, collecting, and organizing data; identifying and controlling variables; formulating and testing hypotheses and explanations; inferring)
> Active, autonomous learning
> Verbal expressiveness
> Tolerance of ambiguity, persistence
> Logical thinking
> Attitude that all knowledge is tentative

The chief learning outcomes of inquiry training are the processes involved—observing, collecting and organizing data, identifying and controlling variables, making and testing hypotheses, formulating explanations, and drawing inferences (see Figure 6.2). The model splendidly integrates these several process skills into a single, meaningful unit of experience.

The format of the model promotes active, autonomous learning as the students formulate questions and test ideas. It takes courage to ask questions, but it is hoped that this type of risk will become second nature to the students. They will also become more proficient in verbal expression as well as in listening to others and remembering what has been said.

Although its emphasis is on process, inquiry training results, too, in the learning of content in any curriculum area from which problems are selected. For example, Suchman developed entire curricula in economics and geology. In our opinion, it is adaptable to all elementary and secondary curriculum areas.

SUMMARY CHART ► **INQUIRY TRAINING MODEL**

Syntax

Phase One: Confrontation with the Problem
  Explain inquiry procedures.
  Present discrepant event.

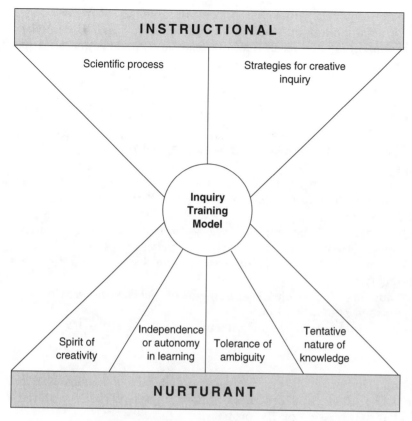

FIGURE 6.2 Instructional and nurturant effects of the inquiry training model.

Phase Two: Data Gathering—Verification
   Verify the nature of objects and conditions.
   Verify the occurrence of the problem situation.

Phase Three: Data Gathering—Experimentation
   Isolate relevant variables.
   Hypothesize (and test) causal relationships.

Phase Four: Organizing, Formulating an Explanation
   Formulate rules or explanations.

Phase Five: Analysis of the Inquiry Process
   Analyze inquiry strategy and develop more effective ones.

Social System

The inquiry training model can be highly structured, with the teacher controlling the interaction and prescribing the inquiry procedures. However, the norms of inquiry are those of cooperation, intellectual freedom, and equality. Interaction among students should be encouraged. The intellectual environment is open to all relevant ideas, and teachers and students should participate as equals where ideas are concerned.

Principles of Reaction

1. Ensure that questions are phrased so they can be answered with yeses or nos, and that their substance does not require the teacher to do the inquiry.
2. Ask students to rephrase invalid questions.
3. Point out unvalidated points—for example, "We have not established that this is liquid."
4. Use the language of the inquiry process—for instance, identify student questions as theories and invite testing (experimenting).
5. Try to provide a free intellectual environment by not evaluating student theories.
6. Press students to make clearer statements of theories and provide support for their generalization.
7. Encourage interaction among students.

Support System

The optimal support is a set of confronting materials, a teacher who understands the intellectual processes and strategies of inquiry, and resource materials bearing on the problem.

CHAPTER 7

MEMORIZATION
Getting the Facts Straight

The only way people come to appreciate the real power of the link-word method is to learn to use it themselves to learn new stuff—the more abstract and unfamiliar the better. Folks can't just put it forward as something that is "good for the kids." You have to feel it to be able to teach it well. Come to think of it, maybe that's true of all the models.
—Mike McKibbin to Bruce Joyce, August 1980

S C E N A R I O

The Phoenix High School social studies department has developed a set of mnemonics that are combined with inductive activities to teach the students the names and locations of the 191 countries plus basic demographic knowledge about each of them—population, per capita GNP, type of government, and life expectancy. The students work in groups using mnemonics like the following one, which is designed to teach the names and locations of the Central American countries.

The exercise begins with the blank map of Central America with the countries numbered (see Map 7.1). The leader describes an imaginary tour they are about to take:

"Imagine that we're about to take a tour of Central America. Our group has learned that there has been a great deal of Spanish influence on the language and the dissemination of a religion based on the Christian Savior—thus, we will see many signs in Spanish and will see mission churches with their distinctive bell towers. We know that the Spanish came for riches and that they expected to find a *rich coast*. We also know we will have to be careful about the water, and we will carry a lot of *nickels* that we will use to buy bottled water. We are going to drive little Hondas, rather than taking a bus, and we will wear Panama hats for identifying our tour group members."

THE TOUR

Imagine that we're about to take a tour of Central America. Our group has learned that there has been a great deal of Spanish influence that has affected the language and the religion based on the Christian savior (we will see mission churches with their distinctive bell towers). We also know that they came for riches. We also know that we have to be careful about the water, except in Panama, and we will carry nickels we will use to buy bottled water. We are going to drive little Hondas and wear Panama hats for identification.

Thus
1. Panama—Panama hat
2. Costa Rica—rich coast
3. Nicaragua—nickel water
4. El Salvador—savior
5. Honduras—Honda race
6. Guatemala—gotta lotta
7. Belize—belleeeeeezzz

CENTRAL AMERICA

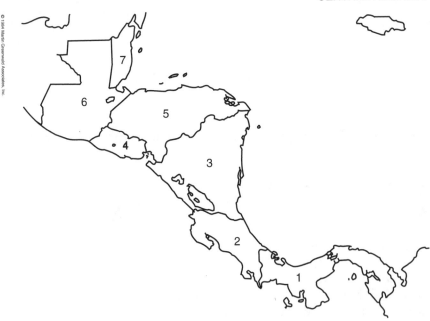

MAP 7.1

Source: Developed by Beverly Showers and Bruce Joyce with the Richmond County, Georgia, Staff Development Cadre. Drawings on this page and on pages 133–135, 141–143, and 147–148 are by Jenna Beard, Eugene, Oregon.

Then the leader points to the first country, Panama, shows the first cartoon, and says,

"The link word for Panama is *Panama hat*" (see Cartoon 7.1). The group repeats the link word. The leader then points to the second country and shows the second cartoon, saying "This country stands for the rich coast the Spanish were looking for, which is Costa Rica. The link word for Costa Rica is *rich coast*" (see Cartoon 7.2).

The group repeats the link word and the names of the countries as the leader points to them: "Panama, Panama hat, Costa Rica, rich coast." The exercise continues. The link word for Nicaragua is "nickel water" or "nickel agua" (see Cartoon 7.3), and El Salvador is "Savior" (see Cartoon 7.4). The group repeats the names of the countries and the link words in order as the leader points to the country. The leader proceeds to introduce the link word for Honduras by saying, "We get bored a little and decide to have a 'Honda Race' in our little cars" (see Cartoon 7.5). Guatemala is next; the leader points out that

CARTOON 7.1

CARTOON 7.2

CARTOON 7.3

CARTOON 7.4

CARTOON 7.5

CARTOON 7.6

it has the largest population in Central America and that the link word is "gotta lotta" (see Cartoon 7.6). Finally, pointing to the seventh country, the leader reminds them about the bell towers and that the sound from them is "belleeeezzz" (see Cartoon 7.7). The group then names the countries and the link words as the leader points to them in turn.

Over the next couple of days the group members study the map, the names of the countries, and the link words until they know them backward and forward. They also consult a database containing information on population, birth and death rates, per capita income, health care, and such, and classify the countries seeking correlations among those variables. (Are level of education and life expectancy correlated? and so forth.)

In this fashion they proceed to examine the regions of the world, comparing and contrasting the countries and learning the names and locations of enough of them that the atlas will seem a familiar place. Eventually, of course, the study goes beyond names, locations, and demographics and proceeds to rich information about a sample of the countries.

CARTOON 7.7

S C E N A R I O

John Pennoyer is bilingual coordinator of Las Pulgas school district. He works with the teachers to ensure that all the students learn Spanish and English simultaneously. Half the students come to school with English as their primary language; the other half speak Spanish. The students work together to generate link words and pronunciation guides for the two languages.

One of the fifth-grade classes has generated the following list as part of an introduction to Spanish for several students who have newly transferred to their school.

SPANISH WORDS II
por favor (poor faBORE) PLEASE [for favor]
gracias (GRA see ahs) THANK YOU [grace to you]
está bién (essTA bee EN) ALL RIGHT; OK [it's be good]
adiós (ahdyOHS) GOODBYE
buenos dias (BWEnos DEEahs) GOOD MORNING [bonnie day]
buenos tardes (BWEnos TARdays) GOOD AFTERNOON [bonnie late day]
buenos noches (BWEnos NOchays) GOOD EVENING [bonnie night]
hasta mañana (AHstah manYAHna) until tomorrow [no haste, man]

The phonetic pronunciation guides are in parentheses, followed by English equivalents. The link words are in brackets and are designed to provide the flavor of the sounds in English and a sense of the meanings.

The new students study the words, associating the new (to them) Spanish words with the English equivalents and the link words.

S C E N A R I O

Imagine a group of students who are presented with the task of learning the names of the presidents of the United States and the order in which they served. Previously, the students have learned to count from 1 to 40 mnemonically. That is, each number is represented by a rhyming word that has an image attached to it. "One" is "bun," "two" is "shoe," and so on. Also, each set of number decades (1 to 10, 11 to 20) is connected to a location or setting. The decade 1 to 10 is represented by a spring garden scene, 11 to 20 by a summer beach scene, 21 to 30 by a fall football scene, and 31 to 40 by a winter snow scene.

Now, capitalizing on this system of number associations, the name and order of each president are presented to the students in terms of the scene, the mnemonic for the number, and a word—called a *link word*—associated with the president's name. Thus Lincoln (link), number sixteen (sticks), is presented with an illustration of a sand castle on a beach encircled by a set of sticks linked together. Similar illustrations are used for the other presidents. The students study the pictures and the words. They are given a test right after they study and again 60 days later.

How effective was this experience? Did the students learn more than other students who tried to memorize the names and their order using the usual procedures for the same length of time? The answer is yes. In this and other studies, students are being taught unfamiliar material much more quickly than usual through the application of various mnemonic devices (Pressley, Levin, and Delaney, 1982, p. 83).

The humble task of memorizing is with us throughout our lives. From the moment of birth, a world of new artifacts and events is presented to us and has to be sorted out. Moreover, many of the elements of our world have been named by those who have come before us. We have to learn large quantities of words, and we have to learn to connect them to the objects, events, actions, and qualities that they represent. In other words, we have to learn a meaningful language.

In any new area of study, a major task is learning the important words and definitions—the languages, if you will—that pertain to the area. To deal with chemistry, we have to learn the names of the elements and their structural properties. To study a continent, we have to learn the names of its countries, its major geographical features, the important events in its history, and so on. Initial foreign language learning involves developing a vocabulary of words that look and sound unfamiliar.

The study of memory has a long history. Although "the goal of a unified coherent and generally satisfying theory of human memory" (Estes, 1976, p. 11) has not yet been achieved, progress has been made. A number of instructional principles are being developed whose goals are both to teach memorization strategies and to help students study more effectively.

For instance, the material on which a particular teacher chooses to focus will affect what information the students retain: "Many items are presented to an individual in a short time, and only those to which attention is directed enter into memory, and only those receiving rehearsal are maintained long enough to secure the processing necessary to establish a basis for long-term recall" (Estes, 1976, p. 7). In other words, if we do not pay attention to something, we are not likely to remember it. Also, we need to attend to it in such a way that we are rehearsing later recall of it. For example, as we wander through a forest, if we do not look carefully at the tree trunks, we are unlikely to remember them, although some visual images may be retained in a haphazard fashion. Even if we notice them, we need to use the information, for example by comparing different trees, to remember it.

When we rehearse, we develop *retrieval cues,* which are the basis for sorting through our memories at later times and locating information.

Short-term memories are often associated with *sensory* experiences of various kinds. When we are exposed to the wine called *Chablis,* we may remember it as straw-colored and tasting a certain way. For long-term recall we may associate things according to *episodic cues*—that is, having to do with the sequences of experience to which we have been exposed. We may remember Andrew Johnson, for instance, as the president who followed Abraham Lincoln. They are connected in time, and their episodes in history are connected to one another. *Categorical* cues, on the other hand, involve conceptualizations of the material. When we compare tree trunks, for example, we form concepts that provide a basis for describing the individual trunks in relation to one another. In other words, we replace specific items with categories, and this categorization provides us with the basis for memory.

Both scholarly and popular sources agree that the ability to remember is fundamental to intellectual effectiveness. Far from being a passive, trivial activity, memorizing and remembering are active pursuits. The capacity to take information, to integrate it meaningfully, and later to retrieve it at will is the product of successful memory learning. Most important, individuals can improve this capacity to memorize material so that they can recall it later. That is the objective of this model.

ORIENTATION TO THE MODEL

GOALS AND ASSUMPTIONS

Our recollection of our early years in school usually includes an image of struggles to master lists of unstructured material such as new words, new sounds, the days of the week, the 50 states, and the nations of the world. Some of us became effective at memorizing. Some did not. As we look back, it is easy to dismiss much of this information as trivial. However, imagine for a moment what our world would be like without the information we acquired in those years of school. We *need* information.

One of the most effective forms of personal power comes from competence based on knowledge; it is essential to success and a sense of well-being. Throughout our lives, we need to be able to memorize skillfully. To improve this ability increases learning power, saves time, and leads to a better storehouse of information.

THE LINK-WORD METHOD

Over the last 25 years an important line of research has been conducted on what is termed the *link-word method.* The result is a considerable advance in knowledge about memorization as well as the development of a system that has practical implications for the design of instructional materials, for classroom teaching and tutoring, and for students.

The method has two components, assuming that the learning task is to master unfamiliar material. The first component provides the students with familiar material to link with the unfamiliar items. The second provides an association to establish the meaning of the new material. For example, when the task involves new foreign language words, one link ties the sounds to those of English words. The second ties the new word to a representation of its meaning. For example, the Spanish word *carta* (postal letter) might be linked to the English word *cart* and a picture showing a letter inside a shopping cart (Pressley, Levin, and Delaney, 1981, p. 62).

An important finding from the research is that people who master material more quickly and who retain it longer generally use more elaborate strategies for memorizing material. They use mnemonics—assists to memorization. The less-effective memorizers generally use "rote" procedures. They "say" what is to be memorized over and over again until they believe it is implanted in their memories.

A second important finding is that devices like the link-word method are even more elaborate than the methods used by the better "natural" memorizers—that is, they require more mental activity than do the rote procedures. When first confronted with the presidential illustrations discussed earlier, many teachers respond, "But why add all the extra stuff? Isn't it hard enough to master the names of the presidents and their order? Why add words like *link* and *stick* and pictures of sand castles on a summer beach?"

The answer is that the additional associations provide a richer mental context, and the linking process increases the cognitive activity. The combination of activity and associations provides better "anchors" within our information-processing systems.

Does the key-word method help students who are ordinarily good, poor, and average memorizers? Apparently so (Pressley and Dennis-Rounds, 1980). Further, it appears to help students who are below average in verbal ability, who might have been expected to have greater difficulty with complex learning strategies. In addition, as students use the method, they seem to transfer it to other learning tasks. In other words, mnemonics can be taught so that students can use them independently of the teacher. The students, in other words, can develop systems for making up their own links.

Finally, even young (kindergarten and first-grade) students can profit from mnemonics (Pressley et al., 1981a). Obviously, they have greater difficulty generating their own links, but they can benefit when links are provided to them.

The effect sizes from this research are impressive. Even in Atkinson's (1975) early studies, the link-word method was about 50 percent more effective than conventional rote methods. That is, students learned half again more material in the same time period as students not using link words. In some of the later studies, it has been twice as efficient or more (Pressley, 1977; Pressley, Levin, and Miller, 1981a, 1981b). Just as important, retention has been facilitated. That is, more is remembered longer when link words are used. A very long line of research by Mastopieri and Scruggs (1993) has adapted mnemonic devices to the curriculum with particular attention to students having learning disabilities.

As we stated earlier, this research has two obvious uses. The first is to arrange instruction so as to make it as easy as possible for students to make associations and to discourage isolated rote drill. The second is to teach students to make their own links when they are studying new material.

Some of the other models can help us here. Concept attainment provides categories that associate exemplars on the basis of attributes and induce students to make contrasts with the nonexemplars. Inductive teaching causes students to build associations on the basis of common characteristics. Advance organizers provide an "intellectual scaffolding" that ties material together, and comparative organizers link the new with the old. The scientific inquiry methods provide an experiential base for terms and an intellectual structure to "glue" material together.

In an interesting study, Levin and Levin (1990) applied the method to teach what are generally considered "higher-order" objectives—in this case, a hierarchical system for classifying plants. They compared the effectiveness of using links to familiar concepts with a traditional graphic representation, with the hierarchy presented in a chart featuring boxes connected by lines. The links not only facilitated the learning and remembering of the hierarchical scheme, but also affected problem solving.

For the teacher, the major labor is preparation. Generating the links, and in some cases creating visual materials or working with students to create them, are the chief activities involved. Once the presentations have been prepared, the delivery is straightforward. Let us look at an example accompanied by cartoon figures.

This exercise is similar to the one described in the Central America scenario at the beginning of the chapter and is part of a global literacy program. The link words are phonetic and are created in a sequence following a made-up story of a career woman in the United States. We begin with the map of the Middle East with seven of the countries numbered in the order in which they will be memorized (see Map 7.2).

Our career woman is recounting the beginning of her day. "I got up," she says, and "*I ran* downstairs." *I ran* and its accompanying cartoon are the links to Iran (see Cartoon 7.8). Then she says, "I took the dishes from the *rack*." *Rack*, with its accompanying cartoon, are links to Iraq (see Cartoon 7.9). She continues, "I fixed the children bowls of *Syrios*." *Syrios*, with the accompanying cartoon, are links to Syria (see Cartoon 7.10).

"I fixed myself some English muffins and took out the *jar of jam*." *Jar of jam*, with its cartoon, are the links to Jordan (see Cartoon 7.11). "I also fixed myself a cup of tea and sliced a *lemon* for it." *Lemon* is the link, with its cartoon, for Lebanon (see Cartoon 7.12). "Finally, I ran for the *rail*road train." *Rail*road, with its cartoon, is the link for Israel (see Cartoon 7.13). "When I

MIDDLE EAST

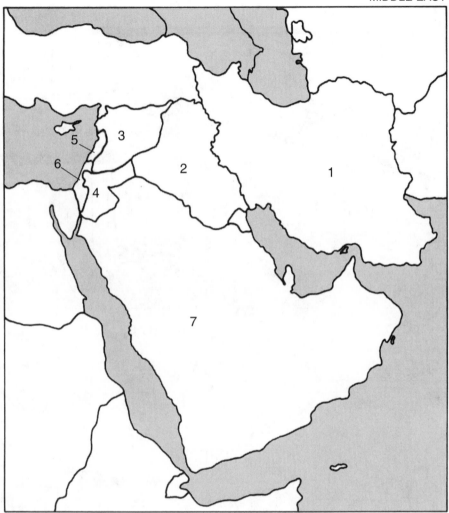

MAP 7.2

got to my office, I was so hot and thirsty I ran straight to the vending machine and got a *soda* to pick me up." *Soda* (*sody*) is the link for Saudi Ara-
bia (see Cartoons 7.14 and 7.15).

These are phonetic links, which, with the illustrations, help the students
connect the words (new to them) with known words and phrases and visu-
alizations to help anchor the new material in association with familiar
words, pictures, and actions. The somewhat humorous and absurd tone
helps make the links vivid.

CARTOON 7.8

CARTOON 7.9

CARTOON 7.10

CARTOON 7.11

CARTOON 7.12

CARTOON 7.13

CARTOON 7.14

CARTOON 7.15

OTHER MEMORY-ASSIST SYSTEMS

A number of popular "memory systems" have been developed, none of them backed by the research that Pressley, Levin, and their associates have generated. However, some of these systems use principles congruent with that research. Lorayne and Lucas's *The Memory Book* (1974) and Lucas's *Learning How to Learn* (2001) are two examples, and we have drawn on them for some suggestions of procedures to use with children.

We repeat first the important maxim that before we can remember something we must first attend to it. An effective memory model needs to induce attention to what is to be learned. Because entities we can see, feel, touch, smell, or taste generate powerful associations for remembering, we remember best those ideas that are represented to several of our sensory channels. Each channel contains old material we can associate with the new. If we "see" a flower, for example, as a visual image, something that feels a certain way, has a distinctive smell, and makes a crunchy noise when its stem is cut, we are linked to it through several types of perception. The likelihood of remembering it (or its name) is greater than if we observe it through one sense only. Lorayne and Lucas (1974) quote Aristotle: "It is the image-making part of the mind which makes the work of the higher processes of thought possible. Hence the mind never thinks without a mental picture. The thinking faculty thinks of its form in pictures" (p. 22).

Lorayne and Lucas built their model to increase (1) *attention* to what is to be learned, (2) the *senses* involved in attending, and (3) the *associations* we make between the new material and things that have previously been learned. A sense of how this is done can be seen in the following vignette:

Boris, who is running for student body president of the elementary school, has prepared a speech to deliver before his schoolmates. But he is having difficulty remembering his speech, so he appeals to his teacher for help and support. The teacher encourages him to use the memory strategies they have applied to other seemingly simple learning tasks such as learning new words and the names of African and Latin American countries. Informally, she guides him through the stages of the model much the same way Lorayne and Lucas do with their clients.

First, the teacher has Boris identify (attend to) the main thoughts of his speech. He carefully numbers each main idea. Next she has him identify one word from each main idea that reminds him of the entire thought. One by one, Boris isolates ideas and underlines a *key word* (one that can stand for the point to be made).

Next the teacher has Boris identify familiar words that have vivid meaning for him and connect those words with the key words. He picks his sister Kate for the term *qualifications* and *pear* for peer. To help him remember those two ideas, she asks him to imagine them in any silly way he can. Boris thinks for a minute and then relays the picture of a gigantic pear chasing his sister Kate. He is on his way to remembering! With each pair of key words and substitute words, Boris imagines some outrageous event combining the two.

After he has gone through all of the key thoughts and generated appropriate images, the teacher has Boris repeat words and describe the images several times. Then she asks him to test his memory by giving the whole speech. He is able to go through it comfortably. He has *attended* to his major points, *visualized* the key words and substitutes, and *associated* the key points with vivid sensory images.

If Boris had been learning new vocabulary or important science concepts, the teacher would have asked him to relate the new material to other *related* material he had learned previously, and she would have suggested that he put the new material to use immediately. This active repetition in a natural setting would help Boris retain the material over the long term. However, Boris's speech is a one-time activity requiring only short-term retention, so it is necessary only to review the associations and test his memory by giving the speech several times.

CONCEPTS ABOUT MEMORY

The following concepts are essentially principles and techniques for enhancing our memory of learning material.

AWARENESS

Before we can remember anything we must give attention to, or concentrate on, the things or idea to be remembered: "Observation is essential to original awareness" (Lorayne and Lucas, 1974, p. 6). According to Lorayne and Lucas, anything of which we are originally aware cannot be forgotten.

ASSOCIATION

The basic memory rule is, "You Can Remember Any New Piece of Information If It Is Associated with Something You Already Know or Remember" (Lorayne and Lucas, 1974, p. 7). For example, to help students remember the spelling of *piece*, teachers will give the cue a *piece of pie*, which helps with both spelling and meaning.

The major limitation of these devices is that they apply only to one specific thing. We can't use the phrase a *piece of pie* for more than the spelling of *piece*. In addition, we usually need to remember a number of ideas. To be broadly applicable, a memory system should apply more than once and should link several thoughts or items.

LINK SYSTEM

The heart of the memory procedure is connecting two ideas, with the second idea triggering yet another one, and so on. Although generally we only expend energy to learn meaningful material, an illustration with material that is not potentially useful helps us see how the method works. Suppose, for example, you want to remember the following five words in order: *house, glove, chair, stove, tree.* (There is no earthly reason why you would want to.) You should imagine an unusual picture, first with a house and a glove, then with a glove and a chair. For example, in the first picture you might imagine a glove opening the front door of a house, greeting a family of gloves. The second picture might be a huge glove holding a tiny chair. Taking the time to concentrate on making up these images and then to visualize them will develop associations that link them in order.

Many memory problems deal with the association of two ideas. We often want to associate names and dates or places, names and ideas, words and their meaning, or a fact that establishes a relationship between two ideas.

RIDICULOUS ASSOCIATION

Even though it is true that association is the basis of memory, the strength of the association is enhanced if the image is vivid and ridiculous, impossible, or illogical. A tree laden with gloves and a family of gloves are examples of ridiculous association.

There are several ways to make an association ridiculous. The first is to apply the rule of substitution. If you have a car and a glove, picture the glove driving the car. Second, you can apply the out-of-proportion rule. You can make small things gigantic or large things miniature—for example, a gigantic baseball glove driving along. The third means is the rule of exaggeration, especially by number. Picture millions of gloves parading down the street. Finally, get action into the association. In the examples discussed earlier, the glove is *ringing* the doorbell and *parading* down the street. Imagining ridiculous associations is not at all difficult for us when we are young children, but making these images gets harder for us as we get older and more logical.

SUBSTITUTE-WORD SYSTEM

The substitute-word system is a way of making "an intangible, tangible and meaningful" (Lorayne and Lucas, 1974, p. 21). It is quite simple. Merely take any word or phrase that seems abstract and "think of something . . . that sounds like, or reminds you of, the abstract material and can be pictured in your mind" (Lorayne and Lucas, 1974, p. 22). As a child you may have said "I'll ask her" to remember the state of Alaska. If you want to remember the name *Darwin* you might visualize a dark wind. The concept of force can be represented by a fork. The pictures you construct represent words, thoughts, or phrases. Cartoons 7.16 and 7.17 illustrate substitute link words and graphics that we use when introducing students to the names of the European countries.

CARTOON 7.16

CARTOON 7.17

KEY WORD

The essence of the key-word system is to select one word to represent a longer thought or several subordinate thoughts. Boris's speech is an example of the use of one word to trigger many verbal statements. Boris chose key-word qualifications to represent a list of his superior qualities. If, as in his case, the key word is abstract, it is necessary to use the substitute-word system before inventing a memorable image.

THE MODEL OF TEACHING

The model of teaching that we have developed from the work of Pressley, Levin, and their associates includes four phases: attending to the material, developing connections, expanding sensory images, and practicing recall. These phases are based on the principle of attention and the techniques for enhancing recall (see Table 7.1).

SYNTAX

Phase one calls for activities that require the learner to concentrate on the learning material and organize it in a way that helps that learner remember it. Generally, this includes focusing on what needs to be remembered—the major ideas and examples. Underlining is one way to do this. Listing the ideas separately and rephrasing them in one's own words is another task that forces attention. Finally, reflecting on the material, comparing ideas, and determining the relationship among the ideas is a third attending activity.

TABLE 7.1 **SYNTAX OF MEMORY MODEL**

Phase One: Attending to the Material	Phase Two: Developing Connections
Use techniques of underlining, listing, reflecting.	Make material familiar and develop connections using key-word, substitute-word, and link-word system techniques.

Phase Three: Expanding Sensory Images	Phase Four: Practicing Recall
Use techniques of ridiculous association and exaggeration. Revise images.	Practice recalling the material until it is completely learned.

Once the material to be learned has been clarified and evaluated, several memory techniques should be used to develop connections with what is to be learned. Phase two includes using such techniques as the link words, substitute words (in the case of abstractions), and key words for long or complex passages. The notion is to connect the new material to familiar words, pictures, or ideas, and to link images or words.

Once the initial associations have been identified, the images can be enhanced (phase three) by asking the student to associate them with more than one sense and by generating humorous dramatizations through ridiculous association and exaggeration. At this time the images can be revised for greater recall power. In phase four the student is asked to practice recall of the material.

SOCIAL SYSTEM

The social system is cooperative: the students and teacher work as a team to shape the new material for commitment to memory.

PRINCIPLES OF REACTION

The teacher's role in this model is to help the student work the material. Working from the student's frame of reference, the teacher helps him or her identify key items, pairs, and images.

SUPPORT SYSTEM

Pictures, concrete aids, films, and other audiovisual materials are especially useful for increasing the sensory richness of the associations. However, no special support system is required for this model. We do recommend, however, that you look up the material by Lucas Education, the "Dr. Memory" series, where books such as *Names and Faces Made Easy* and *Learning How to Learn* are available, along with sets of audio and video cassettes. Although the scholars have documented the considerable effects of the mnemonic techniques, Lucas is the technician of the field and his advice and examples are delightful and effective.

APPLICATION

Mastropieri and Scruggs (1991) provide a large number of applications, including developed materials for a number of areas that have been difficult for students, such as geographical and historical places and people.

The memory model is applicable to all curriculum areas where material needs to be memorized. It can be used with groups (a chemistry class mastering the table of elements) or individuals (a student learning a poem, story, speech, or part in a play).

Although it has many uses in teacher-led "memory sessions," it has its widest application after students have mastered it and can use it independently. Thus, the model should be taught so that dependence on the teacher is decreased and students can use the procedures whenever they need to memorize. The students are taught the following steps:

1. *Organizing information to be learned.* Essentially, the more information is organized, the easier it is to learn and retain. Information can be organized by categories. The concept attainment, inductive, and advance organizer models facilitate memorization by helping students associate the material in the categories. Consider the following list of words from a popular spelling series, in the order in which the spelling book presents them to the children:

soft	plus	cloth	frost	song
trust	luck	club	sock	pop
cost	lot	son	won	

Suppose we ask the students to classify the words by beginnings, endings, and the presence of vowels. The act of classification requires the students to scrutinize the words and associate words containing similar elements. They can then name the categories in each classification (the "c" group and the "st" group), calling further attention to the common attributes of the group. They can also connect words that fit together ("pop song," "soft cloth," and so on). They can then proceed to rehearse the spellings of one category at a time. The same principle operates over other types of material—say, number facts. Whether categories are provided to students or whether they create them, the purpose is the same. Also, information can be selected with categories in mind. The above list is, to outward appearances, almost random. A list that deliberately and systematically provides variations would be easier to organize (it would already have at least implicit categories within it).

2. *Ordering information to be learned.* Information learned in series, especially if there is meaning to the series, is easier to assimilate and retain. For example, if we wish to learn the names of the states of Australia, it is easier if we always start with the same one (say, the largest) and proceed in the same order. Historical events by chronology are more easily learned than events sorted randomly. Order is simply another way of organizing information. We could have the students alphabetize their list of spelling words.

3. *Linking information to familiar material (sounds and meanings are both given consideration).* Suppose we are learning the names of the states. We can connect "Georgia" to "George," "Louisiana" to "Louis," "Maryland" to "Marry" or "Mary," and so on. Categorizing the names of the states or ordering them by size, or ordering them within region, provides more associations.

4. *Linking information to visual representations.* Maryland can be linked to a picture of a marriage, Oregon to a picture of a gun, Maine to a burst water main, and so forth. Letters and numerals can be linked to something that evokes both familiar sounds and images. For example, "one" can be linked to "bun" and a picture of a boy eating a bun, "b" to a bee and a picture of a bee. Those links can be used over and over. "April is the cruelest month, breeding lilacs out of the dead land" is more easily remembered thinking of an ominous metal spring, coiled malevolently over the spring flowers.

5. *Linking information to associated information.* A person's name, linked to information such as a well-known person having the same name, a sound-alike, and some personal information, is easier to remember than the name rehearsed by itself. Louis (Louis Armstrong) "looms" over Jacksonville (his place of birth). Learning the states of Australia while thinking of the points of the compass and the British origins of many of the names (New South Wales) is easier than learning them in order alone.

6. *Devices that make the information vivid are also useful.* Lorayne and Lucas favor "ridiculous association," where information is linked to absurd associations ("The silly two carries his twin two on his back so they are really four"). Others favor the use of dramatization and vivid illustrations (such as counting the basketball players on two teams to illustrate that five and five equal ten).

7. *Rehearsal (practice) is always useful, and students benefit from knowledge of results.* Students who have not had past success with tasks requiring memorization will benefit by having relatively short assignments and clear, timely feedback as they have success.

INSTRUCTIONAL AND NURTURANT EFFECTS

The memory model is specifically designed to increase the capacity to store and retrieve information. It should nurture a sense of intellectual power—a growing consciousness of the ability to master unfamiliar material, as well as imagery skills and attention to one's environment (see Figure 7.1).

One of the most important outcomes of the model is the students' recognition that learning is not a mysterious, innate process over which they have no control. As Ian Hunter (1964) points out:

> The mastery of some simple mnemonic system may lead some people to realize, for the first time, that they can control and modify their own mental activities. And this realization may encourage them to undertake that self-critical

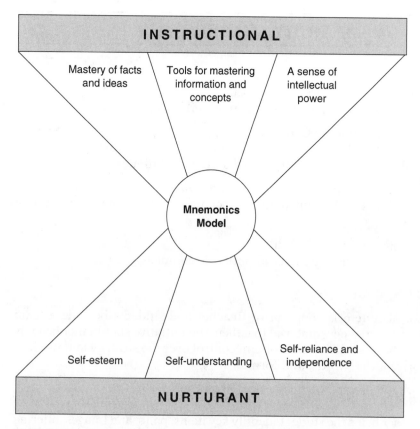

FIGURE 7.1   Instructional and nurturant effects of the mnemonics model.

experimentation with their own learning and remembering procedures which is such an important part of intellectual development. (p. 302)

Thus, awareness of how to learn and how to improve learning results in a sense of mastery and control over one's future.

A second outcome is the improvement of imaging capacity and the realization that creative forms of thinking are an essential part of more convergent, information-oriented learning. In training for imagery, creativity is nourished, and ease with playful, creative thought is encouraged. Imaging requires that we observe and attend to the world around us. Consequently, the use of imaging as part of memory work disciplines us to attend to our surroundings automatically.

Finally, of course, our capacity for remembering particular material is strengthened by this model—we become more effective memorizers.

SUMMARY
CHART ► **MEMORY MODEL**

Syntax

Phase One: Attending to the Material
  Use techniques of underlining, listing, reflecting.

Phase Two: Developing Connections
  Make material familiar and develop connections using key-word, substitute-word, and link-word system techniques.

Phase Three: Expanding Sensory Images
  Use techniques of ridiculous association and exaggeration. Revise images.

Phase Four: Practicing Recall
  Practice recalling the material until it is completely learned.

Social System

The social system is cooperative. Teacher and students become a team working with the new material together. The initiative should increasingly become the students' as they obtain control over the strategy and use it to memorize ideas, words, and formulas.

Principles of Reaction

The teacher helps the student identify key items, pairs, and images, offering suggestions but working from the students' frames of reference. The familiar elements must be primarily from the students' storehouse of material.

Support System

All of the customary devices of the curriculum areas can be brought into play. Pictures, concrete aids, films, and other audiovisual materials are especially useful for increasing the sensory richness of the associations.

SYNECTICS
The Arts of Enhancing Creative Thought

Of all the models, synectics has got to give the most immediate pleasure when you're leading the exercises. We've been teaching kids (both elementary and secondary) to lead synectics. I have to admit that I always have a little touch of green when I turn it over to them, because they're going to have the fun, now.

—Letter from Bruce Joyce to Bill Gordon, January 1971

S C E N A R I O

A tenth-grade class seems to be locked up on a public policy issue. The issue is precipitated by a school board decision that all backpacks and other similar items should be transparent so that all items are easy for security personnel to inspect.

The students appear to agree, without dissent, that security is important, but wonder whether the policy intrudes into their privacy. One student says that having her private items, such as for menstruation (tampons and sanitary pads), visible is a violation of privacy. Ms. Kruger decides to approach the question from a synectics point of view. She leads the students to an analysis of the arguments on both sides, such as "We need to make sure that no student brings dangerous goods into the school" and "We have the right to privacy—to have places where we can bring books, papers, and personal items into the school without scrutinization." The students take relatively "hard lines" on these issues, such as—"Security is paramount" and "Privacy is most important."

Ms. Kruger begins a series of synectics exercises designed to generate original ways of thinking about the problem. She begins with direct analogies: "How are trees like cows?" and proceeds to personal analogies: "Be a tree. How do you feel about storms?" and, finally, has the students accumulate the analogies they have made into compressed conflicts or oxymorons. They come back to the original questions with some of the compressed conflicts—looking at the issues as "Protective turbulence," and "Disciplined freedom," among others, and then review the questions in terms of the ideas that are generated.

Ideas like, "Rules for protection create storms and change the ways we are accustomed to" begin to flow. The compressed conflicts help the students to bridge their disagreements and generate a new set of public policy questions without the emotionality that had locked them into disputes.

That's one of the outcomes we expect from synectics.

S C E N A R I O

A junior high school class is creating a book of short stories and poems. Their English teacher, Tara Hatcher, has gradually become aware that some stories and many of the poems are hackneyed and ordinary. She has been helping individuals rewrite their poems and stories, and some of them have been improved, but on the whole she is disappointed with the work.

Then Tara runs across the work of William Gordon of Cambridge, Massachusetts, who believes that creativity can be enhanced by a series of group exercises. These exercises are designed to help us understand the process of creativity more completely and to use new metaphors and analogies to "break set" and generate new alternatives. Tara decides to try Gordon's methods. One morning, she has each of her students read a poem and a short story. She then says, "Today we're going to try something new that I hope will help us see our stories and poems in a different light. For the next 15 or 20 minutes I want us to play with ideas and then have you go back to your work and see what you can do to improve it. At the end of this exercise, I'm going to ask you to rewrite part or all of your poems and stories." She begins by asking what a poem is. The children give a variety of answers, from which Tara selects key words and writes them on the board.

"It doesn't have to rhyme."

"It lets your feelings come out."

"It uses different kinds of words."

She then asks, "How is a poem like an automobile?" The children are puzzled. Then one ventures, "It takes you on a trip. It's a word trip, and you have to have the road in your imagination."

Someone else observes, "It is self-propelled—you just get in it and it goes." Another student comments, "When you're writing one, sometimes you have trouble getting the motor started."

After a time, Tara says, "Pick an animal—any animal." "How about a giraffe?" someone suggests. "OK," the teacher asks, "how is a poem like a giraffe?"

"It has a lot of parts fastened together in funny ways," one student laughs.

"It kind of stands above everything else and looks at things in a different way," another adds.

The exercise goes on. After a time, Tara asks the students to select one of the words they have dealt with in discussing a poem. They select the word *above*.

"How does it feel," she asks, "to be above?"

"You feel different," replies one. "You can see things you don't ordinarily even notice," says another.

"You'll start feeling superior if you don't watch out," says another.

And so it goes. Finally, Tara asks the students to make lists of words they have been dealing with that seem to be opposite in some fashion—words that apply tension to each other. The students pick giraffe and snail, for they feel that both are animals but that they are very different in the way they live and move.

"Well," she says, "let's come back to your poems and short stories. Think of them as giraffes and snails together; write your poems or stories as if they were a giraffe and a snail holding hands, going through the woods together."

Here are three products of that exercise.

THE GREAT KING

The great king stares out over his kingdom watching admiringly. The king stares out over his subjects, the seagulls, fish, crabs, and everything else in the safe underwater home of his bottomless stomach. He lets out another breeze of his salty breath that can be smelled miles away. Another crash of his arm pushes away the sand to make damp mud that seagulls love. His ever-stretching body wraps around the world of his presence for he is king of earth. He opens his heart to the people who take meaningful walks on his beach as if paying gratitude for everything he has done. Another crash sends a seagull flying as if he was a royal messenger. The Ocean, the king, stares and is proud of what he sees.

by Genevieve

THE MOTORCYCLE

It sounds like an enraged mountain lion.
It looks like a steel horse.
It shifts gears and changes notes.
It goes very fast.
The sound of the motorcycle
    breaks the stillness
        of the night.

THE ADVENTURES OF
SAMUAL O'BRIAN, SECRET SPY _____

It all happened when Samual Watkins O'Brian, an average blond-haired 35-year-old chemist, was working in Laboratory 200, Hartford, Connecticut, for the government. While mixing chemicals in a beaker, the substance started glowing strangely. It also became very hot. At that moment he dropped it to the floor. He turned to run, but before he had time to take a step it crashed to the floor, followed by a blinding explosion! As he started to run, he felt his skin shrinking. As he ran he shrank to a height of 5.5 inches, one-tenth his normal height!

His superior ran in with a fire extinguisher yelling, "What happened in here, Sam?"

While jumping up and down, Sam yelled, "I've shrunk! I've shrunk!" His superior made no reply. He again yelled out his cry for help. Then Sam, realizing that his yelling was useless over the roar of the fire that had now started, tugged at his superior's giant shoelace. His superior bent down to see what was happening with his shoelace, and he saw a very small and scared Samual O'Brian.

Samual yelled, "Hey Jack, pick me up *carefully*!

His superior's reply was *"Cripes*! What happened to you?" Sam explained the story in Jack's ear while Jack ran swiftly with Sam in the palm of his hand to the guard on the second floor.

Jack said (when they got there), "Seal off the building! I need Top Secret government personnel and *speed it up*!!!" Because of the excitement, Sam fainted. The next thing he knew he was in the Central Security President's office lying in a marble ashtray, filled with warm water (and plenty of bubbles, of course). He found himself staring into the face of David Shields, President of C.S.

Sam stated that he was so sorry to clutter up the President's desk but. . . . Then David broke in "Oh, it's nothing, people shrink every day around here, but I guess you wouldn't know because you can't see the rings around the bathtub . . . er, uh, ashtray."

David presented Sam with a small box of cigars and a custom-fitted suit, James Bond style (if you know what I mean). Sam got dressed and David said, "We'd like you to work for us, Sam."

Tara has introduced metaphoric thinking to her students. Synectics, designed by William J. J. Gordon and his associates (1961a), is a very interesting and delightful approach to the development of innovations. The initial work with synectics procedures was to develop "creativity groups" within industrial organizations—that is, groups of people trained to work together to function as problem solvers or product developers. Gordon has adapted synectics for use with schoolchildren, and materials containing many of the synectics activities are now being published. (For a complete list of synectics materials write to Synectics Education Systems, 121 Brattle Street, Cambridge, MA 02138.) The chief element in synectics is the use of analogies. In synectics exercises, students "play" with analogies until they relax and begin to enjoy making more and more metaphoric comparisons, as did Tara's students. Then they use analogies to attack problems or ideas.

Ordinarily, when we are confronted with a task—say, a problem to be solved or a piece of writing to be produced—we consciously become logical. We prepare to write by making an outline of the points to be made. We analyze the elements of a problem and try to think it through. We use our existing storehouse of words and phrases to set down our ideas; we use our storehouse of learned solutions to face a problem.

For many problems and tasks of expressing ourselves, our logic works well enough. What do we do when our old solutions or ways of expressing ourselves are not sufficient to do the job? That is when we use synectics. It is designed to lead us into a slightly illogical world—to give us the opportunity to invent new ways of seeing things, expressing ourselves, and approaching problems.

For example, school officials struggle with the problem of how to deal with absenteeism. When a student repeatedly fails to come to school, what do they do? Frequently, they turn to punishment. And what punishment is available? Frequently, suspension. That is logical, isn't it? To choose a severe punishment to match what is regarded as a severe infraction? The trouble with the solution is that it imposes on the student as a penalty exactly the same condition that the student had chosen in lieu of school. Synectics is used to help us develop fresh ways of thinking about the student, the student's motives, the nature of penalties, our goals, and the nature of the problem. We have to develop empathy for someone who is in conflict with us and recognize that we may have an inadequate definition and may be using a "logical" solution that blinds us to creative alternatives.

When stuck, we have to back away from what appears to be logical thought and then return to see if we can redefine the problem and seek alternative solutions. Through analogies we might conceive of our absentee as an "unhappy lark," as on a "destructive vacation," and the problem as one of ending an "empty feast." Our own needed behaviors may be ones of "seductive strictness," "strong lovingness," and "dangerous peacemaking."

If we can relax the premises that have blocked us, we can begin to generate new solutions. We can consider that we have been taking responsibility for the students in areas where they may need to be responsible for themselves. We can wonder whether the solution lies as much in our administration of the rules as it does in how we teach. We may wonder whether communities of peers might not create the energy and sense of belongingness that would attack the problem from a different perspective.

The social and scientific world in which we live abounds with problems for which new solutions are needed. Problems of poverty, international law, crime, just taxation, and war and peace would not exist if our logic did not fail us. Striving for appropriate self-expression—trying to learn how to write and speak lucidly and compellingly—bedevils all of us. Two problems are persistent: grasping the subject clearly and comprehensively and generating appropriate forms of expression.

Let us consider another example from Martin Abramowitz's classroom in Mill Valley, California.

S C E N A R I O

Abramowitz's 7th-grade class is preparing a campaign in opposition to a change in Forest Service regulations that would permit a large grove of redwood trees to be cut down as part of a lumbering operation. They have made posters that they intend to display around their community and send to the members of the state legislature. They have the rough sketches for the posters and their captions, and they are examining them.

"Well, what do you think?" asks Priscilla.

"Well, they're OK," says Tommy. "They sure say where we stand. Actually, though, I think they're a little dull."

"So do I," adds Maryann. "A couple of them are OK, but the others are real preachy and stiff."

"There's nothing really wrong with them," chimes in another, "they're just not very zingy."

"Also, they don't build any bridges with our opponents. They present our side, but I'm not sure they'll reach anybody but people who already agree with us."

After some discussion, it is obvious that nearly everybody feels the same way. They decide that two or three of the posters are well designed and convey their message, but they need some others that would be more poignant.

"Let's try synectics," suggests one of them.

"With pictures and captions?" asks one of the other children. "I thought we could only use synectics with poetry. Can we use synectics with stuff like this?"

"Why sure we can," says Priscilla. "I don't know why I didn't think of it. We've been doing it with poetry all year long."

"Well we sure have nothing to lose," adds Tommy. "How would it work?"

"Well," says Priscilla, "we could see these posters we've done as the beginning point and then go through a synectics training exercise and see if it gives us some ideas for pictures and captions. We could think of redwood trees in terms of various personal and direct analogies and compressed conflicts."

"Well let's try it," chimes in George.

"Let's start right now," says Sally. "We could go through our exercises and then have lunch time to think about the posters."

"Can I be the leader?" asks Nancy. "I've got some super ideas for some stretching exercises."

"Is that OK?" says Priscilla.

The others agree and Nancy begins.

"How is a redwood tree like a toothpick?" she asks.

"You use the tree to pick the teeth of the gods," laughs George. Everyone joins in the laughter and they are off.

It's clear that Mr. Abramowitz has spent enough time using synectics that the students internalized the process and purpose. They can proceed on their own, drawing on the model when they find it helpful.

S C E N A R I O

One of the present authors struggled for a month to write a single page that would introduce a book on school improvement. The introduction had to express the complexity of the situation the school occupies in society and to convey that it needed improvement, but it had to do so in an upbeat and not discouraging fashion. Finally, after an afternoon of synectics, he produced the following passages:

Richly connected to its social milieu, tightly clasped by tradition and yet the medium of modern ideas and artifacts, the school floats paradoxically in its ocean of social forces. It is a cradle of social stability and the harbinger of cultural change. Throughout history its critics have found it both too backward and too advanced. It falls behind the times and fails to keep us in simultaneous cadence.

Its missions are elusive. Basic education is prized but so are creativity, problem solving, academic excellence, and vocational skills, sometimes by the same people, sometimes not. Liberals and conservatives alike seek to make the school the instrument of social policy. It is the sword of the militant and the warm bosom of the humanist. Its students are varied. Talents and handicaps mingle, sometimes in the same minds and bodies.

The inner city and rural hinterland make their claims on creaky old schoolhouses while shiny suburban schools grope for a coherent mission. Powerful self-concepts march through the front door of the school while timid souls slip in by the back stairs. Cultural differences are mixed together, with problems of identity and adaptation surfacing chaotically to be dealt with.

Technologies strengthen the school's potential and threaten to replace it. Its personnel receive very little training but are asked to manage one of the most complex professional tasks in our society. They have little status but awesome responsibility both for individual children and for the health of the society as a whole.

Because education exerts great influence on the young, society places great constraints on its schools so that they will reflect the prevailing social attitudes and will fit current views about how its children should be trained. Its very size draws attention. (In the United States there are more than 4,000,000 education professionals and about 12 percent of the gross national product is directly or indirectly consumed by the enterprises of education.) The public watches its investment carefully, scrutinizing educational practices, both traditional and innovative.

Efficiency is highly prized, but innovations are watched with apprehension. Our societal patterns of schooling, established in the early 1800s, have become familiar and comfortable, and we want our children to have an education that has continuity with our own. Thus most citizens are cautious about educational innovation. People like the familiar old schoolhouse as much as they criticize it. They tend to believe that current problems in education are caused by changes (perceived as a "lowering of standards") rather than because the old comfortable model of the school may be a little rusty and out-of-date. In fact, our society has changed a great deal since the days when the familiar and comfortable patterns of education were established, and many schools have become badly out of phase with the needs of children in today's world (Joyce, Hersh, and McKibbin, 1983, pp. 3–4).

This passage is by no means perfect, but it is much better than the prosaic passages that were its early drafts (for instance, "The public is somewhat ambivalent about the schools. In some ways they want a forward-looking education for their children and in others they want a familiar, stable education."). The passage was built on a series of compressed conflicts that express the various types of ambivalence that appear in public discussions of the school system.

ORIENTATION TO THE MODEL

GOALS AND ASSUMPTIONS

Gordon grounds synectics in four ideas that challenge conventional views about creativity. First, creativity is important in everyday activities. Most of us associate the creative process with the development of great works of art or music, or perhaps with a clever new invention. Gordon emphasizes creativity as a part of our daily work and leisure lives. His model is designed to increase problem-solving capacity, creative expression, empathy, and insight into social relations. He also stresses that the meanings of ideas can be enhanced through creative activity by helping us see things more richly.

Second, the creative process is not at all mysterious. It can be described, and it is possible to train persons directly to increase their creativity. Traditionally, creativity is viewed as a mysterious, innate, and personal capacity that can be destroyed if its processes are probed too deeply. In contrast, Gordon believes that if individuals understand the basis of the creative process, they can learn to use that understanding to increase the creativity with which they live and work, independently and as members of groups. Gordon's view that creativity is enhanced by conscious analysis led him to describe it and create training procedures that can be applied in schools and other settings.

Third, creative invention is similar in all fields—the arts, the sciences, engineering—and is characterized by the same underlying intellectual processes. This idea is contrary to common belief. In fact, to many people, creativity is confined to the arts. In engineering and the sciences, however, it is simply called by another name: *invention*. Gordon maintains that the link between generative thinking in the arts and in the sciences is quite strong.

Gordon's fourth assumption is that individual and group invention (creative thinking) are very similar. Individuals and groups generate ideas and products in much the same fashion. Again, this is very different from the stance that creativity is an intensely personal experience, not to be shared.

THE CREATIVE STATE AND THE SYNECTICS PROCESS

The specific processes of synectics are developed from a set of assumptions about the psychology of creativity. First, by bringing the creative process to consciousness and by developing explicit aids to creativity, we can directly increase the creative capacity of both individuals and groups.

A second assumption is that the "emotional component is more important than the intellectual, the irrational more important than the rational" (Gordon, 1961a, p. 6). Creativity is the development of new mental patterns. Nonrational interplay leaves room for open-ended thoughts that can lead to a mental state in which new ideas are possible. The basis for decisions, however, is always the rational. The analogistic state is the best mental environment for exploring and expanding ideas, but it is not a decision-making stage. Gordon does not undervalue the linear intellect; he assumes that a logic is used in decision making and that technical competence is necessary to the formation of ideas in many areas. But he believes that creativity is essentially an *emotional* process, one that requires elements of irrationality and emotion to enhance intellectual processes. Much problem solving is rational and intellectual, but by adding the irrational we increase the likelihood that we will generate fresh ideas.

The third assumption is that the "emotional, irrational elements must be understood in order to increase the probability of success in a problem solving situation" (Gordon, 1961a, p. 1). In other words, the analysis of certain irrational and emotional processes can help the individual and the group increase their creativity by using irrationality constructively. Aspects of the irrational can be understood and consciously controlled. Achievement of this control, through the deliberate use of metaphor and analogy, is the object of synectics.

METAPHORIC ACTIVITY

Through the metaphoric activity of the synectics model, creativity becomes a conscious process. Metaphors establish a relationship of likeness, the comparison of one object or idea with another object or idea by using one in place of the other. Through these substitutions the creative process occurs, connecting the familiar with the unfamiliar or creating a new idea from familiar ideas.

Metaphor introduces conceptual distance between the people and the object or subject matter and prompts original thoughts. For example, by asking students to think of their textbook as an old shoe or as a river, we provide a structure, a metaphor, with which the students can think about something familiar in a new way. Conversely, we can ask students to think about a new topic, say the human body, in an old way by asking them to compare it to the transportation system. Metaphoric activity thus depends on and draws from the students' knowledge, helping them connect ideas from familiar content to those from new content, or view familiar content from a new perspective. Synectics strategies using metaphoric activity are designed, then, to provide a structure through which people can free themselves to develop imagination and insight into everyday activities. Three types of analogies are used as the basis of synectics exercises: personal analogy, direct analogy, and compressed conflict.

PERSONAL ANALOGY

To make personal analogies requires students to empathize with the ideas or objects to be compared. Students must feel they have become part of the physical elements of the problem. The identification may be with a person, plant, animal, or nonliving thing. For example, students may be instructed, "Be an automobile engine. What do you feel like? Describe how you feel when you are started in the morning; when your battery goes dead; when you come to a stoplight."

The essence of personal analogy is on empathetic involvement. Gordon gives the example of a problem situation in which the chemist personally identifies with the molecules in action. He might ask, "How would I feel if I were a molecule?" and then feel himself being part of the "stream of dancing molecules."

Personal analogy requires loss of self as one transports oneself into another space or object. The greater the conceptual distance created by loss of self, the more likely it is that the analogy is new and that the students have been creative or innovative. Gordon identifies four levels of involvement in personal analogy:

1. *First-person description of facts.* The person recites a list of well-known facts but presents no new way of viewing the object or animal and shows no empathetic involvement. In terms of the car engine, the person might say, "I feel greasy" or "I feel hot."
2. *First-person identification with emotion.* The person recites common emotions but does not present new insights: "I feel powerful" (as the car engine).
3. *Empathetic identification with a living thing.* The student identifies emotionally and kinesthetically with the subject of the analogy: "When you smile like that, I smile all over."

4. *Empathetic identification with a nonliving object.* This level requires the most commitment. The person sees himself or herself as an inorganic object and tries to explore the problem from a sympathetic point of view: "I feel exploited. I cannot determine when I start and stop. Someone does that for me" (as the car engine).

The purpose of introducing these levels of personal analogy is not to identify forms of metaphoric activity but to provide guidelines for how well conceptual distance has been established. Gordon believes that the usefulness of analogies is directly proportional to the distance created. The greater the distance, the more likely the student is to come up with new ideas.

DIRECT ANALOGY

Direct analogy is the comparison of two objects or concepts. The comparison does not have to be identical in all respects. Its function is simply to transpose the conditions of the real topic or problem situation to another situation in order to present a new view of an idea or problem. This involves identification with a person, plant, animal, or nonliving thing. Gordon cites the experience of the engineer watching a shipworm tunneling into a timber. As the worm ate its way into the timber by constructing a tube for itself and moving forward, the engineer, Sir March Isumbard Brunel, got the notion of using caissons to construct underwater tunnels (Gordon, 1961a, pp. 40–41). Another example of direct analogy occurred when a group was attempting to devise a can with a top that could be used to cover the can once it had been opened. In this instance, the analogy of the pea pod gradually emerged, which produced the idea of a seam placed a distance below the top of the can, thus permitting a removable lid.

COMPRESSED CONFLICT

The third metaphorical form is compressed conflict, generally a two-word phrase in which the words seem to contradict each other. *Tiredly aggressive* and *friendly foe* are two examples. Gordon's examples are *life-saving destroyer* and *nourishing flame*. He also cites Pasteur's expression, *safe attack*. Compressed conflicts, according to Gordon, provide the broadest insight into a new subject. They reflect the student's ability to incorporate two frames of reference with respect to a single object. The greater the distance between frames of reference, the greater the mental flexibility.

STRETCHING EXERCISES: USING METAPHORS

These three types of metaphors form the basis of the sequence of activities in this model of teaching. They can also be used separately with groups, as a warm-up to the creative process—that is, to problem solving. We refer to this use as *stretching exercises.*

Stretching exercises provide experience with the three types of metaphoric activity, but they are not related to any particular problem situation, nor do they follow a sequence of phases. They teach students the process of metaphoric thinking before asking them to use it to solve a problem, create a design, or explore a concept. Students are simply asked to respond to ideas such as the following:

DIRECT ANALOGIES

Direct analogies are elicited with questions that ask for a direct comparison, such as:

An orange is like what living thing?
How is a school like a salad?
How are polar bears like frozen yogurt?
Which is softer—a whisper or a kitten's fur?

PERSONAL ANALOGIES

Personal analogies are elicited by asking people to pretend to be an object, action, idea, or event, such as:

Be a cloud. Where are you? What are you doing?
How do you feel when the sun comes out and dries you up?
Pretend you are your favorite book. Describe yourself.
What are your three wishes?

COMPRESSED CONFLICTS

Compressed conflict practice is elicited by presenting some and asking people to manipulate them, such as:

How is a computer shy and aggressive?
What machine is like a smile and a frown?

THE MODEL OF TEACHING

SYNTAX

There are actually two strategies or models of teaching based on synectics procedures. One of these (*creating something new*) is designed to make the familiar strange, to help students see old problems, ideas, or products in a new, more creative light. The other strategy (*making the strange familiar*) is designed to make new, unfamiliar ideas more meaningful. Although both strategies employ the three types of analogy, their objectives, syntax, and principles of reaction are different. We refer to creating something new as strategy one, and making the strange familiar as strategy two.

Strategy one helps students see familiar things in unfamiliar ways by using analogies to create conceptual distance. Except for the final step, in which the students return to the original problem, they do not make simple comparisons. The objective of this strategy may be to develop a new understanding; to empathize with a show-off or bully; to design a new doorway or city; to solve social or interpersonal problems, such as a garbage strike or two students fighting with each other; or to solve personal problems, such as how to concentrate better when reading. The role of the teacher is to guard against premature analyses and closure. The syntax of strategy one appears in Table 8.1.

The following transcript of a synectics session shows a teacher helping students to see a familiar concept in fresh ways. At the beginning, the students pick the concept of "The Hood," to be described later in a writing

TABLE 8.1 **SYNTAX FOR CREATING SOMETHING NEW, STRATEGY ONE**

Phase One: Description of Present Condition	**Phase Two:** Direct Analogy
Teacher has students describe situation or situation as they see it now.	Students suggest direct analogies, select one, and explore (describe) it further.

Phase Three: Personal Analogy	**Phase Four:** Compressed Conflict
Students "become" the analogy they selected in phase two.	Students take their descriptions from phases two and three, suggest several compressed conflicts, and choose one.

Phase Five: Direct Analogy	**Phase Six:** Reexamination of the Original Task
Students generate and select another direct analogy, based on the compressed conflict.	Teacher has students move back to original task or problem and use the last analogy and/or the entire synectics experience.

composition. The lesson illustrates the six phases of the model (Gordon, 1971, pp. 7–11):

1. Teacher: Now the problem is how to present this hood so that he's the hoodiest of hoods, but also a special, individualized person.
Student: He robs the Rabbinical School.
Student: Let's name him.
Student: Trog.
Student: Al.
Student: Slash.
Student: Eric.
Teacher: His names don't matter all that much. Let's call him Eric. What can we say about Eric?
Student: Black, greasy hair. They all have black, greasy hair.
Student: Long, blonde hair—bleached —peroxided—with baby-blues. Eyes, I mean.
Student: Bitten fingernails.
Student: He's short and muscular.
Student: Maybe he should be scrawny.
Student: Bow-legged   and   yellow teeth and white, tight Levis.

1. *Phase One: Describing the Problem or Present Condition.* Teacher asks students to discuss the familiar idea.

2. Teacher: Is there anything here that's original? If you wrote that and backed off and read it, what would you think?
Class: No! Stereotyped! Standard! No personality! Very general! Same old stuff!
Teacher: I agree. Eric, so far, is like every other hood. Now we have a problem to attack!
Teacher: We must define a personality for this hood, for Eric.
Student: He's got to be individualized.
Student: He has to have a way of getting money.

2. Teacher has students state the problem . . . and define the task.

3. Teacher: That's still an overgeneral idea of Eric. Let's put some strain into this idea. Hold it. Suppose I ask you to

3. *Phase Two: Direct Analogy.* Teacher moves the students into analogies. He asks for a direct analogy. He also spec-

give me a direct analogy, something like Eric, but it's a machine. Tell me about a machine that has Eric's qualities as you see him. Not a human being, a machine.
Student: He's a washing machine. A dishwasher.
Student: An old beat-up car.
Student: I want him to be a rich hood.
Student: A beer factory.
Student: A pinball machine in a dive.
Student: Roulette.

ifies the nature of the analogy—that is, a machine—in order to assure getting one of some distance (organic-inorganic comparison).

4. Teacher: You're focusing on the kinds of machines that Eric plays with. What is the thing that has his qualities in it?
Student: An electric can opener.
Student: A vacuum cleaner.
Student: A neon sign.
Student: A jello mold.

4. Teacher reflects to students what they are doing so that they can be pushed to more creative analogies.

5. Teacher: What is the machine that would make the strangest comparison between it and Eric? Go ahead and vote. (The class voted for the dishwasher.)

5. Teacher lets students select the analogy to develop, but he provides the criterion for selection: "strangest comparison."

6. Teacher: First of all, how does a dishwasher work?
Student: People put in the dirty dishes and the water goes around and around and the dishes come out clean.
Student: There's a blower in the one that's in the common room.
Student: It's all steam inside. Hot!
Student: I was thinking that if you want to make an analogy between the washer and the joy . . .

6. Teacher moves students simply to *explore* (describe) the machine they selected before making comparisons to their original source.

7. Teacher: Hold it. Just stay with me. Don't look backward and make an analogical comparison too soon . . . and now is probably too soon.

7. Teacher controls responses to keep students from pushing to a comparison too soon. No comparisons to original source are made before moving on to another analogy.

8. Teacher: OK. Now, try being the dishwasher. What does it feel like to be

8. *Phase Three: Personal Analogy.* Teacher asks for personal analogy.

a dishwasher? Tell us. Make yourself the dishwasher.

Student: Well, all these things are given to me. Dishes are dirty. I want to get them clean. I'm trying. I throw off some steam and finally I get them clean. That's my duty.

9. Teacher: Come on now people! You've got to put yourselves into the dishwasher and be it. All Lee's told us is what we already know about a dishwasher. There's none of *Lee* in it. It's hard, but try to *be* the dishwasher.

Student: It's very discouraging. You're washing all day long. I never get to know anybody. They keep throwing these dishes at me, and I just throw the steam at them. I see the same type of dishes.

Student: I get mad and get the dishes extra hot, and I burn people's fingers.

Student: I feel very repressed. They keep feeding me dishes. All I can do is shut myself off.

Student: I get so mad at everybody maybe I won't clean the dishes and then everybody will get sick.

Student: I just love garbage. I want more and more. The stuff that falls off the dishes is soft and mushy and good to eat.

10. Teacher: Let's look at the notes I've been making about your responses. Can you pick two words that argue with each other?

Student: "Used" vs. "clean."

Student: "Duty" vs. "what you want to do."

Teacher: How can we put that more poetically?

Student: "Duty" vs. "inclination."

Student: "Duty" vs. "whim."

Student: "Discouraging fun."

Student: "Angry game."

9. Teacher reflects to students the fact that they are describing the dishwasher, not what it *feels* like to be a dishwasher.

10. *Phase Four: Compressed Conflict.* Teacher asks for compressed conflict as outgrowth of the personal analogy: "Can you pick two words that argue with each other?"

11. Teacher: All right. What one do you like best? Which one has the truest ring of conflict?
Class: "Angry game."

11. Teacher ends enumeration of possible compressed conflicts and asks them to select one. The teacher furnishes the criterion: "Which has the truest ring of conflict?"

12. Teacher: All right. Can you think of a direct analogy, an example from the animal world, of "angry game?"
Student: A lion in the cage at the circus.
Student: Rattlesnake.
Student: A pig ready for slaughter.
Student: A bear when it's attacking.
Student: Bullfrog.
Student: A bird protecting its young.
Student: Bullfight.
Student: A fish being caught.
Student: A skunk.
Student: A horse.
Student: A charging elephant.
Student: A fox hunt on horseback.
Student: Rodeo.
Student: Porcupine.
Teacher: Does anyone know where we are?
Student: We're trying to put personality into Eric, trying to make him more original.

12. *Phase Five: Direct Analogy.* Recycling the analogies; compressed conflict is not explored but serves as the basis of the next direct analogy, an example from the animal world of "angry game." There is no mention of the original.

13. Teacher: All right. Which of all the things you just thought of do you think would make the most exciting direct analogy? (Class chooses the bullfight.)
Teacher: Now we go back to Eric. How can we get the bullfight to describe Eric for us. Does anyone know what I mean by that?

13. Teacher ends the enumeration of direct analogies. Again, he has the students select one but he gives the criterion: "Which of all the things you just thought of do you think would make the most *exciting* direct analogy?"

14. (Class doesn't respond.)

14. Students are not into the analogy of the bullfight yet.

15. Teacher: All right. What do we know about a bullfight?
Student: He'll have to be the bull or the matador. I say he's the bull.

15. Teacher gets students to explore the characteristics of the bullfight, the analogy.

Student: Bull runs into the ring and he's surrounded by strangeness.
Student: They stick things into him and goad him . . .
Student: . . . from horses and from the ground.
Student: But sometimes he doesn't get killed.
Student: And everytime the bull is downgraded the crowd yells.

16. Teacher: What happens at the end?
Student: They drag him off with horses.
Student: How do they finish him off?
Student: A short sword.

16. Teacher tries to obtain more information about the analogy.

17. Teacher: How can we use this information to tell us something about Eric? How will you talk about Eric in terms of the material we've developed about a bullfight?
Student: He's the bull.
Student: He's the matador.
Student: If he's the bull, then the matador is society.
Teacher: Why don't you write something about Eric in terms of the bullfight? Talk about his personality and the outward signs of it. The reader opens your story about Eric, and he reads. It is your reader's first introduction to Eric. (A pause while the students write.)
Teacher: All finished? All right, let's read your stuff, from left to right.

17. *Phase Six: Reexamination of the Task.* Getting students to make comparisons; return to the original problem or task.

Here are a few examples of the students' writing.

In rage, running against a red neon flag and blinded by its shadow, Eric threw himself down on the ground. As if they were going to fall off, blood throbbed in his ears. No use fighting anymore. The knife wound in his side; the metallic jeers that hurt worse than the knife; the flash of uniforms and the flushed faces of the crowd made him want to vomit all over their clean robes.

He stood there in the middle of the street staring defiantly at the crowd. Faces leered back at him. Scornful eyes, huge red mouths, twisted laughs; Eric looked back as the crowd approached and drew his hand up sharply as one man began to speak. "Pipe down kid. We don't want any of your nonsense."

He was enclosed in a ring. People cheering all around for his enemy. He has been trained all his life to go out and take what he wanted and now there was an obstacle in his course. Society was bearing down and telling him he was all wrong. He must go to them and he was becoming confused. People should cheer at the matador. The matador hunts his prey. His claim to glory is raised by the approaching approval of the crowd. For although they brought all their holiday finery, the bull is goaded, and the matador smiles complacently. You are but my instrument and I hold the sword. (Gordon, 1970, pp. 7–11)

The synectics model has stimulated the students to see and feel the original idea (a gangster or hood, described in stereotypic terms) in a variety of fresh ways. If they had been solving a problem, we would expect that they would see it more richly and increase the solutions they could explore.

By contrast, strategy two, making the strange familiar, seeks to increase the students' understanding and internalization of substantially new or difficult material. In this strategy, metaphor is used for *analyzing*, not for creating conceptual distance as in strategy one. For instance, the teacher might present the concept of culture to her class. Using familiar analogies (such as a stove or a house), the students begin to define the characteristics that are present and those that are lacking in the concept. The strategy is both analytic and convergent: students constantly alternate between defining the characteristics of the more familiar subject and comparing these to the characteristics of the unfamiliar topic.

In phase one of this strategy, explaining the new topic, the students are provided with information. In phase two the teacher, or the students, suggest a direct analogy. Phase three involves "being the familiar" (personalizing the direct analogy). In phase four, students identify and explain the points of similarity between the analogy and the substantive material. In phase five, students explain the differences between analogies. As a measure of their acquisition of the new information, students can suggest and analyze their own familiar analogies in phases six and seven. The syntax of strategy two appears in Table 8.2.

The following is an illustration of strategy two as it has been used in a programmed workbook. The students are asked to make a comparison between democracy (new topic) and the body (familiar topic). The sample presented here does not include the personal analogy (phase three), which we recommend as part of the strategy. We feel that asking the students to "be the thing" before asking them to make intellectual connections will increase the richness of their thinking. In this example, the students are first presented with a short, substantive paragraph:

Democracy is a form of government that is based on the highest possible respect for the individual. All individuals have equal rights, protected by law. Since each

TABLE 8.2   **SYNTAX FOR MAKING THE STRANGE FAMILIAR,
STRATEGY TWO**

Phase One: Substantive Input	Phase Two: Direct Analogy
Teacher provides information on new topic.	Teacher suggests direct analogy and asks students to describe the analogy.

Phase Three: Personal Analogy	Phase Four: Comparing Analogies
Teacher has students "become" the direct analogy.	Students identify and explain the points of similarity between the new material and the direct analogy.

Phase Five: Explaining Differences	Phase Six: Exploration
Students explain where the analogy does not fit.	Students reexplore the original topic on its own terms.

Phase Seven: Generating Analogy
Students provide their own direct analogy and explore the similarities and differences.

person has a vote, when the people so desire they can change the law to further protect themselves. The role of education in a democracy is critically important because the right to vote carries with it the responsibility to understand issues. An uneducated voting public could be led by a power-hungry political group into voting away their right to freedom. Thus democracy puts all its faith in the individual, in all the people . . . democracy's respect for the individual is expressed in the right of individuals to own property such as industries whose purpose is to make profit in competition with others.

Next the students are told:

List the connections you see between the description of democracy and the human body. Certain elements of the human body are written in the left-hand column. In the right-hand column jot down the elements in the paragraph on democracy that you think are parallel.

BODY	DEMOCRACY
each cell	each individual
muscles	education
brain	law
body as whole	democratic country
disease	loss of freedom

After the students have filled in their connection list, they are asked to "write a short paragraph showing your analogical connections. Be sure to point out where you think the body analogue fits and where it doesn't."

A sample response:

Each body cell is an individual. It may not look like it to the naked eye, but that's how it looks under a microscope. The muscles are educated because they must be taught (except for automatic things such as blinking and digestion, and there may be teaching here that we don't know about) to do certain acts—walking, games, knitting, etc. The brain is the law. If I do something wrong, my mind tells me and my brain is in my mind. The body as a whole is democratic because it depends on the health of all the cells. When there is disease the body loses freedom and a power-hungry disease takes over. The body dies when the disease takes over all the cells. In democracy the people control the government by voting, and then they can always repair bad laws. You can't always repair a body that is growing older . . . it will finally die.

So far in this sample exercise the students have been held by the hand. An analogue was presented to them, and all they had to do was make the connections as they saw them. The final skill taught in this exercise is application. The students' program tells them:

Now think up your own analogue for democracy. Draw on the non-living world to make sure that your analogue is not like the body analogue. Write your choice of analogue on the line below. If your analogue doesn't fit, pick a new one. Remember that analogues never fit exactly, they are just a way of thinking.

Use this list form to get you going. Fill in the elements of your analogue and add more elements about democracy if you want.

YOUR ANALOGUE	DEMOCRACY
automobile	democracy
each part	each individual
education	design of parts
car itself	democracy
no gas	loss of freedom

In the final phase of the programmed exercise the students are told:

> Now write your connections in the best prose you can. First get your connec-
> tive thoughts down; then go back and worry about grammar. Don't let gram-
> mar get in your way while you are trying to say what you mean. Grammar is a
> skill that makes it easier for your reader; so do it later. Try *not* to write more
> than the following lines allow. *Quality not quantity.* Remember, show the fits
> and non-fits.

A student writes:

> All parts of a car are like the individuals in a democracy. When they are all in
> good shape, they are free and the car runs well. The way each part was made
> was its education. God gave men the right to be free, and God gave the car's
> engine the right to run—how the gases explode in the engine is God's gift. If
> democracy is neglected, then no freedom. If the car runs out of gas, then no
> freedom.

One further small phase is necessary to make sure the students realize
that analogues are not exact parallels. . . . The students are told: "On the
lines below, explain where your analogue doesn't fit."
A sample response:

> In a democracy, all the people must not neglect the country. In a car, it is the
> owner who neglects when he forgets to fill her up. Also I tried to find "profit" in
> a car—and couldn't. Any competition is a race in a car—not like competition in
> a democracy. Also, there are so many freedom laws in a democracy, and the only
> law I can think of for a car is the science law that makes the engine run.

The major difference between the two strategies lies in their use of analogy. In strategy one, students move through a series of analogies without
logical constraints; conceptual distance is increased, and imagination is free
to wander. In strategy two, students try to connect two ideas and to identify
the connections as they move through the analogies. The strategy the
teacher selects depends on whether he or she is trying to help students create something new or to explore the unfamiliar.

SOCIAL SYSTEM

Both models or strategies are moderately structured, with the teacher
initiating the sequence and guiding the use of the operational mechanisms.
The teacher also helps the students intellectualize their mental processes.
The students, however, have freedom in their open-ended discussions as
they engage in metaphoric problem solving. Norms of cooperation, "play of
fancy," and intellectual and emotional equality are essential to establishing
the setting for creative problem solving. The rewards are internal, coming
from students' satisfaction and pleasure with the learning activity.

PRINCIPLES OF REACTION

Instructors note the extent to which individuals seem to be tied to regimented patterns of thinking, and they try to induce psychological states likely to generate a creative response. In addition, the teachers themselves must use the nonrational to encourage reluctant students to indulge in irrelevance, fantasy, symbolism, and other devices necessary to break out of set channels of thinking. Because teachers as models are probably essential to the method, they have to learn to accept the bizarre and the unusual. Instructors must accept all student responses to ensure that students feel no external judgments about their creative expression. The more difficult the problem is, or seems to be, to solve, the more necessary it is for teachers to accept farfetched analogies so that individuals develop fresh perspectives on problems.

In strategy two teachers should guard against premature analyses. They also clarify and summarize the progress of the learning activity and, hence, the students' problem-solving behavior.

SUPPORT SYSTEM

Most of all the group needs facilitation by a leader competent in synectics procedures. It also needs, in the case of scientific problems, a laboratory in which it can build models and other devices to make problems concrete and to permit practical invention to take place. The class requires a work space of its own and an environment in which creativity will be prized and utilized. A typical classroom can probably provide these necessities, but a classroom-sized group may be too large for many synectics activities, and smaller groups would need to be created.

APPLICATION _____

USING SYNECTICS IN THE CURRICULUM

Synectics is designed to increase the creativity of both individuals and groups. Sharing the synectics experience can build a feeling of community among students. Students learn about their fellow classmates as they watch them react to an idea or problem. Thoughts are valued for their potential contribution to the group process. Synectics procedures help create a community of equals in which simply having a thought is the sole basis for status. This norm and that of playfulness quickly give support to even the most timid participant.

Synectics procedures may be used with students in all areas of the curriculum, the sciences as well as the arts. They can be applied to both teacher-student discussion in the classroom and to teacher-made materials for the students. The products or vehicles of synectics activity need not always be written: they can be oral, or they can take the form of role plays, paintings and graphics, or simply changes in behavior. When using synectics to look at social or behavioral problems, you may wish to notice situational behavior before and after synectics activity and observe changes. It is also interesting to select modes of expression that contrast with the original topic, such as having students paint a picture of prejudice or discrimination. The concept is abstract, but the mode of expression is concrete.

Some possible uses of the synectics models are discussed in the following paragraphs.

CREATIVE WRITING

Strategy one of the synectics model can be directly applied to creative writing, not only because it stimulates the uses of analogies but because it helps "break set" as writers seek to expand the range of devices they can use to approach expressive tasks in expository and persuasive as well as the narrative genre.

EXPLORING SOCIAL PROBLEMS

Strategy one provides an alternative for exploring social issues, especially ones where the students are vested in definitions and solutions. The metaphor creates distance, so the confrontation does not threaten the learner, and discussion and self-examination are possible. The personal analogy phase is critical for developing insight.

PROBLEM SOLVING

The objective of strategy two is to break set and conceptualize the problem in a new way in order to suggest fresh approaches to it in personal life as well as in the classroom. Social relations in the classroom, conflict resolution, how to overcome math anxiety, how to feel better about wearing glasses, how to stop making fun of people—the list is endless.

CREATING A DESIGN OR PRODUCT

Synectics can also be used to create a product or design. A product is something tangible, such as a painting, a building, or a bookshelf, whereas a design is a plan, such as an idea for a party or a new means of transportation. Eventually, designs or plans become real, but for the purposes of this model they remain as sketches or outlines.

BROADENING OUR PERSPECTIVE OF A CONCEPT

Abstract ideas such as culture, prejudice, and economy are difficult to internalize because we cannot see them in the same way we can see a table or building, yet we frequently use them in our language. Synectics is a good way to make a familiar idea "strange" and thereby obtain another perspective on it.

We have found that synectics can be used with all ages, though with very young children it is best to stick to stretching exercises. Beyond this, adjustments are the same as for any other approach to teaching—care to work within their experience, rich use of concrete materials, attentive pacing, and explicit outlining of procedures.

The model often works effectively with students who withdraw from more "academic" learning activities because they are not willing to risk being wrong. Conversely, high-achieving students who are only comfortable giving a response they are sure is "right" often feel reluctant to participate. We believe that for these reasons alone, synectics is valuable to everyone.

Synectics combines easily with other models. It can stretch concepts being explored with the information-processing family; open up dimensions of social issues explored through role playing, group investigation, or jurisprudential thinking; and expand the richness of problems and feelings opened up by other models in the personal family.

The most effective use of synectics develops over time. It has short-term results in stretching views of concepts and problems, but when students are exposed to it repeatedly, they can learn how to use it with increasing skill—and they learn to enter a metaphoric mode with increasing ease and completeness.

Gordon, Poze, and their associates have developed a wide assortment of materials for use in schools, especially in the language development areas (Gordon and Poze, 1976). The strategy is universally attractive, and its fortunate combination of enhancing productive thinking and nurturing empathy and interpersonal closeness finds it many uses with all ages and most curriculum areas.

INSTRUCTIONAL AND NURTURANT EFFECTS

As shown in Figure 8.1, the synectics model has both instructional and nurturant value. Through his belief that the creative process can be communicated and that it can be improved through direct training, Gordon has developed specific instructional techniques. Synectics is applied, however, not only to the development of general creative power but also to the development of creative responses over a variety of subject-matter domains. Gordon clearly believes that the creative energy will enhance learning in these areas. To this end, he emphasizes a social environment that encourages creativity and uses group cohesion to generate energy that enables the participants to function interdependently in a metaphoric world. The method of synectics has been explicitly designed to improve the creativity of individuals and groups. However, the implicit learning from this model is equally vivid.

Another approach to the stimulation of creativity through metaphoric activity is presented by Judith Sanders and Donald Sanders (1984). Their

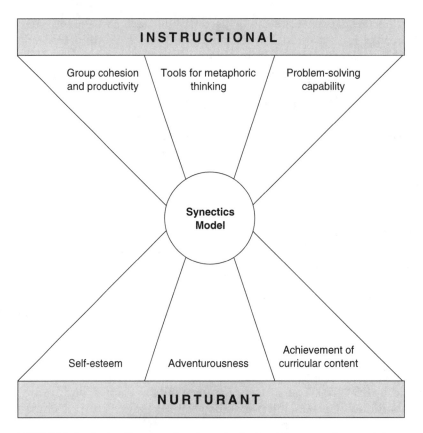

FIGURE 8.1   Instructional and nurturant effects of the synectics model.

book is particularly useful for the range of explicit applications it includes. We have noticed that many educators are not automatically aware of the spectrum of useful applications for models designed to induce divergent thinking. For some reason, many people think of "creativity" as an aptitude that defines talent in the arts, especially writing, painting, and sculpture, whereas the creators of these models believe that this aptitude can be improved and that it has applications in nearly every human endeavor and thus in every curriculum area. The Sanderses provide illustrations in the setting of goals, the development of empathy, the study of values, a variety of areas of problem solving, and the increase of perspectives for viewing topics.

Newby and Ertner (1994) have conducted a nice series of studies where they taught students to use analogies to approach the learning of advanced physiological concepts by college students. Their results confirm the experience we have had with K–12 students: the analogies both enhanced immediate and long-term learning and increased the pleasure the students had in learning the material.

Baer (1993) reports a set of studies exploring specific and general divergent-thinking skills that confirms that general creativity-inducing strategies probably apply across many domains but that domain-specific training may be helpful in some domains. Glynn (1994) has reported a study in science teaching that suggests that using analogies in textual material enhances both short- and long-term learning. The inquiry continues!

ENLARGING CONCEPTS _____

The following transcript illustrates the use of synectics to enlarge on an academic concept. It was preceded by two concept attainment lessons, one on the concept of *oxymorons* and the other on the concept of *small, wealthy countries*. Thus, although this was the students' first experience with synectics, they understood the characteristics of oxymorons and were able to construct them in Phase IV of the lesson.

S C E N A R I O

Teacher's Lesson Plan:

Phase I. Ask students to write a brief characterization of the world's small, wealthy countries. (Students have just finished analyzing a statistical data set on these countries.)

Phase II. Direct analogies (and examples of student responses).

> How is the Panama Canal like a bathtub? [drains]
> How is the Panama Canal like a videotape? [long, encased, continuous, viewed]
> How is a videotape like a book? [information, pictures]
> How is viewing a videotape like dancing? [action, movement]
> How is a dream like a skateboard? [falling, adventurous, accelerating]
> How is a skateboard like a blender? [spinning, wipe-out]

Phase III. Personal analogies (and examples of student responses).

> Be the Panama Canal. It's midnight and a long string of ships has just begun their passage from the Pacific to the Atlantic. How do you feel? [wet, sleepy]
> A huge ship, just barely able to clear both sides of the locks, enters the first lock. How do you feel? [nervous, stop!]
> Pilots are getting on and off of ships. How do you feel about the pilots? [friends, protectors]
> The tide is coming in with the ships from the Pacific. How do you feel about the tides? [smelly, regular, necessary]

Be a raincloud. You're moving into a clear, blue sky. Inside you are hundreds of little people with buckets. How do you feel about these little people? [(laughter), "go for it"]

You move nearer a town. What are you thinking? [Gotcha]

At a signal from you, all the little people begin emptying their buckets. How do you feel? [relieved, light]

You're almost empty. You're starting to break up and you see a little wisp of yourself disappearing on the breeze. How do you feel? [nostalgic, sad]

Phase IV. Form oxymorons (actual student responses).

lonely friendship	accustomed newness
apprehensive relief	encased adventure
archaically new	friendly enemy
descending escalation	fictional facts

Phase V. New direct analogies (and student responses).

What's an example of a "lonely friendship"? [trying to resume a friendship after an argument or fight]

What is a "fictional fact"? [a fantasy, like "Alice in Wonderland"]

Phase VI. Reexamination of the original task.

Think of our small, wealthy nations in terms of "apprehensive relief." [In the case of Kuwait, Hussein is out but it could happen again. Hong Kong is prosperous but worried about China and 1997. Qatar could be swallowed up; they're so small they need a bodyguard; their wealth is based on oil, which could run out or the world market could change with new kinds of fuels; etc.]

The use of synectics following analysis of data on the world's small, wealthy countries enabled students to elaborate their understanding of these countries. Initial data analysis left the students with an impression that these countries have no problems (with the exception of Kuwait). The synectics process moved students toward a more differentiated view of the countries that enabled them to hypothesize weaknesses as well as strengths in their relative world positions.

S C E N A R I O

Indian students, aged 14–17, break set on a social concept.

Another use of synectics is the development of alternative points of view toward social issues, the "breaking of set" when considering solutions. The lesson described below occurred in India with a group of secondary students who were asked to consider the issue of "Career Women" in their modern culture. Often this topic does not even come up for discussion because the traditional cultural prescriptions for male and female roles are so powerful. Ironically, because access to higher education is based solely on merit, women comprise about half the college and university populations of India, although few women attempt to pursue a career after marriage. Since virtually all Indian women marry, an enormous human resource is being lost to a nation that sorely needs it.

[*Note:* This lesson was conducted in English, a second language for all the students in the session. Their native tongues were either Hindi or Marathi.]

Begin!

Phase I. Write a paragraph about "Career Women" in India.

Phase II. Direct analogies (and sample student responses).

How is a feather like a butterfly? [attractive, soft, flight, pursued]
How are scissors like a cactus? [sharp, sting]
How is a snake like a pillow? [slippery, gives you nightmares]
How is Ping-Pong like getting married? [risk, battle, ups and downs]

Phase III. Personal analogies (and sample student responses).

Be a tiger. Good morning, tigers, how do you feel? [grand, kingly, hungry, majestic, untrustworthy]
As you walk through the forest, you come upon a large body of water. You look out over the water and see a whale. What are you thinking, tigers? [greedy, breakfast, threatened, dumbstruck]
Be a feather. Tell me about yourselves, feathers. [no worries, fragile, independent, tramp]

Phase IV. Forming compressed conflicts (oxymorons).

Using words you've generated, construct word pairs that seem to fight each other, word pairs that have a lot of tension or incongruity.

beautiful nightmare   carefully threatened
attractive tramp   dangerously attractive
majestically greedy   grandly majestic

Now select one or two word pairs that have a great deal of incongruity.

beautiful nightmare   dangerously attractive

Phase V. New direct analogies.

What is an example of a beautiful nightmare?
What is dangerously attractive?

Phase VI. Revisiting the original topic.

> Write another paragraph on "Career Women," using the point of view of one of our oxymorons. You don't have to use the actual words of the compressed conflicts but try to capture the meaning of the word pairs.

Here are some of the results, comparing the original (pre) writing with those produced at the end of the exercise:

> **Pre:** If the career woman is married, then the couple gets along with each other only if the husband too pursues an equally good career. Otherwise they tend to split up as the men try to dominate the women, but the women don't like it so they must pursue a career only if it does not interfere with the bringing up of the children.
>
> **Post:** A career woman can succeed if she is dangerously attractive, especially if she is in the science department. People tend to feast their eyes with her in their sight and leave their stubbornness behind. Then the customer or client realizes later that he has had a beautiful nightmare if the material or the product from the dangerously attractive woman proves to be unworthy of being bought.

> **Pre:** Usually a woman should decide before taking up a career because especially in India if a woman decides to take up a career she's obstructed by her family. I think you can't look after your own family and a career together and usually men do not want their wives to have a career.
>
> **Post:** A career woman can be equally dangerous and attractive. She can be dangerous to people in the sense that she threatens them and when she get a task accomplished she can be equally sweet or attractive to them.

> **Pre:** What do men feel about career women? They generally think, rather chauvinistically, that women are stupid, inefficient, miserable, subordinate coworkers. So, it is natural for men to feel when that come face to face with career women that they have been brought down to earth. [An] inferiority complex is expressed, giving vent to anger, jealousy, envy and irritation. But it takes time to realize that career women are generally much more determined and ambitious to make large strides in a severely male-dominated world and once this is realized I think men and women can really work together in one efficient team.
>
> **Post:** A career woman does give most men beautiful nightmares, some because they have to work in close contact with her and some because they do not want to have a female boss. A career woman has, in my opinion, an inbuilt tendency to be charmingly attractive and complimentary when presented with well done tasks and dangerous when work is performed inefficiently and haphazardly.

Participation in a synectics group invariably creates a unique shared experience that fosters interpersonal understanding and a sense of community. Members learn about one another as each person reacts to the common event in his or her unique way. Individuals become acutely aware of their dependence on the various perceptions of other group members. Each thought, no matter how prosaic, is valued for its potential catalytic effect on one's own thoughts. Simply having a thought is the sole basis for status in this community, and the playfulness of synectics activities encourages even the most timid participant.

SUMMARY CHART ► SYNECTICS

Syntax of Strategy One: Creating Something New

Phase One: Description of the Present Condition
Teacher has students describe situation or topic as they see it now.

Phase Two: Direct Analogy
Students suggest direct analogies, select one, and explore (describe) it further.

Phase Three: Personal Analogy
Students "become" the analogy they selected in phase two.

Phase Four: Compressed Conflict
Students take their descriptions from phases two and three, suggest several compressed conflicts, and choose one.

Phase Five: Direct Analogy
Students generate and select another direct analogy, based on the compressed conflict.

Phase Six: Reexamination of the Original Task
Teacher has students move back to original task or problem and use the last analogy and/or the entire synectics experience.

Social System

The model is moderately structured. Teacher initiates phases, but students' responses are quite open. Norms of creativity and "play-of-fancy" are encouraged. Rewards are internal.

Principles of Reaction

Encourage openness, nonrational, creative expression. Model, if necessary.

Accept all student responses.

Select analogies that help students stretch their thinking.

Support System

No special support system.

Syntax of Strategy Two: Making the Strange Familiar

Phase One: Substantive Input
Teacher provides information on new topic.

Phase Two: Direct Analogy
Teacher suggests direct analogy and asks students to describe the analogy.

Phase Three: Personal Analogy
Teacher has students "become" the direct analogy.

Phase Four: Comparing Analogies
Students identify and explain the points of similarity between the new material and the direct analogy.

Phase Five: Explaining Differences
Students explain where the analogy does not fit.

Phase Six: Exploration
Students reexplore the original topic on its own terms.

Phase Seven: Generating Analogy
Students provide their own direct analogy and explore the similarities and differences.

LEARNING FROM PRESENTATIONS
Advance Organizers

> *So why not provide the scaffold (of ideas) at the beginning (of the course)? Let the student in on the secret of the structure, including an understanding of how it continually emerges through further inquiry, so that the mind can be active as the course progresses.*
>
> —David Ausubel to Bruce Joyce, November 1968

S C E N A R I O

A guide, beginning a tour of an art museum with a group of high school students, says, "I want to give you an idea that will help you understand the paintings and sculpture we are about to see. The idea is simply that art, although it is a personal expression, reflects in many ways the culture and times in which it was produced. This may seem obvious to you at first when you look at the differences between Oriental and Western art. However, it is also true that, within each culture, as the culture changes, so the art will change—and that is why we can speak of *periods* of art. The changes are often reflected in the artists' techniques, subject matter, colors, and style. Major changes are often reflected in the forms of art that are produced." The guide then points out examples of one or two changes in these characteristics. She also asks the students to recall their elementary school days and the differences in their drawings when they were five and six, and when they were older. She likens the different periods of growing up to different cultures.

In the tour that follows, as the students look at paintings and sculpture, the guide points out to them the differences that result from changing times. "Do you see here," she asks, "that in this painting the body of the person is almost completely covered by his robes, and there is no hint of a human inside his clothes? In medieval times, the church taught that the body was

187

unimportant and that the soul was everything." Later she remarks, "You see in this painting how the muscularity of the man stands out through his clothing and how he stands firmly on the earth. This represents the Renaissance view that man was at the center of the universe and that his body, his mind, and his power were very important indeed."

The docent is using an *advance organizer*—in this case, a powerful concept used by art historians. This organizer contains many subordinate ideas that can be linked to the particular characteristics of the art objects being viewed. In this scenario, the teacher has thus provided students with what David Ausubel calls an "intellectual scaffolding" to structure the ideas and facts they encounter during their lesson.

S C E N A R I O

Wendy and Keith open their course on chemistry by using a combination of inductive and mnemonics models to teach their students the table of elements. The students learn the names of the elements and their atomic weights and categorize them in terms of their states at 10 degrees Celsius. They learn the concepts *element, atomic weight,* and *chemical bond.*

These concepts and the knowledge of the table itself serve as the conceptual structure of their course. The information to be studied will be linked to this structure, and the concepts themselves will be refined and extended as the course proceeds.

S C E N A R I O

Kelly Young is introducing his students to the difference between the literal and figurative meanings of words, or the difference between *denotative* and *connotative language.* He begins by presenting an organizer, which is simply to point out that words represent things, actions, states of beings, and so on, and, while doing so, often *suggest* things. He uses examples. The word *puppy* refers to a young dog, but it also suggests playfulness and cuddliness because we think of puppies as playful and cuddly. *Limousine* refers to a car, but it suggests status, wealth, and perhaps snobbishness and conspicuous consumption.

He then presents students with a set of short stories and asks them to read them and pick out words that have, in their opinion, only literal or referential meanings and words that also suggest things they do not refer to directly. They develop lists of words and then discuss why some words have only literal and others have literal and figurative meanings. They build categories and then continue their exploration, looking at the works of favorite authors and continuing to develop their lists.

ORIENTATION TO THE MODEL

David Ausubel is an unusual educational theorist. First, he directly addresses the goal of learning subject matter. Second, he advocates the improvement of *presentational* methods of teaching (lectures and readings) at a time when other educational theorists and social critics are challenging the validity of these methods and finding fault with the "passiveness" of expository learning. In contrast to those who advocate discovery methods of teaching, "open education," and experience-based learning, Ausubel stands unabashedly for the mastery of academic material through presentation.

Ausubel is also one of the few educational psychologists to address learning, teaching, and curriculum simultaneously. His theory of meaningful verbal learning deals with three concerns: (1) how knowledge (curriculum content) is organized, (2) how the mind works to process new information (learning), and (3) how teachers can apply these ideas about curriculum and learning when they present new material to students (instruction).

GOALS AND ASSUMPTIONS

Ausubel's primary concern is to help teachers organize and convey large amounts of information as meaningfully and efficiently as possible. He believes that the acquisition of information is a valid, indeed an essential, goal of schooling, and that certain theories can guide teachers in their job of transmitting bodies of knowledge to their students. His stance applies to situations in which the teacher plays the role of organizer of subject matter and presents information through lectures, readings, and providing tasks to the learner to integrate what has been learned. In his approach, the teacher is responsible for organizing and presenting what is to be learned. The learner's primary role is to master ideas and information. Whereas inductive approaches lead the students to discover or rediscover concepts, the advance organizers provide concepts and principles to the students directly. Interestingly, Ausubel believes that students have to be active constructors of knowledge, but his route is to teach them the metalevel of the discipline and the metacognitions relative to how to respond to instruction productively, rather than beginning with their perceptual world and leading them to induce the structures.

The advance organizer model is designed to strengthen students' *cognitive structures*—their knowledge of a particular subject at any given time and how well organized, clear, and stable that knowledge is (Ausubel, 1963, p. 27). In other words, cognitive structure has to do with what kind of knowledge of a field is in our minds, how much of it there is, and how well it is organized.

Ausubel maintains that a person's existing cognitive structure is the foremost factor governing whether new material will be meaningful and how well it can be acquired and retained. Before we can present new material effectively, we must increase the stability and clarity of our students' structures. This is done by giving them concepts that govern the information to be presented to them. The preceding example of the art gallery, where the docent presented the idea that art reflects culture and cultural change, is intended to provide the intellectual scaffolding that will enable the students to see the information in the paintings more clearly. Opening the chemistry course as Wendy and Keith did is another example—the students have little knowledge of chemistry, so the organizing concepts provide a conceptual structure on which the course can be built. Strengthening students' cognitive structure in this way facilitates their acquisition and retention of new information. Ausubel rejects the notion that learning through listening, watching, or reading is necessarily rote, passive, or nonmeaningful. It can be, of course, but it won't be if the students' minds are prepared to receive and process information. If their minds are not prepared, the students must fall back to learning by rote (repeating material over and over), which is arduous and highly subject to forgetting. Any poorly executed teaching methods can lead to rote learning. Expository teaching is no exception. Well done, it promotes the active processing of information.

WHAT IS MEANINGFUL?

According to Ausubel, whether or not material is meaningful depends more on the preparation of the learner and on the organization of the material than it does on the method of presentation. If the learner begins with the right "set," and if the material is solidly organized, then meaningful learning can occur.

IS RECEPTION LEARNING PASSIVE?

Ausubel says "No!" provided the proper conditions are set up. During a lecture or other form of expository teaching, the listeners' or watchers' minds can be quite active. But they must be involved in relating material to their own cognitive structure. Ausubel speaks about the learners' struggle with the material—looking at it from different angles, reconciling it with similar or perhaps contradictory information, and finally translating it into their own frame of reference and terminology. However, this does not happen automatically.

ORGANIZING INFORMATION: THE STRUCTURE OF THE DISCIPLINE AND COGNITIVE STRUCTURE

According to Ausubel there is a parallel between the way subject matter is organized and the way people organize knowledge in their minds (their cognitive structures). He expresses the view that each of the academic disciplines has a structure of concepts (and/or propositions) that are organized hierarchically (Ausubel, 1963, p. 18). That is, at the top of each discipline are a number of very broad, abstract concepts that include the more concrete concepts at lower stages of organization. Figure 9.1 illustrates the hierarchical structure of the discipline of economics, with the more abstract concepts at the top of the pyramid of concepts.

Like Jerome Bruner, Ausubel believes that the structural concepts of each discipline can be taught to students, for whom they become an information-processing system—that is, they become an intellectual map that students can use to analyze particular domains and to solve problems within those domains. For example, students can use economic concepts to analyze events from an economic point of view. Suppose we present filmed case studies depicting activities on a farm, in a grocery store, in a suburban household, and in a brokerage house. Each case contains many pieces of information. The students see people engaged in various activities, observe many behaviors, and listen to several conversations. If the students were then to make an economic analysis of these cases, they would catalog the behaviors and activities of the people in terms of such concepts as supply and demand, wants and needs, goods and services, consumers and producers. These concepts help in several ways. They enable students to make

FIGURE 9.1   Structure of the discipline of economics. Based on Clinton Boutwell, *Getting It All Together* (San Rafael, Calif.: Leswing Press, 1972).

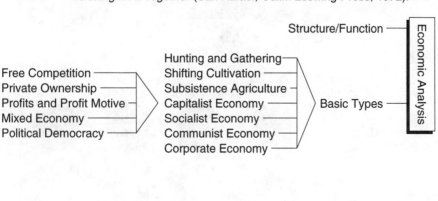

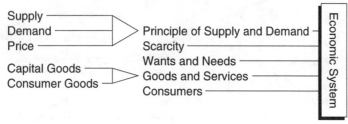

sense of large amounts of data and to compare the four case studies, discovering the underlying commonalities in the apparent differences.

Ausubel describes the mind as an information-processing and information-storing system that can be compared to the conceptual structure of an academic discipline. Like the disciplines, the mind is a hierarchically organized set of ideas that provides anchors for information and ideas and that serves as a storehouse for them. Figure 9.2 shows the hierarchy of cognitive structure in the discipline of economics. The shaded concepts are the most inclusive. They have been "learned" and exist in a hypothetical learner's cognitive structure. The unshaded concepts are potentially meaningful because they can be *linked* to the existing concepts. The black circles are not yet potentially meaningful concepts because suitable anchors for them are not yet incorporated into the cognitive structure. As this information-processing system acquires new information and new ideas, it reorganizes itself to accommodate those ideas. Thus, the system is in a continuous state of change.

Ausubel maintains that new ideas can be usefully learned and retained only to the extent that they can be related to already available concepts or propositions that provide ideational anchors. If the new material conflicts

FIGURE 9.2   An individual's cognitive structure with respect to economics. Based on Clinton Boutwell, *Getting It All Together* (San Rafael, Calif.: Leswing Press, 1972, pp. 180–280).

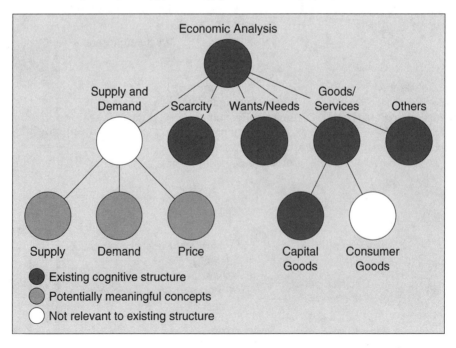

too strongly with the existing cognitive structure *or* is so unrelated that no linkage is provided, the information or ideas may not be incorporated or retained. To prevent this from occurring, the teacher must sequence the material to be learned and present it in such a way that the ideational anchors are provided. In addition, the learner must actively reflect on the new material, think through these linkages, reconcile differences or discrepancies, and note similarities with existing information.

IMPLICATIONS FOR CURRICULUM

Ausubel's ideas about subject matter and cognitive structure have important and direct implications for the organization of curriculum and for instructional procedures. He uses two principles, *progressive differentiation* and *integrative reconciliation*, to guide the organization of content in the subject fields in such a way that the concepts become a stable part of a student's cognitive structure and to describe the student's intellectual role.

Progressive differentiation means that the most general ideas of the discipline are presented first, followed by a gradual increase in detail and specificity. *Integrative reconciliation* simply means that new ideas should be consciously related to previously learned content. In other words, the sequence of the curriculum is organized so that each successive learning is carefully related to what has been presented before. If the entire body of material has been conceptualized and presented according to progressive differentiation, integrative reconciliation follows naturally, though it requires the learner's active cooperation. Gradually, as a result of both principles, the discipline is built into the mind of the learner.

Both the discipline and the sequence of instruction are built from the top down, with the most inclusive concepts, principles, and propositions presented first. Ausubel points out that the organization of most textbooks puts each topic in a separate chapter or subchapter, all at the same level of abstraction and generality. "In most instances," therefore, "students are required to learn the details of new and unfamiliar disciplines before they have acquired an adequate body of relevant subsumers at an appropriate level of inclusiveness" (Ausubel, 1968, p. 153).

At first sight, the approach of providing major ideas and, gradually, subordinate ones, seems opposed to the inductive, concept attainment, and scientific inquiry models, but there is great similarity in that the development of concepts is central and the student is to be actively involved in connecting concepts and information. Also, in a curriculum, one might alternate the construction of ideas with the presentation of ideas.

IMPLICATIONS FOR TEACHING

Advance organizers strengthen cognitive structures and enhance retention of new information. Ausubel describes advance organizers as introductory material presented ahead of the learning task and at a higher level of abstraction and inclusiveness than the learning task itself. Their purpose is to explain, integrate, and interrelate the material in the learning task with previously learned material (and also to help the learner discriminate the new material from previously learned material) (Ausubel, 1968, p. 148). The most effective organizers are those that use concepts, terms, and propositions that are already familiar to the learners, as well as appropriate illustrations and analogies.

Suppose, for example, a teacher wants students to acquire information about current energy problems. The teacher provides learning material containing data about possible power sources, general information about U.S. economic growth and technology, and alternative policies on the energy crisis and future planning. The learning material is in the form of newspaper articles, a lecture, and perhaps a film. The learning task for the students is to internalize the information—that is, to remember the central ideas and perhaps the key facts. Before introducing students to the learning material, however, the teacher provides introductory material in the form of an advance organizer to help them relate to the new data.

In this example, the concept of energy might be used as the basis of the organizer, and related concepts such as energy efficiency and energy conservation can provide auxiliary organizers. Other possibilities are the concept of ecology and its various subsystems dealing with the environment, the economy, the political arena, and social structures. This second set of organizers would focus students' attention on the *impact* of old and new energy sources on the subsystems of our ecological system, whereas the first set would encourage them to process the data through a consideration of energy efficiency and energy conservation.

The organizer is important content in itself and needs to be taught. It may be a concept or a statement of relationship. In either case, teachers must take time to explain and develop the organizer, because only when it is fully understood can it serve to organize the subsequent learning material. For example, students must fully understand the concept of *culture* before the teacher can use it effectively to organize factual information about different culture groups. Advance organizers are generally based on the major concepts, propositions, generalizations, principles, and laws of a discipline. For instance, a lesson or text describing the caste system in India might be preceded by an organizer based on the concept of social stratification. Similarly, the generalization, "Technological changes can produce major changes in society and culture" could be the *basis* for an organizer preceding the study of several historical periods and places.

Usually, the organizer is tied closely to the material it precedes. However, the organizer can also be created from an analogy from another field in order to provide a new perspective. For instance, the concept of balance or form, though generic to the arts, may be applied to literature, to mathematics, to the functioning of the branches of government, or even to our daily activities. A study of churches can be viewed under the rubric of many different organizers: those focusing on the economic implications of the church, cultural or sociological perspectives, or architectural perspectives.

There are two types of advance organizers—expository and comparative. *Expository organizers* provide a basic concept at the highest level of abstraction and perhaps some lesser concepts. These represent the intellectual scaffold on which students will "hang" the new information as they encounter it. Expository organizers are especially helpful because they provide ideational scaffolding for *unfamiliar* material. Thus the basic concepts of economics would be presented prior to the study of the economic condition of a city.

Comparative organizers, on the other hand, are typically used with relatively familiar material. They are designed to discriminate between the old and new concepts in order to prevent confusion caused by their similarity. For example, when the learner is being introduced to long division, a comparative organizer might be used to point out the similarities and differences between division facts and multiplication facts. Whereas in multiplication, the multiplier and multiplicand can be reversed without changing the product—that is, 3 times 4 can be changed to 4 times 3—the divisor and dividend cannot be reversed in division without affecting the quotient—that is, 6 divided by 2 is not the same as 2 divided by 6. The comparative organizer can help the learner see the relationship between multiplication and division and clarify the differences between the two. The learner can then borrow from knowledge about multiplication when learning division without being confused by the differences.

As described in Chapter Two, Ausubel and others have conducted a variety of studies exploring the general theory, and the Lawton (1977a) studies are interesting not only with respect to learning and retention of material but also with respect to the theory's potential for influencing logical operations—that is, to help develop thinking ability.

In general, Lawton's study seems to support the notion that what is taught will be learned. If we present material to students, some of it will be learned. If it is presented with an organizing structure, somewhat more will be learned. If we use a process that helps students develop certain ways of thinking, some of those ways of thinking will be learned. Thus, if we avoid using those models of teaching that provide certain intellectual structures and employ certain thinking processes, we decrease the chances of those structures and thinking processes being acquired. Generally speaking, the development of an *intellectual structure*—whether through presentational or inductive methods—increases the probability that students will learn those structures and the thinking processes associated with them, and that they will retain material more fully. The effects are strongest with respect to older children. Effects, by the way, can be seen in problem-solving behavior as the students bring the structures to bear on problems they have not previously encountered (Bascones and Novak, 1985; Maloney, 1994).

THE MODEL OF TEACHING

The model of teaching developed here is based on Ausubel's ideas about subject matter, cognitive structure, active reception learning, and advance organizers.

SYNTAX

The advance organizer model has three phases of activity. Phase one is the presentation of the advance organizer, phase two is the presentation of the learning task or learning material, and phase three is the strengthening of cognitive organization. Phase three tests the relationship of the learning material to existing ideas to bring about an active learning process. A summary of the syntax appears in Table 9.1

The activities are designed to increase the clarity and stability of the new learning material so that fewer ideas are lost, confused with one another, or left vague. The students should operate on the material as they receive it by relating the new learning material to personal experience and to their existing cognitive structure, and by taking a critical stance toward knowledge.

Phase one consists of three activities: clarifying the aims of the lesson, presenting the advance organizer, and prompting awareness of relevant knowledge.

TABLE 9.1   SYNTAX OF THE ADVANCE ORGANIZER MODEL

Phase One: Presentation of Advance Organizer	Phase Two: Presentation of Learning Task or Material

Clarify aims of the lesson.
Present organizer:
   Identify defining attributes.
   Give examples.
   Provide context.
   Repeat.
Prompt awareness of learner's
relevant knowledge and experience.
	Present material.
	Maintain attention.
	Make organization explicit.
	Make logical order of learning
	material explicit.

Phase Three: Strengthening Cognitive Organization
Use principles of integrative reconciliation. Promote active reception learning. Elicit critical approach to subject matter. Clarify.

Clarifying the aim of the lesson is one way to obtain students' attention and to orient them to their learning goals, both of which are necessary to facilitate meaningful learning. (Clarifying aims is also useful to the teacher in planning a lesson.)

As mentioned earlier, the organizer is not just a brief, simple statement; it is an idea in itself and, like the learning material, must be explored intellectually. It must also be distinguished from introductory comments, which are useful to the lesson but are not advance organizers. For instance, when we teach, many of us begin our instruction by asking students to recall what we did last week or last year or by telling them what we are going to do tomorrow. In this way, we give them a context or orientation for our presentation. Or we may ask students to recall a personal experience and then acknowledge that what we are about to say resembles that situation or will help students understand a previous experience. We may also tell them the objectives of the session—what we hope they will get out of the presentation or discussion. *None of the just-described techniques is an advance organizer.* However, all are part of a well-organized presentation, and some reflect principles that are central to Ausubel's theory of meaningful verbal learning and are part of the model of teaching.

The actual organizer, however, is built around the major concepts and/or propositions of a discipline or area of study. First, the organizer has to be constructed so that the learner can perceive it for what it is—an idea distinct from and more inclusive than the material in the learning task itself. The chief feature of an organizer is thus that it is at a higher level of abstraction and generality than the learning material itself. This higher level of abstraction is what distinguishes organizers from introductory overviews, which are written (or spoken) at the same level of abstraction as the learning material because they are, in fact, previews of the learning material.

Second, whether the organizer is expository or comparative, the essential features of the concept or proposition must be pointed out and carefully explained. Thus, the teacher and students must explore the organizer as well as the learning task. To us, this means citing the essential features, explaining them, and providing examples. The presentation of an organizer need not be lengthy, but it must be perceived (the learner must be aware of it), clearly understood, and continually related to the material it is organizing. This means the learner must already be familiar with the language and ideas in the organizer. It is also useful to illustrate the organizer in multiple contexts and to repeat it several times, particularly any new or special terminology.

Finally, it is important to prompt awareness of the learner's prior knowledge and experiences that might be relevant to this learning task and organizer.

Following the presentation of the advance organizer in phase one, in phase two the learning material is presented in the form of lectures, discussions, films, experiments, or reading. During the presentation, the organization of the learning material needs to be made explicit to the students so that they have an overall sense of direction and can see the logical order of the material and how the organization relates to the advance organizer.

The purpose of phase three is to anchor the new learning material in the students' existing cognitive structure—that is, to strengthen the students' cognitive organization. In the natural flow of teaching, some of these procedures may be incorporated into phase two; however, we want to emphasize that the reworking of new material is a separate teaching task, with its own set of activities and skills. Ausubel identifies four activities: (1) promoting integrative reconciliation, (2) promoting active reception learning, (3) eliciting a critical approach to the subject matter, and (4) clarification.

There are several ways to facilitate reconciliation of the new material with the existing cognitive structure. The teacher can: (1) remind students of the ideas (the larger picture), (2) ask for a summary of the major attributes of the new learning material, (3) repeat precise definitions, (4) ask for differences between aspects of the material, and (5) ask students to describe how the learning material supports the concept or proposition that is being used as organizer.

Active learning can be promoted by: (1) asking students to describe how the new material relates to the organizer, (2) asking students for additional examples of the concept or propositions in the learning material, (3) asking students to verbalize the essence of the material, using their own terminology and frame of reference, and (4) asking students to examine the material from alternative points of view.

A critical approach to knowledge is fostered by asking students to recognize assumptions or inferences that may have been made in the learning material, to judge and challenge these assumptions and inferences, and to reconcile contradictions among them.

It is not possible or desirable to use all these techniques in one lesson. Constraints of time, topic, and relevance to the particular learning situation will guide their use. However, it is important to keep in mind the four goals of this phase and specific techniques for effective expository teaching.

Ideally, the initiation of phase three is shared by teachers and students. At first, however, the teacher will have to respond to the students' need for clarification of some area of the topic and for integration of the new material with existing knowledge.

Essentially, Ausubel has provided us with a method for improving not only presentations, but also students' abilities to learn from them. The more we teach students to become active—to *look* for organizing ideas, reconcile information with them, and generate organizers of their own (engaging in inductive activity while reading or watching)—the greater their potential for profiting from presentations becomes.

SOCIAL SYSTEM

In this model the teacher retains control of the intellectual structure, since it is continually necessary to relate the learning material to the organizers and to help students differentiate new material from previously learned material. In phase three, however, the learning situation is ideally much more interactive, with students initiating many questions and comments. The successful acquisition of the material will depend on the learners' desire to integrate it with prior knowledge, on their critical faculties, and on the teacher's presentation and organization of the material.

PRINCIPLES OF REACTION

The teacher's solicited or unsolicited responses to the learners' reactions will be guided by the purpose of clarifying the meaning of the new learning material, differentiating it from and reconciling it with existing knowledge, making it personally relevant to the students, and helping to promote a critical approach to knowledge. Ideally, students will initiate their own questions in response to their own drives for meaning.

SUPPORT SYSTEM

Well-organized material is the critical support requirement of this model. The effectiveness of the advance organizer depends on an integral and appropriate relationship between the conceptual organizer and the content. This model provides guidelines for building (or reorganizing) instructional materials.

APPLICATION _____

INSTRUCTIONAL USES

The advance organizer model is especially useful to structure extended curriculum sequences or courses and to instruct students systematically in the key ideas of a field. Step by step, major concepts and propositions are explained and integrated, so that at the end of a period of instruction, the learners should gain perspective on the entire area being studied.

We would expect an increase, too, in the learners' grasps of factual information linked to and explained by the key ideas. For instance, the concept of socialization can be drawn on repeatedly in the study of socialization patterns in different cultures and subcultures. This advance organizer thus aids in expanding students' knowledge about cultures.

The model can also be shaped to teach the *skills* of effective reception learning. Critical thinking and cognitive reorganization can be explained to the learners, who receive direct instruction in orderly thinking and in the notion of knowledge hierarchies. Ultimately, they can apply these techniques independently to new learning. In other words, this model can increase effectiveness in reading and watching films, and in other "reception" activities.

Other models are also useful for evaluating or applying the material presented by the advance organizer. For example, the advance organizer model, after introducing new material in a deductive, presentational way, can be followed by inductive concept attainment activities that reinforce the material or that informally evaluate students' acquisition of the material.

INSTRUCTIONAL AND NURTURANT EFFECTS

The probable instructional values of this model seem clear—the ideas themselves that are used as the organizer are learned, as well as information presented to the students. The ability to learn from reading, lectures, and other media used for presentations is another effect, as are an interest in inquiry and precise habits of thinking (see Figure 9.3).

FIGURE 9.3   Instructional and nurturant effects of the advance organizer model.

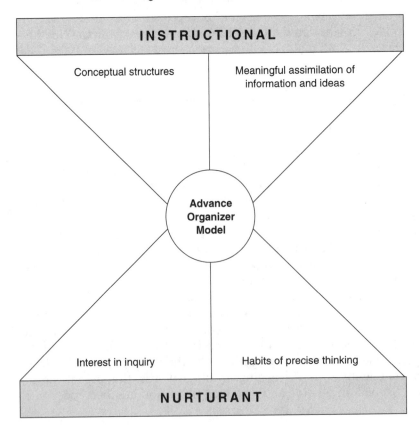

SUMMARY CHART ► ADVANCE ORGANIZER

Syntax

Phase One: Presentation of Advance Organizer
Clarify the aims of the lesson.
Present organizer:
   Identify defining attributes.
   Give examples or illustrations where appropriate.
   Provide context.
   Repeat.
Prompt awareness of learner's relevant knowledge and experience.

Phase Two: Presentation of Learning Task or Material
   Present material.
   Make logical order of learning material explicit.
   Link material to organizer.

Phase Three: Strengthening Cognitive Organization
   Use principles of integrative reconciliation.
   Elicit critical approach to subject matter.
   Clarify ideas.
   Apply ideas actively (such as by testing them).

Social System

Highly structured.
However, requires active collaboration between teacher and learner.

Principles of Reaction

1. Negotiation of meaning.
2. Responsively connecting organizer and material.

Support System

Data-rich, well-organized material.
(*Caution:* Many textbooks do not feature conceptually organized material.)

PART III

THE SOCIAL FAMILY OF MODELS

The models of teaching described in this book come from beliefs about the nature of human beings and how they learn. The social models, as the name implies, emphasize our social nature, how we learn social behavior, and how social interaction can enhance academic learning. Nearly all inventors of social models believe that a central role of education is to prepare citizens to generate integrative democratic behavior, both to enhance personal and social life and to ensure a productive democratic social order. They believe that cooperative enterprise inherently enhances our quality of life, bringing joy and a sense of verve and bonhomie to us and reducing alienation and unproductive social conflict. In addition, cooperative behavior is stimulating not only socially but also intellectually. Thus, tasks requiring social interaction can be designed to enhance academic learning. The development of productive social behavior and academic skills and knowledge are combined.

The social theorists have developed a large number of models that have great potential for our teaching repertoires and for the design of entire school environments as well, for they envision the school as a productive little society, rather than a collection of individuals acquiring education independently. In a cooperative school culture, students can be taught to use the other families of models of teaching to acquire the knowledge and skills for which those models are developed.

Many of the social theorists have not only built rationales for their models, but have raised serious questions about the adequacy of the current dominant patterns of schooling. In many schools the majority of learning tasks are structured by teachers for individuals. Most interaction between teachers and students is in the pattern of recitation—the teacher directs questions about what has been studied, calls on an individual who responds, and then affirms the response or corrects it (Sirotnik, 1983). Patterns of evaluation pit student against student. Many developers of the social models believe that individualistic patterns of schooling, combined with the teacher-dominated recitation pattern of schooling, are actually counterproductive for individuals and for society by depressing learning rates, creating an unnatural and even antisocial climate, and failing to provide opportunities for young people to maximize their potential and that of others by exercising their capacity for cooperation. People are inherently cooperative, they argue, and depressing cooperation drives children from each other and deprives them of an important dimension of their competence (see Johnson and Johnson, 1990; Sharan, 1990; Thelen, 1960).

The ideas of cooperating to learn academic content and of preparing students for citizenship and a satisfying social life are very old. They can be found in the writings of Aristotle, Plato, and Marcus Aurelius, as well as in those of Christian educators such as Thomas Aquinas, in the medieval period, and John Amos Comenius in the Renaissance. The rise of the modern commercial democratic states found expression in the writing of Jean-Jacques Rousseau in France, John Locke in England, and Thomas Jefferson and Benjamin Franklin in America. During the period of the development of the common school in America, Horace Mann and Henry Barnard argued strongly for an active cooperative school.

The concept was announced forcefully by John Dewey throughout the first half of the twentieth century. With his ideas as the primary rationale, it found expression in the development of a number of models for schooling and in the activity of the Progressive Education Association, ushering in the current era of research and development of social models of education.

We will see the themes generated during the evolution of Western civilization in the following chapters as we study the work of the contemporary developers of social models. Three active communities are strongly working to improve the social models. One is led by David and Roger Johnson at the University of Minnesota. The second is led by Robert Slavin at Johns Hopkins University. The third, in Israel, includes Shlomo Sharan, Rachel Hertz-Lazarowitz, and several other teacher-researchers. There are differences in their frames of reference, but they are respectful and cooperative with one another and are appropriately international. Increasingly they are joined by European researchers, and elements of their work are being used and extended by collaborators in Asia.

In Chapter 10 we begin with procedures for developing partnerships in learning and proceed to the contemporary versions of the classic group investigation model. In Chapter 11 we focus on values and social problem solving. Social inquiry and role playing can be used with students of all ages, and the jurisprudential inquiry model emphasizes social policies and issues for older students.

CHAPTER 10

PARTNERS IN LEARNING

From Dyads to Group Investigation

*The most stunning thing about teaching people to help
kids learn cooperatively is that people don't know how to
do it as a consequence of their own schooling and life in this
society. And, if anything is genetically-driven, it's a social instinct.
If it weren't for each other, we wouldn't even know who we are.*

—Herbert Thelen to Bruce Joyce, about 1964

SCENARIO

Jim Wolf's sixth grade is studying Iraq and Afghanistan to try to understand the countries the United States is involved with. Although they have concerns about the current political debates, they have decided that getting information about what is being talked about is essential. In groups, they have developed information to share.

A major source of data has been the Human Development Report CD-ROM 2000, the United Nations Development Program, which contains 300 indicators for 174 countries, plus a set of special reports.

Scanning the report, various groups have found arresting information, such as:

- In Nepal, Hindis have a life expectancy of 61 years, Muslims 49. Adult literacy among Hindis is 58 percent, among Muslims, 22 percent.
- Most developing countries have made significant progress in human development in the last ten years. The exceptions are ones with HIV/AIDS epidemics. Between 1975 and 1997 life expectancy actually fell in 18 countries, 10 of which are in Africa.
- For developing countries, human poverty ranges from a low of 2.6 percent in Barbados to a high of 65 percent in Niger. Among those with less

than 10 percent are Bahrain, Barbados, Chile, Costa Rica, Cuba, Fiji, Jordan, Panama, Trinidad and Tobago, and Uruguay. These countries have overcome severe levels of poverty. The United States is 16.5, the United Kingdom about 15, and Ireland about 15.

- Gender equality is less dependent on income level, stage of development, and culture than is generally supposed. In gender equality, Costa Rica and Trinidad and Tobago are ahead of France and Italy, Israel is ahead of Japan, and the Bahamas outrank Portugal. Greece's index is less than three-fourths that of Costa Rica.

- As they approach Iraq, they learn that it contains over 25 million people, has the fifth largest army in the world, harbored ancient civilizations along the Tigris and Euphrates valleys, that Baghdad contains over five million people and the four next largest cities contain over 10 million people. Only 20 percent of the land is arable. And, the populace is divided among a number of Muslim groups who have significantly different beliefs.

- Afghanistan, they learned, is too chaotic to have reliable data on many demographic variables. However, less than 5 percent of the land is arable and about a third of the population is nomadic tribes.

Dozens of questions emerge. Jim's students are off on a collective inquiry.

S C E N A R I O

Mary Hilltepper opens the year in her 10th-grade English class by presenting the students with 12 poems she has selected from a set of 100 poems that represent the works of prominent contemporary poets. She organizes the students into pairs, asking them to read the poems and then classify them by structure, style, and themes. As they classify the poems (see Chapter 3 for the structure of the inductive model), they are to prepare to report their categories to the other students so that the partnerships can compare their classifications with those of the other students. Working together, the class accumulates a list of the ways they have perceived structure, style, and theme. Then, Ms. Hilltepper presents the pairs of students with another dozen poems that they examine, both fitting them into their existing categories and expanding the categories as necessary. This process is repeated until all students are familiar with four dozen poems. She then gives them several other tasks. One is to decide how particular themes are handled by style and structure and vice versa (whether style and structure are correlated with each other and with themes). Another is to build hypotheses about whether some groups of poems were written by particular authors using distinctive combinations of style, structure, and theme.

Only then does she pass out the anthologies and books of critical analysis that are used as the course textbooks, asking students to test their hypotheses about authorship and also to find out if the scholars of poetry employ the same categories they have been developing in their partnerships.

Mary is organizing her class for partnership-based learning. The cognitive tasks of the classification version of the inductive model of teaching have been used to drive the inquiry. In addition to the substance of this opening unit of study, she is preparing the students to embark cooperatively on their next unit of study—writing poetry or studying the short story. (Which would you use next?) Before long she will introduce them to the more complex activities of group investigation.

S C E N A R I O

As the children enter Kelly Farmer's fifth-grade classroom in Savannah Elementary on the first day of the school year, they find the class roster on each desk. She smiles at them and says, "Let's start by learning all our names and one of the ways we will be working together this year. You'll notice I've arranged the desks in pairs, and the people sitting together will be partners in today's activities. I want each partnership to take our class list and classify the first names by how they sound. Then we will share the groupings or categories each partnership makes. This will help us learn one another's names. It is also to introduce you to one of the ways we will study spelling and several other subjects this year. I know from Mrs. Annis that you have worked inductively last year so you know how to classify, but let me know if you have any problems."

The students *do* know what to do, and within a few minutes they are ready to share their classifications. "We put Nancy and Sally together because they end in 'y.' " "We put George and Jerry together because they sound the same at the beginning even though they're spelled differently." "We put the three 'Kevin's' together." A few minutes later the pairs are murmuring together as they help one another learn to spell the list of names.

Kelly has started the year by organizing the students into a "cooperative set," by which we mean an organization for cooperative learning. She will teach them to work in dyads and triads, which can combine into groups of four, five, or six. (Task or work groups larger than that generally have much lower productivity.) The partnerships will change for various activities. The students will learn to accept any members of the class as their partners and will learn that they are to work with each other to try to ensure that everyone achieves the objectives of each activity.

She begins with pairs because that is the simplest social organization. In fact, much of the early training in cooperative activity will be conducted in groups of two and three because the interaction is simpler than it is in larger groups. She also uses fairly straightforward and familiar cognitive tasks for the initial training for the same reason—it is easier for students to learn to work together when they are not mastering complex activities at the same time. For example, she will have them change partners and have the new partnerships quiz each other on simple knowledge, such as of the states and their capitals, and tutor one another. She will change partnerships again and ask them to categorize sets of fractions by size. Each student will learn how to work with any and all of the other students in the class over a variety of tasks. Later she will teach the children to respond to the cognitive tasks of the more complex information-processing models of teaching as well as more complex cooperative sets. By the end of October she expects that they will be skillful enough that she can introduce them to group investigation.

Both teachers have embarked on the task of building learning communities. They will teach the students to work together impersonally but positively, to gather and analyze information, to build and test hypotheses, and to coach one another as they develop skills. The difference in maturity between the classes will affect the degree of sophistication of their inquiry, but the basic processes will be the same.

Each of these teachers possesses a variety of strategies for educating his or her students to work productively together. On their desks are *Circles of Learning* (Johnson and Johnson, 1994), *Cooperative Learning in the Classroom* (Johnson, Johnson, and Holobec, 1994), and *Cooperative Learning Resources for Teachers* (Kagan, 1990). Each is studying the students, learning how effectively they cooperate, and deciding how to design the next activities to teach them to work more effectively together.

PURPOSES AND ASSUMPTIONS

The assumptions that underlie the development of cooperative learning communities are straightforward:

1. The synergy generated in cooperative settings generates more motivation than do individualistic, competitive environments. Integrative social groups are, in effect, more than the sum of their parts. The feelings of connectedness produce positive energy.

2. The members of cooperative groups learn from one another. Each learner has more helping hands than in a structure that generates isolation.

3. Interacting with one another produces cognitive as well as social complexity, creating more intellectual activity that increases learning when contrasted with solitary study.

4. Cooperation increases positive feelings toward one another, reducing alienation and loneliness, building relationships, and providing affirmative views of other people.

5. Cooperation increases self-esteem not only through increased learning but through the feeling of being respected and cared for by the others in the environment.

6. Students can respond to experience in tasks requiring cooperation by increasing their capacity to work productively together. In other words, the more children are given the opportunity to work together, the better they get at it, which benefits their general social skills.

7. Students, including primary school children, can learn from training to increase their ability to work together.

In the last 30 years, interest has been renewed in research on the cooperative learning models. The more sophisticated research procedures that now exist have enabled better tests of their assumptions and more precise estimates of their effects on academic, personal, and social behavior. Work by three groups of researchers is of particular interest. One is led by David and Roger Johnson of the University of Minnesota (Johnson and Johnson, 1974, 1981, 1990). Another is led by Robert Slavin (1983, 1990) of Johns Hopkins University, and the third by Shlomo Sharan of Tel Aviv University (1980, 1990a). Using somewhat different strategies, the teams of both the Johnsons and Slavin have conducted sets of investigations that closely examine the assumptions of the social family of teaching models. Specifically, they have studied whether cooperative tasks and reward structures affect learning outcomes positively. Also, they have asked whether group cohesion, cooperative behavior, and intergroup relations are improved through cooperative learning procedures. In some of their investigations they have examined the effects of cooperative task and reward structures on "traditional" learning tasks, in which students are presented with material to master.

Important for us is the question of whether cooperative groups do in fact generate the energy that results in improved learning. The evidence is largely affirmative. In classrooms organized so that students work in pairs and larger groups, tutor each other, and share rewards, there is greater mastery of material than with the common individual-study-cum-recitation pattern. Also, the shared responsibility and interaction produce more positive feelings toward tasks and others, generate better intergroup relations, and result in better self-images for students with histories of poor achievement. In other words, the results generally affirm the assumptions that underlie the use of cooperative learning methods (see Sharan, 1990).

Sharan and his colleagues have studied group investigation. They have learned much both about how to make the dynamics of the model work and about its effects on cooperative behavior, intergroup relations, and lower- and higher-order achievement. We will discuss their research as we discuss group investigation later in this chapter.

An exciting use of the cooperative procedures is in combination with models from other families, in an effort to combine the effects of several models. For example, Baveja, Showers, and Joyce (1985) conducted a study in which concept attainment and inductive procedures were carried out in cooperative groups. The effects fulfilled the promise of the marriage of the information-processing and social models, reflecting gains that were twice those of a comparison group that received intensive individual and group tutoring over the same material. Similarly, Joyce, Murphy, Showers, and Murphy (1989) combined cooperative learning with several other models of teaching to obtain dramatic (30 to 95 percent) increases in promotion rates with at-risk students as well as correspondingly large decreases in disruptive activity, an obvious reciprocal of increases in cooperative and integrative behavior. The application of the Picture-Word Model in the studies in Chapter 19, with substantial effects on literacy, is suffused with a cooperative atmosphere and specific cooperative learning strategies.

Those teachers for whom cooperative learning is an innovation find that an endearing feature is that it is easy to organize students into pairs and triads. And it gets effects immediately. The combination of social support and the increase in cognitive complexity caused by the social interaction have mild but rapid effects on the learning of content and skills. In addition, partnerships in learning provide a pleasant laboratory in which to develop social skills and empathy for others. Off-task and disruptive behavior diminish substantially. Students feel good in cooperative settings, and positive feelings toward self and others are enhanced.

Another nice feature is that the students with poorer academic histories benefit so quickly. Partnerships increase involvement, and the concentration on cooperation has the side effect of reducing self-absorption and increasing responsibility for personal learning. Whereas the effect sizes on academic learning are modest but consistent, the effects on social learning and personal esteem can be considerable when comparisons are made with individualistic classroom organization.

Curiously, we have found that some parents and teachers believe that students who are the most successful in individualistic environments will not profit from cooperative environments. Sometimes this belief is expressed as "gifted students prefer to work alone." A mass of evidence contradicts that belief (Slavin, 1991; Joyce, 1991a). Perhaps a misunderstanding about the relationship between individual and cooperative study contributes to the persistence of the belief. Developing partnerships does not imply that individual effort is not required. In the scenario in Ms. Hilltepper's classroom, all the individuals read the poems. When classifying poems together, each individual contributed ideas and studied the ideas of others. Individuals are not submerged but are enhanced by partnerships with others. Successful students are not inherently less cooperative. In highly individualistic environments they are sometimes taught disdain for less-successful students, to their detriment as students and people, both in school and in the future.

INCREASING THE EFFICIENCY OF PARTNERSHIPS: TRAINING FOR COOPERATION

For reasons not entirely clear to us, the initial reaction of some people to the proposition that students be organized to study together is one of concern that they will not know how to work together productively. In fact, partnerships over simple tasks are not very demanding of social skills. Most students are quite capable of cooperating when they are clear about what has been asked of them. However, developing more efficient ways of working together is clearly important, and there are some guidelines for helping students become more practiced and efficient. These guidelines pertain to group size, complexity, and practice.

Our initial illustrations are of simple dyadic partnerships over clear cognitive tasks. The reason is that the pair or dyad is the simplest form of social organization. One way to help students learn to work cooperatively is to provide practice in the simpler settings of twos and threes. Essentially, we regulate complexity through the tasks we give and the sizes of groups we form. If students are unaccustomed to cooperative work, it makes sense to use the smallest groups with simple or familiar tasks to permit them to gain the experience that will enable them to work in groups of larger sizes. Task groups larger than six persons are clumsy and require skilled leadership, which students cannot provide to one another without experience or training. Partnerships of two, three, or four are the most commonly employed.

Practice results in increased efficiency. If we begin learning with partners and simply provide practice for a few weeks, we will find that the students become increasingly productive.

TRAINING FOR EFFICIENCY

There are also methods for training the students for more efficient cooperation and "positive interdependence" (see Kagan, 1990; Johnson and Johnson, 1999). Simple hand signals can be used to get the attention of busy groups. One of the common procedures is to teach the students that when the instructors raise his or her hands, anyone who notices is to give his or her attention to the instructor and raise his or her hand also. Other students notice and raise their hands, and soon the entire instructional group is attending. This type of procedure is nice because it works while avoiding shouting above the hubbub of the busy partnerships and teaches the students to participate in the management process.

Kagan has developed several procedures for teaching students to work together for goals and to ensure that all students participate equally in the group tasks. An example is what he calls "numbered heads." Suppose that the students are working in partnerships of three. Each member takes a number from one to three. Simple tasks are given ("How many metaphors can you find in this page of prose?"). All members are responsible for mastery of each task. After a suitable interval, the instructor calls out one number—for example, "Number twos." The number two persons in all groups raise their hands. They are responsible for speaking for their groups. The instructor calls on one of them. All other persons are responsible for listening and checking the answer of the person who reports. For example, if the response is "seven," the other students are responsible for checking that response against their own. "How many agree? Disagree?" The procedure is designed to ensure that some individuals do not become the "learners" and "spokespersons" for their groups while others are carried along for the ride.

Also, for tasks for which it is appropriate, pretests may be given. An example might be a list of words to learn to spell. After the pretest a number of tasks might be given to help the students study the words. Then an interval might be provided for the students to tutor one another, followed by a posttest. Each group would then calculate its gain scores (the number correct on the posttest minus the number correct on the pretest), giving all members a stake in everyone's learning. Also, cooperative learning aside, the procedure makes clear that learning expressed as gain is the purpose of the exercise. When posttests only are used, it is not clear whether anyone has actually *learned*—students can receive high marks for a score no higher than they would have achieved in a pretest.

Sets of training tasks can help students learn to be more effective partnerships, to increase their stake in one another, and to work assiduously for learning by all.

TRAINING FOR INTERDEPENDENCE

In addition to practice and training for more efficient cooperative behavior, procedures for helping students become truly interdependent are available. The least complex involve reflection on the group process and discussions about ways of working together most effectively. The more complex involve the provision of tasks that require interdependent behavior. For example, there are card games where success depends on "giving up" valuable cards to another player and communication games where success requires taking the position of another. Familiar games like "Charades" and "Pictionary" are popular because they increase cohesion and the ability to put oneself in the place of the other. There are also procedures for rotating tasks so that each person moves from subordinate to superordinate tasks and where members take turns as coordinators.

The Johnsons (1999) have demonstrated that sets of these tasks can increase interdependence, empathy, and role-taking ability and that students can become quite expert at analyzing group dynamics and learning to create group climates that foster mutuality and collective responsibility. The role-playing model of teaching, discussed in the next chapter, is designed to help students analyze their values and to work together to develop interactive frames of reference.

DIVISION OF LABOR: SPECIALIZATION

A variety of procedures has been developed to help students learn how to help one another by dividing labor. Essentially, tasks are presented in such a way that division of labor increases efficiency. The underlying rationale is that dividing labor increases group cohesion as the team works to learn information or skills while ensuring that all members have both responsibility for learning and an important role in the group. Imagine, for example, that a class is studying Africa and is organized into groups of four. Four countries are chosen for study. One member of each team might be designated a "country specialist." The country specialists from all teams would gather together and study their assigned nation and become the tutors for their original groups, responsible for summarizing information and presenting it to the other members. Or similarly, when tasks requiring memorization are presented to the class, the group will divide responsibility for creating mnemonics for aspects of the data. Or teams could take responsibility for parts of the information to be learned.

A procedure known as *jigsaw* (Aronson et al., 1983; Slavin, 1983) has been worked out to develop formal organizations for divisions of labor. It is highly structured and appropriate as an introduction to division-of-labor processes. Whereas individualistic classroom organization allows individuals to exercise their best-developed skills, division of labor procedures require students to rotate roles, developing their skills in all areas.

COOPERATIVE OR COMPETITIVE GOAL STRUCTURES

Some developers organize teams to compete against one another while others emphasize cooperative goals and minimize team competition. Johnson and Johnson (1990) have analyzed the research and argue that the evidence favors cooperative goal structures, but Slavin (1983) argues that competition between teams benefits learning. The fundamental question is whether students are oriented toward competing with one another or with a goal. Recently several of our colleagues have organized whole classes to work cooperatively toward a goal. For example, the science department of a high school began the year in chemistry by organizing the students to master the essential features of the Table of Elements. In teams, they built mnemonics that were used by all teams. Within two weeks, all students knew the table backward and forward, and that information served as the structural organizer (see Chapter 9) for the entire course. In a group of fifth-grade classes the exploration of social studies began with memorization of the states, large cities, river and mountain systems, and other basic information about the geography of the United States. Class scores were computed (for example, 50 states times 30 students is 1,500 items). The goal was for the class as a whole to achieve a perfect score. The classes reached scores over 1,450 within a week, leaving individuals with very few items to master to reach a perfect score for the class.

MOTIVATION: FROM EXTRINSIC TO INTRINSIC?

The issue about how much to emphasize cooperative or individualistic goal structures relates to conceptions of motivation. Sharan (1990) has argued that cooperative learning increases learning partly because it causes motivational orientation to move from the external to the internal. In other words, when students cooperate over learning tasks, they become more interested in learning for its own sake rather than for external rewards. Thus, students engage in learning for intrinsic satisfaction and become less dependent on praise from teachers or other authorities. The internal motivation is more powerful than the external, resulting in increased learning rates and retention of information and skills.

The frame of reference of the cooperative learning community is a direct challenge to the principles that many schools have relied on to guide their use of tests and rewards for student achievement. Unquestionably, one of the fundamental purposes of general education is to increase internal motivation to learn and to encourage students to generate learning for the sheer satisfaction in growing. If cooperative learning procedures (among others) succeed partly because they contribute to this goal, then the testing and reward structures that prevail in most school environments may actually retard learning. As we turn to group investigation—a powerful model that radically changes the learning environment—consider how different are the tasks, cooperative structures, and principles of motivation we observe in many contemporary schools.

GROUP INVESTIGATION: BUILDING EDUCATION THROUGH THE DEMOCRATIC PROCESS ———————

S C E N A R I O

Debbie Psychoyos's 11th-grade social studies class on world geography has been studying demographic data from the computer program PC-GLOBE which has data on 177 nations. Each of the nine groups of four has analyzed the data on about 20 nations and searched for correlations among the following variables: population, per capita GNP, birth rate, life expectancy, education, health care services, industrial base, agricultural production, transportation systems, foreign debt, balance of payments, women's rights, and natural resources.

The groups reported, and what had begun as a purely academic exercise suddenly aroused the students.

"People born in some countries have a life expectancy 20 years less than folks in other countries."

"We didn't find a relationship between levels of education and per capita wealth!"

"Some rich countries spend more on military facilities and personnel than some large poor ones spend on health care!"

"Women's rights don't correlate with type of government! Some democracies are less liberal than some dictatorships!"

"Some little countries are relatively wealthy because of commerce and industry. Some others just have one mineral that is valuable."

"The United States owes other countries an awful lot of money."

The time is ripe for group investigation. Ms. Psychoyos carefully leads the students to record their reactions to the data. They make a decision to bring together the data on all the countries and find out if the conclusions the groups are coming to will hold over the entire data set. They also decide that they need to find a way of getting in-depth information about selected countries to flesh out their statistical data. But which countries? Will they try to test hypotheses?

One student wonders aloud about world organizations and how they relate to the social situation of the world. They have heard of the United Nations and UNESCO but are vague about how they function. One has heard about the "Committee of Seven," but the others have not. Several have heard of NATO and SEATO but are not sure how they operate. Several wonder about the European Economic Community. Quite a number wonder about the ramifications of German reunification. Several wonder about India and China and how they fit into the picture.

Clearly, deciding priorities for the inquiry will not be easy. However, the conditions for group investigation are present. The students are puzzled. They react differently to the various questions. They need information, and information sources are available. Ms. Psychoyos smiles at her brood of young furrowed brows. "Let's get organized. There is information we all need, and let's start with that. Then let's prioritize our questions and divide the labor to get information that will help us."

John Dewey's ideas have given rise to the broad and powerful model of teaching known as *group investigation*. In it, students are organized into democratic problem-solving groups that attack academic problems and are taught democratic procedures and scientific methods of inquiry as they proceed. The movement to practice democracy in the classroom constituted the first major reform effort in American education and generated a great deal of critical reaction. As schools experimented with democratic-process education, they were subjected to serious criticism during the 1930s and 1940s. The first items of research produced by the reformers were actually developed in defense—in response to questions raised by concerned citizens about whether such a degree of reliance on social purposes would retard the students' academic development. The studies generally indicated that social and academic goals are not at all incompatible. The students from those schools were not disadvantaged; in many respects, in fact, they outperformed students from competitive environments where social education was not emphasized (Chamberlin and Chamberlin, 1943). The reaction continued, however, a seeming anomaly in a democracy whose political and commercial institutions depend so much on integrative organizational behavior.

Educational models derived from a conception of society usually envision what human beings would be like in a very good, even utopian, society. Their educational methods aim to develop ideal citizens who could live in and enhance that society, who could fulfill themselves in and through it, and who would even be able to help create and revise it. We have had such models from the time of the Greeks. Plato's *Republic* (1945) is a blueprint for an ideal society and the educational program to support it. Aristotle (1912) also dealt with the ideal education and society. Since their time, many other utopians have produced educational models, including Augustine (*The City of God*, 1931), Sir Thomas More (*Utopia*, 1965), Comenius (*The Great Didactic*, 1907), and John Locke (1927).

It was natural that attempts would be made to use teaching methods to improve society. In the United States, extensive efforts have been made to develop classroom instruction as a model of democratic process; in fact, variations on democratic process are probably more common than any other general teaching method as far as the educational literature is concerned. In terms of instructional models, *democratic process* has referred to organizing classroom groups to do any or all of the following tasks:

1. Develop a social system based on and created by democratic procedures.
2. Conduct scientific inquiry into the nature of social life and processes. In this case the term *democratic procedures* is synonymous with the scientific method and inquiry.
3. Use inquiry to solve a social or interpersonal problem.
4. Provide an experience-based learning situation.

The implementation of democratic methods of teaching has been exceedingly difficult. They require the teacher to have a high level of interpersonal *and* instructional skills. Also, democratic process is cumbersome and frequently slow; parents, teachers, and school officials often fear that it will not be efficient as a teaching method. In addition, a rich array of instructional resources is necessary, and these have not always been available. Probably the most important hindrance is that the school simply has not been organized to teach the social and intellectual processes of democracy. Instead, it has been directed toward and organized for basic instruction in academic subjects, and school officials and patrons have, for the most part, been unwilling to change that direction or organization. Given the positive effects on student learning in all domains, it is a serious mistake not to make group investigation a staple in the repertoire of all schools.

THE PHILOSOPHICAL UNDERPINNINGS

The dominating figure in the effort to develop models for democratic process has been John Dewey, who wrote *How We Think* in 1910. Nearly all the theoreticians dealing with reflective thinking since that time have acknowledged their debt to him. However, those who have emphasized democratic process have by no means been homogeneous, nor have they followed Dewey in the same ways or even directly. For example, in the 1920s Charles Hubbard Judd (1934) emphasized academic scholarship. William Heard Kilpatrick (1919), for many years a major spokesperson for the Progressive movement, emphasized social problem solving. George Counts (1932) stressed not only problem solving but also reconstruction of society. Boyd Bode (1927) emphasized the general intellectual processes of problem solving.

A well-known statement of this group's concern with the democratic process and societal reconstruction was made in 1961 by Gordon H. Hullfish and Philip G. Smith in *Reflective Thinking: The Method of Education*. These authors stress the role of education in improving the capacity of individuals to reflect on the ways they handle information and on their concepts, their beliefs, their values. A society of reflective thinkers would be capable of improving itself and preserving the uniqueness of individuals. This philosophy contains many ideas or propositions common to democratic-process philosophies. It carefully delineates the ties among the personal world of the individual, his or her intellect, social processes, and the functioning of a democratic society.

Hullfish and Smith see intellectual development and skill in social process as inextricably related. For example, the development of skill in social process requires skill in synthesizing and analyzing the viewpoints of those engaged in social interaction.

Next, they believe that knowledge is constructed and continuously reconstructed by individuals and groups. They stress that knowledge is not conveyed to us merely through our sensory interactions with our environment, but that we must operate on experience to produce knowledge. As a result, knowledge has a personal quality and is unique for each individual. For example, a few hours before writing this, one of the authors stood on a rocky point looking at the Pacific Ocean against the brown of the California coast. He felt a quiet excitement and an appreciation of the sea and the rocks and the great peace of the scene about him. Yet the concept *sea*, the concept *rock*, the concept *wave*, and the excitement, peace, and appreciation he felt were not inherent in the experience themselves. These were constructed by the author in relation to that experience and to others he has had. He created some concepts and borrowed some from others. He generated some feelings and some beliefs and had been given some by imitating other people (the vast majority were borrowed in this way).

Thus, individuals' ways of reflecting on reality are what make their world comprehensible to them and give them personal and social meaning. The quality of an individual's ability to reflect on experience becomes a critical factor in determining the quality of the world that individual will construct about himself or herself. Someone who is insensitive to much of his or her experience and does not reflect on it will have a far less richly constructed world than someone who takes in a good deal of experience and reflects fully on it. It becomes critical for education to sensitize the individual to many aspects of the physical and social environment and to increase the individual's capacity to reflect on the environment.

The individual quality of knowledge creates some difficulties, especially when it comes to constructing a society. Nevertheless, Hullfish and Smith maintain that individual differences are the strength of a democracy, and negotiating among them is a major democratic activity. The more an individual learns to take responsibility for reflecting on experience and developing a valid view of the world and a valid set of beliefs, the more it is likely that the resulting network of information, concepts, and values will be unique to the individual. In other words, the more fully reflective an individual is, the more he or she will develop a personal processing system. A democratic society requires that we work together to understand each other's worlds and develop a shared perspective that will enable us to learn from each other and govern ourselves while preserving a pluralistic reality.

The perception of alternative frames of reference and alternative courses of action is essential to social negotiations. But one must have great personal development to understand other people's viewpoints. This sharing of perceptions is necessary, however, if a mutual reality is to be constructed (see Berger and Luckmann, 1966).

The essence of a functioning democracy is the negotiation of problem definitions and problem situations. This ability to negotiate with others also helps each person negotiate his or her own world. Maintaining a sense of meaning and purpose depends on developing a valid and flexible way of dealing with reality. Failure to make life comprehensible or to negotiate reality with others will result in a feeling of chaos. The ability to continually reconstruct one's value stances and the ability to create value systems that are compatible are both essential to mature development.

Most models of teaching assume that one does something in particular to get a specific outcome from the learner. On the contrary, models that emphasize democratic process assume that the outcome of any educational experience is not completely predictable. The democratic model makers reason that if they are successful in persuading students to inquire into the nature of their experiences, and to develop their own ways of viewing the world, it will be impossible to predict just how they will face any given situation or solve any particular problem. Hence, if the students are taught an academic discipline, it is not so that they will know exactly the discipline known by others, but so that this exposure will help each of them create concepts grounded in, but not smothered by, the discipline.

ORIENTATION TO THE MODEL ————————

GOALS AND ASSUMPTIONS

In *Democracy and Education* (1916), John Dewey recommends that the entire school be organized as a miniature democracy. Students participate in the development of the social system and, through experience, gradually learn how to apply the scientific method to improve human society. This, Dewey feels, is the best preparation for citizenship in a democracy. John U. Michaelis (1963) applied Dewey's work to teaching the social studies at the elementary level. Central to his method of teaching is the creation of a democratic group that defines and attacks problems of social significance. Many social studies educators have developed similar approaches.

Herbert Thelen is one of the founders of the National Training Laboratory. In many respects Thelen's group investigation model resembles the methods Dewey and Michaelis recommend. Group investigation attempts to combine in one teaching strategy the form and dynamics of the democratic process with the process of academic inquiry. Thelen is reaching for an experience-based learning situation, easily transferable to later life situations and characterized by a vigorous level of inquiry.

Thelen (1960, p. 80) begins with a conception of a social being: "man [woman] who builds with other men [women] the rules and agreements that constitute social reality." Any view of how people should develop has to refer to the inescapable fact that life is *social*. A social being cannot act without reference to his or her companions on earth; otherwise in the quest for self-maintenance and autonomy each person may well conflict with other people making similar efforts. In establishing social agreements, each individual helps to determine both prohibitions and freedom for action. Rules of conduct operate in all fields—religious, political, economic, and scientific—and constitute the culture of a society. For Thelen, this negotiation and renegotiation of the social order are the essence of social process:

> Thus in groups and societies a cyclical process exists: individuals, interdependently seeking to meet their needs, must establish a social order (and in the process they develop groups and societies). The social order determines in varying degrees what ideas, values and actions are possible, valid, and "appropriate"! Working within these "rules" and stimulated by the need for rules the culture develops. The individual studies his reactions to the rules and reinterprets them to discover their meaning for the way of life he seeks. Through this quest, he changes his own way of life, and this in turn influences the way of

life of others. But as the way of life changes, the rules must be revised, and new controls and agreements have to be hammered out and incorporated into the social order. (Thelen, 1960, p. 80)

The classroom is analogous to the larger society; it has a social order and a classroom culture, and its students care about the way of life that develops there—that is, the standards and expectations that become established. Teachers should seek to harness the energy naturally generated by the concern for creating the social order. The model of teaching replicates the negotiation pattern needed by society. Through negotiation the students study academic knowledge and engage in social problem solving. According to Thelen, one should not attempt to teach knowledge from any academic area without teaching the social process by which it was negotiated.

Thelen rejects the normal classroom order that develops around the basic values of comfort and politeness or of keeping the teacher happy. Rather, the classroom group should take seriously the process of developing a social order.

The teacher's task is to lead the development of the social order in the classroom for the purpose of orienting it to inquiry, and the "house rules" to be developed are the methods and attitudes of the knowledge discipline to be taught. The teacher influences the emerging social order toward inquiring when he "brings out" and capitalizes on differences in the way students act and interprets the role of investigator—which is also the role of member in the classroom. (Thelen, 1960, p. 8)

Life in classrooms takes the form of a series of "inquiries." Each inquiry starts with a stimulus situation to which students

can react and discover basic conflicts among their attitudes, ideas, and modes of perception. On the basis of this information, they identify the problem to be investigated, analyze the roles required to solve it, organize themselves to take these roles, act, report, and evaluate these results. These steps are illuminated by reading, by personal investigation, and by consultation with experts. The group is concerned with its own effectiveness, and with its discussion of its own process as related to the goals of investigation. (Thelen, 1960, p. 82)

In the concentration on the overt activities of the democratic process, we should not overlook the underlying spirit that brings the democratic process to life. The activities, if followed by rote, provide only lifeless applications quite unlike the democratic process and scientific method Dewey and Thelen have in mind. The class should become a miniature democracy that attacks problems and, through problem solving, acquires knowledge and becomes more effective as a social group. Many attempts to use democratic process did little to change educational practice because the implementation was superficial, following the form but not the substance of democracy.

BASIC CONCEPTS

The two concepts of (1) inquiry and (2) knowledge are central to Thelen's strategy.

INQUIRY

Inquiry is stimulated by confrontation with a problem, and knowledge results from the inquiry. The social process enhances inquiry and is itself studied and improved. The heart of group investigation lies in its formulation of inquiry. According to Thelen (1960), the concern of inquiry is

> to initiate and supervise the processes of giving attention to something; of interacting with and being stimulated by other people, whether in person or through their writing; and of reflection and reorganization of concepts and attitudes as shown in arriving at conclusions, identifying new investigations to be undertaken, taking action and turning out a better product. (p. 85)

The first element of inquiry is an event the individual can react to and puzzle over—a problem to be solved. In the classroom the teacher can select content and cast it in terms of problem situations—for example, "How did our community come to be the way it is?" Simply providing a problem, however, will not generate the puzzlement that is a major energy source for inquiry. The students must add an awareness of self and a desire for personal meaning. In addition, they must assume the dual roles of participant and observer, simultaneously inquiring into the problem and observing themselves as inquirers. Because inquiry is basically a social process, students are aided in the self-observer role by interacting with, and by observing the reactions of, other puzzled people. The conflicting viewpoints that emerge also energize the students' interest in the problem.

Although the teacher can provide a problem situation, it is up to the students as inquirers to identify and formulate the problem and pursue its solution. Inquiry calls for firsthand activity in a real situation and ongoing experience that continually generates new data. The students must thus be conscious of method so that they may collect data, associate and classify ideas recalling past experience, formulate and test hypotheses, study consequences, and modify plans. Finally, they must develop the capacity for reflection, the ability to synthesize overt participative behavior with symbolic verbal behavior. The students are asked to give conscious attention to the experience—to formulate explicitly the conclusions of the study and to integrate them with existing ideas. In this way thoughts are reorganized into new and more powerful patterns.

THE MODEL OF TEACHING

SYNTAX

The model begins by confronting the students with a stimulating problem. The confrontation may be presented verbally, or it may be an actual experience; it may arise naturally, or it may be provided by a teacher. If the students react, the teacher draws their attention to the differences in their reactions—what stances they take, what they perceive, how they organize things, and what they feel. As the students become interested in their differences in reaction, the teacher draws them toward formulating and structuring the problem for themselves. Next, students analyze the required roles, organize themselves, act, and report their results. Finally, the group evaluates its solution in terms of its original purposes. The cycle repeats itself, either with another confrontation or with a new problem growing out of the investigation itself (see Table 10.1).

SOCIAL SYSTEM

The social system is democratic, governed by decisions developed from, or at least validated by, the experience of the group—within boundaries and in relation to puzzling phenomena identified by the teacher as objects to study. The activities of the group emerge with a minimal amount of external structure provided by the teacher. Students and teacher have equal status except for role differences. The atmosphere is one of reason and negotiation.

TABLE 10.1   **SYNTAX OF GROUP INVESTIGATION MODEL OF LEARNING AND TEACHING**

Phase One	Phase Two
Students encounter puzzling situation (planned or unplanned).	Students explore reactions to the situation.

Phase Three	Phase Four
Students formulate study task and organize for study (problem definition, role, assignments, etc.).	Independent and group study.

Phase Five	Phase Six
Students analyze progress and process.	Recycle activity.

PRINCIPLES OF REACTION

The teacher's role in group investigation is one of counselor, consultant, and friendly critic. He or she must guide and reflect the group experience over three levels: the problem-solving or task level (What is the nature of the problem? What are the factors involved?), the group management level (What information do we need now? How can we organize ourselves to get it?), and the level of individual meaning (How do you feel about these conclusions? What would you do differently as a result of knowing about . . . ?) (Thelen, 1954, pp. 52–53). This teaching role is difficult and sensitive, because the essence of inquiry is student activity—problems cannot be imposed. At the same time the instructor must: (1) facilitate the group process, (2) intervene in the group to channel its energy into potentially educative activities, and (3) supervise these educative activities so that personal meaning comes from the experience (Thelen, 1960, p. 13). Intervention by the instructor should be minimal unless the group bogs down seriously. Chapters 16 to 18 of *Leadership of Discussion Groups* (1975) by Gertrude K. Pollack provide an excellent advanced discussion of leadership in groups. Although the material was prepared for persons leading therapy groups, it is written at a general level and provides much useful advice for those wishing to build classrooms around group inquiry.

SUPPORT SYSTEM

The support system for group investigation should be extensive and responsive to the needs of the students. The school needs to be equipped with a first-class library that provides information and opinion through a wide variety of media; it should also be able to provide access to outside resources as well. Children should be encouraged to investigate and to contact resource people beyond the school walls. One reason cooperative inquiry of this sort has been relatively rare is that the support systems were not adequate to maintain the level of inquiry.

APPLICATION

Group investigation requires flexibility from the teacher and the classroom organization. Although we assume that the model fits comfortably with the environment of the "open" classroom, we believe it is equally compatible with more traditional classrooms. We have observed successful group investigation teachers in a context in which other subjects, such as math and reading, are carried out in a more structured, teacher-directed fashion. If students have not had an opportunity to experience the kind of social interaction, decision making, and independent inquiry called for in this model, it may take some time before they function at a high level. On the other hand, students who have participated in classroom meetings and/or self-directed, inquiry-oriented learning will probably have an easier time. In any case, it is probably useful for the teacher to remember that the social aspects of the model may be as unfamiliar to students as the intellectual aspects and may be as demanding in terms of skill acquisition.

Although the examples of the model described here tend to be intellectually and organizationally elaborate, all investigations need not be so complex. With young children or students new to group investigation, fairly small-scale investigations are possible; the initial confrontation can provide a narrow range of topics, issues, information, and alternative activities. For example, providing an evening's entertainment for the school is more focused than resolving the energy crisis. Deciding who will care for the classroom pet and how is even narrower. Of course, the nature of the inquiry depends on the interests and ages of the students. Older students tend to be concerned with more complex issues. However, the skillful teacher can design inquiries appropriate to the students' abilities and to his or her own ability to manage the investigation.

As we indicated in the introduction to the social family of models, three recent lines of research by three teams (led by David and Roger Johnson, Robert Slavin, and Shlomo Sharan) have contributed a good deal of knowledge about how to engineer social models and what their effects are likely to be.

The Johnsons have concentrated on cooperative tasks, cooperative rewards, and peer tutoring. They have made extensive reviews of studies with students of all ages working in many substantive areas. As mentioned earlier, their reviews and studies support the contention that working together increases student energy and that rewarding teams of students for performance is effective, appearing to increase the energy of the teams (Johnson, Maruyana, Johnson, Nelson, and Skon, 1981). In addition, their work with peer tutoring appears positive as well, and heterogeneous teams (composed of high and low achievers) appear to be the most productive (Johnson and Johnson, 1972).

Slavin's (1983) work generally confirms that of the Johnsons, and he has added some interesting variations. He has explored ways of differentiating tasks when groups are working on projects and has found that differentiating tasks increases the energy of the students. For example, when students are studying a topic in history, individuals can become "specialists" in certain areas of the topic, with the responsibility of mastering certain information and conveying it to the other students. In addition, he has looked at the effects of team composition on learning and attitudes toward self and others. Generally, the more heterogeneous groups learn more, form more positive attitudes toward the learning tasks, and become more positive toward one another (Slavin, 1983).

Sharan has studied group investigation per se. His team has reported that the more pervasive the cooperative climate, the more positive the students toward both the learning tasks and toward each other (Sharan and Hertz-Lazarowitz, 1980a). In addition, he has hypothesized that the greater social complexity would increase achievement of more complex learning goals (concepts and theories) and both confirmed his hypothesis and found that it increased the learning of information and basic skills as well. A nice small study by teachers in an Oregon high school is worth reading both for its insight into the dynamics of the groups and the effects on the students (Huhtala, 1994).

The purpose of cooperative inquiry is to combine complex social and academic tasks to generate academic and social learning. Properly implemented, it appears to achieve its goals.

INSTRUCTIONAL AND NURTURANT EFFECTS

This model is highly versatile and comprehensive; it blends the goals of academic inquiry, social integration, and social-process learning. It can be used in all subject areas, with all age levels, when the teacher desires to emphasize the formulation and problem-solving aspects of knowledge rather than the intake of preorganized, predetermined information.

Provided that one accepts Thelen's view of knowledge and its reconstruction, the group investigation model (Figure 10.1) can be considered a

FIGURE 10.1   Instructional and nurturant effects of the group
                investigation model.

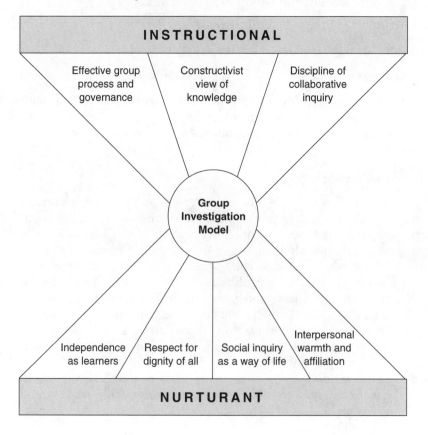

very direct and probably efficient way of teaching academic knowledge as well as social process. It also appears likely to nurture interpersonal warmth and trust, respect for negotiated rules and policies, independence in learning, and respect for the dignity of others.

In deciding whether to use the model, considering the potential nurturant effects may be as important as analyzing the likely direct instructional effects. Another model might be as appropriate for teaching academic inquiry, but a teacher may prefer group investigation for what it might nurture.

SUMMARY CHART ▶ GROUP INVESTIGATION MODEL

Syntax

Phase One: Encounter Puzzling Situation (planned or unplanned)

Phase Two: Explore Reactions to the Situation

Phase Three: Formulate Study Task and Organize for Study (problem definition, role, assignments, and so on)

Phase Four: Independent and Group Study

Phase Five: Analyze Progress and Process

Phase Six: Recycle Activity

Social System

The system is based on the democratic process and group decisions, with low external structure. Puzzlement must be genuine—it cannot be imposed. Authentic exchanges are essential. Atmosphere is one of reason and negotiation.

Principles of Reaction

Teacher plays a facilitative role directed at group process (helps learners formulate plan, act, manage group) and requirements of inquiry (consciousness of method). He or she functions as an academic counselor. The students react to the puzzling situation and examine the nature of their common and different reactions. They determine what kinds of information they need to approach the problem and proceed to collect relevant data. They generate hypotheses and gather the information needed to test them. They evaluate their products and continue their inquiry or begin a new line of inquiry. The central teaching moves to build the cooperative social environment and teach students the skills of negotiation and conflict resolution necessary for democratic problem solving. In addition, the teacher needs to guide the students in methods of data collection and analysis, help them frame testable hypotheses, and decide what would constitute a reasonable test of a hypothesis. Because groups vary considerably in their need for structure (Hunt, 1971) and their cohesiveness (Thelen, 1967), the teacher cannot behave mechanically but must "read" the students' social and academic behavior and provide the assistance that keeps the inquiry moving without squelching it.

Support System

The environment must be able to respond to a variety of learner demands. Teacher and students must be able to assemble what they need when they need it.

CHAPTER 11

THE STUDY OF VALUES

Role Playing and Public Policy Education

> *The analysis of values is what's important. Playing the roles lets the values become visible if the analysis is right. Understanding that what you do is a living out of your values starts the inquiry.*
>
> —Fannie Shaftel to a group of Palo Alto teachers, May 1969

S C E N A R I O

Laurie's eighth grade class is reading David Halberstam's marvelous book, *Firehouse* (2002), which describes the social system of Engine 40 Ladder 35 (known as 40/35) on the West Side of Manhattan before, during, and after September 11, 2001, a day when 13 of the 40/35 men sped down toward the Trade Centers, only one of them to return alive.

Halberstam describes the men, their families, their interaction, and the norms that enabled them, time after time, to go into extremely dangerous situations (incredibly dangerous, when it comes to high rise buildings) and work together while risking their lives.

Laurie's students gradually realize that all over the United States, there are such little communities of people who know what they are doing and do it with pride and loyalty. She lets the students react randomly for a while until they begin to identify issues. She appoints recorders, and they begin a list of questions and statements which will gradually be organized into needs for information, public policy issues, and values. The list begins as a jumble of thoughts and observations.

"How many firemen die in fires in New York in a normal year?"

"Why do we pay them less than they could earn doing something else?"

"What must it be like, heading for a dangerous fire at breakneck speed?"

"How can they make themselves go into a fire?"

"How do they stand their grief?"

"Interesting that many are the sons and even grandsons of firemen."

"What would happen if no one would do their job?"

"Why do we build such tall buildings knowing that they are more dangerous than shorter ones?"

Thus begins an inquiry that will take a while and will lead down many paths. Eventually the class will have identified a number of values that lie under public policy or are compromised as decisions are made. Then Laurie will open up another area with them. The study of values is the core of their social studies program.

In this chapter we are going to lay out two ways of studying values. The first, *role playing*, begins with problem situations in the lives of the students and explores how values drive behavior and raises student consciousness about values. A direct effect is greater understanding about and empathy with differences in values as people interact. Another direct effect is strategies for resolving conflicts in fashions that respect different points of view without giving up the need for agreed on humane values.

The second, *jurisprudential inquiry*, takes us into the world of values as they play out in policy matters. Public policy debates take place because the issues require a balancing of values. For example, debates over whether citizens can possess guns bring together values supporting personal freedom with concerns about the dangers of having an armed populace. Jurisprudential inquiry sensitizes students to public issues and ways of identifying and balancing values as solutions are sought.

We will begin with role playing.

S C E N A R I O

We are in a seventh-grade classroom in East Los Angeles, California. The students have returned to the classroom from a recess period and are complaining excitely to one another. Mr. Williams, the teacher, asks what the matter is and they all start in at once, discussing a series of difficulties that lasted throughout the recess period. Apparently, two of the students began to squabble about who was to take the sports equipment outside. Then all of the students argued about what game to play. Next, there was a dispute about choosing sides for the games. This included a dispute over whether the girls should be included with the boys or whether they should play separately. The class finally began to play volleyball, but very shortly there was a dispute over a line call, and the game was never completed.

At first, Mr. Williams displays his displeasure toward the class. He is angry, not simply over the incidents, but because these arguments have been going on since the beginning of the year. At last he says, "OK, we really have to face this problem. You must be as tired of it as I am, and you really are not acting maturely. So we are going to use a technique that we have been using to discuss family problems to approach our own problems right here in this classroom: we're going to use role playing. Now, what I want you to do is divide into groups and try to identify the types of problems we've been having. Just take today, for example, and outline the problem situations that got us into this fix."

The students begin with the argument over taking the sports equipment outside, and then outline other arguments. Each is a typical situation that people face all the time and that they must learn to take a stand on. After the separate groups of students have listed their problems, Mr. Williams appoints one of the students to lead a discussion in which each group reports the kinds of problem situations that have come up; the groups agree on a half dozen problems that have consistently bothered the class.

The students then group the problems according to type. One type concerns the division of labor. A second type deals with deciding principles for selecting teams. A third type focuses on resolving disputes over the particulars of games, such as whether balls have been hit out of bounds, whether players are out or safe, and so on. Mr. Williams then assigns one type of problem to each group and asks the groups to describe situations in which the problems come up. When they have done this, the class votes on which problem to start with. The first problem they select is disputes over rules; the actual problem situation they select is the volleyball game in which the dispute over a line call occurred.

Together, the class talks about how the problem situation develops. It begins when a ball is hit close to the boundary line. One team believes it is in, and the other believes it is out of bounds. The students then argue with one another, and the argument goes on so that the game cannot continue.

Several students are selected to enact the situation. Others gather around and are assigned to observe particular aspects of the role playing that follows. Some students are to look for the particulars of how the argument develops. Some are to study one role player and others another, to determine how they handle the situation.

The enactment is spirited. The students select as role players those who have been on opposite sides during the game, and they become as involved in the argument during the role playing as they were during the actual situation. Finally, they are standing in the middle of the room shouting at one another. At this point, Mr. Williams calls, "Time!" and asks the students to describe what has gone on.

Everyone is eager to talk. The discussion gradually focuses on how the attitude of the participants prevented resolving the problem. No one was listening to the other person. And no one was dealing with the problem of how to resolve honest disputes. Finally, Mr. Williams asks the students to suggest other ways that people could behave in this kind of conflict. Some students suggest giving in gracefully. But others object that if someone believes he or she is right, that is not an easy thing to do. Finally, the students identify an important question to focus on: "How can we develop a policy about who should make calls, and how should others feel about those calls?" They decide to reenact the scene by having all the participants assume that the defensive team should make the calls only when they see clear evidence that a ball is out and the other team has not seen the evidence.

The enactment takes place. This time, the players attempt to follow the policy that the defensive team has the right to make the call, but the offensive team has the right to object to a call. Once again, the enactment results in a shouting match; however, after it is over, the students who have watched the enactment point out that the role players have not behaved as if there is a resolution to the situation. They recognize that if there are to be games, there has to be agreement about who can make calls as well as a certain amount of trust on both sides.

They decide to try a third enactment, this time with two new role players inserted as dispute referees. The introduction of referees completely changes the third enactment. The referees insist that the other players pay attention to them, which the players do not want to do. In discussing this enactment, the students point out that there has to be a system to ensure reasonable order and the resolution of disputes. The students also agree that as things stand, they probably are unable to resolve disputes without including a referee of some sort, but that no referees will be effective unless the students agree to accept the referees' decisions. They finally decide that in future games, two students will be referees. Those students will be chosen by lot prior to the game; their function will be to arbitrate and to make all calls relevant to the rules of the game, and their decisions will be final. The students agree that they will see how that system works.

The next day Mr. Williams opens up the second set of issues, and the students repeat this process. The exploration of other areas of dispute continues over the next few weeks. At first, many of the notions that are clarified are simply practical ones about how to solve specific problems. Gradually, however, Mr. Williams directs the discussion to a consideration of the basic values governing individual behavior. The students begin to see the problems of communal living, and they develop policies for governing their own behavior, as individuals and as a group. They also begin to develop skills in negotiating. The students who were locked in conflict gradually learn that if they behave in a slightly different way, others may also modify their behavior, and problems become easier to solve.

RATIONALE

In role playing, students explore human relations problems by enacting problem situations and then discussing the enactments. Together, students can explore feelings, attitudes, values, and problem-solving strategies. Several teams of researchers have experimented with role playing, and their treatments of the strategy are remarkably similar. The version we explore here was formulated by Fannie and George Shaftel (1967). We have also incorporated ideas from the work of Mark Chesler and Robert Fox (1966).

Role playing as a model of teaching has roots in both the personal and social dimensions of education. It attempts to help individuals find personal meaning within their social worlds and to resolve personal dilemmas with the assistance of the social group. In the social dimension, it allows individuals to work together in analyzing social situations, especially interpersonal problems, and in developing decent and democratic ways of coping with these situations. We have placed role playing in the social family of models because the social group plays such an indispensable part in human development and because of the unique opportunity that role playing offers for resolving interpersonal and social dilemmas.

ORIENTATION TO THE MODEL

GOALS AND ASSUMPTIONS

On its simplest level, role playing is dealing with problems through action; a problem is delineated, acted out, and discussed. Some students are role players; others observers. A person puts himself or herself in the position of another person and then tries to interact with others who are also playing roles. As empathy, sympathy, anger, and affection are all generated during the interaction, role playing, if done well, becomes a part of life. This emotional content, as well as the words and the actions, becomes part of the later analysis. When the acting out is finished, even the observers are involved enough to want to know why each person reached his or her decision, what the sources of resistance were, and whether there were other ways this situation could have been approached.

The essence of role playing is the involvement of participants and observers in a real problem situation and the desire for resolution and understanding that this involvement engenders. The role-playing process provides a live sample of human behavior that serves as a vehicle for students to: (1) explore their feelings; (2) gain insight into their attitudes, values, and perceptions; (3) develop their problem-solving skills and attitudes; and (4) explore subject matter in varied ways.

These goals reflect several assumptions about the learning process in role playing. First, role playing implicitly advocates an experience-based learning situation in which the "here and now" becomes the content of instruction. The model assumes that it is possible to create authentic analogies to real-life problem situations and that through these re-creations students can "sample" life. Thus, the enactment elicits genuine, typical emotional responses and behaviors from the students.

A related assumption is that role playing can draw out students' feelings, which they can recognize and perhaps release. The Shaftels' version of role playing emphasizes the intellectual content as much as the emotional content; analysis and discussion of the enactment are as important as the role playing itself. We, as educators, are concerned that students recognize and understand their feelings and see how their feelings influence their behavior.

Another assumption, similar to an assumption of the synectics models, is that emotions and ideas can be brought to consciousness and enhanced by the group. The collective reactions of the peer group can bring out new ideas and provide directions for growth and change. The model deemphasizes the traditional role of teacher and encourages listening and learning from one's peers.

A final assumption is that covert psychological processes involving one's own attitudes, values, and belief system can be brought to consciousness by combining spontaneous enactment with analysis. Furthermore, individuals can gain some measure of control over their belief systems if they recognize their values and attitudes and test them against the views of others. Such analysis can help them evaluate their attitudes and values and the consequences of their beliefs, so that they can allow themselves to grow.

THE CONCEPT OF ROLE

Each individual has a unique manner of relating to people, situations, and objects. One person may feel that most people are dishonest and cannot be trusted; someone else may feel that everyone is interesting and may look forward to meeting new people. People also evaluate and behave in consistent ways toward themselves, seeing themselves as powerful and smart, or perhaps afraid and not very able. These feelings about people and situations and about themselves influence people's behavior and determine how they will respond in various situations. Some people respond with aggressive and hostile behavior, playing the part of a bully. Others withdraw and remain alone, playing the part of a shy or sulking person.

These parts people play are called *roles*. A role is "a patterned sequence of feelings, words, and actions. It is a unique and accustomed manner of relating to others" (Chesler and Fox, 1966, pp. 5, 8). Unless people are looking for them, it is sometimes hard to perceive consistencies and patterns in behavior. But they are usually there. Terms such as *friendly, bully, snobby, know-it-all,* and *grouch* are convenient for describing characteristic responses or roles.

The roles individuals play are determined by several factors over many years. The kinds of people someone meets determine his or her general feelings about people. How those people act toward the individual and how the individuals perceive their feelings toward them influence their feelings about themselves. The rules of one's particular culture and institutions help to determine which roles a person assumes and how he or she plays them.

People may not be happy with the roles they have assumed. And they may misperceive the attitudes and feelings of others because they do not recognize *their* role and *why* they play it. Two people can share the same feelings but behave in very different ways. They can desire the same goals, but if one person's behavior is misperceived by others, he or she may not attain that goal.

For a clear understanding of oneself and of others, it is extremely important that a person be aware of roles and how they are played. To do this, each person must be able to put himself or herself in another's place, and to experience as much as possible that person's thoughts and feelings. If someone is able to empathize, he or she can accurately interpret social events and interactions. Role playing is a vehicle that forces people to take the roles of others.

The concept of role is one of the central theoretical underpinnings of the role-playing model. It is also a major goal. We must teach students to use this concept, to recognize different roles, and to think of their own and others' behavior in terms of roles. At the same time, there are many other aspects to this model, and many levels of analysis, which to some extent compete with one another. For example, the content of the problem, the solutions to the problem, the feelings of the role players, and the acting itself all serve to involve students in the role play. Therefore, to be a salient part of the role-playing experience, the concept of role must be interwoven, yet kept in the fore throughout all the role-playing activities. It also helps if, prior to using the model, students have been taught this concept directly.

THE MODEL OF TEACHING

SYNTAX

The benefits of role playing depend on the quality of the enactment and especially on the analysis that follows. They depend also on the students' perceptions of the role as similar to real-life situations. Children do not necessarily engage effectively in role playing or role analysis the first time they try it. Many have to learn to engage in role playing in a sincere way so that the content generated can be analyzed seriously. Chesler and Fox (1966, pp. 64–66) suggest pantomimic exercises as a way of freeing inexperienced students. Role playing is not likely to be successful if the teacher simply tosses out a problem situation, persuades a few children to act it out, and then conducts a discussion about the enactment.

The Shaftels suggest that the role-playing activity consist of nine steps: (1) warm up the group, (2) select participants, (3) set the stage, (4) prepare observers, (5) enact, (6) discuss and evaluate, (7) reenact, (8) discuss and evaluate, and (9) share experiences and generalize. Each of these steps or phases has a specific purpose that contributes to the richness and focus of the learning activity. Together, they ensure that a line of thinking is pursued throughout the complex of activities, that students are prepared in their roles, that goals for the role play are identified, and that the discussion afterward is not simply a collection of diffuse reactions, though these are important too. Table 11.1 summarizes the phases and activities of the model, which are discussed and illustrated in the remainder of this section.

TABLE 11.1   SYNTAX OF ROLE PLAYING

Phase One: Warm Up the Group	Phase Two: Select Participants
Identify or introduce problem. Make problem explicit. Interpret problem story, explore issues. Explain role playing.	Analyze roles. Select role players.

Phase Three: Set the Stage	Phase Four: Prepare the Observers
Set line of action. Restate roles. Get inside problem situation.	Decide what to look for. Assign observation tasks.

Phase Five: Enact	Phase Six: Discuss and Evaluate
Begin role play. Maintain role play. Break role play.	Review action of role play (events, positions, realism). Discuss major focus. Develop next enactment.

Phase Seven: Reenact	Phase Eight: Discuss and Evaluate
Play revised roles; suggest next steps or behavioral alternatives.	As in phase six.

Phase Nine: Share Experiences and Generalize
Relate problem situation to real experience and current problems. Explore general principles of behavior.

Source: Based on Fannie Shaftel and George Shaftel, *Role Playing of Social Values* (Englewood Cliffs, N.J.: Prentice-Hall, Inc., 1967).

Phase one, warming up the group, involves introducing students to a problem so that they recognize it as an area with which everyone needs to learn to deal. The warm-up can begin, for example, by identifying a problem within the group.

Teacher: Do you remember the other day we had a discussion about Jane's lunch money? Because she had put her money in her pocket and had not given it to me when she came into the room, it was lost. We had quite a talk about finding money: whether to keep it or turn it in. Sometimes it's not easy to decide what to do. Do you ever have times when you just don't know what to do? (Shaftel and Shaftel, 1967, p. 67)

The teacher sensitizes the group to a problem and creates a climate of acceptance, so that students feel that all views, feelings, and behaviors can be explored without retribution.

The second part of the warm-up is to express the problem vividly through examples. These may come from student descriptions of imaginary or real situations that express the problem, or from situations selected by the teacher and illustrated by a film, television show, or problem story.

In *Role Playing of Social Values: Decision Making in the Social Studies* (1967), the Shaftels provide a large selection of problem stories to be read to the class. Each story stops when a dilemma has become apparent. The Shaftels feel that problem stories have several advantages. They focus on a particular problem and yet ensure that the children will be able to disassociate themselves from the problem enough to face it. Incidents that students have experienced in their lives or that the group has experienced as a whole, though visually and emotionally involving, can cause considerable stress and therefore be difficult to analyze. Another advantage of problem stories is that they are dramatic and make role playing relatively easy to initiate. The burden of involving the children in the activity is lightened.

The last part of the warm-up is to ask questions that make the children think about and predict the outcome of the story: "How might the story end?" "What is Sam's problem and what can he do about it?" The teacher in the preceding illustration handled this step as follows:

Teacher: I would like to read you a story this afternoon about a boy who found himself in just such a spot. His parents wanted him to do one thing, but his gang insisted he do something else. Trying to please everybody, he got himself into difficulty. This will be one of those problem stories that stop but are not finished.
Pupil: Like the one we did last week?
Teacher: Yes.
Pupil: Oh! But can't you give us one with an ending?

Teacher: When you get into a jam, does someone always come along and tell you how your problems will end?

Pupil: Oh no! Not very often.

Teacher: In life, we usually have to make our own endings—we have to solve our problems ourselves. That's why I'm reading these problem stories—so that we can practice endings, trying out many different ones to see which works the best for us. As I read this story, you might be thinking of what you would do if you were in Tommy Haines's place. (Shaftel and Shaftel, 1967, p. 67)

The story is about a boy caught between his father's views and those of his club. He has committed himself financially to a club project his father does not approve of and would not support. Tommy does not have the money and resorts to a somewhat devious means of getting it. The problem centers on Tommy's opportunity to clear the debt with his gang. He delivers a package for the druggist and is overpaid $5—enough to clear the debt. Tommy stands outside the customer's door, trying to decide whether to return or keep the money. After reading the story, the teacher focuses the discussion on what might happen next, thus preparing for different enactments of the situation:

Teacher: What do you think Tommy will do?

Pupil: I think he'll keep the money.

Teacher: Oh?

Pupil: Because he needs to pay the club.

Pupil: Oh no he won't. He'll get found out, and he knows it. (Shaftel and Shaftel, 1967, p. 69)

In phase two, selecting participants, the children and the teacher describe the various characters—what they are like, how they feel, and what they might do. The children are then asked to volunteer to role play; they may even ask to play a particular role. The Shaftels caution us against assigning a role to a child who has been suggested for it, because the person making the suggestion may be stereotyping the child or putting him or her in an awkward situation. A person must want to play a role. Although he or she takes into account the children's preferences, the teacher should exercise some control in the situation.

We can use several criteria for selecting a child for a role. Roles can be assigned to children who appear to be so involved in the problem that they identify with a specific role, those who express an attitude that needs to be explored, or those who should learn to identify with the role or place themselves in another person's position. The Shaftels warn the teacher not to select children who would give "adult-oriented, socially acceptable" interpretations to the role, because such a quick and superficial resolution of the problem dampens discussion and exploration of the basic issues (Shaftel and Shaftel, 1967, p. 67).

In our illustration, the teacher asks a student to be Tommy and then asks the student what roles need to be filled. He answers that he'll need someone to be the customer and some students to be the gang. The teacher asks several children to fill these roles.

In phase three, setting the stage, the role players outline the scene but do not prepare any specific dialogue. They simply sketch the setting and perhaps one person's line of action. The teacher may help set the stage by asking the students a few simple questions about where the enactment is taking place, what it is like, and so on. It is necessary only that a simple line of action be identified and a general setting clarified so that participants feel secure enough in the roles to begin to act.

The setting is arranged so that one corner of the classroom becomes the school where the gang is waiting for Tommy to bring the money; in another corner, a chair is used to represent the door of the customer's house. The teacher asks the boy playing Tommy where in the action he wants to begin, and the boy decides to start with the scene where he is delivering the packages.

In phase four, preparing the observers, it is important that the observers become actively involved so that the entire group experiences the enactment and can later analyze the play. The Shaftels suggest that the teacher involve observers in the role play by assigning them tasks, such as evaluating the realism of the role playing, commenting on the effectiveness and the sequences of the role players' behavior, and defining the feelings and ways of thinking of the persons being portrayed. The observers should determine what the role players are trying to accomplish, what actions the role players took that were helpful or not helpful, and what alternative experiences might have been enacted. Or they can watch one particular role to define the feelings of that person. The observers should understand that there will be more than one enactment in most cases, and if they would have acted out a certain role in a different way, they may have a chance to do so.

In our illustration, the teacher prepares the observers as follows:

Teacher: Now, as you watch, consider whether you think Jerry's way of ending the story could really happen. How will people feel? You may want to think of what will happen next. Perhaps you'll have different ideas about it, and when Jerry's finished, and we've talked about it, we can try your ideas. (Shaftel and Shaftel, 1967, p. 69)

At phase five, enacting, the players assume the roles and "live" the situation spontaneously, responding realistically to one another. The role playing is not expected to be a smooth dramatization, nor is it expected that each role player will always know how to respond. This uncertainty is part of life, as well as part of feeling the role. A person may have a general idea of what to say or do but not be able to enact it when the time comes. The action now depends on the children and emerges according to what happens in the situation. This is why the preparatory steps are so important.

The Shaftels suggest that enactments be short. The teacher should allow the enactment to run only until the proposed behavior is clear, a character has developed, a behavioral skill has been practiced, an impasse is reached, or the action has expressed its viewpoint or idea. If the follow-up discussion reveals a lack of student understanding about the events or roles, the teacher can then ask for a reenactment of the scene.

The purpose of the first enactment is simply to establish events and roles, which in later enactments can be probed, analyzed, and reworked. In our illustration, the boy playing Tommy chooses not to tell the customer that he has overpaid. During the initial enactment, the players of the major role can be changed to demonstrate variety in the role and to generate more data for discussion.

In phase six, discussing and evaluating, if the problem is important and the participants and observers are intellectually and emotionally involved, the discussion will probably begin spontaneously. At first, the discussion may focus on different interpretations of the portrayal and on disagreements over how the roles should have been carried out. More important, however, are the consequences of the action and the motivations of the actors. To prepare for the next step, a teacher should focus the discussion on these aspects.

To help the observer think along with the role players, the teacher can ask questions such as, "How do you suppose John felt when he said that?" The discussion will probably turn to alternatives, both within the roles and within the total pattern of action. When it does, the stage is set for further enactments in which role players change their interpretations, playing the same roles in a different way.

In our illustration, the discussion of the first enactment goes like this:

Teacher: Well, Jerry has given us one solution. What do you think of it?
Pupil: Uh-uh! It won't work!
Jerry: Why not?
Pupil: That man is going to remember how much money he had. He'll phone the druggist about it.
Jerry: So what? He can't prove anything on me. I'll just say he didn't overpay me.
Pupil: You'll lose your job.
Jerry: When they can't prove it?
Pupil: Yes, even if they can't prove it.
Teacher: Why do you think so, John?
Pupil: Because the druggist has to be on the side of his customer. He can fire Tommy and hire another boy. But he doesn't want his customers mad at him.
Pupil: He's going to feel pretty sick inside, if he keeps the money.
Teacher: What do you mean?
Pupil: Well, it bothers you when you know you've done something wrong.

Teacher: Do you have any other way to solve this problem?

Pupil: Yes. Tommy should knock on the door and tell the customer about being overpaid. Maybe the man'll let Tommy keep the money.

Teacher: All right, let's try it your way, Dick. (Shaftel and Shaftel, 1967, p. 71)

In phase seven, reenacting, the reenactment may take place many times. The students and teacher can share new interpretations of roles and decide whether new individuals should play them. The activity alternates between discussion and acting. As much as possible, the new enactments should explore new possibilities for causes and effects. For example, one role may be changed so that everyone can observe how that change causes another role player to behave. Or at the critical point in the enactment, the participants may try to behave in a different way and see what the consequences are. In this way, the role playing becomes a dramatic conceptual activity.

In our illustration, a second enactment produces the solution in which Tommy alerts the man to his overpayment and gets to keep the money for being so honest. In the discussion that follows the second enactment—phase eight, discuss and evaluate—students are willing to accept the solution, but the teacher pushes for a realistic solution by asking whether they think this ending could really happen. One student has had a similar experience but was overpaid only $1.25, which he was allowed to keep. The teacher asks the class whether they think it might be different with $5. She asks for another solution, and it is suggested that Tommy consult his mother. There follows some discussion of Tommy's father, concepts about family, and parental roles. The teacher suggests that this third solution be enacted. Here's what happens in the third enactment:

Tommy: Mom, I'm in an awful jam!

Mother: What's the trouble, Tommy?

Tommy: (Tells his mother the whole story)

Mother: Why, Tommy, you should have told me sooner. Here, you pay the money (opens purse), and we'll talk this over with Dad when he comes home. (Shaftel and Shaftel, 1967, p. 73)

During the discussion of this enactment, the teacher asks what will happen next, and someone suggests that Tommy will be in the doghouse for a while.

Phase nine, sharing experiences and generalizing, should not be expected to result immediately in generalizations about the human relations aspects of the situation. Such generalizations require much experience. The teacher should, however, attempt to shape the discussion so that the children, perhaps after long experience with the role-playing strategy, begin to generalize about approaches to problem situations and the consequences of those approaches. The more adequate the shaping of the discussion, the more general will be the conclusions reached, and the closer the children will come to hypothetical principles of action they can use in their own lives.

The initial goal, however, is to relate the problem situation to the children's experiences in a nonthreatening way. This goal can be accomplished by asking the class members if they know someone who has had a similar experience. In our illustration with Tommy and the money, the teacher asks if anyone in the class knows of an instance in which a boy or girl was in a situation like Tommy's. One student describes an experience with his father. The teacher then asks about parental attitudes and the role of fathers with respect to their children's money.

From such discussions emerge principles that all students can articulate and use. These principles may be applied to particular problems, or they can be used by the children as a springboard for exploring other kinds of problems. Ideally, the children will gradually master the strategy so that when a problem comes up, either within their group or from a topic they have studied, they will be able to use role playing to clarify and gain insight into the problem. Students might, for example, systematically use role playing to improve the quality of classroom democracy.

SOCIAL SYSTEM

The social system in this model is moderately structured. Teachers are responsible, at least initially, for starting the phases and guiding students through the activities within each phase; however, the particular content of the discussions and enactments is determined largely by the students.

The teachers' questions and comments should encourage free and honest expression of ideas and feelings. Teachers must establish equality and trust between themselves and their students. They can do this by accepting all suggestions as legitimate and making no value judgments. In this way, they simply reflect the children's feelings or attitudes.

Even though teachers are chiefly reflective and supportive, they assume direction as well. They often select the problem to be explored, lead the discussion, choose the actors, make decisions about when the enactments are to be done, help design the enactments, and most significant, decide what to probe for and what suggestions to explore. In essence, the teachers shape the exploration of behavior by the types of questions they ask and, through questioning, establish the focus.

PRINCIPLES OF REACTION

We have identified five principles of reaction that are important to this model. First, teachers should accept student responses and suggestions, especially their opinions and feelings, in a nonevaluative manner. Second, teachers should respond in such a way that they help the students explore various sides of the problem situation, recognizing and contrasting alternative points of view. Third, by reflecting, paraphrasing, and summarizing responses, the teacher increases students' awareness of their own views and feelings. Fourth, the teacher should emphasize that there are different ways to play the same role and that different consequences result as they are explored. Fifth, there are alternative ways to resolve a problem; no one way is correct. The teacher helps the students look at the consequences to evaluate a solution and compare it with alternatives.

SUPPORT SYSTEM

The materials for role playing are minimal but important. The major curricular tool is the problem situation. However, it is sometimes helpful to construct briefing sheets for each role. These sheets describe the role or the character's feelings. Occasionally, we also develop forms for the observers that tell them what to look for and give them a place to write it down.

Films, novels, and short stories make excellent sources for problem situations. Problem stories or outlines of problem situations are also useful. Problem stories, as their name implies, are short narratives that describe the setting, circumstances, actions, and dialogue of a situation. One or more of the characters faces a dilemma in which a choice must be made or an action taken. The story ends unresolved.

Many resource materials now commercially available include stories or problem stories whose endings can be omitted or changed. The books by the Shaftels (1967) and by Chesler and Fox (1966) each contain a section of problem stories.

APPLICATION _____

The role-playing model is extremely versatile and applicable to several important educational objectives. Through role playing, students can increase their abilities to recognize their own and other people's feelings, they can acquire new behaviors for handling previously difficult situations, and they can improve their problem-solving skills.

In addition to its many uses, the role-playing model carries with it an appealing set of activities. Because students enjoy both the action and the acting, it is easy to forget that the role play itself is a vehicle for developing the content of the instruction. The stages of the model are not ends in themselves, but they help expose students' values, feelings, attitudes, and solutions to problems, which the teacher must then explore.

ROLE PLAYING AND THE CURRICULUM

There are two basic reasons why a teacher might decide to use role playing with a group of children. One is to begin a systematic *program of social education* in which a role-playing situation forms much of the material to be discussed and analyzed; for this purpose, a particular kind of problem story might be selected. The second reason is to counsel a group of children to deal with an *immediate human relations problem;* role playing can open up this problem area to the students' inquiry and help them solve the problem.

Several types of social problems are amenable to exploration with the aid of this model, including:

1. *Interpersonal conflicts.* A major use of role playing is to reveal conflicts between people so that students can discover techniques for overcoming them.

2. *Intergroup relations.* Interpersonal problems arising from ethnic and racial stereotyping or from authoritarian beliefs can also be explored through role playing. These problems involve conflict that may not be apparent. Role-playing situations of this type might be used to uncover stereotypes and prejudices or to encourage acceptance of the deviant.

3. *Individual dilemmas.* These arise when a person is caught between two contrasting values or between his or her own interests and the interests of others. Such problems are particularly difficult for young children to deal with, since their moral judgment is still relatively egocentric. Some of the most delicate and difficult uses of role playing make this dilemma accessible to children and help them understand why it occurs and what to do about it. Individual dilemmas that might be explored are ones in which a person is caught between the demands of the peer group and those of his or her parents, or between the pressures of the group and his or her own preferences.

4. *Historical or contemporary problems.* These include critical situations, past or present, in which policymakers, judges, political leaders, or statespeople have to confront a problem or person and make a decision.

Regardless of the particular type of social problem, students will focus naturally on the aspects of the situation that seem important to them. They may concentrate on the feelings that are being expressed, the attitudes and values of the role players as seen through their words and actions, the problem solution, or the consequences of behavior. It is possible for the teacher to emphasize any or all of these areas in the enactments and discussions. In-depth curriculum sequences can be based on each of the following focuses:

Exploration of feelings
Exploration of attitudes, values, and perceptions
Development of problem-solving attitudes and skills
Subject-matter exploration

We have found that a single role-playing session is often very rich. Discussion can go in many directions—toward analyzing feelings, consequences, the roles themselves and ways to play them, and alternative solutions. After several years of working with this model, we have come to believe that if any one of these ideas, or objectives, is to be developed adequately, the teacher must make a concerted effort to explore one particular emphasis. Because all these aspects tend to emerge in the role-playing process, it is easy to consider them only superficially. One difficulty we are faced with, then, is that an in-depth treatment of any one focus requires time. Especially in the beginning, when students are getting accustomed to the model and to exploring their behavior and feelings, we feel it is important to select one major focus, or perhaps two, for any one session. Other aspects, of course, may also need to be considered in the development of ideas, but their place should be secondary. For example, the feelings of the characters will be discussed even when the teacher is trying to get the students to concentrate on alternative solutions to the problem, but in this case, the feelings will tie in to a consideration and evaluation of the solutions.

By choosing one or perhaps two emphases for the enactment, carefully questioning and responding to students' ideas, and building on the ideas of the previous phases, the teacher gradually develops each phase so that it supports the particular objectives that have been selected for that session. This is what we mean by developing a focus (see Table 11.2).

TABLE 11.2 POSSIBLE FOCUSES OF A ROLE-PLAYING SESSION

I. Feelings
  A. Exploring one's own feelings
  B. Exploring others' feelings
  C. Acting out or releasing feelings
  D. Experiencing higher-status roles in order to change the perceptions of others and one's own perceptions
II. Attitudes, values, and perceptions
  A. Identifying values of culture or subculture
  B. Clarifying and evaluating one's own values and value conflicts
III. Problem-solving attitudes and skills
  A. Openness to possible solutions
  B. Ability to identify a problem
  C. Ability to generate alternative solutions
  D. Ability to evaluate the consequences to oneself and others of alternative solutions to problems
  E. Experiencing consequences and making final decisions in light of those consequences
  F. Analyzing criteria and assumptions behind alternatives
  G. Acquiring new behaviors
IV. Subject matter
  A. Feelings of participants
  B. Historical realities: historical crises, dilemmas, and decisions

SELECTING A PROBLEM SITUATION

The adequacy of the topic depends on many factors, such as the age of the students, their cultural background, the complexity of the problem situation, the sensitivity of the topic, and the students' experience with role playing. In general, as students gain experience with role playing and develop a high degree of group cohesiveness and acceptance of one another, as well as a close rapport with the teacher, the more sensitive the topic can be. The first few problem situations should be matters of concern to the students but not extremely sensitive issues. Students themselves may develop a list of themes or problems they would like to work on. Then the teacher can locate or develop specific problem situations that fit the themes.

The gender of the students and their ethnic and socioeconomic backgrounds influence their choice of topic and, according to Chesler and Fox (1966), their expectations for the role play. Different cultural groups experience different sets of problems, concerns, and solutions. Most teachers account for these differences in their curricula all the time. Problems that are typical for a particular ethnic or age group, gender, or socioeconomic class can become the basis of problem situations.

Other ideas for problem situations can be derived from: (1) the age and developmental stage of the student, such as personal and social concerns; (2) value (ethical) themes, such as honesty, responsibility; (3) problem behaviors, such as aggression, avoidance; (4) troublesome situations—for example, making a complaint at a store, meeting someone new; and (5) social issues, such as racism, sexism, labor strikes. These various sources of problem situations are summarized in Table 11.3.

Another consideration in choosing a problem situation is its complexity, which may be a result of the number of characters or the abstractness of the issues. There are no definite rules about levels of difficulty in prob-

---

TABLE 11.3 **SOURCES OF PROBLEM SITUATIONS**

1. Issues arising from developmental stages
2. Issues arising from sexual, ethnic, or socioeconomic class
3. Value (ethical) themes
4. Difficult emotions
5. Scripts or "games people play"
6. Troublesome situations
7. Social issues
8. Community issues

lem situations, but intuitively it seems that the following sequence is a reasonable guide: (1) one main character; (2) two characters and alternative solutions; (3) complex plots and many characters; (4) value themes, social issues, and community issues.

INSTRUCTIONAL AND NURTURANT EFFECTS

Role playing is designed specifically to foster: (1) the analysis of personal values and behavior; (2) the development of strategies for solving interpersonal (and personal) problems; and (3) the development of empathy toward others. Its nurturants are the acquisition of information about social problems and values, and comfort in expressing one's opinions (see Figure 11.1).

FIGURE 11.1 Instructional and nurturant effects of the role-playing model.

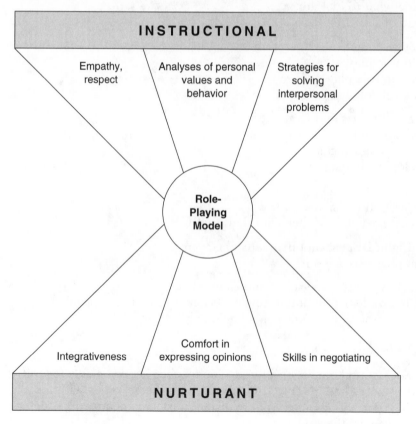

SUMMARY CHART ► ROLE-PLAYING MODEL

Syntax

Phase One: Warm Up the Group
  Identify or introduce problem.
  Make problem explicit.
  Interpret problem story, explore issues.
  Explain role playing.

Phase Two: Select Participants
  Analyze roles.
  Select role players.

Phase Three: Set the Stage
  Set line of action.
  Restate roles.
  Get inside problem situation.

Phase Four: Prepare the Observers
  Decide what to look for.
  Assign observation tasks.

Phase Five: Enact
  Begin role play.
  Maintain role play.
  Break role play.

Phase Six: Discuss and Evaluate
  Review action of role play (events, positions, realism).
  Discuss major focus.
  Develop next enactment.

Phase Seven: Reenact
  Play revised roles.
  Suggest next steps or behavioral alternatives.

Phase Eight: Discuss and Evaluate
  As in phase six.

Phase Nine: Share Experience and Generalize
  Relate problem situation to real experience and current problems.
  Explore general principles of behavior.

Social System

The model is moderately structured. The teacher is responsible for initiating the phases and guiding students through the activities within each phase. The particular content of the discussions and enactments is determined largely by the students.

Principles of Reaction

Accept all student responses in a nonevaluative manner. Help students explore various sides of the problem situation and compare alternative views.

Increase students' awareness of their own views and feelings by reflecting, paraphrasing, and summarizing their responses.

Use the concept of role, and emphasize that there are different ways to play a role.

Emphasize that there are alternative ways to resolve a problem.

Support System

Role playing is an experience-based model and requires minimal support material outside the initial problem situation. The Jurisprudential Model, which we will visit next, requires more complex materials and information sources.

JURISPRUDENTIAL INQUIRY: LEARNING TO THINK ABOUT SOCIAL POLICY

S C E N A R I O

Pat Salcido's senior civics class is examining current cases before the U.S. Supreme Court and the contemporary debates among politicians about social policy. The governor of California has recently made an executive order dismantling the state's provisions for affirmative action. One morning, a few days later, one of the students brings in an article from the *New York Times* discussing the Bakke case. (This case dealt with admission to higher education institutions. Bakke claimed that special preference given to minority candidates had discriminated against him.)

"This case bothers me personally," comments Tammy. "You know a number of us are applying for colleges, and my college board scores aren't too high. It seems to me, though, the important thing is that the actual scores I have are changed depending on how I'm looked at. If I'm looked at as an anonymous person, then my scores are what they are. In some colleges I would be looked at as a woman, and the scores would be higher if they wanted to increase the number of women. In some other places they would be lower because I don't belong to a minority group."

"Wait a minute," says one of the other students, "the Bakke case involved a law student. Are the same kind of issues involved in undergraduate college admissions?"

"You bet they are," comments one of the black students. "We've been shut out of a lot of private universities for years."

"Do medical schools do this kind of thing?" asks another. "Do they admit unqualified students?"

"Now just a minute," says one of the other students, "just because some groups are given a break doesn't mean that they are unqualified."

"Well, what is the story on test scores?" asks another.

"OK, OK," says Pat. "This is obviously going to be a complicated case. It's important in so many ways. I think we'd better sort out the public issues and see where we stand on them."

"Well, how do we begin?" asks Miguel.

"I think we ought to begin by collecting some information. Let's have one group find an abstract of the case to see how it was argued in the lower courts. You can go up to the law library at the university, and I'll call the reference librarian before you get there. Then let's have another group collect what the newspapers have said about it since the case first came to public attention. A third group can collect editorials from the newspapers. I think it would be worthwhile if a fourth group talked to the counselors to find out what information they have about college admissions. Another group might arrange to have one of the college admissions officers talk with us about how they handle scores. Can anybody think of anything else?"

"Yes," adds Sally. "Do the people who sell tests have representatives we can talk to?"

"That's a wonderful idea," says Pat. "Now let's organize ourselves into those groups and begin to get the facts. Then each group can take the material they've collected and start identifying some of the issues. I think it's going to take us quite a long time just to get the issues identified. Then we can proceed to identify the value questions that underlie those issues. Finally we can look at the implications for public policy and try to come up with a statement about where we stand as individuals and possibly as a group."

For the senior civics class at Mervyn Park High School, this discussion initiates exposure to jurisprudential inquiry. During the intervening months, Pat exposed the class to several more important public issues and taught them the framework for jurisprudential inquiry.

Donald Oliver and James P. Shaver (1966/1974) created the jurisprudential inquiry model to help students learn to think systematically about contemporary issues. It requires them to formulate these issues as public policy questions and to analyze alternative positions about them. Essentially, it is a high-level model for citizenship education. In Chapter 18 we will find a cornucopia of educational issues relative to gender, socioeconomic status, race and ethnicity, all of which are food for jurisprudential inquiry for educators and all citizens.

As our society undergoes cultural and social changes, the jurisprudential inquiry model is especially useful in helping people rethink their positions on important legal, ethical, and social questions. The citizenry needs to understand the current critical issues and share in the formulation of policy. By giving them tools for analyzing and debating social issues, the jurisprudential approach helps students participate forcefully in the redefinition of social values (Shaver, 1995).

ORIENTATION TO THE MODEL

GOALS AND ASSUMPTIONS

This model is based on a conception of society in which people differ in their views and priorities and in which social values legitimately conflict with one another. Resolving complex, controversial issues within the context of a productive social order requires citizens who can talk to one another and successfully negotiate their differences.

Such citizens can intelligently analyze and take a stance on public issues. The stance should reflect the concepts of justice and human dignity, two values fundamental to a democratic society. Oliver and Shaver's image of a skillful citizen is very much that of a competent judge. Imagine for a moment that you are a Supreme Court justice hearing an important case. Your job is to listen to the evidence presented, analyze the legal positions taken by both sides, weigh these positions and the evidence, assess the meaning and provisions of the law, and finally, make the best possible decision. This is the role students are asked to take as they consider public issues.

To play the role of inquirer, three types of competence are required. The first is familiarity with the values of the American creed, as embedded in the principles of the Constitution and the Declaration of Independence. These principles form the *values framework*—the basis for judging public issues and for making legal decisions. If policy stances are to be truly derived from ethical considerations, one must be aware of and understand the key values that form the core of our society's ethical system.

The second area of competence is a set of skills for clarifying and resolving issues. Usually, a controversy arises because two important values conflict or because public policies, when examined closely, do not adhere to the core values of our society. Whenever a conflict of value arises, three kinds of problems are likely to be present.

The first kind of problem (*value problem*) involves clarifying which values or legal principles are in conflict, and choosing among them. The second kind of problem (*factual problem*) involves clarifying the facts around which the conflict has developed. The third kind of problem (*definitional problem*) involves clarifying the meanings or uses of words which describe the controversy (Oliver and Shaver, 1966/1974, p. 89; Oliver, 1995).

The process of clarifying and resolving issues involves clarifying definitions, establishing facts, and identifying the values important to each issue.

The third area of competence is knowledge of contemporary political and public issues, which requires that students be exposed to the spectrum of political, social, and economic problems facing American society. Although a broad understanding of the history, nature, and scope of these problems is important, in the jurisprudential inquiry model, students explore issues in terms of a specific legal case rather than in terms of a general study of values.

Oliver and Shaver's work encompasses many ideas: they present us with a model of society, a conception of values, and a conception of productive dialogue. They also detail curriculum and pedagogical considerations (see Oliver and Shaver, 1971, p. 7). It is possible to extrapolate several models of teaching from their work. However, to us, the strategy that seems most reflective of their goals and thinking is one built around a confrontational, or Socratic, mode of discussion. In Socratic dialogue, the students take a position and the teacher challenges the position with questions. The teacher's questions are designed to push students' thinking about their stance and to help them learn:

> Does it hold up well against positions reflecting alternative values?
> Is it consistent across many situations?
> Are the reasons for maintaining the position relevant to the situation?
> Are the factual assumptions on which the position is based valid?
> What are the consequences of this position?
> Will the student hold on to this stance in spite of its consequences?

PUBLIC POLICY ISSUES

Public controversies tend to fill many pages of our newspapers and many hours of television coverage. "A public policy issue is a question involving a choice or a decision for action by citizens or officials in affairs that concern a government or community" (Oliver and Newman, 1967, p. 29).

Policy issues can be phrased as general questions: "Should the United States stay in Afghanistan and try to build its social and economic systems?" "Should capital punishment be abolished?" "Should U.S. citizens be allowed to travel to Cuba?"

"Public policy issues can also be phrased as choices for personal action: 'Should I write my Congressman to protest the draft laws?' 'Should I petition the Governor to commute a criminal's death sentence?'" (Oliver and Newman, 1967, p. 29) "Should I write a candidate asking him to pledge support for abortion rights?"

One of the most difficult tasks for the teacher is to assist students in integrating the details of a case into a public policy question.

A FRAMEWORK OF VALUES

Political and social values, such as personal freedom, equality, and justice, concern Oliver and Shaver (1966/1974, p. 64) in their strategy because these are "the major concepts used by our government and private groups to justify public policies and decisions." When we speak of a framework of values for analyzing public issues, we imply the *legal–ethical* framework that governs American social policies and decisions. A partial list of these principles of American government as found in the Declaration of Independence and the Constitution of the United States is shown in Table 11.4.

Resolving a controversy involves screening the details of the case through this legal–ethical framework and identifying the values and policies in question. Social values help us to analyze controversial situations

TABLE 11.4 **THE LEGAL-ETHICAL FRAMEWORK: SOME BASIC SOCIAL VALUES**

Rule of law. Actions carried out by the government have to be authorized by law and apply equally to all people.

Equal protection under the law. Laws must be administered fairly and cannot extend special privileges or penalties to any one person or group.

Due process. The government cannot deprive individual citizens of life, liberty, or property without proper notice of impending actions (right to a fair trial).

Justice. Equal opportunity.

Preservation of peace and order. Prevention of disorder and violence (reason as a means of dealing with conflict).

Personal liberty. Freedom of speech, right to own and control property, freedom of religion, freedom of personal associations, right of privacy.

Separation of powers. Checks and balances among the three branches of government.

Local control of local problems. Restriction of federal government power and preservation of states' rights.

---

because they provide a common framework that transcends any one particular controversy. However, in most controversial situations, two general rules of ethical conduct conflict with each other. Thus although a framework of social values permits us to speak of diverse conflict situations in common terms, it does not tell us how to go about resolving controversies.

Recent years have witnessed many social problems, frequently involving conflicting values. Some of these problem areas and their underlying value conflicts are listed in Table 11.5. As you read over these topics, note that although the values are identified, the controversies remain. Alternative policy stances are possible on any topic, and most issues can be argued on a number of grounds.

TABLE 11.5   **SOME GENERAL PROBLEM AREAS**

Problem Areas	Sample Unit Topics	Conflicting Values[a]
Racial and ethnic conflict	School desegregation Civil rights for nonwhites and ethnic minorities Housing for nonwhites and ethnic minorities Job opportunities for nonwhites and ethnic minorities Immigration policy	Equal protection Due process Brotherhood of man v. Peace and order Property and contract rights Personal privacy and association
Religious and ideological conflict	Rights of the Communist party in America Religion and public education Control of "dangerous" or "immoral" literature Religion and national security: oaths, conscientious objectors Taxation of religious property	Freedom of speech and conscience v. Equal protection Safety and security of democratic institutions
Security of the individual	Crime and delinquency	Standards of freedom Due process v. Peace and order Community welfare

TABLE 11.5 *(continued)*

Problem Areas	Sample Unit Topics	Conflicting Values[a]
Conflict among economic groups	Organized labor Business competition and monopoly "Overproduction" of farm goods Conservation of natural resources	Equal or fair bargaining Power and competition General welfare and progress of the community v. Property and contract rights
Health, education, and welfare	Adequate medical care: for the aged, for the poor Adequate educational opportunity Old-age security Job and income security	Equal opportunity Brotherhood of man v. Property and contract rights
Security of the nation	Federal loyalty-security programs Foreign policy	Freedom of speech, conscience, and association Due process Personal privacy v. Safety and security of democratic institutions

[a]The *v.* in the listing of values suggests that the top values conflict with the bottom values. Although this is generally true, there are, of course, many exceptions. One can argue, for example, that a minimum-wage law violates property and contract rights and that it is also against the general welfare. *Source:* Donald Oliver and James P. Shaver, *Teaching Public Issues in the High School* (Boston: Houghton Mifflin Company, 1966), pp. 142–143.

DEFINITIONAL, VALUE, AND FACTUAL PROBLEMS

Most arguments center on definitions, values, and facts. Participants in a discussion need to explore each of these to assess the strength of alternative stances. Some controversies can be solved simply by clarifying facts—the controversy may only exist because the facts are not clear.

A frequent problem in discussions of social issues is the ambiguous or confusing use of words. Unless we recognize common meaning in the words we use, discussion is difficult and agreement on issues, policies, or actions is virtually impossible. To resolve these definitional disagreements, it is necessary first to determine whether participants in a discussion are using the same term in a different way or different terms for the same referent, and second to establish a common meaning for terms. Then, to clarify communication, participants may: (1) appeal to common usage by finding out how most people use a word or by consulting a dictionary, (2) stipulate the meaning of the word for purposes of discussion by listing the agreed criteria, and/or (3) obtain more facts about an example to see if it meets the agreed criteria for a definition.

Valuing means classifying things, actions, or ideas as good or bad, right or wrong. If we speak of something as a value (such as honesty), we mean that it is good. As people make choices throughout their lives, they are constantly making value judgments, even if they cannot verbalize their values. The range of items or issues over which each of us makes value judgments is vast—art, music, politics, decoration, clothes, and people. Some of these choices seem less important than others, and the degree of importance has something to do with what we mean by a value. Choices that are not so important are personal preferences, not values. Value issues such as art or the physical environment involve artistic taste or judgment of beauty, and many such choices of ideas, objects, or actions do become subjects of discussion in our society and communities. Currently, U.S. foreign policy is tangled in national and international value questions, specifically the extent to which the United States can act unilaterally or needs to work through the United Nations.

People make decisions on issues involving values because they believe: (1) certain consequences will occur, (2) other consequences will be avoided, or (3) important social values will be violated if the decision is not made. In a values conflict there is often disagreement about the predicted consequences, which can be partially resolved by obtaining evidence to support the prediction; however, to some extent it is always a matter of speculation. "Affirmative action laws will equalize employment opportunity" is an example of predicted consequences. Although there is some evidence that equal employment opportunity results from affirmative action, this is partly a prediction based on logical grounds.

When two *values* conflict, Oliver and Shaver suggest that the best solution is one in which each value is compromised somewhat, or put another way, each value is violated only minimally (see the following section on balancing values). When the value issues conflict because of predicted consequences, the disagreement becomes a *factual* problem.

THE MODEL OF TEACHING ⎯⎯⎯⎯⎯⎯⎯⎯⎯⎯

SYNTAX

Although the exploration of students' stances through confrontational dialogue is the heart of the jurisprudential inquiry model, several other activities are especially important, such as helping students formulate the stance they eventually defend and helping them revise their position after the argumentation. The basic model includes six phases: (1) orientation to the case; (2) identifying the issues; (3) taking positions; (4) exploring the stances underlying the positions taken; (5) refining and qualifying positions; and (6) testing assumptions about facts, definitions, and consequences (see Table 11.6).

TABLE 11.6   **SYNTAX OF JURISPRUDENTIAL INQUIRY MODEL**

Phase One: Orientation to the Case	Phase Two: Identifying the Issues
Teacher introduces materials. Teacher reviews facts.	Students synthesize facts into a public policy issue(s). Students select one policy issue for discussion. Students identify values and value conflicts. Students recognize underlying factual and definitional questions.

Phase Three: Taking Positions	Phase Four: Exploring the Stance(s), Patterns of Argumentation
Students articulate a position. Students state basis of position in terms of the social value or consequences of the decision.	Establish the point at which value is violated (factual). Prove the desirable or undesirable consequences of a position (factual). Clarify the value conflict with analogies. Set priorities. Assert priority of one value over another *and* demonstrate lack of gross violation of second value.

Phase Five: Refining and Qualifying the Positions	Phase Six: Testing Factual Assumptions Behind Qualified Positions
Students state positions and reasons for positions, and examine a number of similar situations. Students qualify positions.	Identify factual assumptions and determine if they are relevant. Determine the predicted consequences and examine their factual validity (will they actually occur?).

In phase one, the teacher introduces the students to case materials by reading a story or historical narrative out loud, watching a filmed incident depicting a value controversy, or discussing an incident in the lives of the students, school, or community. The second step in orienting students to the case is to review the facts by outlining the events in the case, analyzing who did what and why, or acting out the controversy.

In phase two, the students synthesize the facts into a public issue, characterize the values involved (for example, freedom of speech, protecting the general welfare, local autonomy, or equal opportunity), and *identify conflicts between values*. In the first two phases, the students have not been asked to express their opinions or take a stand.

In phase three, they are asked to articulate positions on the issue and state the basis for their positions. In a school finance case, for example, a student might take the position that the state should not legislate how much each school district can spend on each pupil because this would constitute an unacceptable violation of local autonomy.

In phase four, the positions are explored. The teacher now shifts to a confrontational style as he or she probes the students' positions. In enacting the Socratic role, the teacher (or a student) may use one of four patterns of argumentation:

1. Asking the students to identify the point at which a value is violated.
2. Clarifying the value conflict through analogies.
3. Asking students to prove desirable or undesirable consequences of a position.
4. Asking students to set value priorities: asserting priority of one value over another *and* demonstrating lack of gross violation of the second value.

Phase five consists of refining and qualifying the positions. This phase often flows naturally from the dialogue in phase four, but sometimes the teacher may need to prompt students to restate their positions.

SOCIAL SYSTEM

The structure in this model ranges from high to low. At first, the teacher initiates the phases; moving from phase to phase, however, is dependent on the students' abilities to complete the task. After experience with the model the students should be able to carry out the process unassisted, thereby gaining maximum control of the process. The social climate is vigorous and confrontational.

PRINCIPLES OF REACTION

The teacher's reactions, especially in phases four and five, are not evaluative in the sense of being approving or disapproving. They probe substance: the teacher reacts to students' comments by questioning relevance, consistency, specificity or generality, and definitional clarity. The teacher also enforces continuity of thought, so that one thought or line of reasoning is pursued to its logical conclusion before other argumentation begins.

To play this role well, the teacher must anticipate student value claims and must be prepared to challenge and probe. In the Socratic role, the teacher probes one student's opinion at length before challenging other students. Because a Socratic dialogue can easily become a threatening cross-examination or a game of "guess what the teacher's right answer is," the teacher must make it clear that the clarification of issues and the development of the most defensible position are the objectives. The questioning of evidence and assumptions must be tempered with supportiveness. The merits of the case, not of the students, are the basis for evaluation.

SUPPORT SYSTEM

The major material supports for this model are source documents that focus on a problem situation. There are some published case materials, but it is relatively easy to develop one's own case materials. The distinguishing feature of this approach is that the cases are accounts of real or hypothetical situations. It is essential that all pertinent facts of the situation be included in the case material so the case will not be vague and frustrating.

A controversial case describes a specific situation that has conflicting ethical, legal, factual, or definitional interpretations. The case may consist of a classic historical or legal situation, such as *Plessy v. Ferguson* in race relations, or the Wagner Act or the Kohler strike in labor relations; or it may be a short story or fictionalized account of a social controversy, such as Orwell's *Animal Farm*. Generally, each page of the daily newspaper contains three or four articles that either explicitly or implicitly present an important public policy question. Usually some facts of the situation are presented, but the original situation that provoked the controversy is not described in full detail.

APPLICATION

In developing their alternative framework for teaching social studies courses in high schools, Oliver and Shaver were concerned with both the substance of what is taught and the *methods* of teaching it. Consequently, the model provides a framework for developing contemporary course content in public affairs (cases involving public issues) and for developing a process to deal with conflict in the public domain, leading students to an examination of values.

The model is tailored to older students and must be modified considerably for use at the junior high school and middle school levels, even with the most able students. We have successfully carried out the model with extremely able seventh- and eighth-grade students but have had little success with younger children.

The confrontational dialogue that surrounds the argumentation of social issues is apt to be threatening at first, especially to less-verbal students. We have had small groups (three or four students) formulate a stand and collectively argue the stand with another small group. The format allows for time out, reevaluating the stance with one's group, and discussing the issue again. Initially, we presented the case, and after students had selected the policy issue, we asked them to take an initial stand. On this basis we divided them into small groups and told each group to come up with the strongest possible case. The students understood that regardless of the group they were in at first, they might well choose a different stance at the end of the discussion.

Neither the skills of reasoning nor the confidence to take a stance and discuss it are acquired easily or quickly. Teachers should let a single case continue for a long period of time, giving students the opportunity to acquire information, reflect on their ideas, and build their courage. It is self-defeating to set up short, one-time debates over complex questions. Formal instructional sessions teaching students directly about analytic and argumentative techniques may be useful, but these should be introduced naturally and slowly. The initial case materials should be relatively simple and require little previous background. Some should be drawn from the students' experiences, perhaps in the classroom or at home. There are a great many sources of cases that have been adapted for school use. The magazine *Social Education* frequently contains reviews. The Social Science Education Consortium has developed a number of historic cases with extensive background material (Giese, 1989; Glade and Giese, 1989; Greenwald, 1991). Many of the *Jackdaws* contain suitable material for the upper grades and secondary schools. At the Ontario Institute for Studies in Education, a number of faculty members, particularly Malcolm Levin and John Isenberg, have developed interesting cases for use with the jurisprudential inquiry model. Many of these cases are set in Canada and can be quite exciting for students not only because the issues are excellent but because of the somewhat different context and legal system. In addition, their publication, *Ethics in Education*, covers a large number of issues that can stimulate the development of cases and the study of public issues. The Ontario Institute for Studies in Education has a number of well-developed Canadian cases.

For many years instructors have organized social studies courses around cases; the jurisprudential inquiry model heightens the vigor and intensity with which such cases are studied. Of course, cases must have public issues or value conflicts embedded in them to lend themselves readily to the jurisprudential approach. But unless social studies courses deal with values, both personal and public, they will have missed the vital mainstream of social concern.

Once students become fluent in the use of the jurisprudential inquiry model, they can apply it to conflicts that occur in and around their own lives. The scenario on pages 249–250 is an example of students' exploration of an issue that touched their own concerns. Without such application, we speculate that the study of public issues, even vigorously pursued, can seem abstract and irrelevant to the lives of students. Because students live in communities where issues abound, their study of values should not be confined to cases far removed from them, but should be applied to the dynamics of their own lives and the community around them.

INSTRUCTIONAL AND NURTURANT EFFECTS

Mastery of the framework for analyzing issues is the major direct learning outcome. This includes skill in identifying policy questions; application of social values to policy stances; the use of analogies to explore issues; and the ability to identify and resolve definitional, factual, and value problems.

The ability to carry on forceful dialogue with others is another important outcome. It nurtures the capacity for social involvement and arouses the desire for social action.

Finally, the model nourishes the values of pluralism and a respect for the point of view of others. It also advocates the triumph of reason over emotion in matters of social policy, although the strategy itself strongly brings into play the students' emotional responses (see Figure 11.2).

FIGURE 11.2   Instructional and nurturant effects of the jurisprudential inquiry model.

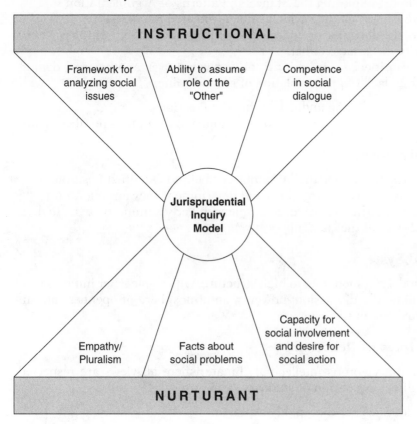

SUMMARY ► **JURISPRUDENTIAL**
CHART ► **INQUIRY MODEL**

Syntax

Phase One: Orientation to the Case
  Introduce materials.
  Review facts.

Phase Two: Identifying the Issues
  Synthesize facts into a public policy issue or issues.
  Select one policy issue for discussion.
  Identify values and value conflicts.
  Recognize underlying factual and definitional questions.

Phase Three: Taking Positions
  Articulate a position.
  State the basis of the position in terms of the social value or consequences of the decision.

Phase Four: Exploring the Stance(s); Patterns of Argumentation
  Establish the point at which value is violated (factual).
  Prove the desirable or undesirable consequences of a position (factual).
  Clarify the value conflict.
  Set priorities. Assert priority of one value over another and demonstrate lack of gross violation of second value.

Phase Five: Refining and Qualifying the Positions
  State position and reasons for position, and examine a number of similar situations.
  Qualify position.

Phase Six: Testing Factual Assumptions behind Qualified Positions
  Identify factual assumptions and determine if they are relevant.
  Determine the predicted consequences and examine their factual validity (will they actually occur?).

Social System

The model has moderate to high structure, with the teacher initiating and controlling the discussion; however, an atmosphere of openness and intellectual equality prevails.

Principles of Reaction

Maintain a vigorous intellectual climate where all views are respected; avoid direct evaluation of students' opinions.

See that issues are thoroughly explored.

Probe the substance of students' thinking through questioning relevance, consistency, specificity, generality, definitional clarity, and continuity.

Support System

Source documents that focus on a problem situation are needed.

The Web is a big help, as issues like stem cell research include sites with a good deal of information and advocacy groups on all sides.

THE PERSONAL FAMILY OF MODELS

From birth, we are acted on by the world. Our social environment gives us our language, teaches us how to behave, and provides love to us. But our individual selves configure themselves relentlessly and create their own interior environments. Within those worlds each of us creates our identity. Our personalities have remarkable continuity from early in life (White, 1980). Yet we have great capacity to change. We can adapt to a wide range of climates and physical environments. We are incomplete without others and can love and receive love, generating perhaps the greatest growth of all.

Paradoxically, we also have the capacity to hold tight to behavior that doesn't work—as if to force the world to yield and make our worst features productive. We are the greatest! And we can be mulish!

Personal models of teaching share several purposes. The first is to lead the student toward greater mental and emotional health by developing self-confidence and a realistic sense of self and by building empathetic reactions to others. The second is to increase the proportion of education that emanates from the needs and aspirations of the students themselves, taking each student as a partner in determining what he or she will learn and how he or she will learn it. The third is to develop specific kinds of qualitative thinking, such as creativity and personal expression.

These models can be used in four ways:

First, the personal models can be used as general models of teaching, even to design a school, when they have adopted a nondirective philosophy as the core approach to education (for example, Aspy and Roebuck, 1973; Neill, 1960) or as a major component (Chamberlin and Chamberlin, 1943).

Second, they can be used to flavor a learning environment designed around other models. For example, we can "carry around with us" concern for the students' self-concepts, and we can think carefully about how to shape everything we do to maximize their positive feelings about self and to minimize the likelihood that our teaching will diminish them as people. In other words, we can use these models to attend to the personal qualities and feelings of our students and to look for opportunities to make them partners with us and to communicate affirmatively with them. We will concentrate on this use of the model.

Third, we can use the unique properties of the personal models to counsel students when we wish to help them learn to reach out to the world more fully and positively.

Fourth, we can build curricula in the academic subjects around students. The "experience" methods for teaching reading, for example, use student-dictated stories as the initial reading materials and student-selected literature as the chief materials once initial competence has been established. Combined with other models, the personal models can be used to design independent study courses, including resource-based programs.

In addition to the belief that enhancing the learner as a person is a worthwhile educational goal in its own right, a major thesis of this family of models is that better-developed, more affirmative, self-actualizing learners have increased learning capabilities. Thus, personal models will increase academic achievement by tending the psyches of the learners. This thesis is supported by a number of studies (Roebuck, Buhler, and Aspy, 1976) that indicate that the students of teachers who incorporate personal models into their repertoires increase their achievement. Sets of studies by Hunt and Joyce and their colleagues (see Joyce, Peck, and Brown, 1981) have indicated how much more effective it is to modulate to the students in the course of using a wide variety of models of teaching.

From the range of personal models, we have selected several to illustrate the genre. The chapter on Carl Rogers's nondirective teaching model illustrates the philosophy and techniques of the major spokesperson for the family, and the chapter on states of growth deals with the organization of the classroom as a self-disciplining community of learners.

CHAPTER 12

NONDIRECTIVE TEACHING
The Learner at the Center

> *The hard part of figuring out how to teach is learning when to keep your mouth closed, which is most of the time.*
>
> —Carl Rogers, to a seminar at Columbia University, about 1960

SCENARIO

We are in a Department of Defense Dependents School (DODDS) in Germany, in Charley Wilson's fifth-grade class of the children of soldiers. Most have just been sent to Afghanistan to secure an airfield against attacking forces. Charley has decided that the best course of action is to busy his students in academic study, and he is ready to begin a unit on writing that begins with a set of film clips that the students will write about.

However, as he readies the VCR and turns to the class, he can see unusual stress on the students' faces. He asks, "What's up?" There is no response. He says, "Are you worried?"

One student responds strongly, "We're worried sick." The others nod.

"OK. Now, shall we deal with it? Do you want to talk about it?"

"I don't know what to say. I'm just frozen," says Pamela. More nodding. "What does frozen feel like?"

"It's like I'm hardly alive. I'm hiding inside a cave."

"That's a good way to put it," says Josh. "It's like I'm somewhere else, trying to freeze out what's happening."

"It's like if you let your fear in—really in—you won't be able to stand it. You have to hide and keep it away," says Nancy.

The students are looking directly at Charley, avoiding each others' eyes. Charley keeps the discussion going, primarily eliciting comments like those above.

"You know what? We all fear," Charley says. Again, everyone nods. "Our fear is a good thing. It's not crazy. There's real danger out there." The students begin to look at each other now, and nod. They are miserable.

"The problem is that we have to support those mothers and fathers and keep ourselves going when we are scared and anxious." More nods and eye contact with Charley. "So, let's directly face how we are going to do that."

Charley is beginning an inquiry into feelings and the very immediate problem of how these children will carry on and help their parents deal with a life-threatening danger.

S C E N A R I O

John Denbro, a 26-year-old high school English teacher in suburban Chicago, is very concerned about Mary Ann Fortnay, one of his students. Mary Ann is a compulsive worker who does an excellent job with literature assignments and writes excellent short stories. She is, however, reluctant to share those stories with other members of the class and declines to participate in any activities in the performing arts.

Mr. Denbro recognizes that the issue cannot be forced, but he wants Mary Ann to understand why she is reluctant to allow any public display of her talents. She will make her own decisions about participation that involves sharing her ideas.

One afternoon she asks him to read some of her pieces and give her his opinion.

Mary Ann: Mr. Denbro, could you take a look at these for me?
Denbro: Why sure, Mary Ann. Another short story?
Mary Ann: No, some poems I've been working on. I don't think they're very good, but I'd like you to tell me what you think.
Denbro: When did you write them?
Mary Ann: One Sunday afternoon a couple of weeks ago.
Denbro: Do you remember what started you thinking that you wanted to write a poem?
Mary Ann: I was feeling kind of sad and I remembered last month when we tried to read "The Waste Land," and it seemed to be trying to say a lot of things that we couldn't say in the usual way. I liked the beginning lines, "April is the cruelest month, breeding lilacs out of the dead land." (T. S. Eliot, "The Waste Land")
Denbro: And this is what you wrote down?

Mary Ann: Yes. It's the first time I've ever tried writing anything like this.

Denbro: (Reads for a few minutes and then looks up.) Mary Ann, these are really good.

Mary Ann: What makes a poem good, Mr. Denbro?

Denbro: Well, there are a variety of ways to judge poetry. Some methods are technical and have to do with the quality of expression and the way one uses metaphors and analogies and other literary devices. Others are subjective and involve the quality of expression, the real beauty of the words themselves.

Mary Ann: I felt very good when I was writing them, but when I read them over, they sound a little dumb to me.

Denbro: What do you mean?

Mary Ann: Oh, I don't know. I guess the main thing is that I feel ashamed if anybody else sees them.

Denbro: Ashamed?

Mary Ann: I really don't know. I just know that if these were to be read aloud, say to my class, I would die of mortification.

Denbro: You really feel that the class would laugh at these?

Mary Ann: Oh sure, they wouldn't understand.

Denbro: How about your short stories? How do you feel about them?

Mary Ann: You know I don't want *anybody* to see what I write.

Denbro: You really feel that you want to put them away somewhere so nobody can see them?

Mary Ann: Yes, I really think so. I don't know exactly why, but I'm pretty sure that no one in my class would understand them.

Denbro: Can you think of anybody else that might understand them?

Mary Ann: I don't know. I kind of think there are people out there who might, but nobody around here, probably.

Denbro: How about your parents?

Mary Ann: Oh, they like everything I write.

Denbro: Well, that makes three of us. Can you think of anybody else?

Mary Ann: I guess I think adults would, but I'm not really so sure about other kids.

Denbro: Kids are somehow different from adults in this respect?

Mary Ann: Well, kids just don't seem to be interested in these kinds of things. I feel they put down anybody who tries to write anything.

Denbro: Do you think they feel this way about the authors we read in class?

Mary Ann: Well, sometimes they do, but I guess a lot of the time they really enjoy the stories.

Denbro: Well then, why do you think they wouldn't like what you write?

Mary Ann: I guess I really don't know, Mr. Denbro. I guess I'm really afraid, but I can't put my finger on it.

Denbro: Something holds you back.

Mary Ann: In a lot of ways, I really would like to find out whether anybody would appreciate what I write. I just don't know how to go about it.

Denbro: How would you feel if I were to read one of your short stories but not tell them who wrote it?

Mary Ann: Would you promise?

Denbro: Of course I would. Then we could talk about how everybody reacted. You would know that they didn't know who had written it.

Mary Ann: I don't know, but it sounds interesting.

Denbro: Depending on what happened, we could cook up some kind of strategy about what to do next.

Mary Ann: Well, I guess you've got me right where I don't have anything to lose.

Denbro: I hope we're always where you don't have anything to lose, Mary Ann; but there's always a risk in telling about ourselves.

Mary Ann: What do you mean, telling about ourselves?

Denbro: I think I should go now—but let me pick one of your stories and read it next week, and then let's get together on Wednesday and talk about what happened.

Mary Ann: OK, and you promise not to tell?

Denbro: I promise. I'll see you next Wednesday after school.

Mary Ann: OK. Thanks a lot, Mr. Denbro. Have a good weekend.

The nondirective teaching model is based on the work of Carl Rogers (1961, 1971) and other advocates of nondirective counseling. Rogers extended to education his view of therapy as a mode of learning. He believed that positive human relationships enable people to grow, and therefore that instruction should be based on concepts of human relations in contrast to concepts of subject matter.

As we mentioned in the introduction to this section of the book, we will concentrate on the use of the model to "flavor" teaching—to keep the students' frames of reference in mind, keep central their growth in self, and help them solve learning problems.

From the nondirective stance, the teacher's role is that of a facilitator who has a counseling relationship with students and who guides their growth and development. In this role, the teacher helps students explore new ideas about their lives, their schoolwork, and their relations with others. The model creates an environment where students and teachers are partners in learning, share ideas openly, and communicate honestly with one another.

The nondirective model nurtures students rather than controlling the sequence of learning. The emphases are more with the development of effective long-term learning styles and the development of strong, well-directed individual personalities than they are with short-term instructional or content objectives. The nondirective teacher is patient and does not sacrifice the long view by forcing immediate results.

ORIENTATION TO THE MODEL

GOALS AND ASSUMPTIONS

We will concentrate on the elements that create a nondirective atmosphere for interacting with the students.

The nondirective teaching model focuses on *facilitating* learning. The environment is organized to help students attain greater personal integration, effectiveness, and realistic self-appraisal. Stimulating, examining, and evaluating new perceptions take a central place, because the reexamination of needs and values—their sources and outcomes—is crucial to personal integration. Students do not necessarily need to change, but the teacher's goal is to help them understand their own needs and values so that they can effectively direct their own educational decisions.

The core rationale comes from Rogers's stance toward nondirective counseling, in which the client's capacity to deal constructively with his or her own life is respected and nurtured. Thus, in nondirective teaching, the teacher respects the students' ability to identify their own problems and to formulate solutions.

When operating nondirectively, the teacher attempts to see the world as the student sees it, creating an atmosphere of empathetic communication in which the student's self-direction can be nurtured and developed. During interaction, the teacher mirrors students' thoughts and feelings. By using reflective comments, the teacher raises the students' consciousness of their own perceptions and feelings, thus helping them clarify their ideas.

The teacher also serves as a benevolent alter ego, one who accepts all feelings and thoughts, even those the students may be afraid of or may view as wrong or perhaps even punishable. In being accepting and nonpunitive, the teacher indirectly communicates to the students that all thoughts and feelings are acceptable. In fact, recognition of both positive and negative feelings is essential to emotional development and positive solutions.

The teacher gives up the traditional decision-making role, choosing instead the role of a facilitator who focuses on student feelings. The relationship between student and teacher in a nondirective interview is best described as a partnership. Thus, if the student complains of poor grades and an inability to study, the teacher does not attempt to resolve the problem simply by explaining the art of good study habits. Instead, the teacher encourages the student to express the feelings that may surround his or her inability to concentrate, as feelings about self and others. When these feelings are fully explored and perceptions are clarified, the student himself or herself tries to identify appropriate changes and bring them about.

The nondirective atmosphere has four qualities. First, the teacher shows warmth and responsiveness, expressing genuine interest in the student and accepting him or her as a person. Second, it is characterized by permissiveness in regard to the expression of feeling; the teacher does not judge or moralize. Because of the importance of emotions, much content is discussed that would normally be guarded against in more customary student relationships with teachers or advisors. Third, the student is free to express feelings symbolically but is not free to control the teacher or to carry impulses into action. Fourth, the relationship is free from any type of pressure or coercion. The teacher avoids showing personal bias or reacting in a personally critical manner to the student. Every learning task is viewed as an opportunity to help the student grow as a person.

A "GROWTH SYNDROME"

A kind of "growth syndrome" emerges as the student (1) releases feelings, (2) develops insight, followed by (3) action and (4) integration that leads to a new orientation (see Figure 12.1).

According to Rogers, responding on a purely intellectual basis to students' problems inhibits the expression of the feelings, which are at the root of the problem of growth. For example, if a student is struggling with writing, an intellectual response would be, "Start by making an outline." An empathetic response would be, "When I get stuck I often feel panicky. How do you feel?" Without the release and exploration of these feelings, students will reject suggestions and be unable to sustain real behavior changes.

Insight is the short-term goal of the process. By expressing feelings the student becomes able to look at a problem—in the case of the scenario at the beginning of the chapter, the problem of allowing others to experience one's writing. Indications of insight come from statements by the students that describe behavior in terms of cause and effect or in terms of personal meaning. In the scenario, the student comes to realize that the problem lies in her own fear, rather than the objective possibility of judgments by others. As they begin to understand the reasons for their behaviors, they begin to see other more functional ways of satisfying their needs. Through the release of emotions, the students can perceive options more clearly. New insights enable the students to select delayed goals that are more satisfying than goals that give immediate but only temporary satisfaction.

FIGURE 12.1   Phases of personal growth in the nondirective interview process.

Ultimately, the test of personal insight is the presence of actions that motivate the students toward new goals. At first, these positive actions may concern minor issues, but they create a sense of confidence and independence in the student. The teacher in the scenario is trying to create "safe space" for the action of sharing the writing. Gradually, the students' positive actions lead to a new, more comprehensive orientation. This is the integration phase. In the first scenario, Charley is redirecting the students from their misery and fear to the problem of helping themselves and others to create a good life in the midst of a really terrible problem. In the second scenario, the long-term goal is a mature ability to share writing derived from a better understanding of the social dynamics of sharing. In other words, the student will gradually find that the action of sharing has more good consequences than bad ones and that satisfaction can come from the integrated understanding of the problem of sharing.

The nondirective approach maintains that the most effective means of uncovering the emotions underlying a problem is to follow the pattern of the students' feelings as they are freely expressed. Instead of asking direct questions for the purpose of eliciting feelings, the teacher lets the students direct the flow of thoughts and feelings. If the students express themselves freely, the problems and their underlying emotions will emerge. This process is facilitated by reflecting the students' feelings, thereby bringing them into awareness and sharper focus. This is a difficult skill for most of us because we are more attuned to the objective content of what people are saying than to the affective dimension of the communications.

TAKING THE LEAD

The student and teacher share the responsibility for the discussion. But, frequently, the teacher must make "lead-taking" responses to direct or maintain the conversation (see Table 12.1). These include statements by the teacher that help start the discussion, establish the direction in an open manner, or give the student some indication as to what he or she should discuss, either specifically or generally.

TABLE 12.1 **NONDIRECTIVE RESPONSES IN INTERVIEW**

A. Nondirective Responses to Feelings	B. Nondirective Lead-Taking Responses
1. Simple acceptance	1. Structuring
2. Reflection of feelings	2. Directive questioning
3. Paraphrasing of content	3. Forcing student to choose and develop a topic
	4. Nondirective leads and open questions
	5. Minimal encouragements to talk

The essential skill is to lead without taking responsibility from the students. Nondirective lead-taking remarks are stated directly in a positive and amiable manner. Some examples are:

"What do you think of that?"
"Can you say more about that?"
"How do you react when that happens?"

Nondirective responses to feelings are attempts to respond either to the feelings the student expresses or to the content of the expressions. In making these comments, the teacher does not interpret, evaluate, or offer advice, but reflects, clarifies, accepts, and demonstrates understanding. The purpose of these comments is to create an atmosphere in which the student is willing to expand the ideas he or she is expressing. Usually, the responses are short statements that are supportive and enable the student to continue the discussion. Some examples are:

"I think I understand."
"It's especially hard to be alone."
"Sort of like it doesn't matter what you do, it will go on the same way."

Interpretation is used sparingly—we want the students to do the interpreting—but occasionally is useful in moving a discussion forward. Interpretation sometimes helps a student who is unable to offer any explanation for his or her behavior. Interpretative responses are attempts to suggest to the student his or her reasons for being unable to continue the discussion. But interpretation is given only to those feelings that can definitely be accepted by the student. The decision to use interpretation is made cautiously by the teacher and is used only in situations in which the teacher feels confident that interpretation will advance rather than close a dialogue. The whole purpose is to help the student inquire into what have been relatively closed areas:

"You do this because . . . "
"Perhaps you feel you won't succeed."
"It sounds like your reasons for your actions this week are . . . "
"You are saying to me that the problem is . . . "

Approval is usually given only when genuine progress has been achieved. It must be used sparingly, or the nondirective relationship is likely to drift rapidly into the traditional teacher-student relationship. But thoughts like the following may help at times:

"That's a very interesting comment and may well be worth considering again."

"That last idea was particularly strong. Could you elaborate on it some
    more?"
"I think you are really making progress."

Directive counseling moves are also to be used rarely—they imply a relationship in which the teacher attempts to change the ideas of the student
or influence his or her attitudes. For example, "Do you think it might be better if . . . " directly suggests a choice to the student. Attempts to support the
student directly are usually made to reduce apparent anxiety, but they do
not contribute to real problem solving.

THE MODEL OF TEACHING

The nondirective stance presents some interesting problems. First, the responsibility is shared. In most models of teaching, the teacher actively
shapes events and can picture the pattern of activities that lies ahead, but
in most nondirective situations, events emerge and the pattern of activities
is more fluid. Second, counseling is made up of a series of responses that
occur in an unpredictable sequence. Thus, to master nondirective teaching,
teachers learn general principles, work to increase their sensitivity to
others, master the nondirective skills, and then practice making contact
with students and responding to them, using skills drawn from a repertoire
of nondirective counseling techniques.

SYNTAX

Despite the fluidity and unpredictability of nondirective teaching, Rogers
points out that the nondirective interview has a sequence. We have divided
this sequence into five phases of activity, as shown in Table 12.2.

In phase one, the helping situation is defined. This includes structuring
remarks that define the student's freedom to express feelings, an agreement
on the general focus of the interview, an initial problem statement, some
discussion of the relationship if it is to be ongoing, and the establishment
of procedures for meeting. Phase one generally occurs during the initial session on a problem. However, some structuring or definition by the teacher
may be necessary for some time, even if this consists only of occasional
summarizing moves that redefine the problem and reflect progress. Naturally, these structuring and definitional comments vary considerably with
the specific problem and the student. For example, negotiating academic
contracts will likely differ from working with behavioral problem situations.

In phase two, the student is encouraged by the teacher's acceptance and
clarification to express negative and positive feelings and to state and explore the problem.

In phase three, the student gradually develops insight: he or she per-
ceives new meaning in personal experiences, sees new relationships of cause

TABLE 12.2   **SEQUENCE OF THE NONDIRECTIVE MODEL**

Phase One: Defining the Helping Situation	Phase Two: Exploring the Problem
Teacher encourages free expression of feelings.	Student is encouraged to define problem. Teacher accepts and clarifies feelings.

Phase Three: Developing Insight	Phase Four: Planning and Decision Making
Student discusses problem. Teacher supports student.	Student plans initial decision making. Teacher clarifies possible decisions.

Phase Five: Integration	Action Outside the Interview
Student gains further insight and develops more positive actions. Teacher is supportive.	Student initiates positive actions.

and effect, and understands the meaning of his or her previous behavior. In most situations, the student seems to alternate between exploring the problem itself and developing new insight into his or her feelings. Both activities are necessary for progress. Discussion of the problem without exploration of feelings would indicate that the student himself or herself was being avoided.

In phase four, the student moves toward planning and decision making with respect to the problem. The role of the teacher is to clarify the alternatives.

In phase five, the student reports the actions he or she has taken, develops further insight, and plans increasingly more integrated and positive actions.

The syntax presented here could occur in one session or, more likely, over a series. In the latter case, phases one and two could occur in the first few discussions, phases three and four in the next, and phase five in the last interview. Or if the encounter consists of a voluntary meeting with a student who has an immediate problem, phases one through four could occur in only one meeting, with the student returning briefly to report his or her actions and insights. On the other hand, the sessions involved in negotiating academic contracts are sustained for a period of time, and the context of each meeting generally involves some kind of planning and decision making, although several sessions devoted entirely to exploring a problem might occur. It is very important that the student comes to understand that he or she is ultimately responsible for his or her affect rather than being helpless in the hands of outside forces.

SOCIAL SYSTEM

The social system of the nondirective strategy requires the teacher to assume the roles of facilitator and reflector. The student is primarily responsible for the initiation and maintenance of the interaction process (control); authority is shared between student and teacher. The norms are those of open expression of feelings and autonomy of thought and behavior. Rewards, in the usual sense of approval of specific behavior—and particularly punishment—do not apply in this strategy. The rewards in a nondirective interview are more subtle and intrinsic—acceptance, understanding, and empathy from the teacher. The knowledge of oneself and the psychological rewards gained from self-reliance are generated by the student personally.

PRINCIPLES OF REACTION

The principles of reaction are based on bringing the student into inquiry on affect. The teacher reaches out to the students, empathizes with their personalities and problems, and reacts in such a way as to help them define their problems and feelings, take responsibility for their actions, and plan objectives and how to achieve them.

SUPPORT SYSTEM

The support system for this strategy varies with the function of the interview. If a session is to negotiate academic contracts, then the necessary resources for self-directed learning must be made available. If the interview consists of counseling for a behavioral problem, no resources beyond the skills of the teacher are necessary. In both cases, the one-to-one situation requires spatial arrangements that allow for privacy, removal from other classroom forces and activities, and time to explore a problem adequately and in an unhurried fashion. For academic curriculum areas—reading, writing, literature, science, and social science—rich arrays of materials are necessary.

APPLICATION ⎯⎯⎯⎯⎯⎯⎯⎯⎯⎯⎯⎯⎯⎯

The nondirective teaching model may be used for several types of problem situations: personal, social, and academic. In the case of personal problems, the individuals explore feelings about self. In social problems, students explore their feelings about relationships with others and investigate how feelings about self may influence these relationships. In academic problems, students explore their feelings about their competence and interests. In each case, however, the interview content is always personal rather than external; it centers on each individual's own feelings, experiences, insights, and solutions.

To use the nondirective teaching model effectively, a teacher must be willing to accept that a student can understand and cope with his or her own life. Belief in the student's capacity to direct himself or herself is communicated through the teacher's attitude and verbal behavior. The teacher does not attempt to judge the student. Such a stance indicates limited confidence in the student's capabilities. The teacher does not attempt to diagnose problems. Instead, the teacher attempts to perceive the student's world as he or she sees it and feels it. And, at the moment of the student's self-perception, the teacher reflects the new understanding to him or her. In this model, the teacher temporarily sets aside personal thoughts and feelings and reflects the student's thoughts and feelings. By doing this, the teacher conveys understanding and acceptance of the feelings.

Nondirective counseling stresses the emotional elements of the situation more than the intellectual. That is, nondirective counseling strives for reorganization through the realm of feeling rather than through purely intellectual approaches. Often this view leads teachers who are considering adopting the nondirective stance to question the possibility of conflicting roles. How (they reason) can I be a disciplinarian, a referee, an instructor, and a friend—and also be a counselor implementing nondirective principles?

One of the important uses of nondirective teaching occurs when a class becomes "stale" and the teacher finds himself or herself just "pushing" the students through exercises and subject matter. One sixth-grade teacher, exhausted by the failure of more traditional attempts to cope with the discipline problems and the lack of interest on the part of her class, decided to experiment with student-centered teaching. She turned to nondirective approaches to help her students take more responsibility for their learning and to ensure that the subject matter would be related to their needs and learning styles. She has provided an account of that experience, from which excerpts are presented here.

MARCH 5, WE BEGIN

A week ago I decided to initiate a new program in my sixth-grade classroom, based on student-centered teaching—an unstructured or nondirective approach. I began by telling the class that we were going to try an "experiment." I explained that for one day I would let them do anything they wanted to do—they did not have to do anything if they did not want to.

Many started with art projects; some drew or painted for most of the day. Others read or did work in math and other subjects. There was an air of excitement all day. Many were so interested in what they were doing that they did not want to go out at recess or noon!

At the end of the day I asked the class to evaluate the experiment. The comments were most interesting. Some were "confused" or distressed without the teacher telling them what to do, without specific assignments to complete.

The majority of the class thought the day was "great," but some expressed concern over the noise level and the fact that a few "goofed off" all day. Most felt that they had accomplished as much work as we usually do, and they enjoyed being able to work at a task until it was completed, without the pressure of a time limit. They liked doing things without being "forced" to do them and liked deciding what to do.

They begged to continue the "experiment" so it was decided to do so, for two more days. We could then reevaluate the plan.

The next morning I implemented the idea of a "work contract." I gave them ditto sheets listing all our subjects with suggestions under each. There was a space provided for their "plans" in each area and for checking work after completion.

Each child was to write his or her contract for the day—choosing the areas in which to work and planning specifically what to do. On completion of any exercise, drill, review, and so on, the student was to check and correct his or her own work, using the teacher's manual. The work was to be kept in a folder with the contract.

I met with each child to discuss his or her plans. Some completed theirs in a very short time; we discussed as a group what this might mean, and what to do about it. It was suggested that the plan might not be challenging enough, that an adjustment should be made—perhaps going on or adding another idea to the day's plan.

Resource materials were provided, suggestions made, and drill materials made available to use when needed.

I found I had much more time, so I worked, talked, and spent the time with individuals and groups. At the end of the third day I evaluated the work folder with each child. To solve the problem of grades, I had each child tell me what he or she had learned.

MARCH 12, PROGRESS REPORT

Our "experiment" has, in fact, become our program—with some adjustments. Some children continued to be frustrated and felt insecure without teacher direction. Discipline also continued to be a problem with some, and I began to realize that, although some of the children may need the program more than others, I was expecting too much from them too soon—they were not ready to assume self-direction yet. Perhaps a gradual weaning from the spoon-fed procedures was necessary.

I regrouped the class—creating two groups. The largest group is the nondirected. The smallest is teacher-directed, made up of children who wanted to return to the former teacher-directed method, and those who, for varied reasons, were unable to function in the self-directed situation. I would have waited longer to see what would happen, but the situation for some disintegrated a little more each day—penalizing the whole class. The disrupting factor kept everyone upset and limited those who wanted to study and work. So it seemed to me best for the group as a whole as well as the program to modify the plan.

Those who continued the "experiment" have forged ahead. I showed them how to program their work, using their texts as a basic guide. They have learned that they can teach themselves (and each other), and that I am available when a step is not clear or advice is needed.

At the end of the week they evaluate themselves in each area—in terms of work accomplished, accuracy, and so on. We have learned that the number of errors is not a criterion of failure or success. Errors can and should be part of the learning process; we learn through our own mistakes. We have also discussed the fact that consistently perfect scores may mean that the work is not challenging enough and perhaps we should move on.

After self-evaluation, each child brings the evaluation sheet and work folder to discuss with me.

Some of the members of the group working with me are most anxious to become "independent" students. We will evaluate together each week their progress toward that goal.

Some students (there were two or three) who originally wanted to return to the teacher-directed program are now anticipating going back into the self-directed program. (I sense that it has been difficult for them to readjust to the old program, as it would be for me to do so.)

FIGURE 12.2   Instructional and nurturant effects of the nondirective teaching model.

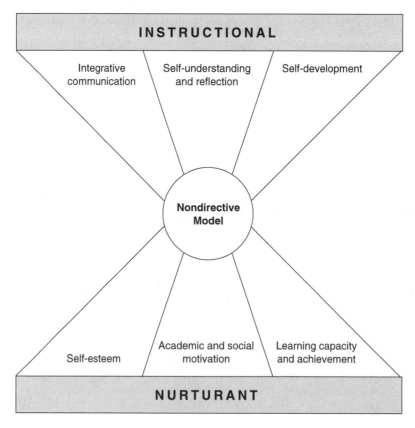

INSTRUCTIONAL AND NURTURANT EFFECTS _____

Since the activities are not prescribed but are determined by the learner as he or she interacts with the teacher and other students, the nondirective environment depends largely on its nurturant effects, with the instructional effects dependent on its success in nurturing more effective self-development (Figure 12.2). The model thus can be thought of as entirely nurturant in character, dependent for effects on experiencing the nondirective environment rather than carrying content and skills through specifically designed activity.

SUMMARY CHART ▶ NONDIRECTIVE TEACHING MODEL

Syntax

Phase One: Defining the Helping Situation
    Teacher encourages free expression of feelings.

Phase Two: Exploring the Problem
    Student is encouraged to define problem.
    Teacher accepts and clarifies feelings.

Phase Three: Developing Insight
    Student discusses problem.
    Teacher supports student.

Phase Four: Planning and Decision Making
    Student plans initial decision making.
    Teacher clarifies possible decisions.

Phase Five: Integration
    Student gains further insight and develops more positive actions.
    Teacher is supportive.

Social System

The model has little external structure: teacher facilitates; student initiates; and the discussion is problem-centered. Rewards, in the usual sense of approval of specific behavior, and punishment do not apply in this strategy. The rewards are intrinsic and include acceptance, empathy, and understanding from the teacher.

Principles of Reaction

Teacher reaches out to students, empathizes, reacts to help students define problems and take action to achieve solutions.

Support System

Teacher needs quiet, private place for one-to-one contacts, resource center for conferences on academic contracts.

CHAPTER 13

DEVELOPING POSITIVE SELF-CONCEPTS

The Inner Person of Boys and Girls, Men and Women

> *We want to make the school rich, but we also want the kids to know that they can't depend on us forever. They've got to be able to take off on their own.*
>
> —Carlene Murphy to Bruce Joyce, Summer 1990

Although people and their growth are the important substance of this book, this is the first chapter that attempts to deal conceptually with the most important underlying element in general education—the states of growth that result from schooling.

We have made a number of statements about people, however, and as we directly approach the subject it is worthwhile to summarize some of them.

First, the research on the spectrum of models of teaching supports the proposition that all students can learn how to learn and they can respond to a great variety of teaching/learning environments. Students can accelerate their ability to learn in a number of ways if we provide them with the opportunity.

Second, the more skills students develop and the more they widen their repertoire, the greater their ability to master an even greater range of skills and strategies. (This is true of teachers as well. The better we get, the better we *can* get!)

Third, the learning community developed in the school and the classroom influences how students feel about themselves, how they interact, and how they learn. The social climate, in other words, is part of the substance of schooling. It provides a "curriculum" that affects the results of the academic curriculum.

The important message is that students can learn, not only academic content and social skills, but how to become integrated selves that reach out into the world and reciprocally contribute to and profit from their transactions with it.

Now we turn to modeling active states of growth for our students. We will examine a framework for looking at the ways children and adults interact with the world—from states of actively seeking growth to more passive interaction to states of pushing experience away. In many ways, students become what we model for them, and part of our influence on them depends on our own states of growth—our own self-concepts—and how we communicate them to children.

INDIVIDUAL DIFFERENCES

We begin with a frame of reference that will enable us to think about individual differences in growth and particularly in the readiness to grow. There are a number of ways of thinking about individual differences that we can rely on at the present time. Some of these have been developed to help us think about the learning styles of children (Dunn and Dunn, 1975; McCarthy, 1981) and can be applied to adults as well. Some are developed to distinguish various styles of thinking (for example, Myers, 1962) and examine how those styles affect problem solving. At least one theory attempts to describe differences between children and adults as learners (Knowles, 1978).

A number of broad conceptualizations of personality can be applied to the behavior of teachers as instructors and as learners (Erikson, 1950; Gregorc, 1982; Harvey, Hunt, and Schroeder, 1961; Maslow, 1962). Conceptual systems theory (Hunt, 1971) has been especially heavily studied and has been a useful predictor of teacher-student interaction, the breadth of styles employed by teachers, sensitivity to students and responsiveness to them, and (most pertinent here) aptitude to acquire the competence to use teaching skills and strategies (see Joyce, Peck, and Brown, 1981).

In this chapter we will discuss a framework developed from the study of the professional and personal lives of teachers in the California Staff Development Study (Joyce, Bush, and McKibbin, 1982; Joyce and Showers, 2002). The framework was developed to guide practice in the organization of human resource development programs and school improvement efforts (McKibbin and Joyce, 1980; Joyce, Hersh, and McKibbin, 1983; Joyce, Calhoun, and Hopkins, 1999) A practical orientation, the findings are correlated with the theories of personality growth and take conceptual development, self-concept, and psychological maturity into account. It owes a particular debt to the work of Abraham Maslow (1962).

THE CONCEPT OF STATE OF GROWTH

The objective of the line of inquiry was to build a picture of the opportunities for growth experienced by teachers from their school setting, the district, universities, intermediate agencies (county offices of education and professional development centers), and other institutions. In the initial investigation, case studies were made of more than 300 teachers from 21 districts in 7 counties, and more than 2,000 others were surveyed through questionnaires. In addition to information about participation in the formal systems of support (courses, workshops, and the services of administrators and supervisors), interaction with peers was examined, as were those aspects of personal lives that might have implications for professional growth. Thus, data were collected on what came to be termed the "formal," the "peer-generated," and the "personal" domains, depending on the origins of the activities that people engaged in.

The focus was the dynamic of individual interaction with the environment. The thesis was that within any given environment (say, a school in the San Francisco Bay Area), the opportunities for productive interaction leading to growth theoretically would be about equal. That is, formal staff development systems, colleagues, and opportunities to read, attend films and events in the performing arts, engage in athletic activity, and so on, would be available to all personnel in profusion. Thus, differences in activity would be a function of the individual's disposition to interact productively with the environment. If we discovered differences, we could proceed to try to understand their origins and develop ideas for capitalizing on them.

THE FORMAL, PEER-GENERATED, AND PERSONAL DOMAINS

The amount of interaction in all three domains varied greatly. The differences were vast in both urban and rural areas and among elementary and secondary teachers. They are easily illustrated in regions like the Bay Area and the Los Angeles Basin where literally thousands of courses and workshops are available, most principals and supervisors have been trained to provide active clinical support, many professional development centers in county offices and other agencies involve teachers in the selection of staff development opportunities, and there are active organizations of teachers of writing, science, and other curriculum areas. In addition, the opportunities for personal activity of all sorts abound in these great metropolitan areas, which also are close to mountain ranges, waterways, and oceans. The nature of the differences in each domain is interesting.

FORMAL STAFF DEVELOPMENT OPPORTUNITIES

Participation ranged from persons who experienced only the activities sponsored and required by the district (possibly only one or two workshops or presentations and one or two visits by supervisors or consultants) and who were aware of very few options, to very active, aware persons with definite plans for professional enhancement. A small number effectively exploited the opportunities in universities and the larger teacher centers.

PEER-GENERATED OPPORTUNITIES FOR GROWTH

The range here was from persons who had virtually no professional discussions with any other teachers, to persons who had close and frequent interaction, who experienced mentoring relationships (on the giving or receiving end or both), and who gathered with others to instigate the introduction of innovations or initiatives for the improvement of the school.

THE PERSONAL DOMAIN

In their personal lives some teachers were extremely active, with one or two well-developed areas of participation, and some others made virtually no use of the rich environments in which they lived. We found some very active readers and others who barely skim the headlines of the daily paper, some Sierra Club activists and others who had never visited Yosemite, some members of performing arts groups and others who have not seen a film or a live performance in 10 or more years.

STATES OF GROWTH ⸻⸻⸻⸻⸻⸻

Somewhat to our surprise, the levels of activity were correlated across domains. That is, those who were more active professionally were also more active personally. Looking for reasons, we concluded that the differences in levels of activity were produced by the individuals' orientations toward their environments, moderated by social influence.

ORIENTATIONS TOWARD THE ENVIRONMENT

The essence of the concept is the degree to which the environment is viewed as an opportunity for satisfying growth. Thus the more active people view the environment as a set of possibilities for satisfying interaction. They initiate contact and exploit the possibilities. Less-active persons are less aware of the possibilities or more indifferent to them. The least-active persons expend energy protecting themselves from what they see as a threatening or unpleasant environment, avoiding contact and fending off the initiatives of others. Also, the persons who are more active and more initiating are also more *proactive*. That is, they *draw* more attention from the environment, bringing more possibilities within their reach. This phenomenon multiplies the opportunities for many people. It was not unusual for us to discover that certain schools that were characterized by a cluster of active people (and generally by an active principal) were regularly approached by central office personnel, teacher centers, and universities to be the "trial" sites for everything from computer technology to community involvement programs. Those people and their schools received more resources and training, while some schools—characterized by a cluster of resistant persons—were approached last, and many initiatives passed them by.

SOCIAL INFLUENCE

Close friends and colleagues, and the social climate of the workplace and the neighborhood, moderate the general dispositions toward growth. Affirmative and active friends and colleagues and positive social climates induce persons to engage in greater activity than they would if left to themselves. This finding provides another dimension to the general theme of Chapter 10. The synergistic environment is not only essential for collective action but to generate the kind of colleagueship that will be productive for the states of growth of individuals.

Also, as we will emphasize later, a major goal of a human resource development system is to increase the states of growth of the personnel in the system, potentially benefiting the individuals as well as the organization and ensuring that the children are in contact with active, seeking personalities.

LEVELS OF ACTIVITY

Although the orientations toward growth are best represented on a continuum, people gradually develop patterns that have more clearly discernible edges, and it is not unreasonable to categorize them—provided we recognize that the categories blend into one another. With that caveat, we present the following prototypes because they can be useful in explaining behavior and in planning staff development programs and organizing faculties to exploit them vigorously.

A GOURMET OMNIVORE

Our prototypes here are mature, high-activity people who have learned to canvass the environment and exploit it successfully. In the formal domain they keep aware of the possibilities for growth, identify high-probability events, and work hard at squeezing them for their growth potential.

They constitute the hard-core clientele for teacher centers and district and intermediate-agency offerings for volunteers. They initiate ideas for programs and find ways of influencing the policymakers. However, they are not negative toward system initiatives. They have the complexity to balance their personal interests with the awareness that they belong to an organization.

Our prototype omnivores find kindred souls with whom to interact professionally. They learn from informal interaction with their peers. A group of omnivores may work together and generate initiatives or attend workshops or courses together. When computers appeared on the educational scene, it was often groups of omnivores who learned to use them and developed the computer centers in their schools.

It is in their personal lives that our prototype omnivores become most clearly defined. They are characterized by a general high level of awareness, but their distinguishing feature is one or two areas in which they are enthusiastically involved. These areas vary quite a bit from person to person. One may be an omnivorous reader; another, a theater-goer; a third, an avid backpacker or skier; a fourth, a maker of ceramics. Some run businesses. In close consort with others, they generate activities. The spouses of omnivore tennis players are likely to find themselves with rackets in their hands, and the close friends of moviegoers will be importuned to share films. Because of their proactivity, our mature omnivores have learned to fend off opportunities and protect time for their chosen avocations. What is striking is their habit of both exploiting and enriching whatever environment they find themselves in. In the workplace, they strive to learn all they can about their craft and give and take energy from their peers. In their private lives they find opportunities for development.

They are also distinguished by their persistence. In McKibbin and Joyce's (1980) study, they sought training that would have a high likelihood for transfer and, once back in the workplace, they practiced and created the conditions of peer support that enabled them to implement a remarkably high proportion of the skills to which they were exposed. They are also more likely than others to bring the ideas they gain in their personal lives into the workplace and use them in their teaching. More recent studies (Hopkins, 1990; Joyce and Showers, 2002) have remarkably similar findings.

A PASSIVE CONSUMER

About 10 percent of the persons we studied fit the profile of our *gourmet omnivores,* and another 10 percent we call *active consumers,* also quite engaged with aspects of their environment. By far the largest number, however (about 70 percent) resembled the prototype we term the *passive consumer.*

The distinguishing characteristics of our passive consumers are a more or less amiable conformity to the environment and a high degree of dependence on the immediate social context. In other words, their degree of activity depends greatly on who they are with. In the company of other passive consumers, our prototype is relatively inactive. We studied one school in which all of the personnel in one "wing" of the building were passive, and their interchange with others was amiable but involved few serious discussions about teaching and learning. They visited one another's classrooms rarely. None attended staff development activities that were not required by the administration. They had no objections to being required to attend those workshops, one day in the fall and one in the spring, and they enjoyed them but did nothing with the content.

In another wing of the school, two passive consumers found themselves in the company of two omnivores and an active consumer and were drawn into many of the activities generated by their more enterprising colleagues. They found themselves helping to set up computer workstations for the students, cooperating in scheduling and the selection of software, and learning word processing and how to teach their students to use self-instructional programs. They attended workshops on the teaching of writing with the study group instigated by the omnivores and began revamping their writing programs.

In personal life our prototype passive consumer is also dependent on consort. If they have relatively inactive spouses and extended families, they will be relatively inactive. If they are with relatives, friends, and neighbors who initiate activity, their levels of activity will increase.

A RETICENT CONSUMER

Whereas our passive consumer has a relatively amiable, if rather unenterprising, view of the world, about 10 percent of the persons we studied expend energy actually pushing away opportunities for growth. We speak of these persons as "reticent" because they have developed an orientation of reluctance to interact positively with their cultural environment. We can observe this dynamic in both professional and domestic settings.

Our prototype reticent attends only the staff development that is required and is often angry about having to be there, deprecates the content, whatever it is, and tries to avoid follow-up activities. Our reticent treats administrative initiatives and those from peers with equal suspicion and tends to believe that negative attitudes are justified because "the system" is inherently oppressive and unfeeling. Thus even peers who make initiatives are deprecated "because they are naive" if they believe that they will gain administrative support for their "idealistic" notions. Hence our reticents tend to view our omnivores as negatively as they do the hated administration. The hard core reticent even rejects opportunities for involvement in decision making, regarding them as co-opting moves by basically malign forces. In discussions about personal lives, the structure of attitudes was similar. Our reticents tend to emphasize what they see as defects in people, institutions, services, and opportunities in a range of fields. Film, theater, athletic activity, state and national parks, books and newspapers—all are suffering rapid decay. ("Only trash gets published these days. . . . Movies are full of sex and violence.") In the richness of an urban environment, they tend to emphasize crowding as an obstacle to participation in events ("If I could get tickets. . . . If you didn't have to wait for a court. . . . You can never get in to the good movies. . . ."). In the rural environments, it is lack of facilities that gets the blame.

Even so, our reticent is not unaffected by the immediate social context. In affirmative school climates they do not "act out" their negative views as much. In the company of omnivores they can be carried along in school improvement efforts. Affirmative spouses who tolerate their jaundiced opinions good-naturedly involve them in a surprising number of activities. In the right circumstances they learn to take advantage of the opportunities in their lives.

CONCEPTUAL STRUCTURE, SELF-CONCEPT, AND STATES OF GROWTH _____

In an attempt to seek reasons for the differences in states of growth manifested by the teachers we were studying, we turned to a number of developmental theories. Two are of particular interest to us here because their descriptions of development appear to correlate with the states of growth we found (Joyce, McKibbin, and Bush, 1983). One is conceptual systems theory (Harvey, Hunt, and Schroder, 1961; Hunt, 1971), and the other is self-concept theory (Maslow, 1962).

CONCEPTUAL DEVELOPMENT

Conceptual systems theory describes people in terms of the structure of concepts they use to organize information about the world. In the lowest developmental stages, people use relatively few concepts for organizing their world, tend to have dichotomous views with few "shades of gray," and much emotion is attached to their views. They tend to reject information that does not fit into their concepts or to distort it to make it fit. Thus people and events are viewed as "right" or "wrong." Existing concepts are preserved.

At higher stages of development, people develop greater ability to integrate new information, are more decentered and can tolerate alternative views better, and their conceptual structure is modified as old concepts become obsolete and new ones are developed. New experiences are tolerated and bring new information and ideas, rather than being rejected or distorted to preserve the existing state.

For an example, let us consider individuals at the lower and higher developmental stages on a first visit to a foreign culture. People characterized by the lower conceptual levels are suspicious of the "different" and tend to find fault with it. ("You can't *believe* what they eat here.") They peer through the windows of the tour buses with increasing gratitude that they will soon be returning to America. They speak loudly to the "stupid" hotel personnel who don't speak English. They clutch their wallets to keep them away from the conniving, dishonest natives and their unclean hands.

Their higher-conceptual-level companions are fascinated by the new sights, sounds, and smells. Gingerly they order the local dishes, comparing them with the familiar, finding some new and pleasing tastes, and bargaining for a recipe. They prefer to walk, avoiding the bus unless time forbids. They ask shopkeepers to pronounce the names of things. They brush off the grime to get a better look at the interesting vase in the corner. They speak quietly and wait for the hotel personnel to indicate the local custom.

There is a substantial correlation between conceptual development and the states of growth of the teachers and administrators we studied. The omnivores are in a continual search for more productive ways of organizing information and have more complex conceptual structures as a result. Their openness to new experience requires an affirmative view of the world and the conceptual sophistication to deal with the new ideas they encounter. Our passive consumers have more limited structures and less ability to figure out how to reach for new experience and deal with it. Our reticents are busy protecting their present concepts and act offended by the presence of the unfamiliar. They can be as negative toward children they do not understand as they are toward the facilitators who try to bring new ideas and techniques into their orbit. Conceptual development is correlated with variety and flexibility in teaching styles (Hunt, 1971), with ease in learning new approaches to teaching, and with ability to understand students and modulate to them (Joyce, Peck, and Brown, 1981).

A change to a more productive orientation involves a structural change—a more complex structure capable of analyzing people and events from multiple points of view and the ability to assimilate new information and accommodate to it.

SELF-CONCEPT

More than 45 years ago, Abraham Maslow (1962) and Carl Rogers (1961) developed formulations of personal growth and functioning that have guided attempts since then to understand and deal with individual differences in response to the physical and social environment. Rather than concentrating on intellectual aptitude and development, their theories focused on individuals' views of self or self-concepts. They took the position that our competence to relate to the environment is greatly affected by the stances we take toward ourselves.

Strong self-concepts are accompanied by "self-actualizing" behavior, a reaching out toward the environment with confidence that the interaction will be productive. The self-actualizing person interacts richly with the milieu, finding opportunities for growth and enhancement and, inevitably, contributing to the development of others.

Somewhat less-developed persons feel competent to deal with the environment but accept it for what it is and are less likely to develop growth-producing relationships from their own initiatives. They work within the environment and what it brings to them rather than generating opportunities from and with it.

The least-developed persons have a more precarious relationship with their surroundings. They are less sure of their ability to cope. Much of their energy is spent in efforts to ensure that they survive in a less-than-generous world.

It is not surprising that we found a relationship between the states of growth of the people we studied and their concepts of self. Our omnivores are self-actualizing. They feel good about themselves and their surroundings. Our passive consumers feel competent but are dependent on the environment for growth-producing opportunities. Our reticents feel that they live in a precarious and threatening world. The faults that they find in their surroundings are products not of being well-developed and able to discern problems the rest of us cannot see, but of an attempt to rationalize their need to protect themselves from a world of which they are afraid.

UNDERSTANDING GROWTH AND THE POTENTIAL FOR GROWTH

The theories of conceptual growth and self-concept both help us understand ourselves as growth-oriented programs are planned and carried out. They help us understand why people respond as they do and provide us with a basis for creating environments that are likely to be productive, in terms of both the content of the programs and the people for whom they are intended.

David Hopkins (1990) and his colleagues reported on a study conducted in England in which they studied the implementation by a group of teachers of a new curriculum in the arts for which they had volunteered to be the forerunners. They were to master the curriculum in their classrooms and then become the disseminators to other teachers. Hopkins and his colleagues studied the states of growth and self-concepts of the teachers and the organizational climates of the schools in which they worked. All were influential, but the states of growth alone were predictors of the teachers' uses of the arts curricula. Essentially, the reticent and passive consumers were unable to achieve implementation in any organizational climate, while climate facilitated the work of the active consumers and gourmet omnivores. Not only were the teachers at the lower states of growth unable to profit from the training they received, but their students were deprived of the opportunities to learn presented by the new curriculum!

DEVELOPING RICHER STATES OF GROWTH

We want to grow as people and also to help our students develop richer orientations for growth. These are closely connected, for our primary influence on our students is what we model as people. If we model passivity, we encourage it. If we model activity and reaching out toward the world, we encourage active states. The good news is that we are far more likely to develop an upward progression than a downward one. Also, we develop by practicing reaching out—we simply "do it!" Thus, the message is that we need to reach out by developing a couple of lines of activity in which we push ourselves for richness and excellence. These areas need to be balanced. Reading or the cinema needs to be balanced by a social or athletic pursuit. We can have confidence that modeling omnivorous reading will not only breed active readers but also will pull students toward different pursuits. The models of teaching described in this book are also strong tools. A cooperative learning community—tooled up with the active models for gathering and interpreting information, examining social issues, and seeking ways of learning more—will have its effect on the students. A rich and active social climate will have its effect.

We are what we eat, not just biologically but socially and emotionally. Rich substance, well organized, in positive circumstances makes us richer, more outreaching, and more productive. And in our professional work, it gives us the tools to develop self-actualizing students.

PART V

THE BEHAVIORAL SYSTEMS FAMILY OF MODELS

To many people, behavior theory *is* psychology. In part, this conception exists because much early psychological research focused on how behavior is learned through conditioning, making the "behaviorists" the founders of psychology and the occupants of the first chapters in most introductory books. Controversy has created the other part, because the science of behavior control, while both illuminating and useful, arouses fears that, should psychological theory become too powerful, malign uses will follow. From *Brave New World* to *Clockwork Orange*, behavior theory has been portrayed as the science of the Dark Side. Also, some find the idea that environmental variables shape behavior to conflict with the idea that we are free to determine ourselves. Educators polarize around programs developed from behavior theory and, at least in academic circles, devotees and critics engage in verbal standoffs.

Our position is that superficial judgment is not wise and that controversy, in this case, is not productive. Behavior theory offers much to teachers and learners, but its models, like the others in this book, are not the treatment of choice in every situation.

Let's begin by sorting out some of the assumptions that have led to the research on which we base several models of learning.

BEHAVIOR IS LAWFUL AND SUBJECT TO VARIABLES IN THE ENVIRONMENT

People respond to variables in their environment with a conditioning effect. These external forces stimulate individuals to engage in or avoid certain behaviors. Once a behavior has been learned, the probability that it will occur again can be strengthened or decreased by responses from the environment. Thus, if a two-year-old sees a table in the room (stimulus), points to it, and verbalizes the word *table* (response behavior), he or she is responding to external forces. If, after the child says the word *table*, the child's mother picks him or her up, gives him or her a big hug, and repeats, "*Table*, that's right" (reinforcing stimuli), the child is likely to say the word again (response behavior). On the other hand, suppose the child sees a menacing-looking toy animal curled nearby (stimulus) and experiences a sudden surge of anxiety and fear (response behaviors). If the child runs away (another response behavior) and thereby avoids the toy, the act reduces his or her anxiety (reinforcing stimulus). The reinforcement increases the likelihood that the child will try to avoid that toy. Both examples illustrate the basic behavioral notion that behavior is acquired or enacted through external variables that serve either as the original stimulus or as the reinforcing stimulus. In one case we are learning to do something; in the other case, to avoid something.

Counterconditioning is related, but slightly different in that it always involves relearning. In counterconditioning, a new behavior incompatible with the old behavior is substituted, such as relaxation for anxiety. To cure a phobia toward public places (agoraphobia), the individual substitutes positive feelings for anxiety. One can even prepare oneself to cope with future situations. The Lamaze approach to birthing prepares the woman to trigger relaxation techniques during delivery.

From this stance the task of the psychologist is to discover what kinds of environmental variables affect behavior in which ways. The task of educators is to translate that knowledge—to design instructional materials and interactions that encourage productive learning and to avoid the environmental variables that can discourage it. If we can do that, so can the student learn to do it. Thus, what appears at first to be a technique for controlling others can be used to free people by increasing their capabilities for self-control.

To capitalize on the behaviorist stance, one doesn't need to accept the idea that *all* behavior is shaped by environmental variables. The position that it has partial truth will do. For example, we can use the behaviorist position to build simulations that work—students interacting with them learn something—and simultaneously accept the personalistic position that students can direct their own behavior.

HISTORY, BRIEFLY TOLD

Behavioral models of learning and instruction have their origins in the classical conditioning experiments of Pavlov (1927), the work of Thorndike (1911, 1913) on reward learning, and the studies of Watson and Rayner

(1921), who applied Pavlovian principles to the psychological disorders of human beings. B. F. Skinner's *Science and Human Behavior* (1953) is in many ways the anchor of the literature in the field and its applications to education. In the late 1950s educators began to employ in school settings some of the behavioral principles, particularly forms of contingency management and programmed learning materials. For some types of learners these have had great success. For example, some youngsters who previously had made no progress in language development and social learning are now trainable and often able to mix with normal individuals. Milder forms of learning problems have responded to behavioral models as well (Becker, 1977; Becker and Carnine, 1980; Becker, Englemann, Carnine, and Rhine, 1981).

During the past 35 years, a great amount of research has demonstrated the effectiveness of behavioral techniques with a wide range of learning problems, from phobias toward subjects such as mathematics, social-skill deficits, behavioral problems, and test anxiety. The research also indicates that these procedures can be used effectively in group settings and by laypeople. We believe that behavior theory presently offers an array of models that are extremely useful to teachers, curriculum planners, and creators of instructional materials.

Terms such as *learning theory, social learning theory, behavior modification,* and *behavior therapy* have been used by various leaders in this field to refer to the models we discuss here (Bandura, 1969; Lazarus, 1971; Salter, Wolpe, and Reyna, 1964; Wolpe, 1969; see also Estes, 1976). Because each term is generally associated with one particular form of the basic theory, we prefer to use the more neutral term *behavior theory* to cover procedures emanating from both operant and counterconditioning principles.

PRINCIPLES

BEHAVIOR AS AN OBSERVABLE, IDENTIFIABLE PHENOMENON

Behavior theory concentrates on observable behavior and takes an optimistic view. Given the right conditions and enough time, we can succeed in learning (and unlearning).

Essentially, a stimulus evokes a behavior (response), which generates consequences, which, if reinforcing, strengthen the likelihood that a similar stimulus will elicit the behavior that was reinforced. Reciprocally, negative consequences will make it less likely that the behavior will be elicited.

Behavior theorists believe that internal responses (such as fear of failure), which mediate our observable responses (such as avoiding areas that arouse fear of failure), can be changed (Rimm and Masters, 1974). The approach involves continuous inquiry—a careful study of the student, the design of the environment, a study of responses, and a continuation or modification of the course of action.

MALADAPTIVE BEHAVIORS ARE ACQUIRED

In our society many people have assumed that many children have "blocks to learning" particular kinds of things (such as math) in the form of internal states that cannot be changed. It turns out that many of these "blocks" are simply learned aversions that the kids can learn to control. If the pattern of avoiding the feared area is left untouched, the aversion becomes more pronounced. The student has greater and greater difficulty as the mathematical content gets more complex. The learning deficit increases. Learning to handle affect in approaching the subject is the key. Some simple techniques can go a long way in mild cases.

BEHAVIORAL GOALS ARE SPECIFIC, DISCRETE, AND INDIVIDUALIZED

Even though behaviorist principles have been used to design instructional materials, like simulations, that have been used by large numbers of students, the behaviorist frame of reference tends toward the discrete, concrete, and individualized. Two externally similar responses do not necessarily proceed from the same original stimulus (one person may be outwardly friendly because friendliness attracts people while another may behave similarly but to avoid being shunned or ignored). Conversely, no two people will respond to the same stimulus in precisely the same way. Consequently, the procedures for encouraging new behaviors involve setting specific, individualized behavioral goals. This does not mean that group training is not possible. It does mean that the goals for each student may differ and that the training process will need to be individualized in terms of pacing or content. The instructional materials prepared from the behaviorist stance are almost always "self-paced" (Becker, 1977; Becker and Carnine, 1980; Becker, Englemann, Carnine, and Rhine, 1981).

BEHAVIORAL THEORY FOCUSES ON THE HERE-AND-NOW

The role of the past in shaping a person's behavior is deemphasized. Poor instruction may have caused a failure to learn to read, but the focus is on learning to read *now*. The behaviorist concentrates on creating conditions or helping students create conditions that will enable them to progress and gain satisfaction quickly. The stance regards human behavior with optimism and does not dwell on the past. The assumption is that past failure did not result in conditions that cannot be corrected. The more difficult problems just take a little longer to fix.

Behavioral practitioners have often reported that they have been able to alter maladaptive behaviors in a short time, even in the case of severe phobias or long-term withdrawal patterns. Many shy people have felt relaxed and socially effective in a short time, and students who had remained virtually illiterate have progressed quickly (Resnick, 1967).

OPERANT CONDITIONING AND COUNTERCONDITIONING

Behaviorists like to arrange instruction so that success is highly probable. Self-instructional programmed material (see below) is sequenced in such small steps as to virtually ensure correct responses, and simulations are designed to generate much successful activity as concepts and skills are being learned. The reinforcement the learner derives from knowledge of his or her correctness both makes the achievement enduring and propels the learner toward new tasks. This is one reason why highly sequenced "programmed" materials often work well with students who previously experienced little success. Finally, students are also *reinforced by controlling their environments.* Part of the attraction of self-instructional computer programs is the reinforcement quality of mechanical manipulation and the ability to control the pace of one's progress.

One should not underestimate the function of social climate to generate reinforcement. The range of naturally occurring positive reinforcers available to teachers is broad—for example, a smile, enthusiasm, show of interest, attention, enjoyment, and casual conversation. Perhaps most powerful is a pervasively positive atmosphere, where just being in that classroom brings pleasure and confidence—an environment filled with little positive events just waiting to attach themselves to appropriate behaviors.

Negative reinforcement, on the other hand, removes something from the situation (possibly by adding something disagreeable). Punishment, such as threats designed to decrease the likelihood of response, is an example of a negative reinforcer (aversive stimulus). The management mode in some classrooms is based on aversive control; students are threatened with reprisals if they do not learn or follow rules. Many years ago the birch rod was used; today the aversive stimuli are less physical (poor grades, disapproval). According to behavior theorists, punishment has several drawbacks. First, its effects are temporary; punished behavior is likely to recur. Second, the aversive stimuli used in punishment may generate unwanted emotions, such as predispositions to escape or retaliate, and disabling anxieties (Skinner, 1953, p. 183). A negative event can actually reinforce the very behavior that it is intended to eliminate or reduce. The use of negative reinforcers can push the student away from the very subject he or she is trying to learn. Wherever possible, positive rather than negative reinforcement should be used.

Some events are devastating because they violate behavioral principles. Retention in grade ("holding back from promotion") is devastating emotionally and frequently has the effect of destroying interest in school. The embarrassment from it continues for a long time and generates aversion to the schooling process and even the social interchange in school. It seriously reduces the probability of later successful schoolwork.

Labeling a child as having learning problems can generate aversion as well. No doubt one of the reasons for the general ineffectiveness of special education is that the child, labeled as having a "learning disability," feels devastated and approaches learning tasks with poor feelings that become attached to learning itself. In the worst cases, the children so labeled "give themselves permission" to avoid relevant learning tasks whenever possible.

The effectiveness of reinforcement programs is determined not only by establishing a close temporal relation between reinforcement and behavior and by the type of reinforcement selected, but also by the scheduling or frequency of reinforcement (*reinforcement schedule*). One of the most difficult skills for teachers, or anyone, to master is to be consistent, immediate, and frequent in rewarding the desired responses when they occur. If a response goes unreinforced it will become less and less frequent until it is extinguished. For example, to teach students to approach writing with confidence and positive feelings, one needs to elicit writing frequently and reinforce production. Eliciting writing too infrequently will diminish positive feelings toward writing tasks and voluntary writing.

Desensitization procedures make use of stimulus control by gradually enlarging the range of stimuli to which individuals can respond without anxiety. Stress reduction models depend on people's recognizing a range of cues indicating body tension or mental stress and taking action to substitute positive for negative feelings in an increasing variety of situations.

Training models using modeling and practice illustrate the basic behavioral concepts. For example, in an excellent tennis lesson, modeling is followed by practice, verbal reinforcement, and self-reinforcement through observation of results. Only a small number of skills are taught in any one lesson, so that the learner has a high probability of mastering them.

OVERCOMING MATH ANXIETY

Sheila Tobias's (1993) nice book on this subject uses several of the behaviorist principles to help people conquer their negative feelings about self-as-learner-of-math. Much of her book is about basic arithmetic and mathematical concepts, because one isn't going to get over the anxiety without studying the subject itself. Learning to approach is an essential part of most programs for the treatment of anxiety. Second is the placement of the responsibility squarely on the individual. Third is the use of support groups and the development of positive social climates in mathematics learning centers. Tobias does a particularly nice job of helping people understand the role the anxiety itself plays in inhibiting effective learning.

A CALL FOR INQUIRY ⸺⸺⸺⸺⸺⸺⸺⸺⸺⸺⸺

Much has been accomplished; much remains to be done. Considering the field as a whole, carefully designed small group studies have generated positive effects in a wide variety of areas. Implementation in school districts is more difficult. Probably the most consistent findings are in programs such as Distar, but each teacher, school, and district needs to conduct action research on implementation and effects when a decision is made to implement a curriculum or process based on behavioral theory. On the other hand, that is not so different from the situation with any other model of teaching or family of models of teaching.

14

LEARNING TO LEARN FROM MASTERY LEARNING

If we can allow them time to learn one thing at a time, and then another, and another, until they can get their feet under them, we can break the cycle of failure.
—Berj Harootunian to Bruce Joyce, March 1993

Mastery learning is a framework for planning instructional sequences, formulated by John B. Carroll (1971) and Benjamin Bloom (1971). Mastery learning provides a compact and interesting way of increasing the likelihood that more students will attain a satisfactory level of performance in school subjects. Recent work has sharpened the idea, and contemporary instructional technology has made it even more feasible.

A CONCEPT OF APTITUDE

The core theoretical idea in mastery learning is based on John Carroll's interesting perspective on the meaning of aptitude. Traditionally, aptitude has been thought of as a characteristic that correlates with a student's achievement. (The more aptitude one has, the more he or she is likely to learn.) Carroll, however, views aptitude as the *amount of time* it takes someone to learn any given material, rather than his or her capacity to master it. In Carroll's view, students with very low aptitude with respect to a particular kind of learning simply take a much longer time to reach mastery than students with a higher aptitude.

This view is optimistic in the sense that it suggests that it is possible for nearly all students to master any given set of objectives, if sufficient time (the opportunity to learn) is provided along with appropriate materials and instruction. Thus viewed, aptitude becomes primarily a guide to how much time a learner will need. Aptitude also suggests *how* to instruct, because learners of different aptitudes will learn more efficiently if the style of instruction is suited to their configurations. (In *our* terms, some aptitudes are model-relevant—they help us choose and adapt models.) For any given objective, according to Carroll, the degree of learning achieved by any given student will be a function of time allowed, the perseverance of the student, the quality of instruction, the student's ability to understand instruction, and his or her aptitude. The problem in managing instruction is deciding how to organize the curriculum and the classroom so that students will have optimal time, benefit from good instruction, be induced to persevere, and receive assistance in understanding the learning tasks.

Bloom transformed Carroll's stance into a system with the following characteristics:

1. Mastery of any subject is defined in terms of sets of major objectives that represent the purposes of the course or unit.
2. The larger substance is then divided into sets of relatively small learning units, each one accompanied by its own objectives, which are parts of the larger ones or thought essential to their mastery.
3. Learning materials are then identified and the instructional strategy (Model of Teaching) selected.
4. Each unit is accompanied by brief diagnostic tests that measure the student's developing progress (the formative evaluation) and identify the particular problems each student is having. Knowledge of progress is fed back to the students to act as a reinforcement. (Praise and encouragement can, if contiguous with correct performance, serve as reinforcement also.)
5. The data obtained from administering the tests are used to provide supplementary instruction to the student to help overcome problems. (Bloom, 1971, pp. 47–63)

If instruction is managed in this way, Bloom believes, time to learn can be adjusted to fit aptitude. Students of lesser aptitude can be given more time and more feedback while the progress of all is monitored with the assistance of the tests.

INDIVIDUALLY PRESCRIBED INSTRUCTION

Bloom, Block, and the other advocates of mastery learning believe that it can be implemented by teachers through modifying traditional group instructional procedures to ensure that some students have more time and that they receive appropriate individual instruction according to the results of the formative evaluation (Carroll, 1971, pp. 37–41).

However, modern instructional technology, especially the development of self-administering multimedia units and the application of programmed learning procedures, has encouraged curriculum developers to invent comprehensive curricular systems and to reorganize schools to provide for a much greater degree of individualized instruction than is generally possible under conventional school organizations.

An early and important example of an application of systems planning to elementary and secondary school instruction is the Individually Pre-scribed Instructional Program (IPI), developed by the Learning Research and Development Center of the University of Pittsburgh, in collaboration with the Baldwin-Whitehall School District. In IPI students usually work in-dependently on the materials prescribed daily (or every few days) for them, depending on their demonstrated level of competence, learning style, and particular learning needs.

STEPS IN THE PROGRAM

IPI illustrates a modular curriculum developed by applying systems analy-sis procedures to curriculum materials development. It is a particularly useful case study because it readily demonstrates the steps the IPI planners took in creating the system. As we examine these steps, we stop briefly to show how each reflects the inner workings of the performance model.

The system is designed to:

1. Enable each pupil to work at his or her own rate through units of study in a learning sequence.
2. Develop in each pupil a demonstrable degree of mastery.
3. Develop self-initiation and self-direction of learning.
4. Foster the development of problem solving through processes.
5. Encourage self-evaluation and motivation for learning. (Lindvall and Bolvin, 1966)

The assumptions regarding the learning process and the related learn-ing environment are as follows:

1. One obvious way pupils differ is in the amount of time and practice that it takes to master given instructional objectives.

2. One important aspect of providing for individual differences is to arrange conditions so that each student can work through the sequence of instructional units at his or her own pace and with the amount of practice he or she needs.

3. If a school has the proper types of study materials, elementary school pupils, working in a tutorial environment that emphasizes self-learning, can with a minimum amount of direct teacher instruction, learn.

4. In working through a sequence of instructional units, a student should not begin work on a new unit until he or she has acquired a specified mini-mum degree of mastery of the material in the units identified as prerequisites.

5. If pupils are to be permitted and encouraged to proceed at individual rates, it is important for both the individual pupil and the teacher that the program provide for frequent evaluations of pupil progress which can provide a basis for the development of individual instructional prescriptions.

6. Professionally trained teachers employ themselves most productively when they are performing such tasks as instructing classes, individual pupils, or small groups, diagnosing pupil needs, and planning instructional programs rather than carrying out such clerical duties as keeping records, scoring tests, and so on. The efficiency and economy of a school program can be increased by employing clerical help to relieve teachers of many non-teaching duties.

7. Each pupil can assume more responsibility for planning and carrying out his own program of study than is permitted in most classrooms.

8. Learning can be enhanced, both for the tutor and the one being tutored, if pupils are permitted to help one another in certain ways. (Lindvall and Bolvin, 1966, pp. 3–4)

Development is crucial. For any curriculum unit, the overall performance model—the objective—is generated.

Then, the performance model is analyzed into a set of sequentially organized behavioral objectives. IPI planners believe that such a listing is fundamental to other aspects of the program and must have the following characteristics:

a. Each objective should tell exactly what a pupil should be able to do to exhibit his mastery of the given content and skill. This should typically be something the average student can master in such a relatively short period as one class period. Objectives should involve such action verbs as *solve, state, explain, list, describe,* etc., rather than general terms such as *understand, appreciate, know,* and *comprehend.*

b. Objectives should be grouped in meaningful streams of content. For example, in arithmetic the objectives will be grouped (typically) into such areas as numeration, place value, addition, subtraction, etc. Such grouping aids in the meaningful development of instructional materials and in the diagnosis of pupil achievement. At the same time, this grouping does not preclude the possibility of having objectives that cut across areas.

c. Within each stream or area, the objectives should, to the extent possible, be sequenced in such an order that each will build on those that precede it, and, in turn, be a prerequisite to those that follow. The goal here is to let the objectives constitute a "scale" of abilities.

d. Within the sequence of objectives in each area, the objectives should be grouped into meaningful subsequences or units. Such units can be designated as representing different levels in progress and can provide break points so that when a student finishes a unit in that area, he or she may either go on to the next unit in that area or may switch to a unit in another area. (For example, on completing Level B addition, the pupil may either go on to Level C addition or move on to Level B subtraction.) (Lindvall and Bolvin, 1966, p. 3).

Over 400 specific behavioral objectives are included in the 13 topics of the IPI mathematics curriculum.

LEVEL E   LEVEL F

ADDITION AND SUBTRACTION

1. Given any two whole numbers, the student adds or subtracts using the short algorithm.

1. Given any two numbers ≤9,999.99 and an operation of addition or subtraction, the student solves. LIMIT: Answers must be positive numbers.

2. Given an addition problem with ≤5 addends, the student solves using the short algorithm.

2. Given ≤5 addends which are mixed decimals with <7 digits, the student adds. LIMIT: Decimals to millionths.

3. Given multiple-step word problems requiring addition and subtraction skills mastered to this point, the student solves them.

3. Given two mixed decimals, the student subtracts. LIMIT: ≤7 digits, decimals to millionths.

4. Solves multiple-step word problems: using addition and subtraction skills mastered to this point.

MULTIPLICATION

1. Given a two-digit number and a one-digit number, the student multiplies in horizontal form by using the distributive principle.

1. Given a two-digit number times a two-digit number, the student multiplies using the standard algorithm.

2. Given a problem with a three-digit multiplicand and a one-digit multiplier, the student solves using partial products.

2. Given a three-digit number times a two-digit number, the student multiplies using the standard algorithm.

3. Given a multiplication problem whose multipliers and multiplicands are whole numbers ≤10 times a multiple of 10, the student solves. LIMIT: Factors ≤9,000.

3. Given a whole number and a mixed decimal to hundredths as factors, the student multiplies. LIMIT: Whole number part ≤100.

4. Given a multiplication problem whose multipliers are whole numbers <10 times a power of 10, and whose multiplicand is three digits, the student solves. LIMIT: Multipliers ≤9,000.

5. Given a multiplication problem with a two-digit number times a two-digit number, the student solves using partial products.

4. Given two pure decimals ≤.99, the student multiplies and shows the equivalent problem in fractional form and converts product to decimal notation, compares answers for check.

5. Given a multiple-step word problem requiring multiplication skills mastered to this point, the student solves.

MULTIPLICATION

6. Given a two-digit number and a one-digit number, the student solves by using the multiplication algorithm.

7. Given a multiplication problem for skills to this point, the student checks the multiplication by commuting the factors and solving again.

8. Given a number ≤100, the student finds the complete factorization for the number. (Lindvall and Bolvin, 1966)

Each of the 13 areas of the mathematics curriculum has nine levels of difficulty, A through I. Within each level for a given topic area, several behavioral objectives are identified and sequentially organized. The breakdown of the 13 topics into levels creates certain options for the student and teacher. The student can cover one area in depth before moving to the next or can go from addition Level E to subtraction Level E.

The materials that the students use to achieve each objective are mostly self-study materials that a student can pursue by himself or herself with minimal assistance from the teacher. In addition to the self-instruction, the program calls on the teacher to offer instruction to small or large groups and to individuals. For instance, if several students are having difficulty successfully completing a particular objective, the teacher may bring them together for small-group instruction. The teacher's role in IPI is a crucial one. He or she serves as

a diagnostician (analyzing the IPI diagnostic data about each student in order to tailor a program to meet the individual learning needs), a selector (drawing on the bank of both human and material resources available to the IPI instructional situation), and a tutor (building meaningful and appropriate learning experiences that lead a student to a more independent and responsible role in his IPI learning setting). (Scanlon and Brown, 1969, p. 1)

LANGUAGE LABORATORY _____

Another prominent example of an instructional system, one in which the machine components paved the way for an entirely different learning environment, is the *language laboratory*. Its development represents vivid application of the combined properties of systems analysis, task analysis, and cybernetic principles in the educational setting. Before the language laboratory became commonplace, the classroom teacher served as the model for foreign speech in a classroom of 25 to 35 students who were trying to reproduce speech sounds. The individual in such a situation might have a maximum of one minute of speech practice per classroom session, hardly enough to produce fluency or accuracy.

Today, in the typical classroom laboratory, learners use electrical equipment to hear, record, and play back spoken materials. The general physical equipment includes student stations and an instructor's central panel. Through this panel, the teacher can broadcast a variety of content materials, new and remedial programs, and instruction to individuals, selected groups, or the entire class. He or she can also monitor the students' performance. The students' stations are often a series of individual, acoustically treated carrels, usually equipped with headphones, a microphone, and a tape recorder. Each student listens through the headphones to live or recorded directions from the instructor to repeat, answer questions, or make other appropriate responses to the lesson. The instructor may also choose to use the chalkboard, textbook, or other visual stimuli to supplement audio inputs. Modern technology has made it possible for almost instantaneous situations in which students might:

1. Hear their own voices more clearly through earphones than they could otherwise.
2. Directly compare their speech with that of a model.
3. Provide themselves with immediate feedback.
4. Isolate items for study.
5. Permit pacing for specific drill.
6. Permit more finely sequenced instructional content.

Learning a foreign language requires that the student hear vocabulary and speech patterns repeatedly. The exercises are carefully sequenced and are followed by new combinations of varying complexity. The ultimate goal is to have the student readily comprehend what he or she hears and make immediate and appropriate responses. From the student's viewpoint, the language laboratory serves as a base for extensive practicing of finely sequenced behavior, matching aural models, and developing speech fluency. From the instructor's viewpoint, it provides the facilities (hardware and software) for a more effective language-learning situation.

In systems analysis terminology, the language laboratory represents the development of a human-machine system based on the performance objectives and requirements of foreign language proficiency. Prior to the development of the language laboratory, it was possible to provide reasonably sequenced visual materials. But the critical elements of language training—individualized audial practice and dynamic feedback—far outran the human management capacities and support facilities of the self-contained classroom teacher with 25 students. With electronic hardware and software support subsystems, instructors can now divide their time more effectively between monitoring (management), diagnosis, and instruction. Students are given immediate, direct sensory feedback so that they can compare their performance with the desired performance and make the necessary self-corrective adjustments.

Many programs now available for personal computers create miniature language laboratories that function in the self-instructional mode. For computers without sound cards, phonetic spelling is used to assist with pronunciation. For computers with sound cards, the computer "speaks" words and phrases. Combined with the use of the Picture-Word Inductive Model (Chapter 5), "talking" dictionaries helped kindergarten students in French immersion to reach levels equal to those of most second and third grade English speaking students in French immersion classes (see Chapter 19).

Mastery learning has been investigated extensively. Slavin's (1990b) reanalysis of the literature generally agrees with Kulik, Kulik, and Bangert-Drowns's (1990) analysis that it usually increases learning modestly but consistently on curriculum-relevant tests. (The average student places about at the 65th percentile when compared with students in control groups studying the same material without the careful sequencing of objectives and modules of instruction.) Standardized tests, however, have been resistant to these gains, for reasons that are not well understood.

A NOTE ON PROGRAMMED INSTRUCTION

Many mastery learning programs use programed instruction, a system for designing self-instructional materials. It is one of the most direct applications of Skinner's writings. It provides for highly systematic stimulus control and immediate reinforcement. Although Skinner's initial programmed instruction format has undergone many transformations, most adaptations retain three essential features: (1) an ordered sequence of items, either questions or statements to which the student is asked to respond; (2) the student's response, which may be in the form of filling in a blank, recalling the answer to a question, selecting from among a series of answers, or solving a problem; and (3) provision for immediate response confirmation, sometimes within the program frame itself but usually in a different location, as on the next page in a programmed textbook or in a separate window in the teaching machine.

Recent research on programmed instruction shows that considerable deviation from these essentials can be made with no significant difference in the amount of learning that takes place. The original linear self-instructional programs in which each student is subjected to the same material, though at his or her own pace, were not sufficiently individualized for some educators. Hence, "branching" programs were developed. The idea in branching is that slower students, unable to respond correctly to a particular frame or sequence of frames, may need additional information or review of background information. On the other hand, the more advanced students could benefit by additional and more difficult material. At various points the branching program directs students to the appropriate material depending on their answer to a particular frame or the number of correct responses within a particular frame sequence. Branching programs will automatically direct the student to a special section depending on his or her choice. If the student selects any of the wrong responses, the particular mistake in reasoning is pointed out; if he or she chooses the correct response, a more difficult example may appear.

Programmed instruction has been successfully employed for a variety of subject matters, including English, math, statistics, geography, and science. It has been used at every school level from preschool through college. Programmed instructional techniques have been applied to a great variety of behaviors: concept formation, rote learning, creativity, and problem solving, for example. Some programs have even led students to discover concepts, using a format reminiscent of inductive thinking.

How is programmed instruction different from traditional workbooks that classroom teachers have used for years with no startling effects? With workbooks the emphasis is on practice (response maintenance) rather than on behavioral acquisition through carefully sequenced material. Workbooks provide endless "frames" of review material. Obviously, review is of little value unless the behavior has first been successfully established; the traditional workbook is not designed to do this. Also, the reinforcing effect of continuous review is bound to suffer diminishing returns; the learner only goes over material already mastered. Finally, most workbooks make no provision for immediate feedback, supplying the answer only in the teacher's copy!

SUMMARY

Mastery learning is straightforward, optimistic, and clear. To create a mastery learning system takes careful development, but in a positive social climate, this system directly approaches many of the learning problems that have vexed teacher-driven instruction. It also places the teacher in an encouraging, assisting role that has a positive effect on the self-esteem of the students.

15

DIRECT INSTRUCTION

The idea that you teach kids how to ask and answer questions, rather than just asking them questions, came as a revelation to me.
—A teacher of 20 years, to Bruce Joyce, May 1995

Although based on the studies of effective teachers, direct instruction has its theoretical origins in the behavioral family, particularly in the thinking of training and behavioral psychologists. Training psychologists have focused on training people to perform complex behaviors that involve a high degree of precision and often coordination with others—for example, being a crew member on a submarine. Their main contributions to learning situations are task definition and task analysis. The instructional design principles they propose focus on conceptualizing learner performance into goals and tasks, breaking these tasks into smaller component tasks, developing training activities that ensure mastery of each subcomponent, and, finally, arranging the entire learning situation into sequences that ensure adequate transfer from one component to another and achievement of prerequisite learning before more advanced learning.

Whereas training psychologists have emphasized the design and planning of instruction, behavioral psychologists address the interaction between teachers and students. They speak of modeling, reinforcement, feedback, and successive approximation. Behaviorists sometimes refer to their approach as "modeling with reinforced guided performance."

GOALS AND ASSUMPTIONS

Direct instruction plays a limited but important role in a comprehensive educational program. Critics of direct instruction caution that the approach should not be used all the time, for all educational objectives, or for all students—cautions we agree with. Despite the cautions and the caveats, direct instruction has a relatively solid empirical track record, getting consistent if modest effects.

THE LEARNING ENVIRONMENT FOR DIRECT INSTRUCTION

The most prominent features are an academic focus, a high degree of teacher direction and control, high expectations for pupil progress, a system for managing time, and an atmosphere of relatively neutral affect. Academic focus means one places highest priority on the assignment and completion of academic tasks. During instruction academic activity is emphasized; the use of nonacademic materials—for example, toys, games, and puzzles—is deemphasized or even discouraged, as is nonacademically oriented student–teacher interaction, such as questions about self or discussions of personal concern. Several studies have shown that a strong academic focus produces greater student engagement and, subsequently, achievement (Fisher et al., 1980; Madaus, Airasian, and Kellaghan, 1980; Rosenshine, 1970, 1971, 1985).

Teacher direction and control occur when the teacher selects and directs the learning tasks, maintains a central role during instruction, and minimizes the amount of nonacademic pupil talk. Teachers who have high expectations for their students and concern for academic progress demand academic excellence and behavior conducive to academic progress. They expect more of their students in terms of quantity and quality of work.

A major goal of direct instruction is the maximization of student learning time. Many teacher behaviors found to be associated with student achievement are in fact associated with student time on task and student rate of success, which in turn are associated with student achievement. Thus, the behaviors incorporated into direct instruction are designed to create a structured, academically oriented learning environment in which students are actively engaged (on task) during instruction and are experiencing a high rate of success (80 percent mastery or better) in the tasks they are given. Time spent by pupils in both these conditions is referred to as *academic learning time* (ALT), which is to be maximized.

Finally, there is substantial evidence that negative affect inhibits student achievement (Rosenshine, 1971; Soar, Soar, and Ragosta, 1971). Teachers should create an academic focus and avoid such negative practices as criticism of student behavior. Research is less clear on the role of positive affect on student outcomes: some students may benefit more from large amounts of praise than others; some types of praise are more effective than others (Brophy, 1981).

In summary, the direct instruction environment is one in which there is a predominant focus on learning and in which students are engaged in academic tasks a large percentage of time and achieve at a high rate of success. The social climate is positive and free of negative affect.

ORIENTATION TO THE MODEL

The term *direct instruction* has been used by researchers to refer to a pattern of teaching that consists of the teacher's explaining a new concept or skill to a large group of students, having them test their understanding by practicing under teacher direction (that is, controlled practice), and encouraging them to continue to practice under teacher guidance (guided practice).

Before presenting and explaining new material, it is helpful to establish a framework for the lesson and orient the students to the new material. Structuring comments made at the beginning of a lesson are designed to clarify for the students the purposes, procedures, and actual content of the subsequent learning experience. Such comments are associated with improved student engagement during the learning activity and with overall achievement (Block, 1980; Medley, Soar, and Coker, 1984; Fisher et al., 1980; Medley, 1977). These orienting comments can take various forms, including: (1) introductory activities that elicit students' relevant existing knowledge structures (Anderson, Evertson, and Brophy, 1979), such as reviewing the previous day's work (Rosenshine, 1985); (2) discussing the objective of the lesson; (3) providing clear, explicit directions about work to be done; (4) telling the students about the materials they will use and the activities they will be engaged in during the lesson; and (5) providing an overview of the lesson.

Once the context for learning has been established, instruction can begin with the presentation of the new concept or skill. Students' success in learning the new material has much to do with the thoroughness and quality of the teacher's initial explanation. Effective teachers spend more time explaining and demonstrating new material than less-effective teachers (Rosenshine, 1985). Presentation practices that appear to facilitate learning include: (1) presenting material in small steps so that one point can be mastered at a time; (2) providing many, varied examples of the new skills or concepts; (3) modeling, or giving narrated demonstrations of the learning task; (4) avoiding digressions, staying on topic; and (5) reexplaining difficult points (Rosenshine, 1985). From research on concept learning we also know that when teaching a new concept it is important to clearly identify the characteristics (attributes) of the concept and to provide a rule or definition (or sequence of steps in skill learning). Finally, providing a visual representation of the concept or skill along with the verbal explanation assists students in following the explanation. Later, at other points in the learning process, the visual representation serves as a cue or prompt.

Following the explanation comes the discussion, in which the teacher checks for students' understanding of the new concept or skill. A common error is simply to ask students if they understand or have any questions and then to assume that if no one or only a few students respond, everyone understands well enough to move on to seatwork. Effective teachers ask more questions that check for student understanding than less-effective teachers (Rosenshine, 1985). Such questions call for specific answers or ask for explanations of how answers were found. According to Rosenshine, effective teachers not only asked more questions, but they also spent more time on teacher-led practice and on repeating the new material they were teaching. Other aspects of effective questioning behavior for direct-instruction approaches are: (1) asking convergent, as opposed to divergent, questions

(Rosenshine, 1971, 1985); (2) ensuring that all students get a chance to respond, not just those who raise their hands or call out the loudest; this can
be accomplished by calling on students in a patterned order, for example by
calling the students' names first, in reading groups, before asking them
questions, or calling for a choral response (Gage and Berliner, 1983; Rosenshine, 1985); (3) asking questions within students' "reach" a high percentage of the time (75 to 90 percent) (Rosenshine, 1985); and (4) avoiding
nonacademic questions during direct instruction (Rosenshine, 1985; Soar,
Soar, and Ragosta, 1971).

Once the teacher has initiated a question and a student has responded,
the teacher needs to give the student feedback on his or her response. Research indicates that effective teachers do a better job of providing feedback
than do noneffective ones (Rosenshine, 1971). They do not let errors go un-
corrected, nor do they simply give the answers to students who have responded incorrectly. They use techniques for correcting responses or they
reteach the material. In addition, effective teachers maintain a brisk pace
during this recitation activity. When they provide corrective feedback or
reteach, they do it efficiently so that many practice opportunities are provided and many students have the opportunity to respond. For example,
when a correct answer has been given, the teacher simply asks a new question. In the early stages of learning, when answers may be correct but somewhat tentative, the teacher provides knowledge of results and quick-process
feedback. ("Very good. You remembered that 'i' goes before 'e' when it comes
after 'c.' ") If the student has carelessly provided an incorrect answer, the
teacher provides corrective feedback and moves on. If the incorrect response indicated lack of understanding, the teacher should provide hints or
clues, such as referring back to the visual representation. It is important to
probe for clarification and improved answers. Effective feedback is academically oriented, not behaviorally oriented (Fisher et al., 1980). It is also
substantive in that it tells students *what* they have done correctly. Feedback
may be combined with praise; however, it is important that praise be deserved based on the quality of the response (Gage and Berliner, 1983). Students differ in the amount of praise they need; some students, particularly
low-achieving students, need a lot, whereas others do not need as much.
Even if a student's need for praise is great, he or she should not be praised
for an incorrect response (Brophy, 1981).

The major point is that the kind of feedback students receive during
structured practice has much to do with their later success. Feedback helps
students find out how well they understand the new material and what their
errors are. To be effective, feedback must be academic, corrective, respectful, and deserved.

The need for students to be given thorough explanations and structured
practice with feedback before they begin their practice seems obvious. However, it is clear both from the research and from the authors' own experiences that students are often asked to work from their texts or workbooks
with almost no explanation and/or practice. Students need to have a high

degree of success when they are engaged in reading or practicing skills. In order for this to occur, they should move from structured practice to open practice only when they have achieved about 90 percent accuracy on the structured-practice examples.

In the average classroom, students spend between 50 and 75 percent of their time working alone on tasks (Rosenshine, 1985). If this large amount of time is to be productively directed toward learning, students need to remain engaged in the learning task. What is most conducive to engagement is being well prepared, by the teacher's presentation and by teacher-led practice. Practice that is directly related to the presentation and that occurs right after teacher-led practice facilitates student engagement. It is also helpful for the teacher to circulate while students are working, monitoring individual students with relatively short contacts (Rosenshine, 1985).

PRACTICE

As its name implies, the "heart" of this teaching strategy is its practice activities; three phases of the model deal with practice under varying conditions of assistance. The three levels of practice function in the following manner: When the students are first introduced to a new skill or concept, the teacher leads the group through each step in working out the problem. The idea is to ensure that few errors are produced in the initial learning stages, when memory is most vulnerable to remembering incorrect practice and when errors reinforce incorrect information. After the highly structured practice, the students practice on their own while the teacher monitors. During this time the teacher provides corrective feedback for any errors produced as well as reinforcement for correct practice. When students are able to practice with accuracy, they are ready for independent practice— that is, for practice under conditions when assistance is not as available. Homework is an example of independent practice. This last step in the practice progression is the mastery level; students are performing the skill independently with minimal error.

The second principle has to do with the length of each practice session. Research indicates that, on the whole, the more a person practices a skill, the longer it takes him or her to forget it. The general principle guiding the length of time recommended for practice is: *Short, intense, highly motivated practice periods produce more learning than fewer but longer practice periods.* For example, with younger students, short, 5- to 10-minute practice sessions interspersed over the day or a series of days will be more effective than long, 30- to 40-minute sessions. Older students are able to handle longer practice sessions, but, for them also, many short sessions with clear feedback about progress pay off.

The third principle is the need to *monitor the initial stage of practice* because incorrect performance at this stage will interfere with learning. Students need corrective feedback to prevent incorrect procedures from becoming embedded in their memories. Immediate corrective feedback (that is, information on how to perform correctly) will reverse misconceptions early in the instructional process. It also reduces performance anxiety because students practice with the assurance of immediate feedback. In addition to catching incorrect performance in the early stages, it is also important to reinforce correct performance. This gives students the knowledge of results that stabilizes the new learning more quickly.

Having students achieve an 85 to 90 percent *level of accuracy* at the current practice level before going to the next level is the fourth practice principle. Paying attention to accuracy rates ensures that students experience success and do not practice errors.

The next guideline is to *distribute practice*, using multiple practice sessions spread out over a period of time. Without practice, as much as 80 percent of new information is forgotten within 24 hours. With periodic reviews spread out over an extended period of time, such as four or five months, nearly all new information can be retained. A common mistake in instruction is to deal with a topic, end the topic, and never review the information or skills again until a "final examination." The important material needs to be reviewed regularly.

And, finally, the general guideline is that practice periods should be close together at the beginning of learning; once learning is at an independent level, the practice sessions can be spaced farther and farther apart. Thus, guided practice sessions should occur immediately after new learning has been introduced and should continue frequently until independence is achieved. When this has occurred, independent practice sessions can be distributed farther apart—that is, for example, 1, 2, 6, and then 15 days apart.

THE MODEL OF TEACHING

SYNTAX

The direct instruction model consists of five phases of activity: orientation, presentation, structured practice, guided practice, and independent practice. However, the use of this model should be preceded by effective diagnosis of students' knowledge or skills to be sure that they have the prerequisite knowledge or skills to achieve high levels of accuracy in the different practice conditions.

Phase one is orientation in which a framework for the lesson is established. During this phase the teacher's expectations are communicated, the learning task is clarified, and student accountability is established. Three steps are particularly important in carrying out the intent of this phase: (1) the teacher provides the objective of the lesson and the level of performance; (2) the teacher describes the content of the lesson and its relationship to prior knowledge and/or experience; and (3) the teacher discusses the procedures of the lesson—that is, the different parts of the lesson and students' responsibilities during those activities.

Phase two is the presentation—explaining the new concept or skill and providing demonstrations and examples. If the material is a new concept, it is important that the teacher discuss the characteristics (or *attributes*) of the concept, the rule or definition, and several examples. If the material is a new skill, it is important to identify the steps of the skill with examples of each step. (Another common mistake is to provide too few demonstrations.) In either case, it is helpful to convey this information both orally and visually so that students will have the visual representation as a reference in the early stages of learning. Another task is to check to see that students have understood the new information before they apply it in the practice phases. Can they recall the attributes of the concept that the teacher has explained? Can they recall the number and list of steps in the skill they have just been shown? Checking for understanding requires that students recall or recognize the information that they have just heard. In structured practice, they will apply it.

Phase three, structured practice, comes next. The teacher leads students through practice examples, working through each step. Usually the students practice as a group, offering to write answers. A good way to accomplish the lockstep technique is to use an overhead projector, doing practice examples on a transparency so that all students can see the generation of each step. The teacher's role in this phase is to give feedback on the students' responses, to reinforce accurate responses, and to correct errors and point out the objective. By referring to it while working the practice examples, the teacher is ensuring that students understand it so that they can use it as a resource during their semi-independent practice phase.

Phase four, guided practice, gives students the opportunity to practice on their own with support. Guided practice enables the teacher to make an assessment of the students' abilities to perform the learning task by assessing the amount and types of errors the students are making. The teacher's role in this phase is to monitor students' work, providing corrective feedback when necessary.

In phase five, we reach independent practice. It begins when students have achieved an accuracy level of 85 to 90 percent in guided practice. The purpose of independent practice is to reinforce the new learning to ensure retention as well as to develop fluency. In independent practice, students practice on their own without assistance and with delayed feedback. The independent practice work is reviewed soon after completion to assess whether the students' accuracy level has remained stable and to provide corrective feedback for those who need it. An independent-practice activity can be short in length of time and number of practice items; however, it should not be a one-time venture. As described earlier, five or six practice sessions distributed over a month or more will sustain retention.

SOCIAL SYSTEM

The social system is highly structured.

PRINCIPLES OF REACTION

The principles of reaction are governed by the need to provide knowledge of results, help students pace themselves, and offer reinforcement. The support system includes sequenced learning tasks, sometimes as elaborate as the sets developed by the individually prescribed instruction team.

APPLICATION ———————————————————

The most common applications are in the study of basic information and skills in the core curriculum areas. A number of large-scale programs built

FIGURE 15.1   Instructional and nurturant effects of the direct
instruction model.

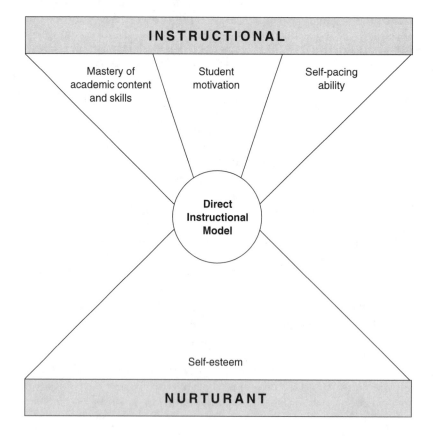

around direct instruction have been directed at economically poor, low-achieving children. In the evaluation of Project Follow Through, a federal program that extended Head Start into the elementary grades, the University of Oregon's direct instruction model produced more significant differences on both cognitive and affective measures than any of the other eight major programs (Becker, 1977). Overall, the students in this program went from being well below the 25th percentile nationally in reading, math, and spelling before starting the program, to being in the 50th percentile or above by the third grade. The program emphasizes "small-group, face to face instruction by a teacher using carefully sequenced, daily lessons in reading, arithmetic and language" (Becker, Engelmann, Carnine, and Rhine, 1981). "A positive self-concept was viewed as a by-product of good teaching rather than as a goal to be achieved in the abstract" (Becker, 1977, pp. 921–922).

INSTRUCTIONAL AND NURTURANT EFFECTS

The model is, as the name applies, "direct." It approaches academic content systematically. Its design is shaped to generate and sustain motivation through pacing and reinforcement. Through success and positive feedback, it tries to enhance self-esteem (see Figure 15.1).

SUMMARY CHART ► **DIRECT INSTRUCTION MODEL**

Phase One: Orientation
  Teacher establishes content of the lesson.
  Teacher reviews previous learning.
  Teacher establishes lesson objectives.
  Teacher establishes the procedures for the lesson.

Phase Two: Presentation
  Teacher explains/demonstrates new concepts or skill.
  Teacher provides visual representation of the task.
  Teacher checks for understanding.

Phase Three: Structured Practice
  Teacher leads group through practice examples in lock step.
  Students respond to questions.
  Teacher provides corrective feedback for errors and reinforces correct practice.

Phase Four: Guided Practice
  Students practice semi-independently.
  Teacher circulates, monitoring student practice.
  Teacher provides feedback through praise, prompt, and leave.

Phase Five: Independent Practice
    Students practice independently at home or in class.
    Feedback is delayed.
    Independent practices occur several times over an extended period.

CHAPTER 16

LEARNING FROM SIMULATIONS
Training and Self-Training

This is a lot better than turning a real chopper upside down.
—Army instructor to Bruce Joyce, June 1953

SCENARIO

Walter Hrycauk is leading his ninth-grade students to find space travel simulations that may be available on the Web. What they find amazes them (and him, for that matter). They begin with NASA and a remarkable array of options appear. Potentially, they can simulate space shuttle trips and other voyages, make world-wide weather forecasts, and visit several dozen websites that are filled with information. There is a National Association of Space Simulating Educators. And Canada continues its efforts that began with Operation Moonshot, a grand simulation that dealt with interpersonal relations and culture as well as space exploration.

Walter and his students find that deciding how to begin is their first complicated problem, and they realize also how much they will have to learn. Walter decides that their study of physics, weather, and the nature of inquiry will be built around the simulators that are available. (Walter suggests that good places for any of us to begin are the Rice University site, which is affiliated with NASA [http://www.rice.edu/armadillo/Simulations/simserver.html], and the Discovery Channel School.)

SCENARIO

Driver education students in a secondary school in Chicago are taking turns driving a simulated car. As the motion picture camera projects an image of the roadway ahead, obstacles appear. A child steps out from behind two parked cars; the "driver" turns the wheel and misses the child. A stop sign appears suddenly beyond a parked truck; the driver slams on the brakes. The driver makes a turn and a roadway narrows suddenly; again the driver brakes. One by one the students experience driving under simulated conditions. As students complete the "course," the instructor and the other students debrief them, questioning their reactions and their defensive driving.

In another classroom, this time in the suburbs of Boston, a class is watching a television show. The actors are portraying the members of the U.S. cabinet facing a crisis. After examining the issues, the class reaches a conclusion. One student reaches for the telephone in the classroom, dials a number, and speaks to the actors in the studio, suggesting how they might play their roles differently to resolve the crisis. Twenty-five other classrooms are simultaneously debating the issues seen on television and they, too, are communicating their views to the actors in the studio. The next day the show resumes. In various ways, the actors play out the suggestions made by the classes. The other members of the cabinet react. Students in the 25 classrooms not only see their ideas brought to life on the television screen, but also see the consequences of their recommendations.

In an inner-city neighborhood in Toronto, an elementary school is also watching a television screen. The announcer portrays a countdown as a rocket attempts to break free from the gravity of the moon but fails to do so. Class members then take the role of members of the spaceship crew. Instructions from the Royal Canadian Space Administration divide them into teams, and they prepare to work together to conserve their life support systems and to manage their relationships in the rocketship until repairs can be made (this is the venerable Operation Moonshot).

In San Antonio, two groups of children enter a room. One group represents the Alpha culture, the other the Beta culture. Their task is to learn how to communicate with others who have learned rules and patterns of behavior from a different society. Gradually, they learn to master communication patterns. Simultaneously, they become aware that, as members of a culture, they have inherited powerful patterns that strongly influence their personalities and ways of communicating with other people.

In Philadelphia, a class is engaged in a caribou hunt. As they progress through the hunt, which the Netsilik Eskimos operate, they learn behavior patterns of the Netsilik and begin to compare those patterns with the ones they carry on in their everyday lives.

In a San Francisco suburb, a group of students faces a problem posed by the secretary of state. Agronomists have developed a nutrient that, when added to the food of beef cattle, greatly increases their weight. Only a limited amount of this nutrient is available, and the students must determine how the nutrient will be divided among the needy nations of the world. Congress has imposed the following restraints: the recipient nations must have a reasonable supply of beef cattle, must not be aligned with the hard core Communist bloc of nations, must not be vegetarians, and must have a population that exceeds a certain size. The students debate the alternatives.

Some countries are ruled out immediately. Of the remaining countries, some seem attractive at first, yet less attractive later. The students grapple with the problems of humanity and ideology and with practical situations. In simulation they face the problems of the committees of scientists who continually advise the U.S. government on various courses of action.

In the quiet of our homes, Carmen Sandiego's gang of thieves takes our children to explore the world and the SIM series has them building neighborhoods and habitats.

These students are all involved in simulations, playing the roles of persons engaged in real-life pursuits. Elements of the real world are simplified and presented in a form that can be contained inside the classroom. The attempt is to approximate realistic conditions as much as possible so that the concepts learned and solutions generated are transferrable to the real world.

To progress through the tasks of the simulation, students must develop concepts and skills necessary for performance in the specified area. The young drivers have to develop concepts and skills for driving effectively. The young caribou hunters have to learn concepts about a certain culture. The young members of the cabinet need to learn about international relations and the problems of governing a major nation.

In simulations, students learn from the consequences of their actions. The driver who does not turn rapidly enough "hits" the child he or she is trying to avoid; he or she must learn to turn more quickly. Yet if the car turns too quickly, it goes out of control and veers to the other side of the street. The driver has to learn to correct the initial move while keeping his or her eyes on the road and looking for yet other obstacles. The students who do poorly in the caribou hunt learn what happens if the culture does not function efficiently, or if its members shrink from carrying out the procedures that enable it to survive.

In this chapter we explore the principles of simulation and discuss examples of various kinds: some games, some not, some competitive, some cooperative, and some are played by individuals against their own standard. Competition is important in the familiar board game, Monopoly. Monopoly simulates the activity of real estate speculators and incorporates many elements of real-life speculation. The winning player learns the "rules" of investment and speculation as embodied in the game. In simulations such as the Life Career game, players attempt to reach their goals in a noncompetitive way. No score is kept, but interactions are recorded and analyzed later. In the Life Career game the students play out the life cycle of a human being: they select mates, choose careers, decide whether to obtain various amounts of education, and learn, through the consequences of their decisions, how these choices can affect their real lives. In the familiar computer simulations like SimCity and SimEarth, students can play alone or together against their own standard for creating a good quality of life.

Nearly all simulations depend on *software*—that is, the game has paraphernalia of various kinds. The simulation model depends on the teacher's blending the already-prepared simulation into the curriculum, highlighting and reinforcing the learning inherent in the game. The teacher's ability to make the activities truly meaningful is critical. That said, however, the self-instructional property of simulations is vital.

ORIENTATION TO THE MODEL

CYBERNETIC PRINCIPLES

Simulations have been used increasingly in education over the last 30 years, but the simulation model did not originate within the field of education. Rather, it is an application of the principles of *cybernetics*, a branch of psychology. Cybernetic psychologists, making an analogy between humans and machines, conceptualize the learner as a self-regulating feedback system. As a discipline, cybernetics "has been described as the comparative study of the human (or biological) control mechanism, and electromechanical systems such as computers" (Smith and Smith, 1966, p. 202). The central focus is the apparent similarity between the feedback control mechanisms of electromechanical systems and human systems: "A feedback control system incorporates three primary functions: it generates movement of the system toward a target or defined path; it compares the effects of this action with the true path and detects error; and it utilizes this error signal to redirect the system (Smith and Smith, 1966, p. 203).

For example, the automatic pilot of a boat continually corrects the helm of the ship, depending on the readings of the compass. When the ship begins to swing in a certain direction and the compass moves off the desired heading more than a certain amount, a motor is switched on and the helm is moved over. When the ship returns to its course, the helm is straightened out again, and the ship continues on its way. The automatic pilot operates in essentially the same way as does a human pilot. Both watch the compass, and both move the wheel to the left or right, depending on what is going on. Both initiate action in terms of a specified goal ("Let's go north"), and depending on the feedback or error signal, both redirect the initial action. Very complex self-regulating mechanical systems have been developed to control devices such as guided missiles, ocean liners, and satellites.

The cybernetic psychologist interprets the human being as a control system that generates a course of action and then redirects or corrects the action by means of feedback. This can be a very complicated process—as when the secretary of state reevaluates foreign policy—or a very simple one—as when we notice that our sailboat is heading into the wind too much and we ease off on our course just a little. In using the analogy of mechanical systems as a frame of reference for analyzing human beings, psychologists came up with the central idea "that performance and learning must be analyzed in terms of the control relationships between a human operator and an instrumental situation." That is, learning was understood to be determined by the nature of the individual, as well as by the design of the learning situation (Smith and Smith, 1966, p. vii).

From this stance, human behavior involves a perceptible pattern of motion. This includes both covert behavior, such as thinking and symbolic behavior, and overt behavior. In any given situation, individuals modify their behavior according to the feedback they receive from the environment. They organize their movements and their response patterns in relation to this feedback. Thus, their own sensorimotor capabilities form the basis of their feedback systems. This ability to receive feedback constitutes the human system's mechanism for receiving and sending information. As human beings develop greater linguistic capability, they are able to use indirect as well as direct feedback, thereby expanding their control over the physical and social environment. That is, they are less dependent on the concrete realities of the environment because they can use its symbolic representations. The essence, then, of cybernetic psychology is the principle of sense-oriented feedback that is intrinsic to the individual (one "feels" the effects of one's decisions) and is the basis for self-corrective choices. Individuals can "feel" the effects of their decisions because the environment responds *in full*, rather than simply "You're right" or "Wrong! Try again." That is, the environmental consequences of their choices are played back to them. *Learning* in cybernetic terms is sensorially experiencing the environmental consequences of one's behavior and engaging in self-corrective behavior. *Instruction* in cybernetic terms is designed to create an environment for the learner in which this full feedback takes place.

SIMULATORS AND SIMULATIONS

The application of cybernetic principles to educational procedures is seen most dramatically and clearly in the development of *simulators*. A simulator is a training device that closely represents reality but in which the complexity of events can be controlled. For example, a simulated automobile has been constructed in which the driver sees a road (by means of a motion picture), has a wheel to turn, a clutch and a brake to operate, a gearshift, and all the other devices of a contemporary automobile. The driver can start this simulated automobile, and by turning the key can hear the noise of a motor running. When the driver presses the accelerator the noise increases in volume, so the driver has the sensation of having actually increased the flow of gas to a real engine. As the person drives, the film shows curves in the road; in turning the wheel, the driver may experience the illusion that the automobile is turning. The simulator can present the student with learning tasks to which he or she can respond, but the responses do not have the same consequences that they would have in a real-life situation—the simulated automobile doesn't crash into anything, although it may look like it is crashing from the driver's point of view. And in the manner of training psychology, the tasks presented can be made less complex than those a driver would have to execute in the real world; this way, it is easier for the student to acquire the skills that would be needed later for actual driving. For instance, in a driving simulator the student can simply practice shifting from one gear to another until he or she has mastered the task. The student can also practice applying the brakes and turning the wheel, thus developing a feel for how the automobile responds when those things are done.

A simulator has several advantages. As we noted earlier, the learning tasks can be made much less complex than they are in the real world, so that the students may have the opportunity to master skills that would be extremely difficult when all the factors of real-world operations impinge on them. For example, learning how to fly a complex airplane without the aid of a simulator leaves little room for error. The student pilot has to do everything adequately the first time, or the plane is in difficulty. With the use of a simulator, the training can be staged. The trainee can be introduced to simple tasks and then more complex ones until he or she builds a repertoire of skills adequate for piloting the plane. In addition, difficulties such as storms and mechanical problems can be simulated, and the student can learn how to cope with them. Thus, by the time the student actually begins flying, a repertoire of necessary skills is available.

A second advantage of simulators is that they permit students to learn from self-generated feedback. As the student pilot turns the wheel of the great plane to the right, for example, he or she can feel the plane bank and feel the loss of speed in some respects and can learn how to trim the craft during the turn. In other words, the trainees can learn the necessary corrective behaviors through their own senses, rather than simply through verbal descriptions. In the driving simulation, if the driver heads into curves too rapidly and then has to jerk the wheel to avoid going off the road, this feedback teaches the driver to turn more gingerly when approaching sharp curves on a real road. The cybernetic psychologist designs simulators so that the feedback about the consequences of behavior enables the learners to modify their responses and develop a repertoire of appropriate behaviors.

An old simulation that we are very fond of illustrates what the model can bring to an academic course. Harold Guetzkow and his associates (1963) developed a complex and interesting simulation for teaching students at the high school and upper elementary levels the principles of international relations. The activity revolves around five "nation" units. In each of these nations, a group of participants acts as decision makers and "aspiring decision makers." The simulated relations among the nations are derived from the characteristics of nations and from principles that have been observed to operate among nations in the past. Each of the decision-making teams has available to it information about the country it represents. This information concerns the basic capability of the national economic systems, the consumer capability, force capability (the ability of the nation to develop military goods and services), and trade and aid information. Together, the nations play an international relations game that involves trading and the development of various agreements. International organizations can be established, for example, or mutual-aid or trade agreements made. The nations can even make war on one another, the outcome being determined by the force capability of one group of allies relative to that of another group.

As students play the roles of national decision makers, they must make realistic negotiations such as those diplomats and other representatives make as nations interact with one another, and they must refer to the countries' economic conditions as they do so. In the course of this game-type simulation, the students learn ways in which economic restraints operate on a country. For example, if they are members of the decision-making team of a small country and try to engage in a trade agreement, they find that they have to give something to get something. If their country has a largely agricultural economy and they are dealing with an industrialized nation, they find that their country is in a disadvantageous position unless the other nation badly needs the product they have to sell. By receiving feedback about the consequences of their decision, the students come to an understanding of the principles that operate in international relations.

THE TEACHER'S ROLE

It is easy to assume that because the learning activity has been designed and packaged by experts, the teacher has a minimal role to play in the learning situation. People tend to believe that a well-designed game will teach itself. But this is only partly true. Cybernetic psychologists find that educational simulations enable students to learn firsthand from the simulated experiences built into the game rather than from teachers' explanations or lectures. However, because of their intense involvement, students may not always be aware of what they are learning and experiencing. Thus, the teacher has an important role to play in raising students' consciousness about the concepts and principles underpinning the simulations and their own reactions. In addition, the teacher has important managerial functions. With more complex games and issues, the teacher's activities are even more critical if learning is to occur. We have identified four roles for the teacher in the simulation model: *explaining, refereeing, coaching,* and *discussing.*

EXPLAINING

To learn from a simulation, the players need to understand the rules sufficiently to carry out most of the activities. However, it is *not* essential that the students have a complete understanding of the simulation at the start. As in real life, many of the rules become relevant only as the activities proceed.

REFEREEING

Simulations used in the classroom are designed to provide educational benefits. The teacher should control student participation in the game to ensure that these benefits are realized. Before the game is played, the teacher must assign students to teams (if the game involves teamwork), matching individual capabilities with the roles in the simulation to assure active participation by all students. Shy and assertive students, for example, should be mixed on teams. One pitfall the teacher should avoid is assigning the apparently more "difficult" roles to brighter students and the more passive roles to less academically talented students.

The teacher should recognize in advance that simulations are active learning situations and thus call for more freedom of movement and more talk among students than do other classroom activities. The teacher should act as a referee who sees that the rules are followed but who does his or her best not to interfere in the game activities.

COACHING

The teacher should act as coach when necessary, giving players advice that enables them to play better—that is, to exploit the possibilities of the simulation more fully. As a coach, the teacher should be a supportive advisor, not a preacher or a disciplinarian. In a simulation, players have the opportunity to make mistakes and take consequences—and learn.

DISCUSSING

After a session there needs to be a discussion about how closely the game simulates the real world, what difficulties and insights the students had, and what relationships can be discovered between the simulation and the subject matter being explored.

THE MODEL OF TEACHING

SYNTAX

The simulation model has four phases: orientation, participant training, the simulation itself, and debriefing (see Table 16.1). In the orientation (phase one), the teacher presents the topic to be explored, the concepts embedded in the actual simulation, an explanation of simulation if this is the students' first experience with it, and an overview of the game itself. This first part should not be lengthy but can be an important context for the remainder of the learning activity.

In phase two the students begin to get into the simulation. At this point the teacher sets the scenario by introducing the students to the rules, roles, procedures, scoring, types of decisions to be made, and goals of the simulation. He or she organizes the students into the various roles and conducts

TABLE 16.1 **SYNTAX OF SIMULATION MODEL**

Phase One: Orientation	Phase Two: Participant Training
Present the broad topic of the simulation and the concepts to be incorporated into the simulation activity at hand. Explain simulation and gaming. Give overview of the simulation.	Set up the scenario (rules, roles, procedures, scoring, types of decisions to be made, goals). Assign roles. Hold abbreviated practice session.

Phase Three: Simulation Operations	Phase Four: Participant Debriefing (Any or All of the Following Activities)
Conduct game activity and game administration. Obtain feedback and evaluation (of performance and effects of decisions). Clarify misconceptions. Continue simulation.	Summarize events and perceptions. Summarize difficulties and insights. Analyze process. Compare simulation activity to the real world. Relate simulation activity to course content. Appraise and redesign the simulation.

an abbreviated practice session to ensure that students have understood all the directions and can carry out their roles.

Phase three is the participation in the simulation. The students participate in the game or simulation, and the teacher functions in his or her role as referee and coach. Periodically the game simulation may be stopped so that the students receive feedback, evaluate their performances and decisions, and clarify any misconceptions.

Finally, phase four consists of participant debriefing. Depending on the outcomes, the teacher may help the students focus on: (1) describing the events and their other perceptions and reactions, (2) analyzing the process, (3) comparing the simulation to the real world, (4) relating the activity to course content, and (5) appraising and redesigning the simulation.

SOCIAL SYSTEM

Because the teacher selects the simulation activity and directs the student through carefully delineated activities, the social system of simulation is rigorous. Within this structured system, however, a cooperative interactive environment can, and ideally should, flourish. The ultimate success of the simulation, in fact, depends partly on the cooperation and willing participation of the students. Working together, the students share ideas, which are subject to peer evaluation but not teacher evaluation. The peer social system, then, should be nonthreatening and marked by cooperation.

PRINCIPLES OF REACTION

The reactions of the teacher are primarily those of a facilitator. Throughout the simulation he or she must maintain a nonevaluative but supportive attitude. It is the teacher's task to first present and then facilitate understanding and interpretation of the rules of the simulation activity. In addition, should interest in the activity begin to dissipate or attention begin to focus on irrelevant issues, the teacher must direct the group to "get on with the game."

SUPPORT SYSTEM

Sources are many. For an example, the *Social Science Education Consortium Data Book* lists more than 50 simulations available for use in social studies alone. Simulations are regularly reviewed in *Social Education*. A vast number of computer simulations have been developed in recent years and are easily available.

APPLICATION

Simulations can stimulate learning about: (1) competition, (2) cooperation, (3) empathy, (4) the social system, (5) concepts, (6) skills, (7) efficacy, (8) paying the penalty, (9) the role of chance, and (10) the ability to think critically (examining alternative strategies and anticipating those of others) and make decisions (Nesbitt, 1971, pp. 35–53).

INSTRUCTIONAL AND NURTURANT EFFECTS

The simulation model, through the actual activity and through discussions afterward, nurtures and instructs a variety of educational outcomes, including concepts and skills; cooperation and competition; critical thinking and decision-making; empathy; knowledge of political, social, and economic systems; sense of effectiveness; awareness of the role of chance; and facing consequences (see Figure 16.1).

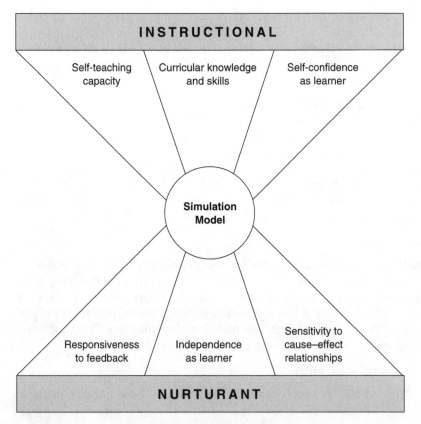

FIGURE 16.1   Instructional and nurturant effects of the simulation model.

SUMMARY
CHART ▶ **SIMULATION MODEL**

Syntax

Phase One: Orientation
   Present the broad topic of the simulation and the concepts to be incorporated into the simulation activity at hand.
   Explain simulation and gaming.
   Provide overview of the simulation.

Phase Two: Participant Training
   Set up the scenario (rules, roles, procedures, scoring, types of decisions to be made, goals).
   Assign roles.
   Hold abbreviated practice session.

Phase Three: Simulation Operations
   Conduct activity.
   Feedback and evaluation (of performance and effects of decisions).
   Clarify misconceptions.
   Continue simulation.

Phase Four: Participant Debriefing
   (Any or all of the following activities:)
   Summarize events and perceptions.
   Summarize difficulties and insights.
   Analyze process.
   Compare simulation activity to the real world.
   Relate simulation activity to course content.
   Appraise and redesign the simulation.

Social System

The social system is structured by the teacher through selecting materials and directing the simulation. The interactive environment of the class, however, should be nonthreatening and marked by cooperation. The teacher has the role of managing the simulation (taking care of organization and logistics), explaining the game, maintaining the rules, coaching (offering advice, prompting), and conducting the debriefing discussion.

Principles of Reaction

A generally supportive role, observing and helping the students cope with problems as they arise.

Support System

Simulation requires a carefully structured base of resource materials, as discussed above.

PART VI

INDIVIDUAL DIFFERENCES, DIVERSITY, AND CURRICULUM

A number of years ago, one of the major U.S. automobile manufacturers announced that its design would take into account the physical dimensions of Americans instead of just building a car and letting people accommodate to it. The company developed a prototype based on statistics about size, including lengths of arms and legs. Unfortunately, they used only averages when they built their dummies. There was no accommodation to variance—to individual differences. Worse, they used averages for males. The consequence was a cockpit in which some people could barely see over the steering wheel, some had to stretch to reach the pedals, and some had to drive with their heads bent forward or sideways and their knees brushing the wheel.

Schooling has a similar problem. Curriculum development involves the formulation of common education—our best judgment about what all students should know and be able to do. However, students are not identical, thank goodness—it is not like we create a curriculum to be experienced by a prototype average student.

In Part VI we open up a set of inquiries into common education and individual differences.

Chapter 17 lays out a general stance toward individual differences. Then we explore gender, ethnicity, and socioeconomic background as variables, including how equity and inequity occur. Literacy is next—we discuss two studies in which multiple model curriculums effectively attacked the problem of the older, struggling reader and the teaching of reading in kindergarten and the other primary grades. We then move to the development of curriculums using the framework created by Robert Gagne.

We close with a brief survey of research on the families of models of teaching—an opening to further inquiries.

CHAPTER 17

LEARNING STYLES AND MODELS OF TEACHING
Making Discomfort Productive

If we get too comfortable, we stop growing. Students can put pressure on us to work within their comfort zone. Let's be kind about that. Kind enough to help them learn to be uncomfortable.
—Herb Thelen to Bruce Joyce, Fall 1963

In this chapter we deal explicitly with the relations between styles of learning and models of teaching. We present a general stance toward individual differences and how to teach students to learn productively from a variety of models.

Learning styles are important because they are the education-relevant expressions of the uniqueness of the individual. Individual differences are to be prized because they are the expression of the uniqueness of personalities. Individually, our configurations give us our personal identities; together, they also exemplify the richness of our culture.

We hope to provide our children with a common education that enhances their individuality and encourages their personalities and simultaneously passes along our culture and its tools. As teachers we need to use our teaching repertoires in such a way that we capitalize on the characteristics of our students to help them achieve increasing control over their own growth.

With respect to models of teaching, we can begin by avoiding two mistakes. The first is to assume that a model of teaching is a fixed, inflexible formula for teaching, which should be employed rigidly for best results. The second is to assume that each learner has a fixed style of learning that is unlikely to change or grow. Both mistakes lead us into an impossible dilemma, for if unyielding teaching methods are mismatched with rigid learners, a destructive collision is inevitable. Fortunately, teaching methods have great flexibility, and students have great learning capacities and, hence, adaptability.

Consider the nature of the models of teaching we have been discussing. By its very nature, the personal family begins with the uniqueness of the learner, and each personal model tries to help the students take charge of their own growth. The social models depend on the synergy caused by the interaction of heterogeneous minds and personalities. The group investigation model explicitly generates the energy for learning from different perceptions of academic and social problems. The behavioral models build into instructional sequences the ability to adjust pace and complexity of tasks to the ability and prior achievement of the student. The information-processing models provide ways of adjusting instruction to cognitive development and style.

Then—perhaps most important to this discussion—we not only employ a model to teach information, concepts, skills, the analysis of values, and other content objectives, but we also teach the students to use the strategies of each model to educate themselves. In the previous chapters we have cast each model as a way of teaching students to learn particular ways of thinking. From that perspective, each model of teaching can be seen as a model of learning—a way of helping students expand their styles of approaching problems now and in their futures.

Yet, as we expose students to content and learning styles that are new to them, we will inevitably cause varying degrees of discomfort. We have to deal with this by teaching our students to manage discomfort productively. The dilemma we have to solve is that real growth often requires us to make our learners uncomfortable, and we have to help them deal with the unfamiliar situations that we must create for them.

DISCOMFORT AND LEARNING

I would like to begin on a personal note (*I* refers to Bruce Joyce, who wrote this section) that explains why discomfort is so prominent in this discussion of learning styles and educational environments. At the University of Chicago, 30 years ago, I ended a conversation with Herbert Thelen by borrowing a copy of his *Education and the Human Quest* (1960); I spent much of the night reading the book. The next day we had a chance to talk again. Among the powerful ideas Thelen had generated, one left me most stimulated and uncomfortable: significant learning is frequently accompanied or impelled by discomfort. Sometimes he put it pungently: "The learner does not learn unless he does not know how to respond" (Thelen, 1960, p. 61). Sometimes he put it in terms of the dynamics of the inquiry process in the approach to teaching he called *group investigation*. Group investigation begins with a "stimulus situation to which students . . . can react and discover basic conflicts among their attitudes, ideas, and modes of perception" (p. 8).

Thelen challenges the effects of the "norms of comfort and accommodation" (p. 80) that exist in so many classrooms and that mitigate against the argumentation and difficult, uncomfortable tasks that characterize effective instruction as he sees it.

My first reaction was confusion. Thelen's ideas appeared to conflict with what I had been taught regarding learners as fragile egos that had to be protected by a supportive environment, so that they would in fact feel *comfortable* enough to stretch out into the world. How can the learner be made comfortable and uncomfortable at the same time? I asked Thelen that question, and he only smiled and replied, "That is a puzzling situation you will have to think about."

Psychologists from otherwise different orientations have dealt with the concept of discomfort for some time, albeit not always using the term as such. Personalistic psychologists are an example. Interpreters of Carl Rogers frequently concentrate on his argument for providing a safe place for learners to explore themselves and their environments. However, Rogers (1956) also emphasizes that our natural tendency as learners is to confine ourselves to domains in which we already feel safe. A major task of counselor/teachers is to help the learner reach into those domains that are shrouded in fear. To grow, learners have to acknowledge discomfort and set tasks to help break the barriers of fear. The educator's task is not simply to unloose the environmental bonds that constrict the learners but to help them become active seekers after new development.

Self-actualization, as described by Maslow (1962), is a state that not only enables people to venture and take risks, but also to endure the inevitable discomfort felt when attempting to use unfamiliar skills. Maslow's constructs apply to adults as well as children. In a four-year study of teachers exposed to a wide variety of staff development activities, it appeared that the teachers' self-concepts were important predictors of their abilities to use new skills and knowledge in their classroom situations (McKibbin and Joyce, 1980), and we have learned that a major part of successful staff development is helping people deal productively with the discomfort attendant to working their way to new levels of competence.

The role of discomfort and the ability to manage it productively appears in a different guise when we consider developmental stage theories (see Erikson, 1950; Harvey, Hunt, and Schroeder, 1961; Piaget, 1952). Most developmental stage theories emphasize not only the naturalness of growth through the stages, but the possibility of arrestation, and the accommodation that is necessary if higher levels of development are to be reached. Consider Piaget: Interpreters of Piaget are often most impressed by the naturalness of growth described from his stance—the position that the assimilation of new information will inevitably force the accommodations that lead to the successive stages of development. However, not everyone makes it upward through the Piagetian stages. Arrestation is possible. Accommodation sufficient to bring about the reconfiguration necessary to a new stage requires a "letting go" of the confines of one level so that the essentials of the next level can be reached. If the comfort of any given level of development is not challenged, the learner may happily forgo the important leaps in cognitive structure.

In conceptual systems theory, Hunt (1971) stresses the relationship of the environment to development. He describes stages of development and the characteristics of environments that permit people to function effectively at each stage while progression to the next stage is facilitated. The next chapter presents synopses of the stages and environments that facilitate progression.

If the environment is perfectly matched to the developmental level of the learners, they may be arrested at that level. The very language that Hunt and his colleagues use is provocative. If the environment is too comfortable or "reliable," the learners may be satisfied at the stage of concrete thinking, where the ability to integrate new information and form new conceptual systems is limited indeed. To impel learners to diverge from the familiar sets of concepts that enable them to view the world in "black and white," the environment must be dissatisfying in some ways. Although he approaches development from a very different perspective from Thelen, Hunt (1971) states explicitly that discomfort is a precursor to growth. To stimulate development, we *deliberately* mismatch student and environment so that the student cannot easily maintain the familiar patterns but must move on toward greater complexity. (But not too much so, for we seek an optimal mismatch where the learner's conceptual systems are challenged but not overwhelmed.)

Research on teacher training has repeatedly uncovered a "discomfort factor" as teachers acquire new repertoires. Between 1968 and 1983 a series of investigations inquired into teachers' abilities to acquire the skills necessary to enable them to use widespread repertoires of teaching strategies (Joyce, Peck, and Brown, 1981; Joyce and Showers, 2002). Teachers could acquire skill by studying the theories of various models of teaching or skills, seeing them demonstrated a number of times (15 or 20, the researchers came to believe), and practicing them about a dozen times with carefully articulated feedback. However, as teachers attempted to use approaches new to them they experienced considerable discomfort. Only a small percentage (about 5 or 10 percent) of the teachers who had learned teaching strategies new to their repertoires were able to handle the discomfort without assistance. Most teachers never tried an unfamiliar strategy at all unless support personnel were available to them. Even then, during the first half dozen trials, most teachers found the use of the new teaching strategies, whatever they were, to be extremely uncomfortable. The explanation was that the discomfort resulted in part because the teachers needed to adapt other, well-ingrained skills in order to use the new strategies; in part because students exposed to the new strategies needed to learn complementary skills so they could relate to them; and in part because the teachers felt less confident with any new strategy than they felt with their older repertoires.

The result was that many teachers would have withdrawn from the use of strategies new to them, even after their training had enabled them to produce these strategies with relative ease. However, after a number of trials with the new strategies, they became more comfortable with and developed power in their use. A major function of peer study groups is to provide the support necessary to work through the period of discomfort. Conceptual level (CL) is a predictor of the ability to acquire new repertoires. The higher-CL teachers mastered sets of new models more fully and also tended to use them more (Joyce, Weil, and Wald, 1981). The relationship between conceptual level and the ability to learn new teaching strategies is partly related to how one manages feelings of discomfort attendant to learning the new repertoire. The more conceptually flexible teachers managed the process of discomfort more effectively. They incorporated the new information from their students, accommodated the discomfort of their students, and—most important—learned how to live through their periods of learning until the new teaching strategies worked in their classrooms.

It also became apparent that a critical part of a teacher's task in learning to use a new teaching strategy has to do with helping the learners acquire the skills necessary to relate to the new approach to teaching. Hunt and his associates initiated a series of studies to investigate the process by which learners respond to unfamiliar teaching strategies (Hunt et al., 1981). These researchers identified students of varying conceptual levels and exposed them to teaching strategies that were matched and mismatched to their levels of development. Nearly all learners were able to respond to a wide variety of teaching strategies, but there were considerable individual differences in their responses. Students with a high need for structure (low CL) were more uncomfortable with teaching strategies that provided low degrees of structure, whereas learners who preferred independent direction were more uncomfortable with teaching strategies that provided higher structure.

Moreover, the students "pulled" the behavior of the teachers toward their preferred styles. Those who required the higher degrees of structure "asked" for that structure, and the teachers responded by adapting the strategies to conform to the personalities of the students. Curiously, the more a given model of teaching was mismatched with the natural learning style of the student, the more it presented a challenge to the student to take an affirmative stance so as to pass through the period of discomfort and develop skills that would permit a productive relationship with the learning environment.

For example, gregarious students are initially the most comfortable with social models and can profit from them quickly. However, the less-gregarious students are in the greatest need of the models least comfortable for them. Hence, the challenge is not to select the most comfortable models but to enable the students to develop the skills to relate to a wider variety of models, many of which appear, at least superficially, to be mismatched with their learning styles.

The formulation gradually developed that significant growth requires discomfort. If the environment and the student are too much in harmony, the student is permitted to operate at a level of comfort that does not require the challenge of growth. To help students grow, we need to generate what we currently term a *dynamic disequilibrium*. Rather than matching teaching approaches to students in such a way as to minimize discomfort, our task is to expose the students to new teaching modalities that will, for some time, be uncomfortable to them.

MARGINALITY IN LEARNERS

Most of the literature on learners and educational environments emphasizes explicit matching, the adjustment of environments to the optimal "comfort level" of the students. The comfort-level matching concept appears frequently in most discussions of learning styles (hemispheric dominance, sensing modalities, cognitive levels, and so on). To consider the productive possibilities of discomfort, let us now discuss the "marginal" learners—students who experience great discomfort in the environments in which they find themselves. Currently many educators are concerned with what are called "marginal" learners and are seeking ways to make the school environment more productive for the people who are regarded as marginal in the environment. (This is often discussed under the concept of "diversity," where students who do not fit in an idea of an ideal mainstream are regarded as difficult to reach.) If we consider the concept of marginality, we can join the issues of discomfort and growth directly. When learners relate only marginally to educational environments, we tend to change the environments and reestablish the "norms of comfort." In fact, the discomfort they feel may be a clue to how we should behave to help them reach new plateaus of growth.

Marginality is a condition that exists when a learner has difficulty relating to an educational environment and profiting from it. Learners may relate marginally to some environments but not others. The theoretically possible range of marginality is from *none* (when learners relate productively to all the environments to which they are exposed) to *all* (when learners experience virtually no environments that are productive for them). Educators create environments, but they clearly cannot do the learning—which is why the condition of the learner accounts for so much of the variance when we consider the productivity of any given environment. If the learner is marginal with respect to a particular environment, educational productivity for that learner is likely to be depressed; worse, if the marginality is acute, serious side effects are likely to occur. The learner becomes frustrated and, very likely, "learns" that he or she cannot be productive in that environment. If the learner generalizes from enough frustrating experiences, a likely derivative lesson may be that the process of education is hopeless (from the perspective of that particular person).

ASSUMPTIONS ABOUT LEARNERS

How do we think about our students? We think about them from a variety of perspectives, each of which gives us assumptions about what they are like.

ENCULTURATION

The first assumption is that our learner has been enculturated to a certain degree, having been exposed to the behavior patterns, artifacts, and cognitions that make up American culture. The learner may (or may not) have a smaller vocabulary than the average person but does possess a vocabulary, has internalized the basic linguistic properties of our language, has been a participant in the cultural process, and has been an observer of adults as they behave in our society. In other words, our learner is not culturally different from the rest of us, although, within the cultural boundaries, the learner may be relatively unsophisticated. This may seem like an obvious point, but much language about marginal learners connotes, if it does not actually denote, that the people who relate marginally to the common educational environments are essentially members of a subculture so different from the mainstream that they have to be treated as foreigners. That is rare indeed. Human beings are born with the capacity to learn a culture, and it is the rare person who develops cultural patterns that do not in some way match the major configurations of his or her society.

INTELLECTUAL CAPACITY AS A TEMPORAL FACTOR

Second, the position about intellectual differences articulated by Carroll (1971) and Bloom (1971) has considerable validity. Specifically, this position is that differences in intellectual ability as we currently measure them translate substantially into temporal differences with respect to the mastery of particular learning objectives. This second assumption relates to the first, for one way of restating Carroll and Bloom's position is that the less "intelligent" learner is not culturally different with respect to what can be learned but may require more time, perhaps *considerably* more time, to acquire a particular cognition that resides within the culture. In other words, the learner is one of us. Some of us are slower than others to acquire some of the elements of the culture in given educational situations. We can make the optimistic assumption that our marginal learner is capable of learning but may require more time than some people do, given the situation.

STIGMATIZATION

A third assumption is that the inability to relate to a given educational environment productively has social stigma attached to it. The learner who does not fit in will be socially stigmatized by other people and, probably more damaging, will internalize the norms of the culture; failing to fit in with these norms, the learner will stigmatize himself or herself. Education, as manifested in formal institutions, is largely a public activity, and the full power of the society comes down on the learner when a marginal condition exists—hence, the latent side effects. The marginal learner is punished twice, first by being frustrated and second by being stigmatized by others (or by self-stigmatization).

FLEXIBILITY

A final assumption about learners is that people are flexible. They are not fixed. They are growing entities and have considerable adaptive capabilities. Nearly all learners have the potential to relate to a wide variety of learning environments, provided they are not made *too* uncomfortable and that they are assisted in relating productively to any given environment.

ASSUMPTIONS ABOUT LEARNING ENVIRONMENTS

ENVIRONMENTS AS WITHIN-CULTURE VARIATIONS

Learning environments, viewed from a cultural perspective, are variations on our basic cultural theme. That is, all of the approaches to teaching that have dominated our literature for the last 25 years have had their origins in Western societies. They belong well within the cultural mainstream. Put another way, all our models of teaching represent variety within the culture, but they are not culturally different. They have originated with scholars and teachers who belong not only to the same genus and species but to the same normative configuration. Thus, both teaching models and learners have the same cultural roots.

INDIVIDUATION AND ENVIRONMENTS

Every learning environment produces a range of responses by students, expressed in terms of the efficiency and comfort with which the learners are able to interact with the environment. Loosely speaking, we can say that learning styles and environments designed to produce learning will interact differentially. No given learning environment will produce exactly the same effects on all students.

ENVIRONMENTS CAN BE ADAPTIVE

Learning environments can be adaptive, potentially at least, if we design them with flexibility in mind. An appropriate model of teaching does not simply bore into the learner in an unyielding and unforgiving fashion. Properly constructed, a learning environment fits soft rather than hard metaphors. It curls around the students, conforming to their characteristics just as, properly treated, learners also better fit soft rather than hard metaphors and can curl around the features of the learning environment.

ALTERNATIVE ENVIRONMENTS AND EDUCATIONAL OUTCOMES

Finally, there exist a good number of approaches to teaching (the construction of learning environments) that are likely to produce different effects on learners. Certain approaches to teaching increase the probability that certain kinds of learning outcomes will eventuate and, probably reciprocally, decrease the probability that others will happen. For example, contrast the role-playing model with the inquiry training model. Shaftel's model of role playing (Shaftel and Shaftel, 1967) is designed to enable students' values to become available for examination by those students. Suchman's (1962) model of inquiry training is designed to increase the probability that students will build capability to make causal inferences. As such, all things being equal, if Shaftel's model is used to design a learning environment, it will increase the probability that students' social values will be made available to them. Suchman's model will increase the probability that the students will become more able to reason causally. We are not dealing with an orthogonal world, however. The examination of values *can* improve causal reasoning, and, vigorously conducted, *ought* to do so. Similarly, there is no law that dictates that Suchman's model cannot be used to increase the ability to reason causally about values. At any given moment it is conceivable that Shaftel's model might be more effective in teaching causal reasoning than Suchman's or that Suchman's might be more effective as an approach to social values. Over the long term, however, each model is more likely to pay off in the direction for which it was designed. Thus, it is wise for educators to have in their repertoires the models of choice for given categories of learning objectives.

DEALING WITH MARGINALITY

Returning now to marginal learners, our problem is to consider what to do when a learner has a marginal reaction to any given learning environment. To keep the discussion within boundaries, let us imagine two learners who are exposed to Shaftel's and Suchman's models. Each learner responds positively to one environment and not to the other. What do we do?

In this example, each learner is marginal in one environment but not in the other. We can predict that one will engage in the study of values in a relatively comfortable way and that the other will increase the capability to engage in causal reasoning. If we do nothing, the differences between the two learners will probably increase. One will get better and better at the study of values and the other better and better in reasoning ability.

For the time being, let us put aside the question of explanation—that is, let us not begin by sorting out the reasons *why* each learner responds to one environment and not to the other; instead, let us concentrate on what we can do.

SOLUTIONS FOR CORRECTING MARGINALITY

First, we reject the "do-nothing" approach. We do not want to leave either of our learners in an unproductive, frustrating, and perhaps phobia-producing situation. A second approach is to remove the learner from the offending environment, thus eliminating the frustration. For each learner we identify the models of comfort. For each learner we eliminate the models of discomfort and choose the ones of greatest comfort. On the positive side, enough models of teaching exist that we can be relatively sure that almost any learner can relate productively to some of them. In our example we already have an initial diagnosis.

THE INDUSTRIAL SOLUTION

In what Hunt (1971) calls the *industrial* solution, we search for the approaches to teaching in which our learners are least marginal, and then we employ them. This approach makes a certain amount of pragmatic sense. Its obvious difficulty is that it eliminates for certain learners the instructional models of choice for the achievement of various kinds of objectives. Consider the case of our two learners. Since Shaftel's model is elegantly constructed to promote the study of values, eliminating it for the learner who is marginal in it means that we are going to have to use a model less elegantly appropriate for the study of values. For any given learner that might be only a moderate loss of efficiency, but if we consider large numbers of learners over a long period of time, the industrial solution has a built-in deficit.

However, this is certainly a more efficient solution than ignoring the problem. It also reduces the likelihood that the most damaging side effects of mismatching will occur. The success of the industrial model depends on the assumption that we can find enough industrial models that accommodate both our students and our objectives.

ADAPTATION OF THE MODELS OF CHOICE

Another solution is to adapt the models to conform to the characteristics of the learners. We identify the reasons why a given learner has trouble relating to a particular learning environment and then modulate the features of that environment to make it easier for the learner to fit in. For example, suppose that we are using inquiry training in elementary science. It is possible that our learner who is not comfortable with the model may be reacting to the ambiguity of inductive reasoning. Our learner may like a direct route to the correct answer and may be uncomfortable asking questions that may be wrong and that surely do not provide quick resolution. We could moderate the task complexity of the inquiry training exercises by providing puzzles for which there are plainly only two or three possible avenues of inquiry and to which the learner can bring considerable knowledge.

Our learner who has trouble relating to role playing may be somewhat embarrassed during the enactments of the puzzling situations, may have difficulty taking the role of the "other," or may find the discussion of values to be uncomfortable. To compensate, we can guide the enactments to make them relatively simple and straightforward, or we can provide practice in the skills necessary to analyze values. Hunt (1971) has pointed out that if we "drill" a model "through" the learner we exacerbate our problem. If we take the trouble to find out what is bothering the learner, we have many options for modifying the environment. We can increase the structure of unstructured models, decrease the structure of highly structured ones, modulate the degree of learner control, manipulate task complexity, and in other ways make the learning environment safe for the person who would otherwise be marginal in it.

The merits of this solution are that it permits us to continue to use the "models of choice" for given objectives—that is, the models likely to produce certain kinds of learning—and that it reduces the likelihood that the student will be acutely uncomfortable. It depends on the assumption that the natural mismatch between the learner and the model is not too great to overcome. Because learners are members of the same culture from which the models of teaching came, we can have some confidence that they will bring some developed tools to the environment. Relatively few learners lack the capacity to function within a fairly wide range of models.

Much research is needed in this area. We need to study how to adapt a wide spectrum of models to learners who, on first contact with the models, display varying degrees of marginality. Without such knowledge, we are left with uncertainty about how far we can go. One of the major findings of the match-mismatch studies mentioned earlier was the extent to which the students exerted modifying influences on the environment. Students who needed more structure asked more questions about procedures and literally forced instructors to provide them with more explicit information about what they were doing, even in the open-ended models. They required teachers to interrupt themselves periodically and to reexplain what was going on. They made teachers break up the model into bite-sized chunks that better fit their intellectual mouths. Other learners vied for control of the procedures, lowering the degree of imposed structure and actually increasing the amount of ambiguity in task complexity. I was the teacher in some of these studies, and I came away from that work with the feeling that many learners will help us out if we let them. They would like to have a productive learning environment and will work with us to adapt the environment if we will give them the opportunity.

LEARNER FLEXIBILITY TRAINING

A third solution for correcting marginality is to attempt to teach the learners to relate to a wide spectrum of learning environments. Maintaining our earlier example, we teach one learner the skills necessary to relate to inquiry training. Again, Hunt's (1971) experiments with direct model-relevant skills training have contributed significantly to our knowledge in this area. To provide skill training requires diagnosing what it is about the learner that makes for a marginal relationship to the instructional model. This training is provided to help that learner become more powerful in that kind of environment. Some of the recent studies in teacher training are instructive on this point. The more a model of teaching is different from the developed and customary teaching style of given teachers, the more uncomfortable they are when beginning to use it. Practice with the model combined with model-relevant skill training appears to make a difference. As we coach teachers who are trying to learn a new model, they identify the particular areas where they are having difficulty, and we provide direct training adapted to their particular learning problems (Showers, 1982a).

We need to learn much about helping learners develop environment-relevant skills. It is interesting to observe students in schools that have distinctive approaches to learning and that pay attention to helping their learners become effective in the environments they are creating. Schools that emphasize self-directed activity need to teach students how to engage in self-direction. Learning laboratories with highly sequenced activities need to help students learn to receive diagnoses and prescriptions and relate to those highly sequenced activities. Again, some of my own clinical experience is relevant. When I was the director of the laboratory at Teachers College, Columbia University, we built a set of learning centers that operated on very different models, and the students contracted for activities within those centers. We became convinced that nearly all of our learners were increasing their capabilities to learn in a variety of ways and that they adapted their learning styles to the requirements of the different centers to which they were exposed (Joyce and Morine, 1977).

If we take the skill-training approach seriously, then we devote substantial energy to teaching students to relate to an appropriate variety of learning environments. We help them master the skills of learning that will enable them to master facts, concepts, and skills, and to solve problems collectively. We include the skills of learning as basic skills in the curriculum, and we measure our success as teachers partly by our abilities to help the students become more effective as learners.

From this perspective, we see individual differences in relating to learning environments in a fresh light. When a learner is uncomfortable with a particular learning environment, we know we have identified an objective—to help the learner become competent in relating to that environment. Rather than giving up, we proceed to give that learner protected practice and the special help necessary for a productive relationship to develop between learner and environment. Thus, our learner who has trouble relating to role playing is not viewed as being immutably unable to study values using that technique but as someone who, through practice, can develop competence. We also modify pace, using Carroll's (1971) and Bloom's (1971) formulations as a heuristic. We assume that all learners can become able to profit from a variety of environments but that some need more time than others to become productive in specific environments. One reason learners become marginal is because they are asked to work at a faster pace than will permit them mastery of the environment. Even though most of the applications of mastery learning have been within the basic skill areas of the elementary school, we suggest that the principles would apply to the ability to master all manner of learning objectives. Hence, some learners will be slower profiting from a Rogerian environment. Others will be slower working their way through the models that are appropriate to divergent thinking. Others will be slower attaining concepts with the models appropriate to concept learning.

There are no special models for marginal learners. All learners are part of this culture and practically all can learn to relate to a considerable array of environments, provided that the environments are adapted to the learners' characteristics and that we pay attention to teaching them how to learn more effectively. Experience with persons with very severe sensory handicaps provides us with a case in point. From a models-of-teaching point of view, there are no special models for the blind or the deaf. They can learn to relate to a great variety of environments and, more important, to profit from them. To fail to help them do this productively is to deny them opportunities for growth in many areas. Learning to relate to an increasing variety of environments is, in itself, growth. That kind of growth leads to a pyramiding array of possibilities for more learning.

THE INTELLIGENCE OF GROWTH

Our nature as learners contains an interesting contradiction: important growth requires change. We have to give up our comfortable ways of thinking and survive the buffeting involved in taking on unfamiliar ideas, skills, and values. The need to grow is built into the fiber of our being. We are impelled upward in a developmental sense. Paradoxically, however, we have an ingrained tendency to conserve our beings as they are or were. Nostalgia is, in fact, a yearning not to have grown or changed. We would like to go on and see things the way we could when we were young and untutored. Curiously, the answer is to produce disequilibrium—to create environments that impel us to change, not discarding what we were at any given stage, but learning to build on it productively. Thelen's advice to us is correct: the learner needs to confront problems and diverse opinions in order to reach beyond the present stage and develop the constructs that will sustain growth at another level.

When we are infants, the process of change is built into us. We do not intend to learn language but we do so, and in so doing we change. We do not expect to walk, but walking leads us where we could not go before. Not very many years later we learn our culture and begin to function at a level so satisfying that we can stay there forever. The purpose of education is to generate the conditions that will enable us to acknowledge the disequilibrium of change as a preequisite to growth, so that we can reach beyond ourselves toward richer understanding and accept the wisdom that lies within ourselves—that discomfort is our lot if we are not to be arrested along our road.

CHAPTER 18

EQUITY
Gender, Ethnicity, and Socioeconomic Background

The belief in the importance of hard work is not alien to Americans. The mystery is why, in the later years of the twentieth century, we have modified this belief in such a destructive way. Why do we dwell on the differences among us, rather than on our similarities? Why are we unwilling to see that the whole society is advanced when all its members, not only the privileged socioeconomic and ethnic groups, are given the opportunity to use their abilities to the fullest?

—Harold Stevenson and Jay Stigler in *The Learning Gap*, 1992.

In the last chapter we dealt with how learning involves discomfort and how we need to ensure that our students move beyond comfort to conditions that stretch them. Now we deal with demography—with how categorical differences affect us as learners and how we can design educational environments that ensure that gender, socioeconomic status, and race and ethnicity never put our students at a disadvantage.

Some differences between learners are purely *individual*. All of us contribute to those differences purely by being distinctive. Other differences are *categorical*: those largely demographic features that operate to advantage or disadvantage groups of people who share some characteristic. With respect to individual differences, our personal and particular complexes of traits interact with every educational environment and our ability to profit from them. Individual characters can greatly affect success in school and life. Some people from unprepossessing school environments educate themselves magnificently while others do only okay or do very poorly in the best of schools. We use our models of teaching, of course, to attempt to reach all students by giving them tools for learning that will be effective regardless of personality.

In this chapter we will examine some of the categorical differences and will give particular attention to gender, socioeconomic status, and ethnicity because normative schooling has resulted in serious differences in educational progress by males and females, students varying in economic background, and students varying in cultural or ethnic background. Then we will consider the function of the various models of teaching in reducing inequities associated with the categorical differences. To begin, let's look at some general data on achievement in the United States. Part, but not all, of our focus will be on data that illuminate our demographic categories or raise questions about the conduct of education.

LARGE-SCALE RESEARCH ON ACHIEVEMENT

The data we will deal with during the next few pages are taken largely from reports generated by the U.S. Department of Education. The reader will find that some of the categories are a bit ambiguous due to problems in defining the attributes of people. For example, much of the data is reported in mixtures of race, ethnic background, and color. Thus, in the government reports, a single table may contain categories such as *Asian,* referring to students whose parents trace their origins to a wide variety of Asian countries; *Hispanic,* which refers to persons whose origins are largely in Mexico, Puerto Rico, and Central and South America; *Black,* referring to African Americans; and *White,* which, in addition to referring to European origins that could be either several hundred years old or very recent, is almost an "all other" category for those remaining after the other categories have been identified. When data are reported for people identified as "White," "Black," "Hispanic," and "Asian," we will refer to these as *ethnic* distinctions, although this is not strictly accurate, because race is mixed with ethnicity, and the white, Hispanic, and Asian categories themselves include people with a wide variety of ethnic origins. Socioeconomic indicators are largely reported in terms of parents' education levels, but sometimes in terms of actual income levels or in terms of whether students receive subsidized lunches. Nonetheless, for our purposes, you will find that the categories are workable in the sense that they provide us with rich information.

DATA ON CATEGORICAL DIFFERENCES

COLLEGE ATTENDANCE: A MYSTERIOUS GENDER GAP

In 1996, 8.2 million (57 percent) of U.S. college students were females, and 6.7 million were males (Lewin, 1998). In 2002, over 60 percent of college students are female. The proportion is about the same for all categories of colleges: public, private, four-year, and two-year, although obviously there are some specific colleges and universities that enroll many more males than females (and vice versa). These remarkable figures, given a long history during which males greatly outnumbered females because society valued education more for men, culminate a long climb. In the mid-1980s, the numbers became roughly equal, and since then the proportion of women has climbed steadily and is expected to continue climbing. In fact, the *num-*

ber of men attending college declined between 1991 and 1996, whereas the number of women rose.

Preparation for college, both academically and motivationally, is obviously a major function of schooling, and, especially given the enormous economic advantages of college attendance and the increasing importance of complex education for increasing numbers of occupations, why would fewer men choose college? There is no mystery about why more women are seeking a college education. There is a considerable mystery about why college enrollment by men is not rising, let alone why there are some declines.

The trend continues in graduate school enrollment, currently about 56 percent female, although mathematics, the sciences, and engineering are lower than parity for females. As the 1990s opened, only about 16 percent of scientists and engineers were women, but at the same time 30 percent of the bachelors degrees and 20 percent of the doctorates in the sciences were awarded to women, indicating an increase that occurred through the 1990s and is continuing. (We will deal with mathematics and science below in greater detail. Ethnicity is also a factor there, and an interesting one.) In the case of first professional degrees, particularly law and medicine, the rising but still unequal enrollment of women is worrisome from an equity perspective, although the ratio of women to men continues to rise. However, in other areas women make up as much as 70 percent of the enrollees. This does not mean that women have achieved equality in all ways. The "glass ceiling" in corporations still exists and denies promotion to many highly qualified women. Women are still paid less on the average for equal work in many occupations.

The society is changing, and the enormous change in gender attendance at college portends even greater changes to come, but, clearly, gender differences are not the only area that should concern us. Think, for example, about this sobering fact. In 1990, U.S. universities awarded 933 doctorates in the mathematical sciences. Only 401 of those degrees were awarded to U.S. citizens! Women received only 87 of those degrees. African Americans received only four of them.

GRADUATION FROM HIGH SCHOOL

Recent information about graduation rates provides some food for thought about the effectiveness of education in general and on differences by category. Here is some information from the report of one of our larger states.

STATE ENROLLMENT, 1996–97

Grade 9	193,000
Grade 10	161,000
Grade 11	128,000
Grade 12	105,000
June Graduates	92,000

The number of graduates is less than half the number of ninth-grade enrollees. The number of students declines year by year—a truly frightening picture. When the figures are broken down by ethnicity, it turns out that there are only small differences among white, African American, and Hispanic students. Half or more are not graduating on time. Broken down by gender, about 55 percent of the females graduate on time compared with about 43 percent of the males (Florida Department of Education, 1998).

Again, we can ask what is going on. Nationally the number of high school graduates in recent years has hovered at a little over 70 percent of the population of 17-year-olds, and the number of graduating females has exceeded the number of graduating males for several years. The gender gap is slowly but gradually widening.

LITERACY

Unquestionably, a major mission of the elementary school is the teaching of reading, and we can ask what the efficiency rate of our schools is, taken as a whole. It is useful to consider the status of reading competence at the end of grades 1, 3, and 5 because grade 1 is when the first mighty effort begins; grade 3 ends the primary years during which literacy is the basic interest and other curriculum areas are not competing for attention to the extent that they will later; and grade 5 is when the elementary school generally ends and an adequate level of reading and writing needs to be reached to enable the students to succeed in secondary education.

From the time that reliable data have been kept, about two-thirds of the students exit first grade able to read informational and narrative picture-prose books and heavily illustrated books competently. They should also have the tools necessary to expand their competence without undue stress under conditions of good instruction in grades 2 and 3. Nearly all of those students do progress at a fairly good pace, exit grade 3 in good shape, and leave the elementary years able to handle the reading tasks of the middle and high school years. The other third is a different story. Very few of them recover from their initial failure, and, in the average elementary school, about 20 to 25 percent of the exiting students read at the level of the average third-grade student or below. These students make up the vast majority of the students who will drop out or will not graduate "on time." And, although there are many females whose problems in reading will hamper them seriously, about three-fourths of the poor readers are males. Few middle and high schools have staff who are equipped to teach "overage beginning readers," an issue we will visit at length in Chapter 19, where we take up the question of developing a multidimensional, multiple-models curriculum for literacy in the upper elementary grades and beyond.

Gender, socioeconomic status, and ethnicity are all involved in this literacy problem. Let's look at some information from the National Assessment of Educational Progress as it bears on achievement in reading, writing, and the other core curriculum areas.

For much of the last two decades, the U.S. Department of Education has been trying to get a handle on the picture of student achievement in the United States by developing tests in the core curriculum areas, administering them to samples of students in all 50 states, analyzing the data, and generating reports that provide a rich database that helps us understand where we are and how we are progressing. We will look at just a few of the findings as they bear on the general picture and issues relating to gender, socioeconomic status, and ethnicity.

READING

The general picture over the last 25 years is different from the picture frequently presented in the media—that literacy has gone to pot in the current generation. In fact, the picture between 1971 and 1996 is relentlessly flat. The National Assessment of Educational Progress (NAEP) scores have hardly changed at all (Campbell, Voelki, and Donohue, 1997; Santapau, 2001) for ages 9, 13, and 17. The bad news is that society—and the educational system—has, during that same 25 years, tried to generate initiatives to increase literacy, and yet the indicators of achievement from the NAEP studies have not shown improvement. (As an aside, there are curricula that incorporate several models of teaching that make a big difference to literacy, so we can be optimistic, but that is a story for Chapter 19.)

In fact, one of the major purposes of this book is to make available to teacher candidates and inservice teachers models of teaching and, to some extent, curriculum, that will change the picture by increasing student capacity to learn.

The NAEP teams have attempted to assess the levels of competence students in grades 4, 8, and 12 have developed. Their 1996 report (Campbell et al., 1996) provides these estimates by gender (see Table 18.1). The categories of competence are rough estimates of whether the students are able to teach themselves easily through reading (advanced and proficient), can respond adequately to assignments requiring reading (basic), or will have a difficult time with the types of reading generally used in the curriculum areas at the particular age or grade level. In interpreting these data, note that the number of twelfth-grade students is smaller than the number in the other grades.

These figures are best interpreted in terms of our goals for the future. We'd like all our students to be at the advanced, or at least at the proficient level. We know that is possible. We have a way to go, but research on curriculum and teaching clearly indicates that we can travel that distance quickly if each of us devotes ourself to that goal and acquires the tools to teach our students to learn at outstanding levels.

Note that from these figures gender has been a factor, but both genders contain many students who will fail to graduate and go on to higher education

TABLE 18.1   **PERCENTAGE OF STUDENTS AT VARIOUS LEVELS OF PROFICIENCY IN READING BY GRADE AND GENDER (CAMPBELL, DONAHUE, REESE, AND PHILLIPS, 1996)**

Grade	Advanced	Proficient (at or above)	Basic (at or above)	Below Basic
4				
Males	4	22	54	46
Females	6	28	64	36
8				
Males	1	22	63	37
Females	3	33	75	25
12				
Males	2	31	70	30
Females	4	42	80	20

unless we teach better. And we have in our midst teachers who do reach all their students. All of us need to reach *their* level of proficiency.

In addition, we need to teach so powerfully that socioeconomic status is eliminated as a factor in student learning. Here is the picture from the same NAEP report. All the grades are similar. For simplicity, let's look only at grade 8. These data are average scores on the NAEP tests by the educational level of the parents, which is highly correlated with family income.

Students one or more of whose parents
   have graduated from college   270

Students one or more of whose parents
   have some education after high school   266

Students one or more of whose parents
   have graduated from high school   252

Students neither of whose parents have
   graduated from high school   238

The gender averages on these same tests are:

Males   252
Females   267

There are gender differences at every level of parents' education. The challenge, of course, is to create schools where curriculum and teaching creates equity of opportunity so that these differences are minimized if not eliminated entirely.

Ethnic and racial differences are largely, but not entirely, ones of economic levels, including the amount of education of the parents. Let's look at selected data, using the same average scores, again at the eighth-grade level.

Asian	273
White	268
Hispanic	240
Black	237

Again, these are serious differences. The average of the black and Hispanic student is about at the 30th percentile of the Asian and white distributions.

The large concentrations of the poor in inner cities generate special problems to inner-city schools, exacerbated by the problem of recruiting teachers to work in them. Essentially, if a student grows up in a neighborhood that contains few highly educated persons, then the school has to be powerful enough to compensate for the culture of poverty that is itself exacerbated by the prejudice minorities are likely to suffer in our society. Taking the nation as a whole, about one-third of the population is now classified as "minority" and about one-fifth of our children are being raised in poverty.

These differences exist in all states and regions. The states differ in socioeconomic status and ethnicity (in California, more students are now classified as "minorities" than as members of the "majority"), and those differences are reflected in the assessment picture for the states.

WRITING

The NAEP studies of achievement in writing parallel the studies of achievement in reading but add some interesting new information (Applebee, 1990). Clearly, competence in reading is necessary for competence in writing to take place, although competence in reading does not by any means guarantee competence in writing.

The gender picture again shows females exceeding males substantially (the average scores for males are at about the 35th percentile of the female scores at grade 4), and the gender difference widens at grades 8 and 12. The average female score at grade 4 is close to the average male score at grade 8. The average female eighth-grade score is *above* the average male score at grade 12!

For both genders, progress in writing competence is slow. The average eighth-grade score is at only the 62nd percentile of the fourth-grade distribution. Ethnicity again plays a role, but to a lesser degree than in reading. The difference between the children of college graduates and children whose parents did not graduate from high school is about the same as the difference in genders.

Again, this situation does not have to exist. Better curriculum and instruction greatly reduces the differences between the genders and alleviates the penalty of poverty.

Reducing differences is not our only objective. Increasing achievement for all is the preemptive goal. Data from Colorado illustrate the point. In 1997, 32 percent of the females were rated "unsatisfactory" in writing at grade four, compared with 50 percent of the males. The rate for whites was 41 percent; African Americans, 50 percent; and Hispanics, 43 percent. All categories had serious problems, indicating an urgent need for school improvement for all categories of students.

SOCIAL STUDIES

The NAEP has concentrated on history and geography, and the findings in these two areas are similar. We will concentrate only on geography (Persky et al., 1996) because some additional information in that area bears on our gender problem.

The total scores for the population as a whole at grades 4, 8, and 12 are close, but slightly higher for males (four points at grade 8 on the same type of scale we examined earlier for reading and writing). The difference is particularly interesting because better reading generally provides an advantage in virtually any subject matter test. Thus, the actual difference in achievement is probably greater than the test scores indicate. Hispanic scores are equal by gender, but males did somewhat better in the white and African American samples. The differences for students at the top and bottom levels of parents' education were about 20 points at each grade. The mean score for African American students was 40 points lower than the average for the white students and 10 points lower than the Hispanic students. This difference is larger than can be explained by socioeconomic differences alone, and we will have to consider it when we make plans to create equity.

MATHEMATICS AND SCIENCE

We will begin our exploration in these areas with the picture from the national assessment, but we will need to visit it again as we examine several serious gender issues. The NAEP average scores in mathematics rose somewhat between 1990 and 1996 (Reese, Miller, Mazzeo, and Dossey, 1997). Gender differences were negligible, as the female average has risen somewhat faster than the male difference (several decades ago male scores were significantly higher). Socioeconomic differences were considerable, with a difference of about 28 points between the lowest and highest levels as judged by parents' education and 32 points at grade 12. The average for white fourth-grade students was 32 points higher than that of African American fourth-graders and 26 points higher than Hispanic students' average. The ethnic differences continued or widened in the higher grades.

In the 1996 assessment in science, gender differences were negligible, with the highest being 4 scale-score points at grade 12 (see below). Socioeconomic differences, again indicated by levels of parents' education, were considerable: 23 scale-score points at grade 4, 29 at grade 8, and 36 at grade 12. Once again, white and Asian students score much higher than African American and Hispanic students.

Ethnicity also operates additionally in terms of opportunity to learn. Although there are few ethnic or racial differences in need to achieve (Cooper and Dorr, 1995), equity in opportunity can take some funny turns. Davenport and her colleagues (1998) examined the course enrollment of students whose achievement was in the top quartile in a large school district. Enrollment in algebra was represented by 100 percent of the Asians, 87.5 percent of the whites, 51 percent of African-Americans, and 42 percent of Hispanics—and these are percents of high-achieving students! Counseling, of course, could and should have corrected this in that setting.

INTERPRETATIONS AND ADDITIONAL INFORMATION

The data clearly indicate that, as a nation, we have not achieved a condition of full categorical equity—far from it. Some think that full equity is an impossibility, an idea we will examine later, but we believe that full or nearly full equity is within reach and that schools, through curriculum and teaching, can ensure it.

Let's look at the various categories and dig into the subject a bit further.

SOCIOECONOMIC STATUS

The data we have been reviewing corroborate what has been clear for many decades: socioeconomic differences are the greatest predictor of success in school in the United States. A massive and well-known study of educational achievement (Coleman et al., 1966) found that parents' education and occupation so greatly influenced academic achievement that the study's authors actually concluded that the influence of differences between schools was so minor in comparison that they did not make a difference. In other words, they argued that if achievement in any given school could be predicted simply by knowing the characteristics of the parents, then schools with poor or high achievement were not in those conditions because of their quality. Instead, change the kids and achievement would change!

Although the Coleman team overinterpreted their findings somewhat— there are schools that make a difference (Brookover et al., 1978)—there is no question that socioeconomic differences affect response to education. Furthermore, the federal government's massive Chapter I program, which provides school districts with resources to improve the education of the economically poor, has failed miserably. Two of the present authors were recently members of a team that studied a large urban school district. We found that the district was receiving Chapter I funds for nearly 70 percent of the students and that the students whom the funds had served in the first grade were still receiving service in the twelfth grade because their educational disadvantage had not been "fixed."

One of the serious problems impeding many programs directed at the economically poor under Chapter I is that the condition of low achievement has existed so long that the children of poverty are stereotyped as inherently poor learners. And, the students tend to stereotype themselves and generate self-handicapping syndromes; essentially, they may give up the fight (Urdan, Midgley, and Anderman, 1998). Not only the general public but also educators can be affected. Studies of instruction in Chapter I programs have indicated that, in many of those programs, the curriculum has been slowed down and watered down and very simple, rather than challenging instructional strategies have been used, further disadvantaging the students those programs were designed to serve. Exactly the opposite medicine is probably optimal—rigorous curriculum with challenging instructional strategies designed to improve the learning capacity of the students. Programs in special education for students with mild disabilities have the same problem. The "LD" stereotype drags down the richness of curriculum and instruction for those who most need an environment abundant in opportunities to grow and to learn tools for learning.

Yet, there are school-improvement programs built around powerful models of teaching that have elevated the achievement of the children of the poor and done it quickly (within a year or two) (Becker and Gersten, 1982; Joyce, Murphy et al., 1989; Levin and Levin, 1990; Slavin, Madden, Karweit, Livermon, and Dolan, 1990; Wallace, Lemahieu, and Bickel, 1990). For general reviews, see Joyce and Calhoun, 1995, 1996; Joyce, Calhoun, and Hopkins, 1999; Joyce, Calhoun, and McKibbin, 1998; Joyce and Showers, 1995; and Joyce and Wolfe, 1996. Again, good teaching can make a huge dent in the problem. And it must, because the failure to learn leaves people with a lifelong self-image that they cannot learn, causing them to avoid learning opportunities and challenges of adulthood, thereby perpetuating the cycles of poverty. The long series of studies by Cohen (1995, 1998) and her associates have shown how feasible it is to generate status equality and how rapidly schools can affect the interactions that generate better self-images and achievement for all students. Although early childhood programs have not been as successful as we had hoped they would when they were inaugurated, there have been some outstanding examples of programs that have made a difference (see, for example, Campbell and Ramey, 1995). How they did so we discuss in relation to the research on specific models of teaching.

Unfortunately, few school districts have prepared their teachers to use the curricular and instructional strategies that provide equity for the poor. We must solve that problem. Again, schooling must lead the society. The massive publicity given to absurd books such as *The Bell Curve* (Herrnstein and Murray, 1994), which argues that the poor are genetically inferior to the rich, indicates how seriously the school has to battle ignorance of the real facts: the children of the poor have as much potential as the children of the rich, but schools haven't learned to use the tools that will reach them, although plenty of those tools exist. As an editorial in the *New York Times* proclaimed in relation to *The Bell Curve*, "Plants grown under ideal conditions will achieve different heights. . . . But, lock half the plants in a dark closet and the difference in average height between the two groups will be due entirely to environment" (Editorial, 1994, p. 16).

ETHNICITY, CULTURE, AND RACE

As indicated earlier, the Department of Education mixes race and ethnicity, and, also, an ethnic category can include people from several cultures (for example, Laotian, Chinese, and Japanese are just three of those included in "Asian"). Thus, we have to be very careful when we reach toward generalizations. At the same time, the achievement data we have been discussing underline the important role that ethnicity plays in terms of response to the educational system in general.

American schools have always been most comfortable with kids who come with the mainstream culture already in place, simply because "mainstream" American society has always been most comfortable with people who are similar to it. (Nearly all world societies share this problem, often to an extreme. Witness the world history of strife between tribes and nations. Just think for a moment of what was once Yugoslavia.)

During the periods of large European immigration to the United States, there was significant strife between those already here and those who were new, even though the European nations share many cultural elements. Linguistic differences were not tolerated in the schools of the nineteenth or early twentieth centuries. "Learn English fast or fail!" was the policy. (In a curious way, the people in residence were treated only a little better. In 1900 the average amount of schooling was seven years. Half of the students had less. While we're considering the subject, it's worth noting that only eight percent of the population before World War II had *any* college experience!)

In America, the European children huddled in ethnic ghettos until they got a handle on English and a handhold on the economic ladder. Schools helped in that they were a major setting where English was learned and where the kids mingled and gradually learned to get along. The schools permitted a cruel cost however; many of those children went through life, as do many of their great-grandchildren today, embarrassed about the origins that gave them life and love and the cultural base that provided them with social meaning.

Leaving out African Americans for the moment (it wasn't until the early 1900s that the Supreme Court ruled that education must be offered to blacks), before 1950 most of the immigration was from Europe. Relatively small numbers of immigrants came from China and Japan, many of whom were imported for hard physical labor, such as building railroads in the West. Few of these immigrants' children had access to education when they arrived. Mexicans came for farm work, often visiting seasonally, and little schooling was offered to the children of those who took up

American residence. Achievement data from the New York City public school system are interesting because the ethnic groups came in considerable numbers, largely to the eastern and midwestern cities and because of the role that native language did and did not play in their progress. D. Cohen (1969) made an analysis of the New York City data in which he compared the achievement of immigrant children with the average of the students who were already there before them. The question he asked was, "How did a new group of immigrant students do in the first few years after they entered school in the United States?" Here are a few of the findings, all in terms of averages:

> British immigrants, who already spoke English as well as coming from a society quite similar to America's, achieved slightly below the level of the "in-place" American population.
>
> Irish immigrants, who also spoke English, achieved far lower than the existing population.
>
> The average of the Scandinavian immigrants was somewhat higher than the norm.
>
> The average of the Italian immigrants was at about the level of the Irish.
>
> The German average was considerably higher than the in-place population.
>
> The average of immigrating Jewish children was quite high.
>
> The few Chinese and Japanese who managed to get any schooling achieved at a very high level.

Perhaps the most arresting aspect of the study is the small role that primary language appeared to play in the achievement of these ethnic groups. Had the English and the Irish been the high achievers at that time, we could hypothesize that having English as a first language provided a considerable advantage in the immigration to a country where English is the language of the schools. However, it did not turn out that way. Level of literacy in any language might have been a factor. The Jewish society has had nearly 100 percent literacy for 2000 years, so Jewish immigrant children, whether from Germany, Russia, Poland, or another country where the language was not English and, in some cases, was quite different from English, were nonetheless the children of literate parents and of a community of literate people. Many of the Italian and Hispanic parents were not educated. The children of Asian immigrants present an interesting picture that continues to this day. Although the Asian languages are very different from English, Asian immigrants have been successful in adapting to and learning the linguistic aspects of American society, even though it contained considerable prejudice against them.

Today, the cultural difference problem is at a crisis stage that has two dimensions. First, a large proportion of American children have immigrated recently from other places, particularly Latin countries and Asia. The schools are not reaching many of them effectively, either in terms of achievement or cultural dignity. Second, the world has changed, and the future prosperity of the nation depends on the ability to mingle productively with the other societies in the world.

The current ethnic and linguistic mix makes our schools a perfect laboratory both to demonstrate that cultural difference is not a barrier to achievement or dignity and to prepare all our kids for the new global society we will have to navigate as a nation as well as individually. The very term minority is becoming obsolete faster than could have been imagined forty years ago. In California and Texas in 1998 the name most frequently given to newborn males was *Jose.*

We have the curricular and instructional technology if we have the will.

MORE ON GENDER

The comparisons of achievement by males and females in the large-scale studies of student learning open up a number of fascinating and serious questions for American education. Gender differences are small in the social studies, sciences, and mathematics. However, in the critical literacy area, clearly males accumulate a tremendous disadvantage, one that no doubt powerfully affects the high school graduation rates as well as college attendance and, eventually, graduate school enrollment. In 20 years we can expect a society where, in the 25- to 40-year-old age bracket, 60 percent of the college graduates and holders of advanced degrees will be females. The gender literacy difference, it should be noted, pervades all socioeconomic levels and most ethnic groups.

Yet, women continue to be disadvantaged, and seriously, in a number of ways that illuminate the process of differentiation and the relationship between the culture, individuals, and schooling. As we indicated earlier, female enrollment in the "first" professional degrees continues to lag. And in the workplace, there are thought-provoking inequities in salaries, women being less well paid for equal work in a host of occupations and passed over for promotion in inequitable proportions.

Education is a part of the society, and the relationship between culture and education is important in general and is illuminated in particular with respect to gender issues. Let us put our imaginations to work on the process.

Imagine society as a massive teacher, imbuing all of us with ways of thinking, values, and patterns of behavior, including relationships. From birth, society begins transmitting its culture to us, and it is relentless. Even in periods of great social change, the culture is with us and it colors and integrates the changes.

Imagine also the family as a powerful teacher, a major educational instrument of society but also bathing its young in its variants of the culture, teaching boys and girls how to be boys and girls, planting habits of relationship, creating readers and nonreaders, building aspirations and strong and weak self-concepts.

Imagine then also the school as a social agent, following cultural norms in its particular way and staffed by people who have been thoroughly socialized. Cultural transmission continues as it operates.

Imagine, finally, the classroom, where teaching is the assigned task.

Now, let us suppose that there is an extreme case in which the thrust of all four levels is in the direction of shaping what turns out to be an inequitable outcome. We have one in the making right now with respect to socioeconomic status as it has been affected by the technological dimension of society and the explosion of computer applications. Low-income workers, with the lowest-technology jobs, have less chance to learn technology in the workplace and fewer resources with which to acquire technological skill at home. The homes reflect economic differences in terms of the technological opportunities they offer to the children. The schools serving the various economic strata differ markedly in technological richness, and that difference carries over to the classrooms, which are, on the whole, less equipped and staffed by teachers who have less access to training in computer applications. What will be the result? The rich will get relatively richer in technological terms.

This is not a subtle example. The examples in terms of gender equity are more subtle and elusive. Myra and David Sadker have written beautifully on the subject (Sadker and Sadker, 1994), and their treatment and bibliographies are a good starting point for a student of the subject.

At the Societal Level.   Although we are a couple of generations beyond the point where general education was prized for males and actually discouraged for females, society still teaches gender differences that are relevant to education. For example, our culture describes men as better at things mechanical and less able in literary matters, and women as having less mathematical aptitude but better at empathy and nurturing. The social weight is maintained despite massive evidence from the behavioral sciences that both genders have plenty of capacity to become quite good at the substance contained in all the major curriculum areas of the school. By the way, the media probably affect both genders in the way scientists are portrayed (Gerbner, 1987). Not only are scientists more likely to be depicted as males but, frequently, as a bit weird. In fact, academics in general are frequently presented as offbeat "eggheads." On the other hand, the space program is probably correcting that image somewhat, especially with the publicity attending female astronauts.

The societal press extends to matters of personality. Although society is somewhat in flux over the matter, males are still taught to make their way by being outwardly self-sufficient and commanding, women by being feminine and charming.

In the Home.   Many homes follow the societal norm. We can see this in the types of careers that are promoted by the home. For example, fewer homes promote careers in the sciences and mathematics or medicine for their daughters than for their sons. In other words, as boys and girls come to school, the social "program" makes it less likely for females to be oriented toward science and mathematics. Asian homes tend to promote science and mathematics for both genders (Burkham, Lee, and Smerdon, 1997).

In the School. For many years males were more likely to elect advanced science and mathematics courses, although females' prior achievement clearly qualified them to do so. The difference has narrowed substantially (Devenport et al., 1998), although some inequity remains. Clearly, school policy and counseling by the staff have much to do with what courses students take. Mathematics is the critical gatekeeper course with respect to the sciences, with respect not only to achievement but also to higher education enrollments. Tobias (1993) refers to a study of women entering the University of California at Berkeley, all of whom had been high achievers in general in order to be admitted. In the year of the study, whereas 57 percent of the males admitted had taken four years of mathematics, only 8 percent of the females had. Without the four years of mathematics courses, students there are not eligible for the calculus sequence, would rarely attempt chemistry or physics, and are disadvantaged for statistics and economics. Because they could not take the entry-level courses, they were ineligible for 10 of the 12 "colleges" and 22 out of the 44 majors the university offered! Many of the high-achieving men had disadvantaged themselves; for women, nine out of ten were at a disadvantage. When males and females were required to take the entire mathematics and science sequence in a study in western Australia, gender differences in achievement dissappeared (female averages actually exceeded those of males somewhat) (Parker and Offer, 1987).

In the Classroom. The nature of teaching comes into play in the science and mathematics courses. The critical issues appear to be whether the courses are conducted with a scientific inquiry model and how the classroom is conducted within that model (Burkham, Lee, and Smerdon, 1997; Staver, 1989). With poor models, not only achievement but also academic self-concept is affected. Sadker and Sadker (1994) report that whereas, in the elementary school, 31 percent of girls feel they are good at math, only 18 percent feel that way by middle school. The active, inquiry-oriented classrooms, with substantial laboratory experiences, appear to increase learning for all students and in a fashion that reduces demographic (categorical) differences for all, including gender differences. Gender differences are greatest where the courses are conducted with the time-honored "chalk and talk" format. Also, even within courses in which laboratory experiences are prominent, participation can be unequal (Jovanovic and King, 1998). Otherwise higher-order learning can become unequal (Bielinski & Davison, 1998; Fennema, Carpenter, Jacobs, Franke, and Levi, 1998).

However, classrooms can generate gender equality quite quickly, even when there are considerable differences as a course begins (Kahle, 1985;

Klein, 1985; Weiss, 1978). Importantly, what was once thought of as a cognitive problem (Maccoby and Jacklin, 1974) is now disappearing from an educational research point of view (Linn and Hyde, 1989), and, when schools and classroom instruction line up with rich curricula taught with rich models, gender differences are minimal in the science and mathematics areas.

The gender difference in literacy is still enormous, and that difference is accepted as normal by many people because it is assumed that a genetic difference is playing its way out. However, again the difference in learning to read disappears under powerful strategies for teaching kids how to read. And, when writing is taught with the most effective curricular and instructional methods, both genders improve their writing markedly, and the gender differences virtually disappear.

We are not arguing that adolescence and early adulthood are not times when young men and women have to learn to come to terms with and capitalize on their real and wonderful biological differences. Far from it. Vive la différence! But the view that gender prevents learning is perverse. With respect to the basic education schools offer, gender differences in academic aptitude, if they exist, need have no effect. There are no gender differences sufficient to prevent boys and girls from having equal degrees of excellence in all areas within the general curriculum.

In an excellent educational system (or classroom), everybody wins. Good education is the key. But the school has to lead the culture on this issue.

THE OPPORTUNITY OF EDUCATION

We are so lucky to be allowed to teach. The rich panoroma of humanity gives us its children to live with and school. We are given boys and girls who come in every human color and bring us the sumptuous cultural and personal differences of their homes. We have the good fortune to nurture the bold and the shy, the tall and the short, the serious and the comic, the confident and the frightened.

And we are given such a luxury of opportunities to show them—science and engineering of unparalleled sophistication, a globe that has shrunk to bring all cultures within reach and whose nations, for the first time in history, are almost all politically free to make their way. We have spectacular media within reach of our fingertips and a phenomenal library that is easier than ever to access.

Our riches enable us to educate in such a way that human variety can be capitalized on and enrich the entire society. Our wealth of educational technology enables us to reach all children and ensure that they are well educated, can make their way in the world of work, and can build a fine quality of life.

GIVING UP SOMETHING IS THE HARD PART OF GROWING UP, FOR A SOCIETY AS WELL AS FOR INDIVIDUALS _____

The really difficult part of our struggle is giving up the idea that gender, monetary, racial, and cultural differences are factors that determine educational potential. They are factors only if we make them so. The powerful models of teaching reach all students and create a much more level playing field because they teach children how to learn and because they possess the adaptive flexibility to accommodate differences productively and capitalize on them. Research that has sought "special" methods for the children of the poor, the racially or culturally different, or for boys and girls has come up empty-handed because our likenesses are far more salient than are our differences—and the differences are superficial. It used to be said that "travel is broadening." World travel certainly is, because as you encounter other cultures and experience new ways of doing things, you find out that there is only one kind of people on Planet Earth.

We have much work to do. Just consider our closing scenarios.

S C E N A R I O

Recently, a team of cheerleaders . . . sat in a circle in their high school cafeteria and looked at the pages of a Frederick's of Hollywood catalogue to see what their competition squad would wear this season. Some of the girls were just a month and a half out of junior high.

When the 44 girls are training, the room buzzes with adolescent energy . . . which is why the hush was so pronounced when the Frederick's catalogue went around. The reason for the stillness was a glossy photograph of a perfectly proportioned woman in a white lace teddy.

"It'll look great," the coach insisted, their silence an implicit rejection of her choice for the uniform. She hadn't yet announced which of the 44 girls would make the competition squad. . . . The squad competes throughout the winter at meets run by private companies.

"The high-waist pants will make your hips look slim," the coach said. "You'll wear a white tank top under the white lace so no one will see your nipples." That, the coach confided, had been something of a problem with past uniforms.

Racial prejudice has been a part of our society for hundreds of years, and intellectual inferiority has been attributed to people of color as a major part of that prejudice. A wonderful review by Professor Jim Banks of the University of Washington traces the studies of psychologists who have studied race and academic ability (Banks, 1995). Although nearly all the scientific community rejects the notion of racially determined intelligence, the idea dies hard in society in general. Although the outstanding achievements of so many people of color have demonstrated the fallacy and despite the wonderful economic progress made in several countries where everybody has color, the ingrained prejudice still leads people to believe that those outstanding achievements are exceptions. The problem is compounded in our society by the fact that so many people of color are also economically poor.

The fact is that race does not predict academic ability, but good education does. The same programs cited in the previous section have demonstrated that, with good curriculum and instruction and a positive social climate, racial differences in academic achievement diminish quite rapidly. We possess the technology. We have only to use it. The problem is complex, however, as we can see in the scenario that summarizes this chapter.

S C E N A R I O

RODNEY POWELL

It had become very clear early on that of the Powell children, Rodney was the one on whom the family's academic hopes would be invested. From the time he was thirteen, he had started taking after school jobs, saving his money so that he could create a college fund of his own. In his way he was a kind of black version of the all-American boy, fresh off a Norman Rockwell cover of the *Saturday Evening Post*, a young man who was well-behaved, extremely polite, got excellent grades, held down responsible jobs, saved his money, and had a compelling purpose in life. . . .

[T]he school tried to route him onto the vocational track instead of an academic one. . . . The guidance counselor was a white woman with a fixed, traditional view of who should go to college and who should not. Rodney was, she pointed out, gifted at shop. That was not a talent to be underestimated nor taken for granted, and if Rodney worked hard, and behaved himself, he might be able to have a very good life. When he argued that it was his family's consuming ambition that he go to college, she let him know that he didn't know his place. "Your father's a laborer, and you have to understand your limits in life. But don't feel badly, there are some valuable things you can do with your life."

Rodney Powell had tried at first to make the case himself, and he had tried to explain about how good his grades were, that it was not only shop in which he did well, and that he and his family had already been saving the requisite money for college, but she remained unmoved. "College is not for everyone," she said. But Rodney persisted. In addition to everything else, he understood that academic excellence affected his self-esteem, that good marks proved something important about himself, about what a young black child could do. But as hard as he tried, he could not move her.

Because his people were simple and poorly educated themselves, they felt unable to go to school and make the case for him. But there was a neighboring black family named Crozier which had taken an interest in him. Edna Crozier's own children were grown and though she did domestic work herself, she had a passion for education. She knew Rodney well, and she was quicker to challenge injustice than his somewhat more cautious mother; as such she went to the school to argue in his behalf. There she listened to the litany of reasons why he was not college material, and she answered that much of this was true, his parents were poor, and no one in his family had ever been to college before. But, she said, this was all the more reason to give him the chance. "Look at how good his marks are," she had said. "If he were white and had those grades and his father was a laborer and he had these exceptional grades, would you be telling him to try the vocational school?" The guidance counsellor was equally dogged. "He can't afford it," she said; "there's no hope there. It's the way life is." But Edna Crozier stood her ground and said, "All we ask is that you give him a chance. Why not do that?" She was a strong woman and she carried the day. Rodney was placed on what was called the X track, which was the academic track, and so he went off to an academic high school and continued to hold several jobs in order to save the money for college. (Halberstam, 1998, pp. 379–380)

THE BATTLE CONTINUES

A recent study in California indicates the extent to which the current generation of Rodneys need advocacy—really simple equity from their schools and districts. The study looked at students whose CTBS scores were in the top quartile and whether they enrolled in algebra. Only 51 percent of the black students and 42 percent of the Latino students were enrolled, compared with 88 percent of the "white" students and 100 percent of the Asian-origin students (Thorson, 2002).

Models of teaching are blind to color, gender, ethnicity, and socio-economic status. The social system is not, but must be made so within the province of our educational system.

CHAPTER 19

ATTACKING THE LITERACY PROBLEM WITH MODELS OF TEACHING

In this chapter we present two curriculum development/action research efforts studies that Emily and Bruce engaged in with the staff of the Northern Lights (Alberta, Canada) school district. The first dealt with struggling readers in the upper elementary grades and beyond. The second was a primary grade curriculum improvement effort that focussed on kindergarten.

As you read these studies, think particularly about the study of student learning—equally important to the use of several models to generate an effective curriculum.

THE OVERAGE BEGINNING READER: AN ACTION RESEARCH TEST OF A MULTIDIMENSIONAL APPROACH*

Whether one judges by examining the studies reported as the National Assessment of Educational Progress (1998), the studies by state and provincial departments of education, or just examines the information available in school districts, the picture is the same: somewhere around one-third of our students have not reached the level of competence needed to educate themselves by accessing the learning resources used in the upper elementary, middle, and high schools. The situation gets worse for those students as their competence falls farther behind their peers, and the massive categorical programs (special education, Chapter I, and ESE initiatives) have in general been able to do little to alleviate the problem (McGill-Franzen and Allington, 1991).

---

*Conducted by Bruce Joyce, Booksend Laboratories; Marilyn Hrycauk, Northern Lights School Division #69; Emily Calhoun, The Phoenix Alliance; and a group of Northern Lights teachers.

Consequently, nearly all school districts face a situation where a substantial proportion of their students in grades four to twelve are virtually "beginning" readers, essentially having only the knowledge and skills characteristic of early or middle primary grade students. In some settings, interventions made in the preschool, kindergarten, and primary years have reduced the number (see Slavin, Madden, Karweit, & Wasik, 1994; Pinnell et al., 1994), but in most districts the number continues to be sizeable and the interventions after the primary grades are largely ineffective.

PERSPECTIVE

The research on how to teach reading is substantial and synthesized, and lays a base from which we can construct curriculums that we can theorize will make a considerable difference. However, these curriculums are not built around off-the-shelf packages of materials that can be adopted with minimal training. To implement these curriculums requires extensive, inquiry-oriented staff development because accomplishing them requires considerable expansion of the repertoire of most teachers. The staff need to study the research, acquire new teaching strategies, and study student learning on a formative as well as a summative basis.

READ TO SUCCEED

In a number of reviews (Calhoun, 1997; Joyce, 1999; and Showers et al., 1998), we have theorized that a multidimensional curriculum containing the following components has a reasonable chance of helping overage beginning readers to accelerate their growth in literacy, regain lost self-esteem, and get in reach of academic success and the capability of teaching themselves through reading and writing. The components include

- Development of sight vocabulary from the developed listening-speaking vocabulary through the picture-word inductive model (Calhoun, 1997) or an "experience-record approach" (Stauffer, 1969) and the study of words encountered through wide reading (Nagy and Anderson, 1984)
- Wide reading at the developed level (Duke and Pearson, undated)
- The study of word patterns, including spelling (Ehri, 1999)
- Regular writing (several times daily) and the study of writing (Englert et al., 1991)
- The study of comprehension strategies (Garner, 1987; Pressley et al., 1995)
- The study of progress, by both teachers and students, on a weekly and monthly basis, including levels of books the students can read, sight words learned, phonetic and structural analytic skills, information learned, and fluency in writing (Calhoun, 1999). Students study their progress and whether they are ready for exit because they are independent readers of grade-appropriate text.

The Read to Succeed curriculum requires about 90 minutes per day. For middle and high school students, the 90 minute period replaces elective and exploratory subjects. Length of enrollment may vary considerably. The gap between their competence on enrollment and the level needed to manage grade-typical learning resources can be substantial. Eighth- or ninth-grade students may enter with the reading level of the average second- or third-grade student. In addition, most of the students arrive with well-developed phobias about reading and writing and, because of their lack of academic success, considerable resistance to instruction and well-developed skills for avoiding instruction of any sort. In several exploratory studies, about half the students made considerable progress in a single semester, moving, for example, to the level of the average fifth-grade student. The other half responded equally well during the second semester (Showers, Joyce, Scanlon, and Schnaubelt, 1998). Thus, enrollment should be for an initial year with exit provided when adequate competence has been achieved. A rule of thumb is the level of the average student at the end of grade six. At that point, most appear to be able to handle middle and high school learning resources, provided that they apply themselves.

MODE OF INQUIRY/DATA SOURCES

In the Northern Lights school district, Read to Succeed is nested in a broader program of initiatives, all of which are conducted from an action research frame of reference whereby the teachers and administrators in each initiative study implementation and student learning on a formative basis. The 20 schools of the district include populations of considerable variance in SES and ethnicity. Both teacher opinion and provincial assessments indicate that the district has been typical of those in North America: about one-third of the students become overage beginning readers.

The components of the program require substantial staff development into research-based curricular and instructional patterns. Some of the components address needs of all students at every level while others address specific levels or students of particular needs:

• *Just Read.* A district-wide program to increase student independent reading, particularly at-home reading (Joyce and Wolf, 1996). The rationale is direct: students need to read widely to consolidate skills, to explore the world that lies within books. Just Read involves the entire school and neighborhood community in an active action research effort to ensure that all students are reading independently.

• *Primary Curriculum (K–3).* The teachers are studying and beginning to implement strategies, particularly the picture-word inductive model (Calhoun, 1999; Joyce and Calhoun, 1998), that are designed to increase vocabulary, enhance phonetic and structural analysis, and increase comprehension strategies. Kindergarten teachers are beginning to study how to teach their students to read. The first emphasis of the action research includes the acquisition of vocabulary and phonetic analysis skills. These teachers engage in 10 to 15 days of staff development that include demonstrations, the study of the literature on literacy, and support by a cadre of teachers and administrators.

• *Early Literacy Tutorial.* The focus of this intervention is on students in the primary grades who are not learning to read from the primary curriculum. The Early Literacy staff study some basic strategies for teaching initial reading. Teachers refer students, and those students receive one-on-one tutoring for a period of up to 20 weeks. The Early Literacy Tutorial is the first safety net for the students who are not responding satisfactorily in the early years.

• *Read to Succeed.* This is the second safety net and is the subject of this chapter.

The present study comprises 12 sections involving 300 students in the Northern Lights School District #69. The Read to Succeed teachers received 10 to 15 days of staff development and studied their implementation and the growth of their students by a variety of measures including standard tests (the Canadian Tests of Basic Skills or the Gates-McGinnitie battery administered on enrollment and at the end of the 1999–2000 academic year). The 20 schools of the district include populations of considerable variance in SES and ethnicity.

In this report, standard tests are the primary source of data and are interpreted, first, in terms of the characteristics of the students and, second, in terms of their progress. Complete data were available for 250 students in the 12 sections. For each student, learning history indices were computed providing estimates of student progress compared with the "average" student. Each of the 12 teachers of the sections studied the growth of each student, the progress of the students in his or her section, and the progress of the Read to Succeed initiative as a whole. The study included the acquisition of sight vocabulary, phonetic and structural analysis skills, and gain scores computed from the standard tests. The overall picture that emerged is the emphasis in this chapter.

Table 19.1 provides an example of the data that were tabulated in one section.

All of these students made substantial gains on the vocabulary subtest, the comprehension subtest, or both subtests of the Canadian Tests of Basic Skills. In this class, there were just four females; thus, there is a big gender difference in enrollment, but no gender difference appears in effects. The mean gain on the vocabulary subtest was 1.2 and on the comprehension subtest, 1.5. Gains relative to initial scores are particularly interesting. The initial vocabulary scores for seven students were in the average range of end-of-first-grade students (1.7–2.3). The average gain for this subgroup of students was 2.1. In their previous four or five years of schooling, the average gain for these seven students had been around 0.25 per year, and the prognosis that that level of gain would rise would normally be poor (Juel, 1992).

TABLE 19.1 **PRE- AND POSTTEST CTBS VOCABULARY AND COMPREHENSION SCORES FOR ONE SECTION**

Student Number and Gender	Grade	Length (mos)	Vocabulary (GLE)			Comprehension (GLE)		
			Initial	Final	Gain	Initial	Final	Gain
1. F	5	9	2.3	4.4	2.1	2.9	4.9	2.0
2. F	5	9	1.9	4.3	2.4	2.9	4.6	1.7
3. M	5	9	1.7	4.2	2.5	1.4	5.0	3.6
4. M	5	5	3.3	3.9	0.6	3.0	4.8	1.8
5. M	5	9	1.4	4.3	2.9	3.0	4.7	1.7
6. M	5	5	2.8	2.9	0.1	3.2	3.7	0.5
7. M	5	5	1.9	4.0	2.1	2.1	3.5	1.4
8. M	5	9	2.3	4.3	2.0	3.5	4.8	1.3
9. M	4/5	7	3.9	3.3	(0.6)	3.0	4.1	1.1
10. M	4/5	5	3.1	4.1	1.0	4.8	5.1	0.3
11. F	4/5	5	3.6	4.4	0.8	3.0	4.6	1.6
12. M	4/5	5	2.6	3.0	0.4	2.9	3.5	0.6
13. F	4/5	5	4.5	4.9	0.4	3.3	5.1	1.8
14. M	4/5	9	3.9	4.9	1.0	2.7	5.3	2.6
15. M	4	5	2.3	3.0	0.7	2.4	3.6	1.2

During this year, or half-year in one case, the student gains in the sub-group were twice the gain of average students for a year, and eight times their own previous average annual gain. For most of these students, another year of this magnitude of gain would bring them to where they "look like" average students, at least from a test-score perspective. As it is, they have experienced a year of considerable growth and have reached a level in reading where, with effort, they can manage typical upper-elementary grade academic tasks. As an aside, all these students were coded as having serious learning disabilities or communication disorders.

Data like those in Table 19.1 were merged into the picture that follows.

RESULTS/EVIDENCE

CHARACTERISTICS OF THE STUDENTS ENROLLED

Each school arranged to identify students and enroll them. The resulting sections of Read to Succeed reflected differences in the process undertaken in the schools, especially the priorities that emerged. In all schools there were more overage beginning readers than could be served at any given time, and the faculties and administrators had to make some tough decisions about whom to enroll. The 250 students are about 10 percent of the district student body from grades four to nine. The overall Read to Succeed student body looks like this:

- *Gender:* Two thirds are males. Some sections were virtually all males (11 of 12, in one case), and a few were relatively even (8 of 14 were females in one case).
- *Coded as having special needs:* Seventy percent. About 30 percent were code 54 (mild to moderate learning disabilities), and another 30 percent were code 57 (communication problems).
- *Standard test scores on entry:* Forty-six percent of the elementary grade students tested at or below the average for graduating grade-two students. For those who were fifth-grade students the gain through their four or more years of schooling was about a quarter the gain of the average student (in GLE terms). A similar picture appeared for the entering middle school students.

What was their progress?

- *Overall:* Fifty-six percent of the gain scores indicated progress of from one and a half times the gains of the average student to three times the gain of average students. Eighteen percent more achieved gains equal to those of average students (approximately two to four times the rate of their previous progress).
- *Gender:* Almost identical progress by males and females as a whole.
- Elementary and middle school sections made almost identical gains. Grade level of students within sections (some included students from two or three grade levels) was not a factor either. For example, grade seven students in sections where there were also grade six and eight students gained about as much as did grade seven students in sections containing only grade seven students.
- Scores on entry were not a factor. Gains were similar for students beginning at 2.0, 3.0, 4.0, and so on.
- *Special needs codes:* Overall, progress of students with and without special needs codes was almost identical across all grades.
- SES of students was not a factor.

EDUCATIONAL IMPORTANCE

Most important is that research on curriculum for overage beginning readers appears to have reached the point where we can design curriculums that can reach those students and provide them with an opportunity to grow better and at normal rates. Further studies will examine students whose response is slower and the academic progress of all the students in order to improve the curricular framework. Also important is that this "bridge" research, where teachers and administrators in a school district apply scholarship to solve a pressing problem and form communities of inquirers, appears feasible, at least in the Northern Lights setting.

SUCCESSFUL READING IN KINDERGARTEN WITH THE PICTURE-WORD MODEL: HAS CURRICULUM DEVELOPMENT BYPASSED THE CONTROVERSIES?*

LITERACY IN THE PRIMARY GRADES

In these pages we discuss the development and implementation of a kindergarten/grade one curriculum in reading where the students, at the end of first grade, are reading at an average grade level equivalent of 3.5, with only a handful of students currently still struggling to read extended text with full comprehension. Typical, of course, at the end of grade one, would be a GLE of 1.9 or 2.0, with about one-third of the students struggling to learn to read extended text.

The real story is the creation of a community of teachers who implemented the curriculum in kindergarten and grade one and studied the achievement of their students. Kindergarten is of special interest because formal reading curriculums are so rare at that level.

In the background is the recognition that the "reading wars" are an obsolete way of doing business. To leap over the controversies and serve their students well, school districts need to make determined efforts to create more powerful curriculums, attending to the growing knowledge base but not being knocked off stride by the strident arguments of vested interests. Our young people have a far greater learning capacity than is served by opinion only (see Gaskins, 1991).

Within schools and school districts, decisions about curriculum and instruction in literacy have to be made on the basis of present knowledge and judgment—those decisions cannot wait until all controversies are resolved and all the evidence is in about available options. In grades one to three, there is little controversy about *whether* to have a formal curriculum in reading, but what should be the shape of the curriculum is debated in the literature, often heatedly. Schooling must proceed nonetheless and with full knowledge that flawless curriculums (ones that ensure that all students read beautifully and voraciously) are not yet in reach. When we in school districts make curricular decisions in literacy, we need to expect imperfection. Whatever we do, we are well advised to study student learning assiduously and to be prepared to modify what we do as we examine the results of curriculums, new and old.

In the case of kindergarten, decisions about curriculum are complicated by controversies about whether there *should be* a formal curriculum in reading or whether components of the kindergarten program should be designed to develop the dimensions of emergent literacy only. Prominent in

*Developed by Bruce Joyce, Marilyn Hrycauk and Lisa Mueller (Northern Lights School Division #69) and Emily Calhoun, with Northern Lights kindergarten teachers Bev Gariepy, Christine Michaud, Melanie Malayney, Carol Kruger, Jennifer Lawton-Godziuk, Elaine Blades, Christine Cairns, Andrea Fama, and Gloria Lane.

the literature on kindergarten is the concern that formal instruction in reading might actully be damaging to some students because they would be overmatched with the task demands of learning to read (see Elkind, 1987), a proposition that makes contemplating a reading curriculum somewhat nerve-racking, to say the least.

The position of the relevant national organizations (NAEYC and IRA, 1998) has been that kindergarten curriculums should promote emerging literacy. Whether to include formal instruction in reading for all or most kindergarten children is problematic because of concern that students will be challenged beyond their capacity to respond to the curriculum. The principle in those position papers is that the kindergarten academic content should be challenging but achievable, and, through the primary grades, that multifaceted curriculums be employed with a variety of instructional models.

Most early childhood literacy specialists favor a rich emergent literacy effort but do not recommend a formal curriculum in reading. Statements like the following are common: "Few kindergartners are developmentally ready for reading on their own" (Snow, Burns, and Griffin, eds., 1998, p. 82). However, we have had to wonder if questions about whether formal instruction is developmentally appropriate are grounded on beliefs that learning to read itself is inappropriate or are fueled by concerns that unpleasant curricular and instructional models might be employed in the kindergarten. For example, while affirming rich emergent literacy programs, Pearson and colleagues (1998, p. 9) comment, "The emphasis on pre-reading knowledge does not mean, however, that our preschool and kindergarten curricula must be workbook-driven skill programs." Such a comment appears to come from a concern that test-driven early childhood practice will devolve into a literacy boot camp mode. The concern is not without foundation; we can imagine all sorts of rote-memory-based curriculums springing up. We see them at the first-grade level in a good many school districts. We want the kindergarten/first-grade experience to be joyfully energetic.

However, the issue of whether to begin a formal reading curriculum cannot be bypassed. We decided to design a formal reading curriculum in kindergarten as well as grade one, prepare the teachers to implement it, and conduct an action research study of student learning. The decision stemmed from our judgment that research on beginning reading had reached the point where an effective, engaging, multidimensional curriculum could be designed and implemented without placing our students at risk in the process. If we were correct, we would be in error if we did *not* teach reading in kindergarten. And, if the curriculum was successful—both effective and engaging—the likelihood of failure in the primary grades should be greatly reduced and the development of all students should be enhanced. If we were wrong, we would learn that we had made an error. We take seriously the statement by Juel (1988) as quoted in the context of the National Research Council report (Snow, Burns, and Griffin, eds., 1998): "Children who struggle in vain with reading in the first grade soon decide that they neither like nor want to read." Undoubtedly, Juel's comment would apply to kindergarten students who do not respond to an intensive kindergarten curriculum. Our teachers who work in our safety net programs for struggling readers (see Joyce, Hrycauk, and Calhoun, 2001; Hrycauk, 2002) confirm that their job is half instruction and half therapy.

INQUIRY INTO EARLY LITERACY

The ideas and studies we reviewed and eventually consolidated were drawn from the fascinating and often convoluted literatures on early literacy and the role of the kindergarten curriculum.

For several decades the early childhood aspect of the controversies in the field of reading has been centered on the question of whether it is appropriate or feasible to provide formal and intensive instruction in reading and writing for entering kindergarten students. All sides agree that no harm be done to the children, that the first experiences in school be socially and affectively positive, that emergent literacy be developed, and that differences in development and early socialization be respected. Virtually all specialists in early childhood oppose a literacy boot camp for infants and young children and oppose drill-and-practice rote training.

In a real sense, those who develop formal reading/writing programs for five year olds are between a rock and a hard place. Building greater literacy is a matter of considerable importance. Not hurting students is of equal importance. If the assumption is made that the most direct avenue to a better start in literacy—formal instruction—is likely to damage the students, then we are stymied. But, it may be that the concerns about hurting the students are based on images of brutal and primitive curriculums rather than humane and sophisticated approaches. We made the decision that there would be no danger to the students if we proceeded carefully and, particularly, if the teachers tracked the responses of the children systematically and were prepared to back off or modulate if a student appeared to be stressed. Not to challenge students might be a larger mistake than challenging them cognitively. Also, we wanted the early experience to be not only effective but joyful—learning to read should be a delightful experience. Our image of a nurturant curriculum appears to differ widely from what many people imagine would be the shape of a curriculum for young children and which causes them to shy away from formal literacy instruction for kindergartners. We did *not* imagine students with workbooks, alphabet flash cards, or letter-by-letter phonics drills. We imagined an environment where students would progress from their developed listening-speaking vocabularies to the reading of words, sentences, and longer text that they had created, where they would examine simple books in a relaxed atmosphere, where they would begin to write with scribbling and simple illustrations (see Heller, 1991; Temple, Nathan, Temple, & Burris, 1993), where they would be read to regularly, and where comprehension strategies would be modelled for them through the reading and study of charming fiction and nonfiction books. If the work of childhood is play, we imagined the students playfully working their way into literacy.

DESIGN

Our image came from developments in curriculum thought about several of the emergent literacy processes. Most of the literature was developed from ideas about and studies centered on first- to sixth-grade students.

DIMENSIONS OF EMERGING LITERACY: DESIGNING THE CURRICULUM

We saw the literature as defining dimensions for early literacy that could be interpolated into components of a curriculum. Essentially, dozens of studies were categorized around the several dimensions. These included

- The development of sight vocabulary from the students' listening-speaking vocabularies (Calhoun, 1997) and the study of words encountered through wide reading (Nagy, Herman, and Anderson, 1985). Words are recognized in terms of their spelling, and once a hundred or so are learned the phonetic and structural categories are available to the students.

- The need for wide reading at the developed level (Duke and Pearson, undated). At the beginning, students can engage at the picture level (see below) and can gradually deal with caption-level books as they learn how meaning is conveyed by the authors.

- The regular study of word patterns, including spelling (Ehri, 1999). The students need to learn to classify words, seeking the phonetic and structural characteristics of words, and seeing the language as comprehensible— understanding that onsets and rhymes are predictable, although not completely consistent.

- The need for regular writing (several times daily) and the study of writing (Englert et al., 1991; Englert and Raphael, 1989). Writing involves expressing ideas through the learned words and patterns—the essential connection between reading and writing. The attempt to write consolidates what is being learned through reading.

- The study of comprehension strategies (Garner, 1987; Pressley et al., 1995). Although most of the research on comprehension is with older students, the search for meaning begins early and the modelling of comprehension strategies (explicit instruction in the literature) is probably important from the beginning.

- The study of progress, by both teachers and students, on a weekly and monthly basis, including, in this case, the levels of books the students can read, sight words learned, phonetic and structural analysis skills, information learned, and fluency in writing (Calhoun, 1999). An example is in the process where the students build their files of words learned and can see what they are learning. Another is where their classifications of words are recorded and they can see that they have developed categories of words (these begin with . . .) and can add to them. Knowing what you know enables you not only to assess progress but to celebrate growth.

Important for our early literacy curriculum was the emergence of the picture-word inductive model from the tradition of the language experience frame of reference with the addition of concept formation and concept attainment models of teaching (see Calhoun, 1999; Stauffer, 1970). Chapter 5 describes the phases of the model.

The literature emphasizing that students need to work with books early—at first getting information primarily from the pictures—was helpful. Several quiet times for independent reading occur daily. And, of course, the students need to be read to a great deal. The research on comprehension strategies helped us design the read aloud, talk aloud, think aloud episodes that can be used from the start.

A major assumption underpinning the image of the curriculum is that students need to become inquirers into language, seeking to build their sight vocabularies and studying the characteristics of those words, trying to build generalizations about phonetic and structural characteristics.

The curriculum was designed to facilitate growth through each of its strands—building vocabulary, classifying, creating sentences and paragraphs, reading—in an integrated fashion so that each strand will support the others. As sight words are developed, phonetic and structural concepts are also developed through the analysis of those words. Similarly, the construction of sentences and paragraphs related to the sight vocabularies that are developed. As they read, the students identify known words and attack new ones through the phonetic, structural, and comprehension skills they are developing.

PROVIDING STAFF DEVELOPMENT
TO SUPPORT IMPLEMENTATION

Once we decided that such a curriculum was feasible, the next stage was designing staff development oriented to help the teachers both implement the curriculum and also to become a positive learning community that would study student learning and take pleasure in colleagueship and inquiry. Eight teachers in three schools in our Grand Centre/Cold Lake area were involved in the initial effort. (The school faculties had formally agreed to participate, and all eight kindergarten teachers had agreed also. Two had taught reading in the primary grades in the past, but none had attempted a formal literacy curriculum in kindergarten. Two were first year teachers. The superintendent, cabinet, and board of trustees were in support, and meetings explaining the curriculum were held with parents in the spring and early fall).

The staff development included demonstrations, the study of early literacy, the analysis of practice, and the study of student learning (see Joyce and Showers, 2002). Altogether, about 15 days per year were provided to build the inquiring community.

THE ACTION RESEARCH INQUIRY

For the eight kindergarten teachers, the action research focused on two questions: Did the multidimensional curriculum work? Did the students learn to read and to what degree, including the extent of their comfort with the process and their feelings about reading? Informal observation was important, but the teachers were also provided with tools for the formal study of the students' learning of the alphabet, acquisition of vocabulary, general language development, including phonetic awareness, books studied or read, and development of the competence to manage unfamiliar books, including extended text, using the procedure developed by Gunning (1998). A team made up of district cadre members and consultants administered the Gunning procedure in June to ensure standardization of the tricky process of measuring the reading competence of very young children.

To what extent is variance in achievement explained by gender, developed language competence as students entered kindergarten, and cohort (class) group, variables that occur repeatedly in the literature and are reported as factors in many studies?

All 141 kindergarten-age students in the three schools were enrolled and are included in the study. The students came from a considerable variety of families (described in SES terms) and about 15 students from First Nations reservations were also included. Teacher judgment indicated that only one of the children entered kindergarten reading at any level. Only one student could recognize all the letters of the alphabet (tested out of the context of words).

Throughout the year the data were collected, summarized, and interpreted with respect to the response of the students. Here we concentrate on the most salient aspects of the student learning. The eight kindergarten sections followed similar patterns. Cohort (section) differences are small by comparison to the general effects. For us, this was very important. Had it been that only half of the teachers had been able to implement the curriculum successfully, we would have had to do some heavy thinking.

THE ALPHABET: RECOGNITION OF LETTERS

Tested in early October, the mean (out of 52 upper- and lowercase letters) was 31. In January, the mean was 46. In March, the mean was 52—all students could recognize all the letters out of context. Letter recognition was associated with the acquisition of sight vocabulary but one was not necessarily a function of the other—the learning of sight vocabulary appeared to pull letter recognition as much as the learning of the letters facilitated the acquisition of sight vocabulary.

ACQUISITION OF SIGHT VOCABULARY

The inquiry focussed on both how many words were being learned and on the students' ability to learn new words. The learning of words was studied in terms of the picture-word cycles, which ranged from about four to six weeks in length. Of interest here is the number of words learned in the cycles and also the increased efficiency developed by the students. The following data are taken from one of the sections.

Cycle One. Twenty-two words were shaken out. At the end of week one, the average number of words identified in an out-of-context assessment was five. By the end of week four, the average was 16 and one student knew all 22.

Cycle Two. Twenty-two words were shaken out. At the end of week one, the average number of words the students could identify out of context was 12. By the end of week three, the average was 20.

Cycle Three. Twenty eight words were shaken out. At the end of week one, the mean recognized in the out-of-context assessment was 20. At the end of week two the mean was 26, with just three students recognizing 24 and *none* recognizing fewer than 24.

All of the students appear to increase in efficiency to the point where by the end of January they were able to add to their sight vocabularies and within the first week or two almost all of the words were shaken out of the picture. For all sections, the mean percent of words recognized after two weeks of the first cycle was 30. By the third cycle, the mean had risen to 90 percent.

RETENTION OF WORDS

In May the focus sample of students was tested with respect to out-of-context recognition of the words shaken out through the year—for example, about 120 words in the previous section. Mean retention was 110. In addition, words added through the generation of titles, sentences, and paragraphs were learned, many of them in the high-frequency "useful little words" category. In that section, used as an example, those additional words added up to over 100.

Had the students had difficulty developing a sight vocabulary or retaining it we would have had a serious warning signal. Such a signal did not develop and, more important, the increase in capability was a positive signal. By mid-winter, the students were mastering words within two weeks that had taken them four or five weeks in the first cycle.

CLASSIFICATION OF WORDS—CATEGORIES DEVELOPED

Once the words were shaken out, they were entered into the computer and sets were given to each student. They could examine them and, if they did not recognize one, could use the picture-word dictionary to identify it. Also, classifying the words was an important component. Students were asked to sort their word cards according to the characteristics of the words. The teachers modeled classifications of various types throughout the year. In the first cycles, most students built categories on the presence of one or more letters. Then, more complex categories emerged, such as multiple syllable words with various sound combinations. The teachers selected categories for instructional emphasis and led the students to develop new words and unlock unfamiliar words using the categories. For example, having dealt with *work, works, worked, worker, working,* the students could hunt for other words from which derivatives could be made. Or, knowing *work* and encountering *working* in their reading, could try to unlock it as they learned how *ing* operates. As a category was selected for instructional emphasis, the instructional mode became quite explicit.

The teachers studied the categories that students were developing, keeping an eye on the phonetic and structural principles that were emerging. The results are too complex to summarize briefly, but, on the whole, about 30 phonetic and about 20 structural concepts were explored intensively.

TRANSITION TO THE READING OF BOOKS

Throughout the year, a profusion of books was available to the students. Books were carried home for "reading to and with," and little books generated from the picture-word activities went home to be read to the parents. As the students began to learn to read independently, books at their developed level accompanied them home. Records were kept: 80 percent of the students encountered 50 or more books in this fashion aside from books from home and library sources.

The assessment of independent reading levels was built around the Gunning framework, where the students attempt to read unfamiliar books at the following levels:

- Picture level—single words on a page are illustrated.
- Caption level—phrases or sentences, most but not all illustrated.
- Easy sight level—longer and more complex, mostly high frequency words.
- Beginning reading—four levels, progressively longer passages, less repetition and predictability.
- Grade 2A—require good-sized sight vocabulary and well-developed word attack skills.

Books at each level, beginning with the simplest, are read aloud. Deviations from print are noted and comprehension questions are asked after the book has been read. Fluency with total comprehension marks a level.

In the December assessment, all the students were able to deal with books at the picture level, and about one-fourth could manage caption level books comfortably. By February, about one-fourth had progressed to the easy sight level, and a handful could manage books at a higher level.

Again, had students not been able to approach any level of text competently, we would have had a warning that the curriculum was failing. However, they were progressing beyond the reading of the sentences and paragraphs developed in each PWIM cycle toward being able to manage simple books almost independently, with help available as they got stuck.

In June, the independent test team administered the assessment using a specially assembled set of books from United Kingdom publishers to reduce the likelihood that the books would be familiar to the students. Table 19.2 presents the June results aggregated for the eight sections. All eight sections apparently succeeded in bringing all the students to some level of print literacy. About 40 percent of the students appeared to be able to read extended text, and another 30 percent manifested emergent ability to read extended text. Twenty percent reached the grade 2A level, which includes long and complex passages and requires the exercise of complex skills both to decode and infer word meanings. All the students could manage at least the simplest level of books. Very important to us was that there were no students who experienced abject failure. Even the student who enters first grade reading independently at the picture level carries alphabet recognition, a substantial storehouse of sight words, and an array of phonetic and structural concepts to the first grade experience. However, a half dozen students need to be watched closely because, even if they were able to handle books at the caption level, they labored at the task, manifesting difficulty either in recognizing text–graphic relationships or using their phonetic or structural generalizations to attack unfamiliar words.

The data were studied to determine whether gender or SES influenced levels of success, and they did not. The distributions of levels for boys and girls were almost identical as were the distributions for students having or not having subsidies for lunch.

COMFORT AND SATISFACTION

During the year, parents voiced their opinions regularly. In May we prepared simple questionnaires for both the parents and the children. We asked

TABLE 19.2 **PERCENT OF STUDENTS REACHING GUNNING LEVELS AT END-OF-YEAR TESTING**

Level	Percent Reaching Level
Picture	2
Caption	26
Sight (emergent to extended text)	30
Above sight (can read extended text)	42

the parents a series of questions about the progress of their children and whether they and the children believed they were developing satisfactorily. The children were just asked whether they were learning to read and how they felt about their progress. Primarily, we were trying to ferret out whether there were levels of discomfort that were not being detected. Apparently not. No student or parent manifested discomfort or dissatisfaction related to the curriculum. However, some parents were anxious at the beginning and still worried at the end of the year. Some were concerned that we had not taken a letter-by-letter synthetic phonics approach and worried that future problems might develop as a consequence, but they appeared to believe that their children were progressing well "so far."

A YEAR LATER: LEAVING AT GRADE ONE

Throughout first grade, the students were followed and, at the end of the year were given the Gray Oral (Pro-Ed, 2001) by a team of external testers. As indicated earlier, the mean GLE was 3.5 (the average for students at the end of grade one is 2.0). Five percent of the students were below 2.0 compared to the typical 40 to 50 percent. In subsequent years the students will continue to be followed to learn their progress, and the lowest achieving students will be followed intensively to determine their progress. Also, at the end of the 2001–2002 academic year, another cohort of kindergarten students, this time from 14 sections, achieved about as well as did the 2000–2001 children in eight sections.

INTERPRETATION

The problem that faced us is whether research on beginning literacy has reached the place where we can design multidimensional curriculums that bring young children into the reading aspect of literacy with comfort and satisfaction. Our first experience is positive. The students will be followed through the grades and the curriculum will remain under scrutiny. The teachers were all new to a formal kindergarten reading curriculum and, with greater experience, will no doubt become increasingly able to provide ideas for its improvement. In this first year, they were scrambling to master a considerable number of unfamiliar instructional models, particularly the picture-word inductive model, and they spent considerable energy tracking the progress of the students and trying to figure out whether they were proceeding optimally and whether the tasks were well matched to the students.

The issues of developmental readiness are moot if the knowledge base permits the design of effective and humane kindergarten curriculums in reading. The progress of the students in these eight sections equals the progress of students in average first-grade classrooms and surpasses it in one very important way: these children did not fail whereas one-third of the students in average first grades do. The half-dozen students who have gained the least are arriving at first grade with substantial knowledge and skill.

We'll find out in the next couple of years how these students do in the other primary grades where similar curriculum change efforts are under way—making another story to tell. Thus far the results are encouraging. But, at the end of the year there are 400 students to follow because more sections have been added. We want outstanding achievement and to close the door on poor achievement either through the primary grade curriculum or the support of our safety net programs.

THOUGHTS

Here we have examples of curriculum development built around a combination of the research on how students acquire literacy and the integration of several models of teaching with built-in studies of student learning. Can other curriculum problems be attacked similarly? You bet they can.

CREATING CURRICULA

The Conditions of Learning

The Japanese teachers teach larger classes, but they have twice as much time to plan. That *might explain some of the variance in achievement.*

—Herb Walberg at the annual meeting of the
American Educational Research Association, 1991

Planning curricula, courses, units, and lessons is a sine qua non of good teaching. In this chapter we study planning with a master and then try to apply his framework to the problem of planning instruction.

One of the most important books on learning and teaching is Robert N. Gagné's *Conditions of Learning* (1965). Gagné gives us a careful analysis of the important variables in learning and how to organize instruction to take these variables into account. His picture of the "varieties of chance called learning" enables us to classify and specify learning objectives and the relationships *between* various kinds of performances.

Gagné identifies six varieties of performances that can be the result of learning:

1. Specific responding
2. Chaining
3. Multiple discrimination
4. Classifying
5. Rule using
6. Problem solving

VARIETIES OF PERFORMANCE _____

Specific responding is making a specific response to a particular stimulus. An example occurs when a first-grade teacher holds up a card (the stimulus) on which the word *dog* is printed and the children say "dog" (the response). Specific responding is an extremely important type of learning and is the basis for much of the information we possess. In order for the student to learn to make correct, specific responses, we must assume he or she has the ability to make connections between things. In the previous example, the printed word dog is associated, or connected, with the verbal statement "dog." Note that we are describing evidence of *learning* here—the student, able to respond, has learned at that level. How the learning was accomplished is a different matter. In other words, whether flashcards are or are not used is immaterial, as is whether any particular model of teaching was or was not used.

Chaining is making a series of responses that are linked together. Gagné uses the example of unlocking a door with a key and of translating from one language to another. Unlocking a door requires us to use a number of specific responses (selecting a key, inserting it, turning it) in an order that will get the job done. When one takes the English words "How are you?" and puts them together into a meaningful phrase, chaining is occurring. Similarly, translating them to "Cómo está usted?" in Spanish is chaining by taking a series of specific responses and linking them into phrases in both languages.

Multiple discrimination is involved in learning a variety of specific responses and chains and in learning how to sort them out appropriately. Discrimination applies to learned responses; one learns to associate colors with their names under similar conditions, such as learning to identify the colors of various objects in a particular room in one's home or in a school. Then one has to sort out the colors and apply them to varieties of objects under different conditions, such as in a shopping center (blue, first learned in relation to a blanket, is applied to a sweater in a store). More complex is sorting out and combining chains. Similarly, when learning a language, one develops a storehouse of words and phrases (chains). Spoken to, one has to sort out the reply, adjusting for gender, number, tense, and so forth. Multiple discrimination, then, involves learning to handle previously learned chains of various sorts.

Classifying is assigning objects to classes denoting like functions. Learning to distinguish plants from animals or automobiles from bicycles involves classifying. The result of this process is *concepts*, ideas that compare and contrast things and events or describe causal relations among them. When learning languages, one builds concepts that pertain to the structure of the language, concepts such as *subject*, *predicate*, *phrase*, *clause*, and the *various parts of speech*. The young language learner, by the age of four or five, has learned many of these concepts without having names for them, including relational concepts, such as modifying nouns with adjectives.

Rule using is the ability to act on a concept that implies action. For instance, in spelling we learn varieties of concepts that describe how words are spelled. Then we apply those concepts in rule form in the act of spelling itself. As an example, one learns that in consonant-vowel words ending in "t," such as *sit*, the consonant is doubled when *ing* is added. This becomes a rule (double the "t") that one usually follows in spelling such words.

Finally, *problem solving* is the application of several rules to a problem not encountered before by the learner. Problem solving involves selecting the correct rules and applying them in combination. For example, a child learns several rules about balancing on a seesaw and then applies them when moving a heavy object with a lever.

FACILITATING THE CLASSES OF LEARNING

Gagné believes that these six classes of learning form an ascending hierarchy; thus, before one can chain, one has to learn specific responses. Multiple discrimination requires prior learning of several chains. Classifying builds on multiple discrimination. Rules for action are forms of concepts learned through classification and the establishment of causal relations. Problem solving requires previously learned rules. Each level of learning requires certain conditions. The task of the instructor is to provide these conditions (by using the appropriate model of teaching).

To facilitate specific responding, a stimulus is presented to the student under conditions that will bring about his or her attention and induce a response closely related in time to the presentation of the stimulus. The response is then reinforced. Thus the teacher may hold up the word *dog*, say "dog," ask the children to say "dog," and then smile and say "good" to the students. A teacher who does this repeatedly increases the probability that the students will learn to recognize words and be able to emit the sounds associated with the symbols. The memory and training models are approaches that facilitate specific responding.

To facilitate the acquisition of chaining, a sequence of cues is offered and appropriate responses are induced. A language teacher may say, "How are you?" followed by "Cómo está usted?" inviting the students to say "How are you?" and "Cómo está usted?" and providing sufficient repetition that the students will acquire the chain and achieve fluency. The memory model, advance organizer, and inductive thinking models are appropriate to helping build chains.

To facilitate multiple discrimination, practice with correct and incorrect stimuli is needed, so that the students can learn to discriminate. For example, suppose the students are learning the Spanish expressions for "How are you?", "Good morning," and "Hello"; they must learn to discriminate which one to use in a given situation. The instructor provides sets of correct and incorrect stimuli until the students learn the appropriate discrimination. Advance organizers and inductive reasoning are useful in this process.

Classification is taught by presenting varieties of exemplars and concepts so that the students can gradually learn bases for distinguishing them. Concept attainment and inductive thinking are appropriate, among other models.

Rule using is facilitated by inducing the students to recall a concept and then apply it to a variety of specific applications. In the earlier spelling example, students recall the rule about doubling the final consonant when adding *ing* and are presented with examples they can practice. Inquiry training can help students move from concepts to rules, as can the application phases of concept attainment and inductive thinking.

Problem solving is largely done by the students themselves, because problem situations are unique. It can be facilitated by providing sets of problems that the students can attempt to attack, especially when the instructor knows that the students have acquired the rules needed to solve the problem. Inquiry training, group investigation, synectics, simulation, and nondirective teaching can be used for problem-solving activities.

FUNCTIONS OF THE INSTRUCTOR

Gagné emphasizes that it is the learner's activity that results in the learning. The function of the instructor is to provide conditions that will increase the probability that the student will acquire the particular performance. Practice is extremely important so that the learner makes the necessary connections, but it is the learner who makes the connections even when they are pointed out to him or her. The instructor cannot substitute his or her own activity for that of the student. We agree completely with Gagné on this point.

Instructors (or perhaps instructional systems) operate through the following instructional functions:

1. Informing the learner of the objectives
2. Presenting stimuli
3. Increasing learners' attention
4. Helping the learner recall what he or she has previously learned
5. Providing conditions that will evoke performance
6. Determining sequences of learning
7. Prompting and guiding the learning

Also, the instructor encourages the student to generalize what he or she is learning so that the new skills and knowledge will be transferred to other situations.

Informing the learner of the performance expected is critical for providing him or her with a definite goal. For example, the teacher might say, "Today we're going to try to learn about three presidents of the United States. We'll learn their names, when they lived, and what they are most known for." The teacher then presents the pictures of Washington, Lincoln, and Theodore Roosevelt. Their names are printed under the pictures. Pointing to the pictures and names and saying the names will draw the students' attention.

To recall previous learning, the teacher may say, "Do you remember that we discussed how the country has grown and changed in various ways? Can you tell me what some of these changes were?" The students can reach into their memories and stimulate themselves with material that will later be connected to the presidents.

To induce performance, a teacher may ask the students to name the three presidents and then read printed material describing the life of each. Then the teacher can ask them to tell him or her what they have learned.

A variety of sequences can be used, depending on the type of learning and the subject matter in question. Generally, however, presenting a stimulus, evoking attention, helping the learner understand the objectives, inducing performance, and then helping the learner to generalize are the major instructional tasks, which follow one another naturally.

Gagné's paradigm reminds us of a variety of important general principles of teaching: informing the learner of the levels of objectives being sought, encouraging generalization, and pushing for application of what is learned.

Gagné emphasizes that we cannot control learning but can only increase the probability that certain kinds of behavior will occur. We can present stimuli in close connection with others and ask the student to perform, but it is the *learner* who makes the connection between the printed and spoken word:

> Essentially, however carefully one controls the aspects of external learning conditions described previously, instruction nevertheless can only make the occurrence of the crucial internal, idiosyncratic event of learning more probable. The careful design of instruction can surely increase its probability, and, by so doing, make the entire process of learning more sure, more predictable and more efficient. But the individual nervous system must still make its own individual contribution. The nature of that contribution is, of course, what defines the need for the study of individual differences (Gagné, 1967, pp. 291–313).

From this point of view, a model of teaching brings structures to the student that change the probability that he or she will learn certain things. The syntax presents tasks to the student, the reactions of the teacher pull the student toward certain responses, and the social system generates a need for particular kinds of interaction with others. The net effect is to make it more likely that various kinds of learning will take place. In Table 20.1, several information-processing models and a few from other families are paired with the six varieties of performance that Gagné has identified.

TABLE 20.1   **MODELS ESPECIALLY APPROPRIATE FOR VARIETIES OF PERFORMANCE**

Types of Performance	Models				
Specific responding	Memory	Inductive thinking	Phase one of concept attainment	Advance organizer	Group investigation (data-gathering activities)
Chaining	Concept attainment	Inductive thinking			
Multiple discrimination	Inquiry training				
Classifying	Concept attainment	Inductive thinking	Advance organizer		
Rule using	Inquiry training	Simulation	Inductive thinking		
Problem solving	Synectics	Scientific thinking	Inquiry training	Group investigation	

Gagné's hierarchy is useful in helping us select models appropriate for varieties of educational objectives. It also reminds us of the multiple types of learning promoted by individual models and the attention that must be given to the varieties of performance as the students engage in the study of any important topic. For example, students using inductive thinking to explore a problem in international relations, such as the balance of imports and exports, will gather data (specific responding and chaining), organize it (multiple discrimination and classifying), and develop principles (rule using) to explore solutions to problems (problem solving).

PLANNING A COURSE: GLOBAL EDUCATION

Let's see what happens when we put Gagné's hierarchy to work. Let's design a global education curriculum that we can use from the primary grades through high school. Such a complex curriculum will give us the opportunity to consider quite a range of models, and we will almost certainly want to use several of them to design the instructional aspects of such a curriculum.

We'll begin with a somewhat arbitrary statement of our overall objectives. Note that we begin with objectives at the problem-solving level because those will guide our selection of objectives at the other levels of Gagné's hierarchy. A common mistake to be avoided in planning is to begin at the response level and then try to "squeeze" the more complex types of learning from responses. Rather, one should begin at the most complex level (problem solving) and then determine what needs to be learned to make problem solving possible.

OVERALL OBJECTIVES

To ensure that the students have a working knowledge of human geography, can think about some of the critical issues facing the peoples of the world, and are prepared to interact productively with people from cultures other than theirs. Our rationale is that the global perspective is essential for personal understanding, for the guidance of our nation, for the betterment of the world, and for economic competence. At one level, we want our students to graduate with the learning that will enable them to spin a globe, put a finger down on a land mass, and know considerable information about the nation it lights on. At another level, we want them to have considerable knowledge of several representative cultures and to be able to think of the world and our nation in terms of cultural history and cultural comparison. At yet another level, we want them to have experience thinking about and generating solutions to important global problems.

A secondary overall objective is to use the study of the globe to further the reading/writing curriculum, especially the reading and writing of expository prose. (This objective appears across all curriculum areas!)

BUILDING OPERATIONAL OBJECTIVES

Several models of teaching can help us clarify our objectives and transform them into goals for which we can plan.

Integrative Complexity, Cognitive Development, and Concept of Self. Let's begin with the models that highlight individual differences. Understanding the globe and its multiple cultures will require a high level of integrative complexity as the students try to develop a perspective on complex problems and how to understand the concept of culture and how to reconcile one's own cultural perspective with that of persons from other cultures.

The framework for studying cognitive development helps us think about the kinds of objectives that can be reasonably aimed for at different ages. The littlest kids can certainly absorb information about one or two other cultures, but thinking abstractly about the cultural spectrum would be a bit much. The upper elementary students can learn to manipulate demographic data about the nations of the world and can search for correlations among variables; they can learn to ask, for example, whether the wealth of nations is correlated with educational levels, fertility, and so on. They can compare cultures with respect to the more visible and concrete variables—housing, family styles, occupations, and so forth. The secondary students can handle complex multicultural problems, compare and contrast cultures with respect to more abstract variables, such as norms, and make inferences about how various nations would respond to particular types of problems, such as population growth, threats of war, and the global ecology.

Studies of self-concept help us in several ways. First, the general orientation reminds us that the entire curriculum should be conducted in a manner to increase the students' sense of ability to learn and to master complex material. Second, it keeps in front of us that self-understanding is vital. Thinking about world cultures is practically ready-made for aspects of self-understanding, for it should help the students think about their own culture in relation to others and to understand how cultural values affect thinking and behavior.

Let us also think from the perspective of the families of models of teaching.

Cooperative Action and Mutual Understanding.   The social family offers the perspective of building a cooperative community of learners (not a bad objective in itself) and helping that community explore the world together and surface the important value questions. Role playing offers us a tool for helping the students study their own values as the inquiry progresses. Jurisprudential inquiry invites us to approach issues by clarifying them and the value positions underlying various alternatives.

Learning Information, Concepts, Hypothesis Building, and Testing. The information-processing family places at our disposal a set of relevant tools. The development of concepts will be necessary to manage the mass of information, and thinking about relationships will give our students many hypotheses to test. Synectics can help students break set and generate alternative solutions to global problems and international relations. The link-word method is there to help the students master unfamiliar terms, and there will be many of them.

Self-Actualization and Self-Direction.   If the makers of the personal models have their way, we will provide much opportunity for self-directed inquiry and will urge our students not just to follow immediate interests or work at their current level of development, but to stretch themselves into new areas and toward "personal bests" in learning. We will make their feelings a part of the subject matter and will recognize always that knowledge is a personal construction.

LITERACY AND THE PICTURE-WORD INDUCTIVE MODEL

Now, let us turn to the picture-word module and plan a sequence of lessons using Gagné's framework. Consider the following scenario.

S C E N A R I O

Judith's five-year-olds at Hempshill Hall Primary School are working on building their reading vocabularies. They are also beginning their study of phonics by analyzing the structures (spelling) of words that are in their listening, speaking, and reading vocabularies.

The children are seated on the floor, facing a poster that features a teddy bear in the countryside. The poster is mounted in the middle of a large blank sheet of paper. Judith says, "We're going to get some of the words for this week's reading vocabulary by shaking words out of this picture. I want you to study the picture carefully and then, when I call on you, come up and point to something in the picture and say what it is. Then I'll write the word and draw a line from the thing in the picture to the word. We'll start learning to read the words as we go along."

The children study the picture. After a while, Judith asks them if they have found something they'd like to share. All the hands go up and Judith calls on Jessica.

Jessica reaches up, points, and says, "That's a ladder." Judith draws a line from the ladder and writes the word, saying the letters as she does so. She then spells "ladder" again, while the children watch and listen.

"Now, I'll spell it again, and you say each letter after me." She does, and then asks another child for a word.

"Sit," says Brian, and points to the teddy bear. "The bear's sitting."

SPECIFIC RESPONDING

Judith draws a letter from the bear and writes. "The bear's sitting." She spells each word as she writes it and then takes the children to each word in turn, saying them, spelling them, and asking the children to spell them after her. She then points to the first word. "What is this word?"

"Ladder," they chorus.

"And if you saw the word and couldn't remember it, what could you do?"

"Go down the line to the ladder in the picture," they say.

"Right. And what's this word?" pointing to the word "the."

"The," they chorus again. She repeats the process with "bear's" and "sitting" and then asks for the whole sentence, but calls on Nancy.

"The bear's sitting," says Nancy.

"Who thinks she's right?" asks Judith. The children's hands go up. Judith continues to elicit words from the children, continuing the pattern as before, examining each word and regularly reviewing all of them.

CHAINING

By the end of the session, the following list has been accumulated, and the children can say each one as she points to it. Judith finishes by asking them to see if they notice any of the words in the books they are taking home for the evening to share with their parents. As they break, an older child who has been recording the words on a computer saves the file and hands her the disk.

ladder	apple	leaf	bear
teddy bear	sitting bear	half-eaten	trunk
tree	apple tree	apples	trees
ate	basket	basketgrass	tree trunk
little trees	ladder	apple core	teddy
core	half-eaten apple	The bear's sitting.	leaves

The following day, as the children enter the classroom, some of them go up to the picture and look at the words, saying them to each other and following words they don't remember down the lines to the objects those words are connected to. Again, the children sit next to the poster and Judith has them read the words, using the picture to help them locate the referents for the words.

MULTIPLE DISCRIMINATION

Judith has taken the file of words that were shaken out of the picture, put them into a large font, and printed them out, making a set of word cards. She gives each child a complete set. Now she asks the children to read their sets and, if they can't remember a word, to go to the poster, find the word, and trace it down to the part of the picture it represents.

Much activity ensues. The children peer at the words, saying them, usually aloud, to themselves. Occasionally, they ask Judith if they are right, and she sends them to the picture to find out for themselves. Soon children are getting up and down, holding a word card and locating the word on the chart.

ELABORATE MULTIPLE DISCRIMINATION _____

Judith then asks them for sentences that describe the picture as a whole, and gets sentences like, "The teddy bear is sitting in the countryside" and "There are apples all over the place." One child asks a question. Pointing to an apple core she wonders, "Who do you suppose ate that apple? Can teddy bears eat apples?" Judith records the sentences, and they read them together before closing the session.

CLASSIFICATION _____

The following morning she again reviews the poster chart with the children. Then she asks them to take out their word cards and put words together according to how they are spelled.

Here are some of the categories they came up with.

Jessica: "'Tree' and 'trees' and 'ladder' have two letters the same in them."

"Super! Can you point to the letters?" Jessica does so. "Did anyone else put words together for the same reason? Nancy?"

"I put 'apple' and 'teddy' together because one has two p's together and the other has two d's together."

Brian adds, "I put 'teddy' and 'ladder' together because they have two d's in the middle."

Judith: "Let's look at 'apple' and 'apples.' How are they the same and how are they different?" Several children volunteer and she calls on Dylan.

"They're spelled the same except for the s's. And 'apple' is just one apple and 'apples' is two apples."

RULE USING _____

Judith asks why "tree" and "trunk" might be put together.

The children are puzzled for a minute, and then hands begin to go up. Judith waits until nearly all the kids have an idea and then calls on Brendan. "Probably because 'tree' and 'trunk' sound the same at the beginning." They discuss Brendan's answer and then Judith writes "sound the same."

Finally, the children read the set of words on the chart once more and end for the day, requested to hunt for the words in their evening's reading.

PROBLEM SOLVING _____

Judith has been using a strategy called the *picture-word inductive model,* as in Chapter 5. This is a model for eliciting words from the children's listening and speaking vocabulary so that those words can be studied and mastered and, through classification, be a basis for the early exploration of phonics. Ultimately, solving the problems of word identification and developing sight vocabularies are the students' problems. But we can help, as in Chapter 19.

CHAPTER 21

INQUIRIES
A Research Brief

> *Educational research has its limitations, but sorting it out is vital.*
> *So is explaining that, thus far, it doesn't lead to one model for*
> *all purposes, but many for the many purposes of teaching.*
> —David Hopkins to Emily Calhoun and Bruce Joyce

S C E N A R I O

The teachers of Kaiser Elementary School in the Newport/Costa Mesa School District have been learning to use the inductive model of teaching to help their students connect reading and writing. The objective is to see if the students can learn to generate better-quality writing by analyzing how expert writers work. For example, when studying how to introduce characters, the students classify the approaches used by authors in the books they are reading. They then experiment with the devices they have identified.

Periodically, the teachers ask the students to produce writing elicited with standardized content and prompts. The students might watch a segment of film that introduces a character and then be asked to provide a written introduction to the character. These samples of writing are scored with an instrument developed at the UCLA Center for Research on Evaluation (Quellmalz and Burry, 1983) to measure quality of writing across the grades. This instrument yields scores on three dimensions of quality.

The year before the teachers began to design the teaching of writing with the inductive model, the average gain during a year was about 20 points on the scale. For example, the fourth-grade average climbed from a score of 180 to 200. The grade-six average moved from about 220 to about 240. As the teachers taught the students to make the connection between reading and writing, the average gain jumped to about 90 points the first year. The average student gained about four and a half times more than the average gain the previous year. No student gained less than 40 points. Some gained as much as 140 points.

The teachers surveyed the research on the teaching of writing and found some examples of what looked like large gains when particular curriculum approaches were implemented. They wondered how they could compare the results of their efforts when some studies used different scales. In this chapter we will explore what the Kaiser teachers found—a tool that will help us as we examine the research underlying various models of teaching. More important, we'll see how that tool can be applied to your inquiries into teaching.

Our Kaiser teachers are inquirers. They conduct teaching as an action research activity, using the knowledge base on teaching as a starting point, then studying student response, preparing to adapt what they are doing and also to seek new models that can enhance their students' learning repertoire.

This chapter is an introduction to the knowledge base and to tools for individual and collective inquiry into teaching. Models of teaching link educational theory and research to contemporary classroom practice. Each model is built on long study of teaching and learning. But they are all in the process of being improved, both through formal research and through the study of teacher-researchers all over the world. Thus, we urge that you use the models as a framework for your study of teaching and as points of departure for your inquiry rather than regarding them as formulas that will work without further need to study student response.

We'll begin our quest with an important tool, one that can be used to assess the existing knowledge base and that will help us conduct inquiry linked to that base.

THE CONCEPT OF EFFECT SIZE

We use the concept of "effect size" (Glass, 1982) to describe the magnitude of gains from any given change in educational practice and thus to predict what we can hope to accomplish by using that practice.

To introduce the idea, let us consider a study conducted by Dr. Bharati Baveja with the authors (1988) in the Motilal Nehru School of Sports about 30 miles northwest of New Delhi, India. Dr. Baveja designed her study to test the effectiveness of an inductive approach (see Chapter 3) to a botany unit compared with an intensive tutorial treatment. All the students were given a test at the beginning of the unit to assess their knowledge before instruction began and were divided into two groups equated on the basis of achievement. The control group studied the material with the aid of tutoring and lectures on the material—the standard treatment in Indian schools for courses of this type. The experimental group worked in pairs and were led through inductive and concept attainment exercises emphasizing classification of plants.

Figure 21.1 shows the distribution of scores for the experimental and control groups on the posttest which, like the pretest, contained items dealing with the information pertaining to the unit.

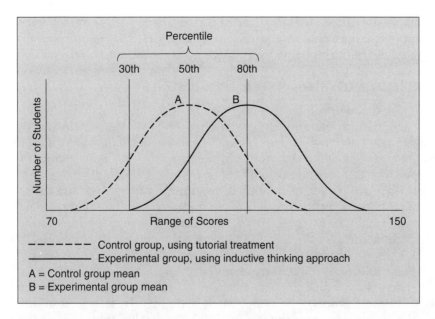

FIGURE 21.1   Distribution of student scores on posttest for a botany unit.
Baveja, 1988.

The difference between the experimental and control groups was a little above a standard deviation. The difference, computed in terms of standard deviations, is the *effect size of the inductive treatment.* Essentially, what
that means is that the experimental-group average score was where the 80th
percentile score was for the control group. The difference increased when a
delayed recall test was given 10 months later, indicating that the information acquired with the concept-oriented strategies was retained somewhat
better than information gained via the control treatment.

Calculations like these enable us to compare the magnitude of the potential effects of the innovations (teaching skills and strategies, curricula, and
technologies) that we might use in an effort to affect student learning. We can
also determine whether the treatment has different effects for all kinds of students or just for some. In the study described just above, the experimental
treatment was apparently effective for the whole population. The lowest score
in the experimental-group distribution was about where the 30th-percentile
score was for the control group, and about 30 percent of the students exceeded the highest score obtained in the control.

Although substantial in their own right, gains in learning and retention
of information were modest when we consider the effect on the students'
ability to identify plants and their characteristics, which was measured on
a separate test. The scores by students from the experimental group were
eight times higher than the scores for the control group. Baveja's inquiry

confirmed her hypothesis that the students, using the inductive model, were able to apply the information and concepts from the unit much more effectively than were the students from the tutorial treatment.

FURTHER INQUIRY INTO EFFECT SIZE

Let's work through some concepts that are useful in describing distributions of scores to deepen our understanding a bit. We describe distributions of scores in terms of the *central tendencies*, which refer to the clustering of scores around the middle of the distribution, and variance, or their dispersion. Concepts describing central tendency include the *average* or arithmetic mean, which is computed by summing the scores and dividing by the number of scores, the *median* or middle score (half of the others are above and half below the median score), and the mode, which is the most frequent score (graphically, the highest point in the distribution). In Figure 21.2 the median, average, and mode are all in the same place, because the distribution is completely symmetrical.

Dispersion is described in terms of the *range* (the distance between the highest and lowest scores), the rank, which is frequently described in *percentiles* (the 20th score from the top in a 100-person distribution is at the 80th percentile because 20 percent of the scores are above and 80 percent are below it), and the *standard deviation*, which describes how widely or

FIGURE 21.2   A sample normal distribution.

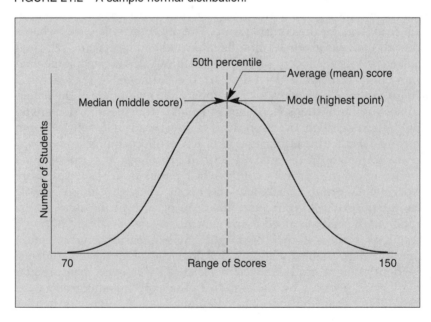

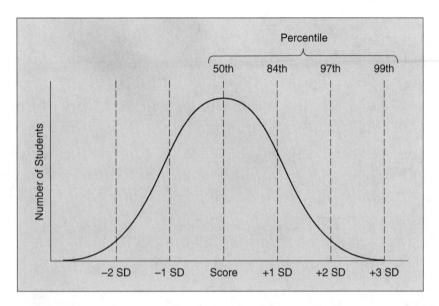

FIGURE 21.3 A sample normal distribution with standard deviations.

narrowly scores are distributed. In Figure 21.3 the range is from 70 (the lowest score) to 150 (the highest score). The 50th-percentile score is at the middle (in this case corresponding with the average, the mode, and the median). The standard deviations are marked off by the vertical lines labeled +1 SD, +2 SD, and so on. Note that the percentile rank of the score 1 standard deviation above the mean is 84 (84 percent of the scores are below that point); the rank 2 standard deviations above the mean is 97; and 3 standard deviations above the mean is 99.

When the mean, median, and mode coincide as in these distributions, and the distribution of scores is as symmetrical as the ones depicted in these figures, the distribution is referred to as *normal*. This concept is useful in statistical operations, although many actual distributions are not symmetrical, as we will see. To explain the concept of effect size, we will use symmetrical, "normal" distributions before illustrating how the concept works with differently shaped distributions.

Thus, in Figure 21.4 we will convert the results of the study of group investigation that appeared in Table 1.1 to graphical form. Figure 21.4 compares the posttest scores of the low-SES students in the "whole-class" and "group investigation" treatments. The average score of the "group investigation" treatment corresponds to about the 92nd percentile of the distribution of the "whole-class" students. The effect size is computed by dividing the difference between the two means by the standard deviation

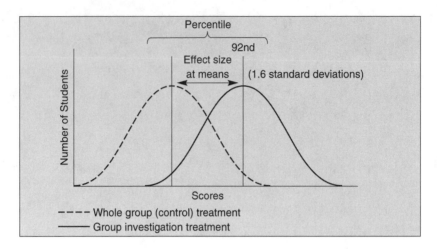

FIGURE 21.4   A sample effect size. Sharan and Shachar, 1988.

of the "control" or "whole-class" group. The effect size in this case is 1.6 standard deviations using the formula

$$ES = \frac{\text{average of experimental group} - \text{average of control group}}{\text{standard deviation of control group}}$$

$$\frac{50.17 - 27.23}{13.73} = 1.6$$

Throughout the chapter figures like these will provide an idea about the relative effects one can expect if one teaches students with each model of teaching compared with using the normative patterns of curriculum and instruction. We will create each figure from an analysis of the research base currently available and will usually build the figure to depict the average effects from large numbers of studies.

When using the research base to decide when to use a given model of teaching it is important to realize that size of effects is not the only consideration. We have to consider the nature of the objectives and the uses of the model. For example, in Spaulding's study described above, the effect size on ability measures was just 0.5, or about a half standard deviation (see Figure 21.5).

However, ability is a powerful attribute, and a model or combination of models that can increase ability will have an effect on everything the student does for years to come, increasing learning through those years. The simplest cooperative learning procedures have relatively modest effect sizes, affecting feelings about self as a learner, social skills, and academic

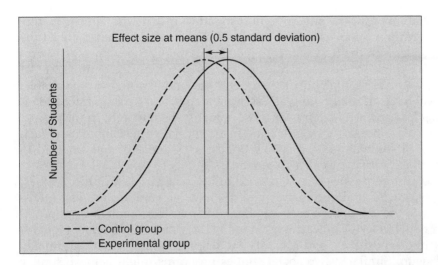

FIGURE 21.5 A sample effect size on measures of ability. Spaulding, 1970.

learning, and they are easy to use and have wide applications. Thus, their modest effect can be felt more regularly and broadly than some models that have more dramatic effect sizes with respect to a given objective.

Some models can help us virtually eliminate dispersion in a distribution. For example, a colleague of ours used mnemonic devices to teach his fourth-grade students the names of the states and their capitals. All his students learned all of them and remembered them throughout the year. Thus the distribution of his class's scores on tests of their ability to supply all the names on a blank map had no range at all. The average score was the highest possible score. There were no percentile ranks because the students' scores were all tied at the top. For some objectives—basic knowledge about the U.S. Constitution, computation skills, a basic reading vocabulary—we want to have a very high degree of success for all our students because anything less is terribly disadvantaging for them—*and* for their society.

Although high effect sizes make a treatment attractive, size alone is not the only consideration when choosing among alternatives. Modest effect sizes that affect many persons can have a large payoff for the population. A comparison with medicine is worthwhile. Suppose a dread disease is affecting a population and we possess a vaccine that will reduce the chances of contracting the disease by only 10 percent. If a million persons might become infected without the vaccine but 900,000 if it is used, the modest effect of the vaccine might save 100,000 lives. In education, some estimates suggest that during the first year of school about one million children each year (about 30 percent) make little progress toward learning to read. We also know that lack of success in reading instruction is in fact a dread educational disease, since for each year that initial instruction is unsuccessful the probability that the student will respond to instruction later is greatly lowered. Would a modestly effective treatment—say, one that reduced the lack of success in the first year for 50,000 children by 5 percent—be worthwhile? We think so. Also, several such treatments might be cumulative. Of course, we prefer a high-effect treatment, but one is not always available. Even when it is, it might not reach some students, and we might need to resort to a less-powerful choice for those students. Fortunately, in the area of literacy, we do possess curricular and instructional patterns that can reach virtually all students (see especially Chapters 19 and 20), and we need to choose those over the weaker treatments.

Also, different types of effects need to be considered. Attitudes, values, concepts, intellectual development, skills, and information are just a few. Keeping to the example of early reading, two treatments might be approximately equal in terms of learning to read in the short run, but one might affect attitudes positively and leave the students feeling confident and ready to try again. Similarly, two social studies programs might achieve similar amounts of information and concepts, but one might excel in attitudes toward citizenship. In the most dramatic instances, when the effect size reaches five or six standard deviations, the lowest-scoring student in the experimental treatment exceeds the highest-scoring student in the control treatment! This is a rare event, of course, but when it does occur, it gives us great hope about the potential of educational practice.

Again, as we describe some practices and the effects that can be expected from them, we should not concentrate on magnitude of effects alone. Self-instructional programs that are no more effective than standard instruction can be very useful because they enable students to teach themselves and can be blended with agent-delivered instruction. Broadcast television, because of its potential to reach so many children, can make a big difference even though it is modestly effective in comparison with standard instruction. *Sesame Street* and the *Electric Company* (Ball and Bogatz, 1970) are examples. They are not dramatically more effective than first-grade instruction without them, but they produce positive attitudes and augment instruction handsomely, enabling a certain percentage of students to virtually teach themselves. In fact, distance education and media-based instruction (learning from television, computer-assisted instruction, and packages of multimedia materials) need not be more effective to be terribly useful. For example, in a high school that does not offer a given foreign language, a student who can learn that language by self-study assisted by television, computer programs, and such can benefit greatly. The British Open University, operated as distance education augmented by tutorial centers, virtually doubled the number of university graduates in the United Kingdom, and the performance of its students on academic tests compared favorably with the performance of "regular" university students.

Some procedures can interact productively with others. One-to-one tutoring has a very large effect size (Bloom, 1984) and might interact productively with some teaching strategies. Or, as is evidently the case within the "Success for All" (Slavin, Madden, Karweit, Livermon, and Dolan, 1990; Slavin, Madden, and Wasik, 1996) and "Reading Recovery" (Pinnell, 1989; 1994) programs, it is incorporated within a curriculum management system that enables short periods of tutoring to pay off handsomely. On the other hand, "tracking" hurts the effectiveness of any procedure (Oakes, 1986).

Simply learning the size of effects of a year's instruction can be very informative, as we learned from the National Assessment of Writing Progress (Applebee et al., 1990). This assessment revealed that the effect size of instruction in writing nationally is such that the average eighth-grade student is about at the 62nd percentile of the fourth-grade distribution! Schools may want to learn how much better they can do than that!

Measures of learning can be of many kinds. School grades are of great importance, as are measures of conduct such as counts of referrals and suspensions. In fact, staff development programs want to give close attention to those measures as well as simple measures such as how many books students read. Content analyses of student work are very important, as in the study of quality of writing. Curriculum-relevant tests (those that measure the content of a unit or course) are important. Finally, the traditional standardized tests can be submitted to an analysis that produces estimates of effect size.

S C E N A R I O

When our Kaiser School faculty discovered the concept of effect size, they were able to calculate the effects of their efforts in such a way that they could compare their results to those of other efforts. They consulted the review of research on writing conducted by George Hillocks (1987) and found that the average effect size of "inquiry" approaches to the teaching of writing was 0.67 compared to textbook-oriented instruction. The average student in the average treatment was at about the 70th percentile of the distributions of students taught by the textbook method. For each grade the teachers carefully calculated the effect size. For example, their sixth grade had gained an average of 90 points compared with an average of 20 the previous year (the control), a difference of 70 points. The standard deviation of the control year was 55. Dividing 55 into 70 they calculated an effect size of 1.27, nearly twice the average in the Hillocks review. The average student in the first year the inductive model was used was at approximately the 90th percentile of the distribution of the control year. Figure 21.6 depicts the two distributions.

As we said before, our Kaiser teachers are inquirers. They picked a model of teaching, learned to use it, and inquired into its effects on the students. The inquiry will lead them to continue to search for ways of using that

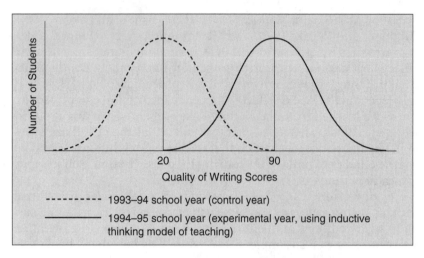

FIGURE 21.6   Comparison of student gains in quality of writing before and after introducing the inductive thinking model of teaching. Kaiser Elementary School, Newport/Costa Mesa School District, California.

model well and for other models that can serve their students. They are classic "teacher-researchers."

The state of the art is not such that any specific curricular or instructional models can solve *all* problems of student learning. Educational research is in its infancy. We hope that the readers of this book will not just use it as a source of teaching and learning strategies, but will learn how to add to the knowledge base. There are millions of teachers in the United States alone. If only 1 percent conducted and reported one study each year, there would be 20,000 new studies every year, a knowledge increment several times larger than the entire current base. But aside from contributing to the larger knowledge base, teachers in any school can, by studying their teaching, share ideas that can help everyone in the school become more effective.

GETTING GOING: SURVEYING THE KNOWLEDGE BASE

The following pages are designed to provide an introduction to some of the research underlying the models of teaching and also some other sources of research on teaching practices. The aspects of research dealt with are ones that we believe can provide some understanding of the yield to date, but the review is not exhaustive. To summarize all the research would require several volumes. This book is about teaching, so most of its space needs to be devoted to the models and how they work. However, the models rely heavily on the knowledge base. We need to consider the nature of that base and how to use it to help us select the models that will best fuel our quest to do our job knowledgeably and well. Our focus is on what can be achieved if any given model is used well. From that starting point, you learn one model and conduct your own inquiry to see how it works and whether you can improve it.

THE NATURE OF INQUIRY
INTO MODELS OF TEACHING

Most models of teaching are designed for specific purposes—the teaching of information, concepts, ways of thinking, the study of social values, and so on—by asking students to engage in particular cognitive and social tasks. The research generally begins with a thesis describing an educational environment, its presumed effects, and a rationale that links the environment and its intended effects—how to develop concepts or to learn them, how to build theories, memorize information, solve problems, learn skills. Some models center on delivery by the instructor while others develop as the learners respond to tasks, and the student is regarded as a partner in the educational enterprise. However, all mature educational models emphasize how to help students learn to construct knowledge—learning how to learn—including learning from sources that are often stereotyped as passive, such as learning from lectures, films, reading assignments, and such.

Testing instructional models requires training teachers to use them. The first step in theory-driven research is often the collection of baseline data about how the teachers normally teach. Then the teachers are prepared to use the new teaching behaviors, including how to teach the students the "learning skills" essential to the model. Since most teachers have used the "recitation" or "lecture-recitation" as the primary mode of teaching (Goodlad, 1984; Goodlad and Klein, 1970; Hoetker and Ahlbrand, 1969; Sirotnik, 1983), training in new strategies must be extensive enough that the new model becomes comfortable. Implementation of the new behavior is monitored, either in the regular classroom or in a laboratory setting, and theory-relevant student behaviors or outcomes are measured. Experimental classrooms are often compared with control classrooms to determine the presence, direction, and magnitude of change, with the use of the concept of effect size. In lines of programmatic research, such as those conducted by Pressley, Levin, and their colleagues on mnemonics (Levin and Levin, 1990) and those by Sharan (1990, 1992) and his colleagues on complex cooperative learning models, repeated studies attempt to engineer increasingly effective ways of helping students learn. One way of looking at this type of research is that the development of a model of teaching is the process of submitting an educational idea to repeated testing and refinement until the idea has matured to the point where fairly precise predictions can be made about how to use it and the effects to be expected if it is implemented well. In nearly all cases, the mastery of a model by the students is the key to effectiveness—the students have to learn how to engage in the particular learning process emphasized by that model.

INQUIRY INTO COOPERATIVE LEARNING MODELS —————————————————

COOPERATIVE LEARNING

There have been three lines of research on ways of helping students study and learn together, one led by David and Roger Johnson, a second by Robert Slavin, and the third by Shlomo and Yael Sharan and Rachel Hertz-Lazarowitz in Israel. Among other things, the Johnsons and their colleagues (1974, 1981, 1990) have studied the effects of cooperative task and reward structures on learning. The Johnsons' (1975a, 1981) work on peers teaching peers has provided information about the effects of cooperative behavior on both traditional learning tasks and on values and intergroup behavior and attitudes. Their models emphasize the development of what they call *positive interdependence*, or cooperation where collective action also celebrates individual differences. Slavin's extensive 1983 review includes the study of a variety of approaches where he manipulates the complexity of the social tasks and experiments with various types of grouping. He reported success with the use of heterogeneous groups with tasks requiring coordination of group members, both on academic learning and intergroup relations, and has generated a variety of strategies that employ extrinsic and intrinsic reward structures. The Israeli team has concentrated on group investigation, the most complex of the social models of teaching.

What is the magnitude of effects that we can expect when we learn to use the cooperative learning strategies effectively? The Johnsons' (1999) recent review estimated that, for the years over which several hundred studies have been accumulated, the average effect size on academic learning is about 0.61, which means that, on tests of academic learning, the average student engaged in cooperative learning (rather than competitive learning) scores a little above the 70th percentile of students instructed in competitive circumstances. Rolheiser-Bennett (1986) compared the effects of the degrees of cooperative structure required by the several approaches (Joyce, Showers, and Rolheiser-Bennett, 1989). On standardized tests in the basic curriculum areas (such as reading and mathematics), the highly structured approaches to teaching students who work together generated effect sizes of an average 0.28 with some studies approaching half a standard deviation. On criterion-referenced tests the average was 0.48, with some of the best implementations reaching an effect of about 1 standard deviation. The more elaborate cooperative learning models generated an average effect size of somewhat more than 1 standard deviation, with some exceeding 2 standard deviations. (The average student was above the 90th percentile student in the control group.) The effects on higher-order thinking were even greater, with an average effect of about 1.25 standard deviations and effects in some studies as high as 3 standard deviations (Figure 21.7).

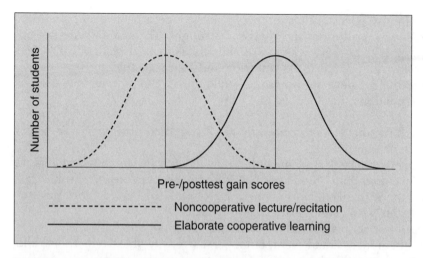

FIGURE 21.7   Effects of elaborate cooperative learning strategies on student achievement compared with noncooperative lecture/recitation procedures.

COOPERATION THROUGH THE SCHOOL

Research that compares schools has gone on for some time. In the early years, these studies were designed on a planned-variation model, where schools operating from different stances toward education were compared with one another. For example, 50 years ago the beautifully designed "eight-year study" (Chamberlin and Chamberlin, 1943) submitted the theses of the Progressive Movement (largely cooperative learning-oriented) to a serious (and generally successful) test and defended it against the suggestion that social and personal models of education were dangerous to the academic health of students. Recent research on unusually effective schools has found that one of their most prominent characteristics is a cooperative social climate in which all faculty and students work together to build a supportive, achievement-oriented climate.

Over the last 10 years, the Johnsons (1991, 1995, 1996) have conducted a series of studies on training students to manage conflict. They have demonstrated that students can learn to manage conflict fairly effectively, engaging fellow students in integrative rather than volatile confrontations over disagreements and reducing the likelihood of unresolved and acrimonious interchanges.

Cohen (1998) has pointed out that cooperative learning has to devote special attention to the equalization of status. In many classrooms, gender and socioeconomic inequalities have to be dealt with directly, and students need to learn how to create equitable situations in which all of their peers are provided with equal opportunities for participation and satisfaction.

The Johnsons stress that teachers using cooperative learning methods need to stress at all times the goals to be sought. The students are not expected simply to cooperate, but to develop focus toward academic or social goals and maintain that focus (Johnson and Johnson, 1999, p. 74).

From their review, the Johnsons (1999; pp. 90–94) have derived a set of recommendations that include:

"Teaching the students how to work together positively and inter-
    dependently,
Ensuring that each student studies how they are progressing—individual
    accountability should not be lost in the cooperative endeavor,
Working with all students cooperatively—there are no categories of stu-
    dents who cannot learn together, and
Creating a cooperative classroom and school—cooperative learning is
    not an occasional event, but a pervasive way of learning to live and
    work together."

SUMMARY

Taken as a whole, research on cooperative learning is overwhelmingly positive—nearly every study has had from modest to very high effects. Moreover, the cooperative approaches are effective over a range of achievement measures. The more intensely cooperative the environment, the greater the effects—and the more complex the outcomes (higher-order processing of information, problem solving), the greater the effects.

The cooperative environment engendered by these models has had substantial effects on the cooperative behavior of the students, increasing feelings of empathy for others, reducing intergroup tensions and aggressive and antisocial behavior, improving moral judgment, and building positive feelings toward others, including those of other ethnic groups. Many of these effect sizes are substantial—1 or 2 standard deviations are not uncommon and one is as high as 8. Hertz-Lazarowitz (1993) used one of the models to create integrative interaction between Israeli and Arab students in the West Bank! Margarita Calderon has worked with Lazarowitz and Jusefina Tinajero to adapt a cooperative integrated reading and composition program for bilingual students with some nice results (Calderon, Hertz-Lazarowitz, and Tinajero, 1991). An adaptation in higher education that organizes students into cooperative study groups reduced a dropout rate in engineering from 40 to about 5 percent (Bonsangue, 1993). Conflict-resolution strategies have taught students to develop integrative behavior and reduced social tension in some very divided environments in inner-city schools (Johnson and Johnson, 1990).

Cooperative learning has a positive effect on a wide array of students. An impressive study of peer-assisted learning strategies (Fuchs, Fuchs, Mathes, and Simmons, 1997) examined the effects on students of various learning histories and found good-sized results for all categories of students. Wentzel (1991) came to the conclusion that the development of social responsibility positively affects achievement due both to the synergy developed and the generally positive personal affect that accompanies cooperative activity.

Good implementation is important. Many schools confuse cooperative learning—the development of goal-directed positive interdependence—with simply having students work together (Antil, Jenkins, Wayne, and Vadasy, 1998), and the students do not receive the benefits that would await them if the basic elements that lead to cooperative synergy had been employed and the students had been taught how to learn together.

INQUIRY ON INFORMATION-PROCESSING MODELS: LEARNING ABOUT THINKING

Quite a number of models of teaching are designed to increase students' ability to process information more powerfully. These include methods for presenting information so that students can learn and retain it more effectively by operating on it more conceptually; systems that assist memorization and teach students how to organize information for mastery; models to teach students to collect and organize information conceptually; and models to teach students to use the methods of the disciplines, to engage in causal reasoning, and to master concepts.

Many of these models have an extensive recent research literature (the number ranges from about a dozen to more than 300). We will discuss just three here: advance organizers, mnemonics, and scientific inquiry, the disciplines-oriented inductive approach.

ADVANCE ORGANIZERS

David Ausubel's formulation (1963) that there would be greater retention of materials from presentations and reading if the material were accompanied by organizing ideas has generated more than two hundred studies. Essentially, lectures, assignments of reading and research, and courses are accompanied by presentations of concepts that help the student increase intellectual activity during and after exposure to information. The early studies involved much experimentation with ways of formulating and delivering organizers. Because of modest findings some reviewers asserted that the line of work was not paying off (Barnes and Clausen, 1975). The technique advanced quite a bit during the 1970s, however, and current reviewers are quite positive (Lawton and Wanska, 1977; Luiten, Ames, and Ackerson, 1980). Rolheiser-Bennett's (1986) review of 18 recent investigations turned up an average effect size of lower-order achievement (such as the recall of information and concepts) of 1.35. (With such an effect the average student studying with the aid of organizers learned about as much as the 90th-percentile student studying the same material without the assistance of the organizing ideas.) The effects on higher-order thinking (transfer of concepts to new material, etc.) averaged 0.42. Longer-term studies obtained somewhat better results than did short-term studies, presumably because the organizing ideas became better anchored in the minds of the students and had greater facilitating effect.

Stone's (1983) analysis indicated that organizers are effective across ages, being somewhat more effective for students at the stage of concrete operations, when students may need more assistance formulating abstract ideas to anchor content, and across curriculum areas. Illustrations add to the effectiveness of organizers and the impact is increased when they lead to activities and generalizations. Although organizers affect several kinds of outcomes, recall of facts and formulas is most affected. The prediction that can be made is that teachers who accompany presentations and written assignments with organizers will have consistent, although sometimes modest, effects on the learning of information and concepts. Because readings and lectures repeatedly reach so many learners, their cumulative potential is great. Also, structuring a course around organizers, organizing presentations and assignments within the course, tying the organizers to activities that require their application, and illustrating them can have effects as high as two standard deviations. (With an effect of that size the lowest-achieving students are about where the average student would be when studying without the help of organizers. The rest of the distribution is comparably above the control.)

In all probability, the effect of organizers is due to the advantage given to students to construct knowledge when reading, watching films and tapes, and listening to lectures. Essentially, students learn how to learn (the metacognitive dimension of learning) and operate at a higher conceptual level than they would without the scaffolding and metacognitive skills that have been provided (Adey and Shayer, 1990). If we consider their behavior from the Piagetian point of view discussed in Chapter 14, the students process information at a more complex level due to the scaffold and their understanding of how to connect that scaffold to the material they are studying. They learn to solve problems by analysis and the application of concepts (Bascones and Novak, 1985).

MNEMONICS (SYSTEMS TO IMPROVE MEMORIZATION)

Although research on memorization and mnemonic strategies has been conducted for more than one hundred years, until a few years ago most of the yield for school practice offered few and very general guidelines, such as advice about when to mass and when to distribute practice. Little research had been conducted on the learning of school subjects. In the mid-1970s a productive line of work was begun by Atkinson (1975) at Stanford University that has been greatly extended by Pressley and Levin at the Universities of Western Ontario and Wisconsin. They have developed a series of systems for organizing information to promote memory and have given particular, although not exclusive attention to one known as the *link-word method*. Atkinson applied the method during experiments with computer-assisted instruction in which he was attempting to increase students' learning of initial foreign language vocabularies. He experimented with what he called "acoustic" and "imagery" links. The first was designed to make associations between foreign pronunciations and the sounds of known English words. The second was used to make the connection vivid (Atkinson, 1975). In one early study the link-word method produced as much learning in two trials as the conventional method did in three. The experimental group learned about half as many words more than the control group and maintained the advantage after several weeks. He also found that the method was enhanced when the students supplied their own imagery.

Further developmental work included experiments with children of various ages and across subjects. Using a link-word system in Spanish vocabulary learning, second- and fifth-grade children learned about twice the number of the words as did children using rote and rehearsal methods (Pressley, 1977). In later work with Levin and Miller, 1981a, Pressley employed a "pictured action" variant of the method with first- and sixth-grade children, who acquired three times as much vocabulary as did control groups. With Dennis-Rounds (1980) he extended the strategy to social studies information (products and cities) and learned that students could transfer the method to other learning tasks with instruction. Pressley, Levin, and McCormick (1980) found that primary school students could generate sentences to enhance memorization. The results were three times as great as for students using their own methods. Similar results were found with kindergarten and preschool children (Pressley, Samuel, Hershey, Bishop, and Dickinson, 1981). With Levin and Miller (1981a) the work was successfully extended to vocabulary with abstract meanings. Levin, Shriberg, and Berry (1983) have also extended the application to abstract prose.

It was important to learn whether better "natural" memorizers, with practice, develop their own equivalent methods. Pressley, Levin, and Ghatala (1984) asked whether students, with age and practice, would spontaneously develop elaborated methods for memorizing material and found that very few did. The better performers had developed more elaborate methods than the majority, who used rote-rehearsal methods alone. However, the newly developed mnemonic methods enhanced learning for the best memorizers, as well as for the others. Hence, it appears that the method or an equivalent one can be beneficial for most students.

The consistency of the findings is impressive. The link-word method appears to have general applicability across subject matters and ages of children (Pressley, Levin, and Delaney, 1982) and can be used by teachers and taught to children. The effect sizes reached by many of the studies are quite high. The average for transfer tasks (where the material learned was to be applied in another setting) was 1.91. Recall of attributes of items (such as towns, cities, and minerals) was 1.5. Foreign language acquisition was 1.3, with many studies reporting very high outcomes. Delayed recall generally maintained the gains, indicating that the mnemonics strategies have a lasting effect.

INDUCTIVE AND CONCEPT-ORIENTED INFORMATION-PROCESSING MODELS: SCIENTIFIC INQUIRY

Models taken directly from the sciences have been the basis for curricula for both elementary and high school children. A description of the teaching skills and the effects of the science-based curricula is included later in this chapter. The results of the research indicate that the scientific method can be taught and has positive effects on the acquisition of information, concepts, and attitudes. More narrowly defined studies have been made on inductive teaching and inquiry training. Beginning with Taba's (1966) exploration of an inductive social studies curriculum, periodic small-scale studies have probed the area. In 1968 Worthen provided evidence to support one of its central theses—that induced concepts facilitate long-term recall. Feeley (1972) reviewed the social science studies and reported that differences in terminology hampered the accumulation of research but that the inductive methods generally lived up to expectations, generating concept development and positive attitudes. Research on Suchman's (1964) model for teaching causal reasoning directly supported the proposition that inquiry training can be employed with both elementary and high school children. Schrenker (1976) reported that inquiry training resulted in increased understanding of science, greater productivity in critical thinking, and skills for obtaining and analyzing information. He reported that it made little difference in the mastery of information, per se, but that it was as efficient as didactic methods or the didactic cum laboratory methods generally employed to teach science. Ivany (1969) and Collins (1969) examined variants in the kinds of confrontations and materials used and reported that the strength of the confrontation as a stimulus to inquiry was important and that richness in instructional materials was a significant factor. Elefant (1980) successfully carried out the strategy with deaf children in an intriguing study that has implications for work with all children. Voss's (1982) general review includes an annotation of a variety of studies that are generally supportive of the approach.

Currently the clearest evidence about the potential effects on students comes from the study of the academically oriented curricula in science and mathematics that were developed and used during the 20-year period from 1955 to 1975 and from the experience with elementary curricula in a variety of subject areas (Becker and Gersten, 1982; Rhine, 1981). The theory of the academic curricula was relatively straightforward. The essence of the position was stated in *The Process of Education* (Bruner, 1961) and Schwab and Brandwein's *The Teaching of Science* (1962). The teaching of science should be as much as possible a simulation of the scientific process itself. The concepts of the disciplines should be studied rigorously in relation to their knowledge base. Thus science would be learned as inquiry. Further, the information thus learned would be retained well because it would be embedded in a meaningful framework, and the student would possess the interrelated concepts that make up the structure of the disciplines.

In the academic reform movement of the 1950s and 1960s, entire curricula in the sciences (e.g., BSCS Biology), social studies (e.g., Man, A Course of Study), mathematics (e.g., School Mathematics Study Group), and language (e.g., the linguistic approaches) were developed and introduced to the schools. These curricula had in common their designers' beliefs that academic subjects should be studied with the tools of their respective disciplines. Most of these curricula therefore required that students learn the modes of inquiry employed by the disciplines as well as factual material. Process was valued equally with content and many of these curricula became characterized as "inquiry oriented."

Much curriculum research resembles the experimental studies of teaching, but the unit under study is a configuration of content, teaching methods, instructional materials and technologies, and organizational forms. In the experiments, any one of the elements of curriculum may be studied separately or in combination with the others, and the yield is expressed in terms of whether a curriculum produces predicted effects. Research on curriculum depends heavily on training in the content of the curriculum and the teaching strategies needed to implement it. Following training, implementation is monitored, either by classroom observation or interviews. Effects are determined by comparing student outcomes in experimental and control classrooms. In a few studies (e.g., Almy, 1970), combinations of curricula are employed to determine effects on cognitive development and intelligence.

In reviewing the studies, El-Nemr (1979) concentrated on the teaching of biology as inquiry in high schools and colleges. He looked at the effects on attainment of information, on the development of process skills, and on attitudes toward science. The experimentally oriented biology curricula achieved positive effects on all three outcomes. The average effect sizes were largest for process skills (0.44 at the high school level and 0.62 at the college level). For information they were 0.27 and 0.11, respectively, and for attitudes, 0.22 and 0.51. Bredderman's (1983) analysis included a broader range of science programs and included the elementary grades. He also reported positive effects for information (0.10), creativity (0.13), scientific process (0.52), and, in addition, reported effects on intelligence tests, where they were included (0.50). From these and other studies we can conclude that it is possible to develop curricula that will achieve model-relevant effects and also will increase learning of information and concepts.

Also, vigorous curricula in one area appear to stimulate growth in other, superficially unconnected areas. For example, Smith's (1980) analysis of aesthetics curricula shows that the implementation of the arts-oriented curricula was accompanied by gains in the basic skills areas. Possibly an active and effective curriculum in one area has energizing effects on the entire school program. Hillocks's (1987) review of the teaching of reading and writing produced similar effects. His conclusion indicated how closely how we teach is connected with what we teach. Essentially, the inductive approaches to the teaching of reading and writing produced average effect sizes of about .60, compared to treatments that covered the same material, but without the inductive approaches to the teaching/learning process.

Reviews (Sternberg, 1986a; Sternberg and Bahna, 1986) of some of the recently developed packages for teaching elements of analytic reasoning to students have reported modest effects for some of them. Bereiter (1984a) produced a fine analysis of various approaches to the teaching of thinking in which he concluded that the teaching of thinking is far better undertaken in a fashion that is integrated with the curriculum areas than in a "separate-skills" approach.

CONSTRUCTIVIST MODELS AND TRADITIONAL PRACTICES

In our culture some people tend to believe that concentration on scientific inquiry will reduce the learning of information in a curriculum. This has definitely not been the case. The more complex, "sciencing" strategies generate increased concept formation and problem solving without a loss of basic information and skills. Studies in mathematics (Brenner et al., 1997; Mevarech and Kramarski, 1997), in the learning of second languages (Fitzgerald, 1995), in general science (Fraser and Walberg, 1995; Fraser and Wummels, 1995; Shymanski, Kyle, and Alport, 1983; Staver, 1989), physics (Maloney, 1994), and other areas of science have found regularly that teaching students to construct knowledge has a positive effect on the learning of information, particularly when compared with highly programed and didactic instruction (Duit and Treagust, 1995). Further, both genders prosper when science is taught as an active, knowledge-construction process (Burkham and Smerdon, 1997; Parker and Offer, 1987), and, as we saw in Chapter 18, the effects of socioeconomic differences are reduced substantially. Many programs for students deemed to be at risk academically have emphasized step-by-step learning of lower-order information and skills, although it appears that the complex, inquiry-oriented models would have much more positive effect (see, for example, Kober, 1981; Rowan and Guthrie, 1988).

Finally, young students can profit greatly from curricula that emphasize authentic sciencing (Almy, 1970; Karplus, 1964). In fact, as Metz (1995) has pointed out strongly, the watering down of inquiry for young children not only underestimates their intelligence but also often results in oversimplified and inaccurate concepts that do the students no good then or later.

INQUIRERS BUILDING ON INQUIRERS

In recent years there has been a new call to arms to help students learn to construct knowledge (Brooks and Brooks, 1993). Three types of student learning are discussed. First is the students' attempts to discover the world from their own perspectives. The second is the work by groups of students to inquire together and construct ideas about the world. The third is inquiry based on the academic disciplines, in which students try on the ideas and approaches to inquiry of the various academic disciplines. Each of these three can be facilitated by the different families of models of teaching. The assumption that if students construct knowledge their learning will be both richer and more enduring is borne out by most of the research. Whether one examines the inquiry approaches to writing (Hillocks, 1987), the inductive approaches to science (Bredderman, 1983), or the development of group investigation in social science (or any other curriculum area), the various themes of constructivism pay off, not only in helping students learn to reason and gain conceptual control over academic substance, but also in the learning of information and skills. The relation to teaching is that, as we help students construct knowledge, we are constructing knowledge about teaching.

INQUIRY ON BEHAVIORAL MODELS

This family, based on the work of B. F. Skinner and the cybernetic training psychologists (Smith and Smith, 1966), has a huge literature. Studies range from programmed instruction to simulations and include training models (Joyce and Showers, 1983) and methods derived directly from therapy (Wolpe and Lazarus, 1966). There is a great deal of research on the application of social learning theory to instruction (Becker and Gersten, 1982), training (Smith and Smith, 1966), and simulations (Boocock and Schild, 1968). The behavioral technologists have demonstrated that they can design programs for both specific and general goals (Becker and Gersten, 1982) and also that the effective application of those techniques requires extensive cognitive activity and precise interactive skills (Spaulding, 1970).

An analysis by White (1986) examined the results of studies on the application of the DISTAR version of social learning theory to special education. The average effect sizes for mathematics and reading ranged from about one-half to one standard deviation. The effects for moderately and severely handicapped students were similar. Perhaps most important, there were a few studies in which the effects on aptitude (measures of intellectual ability) were included, and, where the DISTAR program was implemented for several years, the effect sizes were 1.0 or above, representing an increase of about 10 points in the standard IQ ratio.

Thoreson and his associates (1973) have concentrated on teaching people to change their behavior by developing their own programs. Some of the most interesting work relates to the self-curing of phobias, such as acrophobia, and teaching people to monitor and modify their own behavior in social situations, such as overcoming excessive shyness and agressiveness.

TIPS FOR TEACHING

The optimism and positiveness of the behavioral stance can perhaps best be summarized in these "tips for teaching" that we invite the reader to explore. Here are a few of them. We put these in the form of questions and tips. Try them out and explore them for yourself.

CLASSROOM RULES

Which is best, a list of behaviors to avoid combined with negative reinforcers (a one-time violation results in the "name on the board," a two-time violation results in . . .), or a list of desirable behaviors and rewards (a certificate proclaiming "You Are the Greatest")?

Tip: The high-probability bet is the positive rules and positive reinforcers or nurturers.

OFF-TASK BEHAVIOR

If 28 students are on task and 2 are off task, which teacher behavior has the highest probability of succeeding in bringing the 2 into an on-task mode: reprimanding the off-task students or praising the on-task students?

Tip: Praising the on-task students (positive rather than negative reinforcement).

INSTRUCTION OR SELF-INSTRUCTION

In the computer lab, when introducing a new word-processing program to students who can already use another program, one teacher takes the students step by step through the manual. The other gives the students the program and, after a brief orientation, asks them to teach themselves to use it. Which works best?

Tip: Controlling your own learning schedule arouses positive affect. Also, pacing is under the control of the individual, who can move rapidly or slowly according to individual needs.

ITCHY STUDENTS

Certain kids just don't seem to sit still or pay attention for more than a few minutes. Do you give them extra homework when they wander off task or teach them a relaxation exercise and how to use it when the hyper feeling arises?

Tip: The first solution is a negative reinforcer that also uses academic work as a punishment, which can produce an aversive response. The second provides effective control, makes the students partners in regulating their behavior, and provides the opportunity for positive self-reinforcement as well as external reinforcement.

MOTIVATION

Following a test at the end of a unit in mathematics, one teacher has the students correct their own papers and figure out their gain scores. The other teacher scores the test and provides the students with an analysis of items missed. Which is the best bet for motivating the students?

Tip: Self-scoring, emphasis on progress, and setting of new goals will win almost every time.

Try these, and see if you agree with the tips.

INQUIRY ON PERSONAL MODELS _____

NONDIRECTIVE TEACHING

Carl Rogers's *Freedom to Learn in the Eighties* (1982) includes a chapter summarizing much of the research from the humanistic perspective. Aspy, Roebuck, Willson, and Adams (1974) and Roebuck, Buhler, and Aspy (1976) have been productive in tackling the difficult task of connecting student-centered classrooms to academic learning. They have explored several theses of the personal family of models, particularly that building self-directed, empathetic communities of learners will have positive effects on students' feelings about themselves and others and, consequently, will free energy for learning. Roebuck, Buhler, and Aspy's (1976) study with students identified as having learning difficulties produced positive effects on self-concept, intergroup attitudes and interaction patterns, achievement in reading and mathematics, and increased scores on tests of intelligence. In studies of classroom teachers, they have documented the need for extensive training (Aspy et al., 1974). The students of teachers who had learned the model thoroughly achieved more, felt better about themselves, had better attendance records, and improved their interpersonal skills. The model of nondirective teaching is complex. Teachers have to develop egalitarian relationships with the students, create a cooperative group of students who respect one anothers' differences in personality and ability, help those students develop programs of study (including goals and the means for achieving them), provide feedback about performance and behavior, teach the students to reflect on one anothers' behavior and performance, help individuals and groups evaluate progress, and maintain an affirmative social climate.

The findings run counter to what many people expect. Placing the student at the center of the learning process and paying close attention to personality development and esteem for self, if done properly, apparently enhances learning in the academic as well as the personal domain.

Essentially, growth as a person *should* make a difference to academic learning. Self-esteem can be thought of in terms of a general feeling of well-being and in terms of the feelings of esteem that are connected to particular curriculum areas—domain-specific *academic self-esteem*. Marsh and

Yeung (1997) explored the effects of both general and specific concepts of self on course selection by middle and high school students and concluded that the general feeling of well-being affects student selection of advanced courses. In addition, however, students develop images of themselves with respect to particular curriculum areas. This self-image has a bigger effect on whether they choose more advanced courses. Moreover, and particularly important here, adequate or even high student achievement does not ensure that students will develop a positive self-image with respect to a subject. Quite good students can lack the self-confidence to pursue an academic area.

How instruction is carried on—whether the personal and caring dimension of the classroom and school is given prominence—can have a marked effect on whether students engage in "self-handicapping" (Urdan, Midgley, and Anderman, 1998). Essentially, as students progress, we need to take as much care of their self-esteem as we do of their learning of content.

Gender can be a factor. Female students have frequently developed low academic self-concepts in science and mathematics although achieving about as well as males, and the self-handicapping has caused them to make decisions that have handicapped them in universities and career selection (see Chapter 18 for a thorough discussion of gender as a factor). The most plausible explanation is that the personal dimension of instruction has not been well enough developed to prevent the development of appropriate self-confidence and self-image.

Although we classify synectics as an information-processing model, it generates personal metaphoric growth that is relevant as we consider the personal models simply because personal creativity is so much a part of the model that we think the reader will find it comfortable to think of *creativity* from a personal as well as an information-processing perspective. Synectics (Gordon and Poze, 1971a) is designed both to enhance personal flexibility and creativity and to teach one of the higher-order thinking skills, specifically, the ability to think divergently and generate alternative and relevant solutions to difficult problems and alternative perspectives on important concepts and values.

Research on synectics indicates that it achieves its "model-relevant" purposes, increasing student generation of ideas, divergent solutions to problems, and fluency in expressing ideas. (Effect sizes average 1.5 for generation of ideas and problem solving.) Newby and Ertner (1994) conducted a nice set of studies in which they taught students to generate analogies while studying physiological concepts and confirmed the function of analogies as organizers and generators of mnemonic effects. Glynn's (1994) investigations of learning in science had similar effects—the metaphors brought the students into the subject and increased both short- and long-term recall of information. These recent studies confirm the results of previous inquiries into synectics—that by helping students develop more multidemsional perspectives, synectics increases recall of material from written passages and the information is retained, probably because of the vividness of the metaphoric connections to the content. That teaching students to think creatively is positively related with the learning and retention of information and can increase the lower-order outcomes to a substantial degree runs counter to common sense in our society. Many laymen have the opinion that an emphasis on creativity runs counter to the acquisition of information, concepts, and skills, but it turns out that academic goals are enhanced by the synthesis required to think metaphorically.

THE INQUIRING TEACHER: ADVICE FROM THE AUTHORS

Take nothing for granted. Study student learning often, pay attention to gain, be a critical consumer. Gain is essential. Schools have had a problem grappling with this one, primarily because grading is often based on relative achievement rather than on how much was learned. For example, imagine two students studying mathematics. One begins the class with few prerequisites but struggles toward the objectives of the year, learning the prerequisites and partially achieving those objectives. A second student arrives at the course with the objectives of the year already mastered, but makes little gain, although still ending up looking better than the first student. Who gained the most and needs to be celebrated? Obviously, the first student. Who is likely to get the higher grade?

Let's eliminate that kind of practice, which has two errors built into it: an underestimate of the first student's achievement and a failure to ensure that the higher achieving student grew more.

Finally, pick the models that will most benefit your students, given your objectives, and teach the students to profit from those models.

That's what this book is all about.

APPENDIX

PEER COACHING GUIDES

The following pages contain peer coaching guides for nine of the most commonly used and applicable models of teaching. These forms facilitate planning and communication between members of study groups who observe one another and try to profit from the observational experience.

The forms can also be used to facilitate sharing of ideas by study group members whether or not observation of one anothers' teaching is included.

Hence, they are addressed to both parties in the peer coaching process: the teacher who is planning and directing the teaching episode and the partner who is studying the model. Both parties are involved in a continuing experiment on teaching. Each has the same purpose, which is to increase his or her ability to analyze the transactions between teacher and student, and the ability to teach students how to learn information and concepts. The guide is used both to assist the planning of the teaching episode and in focusing the observation on key features of the model. The teacher prepares the observer by filling out the entries where indicated. The observer fills in the observation checklist and communicates the result to the teacher. Both parties will profit most by making a partnership that studies the student responses and plans how to help the students learn more effectively. The observer is *not* present to advise the teacher on how to teach better but, rather, to learn by observing and help the teacher by providing information about the students' responses.

The communication of the analysis should be conducted in a neutral tone, proceeding matter-of-factly through the phases of the model. The guide draws attention to the syntax of the model—the cognitive and social tasks that are presented to the students and how the students respond, and the principles of reaction—the guidelines for reacting to the students as they try to attain the concept. The teacher may want to orient the coaching partner to look closely at a specific phase of the model, such as student response to a particular cognitive or social task, or reactions to student responses. The coaching partner should avoid giving gratuitous advice.

Normally, the communication about a teaching episode should be completed in five minutes or less. For self-coaching, teachers should use videotape when possible and, during playback, enter the role of partner, analyzing the transactions as dispassionately as possible.

Peer Coaching Guide: Advance Organizer

Teacher: Do you want to suggest a focus for the analysis? If so, what is it?

_____

_____

THE TEACHING PROCESS

Most teaching episodes have both content and process objectives. The content objectives include the information, concepts, theories, ways of thinking, values, and other substance that the students can be expected to learn from the experience that results. The process objectives are the ways of learning—the conduct of the social and intellectual tasks that increase the power to learn. In the case of a model of teaching, the process objectives are those that enable the students to engage effectively in the tasks presented when the model is being used.

CONTENT OBJECTIVES

Teacher: Please state the concepts and information that are the primary objectives of this teaching episode. What kind of information will be presented to the student? What concepts will be presented to organize the information? Are the concepts or information new to the students?

_____

_____

PROCESS OBJECTIVES

Teacher: Please state any process objectives that are of concern during this episode. For example, are you trying to help the students learn how to comprehend and use organizers, how to relate material to the conceptual structure, how to tie new material to the organizers, how to apply what is learned to new information and skills?

_____

_____

_____

Observer: Please comment on the students' familiarity with the model, referring especially to any of the process objectives mentioned above.

_____

_____

_____

_____

PHASE ONE: PRESENTATION OF THE ORGANIZER

The key aspect of the model is the use of organizing ideas to induce students to operate conceptually on the material they are trying to master. The teacher organizes the material with an "intellectual scaffolding" of concepts and presents those concepts to the students so that they can relate the new information to it—or reorganize familiar information within a more powerful conceptual framework. While even the careful organization of information under a series of topics facilitates learning, we attempt to formulate organizing concepts that are at a higher conceptual level, so that they cause the students to process the information beyond associating it with a topic and to think about the material at a more complex level than they would spontaneously.

Phase One is the presentation of the organizer.

Teacher: Please describe the organizer, or system of organizers, stating it (them) if that is practical. Discuss how it (they) will help the student conceptualize the material. How will you present the organizer(s)?

_____

_____

_____

_____

Observer: Please comment on the students' response to the organizer(s). Did they appear to absorb it (them)? Did they appear to understand how organizers are to function and that their task is to learn new material and relate it to the organizer(s)?

_____

_____

PHASE TWO: PRESENTING INFORMATION

The purpose of the model, of course, is to facilitate the learning of material at any level of abstraction: data, concepts, theories, systems of thought—all the possibilities are there. The device is to place the student in the role of active receiver, getting information by reading, watching, or scrabbling around for information from formal resources or the environment. The information can be presented through readings, lectures, films or tapes, or any other mediated form or combination of forms.

Teacher: Please describe the content that will be presented and how it will be presented. Emphasize the content you most want to be retained and how you want it to be applied in the future.

_____

_____

_____

_____

Observer: Please comment on the student responses. Are the students clear about what they are to learn? Is it clear to you (thinking from the point of view of the students) how the organizer(s) may function in relation to the material?

_____

_____

PHASE THREE: CONNECTING THE ORGANIZER TO THE PRESENTATION

The conceptual structure defined by the organizers needs to be integrated with the information that has been presented and also reconciled with the students' personal intellectual structures. While the students, with practice, will accomplish most of these tasks by themselves, it is wise to provide activities that make the relationship between concepts and material explicit and which provide the students with an opportunity to reflect on the organizing structure.

For example, we can illustrate the connection between one of the organizers and some aspect of the information and induce the students to suggest further associations and relationships. Or we can ask the students to reformulate the organizers in their own terms and indicate relationships between them and aspects of the material.

Teacher: How will you make a presentation or provide a task to increase the possibility of the integration of the organizing structure with the students' conceptual structure and also make clear the connection between organizer and the material that has been presented?

_____

_____

_____

_____

Observer: Please comment on this phase. Do the students appear to be clear about the organizing structure and its relation to the material to be learned?

_____

_____

_____

_____

PHASE FOUR: APPLICATION

Sometimes information is presented to students as a precursor to learning a skill (we may teach musical notation to facilitate learning to sing) and sometimes to assist in solving problems (knowledge of mechanics may be applied to problems requiring leverage). We also apply what is learned in subsequent learning tasks (the general concept of *equation* is useful in mastering many mathematical topics).

Teacher: Do you wish to provide an explicit application task at this point? If so, please describe it briefly.

_____

_____

_____

_____

Observer: If an application task is presented, please comment on the students' ability to make the transfer to the new material.

_____

_____

_____

_____

Peer Coaching Guide: Cooperative Learning Organization

Unlike the other guides in this series, this form to assist in the planning and observation of teaching is not built around a model of teaching. The substance is the organization of students into study groups and partnerships. It does not deal with the specific cooperative learning strategies developed by Robert Slavin and his associates (Slavin, 1993) or Roger Johnson and David Johnson (1999), although the philosophy of the approach is similar. Nor does it deal with group investigation (Sharan and Hertz-Lazarowitz, 1980b; Thelen, 1960), the major democratic-process strategy that is covered in another guide.

Rather, cooperative learning organization provides a setting for cooperative study that can be employed in combination with many approaches to teaching.

This guide describes some options and asks the teacher to select from them or to generate others. The observer analyzes the students' productivity and attempts to identify ways of helping the students engage in more productive behavior. The examples provided below are in reference to the inductive model of teaching. Using the two guides simultaneously may be useful.

When other models are used, analogous use can be made of cooperative learning.

OPTIONS FOR ORGANIZATION

Essentially, we want to organize the students so that everyone in the class has a partner with whom he or she can work on instructional tasks. For example, pairs of students can operate throughout the inductive model, collecting information, developing categories, and making inferences about causal relationships. The partnerships (which need not be long-term, although they can be) are collected into teams. For example, if there are 30 students in the class, there can be five teams of six. We do not recommend teams larger than six. These teams can also operate throughout the inductive model, collecting and organizing data and making inferences. The partnerships provide an easy organization through which teams can divide labor. For example, each partnership can collect information from certain sources and then the information can be accumulated into a data set for the team. Similarly, team sets can be accumulated into a class set of data. Teams can then operate on these data sets and compare and contrast the results with those of other teams.

Team membership and partnerships can be organized in a number of ways, ranging from student selection, random selection, or teacher-guided choices to maximize heterogeneity and potential synergy.

Instruction of teams can range from explicit procedures to guide them through the learning activities to general procedures that leave much of the organization to the students.

ORGANIZATION

Teacher: How will you organize the class for this teaching episode? How many groups of what sizes will be selected?

_____

_____

_____

How will memberships be determined?

_____

_____

_____

What approach to teaching/learning will be used? If you are not using a specific model of teaching, what will be your instructional strategy?

_____

_____

_____

How will cooperative groups be used throughout the teaching episode? What cooperative tasks will be given to pairs, study groups, or the whole class? For example, if this were an inductive lesson, partnerships might collect data, classify it, and make inferences. Or, partnerships might collect data, but it might be assembled by the entire class prior to the classification activity. Partnerships might study words, poems, maps, number facts and operations, or other material. What is your plan?

_____

_____

_____

_____

Observer: After you have familiarized yourself with the plan, situate yourself in the room so that you can observe about six students closely. Throughout the teaching episode, concentrate on the behavior of those students, whether they are working in partnerships, study groups, or any other organization. Then comment on their performance.

Did they appear to be clear about the tasks they were to accomplish? if not, can you identify what they were not clear about?

_____

_____

_____

Did they appear to know how to cooperate to accomplish the tasks assigned to them? Is there anything they appear to need to know in order to be more productive?

_____

_____

_____

Do they regulate their own behavior, keeping on task, dividing labor, taking turns? Could they profit from having any aspect of group management modeled for them?

_____

_____

_____

What sort of leadership patterns did they employ? Did they acknowledge one or more leaders? Did they discuss process? Were they respectful to one another?

_____

_____

_____

DISCUSSION

Following the episode, discuss the operation of the groups in which the six students were members. Is their productivity satisfactory? Their relationships? If not, see if you can develop a plan for helping the students become more productive. Remember that:

1. Providing practice is the simplest and most powerful way to help students learn to work productively. This is especially true if they have not had much experience working in cooperative groups.

2. The smaller the group, the more easily students can regulate their own behavior. Reducing the size of study groups often allows students to solve their own problems.

3. Demonstration gets more mileage than exhortation. A teacher can join a group and *show* the students how to work together. In fact, the observer can be a participant in a study group in future sessions.

4. Simpler tasks are easier for students to manage. Breaking complex tasks into several smaller ones often allows students to build their skills through practice.

5. Praising appropriate behavior gets results. If two groups are performing at different levels, it often helps to praise the productive group and then quietly join the less productive one and provide leadership.

Peer Coaching Guide: Jurisprudential Model

The analysis of a jurisprudential case generally takes several class sessions, which often means that the observers will be present for only one or two phases and will have to be briefed about events that occurred during their absence. The process of teaching/learning should not be rushed in an attempt to crowd it into one or two class periods.

Teacher: Do you want to suggest a focus for the analysis? If so, what is it?

_____

_____

THE TEACHING PROCESS

Most teaching episodes have both content and process objectives. The content objectives include the information, concepts, theories, ways of thinking, values, and other substance that the students can be expected to learn from the experience that results. The process objectives are the ways of learning—the conduct of the social and intellectual tasks that increase the power to learn. In the case of a model of teaching, the process objectives are those that enable the students to engage effectively in the tasks presented when the model is being used.

CONTENT OBJECTIVE(S)

Teacher: Please describe the outcomes that have the highest priority. The variety that can be encompassed by the jurisprudential model is considerable, so priority is important. Included are information about the cases to be studied, concepts about the cases, issues, values, and policies.

_____

_____

_____

PROCESS OBJECTIVE(S)

Teacher: Please describe the most important process objectives. This is a model with tasks that have both complex and social dimensions. Will some aspect of the process receive special attention during this episode?

_____

_____

_____

Observer: As the episode progresses, observe the student performance, especially attending to the goals described above. Because the tasks are so complex, it is probably wise to concentrate on just one or two aspects of process for comment.

PHASE ONE: OPENING UP THE ISSUES

Generally, the model is oriented around situations that involve public policy issues. Information about these situations is usually collected in case studies describing circumstances and events. The issues involve dilemmas because there are competing values and interests that need to be reconciled. The core of the model is the identification of those values and interests and the formulation and analysis of policies that could be pursued to deal with the issues.

In phase one the students are presented with the initial case that embodies the issues. Some cases involve lengthy reading and study, even to achieve enough clarity to see what the issues are. Usually, however, a situation that highlights the issues can be presented to the students.

Teacher: Please describe the case briefly. How will you present it to the students? Will you use an enactment of a situation, describe an event or conversation, present readings?

The situation or case is discussed by the students, who are led to identify the problems or dilemmas that inhere in the situation. At this point no attempt is made to press toward conclusions of any kind. Student opinions are identified and respected, but the strongly expressed and mildly put ideas are recorded equally for further consideration later.

Observer: Please comment on the students' reception of the case and their analysis of the problems embodied by it. Are they initiating the inquiry in a cooperative manner? Do they appear to distinguish facts from issues?

PHASE TWO: ISSUES, OPTIONS, AND VALUES

The next step is to bring order to the list of issues and questions that have arisen. Typically, the initial exploration of a problem elicits combinations of statements identifying issues (conflicts of interest or values), assertions of value positions (an assertion of a value that can justify why a certain course of action should be taken), and facts or questions about facts. These need to be sorted out and labeled as issues and values.

Teacher: Please discuss how you will help the students organize the material thus far generated.

_____

_____

_____

_____

Observer: Please comment on the student response. Are they able to distinguish facts, values, issues? Can they tell where they are making assumptions and where they have sufficient information? Until students can employ the model skillfully, they will respond with a melange of opinions, assertions about values, and so on. This is to be expected, but must be noted because it gives cues about how to help them develop more skill.

_____

_____

_____

_____

A decision needs to be made now about whether the students need more information about the case before they can proceed to engage in an analysis of value alternatives. If more information is needed, then it should be provided, or the students should be organized to find it. The observer wants to watch carefully to judge whether the students know enough to proceed. The teacher may decide to provide more information or have students engage in research.

PRELIMINARY IDENTIFICATION OF VALUE POSITIONS

The discussion should now proceed to an identification of the values that are involved. The heart of the dilemma is the difficulty of finding an easy solution that accommodates more than one value. Hence, the students should make an exhaustive list of the values that are represented in the situation. They may work as individuals, small groups, or as an entirety to perform the analysis.

Teacher: How will you have the students work to perform the analysis (individuals, groups, etc.)? What instruction will you give them?

_____

_____

_____

_____

_____

Observer: Please comment on the students' analysis of the situation. Are they able to distinguish between issues and values and to identify the values that are potentially in conflict in the situation?

_____

_____

_____

_____

FOCUSING ON AN ISSUE

Because even the simpler cases generally involve a number of potential issues, it is wise to have the students select a particular issue for the initial focus of the further dialogue, although others may be dealt with subsequently.

Hence, we ask the students to select one issue for focus and to identify the values that are in potential conflict.

Observer: Please comment on the process. Are the issue and values clear?

_____

_____

_____

_____

PHASE THREE: TAKING POSITIONS

The next task is for the students to generate positions that address the issue. The positions may favor one value over another or effect a compromise.

Teacher: Please describe the instructions you will give the students. Also, how will you organize them (individuals, groups, etc.)?

_____

_____

_____

Next, the students share the positions they have generated and indicate the social consequences of their stances.

Observer: Please comment on the products of the analysis. Are the students both able to generate policy positions and see the costs and benefits they entail? Also, are they able to place themselves in the position of their fellow students as they articulate their stances?

_____

_____

_____

_____

PHASE FOUR: EXPLORING THE POSITIONS

Now the students test their positions by discussing the consequences. They may return to the case and see what would be the outcome were each of the policy positions adopted. They should distinguish between the purely practical consequences and the effects on the values. The teacher adopts a Socratic stance, drawing the students out, inducing them to examine their arguments, and assuring fair treatment of each proposal.

Teacher: How will you put this task to the students?

_____

_____

Observer: Please comment on the dialogue. Can the students distinguish between the pragmatic and value-related consequences of their positions? Do they take one another's reasoning seriously?

_____

_____

_____

_____

PHASE FIVE: MODIFYING THE POSITIONS, MAKING RECOMMENDATIONS

What remains is to modify the positions in accordance with the previous discussion and possibly to put forward candidates or a candidate for present policy action.

Teacher: Please describe how you will place this task before the students.

_____

_____

_____

COMMENTS ON STUDENT TRAINING NEEDS

Observer: Please comment on the student responses to the model, identifying any skills that you believe need special attention to improve their performance. If they are new to the model, remember that it involves some very complex social and intellectual tasks and that practice will surely result in an increment of skill. However, are there any particular skills that stand out at this point and might receive special attention in subsequent episodes in which the jurisprudential model is used?

_____

_____

_____

_____

Peer Coaching Guide: Synectics

Teacher: Do you want to suggest a focus for the observer? If so, what is it?

_____

_____

THE TEACHING PROCESS

Most teaching episodes have both content and process objectives. Content objectives include the substance (information, concepts, generalizations, relationships, skills) to be mastered by students. Process objectives include skills or procedures the students need in order to learn productively from the cognitive and social tasks of the model.

CONTENT OBJECTIVE(S)

Teacher: Please state the content objectives of the episode. What kind of learning will come from the activity? What is the nature of the area to be explored?

_____

_____

_____

PROCESS OBJECTIVE(S)

Teacher: Are the students familiar with the model? Is there some aspect of its process where they need practice or instruction, and will you be concentrating on it in this lesson?

_____

_____

_____

Observer: Please comment on the students' response to the model. Do they appear to need specific help with some aspect of the process?

_____

_____

_____

PHASE ONE: THE ORIGINAL PRODUCT

Commonly, synectics is used to generate fresh perspectives on a topic or problem either for clarification or to permit alternative conceptions or solutions to be explored. Thus it generally begins by soliciting from students a product representing their current thinking. They can formulate the problem, speak or write about the topic, enact a problem, draw a representation of a relationship—there are many alternatives. The function of this phase is to enable them to capture their current thoughts about the subject at hand.

Teacher: Please describe how you will elicit the students' conceptions of the area to be explored. What will you say or do to orient them?

_____

_____

Observer: Please comment on the students' response to the originating task. What is the nature of their conceptions?

_____

_____

_____

PHASE TWO: DIRECT AND PERSONAL ANALOGIES

The core of the model requires the development of distance from the original product through exercises inducing the students to make comparisons between sets of stimuli that are presented to them (direct analogy exercises) and to place themselves, symbolically, in the position of various persons, places, and things (personal analogy exercises). The analogistic material generated in these exercises will be used later in the creation of further analogies called *compressed conflicts.*

Teacher: What stimuli will you use to induce the students to make the direct and personal analogies? Please describe the material and the order in which you will proceed to stretch the students toward the more unusual and surprising comparisons.

_____

_____

Observer: Please comment on the stimuli and the student responses. Did the students get "up in the air" metaphorically and generate less literal and more analogistic comparisons?

_____

_____

PHASE THREE: COMPRESSED CONFLICTS
AND OXYMORONIC ANALOGIES

The next task is to induce the students to operate on the material generated in phase two and create compressed conflicts. You need to be prepared to define compressed conflict, even if the students have familiarity with the model and to continue eliciting material until a number of examples clearly contain the logical (illogical?) tension that characterizes a high-quality oxymoron.

Teacher: Please describe how you will initiate phase three and how you will explain compressed conflict if you need to.

_____

_____

_____

_____

Observer: Please comment on the student response to the task. How rich was the product?

_____

_____

_____

Now we ask the students to select some pairs that manifest great tension and to generate some analogies that represent the tension. For example, we might ask them to provide some examples of "exquisite torture."

Teacher: Please describe briefly how you will present these tasks to the students.

_____

_____

_____

Observer: Please discuss the students' understanding of the concept *compressed conflict* and their ability to select the higher-quality ones. Also, comment on the product of their attempt to generate oxymoronic analogies.

_____

_____

_____

_____

PHASE FOUR: GENERATING NEW PRODUCTS

The compressed conflicts and the analogies to them provide material from which to revisit the original problem or topic. Sometimes we select or have the students select just one analogy with which to revisit the original material. At other times multiple perspectives are useful. What course to take depends on a combination of the complexity of the original problem or concept and the students' ability to handle new perspectives. For example, if a secondary social studies class has been trying to formulate potential solutions to a problem in international relations, we are dealing with a very complex problem for which multiple analogies are probably both appropriate and necessary. However, the task of helping the students share and assess a variety of analogies that can be used to redefine the problem and generate alternative solutions is complex, indeed.

Teacher: Please describe how you will present the task of revisiting the original product. What will you ask the students to do?

_____

_____

_____

_____

Observer: Please comment on the student products. What do you think has been the effect of the metaphoric exercises?

_____

_____

Now, the new product needs to be examined. If the students worked as individuals or subgroups, the separate products need to be shared. If a problem is to be solved, new definitions and solutions need to be arranged. If written expression emerged, possibly it needs further editing. Unless the teaching episode is the conclusion of a topic of study, it generally leads to further study.

Teacher: Please describe how the synectics products are to be shared and used. Will they lead to further reading and writing, data collection, or experimentation?

_____

_____

_____

_____

Observer: Please comment on the use of the new products. Are the students able to see the effects of the metaphoric activity? If they are asked to participate in further activities or to generate them, are they bringing to those tasks a "set" toward the development of alternative perspectives or avenues?

_____

_____

_____

COMMENTS ON STUDENT TRAINING NEEDS

It is the student who does the learning, and the greater the skill of the student in responding to the cognitive and social tasks of the model, the greater the learning is likely to be. Practice alone will build skill, and we want to provide plenty of it. After students are thoroughly familiar with the structure of the model, we can begin to develop specific training to improve their ability to perform.

Observer: Please comment on the skills with which the students engaged in the activities and suggest any areas where you believe training might be useful. Think especially of their ability to make comparisons, their ability to take the roles required to make "personal analogies," and their understanding of the structure of compressed conflicts and how to use them. Thinking back on the entire experience, is there any area where specific process training should be considered?

_____

_____

_____

_____

Peer Coaching Guide: Concept Attainment

The guide is designed to assist peer coaching of the concept attainment model of teaching. When planning questions, skip through the guide to the entries marked "Teacher" and fill them in as needed. They will guide you through the model. Observers can use the guide to familiarize themselves with the plans of the teacher and to make notes about what is observed. Please remember, observers, that your primary function is not to give "expert advice" to your colleague, but to observe the students as requested by the teacher and to observe the whole process so that you can gain ideas for your own teaching. The teacher is the coach in the sense that he or she is demonstrating a teaching episode for you. When you teach and are observed, you become the coach.

Teacher: Do you want to suggest a focus for the analysis? If so, what is it?

_____

_____

THE TEACHING PROCESS

Most lessons have both content and process objectives. Content objectives identify subject matter (facts, concepts, generalizations, relationships) to be mastered by students, while process objectives specify skills and procedures students need in order to achieve content objectives or auxiliary social objectives (e.g., cooperation in a learning task).

CONTENT OBJECTIVE

Teacher: Please state the concept that is the objective of the lesson. What are its defining attributes? What kind of data will be presented to the students? Is the information or concept new to the students?

_____

_____

PROCESS OBJECTIVE

Teacher: Are the students familiar with the model? Do they need special assistance or training with respect to any aspect of the process?

_____

_____

PHASE ONE: FOCUS

The focus defines the field of search for the students. It may eliminate nonrelevant lines of inquiry. Often it is pitched at a level of abstraction just above the exemplars (e.g., "a literary device" might serve as a focus for the concept of metaphor).

Teacher: Please write the focus statement here.

_____

_____

Observer: Did the teacher deliver the focus statement?

Yes [ ]   No [ ]

In your opinion, was it clear to the students and did it function to help them focus on the central content of the lesson?

Completely [ ]   Partially [ ]   No [ ]

PHASE TWO: PRESENTING THE DATA SET

The data set should be planned in pairs of positive and negative exemplars, ordered to enable the students—by comparing the positive exemplars and contrasting them with the negative ones—to distinguish the defining attributes of the concept.

Teacher: Please describe the nature of the exemplars. (Are they words, phrases, documents, etc? For example: "These are reproductions of nineteenth-century paintings. Half of them are from the Impressionists [Renoir, Monet, Degas] and the other half are realistic, romantic, or abstract paintings.")

_____

_____

THE SET

Observer: Were approximately equal numbers of positive and negative exemplars presented?

Yes [ ]   No [ ]

Were the early positive exemplars clear and unambiguous?

Yes [ ]   No [ ]

Did the data set contain at least 15 each of positive and negative exemplars?

Yes [ ]   No [ ]

How was the set presented?
A labeled pair at a time? _____
All at once, with labels following? _____
Other (please describe)

_____

_____

Did the teacher provide the labels for the first 8 or 10 pairs before asking the students to suggest a label?

Yes [ ]   No [ ]

DEVELOPING HYPOTHESES ABOUT
THE NATURE OF THE CONCEPT

As the students work through the data set, they are to examine each exemplar and develop hypotheses about the concept. They need to ask themselves what attributes the positive exemplars have in common. It is those attributes that define the concept.
Teacher: How are you going to do this?

_____

_____

Observer: Were the students asked to generate hypotheses but to avoid sharing them?

Yes [ ]   No [ ]

Sometimes students are asked to record the progression of their thinking.
Teacher: Do you want to do this?

_____

Observer: Were the students asked to record their thinking as the episode progressed?

Yes [ ]   No [ ]

As the lesson progresses, we need to get information about whether the students are formulating and testing ideas.

Teacher: How will you do this? _____

_____

_____

_____

Observer: As the episode progressed, did the teacher gather information about whether the students were able to generate hypotheses?

Yes [ ]   No [ ]

Observer: Were the students asked to compare the positives and contrast them with the negatives?

Yes [ ]   No [ ]

PHASE THREE: SHARING THINKING AND HYPOTHESES

When it appears that the students have developed hypotheses that they are fairly sure of, they are asked to describe the progression of their thinking and the concept they have arrived at.

Teacher: When to do this is a matter of judgment. How will you decide, and what will you say?

_____

_____

_____

Observer: Did the teacher ask the students to share their thinking?

Yes [ ]   No [ ]

Were the students able to express their hypotheses?

Yes [ ]   No [ ]

If there were several hypotheses, could the students justify or reconcile them?

Yes [ ]   No [ ]

PHASE FOUR: NAMING AND APPLYING THE CONCEPT

Once concepts have been agreed on (or different ones justified), they need names. After students have generated names, the teacher may need to supply the technical or common term (e.g., "We call this style *Impressionism*").

Application requires that students determine whether further exemplars fit the concept and, perhaps, find examples of their own.

Teacher: Is there a technical or common term the students need to know? How will you provide further experience with the concept?

_____

_____

_____

Observer:
Were the students able to name the concept?

Yes [ ]   No [ ]

Was a technical or common term for the concept supplied (if needed)?

Yes [ ]   No [ ]

Were additional exemplars provided?

Yes [ ]   No [ ]

Were the students asked to supply their own?

Yes [ ]   No [ ]

As the students examined new material, supplying their own exemplars, did they appear to know the concept?

Yes [ ]   No [ ]

An assignment to follow the lesson often involves the application of the concept to fresh material. For example, if the concept of *metaphor* had been introduced, the students might be asked to read a literary passage and identify the uses of metaphor in it.

Teacher: Are you planning such an assignment? If so, please describe it briefly.

_____

_____

_____

_____

COMMENTS ON STUDENT TRAINING NEEDS

In order to improve student performance, the first option we explore is whether it will improve with practice. That is, simple repetition of the model gives the students a chance to learn to respond more appropriately. Second, we directly teach the students the skills they need to manage the cognitive and social tasks of the model.

You might discuss:

HOW THE STUDENTS RESPONDED TO PHASE ONE

Did they pay close attention to the focus statement and apply it to the examination of the exemplars? If not, is it worthwhile to give specific instruction and what might that be?

_____

_____

_____

HOW THE STUDENTS RESPONDED TO PHASE TWO

Did they compare and contrast the exemplars? Did they make hypotheses with the expectation that they might have to change them? Were they using the negative exemplars to eliminate alternatives? Is it worthwhile to provide specific training, and what might that be?

_____

_____

_____

HOW THE STUDENTS RESPONDED TO PHASE THREE

Were they able to debrief their thinking? Were they able to see how different lines of thinking gave similar or different results? Were they able to generate labels that express the concept? Do they understand how to seek exemplars on their own and apply what they have learned? Is it worthwhile to provide specific training, and what might that be?

_____

_____

_____

Peer Coaching Guide: Inquiry Training

Teacher: Do you want to suggest a focus for the analysis? If so, what is it?

_____

_____

_____

THE TEACHING PROCESS

Most lessons have both content and process objectives. Content objectives identify subject matter (facts, concepts, generalizations, relationships) to be mastered by students, while process objectives specify skills and procedures students need in order to achieve content objectives or auxiliary social objectives (e.g., cooperation in a learning task).

The content objectives for inquiry training reside in the information, concepts, and theories embedded in the problem or puzzling situation that is presented to the students. They have to discover the information, form the concepts, and develop the theories. The skills to do those things are the process objectives, as are the social skills of cooperative problem solving.

CONTENT OBJECTIVE(S)

Teacher: What do you want students to gain from this task? What information, concepts, and theories do you wish them to learn?

_____

_____

_____

_____

PROCESS OBJECTIVE(S)

Teacher: Are the students familiar with the model? Do they need special assistance or training with respect to any aspect of the process? (For example, do they know how to obtain information through questioning? Can they work cooperatively with partners on a problem-solving task?)

_____

_____

_____

Observer: Was the process of the model familiar to the students? Do they need help with any aspect of the model?

_____

_____

PHASE ONE: ENCOUNTER WITH THE PROBLEM

The primary activity of phase one of the inquiry training model is the presentation of the problem.

Teacher: Please describe the problem to be used in this lesson and how you will present it.

_____

_____

_____

Observer: Did the students understand the problem and find it puzzling? Were they able to ask questions to clarify it, and could they summarize it when asked to?

_____

_____

_____

PHASE TWO: DATA GATHERING AND VERIFICATION

In this phase the students ask questions to gather information about the problem.

Observer: In your opinion, did the students understand the procedures they were to employ during this phase? Did they ask fact-oriented questions, and were they able to respond when the teacher modeled how to ask them? Could they distinguish between fact and theory-oriented questions? How well could they "caucus" and summarize what they had learned and plan sets of questions to ask? Did they listen to each other?

_____

_____

_____

PHASE THREE: EXPERIMENTATION

If the students do not do so spontaneously, the teacher will introduce this phase by instructing them to begin to develop causal hypotheses.

Observer: Please comment on the students' ability to organize the information and build hypotheses. Describe their social behavior as well as their ability to respond to the cognitive tasks.

_____

_____

_____

PHASE FOUR: FORMULATION OF LIKELY EXPLANATIONS

Now the students weigh the hypotheses and assess what are the most likely explanations of the phenomena. If this does not happen spontaneously the teacher initiates the phase.

Teacher: Please rehearse how you will initiate the phase.

_____

_____

_____

_____

Observer: Discuss the students' response to this task. Were they able to state hypotheses clearly, summarize the evidence, and, where appropriate, weigh competing explanations?

_____

_____

_____

_____

If students were successful in making inferences and conclusions about their data, the teacher may wish to push them a step further and ask them to predict consequences from their data by asking "What would happen if . . ." kinds of questions.

Teacher: Please write one or two examples of hypothetical questions you might ask students about these data.

_____

_____

_____

_____

Observer: Were students able to make logical predictions based on the forgoing categorization and discussion?

PHASE FIVE: ANALYSIS OF THE INQUIRY PROCESS

In phase five the students are led to analyze their inquiry process and contemplate how to improve it. This activity provides the teacher with the opportunity to coach the students, explaining and even modeling how they can work together to collect and verify data, build concepts, and develop hypotheses and test them.

COMMENTS ON STUDENT TRAINING NEEDS

In order to improve student performance, the first option we explore is whether it will improve with practice. That is, simple repetition of the model gives the students a chance to learn to respond more appropriately. Second, we directly teach the students the skills they need to manage the cognitive and social tasks of the model. How to improve student response is the focus of the discussion following the episode.

Observer: Please comment on the skills with which the students engaged in the activities and suggest any areas where you believe training might be useful.

Peer Coaching Guide: Assists to Memory

During the last 20 years there has been renewed research and development on strategies for assisting students to master and retain information. The science of mnemonics, as it is called, has produced some dramatic results (Pressley, Levin, and Delaney, 1982).

Rote repetition (rehearsing something over and over until it is retained) has until recently been the primary method taught to students for memorizing information and the primary method used by teachers as they interact with students. In fact, rote methods have become so used that they have become identified in many people's minds with the act of memorization. To memorize, it is often thought, is to repeat by rote.

MEMORIZATION STRATEGIES

However, although rehearsal of material continues to be one aspect of most mnemonic strategies, a number of other procedures are employed that greatly increase the probability that material will be learned and retained. These procedures are combined in various ways, depending on the material to be learned. Most of the procedures help build associations between the new material and familiar material. Some of the procedures include:

ORGANIZING INFORMATION TO BE LEARNED

Essentially, the more information is organized, the easier it is to learn and retain. Information can be organized by categories. The concept attainment, inductive, and advanced organizer models assist memory by helping students associate the material in the categories. Consider the following list of words from a popular spelling series, in the order the spelling book presents them to the children:

soft	plus	cloth	frost	song
trust	luck	club	sock	pop
cost	lot	son	won	

Suppose we ask the students to classify them by beginnings, endings, and the presence of vowels. The act of classification requires the students to scrutinize the words and associate words containing similar elements. They can then name the categories in each classification (the "c" group and the "st" group), calling further attention to the common attributes of the group. They can also connect words that fit together ("pop song," "soft cloth," etc.). They can then proceed to rehearse the spellings of one category at a time. The same principle operates over other types of material—say, number facts, etc. Whether categories are provided to students or whether they create them, the purpose is the same. Also, information can be selected with categories in mind. The above list is, to outward appearances, almost random. A list that deliberately and systematically provides variations would be easier to organize (it would already have at least implicit categories within it).

ORDERING INFORMATION TO BE LEARNED

Information learned in series, especially if there is meaning to the series, is easier to assimilate and retain. For example, if we wish to learn the names of the states of Australia it is easier if we always start with the same one (say, the largest) and proceed in the same order. Historical events by chronology are more easily learned than events sorted randomly. Order is simply another way of organizing information. We could have the students alphabetize their list of spelling words.

LINKING INFORMATION TO FAMILIAR SOUNDS

Suppose we are learning the names of the states. We can connect *Georgia* to *George*, *Louisiana* to *Louis*, *Maryland* to *Marry* or *Merry*, and so on. Categorizing the names of the states or ordering them by size, or ordering them within region, provides more associations.

LINKING INFORMATION TO VISUAL REPRESENTATIONS

Maryland can be linked to a picture of a marriage, Oregon to a picture of a gun, Maine to a burst water main, and so forth. Letters and numerals can be linked to something that evokes both familiar sounds and images. For example, *one* can be linked to *bun* and a picture of a boy eating a bun, *b* to *bee* and a picture of a bee. Those links can be used over and over again. "April is the cruelest month, breeding lilacs out of the dead land" is easier remembered thinking of an ominous spring, bending malevolently over the spring flowers.

LINKING INFORMATION TO ASSOCIATED INFORMATION

A person's name, linked to information such as a well-known person having the same name, a sound-alike, and some personal information, is easier to remember than the name rehearsed by itself. Louis (Louis Armstrong) "looms" over Jacksonville (his place of birth). Learning the states of Australia while thinking of the points of the compass and the British origins of many of the names (New South Wales) is easier than learning them in order alone.

MAKING THE INFORMATION VIVID

Devices that make the information vivid are also useful. Lorayne and Lucas favor "ridiculous association," where information is linked to absurd associations. ("The silly two carries his twin two on his back so they are really four" and such.) Others favor the use of dramatization and vivid illustrations (such as counting the basketball players on two teams to illustrate that 5 and 5 equal 10).

REHEARSING

Rehearsal (practice) is always useful, and students benefit from knowledge of results. Students who have not had past success with tasks requiring memorization will benefit by having relatively short assignments and clear, timely feedback as they have success.

PLANNING WITH MEMORIZATION IN MIND

The task of the teacher is to think up activities that help the students benefit from these principles.

A teaching episode or learning task that can be organized at least partly by these principles contains information to be learned. Both teacher and students should be clear that a very high degree of mastery is desired. (The students need to be trying to learn all the information and to retain it permanently.)

Teacher: Please identify the information to be learned by your students in some curriculum area within a specified period of time.

_____

_____

_____

_____

Which principles will you emphasize in order to facilitate memorization?

_____

_____

Will these principles be used as the information is presented to the students? If yes, how?

_____

_____

_____

Which principles will be used as the students operate on the information? How?

_____

_____

_____

_____

_____

How will rehearsal and feedback be managed?

_____

_____

_____

_____

Observer: During the teaching/learning episode, situate yourself so that you can observe the behavior of a small number of children (about a half-dozen). Concentrate on their response to the tasks that are given.

Comment on their response to the tasks. Do they appear to be clear about the objectives? Do they engage in the cognitive tasks that have been provided to them? Can they undertake these tasks successfully? Do they appear to be aware of progress?

_____

_____

_____

_____

_____

DISCUSSION

The observer should report the results of the observation to the teacher. Then, the discussion should focus on how the students responded and ways of helping them respond more effectively if that is desirable.

Practice frequently enables students to respond more productively without further instruction. Where instruction is needed, demonstration is useful. That is, the teacher may lead the students through the tasks over small amounts of material.

Tasks can be simplified in order to bring them within the reach of the students. We want the students to develop a repertoire of techniques that enables them to apply the mnemonic principles to learning tasks. Making the process conscious is a step toward independence, so we seek ways of helping the students understand the nature of the tasks and why these should work for them.

Peer Coaching Guide: Role Playing

Teacher: Do you want to suggest a focus for the analysis? If so, what is it?

_____

_____

_____

_____

THE TEACHING PROCESS

Most lessons have both content and process objectives. Content objectives identify subject matter (facts, concepts, generalizations, relationships) to be mastered by students, while process objectives specify skills and procedures students need in order to achieve content objectives or auxiliary social objectives (e.g., cooperation in a learning task).

CONTENT OBJECTIVE

Teacher: Please state the objective of the lesson. What problem will be presented to the students, or in what domain will they construct a problem? Is the problem or domain of values new to the students?

_____

_____

_____

PROCESS OBJECTIVE

Teacher: Are the students familiar with the model? Do they need special assistance or training with respect to any aspect of the process?

_____

_____

_____

PHASE ONE: WARMING UP

Role playing begins with a social problem. The problem may be from a prepared study of a human-relations situation or an aspect of human relations may be presented to the students so they can generate situations involving it. Possibly the problem is one in their lives that simply needs recapitulation.

Teacher: How will you present the problem to the students or help them develop it?

_____

_____

_____

Observer: In your opinion, was the problem clear to the students? Were they able to understand the nature of the problem and the type of human-relations problem it represents? Could they identify the players in the situation and how they act? Can they see the several sides of the problem?

_____

_____

_____

PHASE TWO: SELECTING THE PARTICIPANTS (ROLE PLAYERS AND OBSERVERS)

Teacher: Please describe how the participants will be selected.

_____

_____

_____

_____

PHASE THREE: CREATING THE LINE OF ACTION FOR THE FIRST ENACTMENT

Teacher: How are you going to do this? Do you wish the first enactment to highlight certain aspects of values?

_____

_____

_____

Observer: Were they able to generate a plausible and meaningful story line? Please note any difficulties they had.

_____

_____

_____

PHASE FOUR: PREPARING THE OBSERVERS

Once the characters have been identified and the story line generated, the observers are prepared.

Teacher: What will you ask the observers to focus on?

_____

_____

_____

Sometimes the observers (students) are asked to record the progression of their impressions.

Teacher: Do you want to do this?

_____

PHASE FIVE: THE ENACTMENT

Now the students enact the problem for the first time.

Observer: How well did the students enact the roles? Did they appear to empathize with the positions they were to take? Were the observers attentive and serious? Comment on any problems either role players or observers had.

_____

_____

_____

PHASE SIX: DISCUSSION

Observer: Were the students able to analyze the nature of the conflict and the values that were involved? Did they reveal their own value positions? Did they have any confusion about tactics of argumentation, skill, and values?

_____

_____

_____

From this point, phases five and six are repeated through several enactments (functioning as *phases seven and eight*). The teacher guides the students to ensure that the value questions are brought out.

Observer: Please comment on the student performance in the ensuing cycles of enactments and discussions. Did the students increasingly become able to distinguish value positions?

_____

_____

PHASE NINE: ANALYSIS AND GENERALIZATIONS

When the teacher judges that sufficient material has been generated, a discussion is held (a cooperative learning format can be used for this phase to maximize participation, if desired) to ensure that the value positions are brought out and to put forth positions about what can be done to deal with the particular type of problem from a valuing basis rather than one involving adversarial uses of argumentation and conflict.

Teacher: Please prepare the instructions you will give the students to inaugurate phase nine.

_____

_____

_____

_____

Observer: Please comment on the students' ability to handle the tasks involved in phase nine.

_____

_____

_____

_____

DISCUSSION

Following the teaching episode, the coaching partners might discuss ways of helping the students respond more effectively to the model. Remember that the early trials are bound to be awkward and that practice often does the trick. Also, problems can be adjusted to simplify the issues that have to be dealt with at any one time. Demonstrating the phases of the model to the students is also useful. The coaching partners can play the role of observer or even role player to give the students a model. Or the two teachers can demonstrate together.

Please summarize the results of the discussion—the one or two chief conclusions you have reached to guide what you will next do as you use the model.

_____

_____

_____

_____

Peer Coaching Guide: Inductive Thinking

Teacher: Do you want to suggest a focus for the analysis? If so, what is it?

_____

_____

THE TEACHING PROCESS

Most lessons have both content and process objectives. Content objectives identify subject matter (facts, concepts, generalizations, relationships) to be mastered by students, while process objectives specify skills and procedures students need in order to achieve content objectives or auxiliary social objectives (e.g., cooperation in a learning task).

The content objectives for inductive thinking reside in the information and concepts embedded in a data set. Students categorize items in the data set by attributes held in common by subsets of items. For example, if the data set consisted of a collection of plants, students might classify plants by types of leaves (size, texture, patterns of veins, shape, connection of leaves to stems, etc.). Content objectives for this data set might include both information about specific plants and the building of a typology. Process objectives might include learning the scientific skills of the discipline (observation and classification) as well as the social skills of cooperative problem solving.

CONTENT OBJECTIVE(S)

Teacher: What do you want students to gain from this classification task? What, in your opinion, are the critical attributes of the data set? What categories do you bring to the set?

_____

_____

_____

PROCESS OBJECTIVE(S)

Teacher: Are the students familiar with the model? Do they need special assistance or training with respect to any aspect of the process? (For example, do students understand how to group items by common attributes? Can they work cooperatively with partners on a classification task?)

_____

_____

PHASE ONE: DATA COLLECTION / PRESENTATION

The primary activity of phase one of the inductive thinking model involves collection or presentation of a data set. The teacher may provide a data set or instruct students to collect the data that will be categorized. The data that will be scrutinized by the students are extremely important, for they represent much of the information the students will learn from the episode. The choice between data collection or presentation is also important. To continue the above example, if students collect leaves, a different set of data will result than if they had been presented with them. Once a data set has been collected by or presented to students, the teacher may want to set parameters for the classification activity by orienting students to relevant attributes. For example, if the data are plants, the teacher may wish to narrow the field of observation by having students classify by "types of leaves." On the other hand, the teacher may wish to leave the parameters open and simply instruct students to classify by common attributes. Generally speaking, the more open-ended the instructions, the better the results.

Items from a data set may be included in only one category or in multiple categories. You may want to experiment with different instructions regarding the classification of data and observe differences in the categories that result. Generally speaking, leaving open the possibility of multiple category membership for items from the data set provides the most energy.

Teacher: Please describe the data set to be used in this lesson. Will you provide the data set or have students collect data? If the latter, what will be the sources of information they will use?

_____

_____

_____

ENUMERATION

Data are easier to group if enumerated. Continuing with our example of plants, the teacher might place a numbered card under each plant so that students may discuss plants 1, 4, 7, and 14 as sharing a common attribute rather than by plant names (which students may not yet know).

Observer: Did the teacher/students enumerate the data before attempting to categorize it?

Yes [ ]   No [ ]

PHASE TWO: CONCEPT FORMATION

Once a data set is assembled and enumerated and students have been instructed on procedures for grouping the data, the teacher will need to attend to the mechanics of the grouping activity. Students may work alone, in pairs, in small groups, or as one large group. Working alone requires the least social skill, and working in small groups the greatest social skill. If one objective is to develop students' abilities to work cooperatively, assertively defending their groupings but compromising when appropriate for group consensus, then students will need instruction and practice to develop these skills. If the teacher chooses to work with the entire class as a single group for the categorizing activity, he or she will need to exercise caution so that categories are not inadvertently provided for the students. Structuring students into pairs for the categorizing activity is the simplest way to have all students actively engaged in the task, although the teacher must again use considerable skill in keeping everyone involved while recording and synthesizing reports from the pairs. Teachers will probably want to experiment with different ways of structuring this activity, and pros and cons of each process can be discussed and problem-solved with peer coaches.

Teacher: Please describe how you will organize students for the categorizing activity.

_____

_____

_____

_____

Teacher: Please describe how you will instruct the students to classify the data that you have provided or that they have collected.

_____

_____

_____

_____

Observer: In your opinion, did the students understand the criteria and procedures they were to employ during the categorizing activity? Did the teacher inadvertently give clues about what the "right" groups would be?

_____

_____

_____

_____

Observer: Did the students work productively on the categorizing activity?

Yes [ ]   No [ ]   Partially [ ]

If the teacher had the students work in pairs or small groups, did the students listen as other groups shared their categories?

Yes [ ]   No [ ]   Partially [ ]

Were students able to explain the attributes on which they grouped items within categories?

Yes [ ]   No [ ]   Partially [ ]

Were students able to provide names for their groups which reflected the attributes on which the groups were formed?

Yes [ ]   No [ ]

The names or labels students attach to groups of items within a data set will often accurately describe the group but not coincide with a technical or scientific name. For example, students may label a group of leaves "jagged edges" while the technical term would be "serrated edges." The teacher may choose to provide technical or scientific terms when appropriate, but not before students have attempted to provide their own labels.

For some lessons, the content objectives will be accomplished at the conclusion of phase two. When the teacher wishes to have students learn information by organizing it into categories and labeling it in order to gain conceptual control of the material, he or she may choose to stop here. Or when the objective is to learn what students see within a data set and what attributes they are unaware of, the grouping activity will accomplish that objective. When, however, the objective is the interpretation and application of concepts that have been formed in phase two, the remainder of the inductive thinking model is appropriate. The final phases of the model result in further processing of the information and concepts embedded in the data set and should usually be completed.

PHASE THREE: INTERPRETATION OF DATA

The purpose of phase three is to help students develop understanding of possible relationships between and among categories that they have formed in phase two. The class will need a common set of categories in order to work productively in this kind of discussion. Working off the descriptions of individual groups students have generated in phase two, the teacher asks questions that focus students' thinking on similarities and differences between the groups. By asking "why" questions, the teacher attempts to develop cause-effect relationships between the groups. The success of this phase depends on a thorough categorizing activity in phase two, and the length of phase three is relatively short compared with the time required by phase two.

Teacher: Although you will not know during your planning what groups the students will form, make a guess about possible categories they might construct, and then write two sample questions that would explore cause-effect relationships between those groups.

_____

_____

_____

_____

Observer: Were the students able to discuss possible cause-effect relationships among the groups?

Yes [ ]   No [ ]   Partially [ ]

Did the teacher ask the students to go beyond the data and make inferences and conclusions regarding their data?

Yes [ ]   No [ ]

If yes, were the students able to do so?

Yes [ ]   No [ ]

If students were unable to make inferences or conclusions, can you think of any ideas to share with your partner that might help them do so?

_____

_____

_____

_____

If students were successful in making inferences and conclusions about their data, the teacher may wish to push them a step further and ask them to predict consequences from their data by asking "What would happen if . . ." kinds of questions.

Teacher: Please write one or two examples of hypothetical questions you might ask students about this data set.

_____

_____

_____

_____

Observer: Were students able to make logical predictions based on the foregoing categorization and discussion?

Yes [ ]   No [ ]

Did the teacher ask the students to explain and support their predictions?

Yes [ ]   No [ ]

If students were unable to make logical predictions based on their previous work with their categories, can you think of questions or examples that might assist students in doing so?

_____

_____

_____

For Teacher and Observer Discussion: Are there writing assignments or other activities that would be appropriate extensions of this lesson?

COMMENTS ON STUDENT TRAINING NEEDS

In order to improve student performance, the first option we explore is whether it will improve with practice. That is, simple repetition of the model gives the students a chance to learn to respond more appropriately. Second, we directly teach the students the skills they need to manage the cognitive and social tasks of the model.

Observer: Please comment on the skills with which the students engaged in the activities and suggest any areas where you believe training might be useful. Think especially of their ability to group by attributes, to provide labels for groups that accurately described the groups or synthesized attributes characteristic of a given group, their understanding of possible cause-effect relationships among groups, and their ability to make inferences or conclusions regarding their categories.

_____

_____

_____

_____

Peer Coaching Guide: Picture-Word Inductive Model

School or Agency: _____   Name: _____

Grade Level/Position: _____

Beginning Date of PWIM Cycle: _____

Description of Class (grade level, number of students, special needs):

_____

_____

_____

A. Describe your picture.

_____

_____

B. List of words shaken out of the picture:

_____

_____

_____

_____

_____

Words added to the picture-word chart and word sets after the first round:

_____

_____

_____

C. Examples of categories of words or phrases generated by students:

_____

_____

_____

D. Examples of categories or concepts selected by you for instructional emphasis:

Phonetic analysis categories or concepts:

_____

_____

Structural analysis categories or concepts:

_____

_____

Content categories or concepts:

_____

_____

Other:

_____

_____

E. Examples of titles generated by students

From the picture:

_____

_____

_____

From the picture-word chart:

_____

_____

_____

From sentence groups or categories:

_____

_____

_____

F. Examples of sentences generated by students:

_____

_____

_____

_____

_____

G. One of the informative paragraphs composed by you from student ideas:

_____

_____

_____

_____

Be sure to do a think-aloud with your students about how you put the ideas together to convey your message.

H. Sample(s) of Student Work: You may want to attach examples of student work to the implementation log.

Be sure to take samples of student work, when they are available, to your sessions with your peer-coaching partner and to designated sessions with the team as a learning community. You may take work from your whole class or group; however, we suggest you take, for collective study, the work of six students whose responses you are monitoring more formally and maybe more analytically than those of the whole class.

I. If you used tradebooks with PWIM cycle, list the title, author, and strategy used (if applicable).

Title	Author	F or NF	List Strategy (*Read Aloud, Talk Aloud, Think Aloud, Explicit Instruction*)
1.			
2.			
3.			
4.			
5.			
6.			
7.			
8.			
9.			
10.			
11.			
12.			

Strategies	Total Number during PWIM Cycle
Read Aloud	
Talk Aloud	
Think Aloud	
Explicit Instruction	

Comments and Reflections:

_____

_____

_____

Questions:

_____

_____

Number of lessons in PWIM cycle: _____

Ending date of PWIM cycle: _____

Number of times you planned with your peer coach in this PWIM cycle:

_____

Number of times you demonstrated with your peer coach in this PWIM cycle: _____

Number of times you debriefed with your peer coach in this PWIM cycle:

_____

PWIM: STUDYING STUDENT PERFORMANCE

EMPHASIS: VOCABULARY DEVELOPMENT

Description of six students whose learning is being studied formally as part of studying the picture-word inductive model:

1. Name _____ Birthdate _____ Gender: F/M

Other information that would be useful to understanding the student, such as learning history, etc.

_____

_____

2. Name _____ Birthdate _____ Gender: F/M

Other information that would be useful to understanding the student, such as learning history, etc.

_____

_____

3. Name _____ Birthdate _____ Gender: F/M

Other information that would be useful to understanding the student, such as learning history, etc.

_____

_____

4. Name _____ Birthdate _____ Gender: F/M

Other information that would be useful to understanding the student, such as learning history, etc.

_____

_____

5. Name _____ Birthdate _____ Gender: F/M

Other information that would be useful to understanding the student, such as learning history, etc.

_____

_____

6. Name _____ Birthdate _____ Gender: F/M

Other information that would be useful to understanding the student, such as learning history, etc.

_____

_____

Gender of Student	Total Number of Words	Date Asst.	Number of Words Read	Total Number of Words	Date Asst.	Number of Words Read	Gain
1.							
2.							
3.							
4.							
5.							
6.							

Related Literature and References

Acheson, K. (1967). *The effects of feedback from television recordings and three types of supervisory treatment on selected teacher behaviors.* Unpublished doctoral dissertation, Stanford University.

Adams, A. H., Johnson, M. S., & Connors, J. M. (1980). *Success in kindergarten reading and writing.* Glenview, Ill.: Good Year Books.

Adey, P., & Shayer, M. (1990). Accelerating the development of formal thinking in middle and high school students. *Journal of Research in Science Teaching, 27*(3), 267–285.

Adkins, D. C., Payne, F. D., & O'Malley, J. M. (1974). Moral development. In F. N. Kerlinger & J. B. Carroll (Eds.), *Review of research in education.* Itasca, Ill.: Peacock.

Adler, M. J. (1982). *The Paideia proposal: An educational manifesto.* New York: Macmillan.

Ainscow, M. (1991). Preface. In M. Ainscow (Ed.), *Effective schools for all.* London: Fulton.

Alberti, R. E., & Emmons, F. (1978). *Your perfect right: A guide to assertive behavior* (3rd ed.). San Luis Obispo, Calif.: Impact.

Alfasi, M. (1998). Reading for meaning: The efficacy of reciprocal teaching in fostering reading comprehension in high school students in remedial reading classes. *American Educational Research Journal, 35*(2), 309–332.

Almy, M. (1970). *Logical thinking in second grade.* New York: Teachers College Press.

Anderson, H., & Brewer, H. (1939). Domination and social integration in the behavior of kindergarten children and teachers. *Genetic Psychology Monograph, 21*, 287–385.

Anderson, L. M., Evertson, C. M., & Brophy, J. E. (1979). An experimental study of effective teaching in first grade reading groups. *Elementary School Journal, 79*(4), 191–223.

Anderson, L. W., & Pellicer, L. O. (1990). Synthesis of research on compensatory and remedial education. *Educational Leadership, 48*(1), 10–16.

479

Anderson, L. W., Scott, C., & Hutlock, N. (1976). *The effect of a mastery learning program on selected cognitive, affective, and ecological variables in grades 1 through 6*. Paper presented at the annual meeting of the American Educational Research Association, San Francisco.

Antil, L., Jenkins, J., Wayne, S., & Vadasy, P. (1998). Cooperative learning: Prevalence, conceptualizations, and the relation between research and practice. *American Educational Research Journal, 35*(3), 419–454.

Apple, M. (1979). *Ideology and curriculum*. London: Routledge and Kegan Paul.

Applebee, A., Langer, J., Jenkins, L., Mullis, I., & Foertsch, M. (1990). *Learning to write in our nation's schools*. Washington, D.C.: U.S. Department of Education.

Aquinas, T. (1931). *The city of God*. (J. Healy, Trans.). London: J. M. Dent.

Argyis, C., & Schön, E. (1974). *Theory into practice: Increasing professional effectiveness*. San Francisco: Jossey-Bass.

Aristotle (1912). *The works of Aristotle* (J. A. Smith & W. D. Ross, Eds.). Oxford: Clarendon Press.

Arlin, M. (1984). Time variability in mastery learning. *American Educational Research Journal, 21*(4), 103–120.

Arlin, M., & Webster, J. (1983). Time costs of mastery learning. *Journal of Educational Psychology, 75*(3), 187–196.

Armstrong, T. (1994). *Multiple intelligences in the classroom*. Alexandria, Va.: Association for Supervision and Curriculum Development.

Aronson, E., Blaney, N., Stephan, C., Sikes, J., & Snapp, M. (1978). *The jigsaw classroom*. Beverly Hills, Calif.: Sage.

Aspy, D. N., & Roebuck, F. (1973). An investigation of the relationship between student levels of cognitive functioning and the teacher's classroom behavior. *Journal of Educational Research, 65*(6), 365–368.

Aspy, D. N., Roebuck, F., Willson, M., & Adams, O. (1974). *Interpersonal skills training for teachers*. (Interim Report No. 2 for NIMH Grant No. 5PO 1MH 19871.) Monroe: Northeast Louisiana University.

Atkinson, J. W. (1966). *Achievement motivation*. New York: Wiley.

Atkinson, R. C. (1975). Mnemotechnics in second language learning. *American Psychologist, 30*, 821–828.

Augustine. (1931). *The city of God* (J. Healy, Trans.). London: Dent.

Ausubel, D. P. (1960). The use of advance organizers in the learning and retention of meaningful verbal material. *Journal of Educational Psychology, 51*, 267–272.

Ausubel, D. P. (1963). *The psychology of meaningful verbal learning*. New York: Grune & Stratton.

Ausubel, D. P. (1968). *Educational psychology: A cognitive view*. New York: Holt, Rinehart & Winston.

Ausubel, D. P. (1977). *Behavior modification for the classroom teacher*. New York: McGraw-Hill.

Ausubel, D. P. (1980). Schemata, cognitive structure, and advance organizers: A reply to Anderson, Spiro, and Anderson. *American Educational Research Journal, 17*(3), 400–404.

Ausubel, D. P., & Fitzgerald, J. (1962). Organizer, general background, and antecedent learning variables in sequential verbal learning. *Journal of Educational Psychology, 53*, 243–249.

Ausubel, D. P., Stager, M., & Gaite, A. J. H. (1968). Retroactive facilitation of meaningful verbal learning. *Journal of Educational Psychology, 59,* 250–255.

Baer, J. (1993). *Creativity and divergent thinking.* Hillsdale, N.J.: Erlbaum.

Baker, E., & Saloutas, A. (1974). *Evaluating instructional programs.* Washington, D.C.: Department of Health, Education, and Welfare, National Institute of Education.

Baker, R. G. (1983). *The contribution of coaching to transfer of training: An extension study.* Doctoral dissertation, University of Oregon.

Baker, R. G., & Showers, B. (1984). *The effects of a coaching strategy on teachers' transfer of training to classroom practice: A six-month followup study.* Paper presented at the annual meeting of the American Educational Research Association, New Orleans.

Baldridge, V., & Deal, T. (1975). *Managing change in educational organizations.* Berkeley, Calif.: McCutchan.

Baldridge, V., & Deal, T. (Eds.). (1983). *The dynamics of organizational change in education.* Boston: Addison-Wesley.

Ball, S., & Bogatz, G. A. (1970). *The first year of Sesame Street.* Princeton, N.J.: Educational Testing Service.

Bandura, A. (1969). *Principles of behavior modification.* New York: Holt, Rinehart & Winston.

Bandura, A. (1971a). Psychotherapy based on modeling principles. In A. S. Bergin & S. L. Garfield (Eds.), *Handbook of psychotherapy and behavior change.* New York: Wiley.

Bandura, A. (1971b). *Social learning theory.* New York: General Learning.

Bandura, A., & Perloff, B. (1967). Relative efficacy of self-monitored and externally imposed reinforcement systems. *Journal of Personality and Social Psychology, 7,* 111–116.

Bandura, A., & Walters, R. (1963). *Social learning and personality.* New York: Holt, Rinehart & Winston.

Bangert, R. L., & Kulik, J. A. (1982). *Individualized systems of instruction: A meta-analysis of findings in secondary schools.* Paper presented at the annual meeting of the American Educational Research Association, New York.

Bangert-Drowns, R. L. (1986). *A review of developments in meta-analytic method.* Paper presented at the annual meeting of the American Educational Research Association, San Francisco.

Banks, J. A. (1995). The historical reconstruction of knowledge about race: Implications for transformative teaching. *Educational Researcher, 24*(2), 26–30.

Bany, M., & Johnson, L. V. (1964). *Classroom group behavior: Group dynamics in education.* New York: Macmillan.

Barnes, B. R., & Clausen, E. U. (1973). The effects of organizers on the learning of structured anthropology materials in the elementary grades. *Journal of Experimental Education, 42,* 11–15.

Barnes, B. R., & Clausen, E. U. (1975). Do advance organizers facilitate learning? Recommendations for further research based on an analysis of 32 studies. *Review of Educational Research, 45*(4), 637–659.

Barr, B. (1994). Research on problem-solving. *Elementary School Journal, 5*(3), 237–247.

Barron, F. (1963). *Creativity and psychological health: Origins of personal vitality and creative freedom.* Princeton, N.J.: Van Nostrand.

Barron, R. R. (1971). *The effects of advance organizers upon the reception, learning, and retention of general science concepts.* (DHEW Project No. IB-030.) ERIC Document Reproduction Service, ED 061 554.

Barth, R. (1980). *Run, school, run.* Cambridge, Mass.: Harvard University Press.

Bascones, J., and Novak, J. (1985). Alternative instructional systems and the development of problem-solving in physics. *European Journal of Science Education, 7*(3), 253–261.

Baveja, B. (1988). *An exploratory study of the use of information-processing models of teaching in secondary school biology science classes.* Doctoral dissertation. Delhi, India: Delhi University.

Baveja, B., Showers, B., & Joyce, B. (1985). *An experiment in conceptually based teaching strategies.* Eugene, Ore.: Booksend Laboratories.

Beatty, A., Reese, C., Persky, H., & Carr, P. (1996). *N.A.E.P. 1994 U.S. history report card.* Washington, D.C.: U.S. Department of Education.

Beck, A. T. (1976). *Cognitive therapy and the emotional disorders.* New York: International Universities Press.

Becker, W. (1975). *Classroom management.* Chicago: Science Research Associates.

Becker, W. (1977). Teaching reading and language to the disadvantaged—What we have learned from field research. *Harvard Educational Review, 47,* 518–543.

Becker, W., & Carnine, D. (1980). Direct instruction: An effective approach for educational intervention with the disadvantaged and low performers. In B. Lahey & A. Kazdin (Eds.), *Advances in child clinical psychology* (pp. 429–473). New York: Plenum.

Becker, W., Engelmann, S., Carnine, D., & Rhine, W. (1981). In W. R. Rhine (Ed.), *Making schools more effective.* New York: Academic Press.

Becker, W., & Gersten, R. (1982). A followup of follow through: The later effects of the direct instruction model on children in the fifth and sixth grades. *American Educational Research Journal, 19*(1), 75–92.

Bellack, A. (1962). *The language of the classroom.* New York: Teachers College Press.

Bencke, W. N., & Harris, M. B. (1972). Teaching self-control of study behavior. *Behavior Research and Therapy, 10,* 35–41.

Bennett, B. (1987). *The effectiveness of staff development training practices: A meta-analysis.* Ph.D. thesis, University of Oregon.

Bennis, W. G., & Shepard, H. A. (1964). Theory of group development. In W. G. Bennis, K. D. Benne, & R. Chin (Eds.), *The planning of change: Readings in the applied behavioral sciences.* New York: Holt, Rinehart & Winston.

Bereiter, C. (1984a). Constructivism, socioculturalism, and Popper's World 3. *Educational Researcher, 23*(7), 21–23.

Bereiter, C. (1984b). How to keep thinking skills from going the way of all frills. *Educational Leadership, 42,* 1.

Bereiter, C., & Englemann, S. (1966). *Teaching the culturally disadvantaged child in the preschool.* Englewood Cliffs, N.J.: Prentice-Hall.

Bereiter, C., & Kurland, M. (1981–82). Were some follow-through models more effective than others? *Interchange, 12,* 1–22.

Berger, P., & Luckmann, T. (1966). *Social construction of reality.* Garden City, N.Y.: Doubleday.

Berliner, D. (1992). Effective schools: Teachers make the difference. *Instructor, 99*(3), 14–15.

Berman, P., & Gjelten, T. (1983). *Improving school improvement*. Berkeley, Calif.: Berman, Weiler Associates.

Berman, P., & McLaughlin, M. (1975). *Federal programs supporting educational change: Vol. 4. The findings in review*. Santa Monica, Calif.: Rand Corporation.

Beyer, B. (1988). *Developing a thinking skills program*. Boston: Allyn & Bacon.

Bielinski, J., & Davison, M. (1998). Gender differences by item difficulty interactions in multiple choice mathematics items. *American Educational Research Journal, 35*(3), 455–476.

Black, J. (1989). *Building the school as a center of inquiry: A whole-school approach oriented around models of teaching*. Ph.D. thesis, Nova University.

Blatt, B. (Ed.). (1980). *Providing leadership for staff development*. Syracuse, N.Y.: National Council for the States in Inservice Education.

Block, J. W. (1971). *Mastery learning: Theory and practice*. New York: Holt, Rinehart & Winston.

Block, J. W. (1980). Success rate. In C. Denham & A. Lieberman (Eds.), *Time to learn*. Washington, D.C.: Program on Teaching and Learning, National Institute of Education.

Block, J. W., & Anderson, L. W. (1975). *Mastery learning in classrooms*. New York: Macmillan.

Bloom, B. S. (1971). Mastery learning. In J. H. Block (Ed.), *Mastery learning: Theory and practice*. New York: Holt, Rinehart & Winston.

Bloom, B. S. (1974). Time and learning. *American Psychologist, 29*, 682–688.

Bloom, B. S. (1976). *Human characteristics and school learning*. New York: McGraw-Hill.

Bloom, B. S. (1981). *The new direction in educational research and measurement: Alterable variables*. Paper presented at the annual meeting of the American Educational Research Association, Los Angeles.

Bloom, B. S. (1982). *Human characteristics and school learning*. New York: McGraw-Hill.

Bloom, B. S. (1984). The 2 sigma problem: The search for methods of group instruction as effective as one-to-one tutoring. *Educational Leadership, 41*, 4–17.

Bloom, B. S., et al. (1956). *Taxonomy of educational objectives. Handbook I: Cognitive domain*. New York: McKay.

Bode, B. (1927). *Modern educational theories*. New York: Macmillan.

Bonsangue, M. (1993). Long term effects of the Calculus Workshop Model. *Cooperative Learning, 13*(3), 19–20.

Bonstingl, J. J. (1992). *Schools of quality: An introduction to total quality management in education*. Alexandria, Va.: Association for Supervision and Curriculum Development.

Boocock, S. S. (1973). The school as a social environment for learning social organization and micro-social process in education. *Sociology of Education, 4*, 49–63.

Boocock, S. S., & Schild, E. (1968). *Simulation games in learning*. Beverly Hills, Calif.: Sage.

Borg, W. R., Kallenbach, W., Morris, M., & Friebel, A. (1969). Videotape feedback and microteaching in a teacher training model. *Journal of Experimental Research, 37*, 9–16.

Borg, W. R., Kelley, Langer, P., & Gall, M. (1970). *The minicourse.* Beverly Hills, Calif.: Collier-Macmillan.

Boutwell, C. (1972). *Getting it all together.* San Rafael, Calif.: Leswing Press.

Braden, V., & Bruns, B. (1977). *Vic Braden's tennis for the future.* Boston: Little, Brown.

Bradford, L. P., Gibb, J. R., & Benne, K. D. (Eds.). (1964). *T-Group theory and laboratory method.* New York: Wiley.

Brandt, R. (1982). Overview. *Educational Leadership, 40*(4), 3.

Brandt, R. (1987). On cooperation in schools: A conversation with David and Roger Johnson. *Educational Leadership, 45*(3), 14–19.

Bransford, J., Brown, A., & Cocking, R. (1999). *How people learn: Brain, mind, experience, and school.* Washington, D.C.: National Academy Press.

Brashear, R. M., & Davis, O. L. (1970). *The persistence of teaching laboratory effects into student teaching: A comparative study of verbal teaching behaviors and attitudes.* Paper presented at the annual meeting of the American Educational Research Association, New York.

Bredderman, T. (1981). *Elementary school process curricula: A meta-analysis.* ERIC Document Reproduction Service, ED 170-333.

Bredderman, T. (1983). Effects of activity-based elementary science on student outcomes: A quantitative synthesis. *Review of Educational Research, 53*(4), 499–518.

Brenner, M., Mayer, R., Moseley, B., Barr, T., Duran, R., Reed, B., & Webb, D. (1997). Learning by understanding: The role of multiple representations in learning algebra. *American Educational Research Journal, 34*(4), 663–689.

Brookover, W., Schwitzer, J. H., Schneider, J. M., Beady, C. H., Flood, P. K., & Wisenbaker, J. M. (1978). Elementary school social climate and school achievement. *American Educational Research Journal, 15*(2), 301–318.

Brooks, J. G., & Brooks, M. G. (1993). *The case for constructivist classrooms.* Alexandria, Va.: Association for Supervision and Curriculum Development.

Brophy, J. E. (1973). Stability of teacher effectiveness. *American Educational Research Journal, 10*, 245–252.

Brophy, J. E. (1981). Teacher praise: A functional analysis. *Review of Educational Research, 51*, 5–32.

Brophy, J. E., & Evertson, C. (1974). *The Texas teacher effectiveness project: Presentation of non-linear relationships and summary discussion.* Austin: Research and Development Center for Teacher Education, University of Texas.

Brophy, J. E., & Good, T. (1986). Teacher behavior and student achievement. In M. Wittrock (Ed.), *Handbook of research on teaching* (3rd ed., pp. 328–375). New York: Macmillan.

Brothers, L. (1997). *Friday's footprint: How society shapes the human mind.* New York: Oxford.

Broudy, H. (1963). Historic exemplars of teaching methods. In N. L. Gage (Ed.), *Handbook of research on teaching.* Chicago: Rand McNally.

Brown, A. (1985). Reciprocal teaching of comprehension strategies (Technical Report No. 334). Urbana-Champaign: University of Illinois, Center for the Study of Reading.

Brown, A., & Palincsar, A. (1989). Guided, cooperative learning individual knowledge acquisition. In L. Resnick (Ed.), *Knowing, learning, and instruction* (pp. 393–451). Hillsdale, N.J.: Erlbaum.

Brown, A. L. (1995). Guided discovery in a community of learners. In K. McGilly (Ed.), *Classroom lessons: Integrating cognitive theory and classroom practice* (pp. 229–270). Cambridge, Mass.: MIT/Bradford Press.

Brown, C. (1967). *A multivariate study of the teaching styles of student teachers.* Ph.D. dissertation, Teachers College, Columbia University.

Brown, C. (1981). The relationship between teaching styles, personality, and setting. In B. Joyce, L. Peck, & C. Brown (Eds.), *Flexibility in teaching* (pp. 94–100). New York: Longman.

Brown, G. (1968). *Humanistic education.* Report to the Ford Foundation on the Ford-Esallen project: A pilot project to explore ways to adapt approaches in the affective domain to the school curriculum.

Brown, G. (1971). *Human teaching for human learning.* New York: Viking Penguin.

Bruce, W. C., & Bruce, J. K. (1992). *Learning social studies through discrepant event inquiry.* Annapolis, Md.: Alpha Press.

Bruer, J. T. (1997). Education and the brain: A bridge too far. *Educational Researcher, 26*(8), 4–16.

Bruer, J. T. (1998). Brain science, brain fiction. *Educational Leadership, 56*(3), 14–18.

Bruner, J. (1961). *The process of education.* Cambridge, Mass.: Harvard University Press.

Bruner, J., Goodnow, J. J., & Austin, G. A. (1967). *A study of thinking.* New York: Science Editions.

Bruno, J. E., & Ellett, F. S. (1986). *A core-analysis of meta-analysis.* Paper presented at the annual meeting of the American Educational Research Association, San Francisco.

Burgess, E. W., & Bogue, D. J. (1962). The delinquency research of Clifford R. Shaw and Henry D. McKay and Associates. In E. W. Burgess (Ed.), *Urban sociology.* Chicago: University of Chicago Press.

Burkham, D., Lee, V., & Smerdon, B. (1997). Gender and science learning early in high school: Subject matter and laboratory experiences. *American Educational Research Journal, 34*(2), 297–331.

Burns, S., Griffin, P., & Snow, C. (1998). *Starting out right.* Washington, D.C.: National Academy Press.

Bushell, D., Jr. (1970). *The behavior analysis classroom.* Lawrence: University of Kansas, Department of Human Development.

California Department of Education. (1998). *Fact Book: 1997–98.* Sacramento: California Department of Education.

Calderon, M., Hertz-Lazarowitz, R., & Tinajero, J. (1991). Adapting CIRC to multi-ethnic and bilingual classrooms. *Cooperative Learning, 12,* 17–20.

Calhoun, E. (1997). *Literacy for all.* Saint Simons Island, Ga.: The Phoenix Alliance.

Calhoun, E. (1998). *Literacy for the primary grades: What works, for whom, and to what degree.* Saint Simons Island, Ga.: The Phoenix Alliance.

Calhoun, E. F. (1994). *How to use action research in the self-renewing school.* Alexandria, Va.: Association for Supervision and Curriculum Development.

Calhoun, E. F. (1999). *Teaching beginning reading and writing with the picture word model.* Alexandria, Va.: Association for Supervision and Curriculum Development.

Calvin, W. (1996). *How brains think: Evolving intelligence, then and now.* New York: Basic Books.

Cambourne, B. (2002). Holistic, integrated approaches to reading and language arts instruction: The constructivist framework of an instructional theory. In A. Farstrup & J. Samuels (Eds.), *What research has to say about reading instruction.* Newark, Del.: International Reading Instruction.

Cameron, J., & Pierce, W. (1994). Reinforcement, reward, and intrinsic motivation: A meta-analysis. *Review of Educational Research, 64*(2), 363–423.

Campbell, F., & Ramey, C. (1995). Cognitive and school outcomes for high-risk African-American students at middle adolescence: Positive effects of early intervention. *American Educational Research Journal, 32*(4), 743–772.

Campbell, J., Donahue, P., Reese, C., & Phillips, G. (1996). *NAEP 1994 reading report card for the nation and the states.* Washington, D.C.: U.S. Department of Education.

Campbell, J., Voelki, K., & Donohue, P. (1997). *Report in brief: NAEP 1996 trends in reading progress.* Washington, D.C.: National Center for Educational Statistics.

Canfield, L. H., & Wilder, H. B. (1966). *The making of modern America.* Boston: Houghton Mifflin.

Canter, L., & Canter, M. (1976). *Assertive discipline: A take-charge approach for today's educator.* Seal Beach, Calif.: Canter and Associates.

Carroll, J. B. (1963). A model of school learning. *Teachers College Record, 64,* 722–733.

Carroll, J. B. (1964). *Language and thought.* Englewood Cliffs, N.J.: Prentice-Hall.

Carroll, J. B. (1971). Problems of measurement related to the concept of learning for mastery. In J. H. Block (Ed.), *Mastery learning: Theory and practice.* New York: Holt, Rinehart & Winston.

Carroll, J. B. (1977). A revisionist model of school learning. *Review of Educational Research, 3,* 155–167.

Cawelti, G. (Ed.). (1995). *Handbook of research on improving student achievement.* Arlington, Va.: Educational Research Service.

Center for Research on Elementary and Middle Schools. (1989, February). *Success for all.* Johns Hopkins, Baltimore, Md.: Author.

Ceram, C. W. (1951). *Gods, graves, and scholars: The story of archeology.* New York: Random House.

Chall, J. S. (1983). *Stages of reading development.* New York: McGraw-Hill.

Chamberlin, C., & Chamberlin, E. (1943). *Did they succeed in college?* New York: Harper & Row.

Charles, C. M. (1985). *Building classroom discipline: From models to practice.* White Plains, N.Y.: Longman.

Chesler, M., & Fox, R. (1966). *Role-playing methods in the classroom.* Chicago: Science Research Associates.

Clark, C., & Peterson, P. (1986). Teachers' thought processes. In M. Wittrock (Ed.), *Handbook of research on teaching* (pp. 225–296). New York: Macmillan.

Clark, C., & Yinger, R. (1979). *Three studies of teacher planning.* (Research Series No. 55.) East Lansing: Michigan State University.

Clark, H. H., & Clark, E. V. (1977). *Psychology and language: An introduction to psycholinguistics.* New York: Harcourt, Brace, Jovanovich.

Clauson, E. V., & Barnes, B. R. (1973). The effects of organizers on the learning of structured anthropology materials in the elementary grades. *Journal of Experimental Education, 42,* 11–15.

Clauson, E. V., & Rice, M. G. (1972). *The changing world today.* (Anthropology Curriculum Project Publication No. 72-1.) Athens: University of Georgia.

Codianni, A. V., & Wilbur, G. (1983). *More effective schools: From research to practice.* New York: Teachers College Press.

Cogan, M. (1973). *Clinical supervision.* Boston: Houghton Mifflin.

Cohen, D. (1969). *Immigrants and the schools: A review of research* (Report No. AA000433). New York: ERIC-IRCD Urban Disadvantaged Series, Number 8. (ERIC Document Reproduction Service No. ED 033 263).

Cohen, E. (1986). *Designing groupwork.* New York: Teachers College Press.

Cohen, E. (1995). Producing equal-status interaction in the heterogeneous classroom. *American Educational Research Journal, 32*(1), 99–120.

Cohen, E. (1998). Making cooperative learning equitable. *Educational Leadership, 56*(1), 18–21.

Cohen, J. (1977). *Statistical power analysis for the behavioral sciences* (Rev. ed.). New York: Academic Press.

Cohen, M. (1982, January/February). Effective schools: Accumulating evidence. *American Education,* 13–16.

Coleman, J. S., Campbell, E. Q., Hobson, C. J., McPortland, J., Mood, A. M., Weinfield, E. D., & York, R. L. (1966). *Equality of educational opportunity.* Washington, D.C.: U.S. Government Printing Office.

Coles, G. (2001). Reading taught to the tune of the "scientific" hickory stick. *Phi Delta Kappan, 83*(3), 204–212.

Collins, K. (1969). The importance of strong confrontation in an inquiry model of teaching. *School Science and Mathematics, 69*(7), 615–617.

Collins standard dictionary. (1978). New Delhi, India: Oxford and IBH Publishing Co.

Cook, L., & Cook, E. (1954). *Intergroup education.* New York: McGraw-Hill.

Cook, L., & Cook, E. (1957). *School problems in human relations.* New York: McGraw-Hill.

Cook, T., & Leviton, L. (1980). Reviewing the literature: A comparison of traditional methods with meta-analysis. *Journal of Personality, 48*(4), 449–472.

Cook, W., Leeds, C. H., & Callis, R. (1951). *The Minnesota Teacher Attitude Inventory.* New York: Psychological Corporation.

Cooper, H., & Dorr, N. (1995). Race comparisons on need for achievement. *Review of Educational Research, 65*(4), 483–508.

Cooper, H. M. (1982). Scientific guidelines for conducting integrative research reviews. *Review of Educational Research, 52,* 291–302.

Cooper, H. M. (1984). *The integrative research review: A systematic approach.* Beverly Hills, Calif.: Sage.

Cooper, H. M., & Arkin, R. (1981). On quantitative reviewing. *Journal of Personality, 49,* 225–230.

Cooper, H. M., & Rosenthal, R. (1980). Statistical versus traditional procedures for summarizing research findings. *Psychological Bulletin, 87*(3), 442–449.

Cooper, L., Johnson, D. W., Johnson, R., & Wilderson, F. (1980). The effects of cooperative, competitive, and individualistic experiences on interpersonal attraction among heterogeneous peers. *Journal of Social Psychology, 111,* 243–252.

Copeland, W. D. (1975). The relationship between micro teaching and student teacher classroom performance. *Journal of Educational Research, 68,* 289–293.

Coppel, C., & Sigel, I. E. (1981). *Educating the young thinker: Classroom strategies for cognitive growth.* Boston: Krieger.

Costa, A. (1985). *Developing minds: A resource book for teaching thinking.* Alexandria, Va.: Association for Supervision and Curriculum Development.

Counts, G. (1932). *Dare the school build a new social order?* New York: John Day.

Courmier, S., & Hagman, J. (Eds.). (1987). *Transfer of learning.* San Diego, Calif.: Academic Press.

Crandall, D., et al. (1982). *People, policies, and practices: Examining the chain of school improvement* (Vols. 1–10). Andover, Mass.: The Network.

Crawford, J., Gage, N., Corno, L., Stayrook, N., Mittman, A., Schunk, D., Stallings, J., Baskin, E., Harvey, P., Austin, D., Cronin, D., & Newman, R. (1978). *An experiment on teacher effectiveness and parent-assisted instruction in the third grade* (Vols. 1–3). Stanford, Calif.: Stanford University, Center for Educational Research.

Crosby, M. (1965). *An adventure in human relations.* Chicago: Follet Corporation.

Cruickshank, D. R. (1986). *Simulations and games: An ERIC bibliography.* Washington, D.C.: ERIC Clearinghouse on Teacher Education.

Cuban, L. (1984). *How teachers taught.* White Plains, N.Y.: Longman.

Cuban, L. (1986). *Classroom use of technology since 1920.* New York: Teachers College Press, Columbia University.

Cummings, C. B. (1985). *The effect of training on interactive and classroom management in non-volunteer teacher behavior.* Paper presented at the annual meeting of the American Educational Research Association, Chicago.

Dale, P. (1988). *Ten in the Bed.* New York: Candlewick.

Dalton, M. (1986). *The thought processes of teachers when practicing two models of teaching.* Doctoral dissertation, University of Oregon.

Dalton, M., & Dodd, J. (1986). *Teacher thinking: The development of skill in using two models of teaching and model-relevant thinking.* Paper presented at the annual meeting of the American Educational Research Association, San Francisco.

Damon, W. (1977). *The social world of the child.* San Francisco: Jossey-Bass.

Data Handbook. (1971, 1972, 1973). Boulder, Colo.: Social Science Consortium.

Davenport, E., Davison, M., Kuang, H., Ding, S., Kim, Se.-K., and Kwak, N. (1998). High-school mathematics course-taking by gender and ethnicity. *American Educational Research Journal, 35*(3), 497–514.

Deal, T. E., & Kennedy, A. A. (1984). *Corporate cultures: The rites and rituals of corporate life.* Boston: Addison-Wesley.

Dean, V. M. (1960). *The nature of the non-Western world.* New York: New American Library of World Literature.

Decker, R. E., & Alperin, R. (n.d.). *Emotional rating supplement.* Unpublished manual, Palo Alto, Calif.

de Jong, T., and van Joolingen, W. (1998). Scientific discovery learning with computer simulations of conceptual domains. *Review of Educational Research, 68*(2), 179–201.

Denham, C., & Liederman, A. (Eds.) (1980). *Times to learn.* Washington, D.C.: National Institute of Education, Program on Teaching and Learning.

Derry, S. J., & Murphy, D. A. (1986). Designing systems that train learning ability: From theory to practice. *Review of Educational Research, 56,* 1–40.

Devaney, K., & Thorn, L. (1975). *Exploring teacher centers.* San Francisco: Far West Laboratory for Educational Research and Development.

Dewey, J. (1910). *How we think.* Boston: Heath.

Dewey, J. (1916). *Democracy and education.* New York: Macmillan.

Dewey, J. (1920). *Reconstruction in philosophy.* New York: Holt.

Dewey, J. (1937). *Experience and education.* New York: Macmillan.

Dewey, J. (1956). *The school and society.* Chicago: University of Chicago Press.

Dewey, J. (1960). *The child and the curriculum.* Chicago: University of Chicago Press.

Donahue, P., Flanagan, R., Lutkus, A., Allen, N., & Campbell, J. (1999). *1998 NAEP reading report card for the nation and the states.* Washington, D.C.: U.S. Department of Education.

Donahue, P., Flanagan, R., Lutkus, A., Allen, N., & Campbell, J. (2001). *The national report card: Fourth grade reading 2000.* Washington, D.C.: U.S. Department of Education, Office of Educational Research and Improvement, National Center for Educational Statistics.

Downey, L. (1967). *The secondary phase of education.* Boston: Ginn and Co.

Duit, R., & Treagust, D. (1995). Student conceptions and constructivist teaching approaches. In Fennema and Carpenter, eds. 46–67.

Duke, N., & Pearson, P. D. (undated). *Effective practices for developing reading comprehension.* East Lansing: College of Education, Michigan State University.

Dunn, R., Beaudry, J., & Klavas, A. (1989). Survey of research on learning styles. *Educational Leadership, 46*(6), 50–58.

Dunn, R., & Dunn, K. (1975). *Educator's self-teaching guide to individualizing instructional programs.* West Nyack, N.Y.: Parker.

Dunn, R., Dunn, K., & Price, G. E. (1989). *The learning styles inventory.* Lawrence, Kan.: Price Systems.

Durkin, D. (1966). *Children who read early.* New York: Teachers College Press.

Eastman, P. (1961). *Go, dog, go!* New York: Random House.

Editorial. (1994, October 24). *The New York Times.*

Edmonds, R. (1979). Some schools work and more can. *Social Policy, 9*(5), 28–32.

Ehri, L. C.(1999). *Phases of acquisition in learning to read words and instructional implications.* Paper presented to the Annual Meeting of the American Educational Research Association, Montreal.

Elefant, E. (1980). Deaf children in an inquiry training program. *Volta Review, 82,* 271–279.

Elementary Science Study (ESS). (1971). *Batteries and bulbs: An electrical suggestion book.* New York: Webster-McGraw-Hill.

Eliot, T. S. The wasteland. In *Collected Poems 1909–1962.* New York: Harcourt Brace Jovanovich.

Elkind, D. (1987). *Miseducation: Preschoolers at risk.* New York: Knopf.

Ellis, A., & Harper, R. (1975). *A new guide to rational living.* Englewood Cliffs, N.J.: Prentice-Hall.

Elmore, R. (1990). On changing the structure of public schools. In R. Elmore (Ed.), *Restructuring schools.* San Francisco: Jossey-Bass.

El-Nemr, M. A. (1979). *Meta-analysis of the outcomes of teaching biology as inquiry.* Boulder: University of Colorado.

Emmer, E., & Evertson, C. (1980). *Effective classroom management at the beginning of the year in junior high school classrooms.* (Report No. 6107.) Austin: Research and Development Center for Teacher Education, University of Texas.

Emmer, E., Evertson, C., & Anderson, L. (1980). Effective classroom management at the beginning of the school year. *Elementary School Journal, 80,* 219–231.

Englemann, S., & Osborn, J. (1972). *DISTAR language program.* Chicago: Science Research Associates.

Englert, C., & Raphael, T. (1989). Developing successful writers through cognitive strategy instruction. In J. Brophy (Ed.), *Advances in research in teaching* (pp. 105–151). Greenwich, Conn.: JAI Press.

Englert, C. S., Raphael, T. E., Anderson, L. M., Anthony, H. M., & Stevens, D. D. (1991). Making strategies and self-talk visible: Writing instruction in regular and special education classrooms. *American Educational Research Journal, 28*(2), 337–372.

Erikson, E. (1950). *Childhood and society.* New York: Norton.

Estes, W. E. (Ed.). (1976). *Handbook of learning and cognitive processes: Vol. 4. Attention and memory.* Hillsdale, N.J.: Erlbaum.

Evans, M., & Hopkins, D. (1988). School climate and the psychological state of the individual teacher as factors affecting the use of educational ideas following an inservice course. *British Educational Research Journal, 14*(3), 211–230.

Evertson, C. (1982). Differences in instructional activities in higher- and lower-achieving junior high English and math classes. *Elementary School Journal, 82*(4), 329–350.

Evertson, C., Anderson, C., Anderson, L., & Brophy, J. (1980). Relationships between classroom behaviors and student outcomes in junior high mathematics and English classes. *American Educational Research Journal, 17*(1), 43–60.

Eysenck, H. J. (1978). An exercise in mega-silliness. *American Psychologist, 33*(5), 517.

Feeley, T. (1972). *The concept of inquiry in the social studies.* Doctoral dissertation, Stanford University.

Fennema, E., Carpenter, T., Jacobs, V., Franke, M., & Levi, L. (1998). A longitudinal study of gender differences in young children's mathematical thinking. *Educational Researcher, 27*(5), 6–11.

Fensterheim, H., & Baer, J. (1975). *Don't say yes when you want to say no.* New York: Dell.

Festinger, C. L. (1964). Behavior support for opinion change. *Public Opinion Quarterly, 28,* 404–417.

Fisher, C. W., Berliner, D. C., Filby, N. N., Marliave, R., Ghen, L. S., & Dishaw, M. M. (1980). Teaching behaviors, academic learning time, and student achievement: An overview. In C. Denham & A. Lieberman (Eds.), *Time to learn.* Washington, D.C.: National Institute of Education.

Fitzgerald, J. (1995). English-as-a-second-language learners' cognitive reading processes: A review of research in the United States. *Review of Educational Research, 65*(2), 145–190.

Flanders, N. (1970). *Analyzing teaching behavior.* Reading, Mass.: Addison-Wesley.

Flavell, J. H. (1963). *The developmental psychology of Jean Piaget.* Princeton, N.J.: Van Nostrand Reinhold.

Flesch, R. (1955). *Why Johnny can't read.* New York: Harper Brothers.

Flint, S. (1965). *The relationship between the classroom verbal behavior of student teachers and the classroom verbal behavior of their cooperating teachers.* Doctoral dissertation. New York: Teachers College Press.

Florida Department of Education. (January, 1998). *Profiles of Florida School Districts: Student and Staff Data.* Tallahassee, Fla: Author.

Fraser, B., & Walberg, H. (Eds.). (1995). *Improving science education.* Chicago: University of Chicago Press.

Fraser, B., & Wubbels, T. (1995). Classroom learning environments. Fennema and Carpenter, 117–144.

Friedman, L. (1995). The space factor in mathematics: Gender differences. *Review of Educational Research, 65*(1), 22–50.

Fromm, E. (1941). *Escape from freedom.* New York: Farrar & Rinehart.

Fromm, E. (1955). *The sane society.* New York: Rinehart.

Fromm, E. (1956). *The art of loving.* New York: Harper.

Fuchs, D., Fuchs, L., Mathes, P., & Simmons, D. (1997). Peer-assisted learning strategies. *American Educational Research Journal, 34*(1), 174–206.

Fullan, M. (1982). *The meaning of educational change.* New York: Teachers College Press.

Fullan, M. (1983). Evaluating program implementation: What can be learned from follow through. *Curriculum Inquiry, 13*(2), 215–227.

Fullan, M. (1990). Staff development, innovation, and institutional development. In B. R. Joyce (Ed.), *ASCD yearbook on staff development.* Alexandria, Va.: Association for Supervision and Curriculum Development.

Fullan, M., Miles, M., & Taylor, G. (1980). Organization development in schools: The state of the art. *Review of Educational Research, 50*(1), 121–184.

Fullan, M., & Park, P. (1981). *Curriculum implementation: A resource booklet.* Toronto: Ontario Ministry of Education.

Fullan, M., and Pomfret, A. (1977). Research on curriculum and instruction implementation. *Review of Educational Research, 47*(2), 335–397.

Fullan, M. G., Bennett, B., & Bennett, C. R. (1990). Linking classroom and school improvement. *Educational Leadership, 47*(8), 13–19.

Furth, H. G. (1969). *Piaget and knowledge.* Englewood Cliffs, N.J.: Prentice-Hall.

Gabel, D. L. (Ed.). (1994). *Handbook of research on science teaching and learning.* New York: MacMillan.

Gage, N. L. (1963). Paradigms for research on teaching. In N. L. Gage (Ed.), *Handbook of research on teaching* (pp. 94–141). Chicago: Rand McNally.

Gage, N. L. (1979). *The scientific basis for the art of teaching.* New York: Teachers College Press.

Gage, N. L., & Berliner, D. (1983). *Educational psychology.* Boston: Houghton Mifflin.

Gagné, R. (1962a). Military training and principles of learning. *American Psychologist, 17*, 46–67.

Gagné, R. (1962b). *Psychological principles in system development.* New York: Holt, Rinehart & Winston.

Gagné, R. (1965a). *The conditions of learning.* New York: Holt, Rinehart & Winston.

Gagné, R. (1965b). The learning of concepts. *School Review, 75,* 187–196.

Gagné, R. (1967). Instruction in the conditions of learning. In L. Siegel (Ed.), *Instruction: Some contemporary viewpoints.* New York: Harper & Row.

Gagné, R., & Briggs, L. (1979). *Principles of instructional design.* New York: Holt, Rinehart & Winston.

Gagné, R., et al. (1962). *Psychological principles in systems development.* New York: Holt, Rinehart & Winston.

Gall, M. D., Haisley, F. B., Baker, R. G., & Perez, M. (1982). *The relationship between inservice education practices and productivity of basic skills instruction.* Eugene: University of Oregon, Center for Educational Policy and Management.

Gall, M. D., & Renchler, R. S. (1985). *Effective staff development practices: A research-based model.* Eugene: University of Oregon, Center for Educational Policy and Management. (ERIC Document Reproduction Service No. ED 017 615).

Gallway, W. T. (1977). *Inner skiing.* New York: Random House.

Gardner, H. (1983). *Frames of mind: The theory of multiple intelligences.* New York: Basic Books.

Gardner, J. (1978). *Excellence and education.* New York: Harper & Row.

Garmston, R. J., & Eblen, D. R. (1988). Visions, decisions, and results: Changing school culture through staff development. *Journal of Staff Development, 9*(2), 22–29.

Garner, R. (1987). *Metacognition and reading comprehension.* Norwood, N.J.: Ablex.

Gaskins, I., & Elliot, T. (1991). *Implementing cognitive strategy instruction across the school.* Cambridge, Mass.: Brookline Books.

Gentile, J. R. (1988). *Instructional improvement: Summary and analysis of Madeline Hunter's essential elements of instruction and supervision.* Oxford, Ohio: National Staff Development Council.

Gerbner, G. (1987). Science on television: How it affects public conceptions. Issues in *Science and Technology 3*(2), 109–115.

Gideonse, H. D. (1982). The necessary revolution in teacher education. *Phi Delta Kappan, 64*(1), 15–18.

Giese, J. R. (1989). *The progressive era: The limits of reform.* Boulder, Colo.: Social Science Education Consortium.

Gilbert, J. P., McPeek, B., & Mosteller, P. (1977). Statistics and ethics in surgery and anesthesia. *Science, 198,* 684–689.

Glade, M. E., & Giese, J. R. (1989). *Immigration, pluralism, and national identity.* Boulder, Colo.: Social Science Education Consortium.

Glaser, R. (Ed.). (1962). *Training research and education.* Pittsburgh: University of Pittsburgh Press.

Glass, G. V. (1975). Primary, secondary, and meta-analysis of research. *Educational Researcher, 7*(3), 33–50.

Glass, G. V. (1982). Meta-analysis: An approach to the synthesis of research results. *Journal of Research in Science Teaching, 19*(2), 93–112.

Glass, G. V., Cahan, L. S., Smith, M. L., & Filby, N. N. (1982). *School class size: Research and Policy.* Beverly Hills, Calif.: Sage.

Glass, G. V., McGaw, B., & Smith, M. L. (1981). *Meta-analysis in social research.* Beverly Hills, Calif.: Sage.

Glassbury, S., & Oja, S. N. (1981). A developmental model for enhancing teachers' personal and professional growth. *Journal of Research and Development in Education, 14*(2), 59–70.

Glasser, W. (1965). *Reality therapy.* New York: Harper & Row.

Glasser, W. (1969). *Schools without failure.* New York: Harper & Row.

Glasser, W. (1984). *Take effective control of your life.* New York: Harper & Row.

Glasser, W., & Powers, W. T. (1981). *Stations of the mind: New directions for reality therapy.* New York: Harper & Row.

Glickman, C. D. (1993). *Renewing America's schools: A guide for school-based action.* San Francisco: Jossey-Bass.

Gliessman, D. H., & Pugh, R. C. (1978). Acquiring teacher behavior concepts through the use of high-structure and low-structure protocol films. *Journal of Educational Psychology, 70*(5), 779–787.

Glynn, S. M. (1994). *Teaching science with analogies.* Athens: National Reading Research Center, University of Georgia.

Gnott, H. (1971). *Teacher and child.* New York: Macmillan.

Goffman, I. (1986). *Gender advertisements.* New York: Harper.

Golemiewski, R. T., & Blumberg, A. (1970). *Sensitivity training and the laboratory approach.* Itaska, Ill.: Peacock.

Good, T., & Brophy, G. (1974). An empirical investigation: Changing teacher and student behavior. *Journal of Educational Psychology, 66,* 399–405.

Good, T., & Grouws, D. (1977). Teaching effects: A process-product study in fourth grade mathematics classrooms. *Journal of Teacher Education, 28,* 49–54.

Good, T., Grouws, D., & Ebmeier, H. (1983). *Active mathematics teaching.* New York: Longman.

Goodlad, J. (1984). *A place called school.* New York: McGraw-Hill.

Goodlad, J., & Klein, F. (1970). *Looking behind the classroom door.* Worthington, Ohio: Charles A. Jones.

Goodman, P. (1964). *Compulsory miseducation.* New York: Horizon Press.

Gordon, W. J. J. (1952). *The integration of creative persons.* Paper delivered to Sloan Fellows, MIT.

Gordon, W. J. J. (1955, December). *Some environmental aspects of creativity.* Paper delivered to the Department of Defense, Fort Belvoir, Va.

Gordon, W. J. J. (1956a). *Creativity as a process.* Paper delivered at the First Arden House Conference on Creative Process.

Gordon, W. J. J. (1956b). Operational approach to creativity. *Harvard Business Review, 34*(6), 41–51.

Gordon, W. J. J. (1957). *The role of irrelevance in art and invention.* Paper delivered at the Third Arden House Conference on Creative Process.

Gordon, W. J. J. (1961a). *Synectics.* New York: Harper & Row.

Gordon, W. J. J. (1961b, November 4). Director of research. *New Yorker.*

Gordon, W. J. J. (1962a, May). The Pures. *Atlantic Monthly.*

Gordon, W. J. J. (1962b, August). The Nobel prizewinners. *Atlantic Monthly.*

Gordon, W. J. J. (1963a, March). *How to get your imagination off the ground.* Think (IBM Press).

Gordon, W. J. J. (1963b, April). Mrs. Schyler's plot. *Atlantic Monthly.*

Gordon, W. J. J. (1965). The metaphorical way of knowing. In G. Kepes (Ed.), *Education of vision.* New York: Braziller.

Gordon, W. J. J. (1970). The metaphorical development of man. In C. McC. Brooks (Ed.), *The changing world and man.* New York: New York University Press.

Gordon, W. J. J. (1971). Architecture—The making of metaphors. *Main Currents in Modern Thought, 28*(1), 21–30.

Gordon, W. J. J. (1972, Spring). Use of metaphor increases creative learning efficiency. *Trend,* 11–14.

Gordon, W. J. J. (1973). On being explicit about the creative process. *Journal of Creative Behavior, 6*(4), 295–300.

Gordon, W. J. J. (1974). Some source material in discovery-by-analogy. *Journal of Creative Behavior, 8*(4), 239–257.

Gordon, W. J. J. (1975). *Training for creativity. International handbook of management development and training.* London: McGraw-Hill.

Gordon, W. J. J. (1977a). Connection-making is universal. *Curriculum Product Review, 9*(4), 21–30.

Gordon, W. J. J. (1977b). *Toward understanding "the moment of inspiration."* Paper delivered at the Creativity Symposium for the American Association for the Advancement of Science.

Gordon, W. J. J. (with J. Bruner). (1957, May). *Motivating the creative process.* Paper delivered at the Second Arden House Conference on Creative Process.

Gordon, W. J. J. (Poze, T., Project Director). (1968). *Making it strange* (Books 1 & 2). Evanston, Ill.: Harper & Row.

Gordon, W. J. J. (Poze, T., Ed.). (1969). *Making it strange* (Books 3 & 4). Evanston Ill.: Harper & Row.

Gordon, W. J. J. (Poze, T., Ed.). (1971). *What color is sleep?* Cambridge, Mass.: Porpoise Books.

Gordon, W. J. J., & Poze, T. (1971a). *The art of the possible.* Cambridge, Mass.: Porpoise Books.

Gordon, W. J. J., & Poze, T. (1971b). *The basic course in synectics.* Cambridge, Mass.: Porpoise Books.

Gordon, W. J. J., & Poze, T. (1971c). *Facts and guesses.* Cambridge, Mass.: Porpoise Books.

Gordon, W. J. J., & Poze, T. (1971d). *Invent-o-rama.* Cambridge, Mass.: Porpoise Books.

Gordon, W. J. J., & Poze, T. (1971e). *Making it whole.* Cambridge, Mass.: Porpoise Books.

Gordon, W. J. J., & Poze, T. (1971f). *The metaphorical way of learning and knowing.* Cambridge, Mass.: Porpoise Books.

Gordon, W. J. J., & Poze, T. (1972a). *Activities in metaphor.* Cambridge, Mass.: Porpoise Books.

Gordon, W. J. J., & Poze, T. (1972b). *Introduction to synectics* (Problem-solving). Cambridge, Mass.: Porpoise Books.

Gordon, W. J. J., & Poze, T. (1972c). *Strange and familiar* (Book 6). Cambridge, Mass.: Porpoise Books.

Gordon, W. J. J., & Poze, T. (1972d). *Teaching is listening.* Cambridge, Mass.: Porpoise Books.

Gordon, W. J. J., & Poze, T. (1974a). Creative training in an occupational context. *Technical Education Reporter, 1*(1), 52–57.

Gordon, W. J. J., & Poze, T. (1974b). *From the inside.* Cambridge, Mass.: Porpoise Books.

Gordon, W. J. J., & Poze, T. (1974c). *Learning is connection-making.* Professional Report (Croft Publications).

Gordon, W. J. J., & Poze, T. (1975a). *Strange and familiar* (Book 1). Cambridge, Mass.: Porpoise Books.

Gordon, W. J. J., & Poze, T. (1975b). *Strange and familiar* (Book 3). Cambridge, Mass.: Porpoise Books.

Gordon, W. J. J., & Poze, T. (1976). *The art of the possible.* Cambridge, Mass.: Porpoise Books.

Gottfredson, D. C., Fink, C. M., & Graham, N. (1994). Grade retention and student behavior. *American Educational Research Journal, 31*(4), 761–784.

Grant, G. (1988). *The world we created at Hamilton High.* Cambridge, Mass.: Harvard University Press.

Graves, M., Watts, S., & Graves, B. (1994). *Essentials of classroom teaching: Elementary reading methods.* Boston: Allyn & Bacon.

Graves, N., & Graves, T. (1990). *Cooperative learning: A resource guide.* Santa Cruz, Calif.: International Association for the Study of Cooperation in Education.

Gray, J. (1992). *Men are from Mars and women are from Venus.* New York: HarperCollins.

Greenwald, G. D. (1991). *The railroad era: Business competition and the public interest.* Boulder, Colo.: Social Science Education Consortium.

Gregorc, A. F. (1982). *An adult's guide to style.* Maynard, Mass.: Gabriel Systems.

Griffin, G. A. (1983). *Staff development: Eighty-second yearbook of the National Society for the Study of Education.* Chicago: University of Chicago Press.

Griffin, G. A., & Barnes, S. (1984). School change: A craft-derived and research-based strategy. *Teachers College Record, 86*(1), 103–123.

Griffin, G. A., & Lieberman, A. (1974). *Behavior of innovative personnel.* Washington, D.C.: ERIC Clearinghouse on Teacher Education.

Guetzkow, H., et al. (1963). *Simulation in international relations.* Englewood Cliffs, N.J.: Prentice-Hall.

Guetzkow, H., & Valdez, J. J. (Eds.). (1966). *Simulated international processes: Theories and research in global modeling.* Beverly Hills, Calif.: Sage.

Gunning, T. (1998). *Best books for beginning readers.* Boston: Allyn & Bacon.

Guskey, T. (1986). Staff development and the process of change. *Educational Researcher, 15*(5), 5–12.

Haberman, M. (1995). *Star teachers in poverty.* West Lafayette, Ind.: Kappa Delta Phi.

Halberstam, D. (1998). *The children.* New York: Random House.

Halberstam, D. (2002). *Firehouse.* New York: Hyperion.

Hall, G. (1986). *Skills derived from studies of the implementation of innovations in education.* Paper presented at the annual meeting of the American Educational Research Association, San Francisco.

Hall, G., & Loucks, S. (1977). A developmental model for determining whether the treatment is actually implemented. *American Educational Research Journal, 14*(3), 263–276.

Hall, G., & Loucks, S. (1978). Teacher concerns as a basis for facilitating and personalizing staff development. *Teachers College Record, 80*(1), 36–53.

Halpin, A. W. (1966). *Theory and research in administration.* New York: Macmillan.

Hanson, R., & Farrell, D. (1995). The long-term effects on high school seniors of learning to read in kindergarten. *Reading Research Quarterly, 30*(4), 908–933.

Harvey, O. J., Hunt, D., & Schroeder, H. (1961). *Conceptual systems and personality organization.* New York: Wiley.

Hatcher, P., Hulme, C., & Ellis, A. (1994). Ameliorating reading failure by integrating the teaching of reading and phonological skills. *Child Development, 65,* 41–57.

Hawkes, E. (1971). *The effects of an instruction strategy on approaches to problem-solving.* Unpublished doctoral dissertation, Teachers College, Columbia University.

Heard, S., & Wadsworth, B. (1977). *The relationship between cognitive development and language complexity.* Unpublished paper, Mount Holyoke College.

Hedges, L. V., & Olkin, I. (1986). Meta-analysis: A review and a new view. *Educational Researcher, 15*(8), 14–21.

Hedgeson, S. (1994). Research on problem solving: Middle school. In D. L. Gabel (Ed.), *Handbook of research on science teaching and learning* (pp. 248–269). New York: MacMillan.

Heller, M. (1991). *Reading-writing connections.* White Plains, N. Y.: Longman.

Hendrickson, R. (1987). *The Henry Holt encyclopedia of word and phrase origins.* New York: Henry Holt.

Herrnstein, R., & Murray, C. (1994). *The bell curve.* New York: Free Press.

Hersh, R. H. (1984). *What makes some schools and teachers more effective?* Eugene: Center for Educational Policy and Management, University of Oregon.

Hertz-Lazarowitz, R. (1993). Using group investigation to enhance Arab-Jewish relationships. *Cooperative Learning, 11*(2), 13–14.

Hiebert, E., Pearson, P., Taylor, B., Richardson, V., & Paris, S. (1998). *Concepts of print, letter naming, and phonetic awareness.* Ann Arbor: University of Michigan School of Education, CIERA.

Hiebert, E., & Taylor, B. (2000). Beginning reading instruction: Research on early inventions. In L. Kamil, P. Mosenthal, P. Pearson, & R. Barr, *Handbook of reading research, Vol. III* (pp. 455–482). Mahwah, N.J.: Erlbaum.

Hiebert, E., & Taylor, B., eds. (1994). *Getting reading right from the start.* Boston: Allyn & Bacon.

Hillocks, G. (1987). Synthesis of research on teaching writing. *Educational Leadership, 44*(8), 71–82.

Hoetker, J., & Ahlbrand, W. (1969). The persistence of the recitation. *American Educational Research Journal, 6,* 145–167.

Holloway, S. D. (1988). Concepts of ability and effort in Japan and the United States. *Review of Educational Research, 58*(3), 327–345.

Holms, T. H., & Rahe, R. H. (1967). The social readjustment rating scale. *Journal of Psychosomatic Research, 11,* 213–218.

Hooper, F. H. (1974). An evaluation of logical operations in instruction in the preschool. In R. K. Parker (Ed.), *The preschool in action: Exploring early childhood education programs* (pp. 134–186). Boston: Allyn & Bacon.

Hopkins, D. (1987). *Improving the quality of schooling.* London: Falmer Press.

Hopkins, D. (1990). Integrating staff development and school improvement: A study of teacher personality and school climate. In B. Joyce (Ed.), *Changing school culture through staff development. 1990 Yearbook of the Association for Supervision and Curriculum Development.* Alexandria, Va.: ASCD.

Hopkins, I. (1982). The unit of analysis: Group means versus individual observations. *American Educational Research Journal, 19,* 5–18.

Howey, K., Yarger, S., & Joyce, B. (1978). *Improving teacher education.* Washington, D.C.: Association for Teacher Education.

Hrycauk, M. (2002). A safety net for second grade students. *Journal of Staff Development, 23*(1), 55–58.

Huberman, A. M., & Crandall, D. P. (1983). *A study of dissemination efforts supporting school improvement: Implications for action* (Vol. 9). Andover, Mass.: The Network.

Huberman, M., & Miles, M. (1984). *Innovation up close.* New York: Plenum.

Huhtala, J. (1994). *Group investigation structuring an inquiry-based curriculum.* Paper presented at the annual meeting of the American Educational Research Association, New Orleans.

Hullfish, H. G., & Smith, P. G. (1961). *Reflective thinking: The method of education.* New York: Dodd, Mead.

Human relations laboratory training student notebook. (1961). Washington, D.C.: U.S. Office of Education. ERIC Document Reproduction Service, ED 018 834.

Hunt, D. E. (1970a). Adaptability in interpersonal communication among training agents. *Merrill Palmer Quarterly, 16,* 325–344.

Hunt, D. E. (1970b). A conceptual level matching model for coordinating learner characteristics with educational approaches. *Interchange: A Journal of Educational Studies, 1*(2), 1–31.

Hunt, D. E. (1971). *Matching models in education.* Toronto: Ontario Institute for Studies in Education.

Hunt, D. E. (1975a). The B-P-E paradigm in theory, research, and practice. *Canadian Psychological Review, 16,* 185–197.

Hunt, D. E. (1975b). Person-environment interaction: A challenge found wanting before it was tried. *Review of Educational Research, 45,* 209–230.

Hunt, D. E. (1975c). *Teachers' adaptation to students: Implicit and explicit matching.* (Research and Development Memorandum No. 139.) Stanford, Calif.: SCRDT.

Hunt, D. E. (1976). Teachers are psychologists, too: On the application of psychology to education. *Canadian Psychological Review, 8,* 14–46.

Hunt, D. E., Butler, L. F., Noy, J. E., & Rosser, M. E. (1978). *Assessing conceptual level by the paragraph completion method.* Toronto: Ontario Institute for Studies in Education.

Hunt, D. E., Greenwood, J., Brill, R., & Deineka, M. (1972). *From psychological theory to educational practice: Implementation of a matching model.* Symposium presented at the annual meeting of the American Educational Research Association, Chicago.

Hunt, D. E., & Hardt, R. H. (1967). *The role of conceptual level and program structure in summer Upward Bound programs.* Paper presented at the Eastern Psychological Association, Boston.

Hunt, D. E., & Joyce, B. (1967). Teacher trainee personality and initial teaching style. *American Educational Research Journal, 4,* 253–259.

Hunt, D. E., Joyce, B., & Del Popolo, J. (1964). *An exploratory study of the modification of student teachers' behavior patterns.* Unpublished paper, Syracuse University.

Hunt, D. E., Joyce, B., Greenwood, J., Noy, J., Reid, R., & Weil, M. (1981). Student conceptual level and models of teaching. In B. Joyce, L. Peck, & C. Brown (Eds.), *Flexibility in teaching*. White Plains, N.Y.: Longman.

Hunt, D. E., & Sullivan, E. V. (1974). *Between psychology and education*. Hinsdale, Ill.: Dryden.

Hunt, J. McV. (1961). *Intelligence and experience*. New York: Ronald Press.

Hunter, I. M. L. (1964). *Memory*. Harmondsworth, Middlesex, England: Penguin Books.

Hunter, J. E., Schmidt, F. L., & Jackson, G. B. (1982). *Meta-analysis: Cumulating research findings across studies*. Beverly Hills, Calif.: Sage.

Hunter, M. (1980). Six types of supervisory conferences. *Educational Leadership, 37*, 408–412.

Hunter, M., & Russell, D. (1981a). *Increasing your teaching effectiveness*. Palo Alto, Calif.: Learning Institute.

Hunter, M., & Russell, D. (1981b). Planning for effective instruction: Lesson design. In *Increasing your teaching effectiveness*. Palo Alto, Calif.: Learning Institute.

Hunziker, J. C. (1972). *The use of participant modeling in the treatment of water phobias*. Tempe: Arizona State University.

Individually Prescribed Instruction. (1966). Unpublished manuscripts. Philadelphia: Research for Better Schools.

International Reading Association. (1998). *Position statement on phonemic awareness and the teaching of reading*. Newark, Del.: Author.

International Reading Association and the National Association for the Education of Young Children. (1998). *Position statement on learning to read and write: Developmentally appropriate practices for young children*. Newark, Del.: International Reading Association.

Ivany, G. (1969). The assessment of verbal inquiry in elementary school science. *Science Education, 53*(4), 287–293.

Jackson, G. B. (1980). Methods for integrative reviews. *Review of Educational Research, 50*, 438–460.

Jackson, P. W. (1966). *The way teaching is*. Washington, D.C.: National Education Association.

Jackson, P. W. (1968). *Life in classrooms*. New York: Holt, Rinehart & Winston.

Jacobson, E. (1979). *Progressive relaxation*. Chicago: University of Chicago Press.

James, H. H. (1971). Attitude and attitude change: Its influence upon teaching behavior. *Journal of Research in Science Teaching, 8*, 234–249.

Jencks, C., Smith, M., Acland, H., Bane, M. J., Cohen, D., Gintis, H., Hayns, B., & Michelsohn, S. (1972). *Inequality: A reassessment of the effect of family and schooling in America*. New York: Basic Books.

Johnson, D. W., & Johnson, R. T. (1974). Instructional goal structure: Cooperative, competitive, or individualistic. *Review of Educational Research, 44*, 213–240.

Johnson, D. W., & Johnson, R. T. (1975a). *Circles of learning*. Englewood Cliffs, N.J.: Prentice-Hall.

Johnson, D. W., & Johnson, R. T. (1975b). *Learning together and alone*. Englewood Cliffs, N.J.: Prentice-Hall.

Johnson, D. W., & Johnson, R. T. (1979). Conflict in the classroom: Controversy in learning. *Review of Educational Research, 49*(1), 51–70.

Johnson, D. W., & Johnson, R. T. (1981). Effects of cooperative and individual-istic learning experiences on inter-ethnic interaction. *Journal of Educational Psychology, 73*(3), 444–449.

Johnson, D. W., & Johnson, R. T. (1990). *Cooperation and competition: Theory and research.* Edina, Minn.: Interaction Book Company.

Johnson, D. W., & Johnson, R. T. (1996). Conflict resolution and peer mediation programs in elementary and secondary schools: A review of the research. *Review of Educational Research, 66*(4), 459–506.

Johnson, D. W., & Johnson, R. T. (1999). *Methods of cooperative learning: What can we prove works?* Edina, Minn.: Cooperative Learning Institute.

Johnson, D. W., Johnson, R. T., Dudley, B., Ward, M., & Magnusen, D. (1995). The impact of peer mediation training on the management of school and home conflicts. *American Educational Research Journal, 32*(4), 829–844.

Johnson, D. W., Johnson, R. T., & Holobec, E. (1994). *Circles of learning.* Alexandria, Va.: ASCD.

Johnson, D. W., Johnson, R. T., Johnson, J., & Anderson, D. (1976). The effects of cooperative vs. individualized instruction on student prosocial behavior, attitudes toward learning, and achievement. *Journal of Educational Psychology, 68,* 446–452.

Johnson, D. W., Johnson, R. T., & Scott, L. (1978). The effects of cooperative and individualized instruction on student attitudes and achievement. *Journal of Social Psychology, 104,* 207–216.

Johnson, D. W., Johnson, R. T., & Skon, L. (1979). Student achievement on different types of tasks under cooperative, competitive, and individualistic conditions. *Contemporary Educational Psychology, 4,* 99–106.

Johnson, D. W., & Johnson, S. (1972). The effects of attitude similarity, expectation of goal facilitation, and actual goal facilitation on interpersonal attraction. *Journal of Experimental Social Psychology, 8,* 197–206.

Johnson, D. W., Maruyana, G., Johnson, R., Nelson, D., & Skon, L. (1981). Effects of cooperative, competitive, and individualistic goal structures on achievement: A meta-analysis. *Psychological Bulletin, 89*(1), 47–62.

Johnson, J. L., & Sloat, K. M. (1980). Teacher training effects: Real or illusory? *Psychology in the Schools Journal, 17*(1), 109–114.

Jovanovic, J., & King, S. (1998). Boys and girls in the performance-based science classroom: Who's doing the performing? *American Educational Research Journal, 35*(3), 455–477.

Joyce, B. (1975). The models of teaching community: What have we learned? *Texas Tech Journal of Education, 22,* 95–106.

Joyce, B. (Ed.). (1978). *Involvement: A study of shared governance of teacher education.* Washington, D.C.: ERIC Clearinghouse on Teacher Education.

Joyce, B. (1978–79). Toward a theory of information processing in teaching. *Educational Research Quarterly, 3*(4), 66–77.

Joyce, B. (1980). *Teacher innovator system: Observer's manual.* Eugene, Ore.: Booksend Laboratories.

Joyce, B. (1987). Essential reform in teacher education. In L. Newton, M. Fullan, & J. W. MacDonald (Eds.), *Rethinking teacher education* (pp. 1–27). Toronto: Ontario Institute for Studies in Education.

Joyce, B. (1991a). Common misconceptions about cooperative learning and gifted students. *Educational Leadership, 48*(6), 72–74.

Joyce, B. (1991b). Doors to school improvement. *Educational Leadership, 48*(8), 59–62.

Joyce, B. (1999). Reading about reading. *The Reading Teacher, 36,* 220–227.

Joyce, B., Bush, R., & McKibbin, M. (1982). *The California staff development study: The January 1982 report.* Palo Alto, Calif.: Booksend Laboratories.

Joyce, B., & Calhoun, E. (1995). *Learning experiences in school renewal.* Eugene, Ore.: The ERIC Clearinghouse in Educational Management.

Joyce, B., & Calhoun, E. (1996). *Creating learning experiences.* Alexandria, Va.: Association for Supervision and Curriculum Development.

Joyce, B., & Calhoun, E. (1998). *Learning to teach inductively.* Boston: Allyn & Bacon.

Joyce, B., Calhoun, E., Carran, N., Simser, J., Rust, D., & Halliburton, C. (1996). University town. In B. Joyce & E. Calhoun (Eds.), *Learning experiences in school renewal.* Eugene, Ore.: ERIC Clearinghouse for Educational Management.

Joyce, B., Calhoun, E., & Hopkins, D. (1998). *Models of learning: Tools for teaching.* Buckingham, U.K.: Open University Press.

Joyce, B., Calhoun, E., & Hopkins, D. (1999). *The new structure of school improvement.* Buckingham, U.K.: Open University Press.

Joyce, B., Calhoun, E., & McKibben, M. (1998). *Going for the gold in school renewal.* Pauma Valley, CA: Booksend Laboratories.

Joyce, B., & Clift, R. (1983). *Generic training problems: Training elements, socialization, contextual variables, and personality disposition across occupational categories that vary in ethos.* Paper presented at the annual meeting of the American Educational Research Association, Montreal.

Joyce, B., & Clift, R. (1984). The Phoenix agenda: Essential reform in teacher education. *Educational Researcher, 13*(4), 5–18.

Joyce, B., & Harootunian, B. (1967). *The structure of teaching.* Chicago: Science Research Associates.

Joyce, B., Hersh, R., & McKibbin, M. (1983). *The structure of school improvement.* New York: Longman.

Joyce, B., Howey, K., & Yarger, S. (1975). *Issues to face.* Syracuse, N.Y.: National Dissemination Center, Syracuse University.

Joyce, B., Howey, K., & Yarger, S. (1976). *Issues to face, report one: Inservice teacher education.* Palo Alto, Calif.: Educational Research and Development Center.

Joyce, B., Hrycauk, M., & Calhoun, E. (2001). A second chance for struggling readers. *Educational Leadership, 58*(6), 42–47.

Joyce, B., McKibbin, M., & Bush, R. (1983). *The seasons of professional life: The growth states of teachers.* Paper presented at the annual meeting of the American Educational Research Association, Montreal.

Joyce, B., McKibbin, M., & Bush, R. (1984). *Predicting whether an innovation will be implemented: Four case studies.* Paper presented at the annual meeting of the American Educational Research Association, New Orleans.

Joyce, B., & Morine, G. (1977). *Creating the school.* Boston: Little, Brown.

Joyce, B., Murphy, C., Showers, B., & Murphy, J. (1989). School renewal as cultural change. *Educational Leadership, 47*(3), 70–78.

Joyce, B., Peck, L., & Brown, C. (1981). *Flexibility in teaching.* New York: Longman.

Joyce, B., & Showers, B. (1980). Improving inservice training: The message of research. *Educational Leadership, 37,* 163–172.

Joyce, B., & Showers, B. (1981a). *Teacher training research: Working hypothesis for program design and directions for further study.* Paper presented at the annual meeting of the American Educational Research Association, Los Angeles.

Joyce, B., & Showers, B. (1981b). Transfer of training: The contribution of coaching. *Journal of Education, 163,* 163–172.

Joyce, B., & Showers, B. (1982). The coaching of teaching. *Educational Leadership, 40*(1), 4–10.

Joyce, B., & Showers, B. (1983). *Power in staff development through research on training.* Washington, D.C.: Association for Supervision and Curriculum Development.

Joyce, B., & Showers, B. (1984, April). *Persuasion-oriented studies of teaching.* Paper presented at the annual meeting of the American Educational Research Association, New Orleans.

Joyce, B., & Showers, B. (1986). *Peer coaching guides.* Eugene, Ore.: Booksend Laboratories.

Joyce, B., & Showers, B. (2002). *Student achievement through staff development* (3rd ed.). Alexandria, VA: Association for Supervision and Curriculum Development.

Joyce, B., Showers, B., Beaton, C., & Dalton, M. (1984). *The search for validated objectives of teacher education: Teaching skills derived from naturalistic and persuasion oriented studies of teaching.* Paper presented at the annual meeting of the American Educational Research Association, New Orleans.

Joyce, B., Showers, B., & Bennett, B. (1987). Synthesis of research on staff development: A framework for future study and a state-of-the-art analysis. *Educational Leadership, 45*(3), 77–87.

Joyce, B., Showers, B., Dalton, M., & Beaton, C. (1985). *Theory-driven and naturalistic research as sources of teaching skills: A classification.* Paper presented at the annual meeting of the American Educational Research Association, Chicago.

Joyce, B., Weil, M., & Wald, R. (1981). Can teachers learn repertoires of models of teaching? In B. Joyce, L. Peck, & C. Brown, *Flexibility in teaching.* New York: Longman.

Joyce, B., & Wolf, J. (1996). Readersville: Building a culture of readers and writers. In B. Joyce and E. Calhoun (Eds.), *Learning experiences in school renewal.* Eugene, Ore.: The ERIC Clearinghouse in Educational Management.

Joyce, B., Wolf, J., & Calhoun, E. (1993). *The self-renewing school.* Alexandria, Va.: Association for Supervision and Curriculum Development.

Judd, C. H. (1934). *Education and social progress.* New York: Harcourt Brace Jovanovich.

Juel, C., (1988). Learning to read and write. *Journal of Educational Psychology, 80*(4), 437–447.

Juel, C. (1992). Longitudinal research on learning to read and write with at-risk students. In M. Dreher & W. Slater (Eds.), *Elementary school literacy: Critical issues* (pp. 73–99). Norwood, Mass.: Christopher-Gordon.

Kagan, J. (1994). *Galen's prophecy.* New York: Basic Books.

Kagan, S. (1990). *Cooperative learning resources for teachers.* San Juan Capistrano, Calif.: Resources for Teachers.

Kahle, J. (1985). *Women in science: A report from the field.* Philadelphia: Falmer Press.

Kahle, J., & Meece, R. (1994). Research on gender issues in the classroom. In D. L. Gabel (Ed.), *Handbook of research on science teaching and learning* (pp. 542–557). New York: MacMillan.

Kahn, S. B., & Weiss, J. (1973). The teaching of affective responses. In R. M. W. Travers (Ed.), *The second handbook of research on teaching.* Chicago: McNally & Company.

Kamii, C., & DeVries, R. (1974). Piaget-based curricula for early childhood education. In R. Parker (Ed.), *The preschool in action.* Boston: Allyn & Bacon.

Karplus, R. (1964). *Theoretical background of the science curriculum improvement study.* Berkeley: University of California Press.

Kenworthy, L. S. (1955). *Introducing children to the world.* New York: Harper.

Kerman, S. (1979). Teacher expectations and student achievement. *Phi Delta Kappan, 60*(10), 716–718.

Kidron, M., & Segal, R. (2001). *The state of the world atlas.* New York: Simon & Schuster Touchstone.

Kilpatrick, W. H. (1919). *The project method.* New York: Teachers College Press.

Kincaid, E. (1959). *In every war but one.* New York: Norton.

Klausmeier, H. J. (1980). *Learning and teaching concepts.* New York: Academic Press.

Klausmeier, H. J., & Harris, C. W. (1966). *Analysis of concept learning.* New York: Academic Press.

Klausmeier, H. J., & Hooper, F. H. (1974). Conceptual development on instruction. In F. N. Kerlinger & J. B. Carroll (Eds.), *Review of research in education* (pp. 3–54). Itasca, Ill.: Peacock.

Klein, S. (1985). *Handbook for achieving sex equity through education.* Baltimore: Johns Hopkins University Press.

Kleitsch, R. G. (1969). *Directory of educational simulations, learning games, and didactic units.* St. Paul, Minn.: Instructional Simulations.

Klinzing, G., & Klinzing-Eurich, G. (1985). Higher cognitive behaviors in classroom discourse: Congruencies between teachers' questions and pupils' responses. *Australian Journal of Education, 29*(1), 63–74.

Knowles, M. (1978). *The adult learner: A neglected species* (2nd ed.). Houston: Gulf.

Kober, N. (1981). *The role and impact of Chapter I.* Washington, D.C.: Office of Technology Assessment, U.S. Department of Education.

Kohlberg, L. (1966). Moral education and the schools. *School Review, 74,* 1–30.

Kohlberg, L. (1976). The cognitive developmental approach to moral education. In D. Purpel & K. Ryan (Eds.), *Moral education . . . It comes with the territory.* Berkeley, Calif.: McCutchan.

Kohlberg, L. (Ed.). (1977). *Recent research in moral development.* New York: Holt, Rinehart & Winston.

Kourilsky, M. (1974). *Beyond simulation: The mini-society approach to education and other social sciences.* Los Angeles: Educational Research Associates.

Kozol, J. (1992). *Savage inequalities.* New York: HarperCollins.

Kuhn, D., Amsel, E., & O'Loughlin, M. (1988). *The development of scientific thinking skills.* New York: Academic Press.

Kulik, C. C., Kulik, J. A., & Bangert-Drowns, R. L. (1990). Effectiveness of mastery learning programs: A meta-analysis. *Review of Educational Research, 60,* 265–299.

Lavatelle, C. (1970). *Piaget's theory applied to an early childhood education curriculum.* Boston: American Science and Engineering.

Lawson, A. E., et al. (1984). Proportional reasoning and linguistic abilities required for hypothetico-deductive reasoning. *Journal of Research in Science Teaching, 21*(4), 377–384.

Lawton, J. T. (1977a). Effects of advance organizer lessons on children's use and understanding of the causal and logical "Because." *Journal of Experimental Education, 46*(1), 41–46.

Lawton, J. T. (1977b). The use of advance organizers in the learning and retention of logical operations in social studies concepts. *American Educational Research Journal, 14*(1), 24–43.

Lawton, J. T., & Wanska, S. K. (1977a). Advance organizers as a teaching strategy: A reply to Barnes and Clawson. *Review of Educational Research, 47*(1), 233–244.

Lawton, J. T., & Wanska, S. K. (1977b, Summer). The effects of different types of advance organizers on classification learning. *American Educational Research Journal, 16*(3), 223–239.

Lepper, M., Keavney, M., & Drake, M. (1996). Intrinsic motivation and extrinsic rewards. *Review of Educational Research, 66*(1), 5–32.

Levin, J. R., McCormick, C., Miller, H., & Berry, J. (1982). Mnemonic versus nonmnemonic strategies for children. *American Educational Research Journal, 19*(1), 121–136.

Levin, J. R., Shriberg, L., & Berry, J. (1983). A concrete strategy for remembering abstract prose. *American Educational Research Journal, 20*(2), 277–290.

Levin, M. E., & Levin, J. R. (1990). Scientific mnemonics: Methods for maximizing more than memory. *American Educational Research Journal, 27,* 301–321.

Levine, D. (1991). Creating effective schools. *Phi Delta Kappan, 72*(5), 389–393.

Levy, D. V., & Stark, J. (1982). *Implementation of the Chicago mastery learning reading program at inner-city elementary schools.* Paper presented at the annual meeting of the American Educational Research Association, New York.

Lewin, T. (1998, December 6). U.S. colleges begin to ask, Where have the men gone? *The New York Times,* pp. 1, 28.

Lewis, H., & Streitfeld, H. (1970). *Growth games.* New York: Harcourt Brace Jovanovich.

Lindvall, C. M., & Bolvin, J. O. (1966). *The project for individually prescribed instruction.* Oakleaf Project. Unpublished manuscript, Learning Research and Development Center, University of Pittsburgh.

Linn, M., & Hyde, J. (1989). Gender, mathematics, and science. *Educational Researcher, 18*(8), 17–19, 22–27.

Lippitt, R., Fox, R., & Schaible, L. (1969a). *Cause and effect: Social science resource book.* Chicago: Science Research Associates.

Lippitt, R., Fox, R., & Schaible, L. (1969b). *Social science laboratory units.* Chicago: Science Research Associates.

Little, J. W. (1986). *The persistence of privacy: Autonomy and initiative in teachers' professional opportunities.* Paper presented at the annual meeting of the American Educational Research Association, San Francisco.

Little, J. W., et al. (1987). *Staff development in California.* San Francisco: Far West Laboratories.

Locke, J. (1927). *Some thoughts concerning education* (R. H. Quick, Ed.). Cambridge, England: Cambridge University Press.

Lorayne, H., & Lucas, J. (1974). *The memory book.* Briercliff Manor, N.Y.: Lucas Educational Systems.

Lortie, D. (1975). *Schoolteacher.* Chicago: University of Chicago Press.

Loucks, S. F., Newlove, B. W., & Hall, G. E. (1975). *Measuring levels of use of the innovation: A manual for trainers, interviewers, and raters.* Austin: Research and Development Center for Teacher Education, University of Texas.

Louis, K. S., & Miles, M. B. (1990). *Improving the urban high school.* New York: Teachers College Press.

Lucas, J. (2001). *Learning how to learn.* Frisco, Tex.: Lucas Educational Systems.

Lucas, S. B. (1972). *The effects of utilizing three types of advance organizers for learning a biological concept in seventh grade science.* Doctoral dissertation, Pennsylvania State University.

Ludlum, R. P., et al. (1969). *American government.* Boston: Houghton Mifflin.

Luiten, J., Ames, W., & Ackerson, G. A. (1980). A meta-analysis of the effects of advance organizers on learning and retention. *American Educational Research Journal, 17,* 211–218.

Lundquist, G., & Parr, G. (1978). Assertiveness training with adolescents. *Technical Journal of Education, 5,* 37–44.

Maccoby, E., & Jacklin, C. (1974). *The Psychology of Sex Differences.* Stanford, Calif.: Stanford University Press.

Madaus, G. F., Airasian, P. W., & Kellaghan, T. (1980). *School effectiveness: A review of the evidence.* New York: McGraw-Hill.

Madden, N. A., & Slavin, R. E. (1983). Cooperative learning and social acceptance of mainstreamed academically handicapped students. *Journal of Special Education, 17,* 171–182.

Mahoney, M., & Thorensen, C. (1972). Behavioral self-control-power to the person. *Educational Researcher, 1,* 5–7.

Maloney, D. (1994). Research on problem solving: Physics. In D. L. Gabel (Ed.), *Handbook of research on science teaching and learning* (pp. 327–354). New York: MacMillan.

Mandeville, G. K., & Rivers, J. L. (1989). Effects of South Carolina's Hunter-based PET program. *Educational Leadership, 46*(4), 63–66.

Marcuse, H. (1955). *Eros and civilization.* Boston: Beacon Press.

Marsh, H., & Yeung, A. (1997). Coursework selection: Relations to academic self-concept and achievement. *American Educational Research Journal, 34*(4), 691–720.

Marzano, R., Brandt, R., Hughes, C., Jones, B., Presseisen, B., Rankin, S., & Suhor, C. (1987). *Dimensions of thinking.* Alexandria, Va.: Association for Supervision and Curriculum Development.

Maslow, A. (1962). *Toward a psychology of being.* New York: Van Nostrand.

Massialas, B., & Cox, B. (1966). *Inquiry in social studies.* New York: McGraw-Hill.

Mastropieri, M. A., & Scruggs, T. E. (1991). *Teaching students ways to remember.* Cambridge, Mass.: Brookline Books.

Mastropieri, M. A., & Scruggs, T. E. (1994). *A practical guide for teaching science to students with special needs in inclusive settings* Austin, Tex.: Pro-Ed.

Mayer, R. F. (1979). Can advance organizers influence meaningful learning? *Review of Educational Research, 49*(2), 371–383.

McCarthy, B. (1981). *The 4mat system: Teaching to learning styles with right/left mode techniques.* Barrington, Ill.: Excel.

McDonald, F. J., & Elias, P. (1976a). *Beginning teacher evaluation study: Phase II, 1973–74. Executive summary report.* Princeton, N.J.: Educational Testing Service.

McDonald, F. J., & Elias, P. (1976b). *Executive summary report: Beginning teacher evaluation study, phase II.* Princeton, N.J.: Educational Testing Service.

McGill-Franzen, A., & Allington, R. (1991). The gridlock of low achievement. *Remedial and Special Education, 12,* 20–30.

McGill-Franzen, A., & Goatley, V. (2001). Title I and special education: Support for children who struggle to learn to read. In S. Neuman & D. Dickinson (Eds.), *Handbook of early literacy research* (pp. 471–484). New York: Guilford.

McGill-Franzen, A., Lanford, C., & Killian, J. (undated). *Case studies of literature-based textbook use in kindergarten.* Albany: State University of New York.

McKibbin, M., & Joyce, B. (1980). Psychological states and staff development. *Theory into Practice, 19*(4), 248–255.

McKinney, C., Warren, A., Larkins, G., Ford, M. J., & Davis, J. C. III. (1983). The effectiveness of three methods of teaching social studies concepts to fourth-grade students: An aptitude-treatment interaction study. *American Educational Research Journal, 20,* 663–670.

McNair, K. (1978–1979). Capturing in-flight decisions. *Educational Research Quarterly, 3*(4), 26–42.

Medley, D. M. (1977). *Teacher competence and teacher effectiveness.* Washington, D.C.: American Association of Colleges of Teacher Education.

Medley, D. M. (1982). Teacher effectiveness. In H. Mitzel (Ed.), *Encyclopedia of educational research* (pp. 1894–1903). N.Y.: Macmillan.

Medley, D. M., Coker, H., Coker, J. G., Lorentz, J. L., Soar, R. S., & Spaulding, R. L. (1981). Assessing teacher performance from observed competency indicators defined by classroom teachers. *Journal of Educational Research, 74,* 197–216.

Medley, D., Soar, R., & Coker, H. (1984). *Measurement-based evaluation of teacher performance.* New York: Longman.

Melamed, B., & Siegel, L. (1973). Reduction of anxiety in children facing hospitalization and surgery by use of filmed modeling. *Journal of Consulting and Clinical Psychology, 43,* 511–520.

Merrill, M. D., & Tennyson, R. D. (1977). *Concept teaching: An instructional design guide.* Englewood Cliffs, N.J.: Educational Technology.

Metz, K. E. (1995). Reassessment of developmental constraints on children's science instruction. *Review of Educational Research, 65*(2), 93–127.

Mevarech, Z., & Kramarski, B. (1997). IMPROVE: A multidimensional method for teaching mathematics in heterogeneous classrooms. *American Educational Research Journal, 34*(2), 365–394.

Meyer, L. (1984). Long-term academic effects of the direct instruction project follow through. *Elementary School Journal, 84,* 380–394.

Miles, M., & Huberman, M. (1984). *Innovation up close.* New York: Praeger.

Millar, G. (1956). The magical number seven, plus or minus two: Some limits on our capacity to process information. *Psychological Review, 63,* 81–87.

Mitchell, L. S. (1950). *Our children and our schools.* New York: Simon & Schuster.

More, T. (1965). *Utopia.* New York: Dutton.

Morris, R. (1999). *How new research on brain development will influence educational policy.* Presentation to the Policy Makers Institute. Georgia Center for Advanced Telecommunications Technology, Atlanta.

Nagy, W., & Anderson, R. (1984). How many words are there in printed English? *Reading Research Quarterly, 19,* 304–330.

Nagy, W., Herman, P., & Anderson, R. (1985). Learning words from context. *Reading Research Quarterly, 20,* 233–253.

National Assessment of Educational Progress (NAEP). (1992). *The reading report card.* Washington, D.C.: National Center for Educational Statistics, U.S. Department of Education.

National Center for Education Statistics. (2000). *The condition of education.* Washington, D.C.: U.S. Department of Education.

National Council for the Social Studies. (1964). *The Glen Falls story.* Washington, D.C.: National Education Association.

National Institutes of Education. (1975). *National conference on studies in teaching (Vols. 1–10).* Washington, D.C.: U.S. Department of Health, Education and Welfare.

National Reading Panel. (1998). *Teaching children to read.* Washington, D.C.: U.S. Department of Education.

Neill, A. S. (1960). *Summerhill.* New York: Holt, Rinehart & Winston.

Nesbitt, W. A. (1971). *Simulation games for the social studies classroom.* New York: Foreign Policy Association.

Neuman, S., & Dickinson, D., eds. (2001). *Handbook of early literacy research.* New York: Guilford Press.

New Standards Primary Literacy Committee. (1999). *Reading and writing: Grade by grade.* Pittsburgh, Penn.: National Center on Education and the Economy and the University of Pittsburgh.

New Webster's dictionary of the English language (Deluxe Encyclopedia Edition). (1981). New York: Delair.

Newby, T. J., & Ertner, P. A. (1994). *Instructional analogies and the learning of concepts.* Paper presented at the annual meeting of the American Educational Research Association, New Orleans.

Nicholson, A. M., & Joyce, B. (with D. Parker & F. Waterman). (1976). *The literature on inservice teacher education.* (ISTE Report No 3.) Syracuse, N.Y.: National Dissemination Center, Syracuse University.

Nucci, L. P. (Ed.). (1989). *Moral development and character education.* Berkeley, Calif.: McCutchan.

Oakes, J. (1986). *Keeping track: How schools structure inequality.* New Haven, Conn.: Yale University Press.

Oliver, D., & Shaver, J. P. (1966/1974). *Teaching public issues in the high school.* Boston: Houghton Mifflin.

Oliver, D. W., & Shaver, J. P. (1971). *Cases and controversy: A guide to teaching the public issues series.* Middletown, Conn.: American Education Publishers.

Olson, D. R. (1970). *Cognitive development: The child's acquisition of diagonality.* New York: Academic Press.

Orme, M., & Purnell, R. (1968). *Behavior modification and transfer in an out-of-control classroom.* Cambridge, Mass.: R & D Center on Educational Differences, Harvard University.

O'Sullivan, C., Reese, C., & Mazzeo, J. (1997). *NAEP 1996 Science report card for the nation and the states*. Washington, D.C.: U.S. Department of Education.

Palomares, U., Ball, G., & Bessell, H. (1976). *Magic circle: Human development program*. La Mesa, Calif.: Human Development Institute.

Parker, L., & Offer, J. (1987). School science achievement: Conditions for equality. *International Journal for Science Education, 8*(2), 173–183.

Pavlov, I. (1927). *Conditioned reflexes: An investigation of physiological activity of the cerebral cortex* (G. V. Anrep, Trans.). London: Oxford University Press.

Pearson, D. (1998). *New York State Reading Symposium*. Albany: The New York State Education Department.

Perkins, D. N. (1984). Creativity by design. *Educational Leadership, 42*(1), 18–25.

Perls, F. (1968). *Gestalt therapy verbatim*. Lafayette, Calif.: Real People Press.

Persing, P., Bailey, W. C., & Kleg, M. (1969). *Life-cycle*. (Anthropology Curriculum Project, Publication No. 49.) Athens: University of Georgia.

Persky, H., Reese, C., O'Sullivan, C., Lazer, S., Moore, J., & Shakrani, S. (1996). *NAEP 1994 geography report card*. Washington, D.C.: U.S. Department of Education.

Peterson, P., & Clark, C. (1978). Teachers' reports of their cognitive processes while teaching. *American Educational Research Journal, 15*(4), 555–565.

Peterson, P., Marx, R., & Clark, C. (1978). Teacher planning, teacher behavior, and student achievement. *American Educational Research Journal, 15*(4), 417–432.

Phenix, P. (1961). *Education and the common good*. New York: Harper.

Phillips, D. (1995). The good, the bad, and the ugly. *Educational Researcher, 24*(7), 5–12.

Piaget, J. (1952). *The origins of intelligence in children*. New York: International University Press.

Piaget, J. (1960). *The child's conception of the world*. Atlantic Highlands, N.J.: Humanities Press.

Piksulski, J., with Taylor, B. (1999). *Emergent literacy survey/K–2*. Boston: Houghton Mifflin.

Pinnell, G. S. (1989). Helping at-risk children learn to read. *Elementary School Journal, 90*(2), 161–184.

Pinnell, G. S., & McCarrier, A. (1994). Interactive Writing. In E. Hiebert & B. Taylor (Eds.), *Getting reading right from the start* (pp. 149–170). Boston: Allyn & Bacon.

Plato. (1945). *The Republic* (F. M. Cornford, Trans.). New York: Oxford University Press.

Premack, D. (1965). Reinforcement theory. In D. Levine (Ed.), *Nebraska Symposium on Motivation*. Lincoln: University of Nebraska Press.

Pressley, M. (1977). Children's use of the keyword method to learn simple Spanish vocabulary words. *Journal of Educational Psychology, 69*(5), 465–472.

Pressley, M. (1995). *Cognitive strategy instruction that really improves student performance*. Cambridge, Mass: Brookline.

Pressley, M. (2002). Metacognition and self-regulated comprehension. In A. Farstrup & J. Samuels (Eds.), *What research has to say about reading instruction* (pp. 291–310). Newark, Del.: International Reading Instruction.

Pressley, M., & Dennis-Rounds, J. (1980). Transfer of a mnemonic keyword strategy at two age levels. *Journal of Educational Psychology, 72*(4), 575–582.

Pressley, M., & Levin, J. R. (1978). Developmental constraints associated with children's use of the keyword method of foreign language learning. *Journal of Experimental Child Psychology, 26*(1), 359–372.

Pressley, M., Levin, J. R., & Delaney, H. D. (1982). The mnemonic keyword method. *Review of Educational Research, 52*(1), 61–91.

Pressley, M., Levin, J., & Ghatala, E. (1984). Memory-strategy monitoring in adults and children. *Journal of Verbal Learning and Verbal Behavior, 23*(2), 270–288.

Pressley, M., Levin, J. R., & McCormick, C. (1980). Young children's learning of foreign language vocabulary: A sentence variation of the keyword method. *Contemporary Educational Psychology, 5*(1), 22–29.

Pressley, M., Levin, J., & Miller, G. (1981a). How does the keyword method affect vocabulary, comprehension, and usage? *Reading Research Quarterly, 16,* 213–226.

Pressley, M., Levin, J., & Miller, G. (1981b). The keyword method and children's learning of foreign vocabulary with abstract meanings. *Canadian Psychology, 35*(3), 283–287.

Pressley, M., Samuel, J., Hershey, M., Bishop, S., & Dickinson, D. (1981). Use of a mnemonic technique to teach young children foreign-language vocabulary. *Contemporary Educational Psychology, 6,* 110–116.

Pressley, M., and Associates. (1990). *Cognitive instruction that really improves children's academic performance.* Cambridge, Mass.: Brookline Books.

Purkey, S., & Smith, M. (1983). Effective schools: A review. *Elementary School Journal, 83*(4), 427–452.

Purpel, D., & Ryan, K. (Eds.). (1976). *Moral education: It comes with the territory.* Berkeley, Calif.: McCutchan.

Qin, Z., Johnson, D. W., & Johnson, R. T. (1995). Cooperative versus competitive efforts and problem solving. *Review of Educational Research, 65*(2), 82–102.

Quellmalz, E. S., & Burry, J. (1983). *Analytic scales for assessing students' expository and narrative writing skills.* (CSE Resource Paper No. 5.) Los Angeles: Center for the Study of Evaluation, Graduate School of Education, University of California at Los Angeles.

Ralph, J., & Fennessey, J. (1983). Science or reform: Some questions about the effective schools model. *Phi Delta Kappan, 64*(10), 689–694.

Reese, C., Miller, K., Mazzeo, J., and Dossey, J. (1997). *NAEP 1996 mathematics report card for the nation and the states.* Washington, D.C: U.S. Department of Education.

Resnick, L. B. (1967). *Design of an early learning curriculum.* Pittsburgh, Pa.: Learning Research and Development Center, University of Pittsburgh.

Resnick, L. B. (1987). *Education and learning to think.* Washington, D.C.: Academic Press.

Rhine, W. R. (Ed.). (1981). *Making schools more effective: New directions from follow through.* New York: Academic Press.

Richardson, V. (1990). Significant and worthwhile change in teaching practice. *Educational Researcher, 19*(7), 10–18.

Rimm, D. C., & Masters, J. C. (1974). *Behavior therapy: Techniques and empirical findings.* New York: Academic Press.

Ripple, R., & Drinkwater, D. (1981). Transfer of learning. In H. E. Mitzel (Ed.), *Encyclopedia of educational research* (Vol. 4, pp. 1947–1953). New York: Free Press, MacMillan.

Roberts, J. (1969). *Human relations training and its effect on the teaching-learning process in social studies.* (Final Report.) Albany: Division of Research, New York State Education Department.

Roebuck, F., Buhler, J., & Aspy, D. (1976). *A comparison of high and low levels of humane teaching/learning conditions on the subsequent achievement of students identified as having learning difficulties.* (Final Report: Order No. PLD 6816-76 re the National Institute of Mental Health.) Denton: Texas Woman's University Press.

Rogers, C. (1961). *On becoming a person.* Boston: Houghton Mifflin.

Rogers, C. (1969). *Freedom to learn.* Columbus, Ohio: Merrill.

Rogers, C. (1971). *Client centered therapy.* Boston: Houghton Mifflin.

Rogers, C. (1981). *A way of being.* Boston: Houghton Mifflin.

Rogers, C. (1982). *Freedom to learn in the eighties.* Columbus, Ohio: Merrill.

Rolheiser-Bennett, C. (1986). *Four models of teaching: A meta-analysis of student outcomes.* Ph.D. thesis, University of Oregon.

Romberg, T. A., & Wilson, J. (1970). *The effect of an advance organizer, cognitive set, and postorganizer on the learning and retention of written materials.* Paper presented at the annual meeting of the American Educational Research Association, Minneapolis, Minn.

Roper, S., Deal, T., & Dornbusch, S. (1976, Spring). Collegial evaluation of classroom teaching: Does it work? *Educational Research Quarterly,* 56–66.

Rosenholtz, S. J. (1989). *Teachers' workplace: The social organization of schools.* White Plains, N.Y.: Longman.

Rosenshine, B. (1970). The stability of teacher effects upon student achievement. *Review of Educational Research, 40,* 647–662.

Rosenshine, B. (1971). *Teaching behaviours and student achievement.* London: National Foundation for Educational Research.

Rosenshine, B. (1985). *Direct instruction. International Encyclopedia of Education* (T. Husen & T. N. Postlethwaite, Eds.) (Vol. 3, 1395–1400). Oxford: Pergamon Press.

Rosenshine, B., & Meister, C. (1994). Reciprocal teaching: A review of the research. *Review of Educational Research, 64*(4), 479–530.

Rosskopf, M. (1971). *Piagetian cognitive development research in mathematical education.* Washington, D.C.: National Council of Teachers of Mathematics.

Rousseau, J. J. (1983). *Emile.* New York: Dutton. (Original work published 1762.)

Rowan, S., & Guthrie, L. (1988). *The quality of Chapter I instruction: Results from a survey of 24 schools.* San Francisco: The Far West Laboratory.

Rowe, M. B. (1969). Science, soul, and sanctions. *Science and Children, 6*(6), 11–13.

Rowe, M. B. (1974). Wait-time and rewards as instructional variables: Their influence on language, logic, and fate control. *Journal of Research in Science Teaching, 11,* 81–94.

Rowen, B., Bossert, S. T., & Dwyer, D. C. (1983). Research on effective schools: A cautionary note. *Educational Researcher, 12*(4), 24–31.

Rutter, M., Maughan, R., Mortimer, P., Oustin, J., & Smith, A. (1979). *Fifteen thousand hours: Secondary schools and their effects on children.* Cambridge, Mass.: Harvard University Press.

Sadker, M., & Sadker, D. (1994). *Failing at fairness.* New York: Touchstone (Simon & Schuster).

Salter, A. (1964). The theory and practice of conditioned reflex therapy. In A. Salter, J. Wolpe, & L. J. Reyna (Eds.), *Conditioning therapies: The challenge in psychotherapy.* New York: Holt, Rinehart & Winston.

Salter, A., Wolpe, J., & Reyna, J. (Eds.). (1964). *The conditioning therapies: The challenge in psychotherapies.* New York: Holt, Rinehart & Winston.

Sanders, D. A., & Sanders, J. A. (1984). *Teaching creativity through metaphor.* New York: Longman.

Sanders, W., & Rivers, J. (1996). *Cumulative and residual effects of teachers on future student academic achievement. Research progress report.* Knoxville: University of Tennessee Value-Added Research and Assessment Center.

Sarason, S. (1982). *The culture of the school and the problem of change* (2nd ed.). Boston: Allyn & Bacon.

Scanlon, R., & Brown, M. (1969). *In-service education for individualized instruction.* Unpublished manuscript. Philadelphia: Research for Better Schools.

Schacter, J. (undated). *Reading programs that work: A review of programs from pre-kindergarten to 4th grade.* Santa Monica, Calif.: Milken Family Foundation.

Schaefer, R. (1967). *The school as a center of inquiry.* New York: Harper & Row.

Schaubel, L., Klopfer, L. E., & Raghavan, K. (1991). Students' transition from an engineering model to a science model of experimentation. *Journal of Research on Science Teaching, 28*(9), 859–882.

Schein, E. H., & Bennis, W. G. (1965). *Personal and organizational change through group methods.* New York: Wiley.

Schiffer, J. (1980). *School renewal through staff development.* New York: Teachers College Press.

Schlenker, R. M. (1991). Learning about fossil formulation by classroom simulation. *Science Activities, 28*(3), 17–20.

Schmuck, R. A., & Runkel, P. J. (1985). *The handbook of organizational development in schools* (3rd ed.). Palo Alto, Calif.: Mayfield Press.

Schmuck, R. A., Runkel, P. J., Arends, R., & Arends, J. (1977). *The second handbook of organizational development in schools.* Palo Alto, Calif.: Mayfield Press.

Schön, D. (1982). *The reflective practitioner.* New York: Basic Books.

Schrenker, G. (1976). *The effects of an inquiry-development program on elementary schoolchildren's science learning.* Ph.D. thesis, New York University.

Schroeder, H. M., Driver, M. J., & Streufert, S. (1967). *Human information processing: Individuals and groups functioning in complex social situations.* New York: Holt, Rinehart & Winston.

Schroeder, H. M., Karlins, M., & Phares, J. (1973). *Education for freedom.* New York: Wiley.

Schutz, W. (1967). *Joy: Expanding human awareness.* New York: Grove Press.

Schutz, W. (1982). *Firo.* New York: Holt, Rinehart & Winston.

Schutz, W., & Turner, E. (1983). *Body fantasy.* Irvington, Ill.: Irvington Press.

Schwab, J. (1965). *Biological sciences curriculum study: Biology teachers' handbook.* New York: Wiley.

Schwab, J. (1982). *Science, curriculum, and liberal education: Selected essays.* Chicago: University of Chicago Press.

Schwab, J., & Brandwein, P. (1962). *The teaching of science.* Cambridge, Mass.: Harvard University Press.

Seperson, M. (1970). *The relationship between the teaching styles of student teachers and those of their cooperating teachers.* Ph.D. dissertation. New York: Teachers College, Columbia University.

Seperson, M., & Joyce, B. (1981). The relationship between the teaching styles of student teachers and those of their cooperating teachers. In B. Joyce, L. Peck, & C. Brown (Eds.), *Flexibility in teaching* (pp. 101–108). New York: Longman.

Shaffer, J. B. P., & Galinsky, J. D. (1974). *Models of group therapy and sensitivity training.* Englewood Cliffs, N.J.: Prentice-Hall.

Shaftel, F., & Shaftel, G. (1967). *Role playing of social values: Decision making in the social studies.* Englewood Cliffs, N.J.: Prentice-Hall.

Shaftel, F., & Shaftel, G. (1982). *Role playing in the curriculum.* Englewood Cliffs, N.J.: Prentice-Hall.

Shane, H. (1977). *Curriculum change: Toward the 21st century.* Washington, D.C.: National Education Association.

Sharan, S. (1980). Cooperative learning in small groups: Recent methods and effects on achievement, attitudes, and ethnic relations. *Review of Educational Research, 50*(2), 241–271.

Sharan, S. (1990). *Cooperative learning: Theory and research.* New York: Praeger.

Sharan, S., & Hertz-Lazarowitz, R. (1980a). Academic achievement of elementary school children in small group versus whole-class instruction. *Journal of Experimental Education, 48*(2), 120–129.

Sharan, S., & Hertz-Lazarowitz, R. (1980b). A group investigation method of cooperative learning in the classroom. In S. Sharan, P. Hare, C. Webb, & R. Hertz-Lazarowitz (Eds.), *Cooperation in education* (pp. 14–46). Provo, Utah: Brigham Young University Press.

Sharan, S., & Hertz-Lazarowitz, R. (1982). Effects of an instructional change program on teachers' behavior, attitudes, and perceptions. *Journal of Applied Behavioral Science, 18*(2), 185–201.

Sharan, S., & Shachar, H. (1988). *Language and learning in the cooperative classroom.* New York: Springer-Verlag.

Sharan, S., & Shaulov, A. (1990). Cooperative learning, motivation to learn, and academic achievement. In S. Sharan (Ed.), *Cooperative learning: Theory and research* (pp. 173–202). New York: Praeger.

Sharan, S., Slavin, R., & Davidson, N. (1990). The IASCE: An agenda for the 90's. *Cooperative Learning, 10,* 2–4.

Shaver, J. P. (1995). Social studies. In G. Cawelti (Ed.), *Handbook of research on improving student achievement.* Arlington, Va.: Educational Research Service.

Shaver, J. P., & Strong, W. (1982). *Facing value-decisions: Rationale-building for teachers.* New York: Teachers College Press.

Shepard, H. A. (1964). The T-Group as training in observant participation. In W. G. Bennis, K. D. Benne, & R. Chin (Eds.), *The planning of change: Readings in the applied behavioral sciences.* New York: Holt, Rinehart & Winston.

Showers, B. (1980). *Self-efficacy as a predictor of teacher participation in school decision-making.* Ph.D. thesis, Stanford University.

Showers, B. (1982a). *A study of coaching in teacher training.* Eugene: Center for Educational Policy and Management, University of Oregon.

Showers, B. (1982b). *Transfer of training: The contribution of coaching.* Eugene: Center for Educational Policy and Management, University of Oregon.

Showers, B. (1984). *Peer coaching and its effect on transfer of training.* Paper presented at the annual meeting of the American Educational Research Association, New Orleans.

Showers, B. (1985). Teachers coaching teachers. *Educational Leadership, 42*(7), 43–49.

Showers, B. (1989, March). *Implementation: Research-based training and teaching strategies and their effects on the workplace and instruction.* Paper presented at the annual meeting of the American Educational Research Association, San Francisco.

Showers, B., Joyce, B., & Bennett, B. (1987). Synthesis of research on staff development: A framework for future study and a state-of-the-art analysis. *Educational Leadership, 45*(3), 77–87.

Showers, B., Joyce, B., Scanlon, M., & Schnaubelt, C. (1998). A second chance to learn to read. *Educational Leadership, 55*(6), 27–31.

Shymanski, J., Kyle, W., & Alport, E. (1983). The effects of new science curricula on student performance. *Journal of Research on Science Teaching, 20*(5), 387–404.

Siegel, I. E. (1984). *Advances in applied developmental psychology.* New York: Ablex.

Sigel, F. E. (1969). The Piagetian system and the world of educational studies. In J. Hunt (Ed.), *Intelligence and experience.* N.Y.: Ronald.

Sigel, I. E., & Hooper, F. H. (1968). *Logical thinking in children.* New York: Holt, Rinehart & Winston.

Simon, A., & Boyer, E. G. (1967). *Mirrors for behavior: An anthology of classroom observation instruments.* Philadelphia: Research for Better Schools, Inc.

Sitotnik, K. (1983). What you see is what you get: Consistency, persistence, and mediocrity in classrooms. *Harvard Educational Review, 53*(1), 16–31.

Sizer, T. R. (1985). *Horace's compromise: The dilemma of the American high school.* Boston: Houghton Mifflin.

Skinner, B. F. (1953). *Science and human behavior.* New York: Macmillan.

Skinner, B. F. (1957). *Verbal behavior.* New York: Appleton-Century-Crofts.

Skinner, B. F. (1968). *The technology of teaching.* Englewood Cliffs, N.J.: Prentice-Hall.

Skinner, B. F. (1971). *Beyond freedom and dignity.* New York: Knopf.

Skinner, B. F. (1978). *Reflections on behaviorism and society.* Englewood Cliffs, N.J.: Prentice-Hall.

Slavin, R. E. (1977a). Classroom reward structure: An analytic and practical review. *Review of Educational Research, 47*(4), 633–650.

Slavin, R. E. (1977b). How student learning teams can integrate the desegregated classroom. *Integrated Education, 15*(6), 56–58.

Slavin, R. E. (1977c). *Student learning team techniques: Narrowing the achievement gap between the races.* (Report No. 228.) Baltimore, Md.: Center for Social Organization of Schools, Johns Hopkins University.

Slavin, R. E. (1977d). A student team approach to teaching adolescents with special emotional and behavioral needs. *Psychology in the Schools, 14*(1), 77–84.

Slavin, R. E. (1978a). Separating incentives, feedback, and evaluation: Toward a more effective classroom system. *Educational Psychologist, 13*, 97–100.

Slavin, R. E. (1978b). Student teams and achievement divisions. *Journal of Research and Development in Education, 12*, 39–49.

Slavin, R. E. (1983). *Cooperative learning.* New York: Longman.

Slavin, R. E. (1990a). Achievement effects of ability grouping in secondary schools. *Review of Educational Research, 60*(3), 471–500.

Slavin, R. E. (1990b). Mastery learning reconsidered. *Review of Educational Research, 60*, 300–302.

Slavin, R. E. (1991). Are cooperative learning and "untracking" harmful to the gifted? *Educational Leadership, 48*(6), 68–70.

Slavin, R. E., and Madden, N. A. (1995). Success for all: Creating schools and classrooms where all children can read. In J. Oakes and K. Quartz (Eds.), *Creating new educational communities: The ninety-fourth yearbook of the National Society for the Study of Education,* 70–86. Chicago: University of Chicago Press.

Slavin, R. E., Madden, N. A., Karweit, N., Livermon, B. J., & Dolan, L. (1990). Success for all: First-year outcomes of a comprehensive plan for reforming urban education. *American Educational Research Journal, 27*, 255–278.

Smith, K., & Smith, M. (1966). *Cybernetic principles of learning and educational design.* New York: Holt, Rinehart, & Winston.

Smith, L., & Keith, P. (1971). *Anatomy of an innovation.* New York: Wiley.

Smith, M. L. (1980). *Effects of aesthetics educations on basic skills learning.* Boulder, Colo.: Laboratory of Educational Research, University of Colorado.

Snow, C., Burns, M., & Griffin, P., eds. (1998). *Preventing reading difficulties in young children.* Washington, D.C.: National Academy Press.

Snow, R. (1982). *Intelligence, motivation, and academic work.* Paper presented at a symposium on "The Student's Role in Learning," conducted by the National Commission for Excellence in Education, U.S. Department of Education, San Diego, Calif.

Soar, R. S. (1973). *Follow through classroom process measurement and pupil growth (1970–71).* (Final Report.) Gainesville: College of Education, University of Florida.

Soar, R. S., Soar, R. M., & Ragosta, M. (1971). *Florida climate and control system: Observer's manual.* Gainesville: Institute for Development of Human Resources, University of Florida.

Social Science Consortium. (1971, 1972, 1973). *Data Handbook.* Boulder, Colo.: Author.

Spaulding, R. L. (1970). E. I. P. Durham, NC: Duke University Press.

Sprinthall, M. A., & Thies-Sprinthall, L. (1983). Teachers as adult learners. In *Evaluation of the implementation of Public Law 94-142: Eighty-second yearbook of the National Society for the Study of Education.* Menlo Park, Calif.: SRI International.

Stallings, J. (1980). Allocating academic learning time revisited: Beyond time on task. *Educational Researcher, 9*, 11–16.

Stallings, J. (1985). A study of implementation of Madeline Hunter's model and its effects on students. *Journal of Educational Research, 78*, 325–337.

Starr, J. (1965). *Programmed modern arithmetic: Introduction to sets.* Boston: Heath.

Stauffer, R. (1970). *The language-experience approach to the teaching of reading.* New York: Harper and Row.

Staver, J. (1989). A summary of research in science education. *Science Education, 70*(3), 245–341.

Stenhouse, L. (1975). *An introduction to curriculum research and development.* London: Heinemann.

Stenhouse, L. (1980). *Curriculum research and development in action.* London: Heinemann.

Sternberg, R. (1986a). *Intelligence applied: Understanding and increasing your intellectual skills.* San Diego, Calif.: Harcourt Brace Jovanovich.

Sternberg, R. (1986b). Synthesis of research on the effectiveness of intellectual skills programs. *Educational Leadership, 44,* 60–67.

Sternberg, R., & Bahna, K. (1986). Synthesis of research on the effectiveness of intellectual skills programs: Snake-oil remedies or miracle cures? *Educational Leadership, 44*(2), 60–67.

Stevens, R. J., & Slavin, R. E. (1995). The cooperative elementary school: Effects on students' achievement, attitudes, and social relations. *American Educational Research Journal, 32*(2), 321–351.

Stevenson, H. W., Lee, S., & Stigler, J. W. (1986). Mathematics achievement of Chinese, Japanese, and American children. *Science, 231,* 693–699.

Stevenson, H. W., & Stigler, J. (1992). *The learning gap.* New York: Summit Books.

Stone, C. L. (1983). A meta-analysis of advance organizer studies. *Journal of Experimental Education, 51*(4), 194–199.

Stone, J. (2001). Comment on "An open letter to Reid Lyon." *Educational Researcher, 30*(7), 31–32.

Strauss, S. (2001). Methodology, metaphors, and mental health. *Educational Researcher, 30*(7), 32–33.

Suchman, R. J. (1962). *The elementary school training program in scientific inquiry. Report to the U.S. Office of Education, Project Title VII.* Urbana: University of Illinois.

Suchman, R. J. (1964). Studies in inquiry training. In R. Ripple & V. Bookcastle (Eds.), *Piaget reconsidered.* Ithaca, N.Y.: Cornell University Press.

Suchman, R. J. (1981). *Idea book for geological inquiry.* Chicago: Trillium Press.

Sullivan, E. (1967). *Piaget and the school curriculum: A critical appraisal.* (Bulletin No. 2.) Toronto: Ontario Institute for Studies in Education.

Sullivan, E. V. (1984). *A critical psychology: Interpretations of the personal world.* New York: Plenum.

Swanson, H., & Hoskyn, M. (1998). Experimental intervention research on students with learning disabilities: A meta-analysis of treatment outcomes. *Review of Educational Research, 68*(3), 277–321.

Taba, H. (1966). *Teaching strategies and cognitive functioning in elementary school children.* (Cooperative Research Project 2404.) San Francisco: San Francisco State College.

Taba, H. (1967). *Teacher's handbook for elementary school social studies.* Reading, Mass.: Addison-Wesley.

Taber, J., Glaser, R., & Halmuth, H. S. (1967). *Learning and programmed instruction.* Reading, Mass.: Addison-Wesley.

Taylor, C. (Ed.). (1964). *Creativity: Progress and potential.* New York: McGraw-Hill.

Temple, C., Nathan, R., Temple, F., & Burris, N. (1993). *The beginnings of writing.* Boston: Allyn & Bacon.

Tennyson, R. D., & Cocchiarella, M. (1986). An empirically based instructional design theory for teaching concepts. *Review of Educational Research, 56,* 40–71.

Thelen, H. (1954). *Dynamics of groups at work.* Chicago: University of Chicago Press.

Thelen, H. (1960). *Education and the human quest.* New York: Harper & Row.

Thelen, H. (1981). *The classroom society: The construction of education.* N.Y.: Halsted Press.

Thoreson, C. (Ed.). (1973). *Behavior modification in education.* Chicago: University of Chicago Press.

Thorndike, E. L. (1911). Animal intelligence: An experimental study of the associative process in animals. In *Psychological Review, 8*(Suppl. 2). New York: Macmillan.

Thorndike, E. L. (1913). *The psychology of learning: Vol. II. Educational psychology.* New York: Teachers College.

Thorson, A. (2002). More from the education trust. *ENC Focus, 9*(4), 32.

Tobias, S. (1993). *Overcoming math anxiety.* New York: Norton.

Tobin, K. (1986). Effects of teacher wait time on discourse characteristics in mathematics and language arts classes. *American Educational Research Journal, 23*(2), 191–200.

Torrance, E. P. (1962). *Guiding creative talent.* Englewood Cliffs, N.J.: Prentice-Hall.

Torrance, E. P. (1965). *Gifted children in the classroom.* New York: Macmillan.

"The Urban Simulator." (1972). Washington, D.C.: Washington Center for Metropolitan Studies.

Urdan, T., Midgley, C., and Anderman, E. (1998). The role of classroom goal structure in students' use of self-handicapping strategies. *American Educational Research Journal, 35*(1), 101–102.

U.S. Department of Education. (1986). *What works: Research about teaching and learning.* Washington, D.C.: U.S. Department of Education.

U.S. Department of Education. (1998). *NAEP Facts, 3*(1), 1.

Useem, E. (1990). "You're good, but you're not good enough." *American Educator, 14*(3), 24–46.

Vance, V. S., & Schlechty, P. C. (1982). The distribution of academic ability in the teaching force: Policy implications. *Phi Delta Kappan, 64*(1), 22–27.

Varenhorst, B. B. (1968). The life career game: Practice in decision-making. In S. Boocock & E. O. Schild (Eds.), *Simulating games in learning.* Beverly Hills, Calif.: Sage.

Vellutino, F., & Scanlon, D. (2001). Emergent literacy skills, early instruction, and individual differences as determinants of difficulties in learning to read: The case for early intervention. In S. Neuman & D. Dickinsons (Eds.), *Handbook of early literacy research* (pp. 295–321). New York: Guilford.

Voss, B. A. (1982). *Summary of research in science education.* Columbus, Oh.: ERIC Clearinghouse for Science, Mathematics, and Environmental Education.

Wade, N. (2002, June 18). Scientist at work/Kari Stefansson: Hunting for disease genes in Iceland's genealogies. *The New York Times,* p. 4.

Wadsworth, B. (1978). *Piaget for the classroom teacher.* New York: Longman.

Walberg, H. J. (1985). *Why Japanese educational productivity excels.* Paper presented at the annual meeting of the American Educational Research Association, Chicago.

Walberg, H. J. (1986). What works in a nation still at risk. *Educational Leadership, 44*(1), 7–11.

Walberg, H. J. (1990). Productive teaching and instruction: Assessing the knowledge base. *Phi Delta Kappan, 71*(6), 70–78.

Wallace, R. C., Lemahieu, P. G., & Bickel, W. E. (1990). The Pittsburgh experience: Achieving commitment to comprehensive staff development. In B. Joyce (Ed.), *Changing school culture through staff development.* Alexandria, Va.: Association for Supervision and Curriculum Development.

Wasik, B. A., & Slavin, R. E. (1993). Preventing early reading failure with one-to-one tutoring: A review of five programs. *Reading Research Quarterly, 28*(2).

Waterman, F. (1977). *Interviews.* (ISTE Report No. 4.) Syracuse, N.Y.: National Dissemination Center in Education, Syracuse University.

Watson, J. B. (1916). The place of conditioned reflex in psychology. *Psychological Review, 23*, 89–116.

Watson, J. B., & Rayner, R. (1921). Conditioned emotional reactions. *Journal of Experimental Psychology, 3*, 1–14.

Webster's New Collegiate Dictionary. (1975). Springfield, Mass.: G. & C. Merriam.

Weikart, D., et al. (1971). *The cognitively oriented curriculum: A framework for pre-school teachers.* Washington, D.C.: National Association for Education of Young Children.

Weil, M., Marshalek, B., Mittman, A., Murphy, J., Hallinger, P., & Pruyn, J. (1984). *Effective and typical schools: How different are they?* Paper presented at the annual meeting of the American Educational Research Association, New Orleans.

Weiler, H. (1983). Hunter's model and its effects on students. *Journal of Educational Research, 78*, 325–337.

Weinstein, G., & Fantini, M. (Eds.). (1970). *Toward humanistic education: A curriculum of affect.* New York: Praeger.

Weiss, I. R. (1978). *Report of the 1977 national survey of science, social science, and mathematics education. National Science Foundation.* Washington, D.C.: U.S. Government Printing Office.

Wentzel, K. (1991). Social competence at school: Relation between social responsibility and academic achievement. *Review of Educational Research, 61*(1), 1–24.

Wertheimer, M. (1945). *Productive thinking.* New York: Harper.

White, B. Y. (1993). ThinkerTools: Causal models, conceptual change, and science education. *Cognition and Instruction, 10*(1), 1–100.

White, W. A. T. (1986). *The effects of direct instruction in special education: A meta-analysis.* Ph.D. thesis, University of Oregon.

Whitehead, A. (1929). *The aims of education.* New York: Macmillan.

Wing, R. (1965). *Two computer-based economic games for sixth graders.* Yorktown Heights, N.Y.: Board of Cooperative Educational Services, Center for Educational Services and Research.

Wittrock, M. C., & Alesandrini, K. (1990). Generation of summaries and analogies and analytic and holistic abilities. *American Educational Research Journal, 27*(3), 489–502.

Wolfe, P., & Brandt, R. (1998). What do we know from brain research? *Educational Leadership, 56*(3), 8–13.

Wolpe, J. (1969). *The practice of behavior therapy.* Oxford: Pergamon Press.

Wolpe, J., & Lazarus, A. (1966). *Behavior therapy techniques: A guide to the treatment of neuroses.* Oxford: Pergamon Press, Inc.

Wolpe, J., & Wolpe, D. (1981). *Our useless fears.* Boston: Houghton Mifflin.

Wood, K., & Tinajero, J. (2002, May). Using pictures to teach content to second language learners. *Middle School Journal,* 47–51.

Worthen, B. (1968). A study of discovery and expository presentation: Implications for teaching. *Journal of Teacher Education, 19,* 223–242.

Young, D. (1971). Team learning: An experiment in instructional method as related to achievement. *Journal of Research in Science Teaching, 8,* 99–103.

Ziegler, S. (1981). The effectiveness of cooperative learning teams for increasing cross-ethnic friendship: Additional evidence. *Human Organization, 40,* 264–268.

Zuckerman, D. W., & Horm, R. E. (1970). *The guide to simulation games for education and training.* Cambridge, Mass.: Information Resources.

Zumwalt, K. (Ed.). (1986). *Improving teaching: 1986 yearbook of the Association for Supervision and Curriculum Development.* Washington, D.C.: Association for Supervision and Curriculum Development.

INDEX

Academic learning time (ALT), 314
Academic reform movement, 419
Academic self-esteem, 423–424
Ackerson, G. A., 415
Active consumers, 287–288
Adams, A. H., 83
Adams, O., 423
Adaptation of teaching models
    to age level of students, 126–127
    inquiry training, 126–127
    to learning environment, 127–128
    to learning styles of students, 337–350
    marginality of learners and, 344
    to personality of students, 337–350
Adey, P., 416
Advance organizers, 13, 26, 29, 37, 187–201
    application of, 199–200
    instructional and nurturant effects of, 200
    model of teaching, 196–199, 201
    orientation to, 189–195
    peer coaching guide, 429–432
    research on, 415–416
    scenarios, 187–189
    summary chart, 201
Age level
    adaption of inquiry training to, 126–127
    overage beginning reader, 371–376
Ahlbrand, W., 411
Airasian, P. W., 314
Alfasi, M., 16
Allington, R., 371
Almy, M., 419, 420
Alport, E., 420
Ames, W., 415
Analogies, in synectics, 159, 164–165, 166, 445
Anderman, E., 360, 424

Anderson, L. M., 315, 372, 380
Anderson, Richard, 26, 372, 380
Anthony, H. M., 372, 380
Antil, L., 415
Applebee, A., 357, 409
Aptitude, concept of, 303–304
Aquinas, Thomas, 204
Aristotle, 12–13, 144, 204, 216
Aronson, 29
Aspy, D. N., 32, 265, 266, 423
Associations, 144–145
Atkinson, R. C., 139, 416, 417
Attributes
    in concept attainment model, 62–63, 66–68, 69
    in direct instruction, 319
    multiple, 67–68, 69
    types of, 66–68
Attribute value, 66–67
Austin, G. A., 27, 62
Ausubel, David P., 26, 29, 187–194, 197, 415
Average, 404
Awareness, memorization and, 145

Baer, J., 181
Bahna, K., 420
Ball, S., 408
Bandura, Albert, 34, 297
Bangert-Drowns, R. L., 310
Banks, J. A., 367–368
Barnes, B. R., 415
Barr, T., 420
Bascones, J., 195, 416
Baveja, Bharati, 69, 210, 402–404
Beady, C. H., 359
Becker, Wes, 34, 297, 298, 321, 360, 418, 421

Behavioral modification, 33
Behavioral systems family of models,
    295–334
  direct instruction, 34, 313–322
  history of, 296–297
  learning environment and, 295–296,
    305–306
  learning style and, 338
  mastery learning, 33–34, 303–311
  principles of, 297–299
  programmed learning, 33–34, 310–311
  research on, 421–423
  simulation, 34–35, 323–334, 421
  social learning, 33, 34, 421
Behavior therapy, 33
Bereiter, Carl, 34, 420
Berger, P., 218
Berliner, D. C., 314–316
Berry, J., 417
Bickel, W. E., 360
Bielinski, J., 365
Biological Sciences Curriculum (BSC)
    study, 27, 28, 104–111
Bishop, S., 417
Block, James W., 34, 315
Blocks to learning, 298
Bloom, Benjamin S., 33, 34, 303, 304, 343,
    348, 408
Bode, Boyd, 217
Bogatz, G. A., 408
Bolvin, J. O., 305–308
Bonsangue, M., 414
Boocock, S. S., 421
Boutwell, Clinton, 192
Branching programs, 311
Brandwein, P., 418
Bredderman, T., 36–37, 46, 115, 419,
    421
Brenner, M., 420
British Open University, 408
Brookover, W., 359
Brooks, J. G., 420
Brooks, M. G., 420
Brophy, Jere E., 34, 314–316
Brown, A., 15–16
Brown, C., 266, 284, 291, 340
Brown, M., 308
Bruce, J. K., 127
Bruce, W. C., 127
Brunel, March Isumbard, 165

Bruner, Jerome, 26, 27, 62, 65–66, 74, 118,
    191, 418
Buhler, J., 266, 423
Burkham, D., 365, 420
Burns, M., 378
Burris, N., 379
Burry, J., 401
Bush, R., 284, 290

Calderon, Margarita, 29, 414
Calhoun, Emily F., 3, 20, 26, 27, 30, 47, 77,
    81–83, 96, 97, 284, 360, 372, 373, 379,
    380, 381, 401
California Staff Development Study,
    284–293
Campbell, E. Q., 359
Campbell, F., 360
Campbell, J., 355, 356
Canadian Tests of Basic Skills, 374
Carnine, D., 297, 298, 321
Carpenter, T., 365
Carran, N., 47
Carroll, John B., 303, 304, 343, 348
Categorical cues, 138
Categorical differences, 351–369
  cultural, 361–363, 364
  data on, 352–359
  educational opportunity and, 365
  ethnic and racial, 354–359, 361–363,
    367–369
  gender, 352–359, 363–366
  scenarios, 367–369
  socioeconomic status, 7–9, 354–359, 363
Causal reasoning, 345
Central tendencies, 404–410
Chaining, 390, 391, 394, 398
Chall, J. S., 83
Chamberlin, C., 30, 32, 216, 265, 413
Chamberlin, E., 30, 32, 216, 265, 413
Change, in instruction methods, 7–9
Chapter I programs, 359–360
Checking for understanding (CFU), 319
Chesler, Mark, 233–235, 243, 246
Clark, E. V., 83
Clark, H. H., 83
Classification, 50, 390, 392, 394, 399
Classroom level, gender at, 365–366
Classroom rules, 422
Classrooms, open, 223
Clausen, E. U., 415

Coaching, in simulation, 330
Cocchiarella, M., 26, 27, 70
Cognitive development, 395–396
Cognitive structures, 189–193
　organizing information and, 190–193, 198
　synectics and, 189–190, 198
Cohen, D., 362
Cohen, Elizabeth, 29, 360, 413
Coker, H., 315
Coleman, J. S., 359
College attendance, gender gap and,
　352–353
Collins, K., 118, 418
Comenius, John Amos, 204, 216
Comparative organizers, 195
Compressed conflict, 165, 166
Concept attainment model, 26, 27, 59–76
　application of, 73–74
　attributes in, 62–63, 66–68, 69
　exemplars in, 62–71
　instructional and nurturant effects of,
　　74–76
　memorization and, 140
　model of teaching, 71–73, 75
　peer coaching guide, 448–453
　research on, 70–71
　scenarios, 59–62, 64–65
　student strategies for concept
　　attainment, 68–71
　summary chart, 76
　varieties of performance and, 394
Concept formation
　in concept attainment model, 62–68
　in inductive-thinking model, 52
Conceptual development, 290–291, 396
Conceptual systems theory, 284
　conceptual development and, 290–291
　discomfort in learning and, 340–341
　levels of integrative complexity, 395–396
　self-concept and, 291–292
Condition questions, 123
Conditions of learning, 389–400
Conflict management, 413–414
Conjunctive concepts, 68
Connors, J. M., 83
Connotative language, 188
Constructivism, 12–13
　inquiry building inquirers, 420–421
　metacognition and, 14, 15–16
　scientific inquiry and, 420

Control groups, 403
Cooper, H., 359
Cooperative learning, 37, 396. See also
　Group investigation model; Partners
　in learning
　peer coaching guide, 433–436
　research on, 412–414
　through the school, 413–414
Cooperative set, 207
Counterconditioning, 296, 299–300
Counts, George, 217
Covert behavior, 327
Creativity, 26, 28, 37–38, 162–163, 179–181
Criterion-referenced tests, 412
Critical thinking, 198, 199
Culture
　constructivism and, 13
　enculturation process, 343
　equity and, 361–363
　language and, 361–363
　learning environment and, 344
　marginality in learners and, 347
Curriculum
　classes of learning in, 397–400
　conditions of learning and, 389–400
　designing for early literacy, 380–381
　direct instruction and, 320–321
　functions of instructor in, 392–396
　implications of advance organizers for,
　　193
　multidimensional, 371–376, 386–387
　objectives and, 20
　planning a course, 394–396
　role playing in, 243–245
　synectics in, 177–179, 193
Cybernetics, 33, 326–327

Dale, P., 84–85
Data collection, 49–51
Data enumeration, 50
Data examination, 50
Data interpretation, 470–472
Data presentation, 49–51
Davis, J. C., III, 75
Davison, M., 365
Delaney, H. D., 28, 36, 38, 137, 139, 417,
　458
Democratic process, in group
　investigation, 216–219
Dennis-Rounds, J., 139

Denotative language, 188
Desensitization, 300
Developmentally appropriate practice, 378
Dewey, John, 13, 24–25, 29, 30, 204,
    215–217, 219
Dickinson, D., 417
Direct analogy, 165, 166, 173
Direct instruction, 34, 313–322
    application of, 320–321
    instructional and nurturant effects of,
        320–321
    learning environment for, 314
    model of teaching, 318–320, 321–322
    orientation to, 314–317
    practice theory, 317–318
    summary chart, 321–322
Discussing, in simulation, 330
Dishaw, M. M., 314–316
Disjunctive concepts, 68
DISTAR version of social learning theory,
    421
Division of labor, in partners in learning,
    213
Dolan, L., 360, 408–409
Donahue, P., 355, 356
Dorr, N., 359
Dossey, J., 358
Duit, R., 420
Duke, N., 372, 380
Dunn, K., 284
Dunn, R., 284
Duran, R., 420
Durham, E. I. P., 421
Dyads. *See also* Partners in learning
Dynamic disequilibrium, 342

Early Literacy Tutorial, 374
Eastman, P., 84–85
Educational opportunity, 365
Effective teachers, 7–9, 313, 315–316. *See
    also* Direct instruction
Effect size, 139–140, 402–410
    concept of, 402–404
    further inquiry into, 404–410
Efficiency, of partners in learning,
    211–212
Ehri, L. C., 20, 85, 372, 380
Eisner, Eliot, 101
Elefant, E., 118, 418
Elkind, D., 378

Elliot, T., 14
El-Nemr, M. A., 36, 46, 115, 419
Emergent literacy, 378
Enculturation, 343
Engelmann, S., 297, 298, 321
Engleman, Ziggy, 34
Englert, C. S., 372, 380
Episodic cues, 138
Equity, 351–369. *See also* Scientific inquiry
    cultural, 361–363
    data on categorical differences, 352–359
    educational opportunity and, 365
    ethnic and racial, 354–359, 361–363,
        367–369
    gender, 352–359, 363–366
    scenarios, 367–369
    socioeconomic status, 354–359, 363
Erikson, E., 284, 339
Ertner, P. A., 180, 424
Essential attributes, 66–67
Estes, W. E., 137, 297
Ethnicity and race, 361–363
    categories, 352
    high school graduation and, 353–354
    literacy and, 354–355
    mathematics and science and, 358–359
    reading and, 357
    social studies and, 358
    writing and, 357–358
Event questions, 123
Evertson, C. M., 315
Exemplars, in concept attainment model,
    62–71
Experimental groups, 403, 417
Expert performance, 20–21
Explaining, in simulation, 329
Expository organizers, 195

Feedback
    in direct instruction, 316–317, 318
    in simulations, 326–327
Feeley, T., 418
Fennema, E., 365
Filby, N. N., 314–316
Fisher, C., 314–316
Fitzgerald, J., 420
Flexibility of learners, 344, 347–349
Flood, P. K., 359
Foertsch, M., 409
Ford, M. J., 75

Formal staff development, 286
Fox, Robert, 104, 112, 113, 233–235, 243, 246
Franke, M., 365
Franklin, Benjamin, 204
Fraser, B., 420
Fuchs, D., 414–415
Fuchs, L., 414–415

Gabel, D. L., 36
Gage, N. L., 316
Gagné, Robert N., 75, 336, 389, 394
Garner, R., 372, 380
Gaskins, I., 14, 377
Gates-McGinnitie battery, 374
Gender
    academic self-esteem and, 424
    college attendance and, 352–353
    equity and, 352–359, 363–366
    high school graduation and, 353–354
    literacy and, 354–355
    mathematics and science and, 353, 358–359, 364–365. See also Scientific inquiry
    reading and, 355–357
    Read to Succeed and, 376
    social studies and, 358
    writing and, 357–358
Gerbner, George, 50, 364
Gersten, R., 360, 418, 421
Ghatala, E., 417
Ghen, L. S., 314–316
Giese, J. R., 260
Glade, M. E., 260
Glass, G. V., 402
Glynn, S. M., 181, 424
Goals
    of advance organizers, 189–190
    behavioral, 298
    of direct instruction, 313
    of group investigation, 219–221
    of inquiry training, 118–119
    of jurisprudential inquiry, 251–252
    of memorization, 138, 162–163
    of nondirective teaching, 271–273
    of partners in learning, 213–214
    of role playing, 233–234
Goffman, Irving, 49–50
Good, Tom, 34
Goodlad, J., 411

Goodnow, J. J., 27, 62
Gordon, William J. J., 26, 28, 155, 158, 163–165, 167–173, 179, 424
Grammar, in Picture-Word Inductive Model (PWIM), 98
Graves, B., 85
Graves, M., 85
Greenwald, G. D., 260
Greenwood, J., 54, 341
Gregorc, A. F., 284
Griffin, P., 378
Group investigation model, 7–9, 29, 30, 214–227, 338–339, 405–406
    application of, 223–225
    instructional and nurturant effects of, 225–226
    model of teaching, 222–223, 226–227
    orientation to, 219–225
    philosophical underpinnings of, 217–219
    scenarios, 5–6, 214–215
    summary chart, 226–227
Growth
    concept of state of, 285
    discomfort in learning and, 338–342
    intelligence of, 349–350
    nondirective teaching and, 272–273
    self-concept and, 292–293
    states of, 286–287, 292–293
Guetzkow, Harold, 328
Guided practice, in direct instruction, 319
Gunning, T., 382
Gunning framework, 384–385
Guthrie, L., 420

Halberstam, David, 229, 369
Halliburton, C., 47
Harootunian, Berj, 303
Harvey, O. J., 18, 284, 290, 339
Head Start, 321
Heller, M., 379
Herman, P., 380
Herrnstein, R., 360
Hersh, R., 161–162, 284
Hershey, M., 417
Hertz-Lazarowitz, Rachel, 204, 224, 412, 414, 433
High school graduation, ethnicity and, 353–354
Hillocks, George, 46, 409, 421
Hobson, C. J., 359

Hoetker, J., 411
Holistic strategies, 68
Holobec, E., 208
Home level, gender at, 364–365
Hopkins, David, 30, 284, 288, 292, 360, 401
Hrycauk, M., 27, 379
Huhtala, J., 224–225
Hullfish, Gordon H., 217–218
Human Development Report CD-ROM
    2000, The United Nations
    Development Program, 205–206
Hunt, D. E., 18, 54, 226–227, 284, 290,
    291, 339, 340, 341, 346, 347
Hunter, Ian, 152–153
Hyde, J., 366
Hypothesis formation
    in concept attainment, 450–451
    in inductive-thinking model, 50–51
    in inquiry training, 120

Independent practice, in direct
    instruction, 319
Individual differences
    adapting instruction to, 126–127,
        337–350
    in age-level of students, 126–127
    categorical differences versus, 351
    in learning styles, 284, 337–350
    operational objectives and, 395–396
    in personality, 284
    in relating to learning environments,
        348–349
Individually Prescribed Instruction (IPI),
    304–308
Individuation, 344
Inductive-thinking model, 26, 27, 41–58,
    207
    application of, 52
    concept formation in, 52
    instructional and nurturant effects of,
        56–58
    model of teaching, 57–58
    orientation to, 44–46
    peer coaching guide, 467–472
    research on, 46–48
    scenarios, 4, 41–44, 52–54
    summary chart, 58
    teaching strategy and, 51, 54–56
Industrial solution, marginality in learners
    and, 346

Information-processing family of models,
    26–29, 39–201
    advance organizers, 13, 26, 29, 37,
        187–201, 415–416, 429–432
    concept attainment, 26, 27, 59–76,
        448–453
    inductive thinking, 26, 27, 41–58,
        467–472
    inquiry training, 3–4, 26, 28, 116–130,
        344–345, 454–457
    learning style and, 338
    memorization, 26, 28, 131–154,
        416–418, 458–462
    operational objectives and, 396
    overview, 39
    Picture-Word Inductive Model (PWIM),
        26, 27, 37, 77–99, 210, 373–374
    research on, 415–421
    scientific inquiry, 26, 27–28, 103–116,
        418–420
    synectics, 26, 28, 37–38, 155–186, 396,
        424–425, 443–447
Inquiry, 401–425
    on behavioral models, 421–423
    concept of effect size, 402–410
    on cooperative learning models,
        412–414
    in group investigation, 220, 221,
        224
    on information-processing models,
        415–421
    into models of teaching, 411
    on personal models, 423–425
    scenarios, 401–402, 409
    surveying the knowledge base, 410–
        411
    teacher, 425
Inquiry training, 3–4, 26, 28, 116–130
    application of, 124–125
    instructional and nurturant effects of,
        128–129
    learning environment and, 344–345
    marginality in learners and, 345
    model of teaching, 121–124, 128–130
    orientation to, 118–121
    peer coaching guide, 454–457
    research on, 117–118
    scenarios, 3–4, 116–117, 125–126
    summary chart, 128–129
    varieties of performance and, 394

Integrative complexity, 395
Integrative reconciliation, 193
Intellectual capacity, as temporal factor, 343
Intellectual scaffolding, 140, 188, 190, 430
Intellectual structure, 195
Interaction, in Picture-Word Inductive Model (PWIM), 82
Interpretation, in nondirective teaching, 274
Invitations to Enquiry (BSC study), 106–111
Isenberg, John, 260
Israel, group investigation model in, 7–9, 412
Itchy students, 422
Ivany, G., 118, 418

Jacklin, C., 366
Jacobs, V., 365
Jefferson, Thomas, 204
Jenkins, J., 415
Jenkins, L., 409
Jigsaw, 213
Johnson, David W., 29, 30, 204, 208, 209, 211–213, 224, 412–414, 433
Johnson, M. S., 83
Johnson, Roger T., 29, 30, 204, 208, 209, 211–213, 224, 412–414, 433
Johnson, S., 224
Jones, Howard, 26
Jovanovic, J., 365
Joyce, Bruce, 3, 23, 26, 27, 29, 30, 32, 37, 47, 54–56, 59, 69, 77, 79, 82, 97, 131, 132, 155, 161–162, 187, 205, 210, 266, 283, 284, 288, 290, 291, 303, 313, 323, 337–341, 348, 360, 372, 373, 379, 382, 401, 412, 421
Judd, Charles Hubbard, 217
Juel, C., 374, 378
Jurisprudential inquiry, 29, 31, 230, 249–263, 396
  application of, 259–261
  instructional and nurturant effects of, 261
  model of teaching, 256–259, 262–263
  orientation to, 251–256
  peer coaching guide, 437–442
  scenarios, 4–5, 249–250
  Socratic dialogue in, 252
  summary chart, 262–263
  values conflict and, 251–252, 254–256
  values framework and, 253–256
Just Read, 373

Kagan, S., 208, 211–212
Kahle, J., 365
Kaiser Elementary School (Costa Mesa, California), 409–410
Karplus, R., 420
Karweit, N., 360, 408–409
Kellaghan, T., 314
Key-word system, memorization and, 149
Kilpatrick, William Heard, 217
Kindergarten, Picture-Word Inductive Model (PWIM) and, 377–387
King, S., 365
Klein, F., 411
Klein, S., 365–366
Klopfer, L. E., 111
Knowledge, surveying knowledge base, 410–411
Knowles, M., 284
Kober, N., 420
Kramarski, B., 420
Kulik, C. C., 310
Kulik, J. A., 310
Kyle, W., 420

Labeling, 300
Langer, J., 409
Language
  connotative, 188
  denotative, 188
  equity and, 361–363
  in Picture-Word Inductive Model (PWIM), 83–84
Language laboratory, 309–310
Larkins, G., 75
Lawton, J. T., 26, 195, 415
Lazarus, R., 421
Lazer, S., 358
Lead-taking responses, 273–275
Learning communities. See also Social family of models
  inductive-thinking model, 45–46
  nature of, 10–11
  scenarios, 3–6, 10–11
Learning deficits, 298, 299–300

Learning environment
  adaptation of inquiry training to,
    127–128
  in behavioral systems family of models,
    295–296, 305–306
  conceptual levels and, 18–19, 340
  for direct instruction, 314
  for inductive-thinking model, 51
  marginality and, 344–345
  models of teaching and, 24–26
  optimal, 18–20
  orientations toward, 286–287
Learning histories, of students, 36
Learning skills, 411
Learning styles, 25
  adaptation of teaching models for,
    337–350
  discomfort and, 338–342
  flexibility training and, 344, 347–349
  individual differences in, 284,
    337–350
  marginality in learners and, 342
Lee, V., 365
Legal-ethical framework, 253–254
Lemahieu, P. G., 360
Letters/sounds, in Picture-Word Inductive
    Model (PWIM), 85–86, 383, 392
Levi, L., 365
Levin, Joel R., 26, 28, 36, 38, 137, 139,
    140, 149, 360, 411, 417, 458
Levin, Malcolm E., 28, 38, 140, 260, 360,
    411
Lewin, T., 352
Lighthall, Fred, 26
Lindvall, C. M., 305–308
Link-word method, 38, 138–143, 145–146,
    151–152, 417
Linn, M., 366
Lippitt, Ronald, 104, 112, 113
Literacy, 354–355
  action research on, 371–387
  inquiry into early, 379–380
  in language, 362
  in primary grades, 377–379
Livermon, B. J., 360, 408–409
Locke, John, 204, 216
Lorayne, H., 28, 144–146
Lucas, J., 28, 144–146
Luckmann, T., 218
Luiten, J., 415

Maccoby, E., 366
Madaus, G. F., 314
Madden, N. A., 360, 408–409
Magnitude of effects, 408
Mainstream society, 361
Maloney, D., 195
Marcus Aurelius, 204
Marginality in learners
  assumptions about learners, 342
  assumptions about learning
    environments, 343–344
  dealing with, 345
  solutions for correcting, 346–349
Marliave, R., 314–316
Marsh, H., 423–424
Maruyama, G., 224
Maslow, Abraham, 32, 284, 290, 291, 339
Masters, J. C., 297
Mastery learning, 33–34, 303–311
  aptitude in, 303–304
  Individually Prescribed Instruction
    (IPI), 304–308
  language laboratory, 309–310
  programmed instruction, 33–34,
    310–311
Mastropieri, M. A., 139–140, 150
Mathematics and science. See also
    Scientific inquiry
  ethnicity and race and, 358–359
  gender equity, 353, 358–359, 364–365
  Individually Prescribed Instruction
    (IPI), 304–308
  math anxiety, 300
  NAEP findings, 358–359
  in Picture-Word Inductive Model
    (PWIM), 82
  scientific inquiry and, 418–419, 420
Mathes, P., 414–415
Mayer, R., 420
Mazzeo, J., 358
McCarthy, B., 284
McCormick, C., 417
McGill-Franzen, A., 371
McKibbin, Mike, 131, 161–162, 284, 288,
    290, 339, 360
McKinney, C., 75
McPortland, J., 359
Mean, 404–405
Meaning, in Picture-Word Inductive Model
    (PWIM), 82

Mechanics, in Picture-Word Inductive Model (PWIM), 98
Median, 404–405
Medley, D. M., 315
Meister, C., 16
Memorization, 26, 28, 131–154
    application of, 150–152
    concepts about memory and, 144–149
    instructional and nurturant effects of, 152–153
    link-word method, 38, 138–143, 145–146, 151–152, 417
    model of teaching, 149–150, 154
    orientation to, 138–149
    other memory-assist systems, 144–149
    peer coaching guide, 458–462
    research on, 138–140, 416–418
    scenarios, 131–137
    summary chart, 154
    varieties of performance and, 394
Merrill, M. D., 75
Metacognition, 14, 15–16
Metaphoric activity, 165–166
    compressed conflict, 165, 166
    direct analogy, 165, 166, 173
    personal analogy, 163–165, 166
    stretching exercises, 165–166
Metz, K. E., 28, 115
Mevarech, Z., 420
Michaelis, John U., 219
Michigan Social Science Curriculum Project, 104, 112–113
Midgley, C., 360, 424
Miller, G., 139, 417
Miller, K., 358
Mnemonics, 138–143, 411, 416–418. See also Memorization
Mode, 405
Models of learning. See Models of teaching
Models of teaching, 7, 23–38. See also Behavioral systems family of models; Information-processing family of models; Personal family of models; Social family of models
    applications of, 371–387
    concepts applied to, 12–21
    guidelines for using, 21–22
    learning environments, 24–26
    scenario, 23–24
    using teaching repertoire, 35–38

Mood, A. M., 359
Moore, J., 358
More, Thomas, 216
Morine, G., 348
Moseley, B., 420
Motilal Nehru School of Sports (India), 402–404
Motivation, 214, 423
Mullis, I., 409
Multidimensional curriculum, 371–376, 386–387
Multiple attributes, 67–68, 69
Multiple discrimination, 390, 391, 394, 398–399
Murphy, Carlene, 210, 283, 360
Murphy, J., 210, 360
Murray, C., 360

Nagy, W., 372, 380
Nathan, R., 379
National Assessment of Educational Progress (NAEP), 354–359, 371–372
National Assessment of Writing Progress, 409
National Research Council (NRC), 378–379
National Training Laboratory, 219
Negative reinforcement, 299–300
Neill, A. S., 32, 265
Nelson, D., 224
Nesbitt, W. A., 332
Newby, T. J., 180, 424
Nondirective teaching, 31–32, 267–282
    application of, 277–280
    growth and, 272–273
    instructional and nurturant effects of, 280–281
    model of teaching, 275–277, 281–282
    orientation to, 271–275
    research on, 423–425
    scenarios, 267–270
    summary chart, 281–282
Novak, J., 195, 416
Noy, J., 54, 341
Numbered heads, 211–212

Oakes, J., 409
Objectives, role of expert performance in selecting, 20–21
Object questions, 123

Offer, J., 28, 365, 420
Off-task behavior, 422
Oliver, Donald, 29, 31, 250–252, 255, 259
Ontario Institute for Studies in Education, 260
Open classrooms, 223
Operant conditioning, 299–300
Optimal environments, 18–20
O'Sullivan, C., 358
Overage beginning reader, teaching models for, 371–376
Overt behavior, 327

Palincsar, A., 15–16
Parker, L., 28, 365, 420
Partistic strategies, 68
Partners in learning, 29, 30, 205–227. *See also* Group investigation model
    positive interdependence, 29, 412
    purposes and assumptions of, 208–210
    scenarios, 205–208
    training for cooperation in, 211–214
Passive consumers, 288–289
Pavlov, I., 296
Pearson, D., 378
Pearson, P. D., 372, 380
Peck, L., 266, 284, 291, 340
Percentiles, 404
Perls, Fritz, 23
Persistence, 288
Persky, H., 358
Personal analogy, 163–166
Personal family of models, 31–32, 265–311
    learning style and, 338
    nondirective teaching, 31–32, 267–282, 423–425
    overview, 265–266
    research on, 423–425
    self-concept, 32, 33, 283–293, 396, 423–424
Personality
    adaptation of social models for, 337–350
    individual differences in, 284
Phillips, G., 356
Phonics, in Picture-Word Inductive Model (PWIM), 80, 98
Piaget, Jean, 17, 339
Picture-Word Inductive Model (PWIM), 26, 27, 37, 77–99, 210, 310, 373–374
    application in kindergarten, 377–387

development of, 81–82
instructional and nurturant effects of, 98–99
peer coaching guide, 473–478
research on, 81, 83–87, 377–387
scenarios, 77–81, 88–96
structure of, 87–96, 97–99
Pinnell, G. S., 372, 409
Plato, 12–13, 204, 216
Pollack, Gertrude K., 223
Positive interdependence, 29, 412
Poze, T., 179, 424
Presentational methods. *See* Advance organizers
Pressley, Michael, 14, 26, 28, 36, 38, 137, 139, 149, 372, 380, 417, 458
Principle of optimal mismatch, 16–17
Problem solving, 391, 392, 394, 399–400. *See also* Role playing; Synectics
Programmed learning, 33–34, 310–311
Progressive differentiation, 193
Progressive Education Association, 204
Progressive Movement, 413
Project Follow Through, 321
Property questions, 123
Public policy issues, 252–253
Punishment, 299

Quellmalz, E. S., 401

Race. *See* Ethnicity and race
Raghavan, K., 111
Ragosta, M., 314, 316
Ramey, C., 360
Range, 404
Raphael, T. E., 380
Rayner, R., 296–297
Reaction
    in advance organizers, 199, 201
    in concept attainment model, 73, 76
    in direct instruction, 320
    in group investigation, 223, 226–227
    in inductive-thinking model, 51, 58
    in inquiry training, 124, 130
    in jurisprudential inquiry, 258–259, 262–263
    in memorization, 150, 154
    in nondirective teaching, 277, 281
    in role playing, 242–243, 249
    in scientific inquiry, 112, 115

in simulation, 332, 334
in synectics, 177, 185
Reading, 355–357. *See also* Literacy
curriculum objectives, 20
effect size and, 408
NAEP findings, 355–357
in Picture-Word Inductive Model
(PWIM), 80–81, 84–87, 380, 384–385
reciprocal teaching of reading
comprehension, 15–16
Reading Recovery, 409
Reading wars, 377
Read to Succeed, 372–373, 374, 375–376
Reciprocal teaching, 15–16
Reed, B., 420
Reese, C., 356, 358
Refereeing, in simulation, 330
Reid, R., 54, 341
Reinforcement, 299–300
Resnick, L. B., 298–299
Retention in grade, 299–300
Reticent consumers, 289–290
Retrieval cues, 138
Reyna, J., 297
Rhine, W. R., 297, 298, 321, 418
Ridiculous association, memorization and,
146
Rimm, D. C., 297
Roebuck, F., 32, 265, 266, 423
Rogers, Carl, 31–32, 266, 267, 270–272,
275, 291, 339, 423
Role playing, 29, 30–31, 229–249, 396
application of, 243–247
instructional and nurturant effects of,
247
learning environment and, 343–344
model of teaching, 235–243, 248–249
orientation to, 233–235
peer coaching guide, 463–466
scenarios, 229–232
summary chart, 248–249
Rolheiser-Bennett, C., 412, 415
Rosenshine, B., 16, 314–317
Rousseau, Jean-Jacques, 204
Rowan, S., 420
Rule using, 390–391, 392, 394, 399
Rust, D., 47

Sadker, D., 364–365
Sadker, M., 364–365

Salter, A., 297
Samuel, J., 417
Sanders, Donald A., 179–180
Sanders, Judith A., 179–180
Scaffolding, 14–16
reciprocal teaching of reading
comprehension, 15–16
scenario, 14–15
Scaffolding, intellectual, 140, 188, 190,
430
Scanlon, M., 372, 373
Scanlon, R., 308
Schaible, L., 104, 113
Schaubel, L., 111
Schild, E., 421
Schnaubelt, C., 372, 373
Schneider, J. M., 359
School level, gender at, 365
Schrenker, G., 418
Schroeder, H., 18, 284, 290, 339
Schwab, Joseph J., 26, 27–28, 104–109,
111, 418
Schwitzer, J. H., 359
Science. *See* Mathematics and science
Scientific inquiry, 26, 27–28, 103–116
application of, 112–114
future of inductive models of teaching,
116
instructional and nurturant effects of,
114–115
model of teaching, 111–112, 114,
115–116
orientation to, 104–111
research on, 418–420
scenarios, 101–103
summary chart, 115–116
Scruggs, T. E., 139–140, 150
Self-actualization, 291–292, 339, 396
Self-concept, 32, 33, 283–293, 396,
423–424
conceptual systems theory and, 291–292
domains and, 285–286
growth and, 292–293
individual differences and, 284
learning environment and, 286–287
levels of activity, 287–290
Self-directed inquiry, 396
Self-esteem. *See* Self-concept
Self-instruction programs, 299, 422. *See
also* Mastery learning

Self-monitoring, 15–16
Shachar, Hana, 7–8, 30, 406
Shaftel, Fannie, 29, 31, 229, 232–243, 345, 346
Shaftel, George, 31, 232–243, 345, 346
Shakrani, S., 358
Shaping, 317–318
Sharan, Shlomo, 7–8, 29, 30, 204, 209, 214, 224, 406, 411, 412, 433
Sharan, Yael, 412
Shaver, James P., 29, 31, 250–252, 255, 259
Shayer, M., 416
Showers, Beverly, 32, 37, 69, 79, 132, 210, 284, 288, 340, 348, 360, 372, 373, 382, 412, 421
Shriberg, L., 417
Shymanski, J., 420
Sight words, in Picture-Word Inductive Model (PWIM), 80
Simmons, D., 414–415
Simser, J., 47
Simulation, 34–35, 323–334, 421
    application, 332
    instructional and nurturant effects of, 332–333
    model of teaching, 330–332, 333–334
    orientation to, 326–330
    scenario, 323–325
    summary chart, 333–334
Sirotnik, K., 203, 411
Skill-training approach, 347–349
Skinner, B. F., 33, 34, 297, 299, 310–311
Skon, L., 224
Slavin, Robert E., 29, 30, 204, 209, 210, 213, 224, 360, 408–409, 412, 433
Slavin, Robert T., 310
Smerdon, B., 365, 420
Smith, Carl, 34
Smith, K., 326–327, 421
Smith, Mary L., 34, 47, 326–327, 419, 421
Smith, Philip G., 217–218
Snow, C., 378
Soar, R. M., 314, 315, 316
Soar, R. S., 314, 316
Social family of models, 29–31, 203–263
    adaptation of, 337–350
    group investigation, 7–9, 29, 30, 214–227, 338–339, 405–406
    jurisprudential inquiry, 29, 31, 230, 249–263, 396, 437–442

learning style and, 338
    overview, 203–204
    partners in learning, 29, 30, 205–227
    rationale for, 232–233
    role playing, 29, 30–31, 229–249, 396, 463–466
Socialization, in Picture-Word Inductive Model (PWIM), 82
Social learning theory, 33, 34, 421
Social Science Education Consortium, 260
Social skills, 37
Social studies. *See also* Inquiry training; Jurisprudential inquiry
    curriculum objectives, 20
    effect size and, 408
    ethnicity and race, 358
    jurisprudential inquiry and, 260–261
    memorization and, 417
    NAEP findings, 358
    in Picture-Word Inductive Model (PWIM), 82
    synectics in, 178
Social system
    in advance organizers, 198–199, 201
    in concept attainment model, 72–73, 76
    in direct instruction, 320
    in group investigation, 222, 226
    in inductive-thinking model, 51, 58
    in inquiry training, 123–124, 129–130
    in jurisprudential inquiry, 258, 262
    in memorization, 150, 154
    in nondirective teaching, 277, 281
    in role playing, 242, 248
    in scientific inquiry, 111–112, 115
    in simulation, 331–332, 334
    in synectics, 176, 185
Societal level, gender at, 364
Socioeconomic status (SES)
    equity and, 359–361, 363
    group investigation model and, 7–9
    literacy and, 354–355
    mathematics and science and, 359
    reading and, 356, 357
Socratic dialogue, 252
Sounds/symbols, in Picture-Word Inductive Model (PWIM), 85–86, 97–99
Spaulding, Robert L., 37, 406, 407, 421
Specialization, in partners in learning, 213

Special needs
    partners in learning and, 210
    Read to Succeed and, 376
Specific responding, 389–390, 391, 394,
    397–398
Spelling, in Picture-Word Inductive Model
    (PWIM), 86
Staff development. *See also* Teacher training
    formal, 286
    for Picture-Word Inductive Model
        (PWIM), 381–382
Standard deviation, 404–405
Standardized tests, 376, 412
Stanford University, 416–417
Stauffer, R., 372, 381
Staver, J., 365, 420
Sternberg, R., 420
Stevens, D. D., 380
Stevenson, Harold, 351
Stigler, Jay, 351
Stigmatization, 343–344
Stone, C. L., 416
Structured inquiry, 29
Structured practice, in direct instruction,
    319
Student-centered teaching. *See*
    Nondirective teaching
Students at risk, partners in learning and,
    210
Substitute-word system, memorization
    and, 146–148
Success for All, 408–409
Suchman, Richard J., 26, 28, 117–121,
    345, 418
Support system
    in advance organizers, 199, 201
    in concept attainment model, 73, 76
    in group investigation, 223, 227
    in inductive-thinking model, 51, 58
    in inquiry training, 124, 130
    in jurisprudential inquiry, 259, 263
    in memorization, 150, 154
    in nondirective teaching, 277, 282
    in role playing, 243, 249
    in scientific inquiry, 112, 116
    in simulation, 332, 334
    in synectics, 177, 185
Synectics, 26, 28, 37–38, 155–186, 396,
    424–425
    application of, 177–179

instructional and nurturant effects of,
    179–181
model of teaching, 166–177, 185–186
orientation to, 162–166
peer coaching guide, 443–447
scenarios, 155–158, 160–162, 181–184
summary chart, 185–186
varieties of performance and, 394
Synergy, 208, 338
Syntax
    in advance organizers, 196–198, 201
    in concept attainment model, 71–72, 76
    in direct instruction, 318–319
    in group investigation, 222, 226
    in inductive-thinking model, 48–51,
        57–58
    in inquiry training, 121–123, 128
    in jurisprudential inquiry, 256–258, 262
    in memorization, 149–150, 154
    in nondirective teaching, 275–277, 281
    in role playing, 235–242, 248
    in scientific inquiry, 111–112, 115
    in simulation, 330–331, 333–334
    in synectics, 166–176, 185, 186

Taba, Hilda, 26, 27, 41, 48–49, 51, 118, 418
Teacher training. *See also* Staff
    development
    discomfort in learning and, 340–341
    marginality in learners and, 347–349
Teaching strategy
    advance organizers and, 193–195
    concept formation, 52
    conditions of learning and, 389–396
    in direct instruction, 315–317
    in group investigation, 222–223
    in inductive-thinking model, 51, 54–56
    in inquiry training, 119–121
    interpretation of data, 470–472
    in nondirective teaching, 273–275
    in simulation, 329–330
    thinking processes and, 48
Temple, C., 379
Temple, F., 379
Temporal differences, 343
Tennyson, R. D., 26, 27, 70, 75
Thelen, Herbert, 29, 30, 204, 205, 219–223,
    226–227, 337–340
Thinking processes, 48
Thoresen, Carl, 34, 421

Thorndike, E. L., 296
Thorson, A., 369
Tinajero, Jusefina, 414
Tobias, Sheila, 300, 365
Training. *See also* Simulation; Teacher
    training
    behavioral practices in, 300
    for efficiency, 211–212
    for interdependence, 212
    simulations and, 323–334
Treagust, D., 420

United Kingdom, 385
U.S. Department of Education, 352, 355,
    361
University of California at Berkeley,
    365
University of California at Los Angeles,
    Center for Research on Evaluation,
    401
Urdan, T., 360, 424
Usage, in Picture-Word Inductive Model
    (PWIM), 98

Vadasy, P., 415
Values framework, 253–256. *See also* Role
    playing
    conflict of values and, 251–252, 254–256
Valuing, 256
Vandergrift, Kay, 59
Visual representation of tasks (VRTs),
    319
Vocabulary, in Picture-Word Inductive
    Model (PWIM), 80, 85, 99, 380, 383
Voelki, K., 355
Voss, B. A., 118, 418
Vygotsky, Lev, 13, 17

Wade, N., 101
Walberg, Herb, 389, 420
Wald, R., 341
Wallace, R. C., 360
Wanska, S. K., 26, 415
Warren, A., 75
Watson, J. B., 296–297
Watts, S., 85
Wayne, S., 415
Webb, D., 420
Weil, M., 54, 341
Weinfield, E. D., 359
Weiss, I. R., 365–366
Wentzel, K., 415
White, W. A. T., 421
Willson, M., 423
Wisenbaker, J. M., 359
Wolf, J., 360, 373
Wolpe, J., 297, 421
Words
    classification of, in Picture-Word
        Inductive Model (PWIM), 383–384
    retention of, in Picture-Word Inductive
        Model (PWIM), 383
Writing. *See also* Synectics
    curriculum objectives, 20, 21
    NAEP findings, 357–358
    in Picture-Word Inductive Model
        (PWIM), 84–87, 380
Wubbels, T., 420

Yeung, A., 423–424
York, R. L., 359

Zone of proximal development, 16–17
    finding, 17
    principle of optimal mismatch, 16–17